MW00813710

ILLUMINATING THE INTENT

The Library of Tibetan Classics is a special series being developed by the Institute of Tibetan Classics aimed at making key classical Tibetan texts part of the global literary and intellectual heritage. Eventually comprising thirty-two large volumes, the collection will contain over two hundred distinct texts by more than a hundred of the best-known authors. These texts have been selected in consultation with the preeminent lineage holders of all the schools and other senior Tibetan scholars to represent the Tibetan literary tradition as a whole. The works included in the series span more than a millennium and cover the vast expanse of classical Tibetan knowledge—from the core teachings of the specific schools to such diverse fields as ethics, philosophy, linguistics, medicine, astronomy and astrology, folklore, and historiography.

Illuminating the Intent
An Exposition of Candrakīrti's Entering the Middle Way
Tsongkhapa (1357–1419)

This work is an authoritative exposition of Candrakīrti's seventh-century classic *Entering the Middle Way*. Written primarily as a supplement to Nāgārjuna's *Fundamental Verses on the Middle Way*, Candrakīrti's text integrates the central insight of Nāgārjuna's thought—the rejection of any metaphysical notion of intrinsic, objective being—with the ethical and edifying elements of the Buddha's teachings. He undertakes this by correlating the progressive stages of insight into the emptiness of intrinsic existence with the well-known Mahayana framework of the ten levels of the bodhisattva.

Completed the year before the author's death, Tsongkhapa's exposition of Candrakīrti's text is recognized by the Tibetan tradition as the final standpoint of Tsongkhapa on many of the questions of Buddhist Madhyamaka philosophy. Written in lucid exemplary Tibetan, Tsongkhapa's work presents a wonderful marriage of rigorous Madhyamaka philosophical analysis with a detailed and subtle account of the progressively advancing mental states and spiritual maturity realized by sincere Madhyamaka practitioners. The work is still used as the principal textbook in the study of Indian Madhyamaka philosophy in many Tibetan monastic colleges. Tsongkhapa's extensive writings on Madhyamaka philosophy, including the present text, ushered in a new phase of engagement with the philosophy of emptiness in Tibet, giving rise to a great flowering of literary activity on the subject by subsequent Tibetan scholars like Gyaltsab Jé, Khedrup Jé, and the First Dalai Lama, as well as the critiques of Taktsang Lotsāwa, Gorampa, Shākya Chokden, and Karmapa Mikyö Dorjé and the subsequent responses to these by Tsongkhapa's followers, such as Jamyang Galo, Jetsun Chökyi Gyaltsen, and Panchen Losang Chögyen.

THE LIBRARY OF TIBETAN CLASSICS • VOLUME 19
Thupten Jinpa, General Editor

ILLUMINATING THE INTENT

An Exposition of Candrakīrti's
Entering the Middle Way

Tsongkhapa

Translated by Thupten Jinpa

in association with the Institute of Tibetan Classics

Wisdom Publications
199 Elm Street
Somerville, MA 02144 USA
wisdomexperience.org

Library of Congress Cataloging-in-Publication Data
Names: Tsong-kha-pa Blo-bzang-grags-pa, 1357–1419, author. |
    Thupten Jinpa, translator.
Title: Illuminating the intent: an exposition of Candrakīrti's Entering the middle way /
    Tsongkhapa; translated by Thupten Jinpa.
Other titles: Dbu ma la 'jug pa'i rgya cher bśad pa dgoṅs pa rab gsal. English
Description: Somerville, MA, USA: Wisdom Publications, 2021. | Series: Library of
    Tibetan classics; volume 19 | Includes bibliographical references and index.
Identifiers: LCCN 2020013718 (print) | LCCN 2020013719 (ebook) |
    ISBN 9780861714582 (hardback) | ISBN 9781614297307 (ebook)
Subjects: LCSH: Candrakīrti. Madhyamakāvatāra. | Mādhyamika (Buddhism)—Early
    works to 1800.
Classification: LCC BQ2910.M365 T7723613 2021 (print) |
    LCC BQ2910.M365 (ebook) | DDC 294.3/85—dc23
LC record available at https://lccn.loc.gov/2020013718
LC ebook record available at https://lccn.loc.gov/2020013719

ISBN 978-0-86171-458-2 ebook ISBN 978-1-61429-730-7

25 24 23 22 21
5 4 3 2 1

Cover and interior design by Gopa&Ted2. Typeset by Kristin Goble. Set in Adobe
Garamond Premier Pro 10.5/13.5.

Printed on acid-free paper that meets the guidelines for permanence and durability of
the Production Guidelines for Book Longevity of the Council on Library Resources.

Printed in Canada.

Message from the Dalai Lama

THE LAST TWO MILLENNIA witnessed a tremendous proliferation of cultural and literary development in Tibet, the "Land of Snows." Moreover, due to the inestimable contributions made by Tibet's early spiritual kings, numerous Tibetan translators, and many great Indian paṇḍitas over a period of so many centuries, the teachings of the Buddha and the scholastic tradition of ancient India's Nālandā monastic university became firmly rooted in Tibet. As evidenced from the historical writings, this flowering of Buddhist tradition in the country brought about the fulfillment of the deep spiritual aspirations of countless sentient beings. In particular, it contributed to the inner peace and tranquility of the peoples of Tibet, Outer Mongolia—a country historically suffused with Tibetan Buddhism and its culture—the Tuva and Kalmuk regions in present-day Russia, the outer regions of mainland China, and the entire trans-Himalayan areas on the southern side, including Bhutan, Sikkim, Ladakh, Kinnaur, and Spiti. Today this tradition of Buddhism has the potential to make significant contributions to the welfare of the entire human family. I have no doubt that, when combined with the methods and insights of modern science, the Tibetan Buddhist cultural heritage and knowledge will help foster a more enlightened and compassionate human society, a humanity that is at peace with itself, with fellow sentient beings, and with the natural world at large.

It is for this reason I am delighted that the Institute of Tibetan Classics in Montreal, Canada, is compiling a thirty-two-volume series containing the works of many great Tibetan teachers, philosophers, scholars, and practitioners representing all major Tibetan schools and traditions. These important writings are being critically edited and annotated and then published in modern book format in a reference collection called *The Library of Tibetan Classics*, with their translations into other major languages to follow later. While expressing my heartfelt commendation for this noble project, I pray and hope that *The Library of Tibetan Classics* will not only make these important Tibetan treatises accessible to scholars of Tibetan studies, but will create a new opportunity for younger Tibetans to study and take interest in their own rich and profound culture. Through translations into other languages, it is my sincere hope that millions of fellow citizens of the wider human family will also be able to share in the joy of engaging with Tibet's classical literary heritage, textual riches that have been such a great source of joy and inspiration to me personally for so long.

The Dalai Lama
The Buddhist monk Tenzin Gyatso

Special Acknowledgments

THE INSTITUTE OF TIBETAN CLASSICS expresses its deep gratitude to Tsadra Foundation for the core funding for the translation of this important volume. We also thank the Ing Foundation for its long-standing patronage of the Institute of Tibetan Classics and the Scully Peretsman Foundation for its support of the work of the Institute's chief editor, Dr. Thupten Jinpa; these together made it possible for the translator of the present volume to devote the time and attention necessary to bring this project to a successful completion.

Publisher's Acknowledgment

THE PUBLISHER WISHES TO extend a heartfelt thanks to the following people who have contributed substantially to the publication of *The Library of Tibetan Classics*:

Pat Gruber and the Patricia and Peter Gruber Foundation
The Hershey Family Foundation
The Ing Foundation

We also extend deep appreciation to our other subscribing benefactors:

Anonymous, dedicated to Buddhas within
Anonymous, in honor of Dzongsar Khyentse Rinpoche
Anonymous, in honor of Geshe Tenzin Dorje
Anonymous, in memory of K. J. Manel De Silva—may she realize the truth
Dr. Patrick Bangert
Nilda Venegas Bernal
Serje Samlo Khentul Lhundub Choden and his Dharma friends
Nicholas Cope
Kushok Lobsang Dhamchöe
Tenzin Dorjee
Richard Farris
Gaden Samten Ling, Canada
Evgeniy Gavrilov & Tatiana Fotina
Great Vow Zen Monastery
Ginger Gregory
The Grohmann family, Taiwan
Rick Meeker Hayman
Steven D. Hearst
Jana & Mahi Hummel

Julie LaValle Jones
Heidi Kaiter
Paul, Trisha, Rachel, and Daniel Kane
Land of Medicine Buddha
Diane & Joseph Lucas
Elizabeth Mettling
Russ Miyashiro
Kestrel Montague
the Nalanda Institute, Olympia, WA
Craig T. Neyman
Kristin A. Ohlson
Arnold Possick
Magdalene Camilla Frank Prest
Quek Heng Bee, Ong Siok Ngow, and family
Randall-Gonzales Family Foundation
Erick Rinner
Andrew Rittenour
Dombon Roig Family
Jonathan and Diana Rose
the Sharchitsang family
Nirbhay N. Singh
Tibetisches Zentrum e.V. Hamburg
Richard Toft
Alissa KieuNgoc Tran
Timothy Trompeter
Tsadra Foundation
the Vahagn Setian Charitable Foundation
Ellyse Adele Vitiello
Jampa (Alicia H.) Vogel
Nicholas C. Weeks II
Claudia Wellnitz
Bob White
Kevin Michael White, MD
Eve and Jeff Wild

and the other donors who wish to remain anonymous.

Contents

Preface

IT'S A SOURCE OF both profound joy and great honor to be able to finally offer in this volume a full translation of one of the most important philosophical works in the Tibetan language, *Illuminating the Intent: An Exposition of Entering the Middle Way*. Authored by Tsongkhapa, arguably the most influential figure in the history of Tibetan Buddhism, the work represents the mature standpoint of this great Tibetan thinker on the Madhyamaka philosophy of emptiness. This work is volume 19 in *The Library of Tibetan Classics* series and, in my view, truly deserving of its place in any collection that claims some degree of completeness with respect to representing Tibet's classical culture. Ever since its first appearance in 1418, a year before Tsongkhapa's death, numerous materials—commentaries, expositions of the general points, analytic explanations, annotations, as well as critiques—have appeared in Tibetan substantially expanding the literature for studying and understanding this work.

Acknowledging the text's status as a major textbook in the Tibetan monastic curriculum, I have striven to prepare this translation to help the reader, especially the student, engage with it in an efficient but comprehensive manner. I have inserted the lines of the root text in the relevant sections of the text, taking my cues from Candrakīrti's own placement of the verses in his autocommentary. In editing my translation of Candrakīrti's root text, I have benefited from two earlier translations of the text, one by C. W. Huntington with Geshe Namgyal Wangchen in *The Emptiness of Emptiness* and the other by the Padmakara Translation Group in *Introduction to the Middle Way*. Where I deemed it helpful, I have offered explanations of difficult passages in my notes so that what is at issue in a given passage is clear to the reader. In my notes, I have also referenced passages in Tsongkhapa's other Madhyamaka writings to aid the reader who wishes to delve into the specific topics further. I have also provided as an appendix Tsongkhapa's entire topical outline, which provides a bird's-eye view of how the text was conceived by the author and also serves as an expanded table of contents. It is my sincere hope that, with these tools offered with care, you, the reader, will be able to embark on a meaningful journey—intellectual, philosophical, and spiritual.

I wish first of all to express my deep personal gratitude to His Holiness the Dalai Lama for always being such a profound source of inspiration and an exemplary embodiment of the best of the Tibetan tradition, including that of Tsongkhapa. I acknowledge my two teachers at Ganden, Kyabjé Zemey Rinpoché and Khensur Lati Rinpoché, who taught me, among others, the great works of Tsongkhapa. To the following individuals and organizations, I owe my sincere thanks: to David Kittelstrom at Wisdom for his incisive editing; to Beth Newman for her thorough and careful reading of the entire manuscript of my draft translation and making extensive editorial suggestions; to my fellow Tibetan editor Geshé Lobsang Choedar for assisting me sourcing all citations; and to my wife, Sophie Boyer-Langri, for taking on the numerous administrative chores that are part of a collaborative project such as this. I thank the Buddhist Digital Resource Center (tbrc.org) for providing me access to its immense library of digitized Tibetan texts, including the rare Madhyamaka writings of Tsongkhapa's teacher Rendawa, his senior colleague Lochen Kyabchok Palsang, and his student Lodrö Rinchen Sengé.

Finally, I would like to express my heartfelt thanks to the benefactors whose generosity has made the realization of this important project possible: to the Tsadra Foundation for its core funding of several projects from *The Library of Tibetan Classics*, including this present volume; to the Ing Foundation for its generous long-standing patronage of the Institute of Tibetan Classics; and to the Scully Peretsman Foundation for its support of my work for the institute, all of which allowed me to devote the time and attention necessary to bring this important work into English.

May the experience of engaging with this seminal work from one of the greatest philosophical minds of Tibet be meaningful and transformational to all readers, as it has been for so many Tibetans over the last six centuries.

Thupten Jinpa
Montreal, 2020

Introduction

TSONGKHAPA, THE AUTHOR OF the text contained in this volume, is arguably the most influential figure in the history of Tibetan Buddhism. Born in northeastern Tibet in 1357 and educated in central Tibet, Tsongkhapa rose to prominence rapidly through his mastery of the Indian Buddhist classics that formed the core of Tibetan monastic curriculum at the time. His first major work, the *Golden Rosary*, completed at the age of thirty-one, is a two-volume exposition of Perfection of Wisdom studies that cemented his reputation as a great scholar. Tsongkhapa was a maverick with an independent mind who shunned formal affiliation with any of the established Tibetan schools of his time, including that of his primary teacher, Rendawa. Through close reading of key Buddhist texts, sustained critical reflection, and extensive meditative cultivation over prolonged periods, Tsongkhapa by the end of the fourteenth century had synthesized the vast Indian Buddhist heritage—philosophical, psychological, and spiritual—into a unique and remarkable system of Buddhist thought and practice that came to be known as the Geluk tradition.

One area where Tsongkhapa's original contribution is most pronounced is his interpretation of the Indian Madhyamaka philosophy that rejects any notion of ultimate existence, stating that all things and events are empty of intrinsic existence. This is the philosophical standpoint first defined systematically by the second-century Indian Buddhist thinker Nāgārjuna and developed further by Āryadeva (second century), Buddhapālita (fifth century), Bhāviveka (sixth century), and Candrakīrti (seventh century).

Completed a year before his death, our text, Tsongkhapa's *Illuminating the Intent*, embodies the author's mature and final standpoint on central issues of Madhyamaka philosophy. Soon after its appearance in 1418, *Illuminating the Intent* became the primer on the subject for Tsongkhapa's followers, especially for the rapidly growing population of Ganden Monastery, which Tsongkhapa founded in 1409, as well as for Drepung and Sera, the two major monasteries near Lhasa founded by senior students—Drepung founded by Jamyang Chöjé in 1416 and Sera by Jamchen Chöjé in 1419. After Tsongkhapa's death in 1419, the adoption of *Illuminating the Intent* as the key textbook on Madhyamaka philosophy gained momentum as more monasteries upholding Tsongkhapa's tradition sprang up across the Tibetan plateau. *Illuminating the Intent's* status as the primary reference on Madhyamaka philosophy within the monastic curriculum in the Geluk tradition remains unchanged to this day.[1]

Formally, Tsongkhapa's *Illuminating the Intent* is not an independent work; it is a commentary on an Indian text, *Entering the Middle Way* (*Madhyamakāvatāra*), authored by Candrakīrti in the seventh century. Candrakīrti's own text, though an independent work, was composed as a supplement to yet another Indian work, *Treatise on the Middle Way*, also known as *Fundamental Verses on the Middle Way* (*Mūlamadhyamkakārikā*) or *Fundamental Wisdom*, by Nāgārjuna, one of the greatest Indian philosophers of antiquity. Nāgārjuna's *Treatise* too was, in turn, written as a systematic exposition of the teaching on emptiness as presented in Mahayana scriptures attributed to the Buddha, especially the collection known as the Perfection of Wisdom sutras, which includes the famed *Heart Sutra*. So in *Illuminating the Intent*, we have Tsongkhapa reading Candrakīrti reading Nāgārjuna, who in turn was reading teachings handed down from the Buddha.

Candrakīrti's Entering the Middle Way

Candrakīrti's *Entering the Middle Way*, the root text for Tsongkhapa's *Illuminating the Intent*, is entirely in verse, and Candrakīrti himself wrote a lengthy prose commentary on it, which Tsongkhapa also reads closely in our volume. The root text runs into some 330 four-line stanzas, with chapter 6, by far the longest chapter, forming about 70 percent of the text. The first ten of the eleven total chapters take their names as well as their themes from the characteristics of the ten bodhisattva grounds (*bodhisattvabhūmi*), from the first, "Perfect Joy," to the tenth, "Cloud of Dharma." The final chapter presents the attributes of the ten grounds followed by the resultant ground of buddhahood. In structuring his *Entering the Middle Way* in this way, Candrakīrti follows the well-known Mahayana scripture the *Ten Grounds Sutra*, which is part of the extensive *Avataṃsaka Sutra*. That this sutra is the basis for Candrakīrti's text is evident especially from the author's own commentary, which beyond extensive quotes from the sutra, contains language, tone, and sequencing of ideas that are strikingly similar.

Following this sutra, each chapter of *Entering the Middle Way* is structured broadly around three elements: (1) the name of the specific ground and what it means, (2) an extensive presentation of the attributes of the ground, and (3) a summary. The ten bodhisattva grounds, the themes of the first ten chapters, are associated each with a specific perfection—generosity, morality, forbearance, diligence, meditative absorption, wisdom, skillful means, aspiration, power, and gnosis—and these ten grounds represent progressive stages on the bodhisattva's path to the full awakening of buddhahood. The ten grounds are themselves part of a broader structure of the path to enlightenment that consists of five stages: the paths of accumulation, of preparation, of seeing, of meditation, and of no-more-learning. The first bodhisattva ground begins when the bodhisattva reaches the path of seeing and first gains direct realization of the ultimate truth, emptiness. Given Candrakīrti's text is primarily a work on Madhyamaka philosophy and also an essential supplement to Nāgārjuna's *Treatise on the Middle Way*, the primary subject matter of the work is clearly the philosophy of emptiness. And it is because emptiness, which Nāgārjuna says is the ultimate truth, comprises the content of the sixth perfection that the sixth chapter attracts the lengthiest treatment in Candrakīrti's text.

Why did Candrakīrti call his text *Entering the Middle Way*? According to Tsongkhapa, Candrakīrti's text "enters" Nāgārjuna's treatise in two crucial ways: from the perspective of *profound emptiness* and from the perspective of the *vast aspect of the path*. The first entails an interpretation of Nāgārjuna's *Treatise* that is unique compared to other commentators, as well as an extensive refutation of the Cittamātra (Mind Only) standpoint (6.45–97). The second manner of "entering," according to Tsongkhapa, involves complementing Nāgārjuna's treatise by explicitly bringing in other dimensions of the Mahayana path drawing on Nāgārjuna's other writings, especially his *Precious Garland* (*Ratnāvalī*). These include the three factors on the ground of the ordinary being, the ten bodhisattva grounds, the resultant ground of buddhahood, and the method for cultivating insight grounded in meditative absorption.

Since Candrakīrti's text begins with the first bodhisattva ground, he uses his salutation verse to present the key factors of the path on the beginner's stage—the stage that precedes the first ground. These are compassion, the altruistic awakening mind, and the knowledge of emptiness, the last of which he refers to as *nondual awareness*. Compassion is, in fact, presented as the object of salutation at the beginning of the text, where he compares its importance, with respect to the attainment of buddhahood, to the seed at the outset, the moisture in the middle, and the ripened fruit at the end. By using these three analogies, Candrakīrti underlines compassion's centrality to the entire path, not just at the beginning as a motivation. Chapters 1 to 5 present key attributes of the first five perfections, with the presentations on the first two, generosity and forbearance, the most extensive.

The sixth and chief chapter of Candrakīrti's text begins with a statement about how the bodhisattva on the fifth ground, having attained excellence in meditative absorption, progresses onto the sixth ground and "attains true cessation by dwelling in wisdom" (6.1d). Following the presentation in the *Ten Grounds Sutra*, the chapter explains how the bodhisattva abides in wisdom by attaining "ten perfect equanimities," the first being the perfect equanimity of the *absence of signs*, or nonarising.[2] The rest of the chapter then is an extensive exploration of what this perfect equanimity means. Incidentally, nonarising is also the topic of the first chapter of Nāgārjuna's *Treatise on the Middle Way*. Here, then, is a broad outline of Candrakīrti's sixth chapter, which is treated in chapters 8–19 of the present volume:

Name of the ground and how the perfection of wisdom excels on the ground (6.1)

Praise of the perfection of wisdom (6.2)

Extensive presentation of the ultimate nature of reality

Preliminary points (6.3–7)

Actual presentation of the ultimate nature of reality

Selflessness of phenomena

Refuting arising from four possibilities

Refuting arising from self (6.8–13)

Refuting arising from what is other

Refuting arising from other in general

Actual refutation of arising from other (6.14–21)

Rejecting objections to such refutation from the worldly perspective (6.22–32)

Presentation of the two truths (6.23–29)

Chapters 7 to 10 are all quite brief. The eleventh chapter, on attributes of the ten grounds and the resultant ground, runs to more than fifty stanzas. In particular, the part on the resultant ground of buddhahood offers not only an account of buddhahood—the buddha bodies (*kāya*), the unique attributes of the buddha such as ten powers—but also addresses critical questions, such as, If emptiness is the ultimate truth, how can there be knowledge of it? And, If the buddha's gnosis is fused inseparably with emptiness, how can it be a knower of such truth? Candrakīrti ends his seminal work with the following stanzas (11.52–53):

This system has been explained by the monk Candrakīrti
drawing from the *Treatise on the Middle Way*,
in perfect accord with the scriptures,
and in accord with oral instructions.

Just as outside this [tradition of the] *Treatise*,
no scriptures set forth this teaching as it is,
likewise the system found here is not found elsewhere.
O learned ones, be sure of this fact!

Indian and Tibetan commentators on Candrakīrti ascribe to him a number of distinctive philosophical views. These include (1) rejection of formal inference based on criteria grounded in objective facts of the world, relying instead on *consequential reasoning* that reveals logical contradictions and absurd consequences entailed by an opponent's positions, (2) rejection of the key tenets of the Buddhist epistemology initiated by Dignāga and developed further by Dharmakīrti,[3] (3) a radical understanding of the inaccessibility of ultimate truth through language and thought, (4) an understanding of conventional truth that appeals for its validity to everyday intuitions of the world instead of philosophical grounding, (5) a unique interpretation of Nāgārjuna's statement about his having no thesis, and (6) the possible cessation of mind and mental factors in buddhahood.[4]

The first, rejection of formal inference based on criteria grounded in objective facts, emerges in Candrakīrti's *Clear Words* (*Prasannapadā*), where he mounts a defense of Buddhapālita, a fifth-century commentator on Nāgārjuna who was critiqued by Bhāviveka for failing to formulate probative inferences in presenting the master's argument and for relying on a *reductio ad absurdum* style of reasoning. This debate on the appropriateness of formal inference in the context of establishing the truth of emptiness came to be seen, by Tibetan commentators, as the starting point for the emergence of two major strands of Madhyamaka philosophy. The second point, Candrakīrti's refutation of Dignāga's influential epistemology, is also found in *Clear Words*, which takes two key ideas of Dignāga to task: unique particulars (*svalakṣaṇa*) and the definition of perception (*pratyakṣa*). The third, inaccessibility of ultimate truth to thought and language, is most clearly articulated in *Entering the Middle Way* 6.29–31b and its relevant sections in the autocommentary. The fourth, a unique understanding of conventional truth grounded in appeal to everyday worldly conventions, emerges throughout important parts of chapter 6 of *Entering the Middle Way*, especially 6.31c–32, 35, and 159. The fifth, Candrakīrti's interpretation of Madhyamaka's lack of a thesis, emerges in 6.173–76 and elsewhere, such as in his *Commentary on Sixty Stanzas of Reasoning*. The final issue, about the possible cessation of mind and mental factors in buddhahood, can be found in the final chapter of *Entering the Middle Way*.

To Candrakīrti's critics, such as Chapa Chökyi Sengé (1106–69), it is these views that make him suspect when it comes to interpreting Nāgārjuna's teachings on emptiness.[5] Among his enthusiasts, some, like Jayānanda[6] (and possibly Thangsakpa, a student of Patsab Lotsāwa [b. 1055]), would embrace these views unreservedly. Others, like Tsongkhapa, would offer a more nuanced reading of Candrakīrti, so that he is not seen as rejecting epistemology and not seen as denying the possibility of the knowledge of ultimate truth by human cognition—that is, suggesting that there remains no cognition whatsoever, including gnosis, in buddhahood.[7]

Reception of Candrakīrti's Works in India and Tibet

One curious historical fact about Candrakīrti's *Entering the Middle Way*, like all his writings on Madhyamaka, is the near silence about it on the part of his contemporaries and immediate successors in India.[8] Although Tibetan tradition recognizes Śāntideva, author of the famed *Guide to the Bodhisattva Way*, as belonging to the same Madhyamaka lineage as Candrakīrti, nowhere does the influential eighth-century master reveal cognizance of Candrakīrti's works. Similarly, neither Śāntarakṣita nor his student Kamalaśīla—two hugely influential eighth-century authors on Madhyamaka and *pramāṇa* epistemology—appear to engage with Candrakīrti's Madhyamaka writings. Even those who do evince awareness of his writing, such as Avalokitavrata (eighth century), do not substantively engage him in their texts. We know, however, that Candrakīrti's commentary on Nāgārjuna's *Sixty Stanzas of Reasoning* was translated into Tibetan sometime between the end of the eighth and the beginning of ninth century, suggesting that he was not an entirely unknown figure in Indian Buddhism at the time. However, only around the tenth century, more than two centuries after Candrakīrti's death, does one notice real recognition of the master's writings in India. Prajñākaramati (950–1030), the author of an influential commentary on Śāntideva's *Guide*, plus the so-called Bhāviveka II, author of *Precious Lamp on the Middle Way* (*Madhyamakaratnapradīpa*), along with Maitripa and Atiśa all took Candrakīrti to be an important authority on Madhyamaka philosophy. One possible explanation for this near silence about Candrakīrti's Madhyamaka writings before the tenth century could be owing to the fact that his approach to interpreting Nāgārjuna's philosophy was an outlier at a time when the dominant pattern was to read Madhyamaka's ontology of emptiness in consonance with the sophisticated Buddhist epistemology of Dignāga and Dharmakīrti. As we saw above, this is something Candrakīrti not only shunned but explicitly critiqued.[9]

Whatever the historical reasons for the late recognition of Candrakīrti in India, Candrakīrti's interpretation of Nāgārjuna came to be celebrated in Tibet as the apex of Madhyamaka philosophy. My own sense is that the Indian Bengali missionary to Tibet, Atiśa, may have been pivotal in elevating Candrakīrti's status. This stanza from his *Entering the Two Truths* (*Satyadvayāvatāra*) is often cited by Tibetan authors to link Nāgārjuna and Candrakīrti in a special lineage of Madhyamaka philosophy:

> If you ask who realized emptiness,
> it was Nāgārjuna, who was prophesized by the Tathāgata
> and saw the truth of ultimate nature,
> and his disciple Candrakīrti.[10]

Atiśa's student and translator Naktso Lotsāwa produced the first translation of Candrakīrti's *Entering the Middle Way* and its lengthy autocommentary. Later, in the early twelfth century, Patsab Lotsāwa produced influential translations of most of Candrakīrti's major writings, including especially his *Clear Words* commentary of Nāgārjuna's treatise, a new translation of *Entering the Middle Way* and its autocommentary, and his commentary on Āryadeva's *Four Hundred Stanzas on the Middle Way* (*Catuḥśatakaśāstra*). Patsab is also credited by scholars, both Tibetan as well as Western, for coining the labels Prāsaṅgika and Svātantrika to refer to two subschools of Madhyamaka associated, respectively, with Buddhapālita and Candrakīrti, on the one hand, and Bhāviveka and others, on the other. As we saw above, enthusiasm for Candrakīrti's Madhyamaka writings in Tibet in the twelfth century was by no means universal, and foremost among his Tibetan critics was the influential logician Chapa Chökyi Seṅgé of Sangphu Monastery. According to a fifteenth-century source, Chapa challenged the monk Jayānanda in a formal debate, where the latter is said to have failed to defend Candrakīrti's views. In any case, by Tsongkhapa's time in the second half of the fourteenth century, recognition of Candrakīrti's reading of Nāgārjuna as the apex of Buddhist philosophical thinking was near universal in Tibet.

Part of the enthusiasm for and long-standing loyalty to *Entering the Middle Way* as the key textbook in Tibet on Madhyamaka philosophy may have to do with its comprehensiveness. Unlike other Madhyamaka texts like Nāgārjuna's *Treatise on the Middle Way*, Candrakīrti's *Entering* spans the entire path to enlightenment, from the beginner's stage, through the ten bodhisattva grounds, to the resultant state of buddhahood. With its treatment of all the perfections, combined with its extensive presentation of emptiness in chapter 6, *Entering the Middle Way* offers a framework that embraces, and in fact unites, both the wisdom of emptiness and the compassion-based method dimension of the path, including the cultivation of the altruistic awakening mind and the perfections of generosity, morality, and forbearance. Monastic students would memorize the entire root text, as I myself did when I was a student at Ganden Monastery; receive classes on it with the aid of an authoritative commentary, such as Tsongkhapa's *Illuminating the Intent*; and debate its meaning, especially the more challenging parts. Finally, students would sit down for formal debate on the text, demonstrating their mastery of the text, its meaning, and the philosophical issues it raises.

Key Aspects of Tsongkhapa's Commentary

Tibetan exegetical tradition speaks of different types of commentarial texts: commentary in the form of annotation, word-by-word commentary, commentary on the essential points, and extensive commentary. Tsongkhapa's *Illuminating the Intent* belongs to the final category, faithfully following the structure of its root text, *Entering the Middle Way*. However, Tsongkhapa sees his *Illuminating the Intent* to be an exposition of Candrakīrti's autocommentary as well. So, in terms of structure, content, and scope, *Illuminating the Intent* is a three-layered text. First there is Candrakīrti's root text in verse, next we have the text of Candrakīrti's own commentary on the verses, and finally we have Tsongkhapa's exposition of the meaning of these two layers. To assist the reader, I have inserted the actual verses of the root text into the translation of *Illuminating the Intent*; Tsongkhapa does not set them off in his own work. And when the words of the root text are repeated within Tsongkhapa's commentary, I have bolded them so that they are easily identifiable.[11]

When glossing the words of the root text, Tsongkhapa not only strives to explain the meaning of every single word of the verses, he draws heavily on Candrakīrti's own explanation of the verses from the autocommentary. I have chosen not to highlight such transcriptions of the autocommentary, as it would have led to an aesthetically unappealing reader experience. Quite often, especially when addressing issues he deems of particular philosophical importance, Tsongkhapa reproduces specific sections of the autocommentary that are not part of Candrakīrti's gloss on the verses but treat related philosophical or soteriological questions. With some of these, Tsongkhapa does not explicitly indicate that they are reproduced from the autocommentary with a few explanatory words interspersed, and so I have annotated all these citations to alert the reader. Unavoidably, when an author expounds on a verse text by including every single word of the verse in his gloss, this constrains the commentator's ability to employ a natural and fluid prose. Thus my hope in bolding the words of the root text and annotating the transcriptions of the autocommentary is that the reader will engage with those parts of the text with greater patience.

What might be considered a fourth layer of our text are Tsongkhapa's own independent sections. In this layer, Tsongkhapa provides a wider philosophical context for important topics addressed by Candrakīrti—for instance, the nature and types of compassion, the first three perfections, the outset of the presentation of emptiness, the two truths, and the critique of the Mind Only standpoint. Part of this contextualization involves offering what is known as "explaining the general points" (*spyi don*) and relating the treatment, where essential, to earlier sources. It might also involve Tsongkhapa's independent observations and unique methodological approaches, such as the section on what he calls "identifying what is to be negated" (see chapter 9).

A second element Tsongkhapa introduces in these more independent sections is the cross-references he makes to relevant passages in the root-text author's other philosophical works. Tsongkhapa refers extensively to Candrakīrti's commentaries on Nāgārjuna's *Treatise on the Middle Way*, *Sixty Stanzas of Reasoning*, and *Seventy Stanzas on Emptiness* and to Candrakīrti's last-known major work, a commentary on Āryadeva's *Four Hundred Stanzas*. In so doing, Tsongkhapa ensures that his reading of Candrakīrti's root text is not confined to just the root text and its autocommentary. And even when reading the root text and its autocommentary directly, Tsongkhapa carefully compares the two Tibetan translations of the text—the earlier one by Naktso Lotsāwa and the later one by Patsab Lotsāwa—and he is explicit in stating which version he prefers in a given context. He also carefully consults Jayānanda, the only known Indian commentator on Candrakīrti's *Entering the Middle Way*, citing him favorably where appropriate and critiquing his reading elsewhere.

Third, every now and then, when the texts address a question of philosophical or soteriological significance, Tsongkhapa takes the opportunity to draw out its wider implications, especially in relation to matters that historically have attracted divergent opinions among commentators. Fourth, an important strategy in Tsongkhapa's interpretation of Madhyamaka philosophy is his appeal to experience (both ordinary and meditative), our common-sense intuitions, and, in some cases, thought experiments. Finally, Tsongkhapa exhibits a high degree of innovation in his topical outline (*sa bcad*) of the text, a textual hermeneutic that became integral to Tibetan works beginning in the eleventh century. These methodological approaches make Tsongkhapa's readings of Indian sources innovative and yet, as one modern scholar on Madhyamaka puts it, "authentically grounded in careful philosophical thinking and analysis."[12]

A Summary of Key Discussions

In the summary that follows, my aim is to spotlight those sections of *Illuminating the Intent* where Tsongkhapa offers a substantive presentation to help his reader develop deeper appreciation of a topic's philosophical or soteriological significance. As already stated, Tsongkhapa's *Illuminating the Intent* is divided into eleven parts, each corresponding to a specific chapter in the root text, which is mapped to the ten bodhisattva grounds and the resultant ground of a buddha. But these chapters differ dramatically in length: in the Tibetan edition of Tsongkhapa's text, the sixth ground comes to 271 pages, while the eighth and ninth grounds are only 2 pages apiece. To assist the reader, we have introduced a structure to make the text more manageable and more closely aligned with modern expectations for a major book like this. The entire text is divided into three parts, preceded by a chapter on the preliminaries: part 1 contains the introductory section and presentation of the first five grounds, part 2 contains the lengthy sixth ground, and part 3 contains the seventh to the tenth grounds and the resultant ground. All together, there are twenty-five chapters, with twelve devoted to the sixth ground alone. So when I refer to chapter numbers below, I use the numbers in our new format devised for this volume.

In chapter 1, when explaining the salutation verse of Candrakīrti's text, Tsongkhapa offers an extensive exploration of the concept of compassion in Mahayana Buddhism (pp. 47–55). In doing so, he observes insightfully that compassion requires a sense of identification with your object of concern. In present-day parlance, this is the crucial concept of empathy. He cites two primary methods in Buddhist tradition for extending our empathy outside our normal narrow circle of concern. The first is to view all beings as kin—as our mothers, in fact—and the other is to identify with others grounded in the recognition of our shared sentient nature (pp. 49–50). Commenting on three types of compassion differentiated by their focus—sentient beings, phenomena, and no object—Tsongkhapa shows how they reflect the progressive lessening of grasping on the part of one who experiences compassion for others (pp. 52–55). In chapter 2, "General Presentation of the Grounds," Tsongkhapa defines what is meant by a *bodhisattva ground* and overviews the stages of the path to awakening as understood in Nāgārjuna's Madhyamaka tradition. In doing so, he draws on Nāgārjuna's own *Precious Garland* and on the seminal *Ten Grounds Sutra*. In chapter 3, on the first ground, Tsongkhapa addresses extensively the question of whether realization of ultimate truth defined in terms of the emptiness of intrinsic existence is indispensable for attaining nirvana (pp. 82–106). Part of this entails a detailed exposition of a key section of Śāntideva's *Guide*, which Tsongkhapa sees as consonant with Candrakīrti's *Entering the Middle Way* (pp. 83–88). An important upshot of this analysis is the suggestion that Candrakīrti differs significantly from other Buddhist schools in his interpretation of the selflessness of persons. In chapter 5, as part of defining *forbearance* as the antidote to anger, Tsongkhapa examines what characteristics of virtue are destroyed in the wake of anger (pp. 133–37). Furthermore, what exactly is meant by *destruction* when it is said that an instance of anger destroys virtuous karma accumulated over a span of eons? On the flip side, he examines the mechanism for how negative karma is purified through declaration and purification rites (pp. 139–40).

In part 2, chapter 9, Tsongkhapa presents the important topic of *what is to be negated* in the context of understanding emptiness. Delineating the scope of negation is, for him, crucially important, for failure to do so could lead to the extreme of nihilism. Tsongkhapa, in fact, defines the object of negation differently depending on whether the standpoint is that of the Svātantrika (pp. 174–80) or the Prāsaṅgika (pp. 181–89). His conclusion is that what is negated according to Candrakīrti is the *intrinsic existence* that we instinctively project onto anything we perceive. Part of this discussion involves distinguishing "innate grasping" from "acquired grasping," the former being the ultimate target of meditation on emptiness. In chapter 11, in expounding on Candrakīrti's extensive presentation of the two truths—ultimate truth and conventional truth—Tsongkhapa examines the following questions: What exactly is the basis upon which this division into two truths is conceived? What is meant by the word *truth* in the context of the two (pp. 223–25)? How are they defined and from whose perspectives (pp. 234–54)? What is the relation between the two (pp. 225–29)? And, What is meant by the statement that ultimate truth is beyond knowledge and language (pp. 247–54)? As an aside, Tsongkhapa notes how Candrakīrti's identification of subtle grasping suggests a unique Madhyamaka understanding of the nature of subtle afflictions (pp. 239–44).

Chapter 12 deserves special attention for understanding Tsongkhapa's reading of Candrakīrti. Here, Tsongkhapa reads three stanzas, 6.34–36, as presenting three important arguments for negating the arising of things through their intrinsic characteristics. As we will see below, the phrase "existence through intrinsic characteristic" or "the arising of things through their intrinsic characteristics" occupies an extremely important place in Tsongkhapa's interpretation of the Madhyamaka philosophy of Nāgārjuna and Candrakīrti. Tsongkhapa understands the text as presenting three unwanted consequences (four if we add the one additional consequence mentioned in Candrakīrti's autocommentary)[13] if one subscribes to the notion of existence through intrinsic characteristic: (1) the wisdom realizing emptiness would become the cause for annihilation of conditioned things (pp. 261–64), (2) the facts of conventional truth would be able to withstand ultimate analysis (pp. 264–68), and (3) ultimate arising would remain unnegated (pp. 268–71). Here in relation to these three objections, Tsongkhapa sees Bhāviveka's brand of Svātantrika Madhyamaka to be an object of critique by Candrakīrti. To my knowledge, grouping these three stanzas together as formally presenting three arguments, all against the notion of intrinsic arising, is unique. Tsongkhapa's own teacher Rendawa, for example, reads 6.34–36 as part of a section that includes 6.33 and presents the benefit of being able to establish dependent origination as free of the extremes of eternalism and nihilism. Similarly, Lochen Kyabchok Palsang, a senior colleague of both Rendawa and Tsongkhapa, reads 6.35–36 as part of a rebuttal of objections against refuting arising from another.[14] Also in chapter 12 (6.39–43) is Tsongkhapa's detailed analysis of Candrakīrti's refutation of foundation consciousness (*ālayavijñāna*) and his explanation of how Madhyamaka accounts for the functioning of karma in its absence.

Chapter 14, "Refuting the Proof of Intrinsic Existence of Dependent Nature," features two key analyses from Tsongkhapa. One is his rejection of the concept of self-cognition or reflexive awareness (*svasaṃvitti*) proposed by Cittamātra as their "proof" of intrinsically existent dependent nature (pp. 340–45). Since the opponent's argument for reflexive awareness draws on the fact of subsequent recollection, Tsongkhapa presents two distinct accounts of recollection from the Madhyamaka perspective (pp. 345–49). The second issue Tsongkhapa addresses in this chapter is Candrakīrti's views on epistemology, with special attention paid to the definition of what constitutes *manas*, or mental cognition (pp. 351–57). In chapter 17, "The Selflessness of Persons," Tsongkhapa asks the crucial question of what object exactly is grasped when it comes to the intrinsic existence of persons. Is it the physical and mental aggregates that make up the person's existence? Or is it the sense of self projected onto the physical and mental aggregate? (pp. 421–38) What distinguishes grasping at an "I" from grasping at "mine"? Related to this is the basic question of what exactly is negated in the context of the Buddhist view of no-self. Finally, in chapter 19, "Enumerations of Emptiness," Tsongkhapa examines the meaning of the crucial Sanskrit term *svabhāva*—intrinsic nature—and concludes that although *svabhāva* in the sense of intrinsic *existence* must be negated, *svabhāva* in the sense of intrinsic *nature*—as referring to an object's emptiness—must be accepted, for only through its knowledge can true release from grasping be attained (pp. 490–94).

In part 3, in the final chapter, Tsongkhapa presents his analysis of the nature of a buddha's gnosis and addresses the question of how a buddha's gnosis can be understood to know the facts of conventional truth (pp. 533–38). In doing so, Tsongkhapa relates the topic of how a buddha's gnosis perceives the two truths within a single instance of cognition with no traces of dualistic perception to the definition of the two truths presented earlier. For Tsongkhapa, the two facets of the buddha's gnosis—perceiving ultimate truth (the way things really are) and perceiving conventional truth (things in their diversity)—are conceptually distinguished not in actual reality but only from the perspectives of their objects, in relation to which they are thus defined. Tsongkhapa rejects the idea, suggested by some, that a buddha's gnosis sees only emptiness, not the world of conventional truth, on the assumption that perceiving the latter would imply that a buddha's gnosis would be tainted by the delusion of duality. For Tsongkhapa, however, if conventional truth—the world of everyday reality, of our experience, of cause and effect—is not perceived by a buddha's gnosis, this would incur the unwanted consequence that a buddha's gnosis is not omniscient. One would be unable to explain a buddha's ten powers defined in terms of knowledge of specific facts. Elsewhere, Tsongkhapa observes that a buddha's gnosis knows when and how an unenlightened being is perceiving the world in a distorted manner by attributing intrinsic existence to things but that such perception is purely mirroring what is being perceived by the deluded being; it does not occur due to the buddha's own residual imprints of delusion.[15] Tsongkhapa identifies the ability to maintain a coherent account of how a buddha's gnosis perceives the world of diversity that constitutes conventional truth, in the wake of rejecting the intrinsic existence of everything, as a formidable but crucial challenge for Madhyamaka.

Tsongkhapa's Madhyamaka Philosophy

According to his biographies, gaining full insight into Madhyamaka's profound view of emptiness took time, effort, and extensive meditative cultivation on Tsongkhapa's part.[16] He had studied the great Indian treatises on Madhyamaka with Rendawa, the then greatest known authority on the subject in Tibet. He had read, critically reflected on, and meditated on the meaning of these important texts. Thanks to existing records, we know that he had also engaged in a prolonged dialogue on the view of emptiness with Rendawa. In addition, according to the biographies, Tsongkhapa had "access" to the meditation deity Mañjuśrī through the medium of Lama Umapa at first and later Tokden Jampal Gyatso.[17] However, even after his three-year intensive retreat in the Wölkha Valley, 1393–95, gaining the Madhyamaka view was one area where he felt he needed further effort. When he did finally experience the breakthrough in 1397, at the age of forty, Tsongkhapa had developed a unique understanding of Nāgārjuna's Madhyamaka philosophy as read through Candrakīrti. In the immediate aftermath, Tsongkhapa wrote a hymn to the Buddha, praising him for his revelation of the truth of dependent origination. In 1401, Tsongkhapa completed his *Great Treatise on the Stages of the Path to Enlightenment*, which contained, in the final insight section, an extensive presentation on the Madhyamaka philosophy of emptiness. This lengthy work would be followed by four other major works on Madhyamaka: the hermeneutic text *Essence of True Eloquence* in 1407, his extensive commentary on Nāgārjuna's *Treatise on the Middle Way* in 1408, the insight section in his *Middle-Length Treatise on the Stages of the Path to Enlightenment* in 1415, and finally our present volume, *Illuminating the Intent*, in 1418. Together, these five are known as the five great Madhyamaka works of Jé Tsongkhapa.

To understand Tsongkhapa's Madhyamaka, it is important to appreciate the concerns and questions underlying his deep inquiry into this philosophy. Recognizing its crucial importance as the only way to liberation, "with no second alternative door," as Nāgārjuna's disciple Āryadeva puts it,[18] Tsongkhapa was nonetheless deeply concerned about the nihilistic implications of the view of emptiness if not properly understood. After all, Nāgārjuna himself had warned against this, comparing the erroneous understanding of emptiness to mishandling a venomous snake.[19] In particular, Tsongkhapa was concerned about certain Tibetan readings of Candrakīrti that advocated such views as the following: a Mādhyamika is concerned only with refuting other's views but presents no positions of his own; the facts of conventional truths are perceived only by the deluded mind; the existence of things can be accepted purely for another's sake and also from the other's perspective;[20] there can be no knowledge of the ultimate truth except in a metaphorical sense; and the buddha's gnosis does not perceive the world of conventional truth (with some in fact reading Candrakīrti to suggest that gnosis itself ceases to exist at the point of buddhahood).[21] Tsongkhapa was concerned about the nihilistic implications of these views with respect to both ethics and soteriology. In harboring these concerns, Tsongkhapa seemed to sympathize with Chapa's critiques of Candrakīrti, but he did not like the former's proposed solution. There was, however, another alternative in Tibet with respect to Madhyamaka philosophy. By this I am referring to the so-called *extrinsic emptiness* (*gzhan stong*) view of Jonang masters like Dölpopa Sherab Gyaltsen (1292–1361). Tsongkhapa was never attracted to this extrinsic emptiness view, which involved accepting the idea of emptiness itself as being absolute with intrinsic existence. His critique of this view dates from his early writings. What Tsongkhapa strove for, in his deep inquiry into Madhyamaka philosophy, was an integrated view, wherein Madhyamaka's emptiness ontology serves as a robust basis for ethics and soteriology and is consonant as well with a coherent system of logic and epistemology based on common-sense intuitions of epistemic practice.[22]

Below are some key elements of Tsongkhapa's quest to develop a more integrated understanding of Madhyamaka philosophy:[23]

1. Identifying *what is to be negated* in the context of philosophical analysis of and meditation on emptiness (pp. 171–90)
2. Distinguishing the domains of discourse of *conventional analysis* from those of *ultimate analysis* (pp. 264–68)
3. Clarifying the meaning of the key modifier *ultimate* in the statement that things do not exist on the ultimate level (pp. 175–76)
4. Drawing a critical conceptual distinction between *existence* and *intrinsic existence*, the latter rejected even on the conventional level (pp. 271–74)
5. Defining emptiness in terms of the categorical negation of intrinsic existence: in other words, saying that emptiness must be defined, in technical Buddhist language, in terms of *nonimplicative negation* (pp. 195–96)
6. Interpreting emptiness in terms of *dependent origination* (that is,

emptiness = dependent origination) (pp. 412–14; *Great Treatise,* 135–53)

7. Asserting that though emptiness lies beyond thought, insofar as its total knowledge is concerned, its truth is accessible to human cognition: in other words, saying there can be a legitimate knowledge of emptiness through *inferential cognition* (pp. 252–54)

8. Respecting the *apparent world of conventional truth* and not denigrating it through taking it to be mere illusion with no causal efficacy; saying that, in fact, a criteria of validity can be brought to bear within the domain of conventional truth so that a robust differentiation can be drawn between the truth of water as water and the falsity of mirage as water (pp. 236–38; *Great Treatise,* 177–94)

9. Differentiating the Svātantrika and Prāsaṅgika standpoints on the basis of not just a methodological difference on whether to employ formal inference or consequence-demonstrating reasoning, but also a substantive philosophical difference over whether intrinsic existence should be accepted or rejected on the conventional level (pp. 264–68; *Essence of True Eloquence,* 306–44; *Great Treatise,* 233–66)

10. Clearly differentiating three distinct uses of the crucial Sanskrit term *svalakṣaṇa* (*rang mtshan*): (1) the *defining characteristics* of a phenomenon, (2) the *unique particulars* found in Dignāga and Dharmakīrti's epistemology, and (3) *intrinsic characteristics*, which Tsongkhapa understands to be equivalent to the notion of *intrinsic nature* (*svabhāva* or *svarūpa*), a central object of critique for Candrakīrti's Madhyamaka philosophy (*Essence of True Eloquence,* 291–92)

11. Developing a *unique Prāsaṅgika standpoint* on key questions of ontology, epistemology, and soteriology in the wake of rejecting intrinsic existence even at the conventional level

Let me expand a little on numbers 9 and 10, which are interrelated. For Tsongkhapa, Candrakīrti's critique of Bhāviveka's use of formal inference in the context of establishing Nāgārjuna's emptiness is not simply a dispute over a methodological choice. That is to say, it is not just about how best to establish the truth about emptiness. This methodological difference belies a substantive philosophical difference centered on whether a Mādhyamika could subscribe to any notion of objective intrinsic existence, even on the conventional level, that would entail a degree of realism.[24] For Tsongkhapa, when Bhāviveka (and his Svātantrika colleagues) accept Dignāga and

Dharmakīrti's definition of perception as the absence of conceptuality and as having a nonerroneous relation to its objects, which are unique particulars, this indicates admission of some kind of residual realism. There are at least three important contexts that Tsongkhapa cites as evidence that Bhāviveka holds such a view. One is Bhāviveka's assumption that, in formulating a formal inference establishing emptiness by the Mādhyamika, three elements of the syllogism—subject, logical reason, and example—can be established commonly by both parties. Candrakīrti rejects such commonly established factors, while Bhāviveka accepts them; for him, there are such things as subjects, logical reasons, and examples as perceived by ordinary perceptions. The second relates to Bhāviveka's charge of nihilism against the Cittamātra claim, within their "three natures" theory, that the imputed nature lacks existence by virtue of intrinsic characteristics while the other two—dependent nature and perfected nature—exist by virtue of their intrinsic characteristics.[25] The third context relates to Bhāviveka's distinction between veridical conventional truths, such as water, faces, and real elephants, versus nonveridical or distorted conventional truths, such as mirages, mirror reflections, and magical conjurations. For Candrakīrti, no such objective distinction can be made within conventional truth, since the entire world of conventional truth is defined from the deluded perspective of the unenlightened mind. Differentiation within conventional truth can be made only in a limited sense, purely from the everyday-world perspective, and not in terms of objectively real intrinsic existence.[26] What Candrakīrti is rejecting here, according to Tsongkhapa, is not the reality of conventional truth itself; rather, he is refuting any attempt to ground its existence and validity in objective facts that possess intrinsic existence.

In a memorable line in his commentary on Nāgārjuna's *Seventy Stanzas on Emptiness*, in responding to a question raised by an opponent as to why, being equally devoid of intrinsic arising, we can observe dependent origination in relation to ignorance but not in relation to the son of a barren woman, Candrakīrti says, "You should ask this question to the world alone, not to me."[27] In the same text, in rejecting Cittamātra's intrinsically real consciousness but admitting external reality, Candrakīrti states, "I accept the conventions of the world, but as to the status of its contents and cognitions about them, it is the world that knows about them, not me. On your part too, you [Cittamātra] will not be able to negate this fact of the world associated with us [Madhyamaka]."[28] In brief, Candrakīrti seems to be saying that he accepts the reality of conventional truth as the world defines it, including the truths of such things as the laws of cause and effect, noncontradiction, and so on. It is not the task of a Mādhyamika like him, or for that matter any philosopher, to define the criteria for the reality of conventional truth. For him, what philosophers such as Cittamātras, Sautrāntikas, and Bhāviveka are asking with respect to conventional truth—grounding it in some objective facts affirmed by incontrovertible knowledge—is impossible. When it comes to conventional truth, philosophers need to defer to the world, not formulate their own metaphysical views. Tsongkhapa strives to flesh out what such "deferring to the world" might entail, and he proposes three criteria for existence on the conventional level: (1) a given fact is known to, or acknowledged within, a conventional cognition, (2) it is not invalidated by another valid conventional knowledge, and (3) it is also not invalidated by analysis probing the ultimate nature of reality.[29] "Conventional cognition" (*tha snyad pa'i shes pa*), as Tsongkhapa understands it, refers to what Candrakīrti calls "unexamined cognition" (*ma dpyad pa'i shes pa*) and "worldly convention" (*'jig rten pa'i grags pa*). In summarizing his understanding of what is meant by these crucial terms associated with conventional truth, Tsongkhapa writes:

> *Conventional cognitions* are cognitions that operate without analysis, such as those that engage their objects only within the context of how a given phenomenon appears to it, without analyzing in terms such as, "Is this how the thing actually exists, or does it just appear this way to my mind?" These are called unanalyzed perspectives, but it is not the case that they do not engage in any form of inquiry. Given that they operate within the context of how things appear and are known to a worldly or conventional knowledge, they also constitute what is meant by *worldly convention*. And this kind of cognition occurs in everyone, whether or not their minds have been exposed to philosophical systems. Thus, no matter whose mindstream they occur in, they are called *worldly conventions* or *unanalyzed perspectives*.[30]

For Tsongkhapa, "deferring to the world" when it comes to defining conventional truth does not mean looking for the commonest denominator and taking the word of "cowherds" and their like. Nor does it entail a kind of defeatism, throwing one's arms in the air saying, "It is impossible to say." Furthermore, if Candrakīrti is to be taken seriously when he is presenting

the various stages and attributes of the bodhisattva grounds with such diligence, and when he is presenting what he understands to be the heart of wisdom that leads to true freedom, then to leave the issue of validity and truth
of statements pertaining to these presentations simply to the perspectives
of cowherds (no disrespect to cowherds) seems at best naive! Something
like this is what Tsongkhapa has in mind when he says that the unexamined perspective of worldly convention exists not just in common people
but also in reflective philosophers.[31] In brief, he is saying that what is called
worldly convention exists in all of us and relates to our shared intuitions
concerning everyday epistemic practice.[32] In critiquing Svātantrika views
on conventional truth, Tsongkhapa writes: "Those who are at such odds
with the manner in which the world understands the referents of everyday
conventions, even if they say, 'Things exist on the level of worldly conventions,' they do not actually hold such a view. Theirs is merely an utterance."[33]
Tsongkhapa's insistence that even Candrakīrti's Madhyamaka ontology
must be reconcilable with fundamental elements of *pramāṇa* (logic and
epistemology)—rules of inference, principles of logic (such as the laws of
noncontradiction and the excluded middle), facts about human cognition,
and the shared experience of emotions—is premised on the understanding
that their acceptance is indispensable for any coherent account of the world
of conventional truth.

Noted above as element 10 of Tsongkhapa's approach to Madhyamaka, a
key difference between Candrakīrti and other Mādhyamikas like Bhāviveka
is the crucial term *svalakṣaṇa*—literally, "self-characteristic"—a term with
multiple senses in Buddhist sources. Tsongkhapa identifies three distinct
uses of the term: (1) as *defining characteristics*, such as heat being the defining
characteristic of fire, as found in the Abhidharma texts; (2) as *unique particulars* in the context of Dignāga and Dharmakīrti's epistemology, where they
serve as objects of direct perception; unique particulars are distinguished
from *universal properties* in being causally efficacious; and finally, (3) as
intrinsic characteristic, a kind of fixed, defining essence by virtue of which a
given thing is thought to acquire its existence and identity.[34]

In this third sense, intrinsic characteristic becomes equivalent to *intrinsic nature* (*svabhāva*), which is well known as an important object of critique for Nāgārjuna's Madhyamaka. Tsongkhapa suggests that one of the key
differences between Candrakīrti and Bhāviveka is the former's rejection of
intrinsic characteristic and the latter's acceptance of it on the conventional
level. For Madhyamaka, according to Candrakīrti as read by Tsongkhapa,

there can be existence only in the conventional sense and only on the conventional level; there is no ultimate existence, no irreducible, ultimate "primitives," no existence defined by some intrinsic nature or essence. And what constitutes conventional existence is nothing but dependent originations, which are referred to also as *dependent designations* (*rten nas btags pa*). Even emptiness, which is the ultimate truth, is a conventional existent, not an ultimate existent. Though emptiness *is* the ultimate truth, paradoxically, it has no ultimate existence—hence the emptiness of emptiness.

Some present-day scholars seem to suggest that this third sense of the term, *intrinsic characteristic*, is Tsongkhapa's innovation and is not found in Candrakīrti's own writings. They contend that when Candrakīrti is critiquing *svalakṣaṇa*, he has in mind how the term is defined in the Dignāga and Dharmakīrtian sense—namely, as unique particulars—and the sense in which Tsongkhapa is reading "is not present in Candrakīrti."[35] It is perhaps too early to make such unequivocal judgment. No doubt Dignāga's unique particulars are an important object of critique for Candrakīrti when he is refuting *svalakṣaṇa*. There are, however, also numerous passages in Candrakīrti's writings where it would be problematic, to say the least, to read the usage of the term in this *unique particulars* sense. We find phrases like "the *svalakṣaṇa* of conditioned things"[36] or "some Buddhist schools accept *svalakṣaṇa* for conditioned things,"[37] where the term appears as if referring to an attribute or characteristic of things, and "if things endure in the three times through their *svalakṣaṇa*,"[38] and "in that very *Ten Grounds Sutra*, consciousness is stated to be a result of ignorance and volition, not existing by virtue of *svalakṣaṇa*,"[39] where the term is used with the instrumental case, suggesting clearly that what is referred to is akin to a defining essence by virtue of which a given thing might be thought to exist and derive a unique identity. To read these usages in terms of unique particulars would stretch the limits of both readability and philosophical coherence. In any case, the supposition that Tsongkhapa was the first to distinguish the two Madhyamaka subschools by their acceptance or rejection of intrinsic characteristics on the conventional level is unfounded. We have textual evidence to show that Maja Jangchup Tsöndrü, an important student of both Chapa and Patsab, also maintained such a view.[40]

Tsongkhapa's Madhyamaka, because of what some perceive as its innovative and "controversial" interpretations, generated extensive debate in fifteenth-century Tibet. Some, such as Taktsang Lotsāwa, took issue with Tsongkhapa's insistence on the criteria of validity for the facts of conventional truth, accusing him of adhering to a form of realism. Famously, Taktsang leveled against Tsongkhapa "eighteen heavy loads of contradiction."[41] Others critiqued Tsongkhapa's exclusively *via negativa* approach to defining emptiness in terms of nonimplicative negation—its categorical negation of intrinsic existence. They accuse Tsongkhapa of having fallen into the extreme of nihilism.[42] For some, Tsongkhapa's acceptance of the possibility for knowledge of ultimate truth on the ordinary person's stage through inference is tantamount to violating Candrakīrti's important point about the ultimate truth being inaccessible to conventional cognitions. At the same time, some Tibetan authors found Tsongkhapa's reading of Candrakīrti to be too literal when the former rejects, even on the conventional level, reflexive awareness and foundation consciousness—two key concepts of Yogācāra.[43] Tsongkhapa's insistence on a substantive philosophical difference between the two subschools of Madhyamaka was a particular target of his critics. That Candrakīrti himself admits there being substantive philosophical difference between him and other Madhyamaka commentators of Nāgārjuna is evidenced from the following quote from the autocommentary: "Some Mādhyamikas speak of how what the Sautrāntikas assert to be ultimate realities are accepted by Madhyamaka as conventional existents. He who says this fails to understand the true intent of the *Treatise on the Middle Way*."[44] Members of Tsongkhapa's own Geluk school responded to these critiques, which, in turn, generated further critical discussions, with the result that Madhyamaka discourse remained a fertile philosophical enterprise in the Tibetan language for a long time.

What Is at Stake in Getting Madhyamaka's Emptiness Right?

One may wonder why deep thinkers like Nāgārjuna, Candrakīrti, and Tsongkhapa, like so many Indian and Tibetan Buddhist philosophers, made such a fuss about emptiness. For these great Buddhist minds, Madhyamaka philosophy is not a speculative metaphysics competing for acceptance as a worldview. Nor is it a descriptive philosophy attempting to establish a clear description of reality so that humans might build their knowledge upon an incontrovertible foundation. Madhyamaka philosophy is, in the best sense of the word, therapeutic, so that the insights it reveals can cure us of deeply ingrained habits of grasping. So, unsurprisingly, the Madhyamaka philosophical project involves to a large extent a form of deconstruction—revealing, through careful analysis, every concept, every existent, to be ultimately contingent, composite, and relational. This is quite contrary to our naive view of the world, wherein, deeply conditioned by our experience and language and thought structured around things and properties reflected in our language of nouns and adjectives, we instinctively assume that things possess objective existence definable through some kind of essence that establishes their unique existence and identity. It is this deep innate assumption of the intrinsic existence of things, according to Madhyamaka philosophy, that forms the basis for our grasping and subsequent attachment to the people and things in our lives. And this deep innate assumption is the fundamental ignorance (*avidyā*) that is the target for removal by anyone who seeks the true freedom of nirvana. The absence of such intrinsic existence, described as *emptiness*, represents the ultimate truth and therefore constitutes the content of true wisdom that can lead to freedom. There is, according to Madhyamaka thought, simply no other way to liberation. So, for the Mādhyamika, a lot is at stake in getting emptiness right.

For Tsongkhapa, what is required is an active realization of emptiness, one based initially on a reasoned knowledge obtained through careful inquiry. Simply suspending our grasping or remaining nondiscursive without any judgment—as in the single-pointed state of tranquil abiding (*śamatha*)—is not adequate. He takes this to be, in fact, the central message of Kamalaśīla's *Stages of Meditation*, echoed in the following crucial passage from the *King of Meditations Sutra*, an important source scripture for Nāgārjuna:

> Though one pursues meditative concentration,
> if one does not destroy the notion of selfhood,
> afflictions will resurface, and one will be perturbed.
> This is analogous to Udraka's meditative concentration.
>
> But when one probes phenomena and self with discriminative
>   wisdom
> and meditates on what had been analyzed in such manner,
> this then becomes the cause for attaining nirvana.
> No other cause can lead to such a state of peace.[45]

Tsongkhapa's insistence on cultivating the knowledge or insight into emptiness is based on the recognition that our habitual grasping at intrinsic existence is so deeply ingrained that no amount of suspension of discursive thought can undo it. In fact, according to Tsongkhapa, for most of us who have not internalized the knowledge of emptiness, it remains impossible to differentiate, perceptually or cognitively, between the mere existence of things and their assumed intrinsic existence.[46] Furthermore Tsongkhapa tells us that our habitual grasping, fundamental ignorance, is not a case of simple unknowing; it is a case of active "misknowing." This means that only a sustained deconstruction of its object—assumed intrinsic existence—through reasoned analysis combined with meditative internalization of that insight could begin the process of such undoing. More plainly, it requires a prolonged "unlearning" to remove layers and layers of grasping that we take for granted in our normal everyday perception and experience. As we deepen our insight into emptiness, we begin to view our own existence and the world in a manner that resembles our engagement with an illusion, where we are conscious of what we perceive yet we are simultaneously cognizant of its unreality. In this way, our instinct for grasping and attachment comes to be thinned to the point where what Śāntideva says toward the end of his lengthy "Wisdom" chapter will ring true for us:

> When all things are empty in this way,
> what can be obtained, what can be lost?
> Who can be honored by whom?
> Who can be insulted by whom?
>
> From what can there be happiness or misery?
> What is there to be liked or loathed?
> And when examined in reality,
> who is craving and what is craved?[47]

For Tsongkhapa the knowledge of emptiness, like knowledge of any other important truths of existence such as impermanence, first arises at the level of hearsay, meaning it is derived from studying or hearing about it. Gradually, as one's understanding of emptiness is deepened through critical reflection, which involves constantly relating the truth of emptiness to one's personal everyday experience, genuine ascertainment of the truth will at some point arise accompanied by a powerful conviction. This ascertainment (*nges pa*; Skt. *niścaya*) will be tinged also with a sense of wonder at how emptiness and dependent origination arise as one and the same truth, and how emptiness constitutes both the cause and effect. Both Candrakīrti and Tsongkhapa aim to inspire this sense of wonder in us by quoting specifically, at the end of their commentaries on many of the chapters of Nāgārjuna's *Treatise on the Middle Way*, some of the most poetic and memorable verses from the Mahayana sutras that convey what it feels like to experience the world in an illusion-like manner. In any case, at this stage, in Tsongkhapa's language, inferential cognition of emptiness has occurred for the person. This then is the second stage in the progression of one's understanding of emptiness, and a key indication of this would be progressive ebbing in the force of the afflictions, especially attachment and anger.

Now for this knowledge of emptiness to become fully incorporated into one's very being, it must be grounded in the attainment of tranquil abiding focused on emptiness. That is, one combines the tranquil abiding of single-pointed concentration with the cultivation of insight (*vipaśyanā*) into emptiness so that one's realization of emptiness becomes what is called the *union of tranquil abiding and insight*. As one cultivates this union, one eventually reaches a point when, suddenly, one's insight into emptiness acquires the quality of direct experience. Such direct realization of emptiness, characterized by an absence of conceptuality and of subject-object duality, involves a total fusion of the mind with emptiness, "like water poured into water." One who has gained such a state is known as an *ārya*, a noble being.

Even in advanced highest yoga tantra, for Tsongkhapa, emptiness remains the same as that defined by Nāgārjuna and Candrakīrti in terms of the absence of intrinsic existence. There is no further, deeper truth to be revealed in Vajrayāna. Where tantra's profundity comes is in the domain of the knowing subject, not the object emptiness. Unlike in the non-Vajrayāna Madhyamaka sources, tantra emphasizes techniques for generating the insight into emptiness at the level of subtle consciousness, which results in bliss when duality and discursivity are progressively dissolved. Insofar as emptiness itself is concerned, however, tantra has nothing more to add.[48]

So for those who take Tsongkhapa seriously, a lot is at stake—not just philosophy but also ethics and soteriology—in getting one's understanding of emptiness according to Madhyamaka philosophy right. And taking the time and making the effort to deeply engage with our volume, *Illuminating the Intent*, is an effective way to getting emptiness right according to Tsongkhapa.

Technical Note

THE TIBETAN TITLE OF the volume translated here is *Dbu ma la 'jug pa'i rgya cher bshad pa dgongs pa rab gsal*, which means *Illuminating the Intent: An Exposition of Entering the Middle Way*. This edition of Tsongkhapa's work was prepared specifically for *The Library of Tibetan Classics* and its Tibetan equivalent, the *Bod kyi gtsug lag gces btus*. Bracketed numbers embedded in the text refer to page numbers in the critical and annotated Tibetan edition published in New Delhi in modern book format by the Institute of Tibetan Classics (2011, ISBN 978-81-89165-21-5) as volume 19 of the *Bod kyi gtsug lag gces btus* series. In preparing this translation, the Institute of Tibetan Classics edition served as the primary source, with reference also to other editions.

In the Tibetan original, Tsongkhapa's text is structured around eleven chapters refered to as "grounds"—the first to tenth grounds followed by a chapter entitled "Qualities of the Ten Grounds and the Resultant Ground." In this English volume, however, we have provided a slightly different structure, with the entire text divided into three parts preceded by a chapter on the preliminaries: part 1 contains the introductory section and the presentation of the first five grounds, part 2 contains the lengthy sixth ground, and part 3 contains the seventh to the tenth grounds and the resultant ground.

To assist readers who wish to view the hierarchical structure of Tsongkhapa's outline of the text, the entire outline appears as an appendix. In the main body of the text, the individual entries in the outline appear as subheadings subsumed within the twenty-five-chapter structure devised for this English translation.

The titles of all texts referred to in the main body of this book are rendered in English, regardless of whether translations of those texts have been published in English. When those texts are available in translation, we have tried to provide the relevant information in the bibliography.

The conventions for phonetic transcription of Tibetan words are those developed by the Institute of Tibetan Classics and Wisdom Publications. These reflect approximately the pronunciation of words by a modern Central Tibetan; Tibetan speakers from Ladakh, Kham, or Amdo, not to mention Mongolians, might pronounce the words quite differently. Transliterated spellings of the phoneticized Tibetan terms and names used in the text can be found in the table in the appendixes. Sanskrit diacritics are used throughout, except for certain terms that have entered the English language, such as Mahayana, sutra, samsara, and nirvana.

PRONUNCIATION OF TIBETAN PHONETICS

ph and *th* are aspirated *p* and *t*, as in *pet* and *tip*.
ö is similar to the *eu* in the French *seul*.
ü is similar to the *ü* in the German *füllen*.
ai is similar to the *e* in *bet*.
é is similar to the *e* in *prey*.

PRONUNCIATION OF SANSKRIT

Palatal *ś* and retroflex *ṣ* are similar to the English unvoiced *sh*.
c is an unaspirated *ch* similar to the *ch* in *chill*.
The vowel *ṛ* is similar to the American *r* in *pretty*.
ñ is somewhat similar to the nasalized *ny* in *canyon*.
ṅ is similar to the *ng* in *sing* or *anger*.

ILLUMINATING THE INTENT

An Exposition of
Entering the Middle Way

Tsongkhapa Losang Drakpa (1357–1419)

1. Preliminaries

Salutation

[3] With deep respect, I pay homage at the feet of and go for refuge to my revered guru, Mañjuśrī, and to the noble Nāgārjuna and his sons.

You are the treasure of all excellent insights profound and vast,
the unacquainted friend of everyone in this world,
the eyes for beings of the three realms to see the excellent path.
Munīndra [the Buddha], the sun among preachers, sustain us at all times.

You are unrivaled among the myriad conquerors
in proclaiming everywhere the lion's roar,
the perfect and excellent tale of the profound truth.
Guru Mañjuśrī, bless us throughout all times.

You were prophesized to expound as they are
the distilled essence of the mind of the sugatas of three times,
the middle way free of extremes, and the path of dependent origination.
Nāgārjuna, I bow to you from my heart; seize me with your hook of
    compassion.

Through Nāgārjuna's instructions you have reached great heights,
you reveal to other beings what you have yourself seen,
you have gained mastery over the tale revealing the excellent path.
Glorious Āryadeva, I bow at your feet.

You have fulfilled the sacred words of the revered Mañjuśrī,
you have illuminated the ultimate intent of the noble Nāgārjuna,
you have traveled to the state of a perfected knowledge-holder.
Buddhapālita, I bow my head at your feet.

You have revealed in its perfect fullness
the path of the great sage subtle and difficult to fathom,
the way of Nāgārjuna's with its singular traits.
Candrakīrti and Śāntideva, I bow at your feet.

Having properly seen with eyes of untainted intelligence
the well-established system of Nāgārjuna and Āryadeva
in its entirety, with all its unique and essential points
as elucidated by the three great charioteers,[49]
and so that I may remove the stains of erroneous explanations of many
who strove to expound this tradition here in this region,
and also because I have been urged to by others,
I will correctly and extensively present *Entering the Middle Way*.

Preamble

[4] Here I will explain *Entering the Middle Way*, the great treatise that presents without error the meaning of the two aspects of the path—the profound and the vast—in accordance with the *Commentary*.[50] This has four parts: (1) the meaning of the title, (2) the translator's homage, (3) the meaning of the treatise itself, and (4) the concluding matter.

The meaning of the title

In Sanskrit, one of the four great languages that existed in India, the title of this treatise is *Madhyamakāvatāra*. When translated into Tibetan, it is rendered as *Dbu ma la 'jug pa* (*Entering the Middle Way*). Here, the "middle way" that is being entered into is found in the statement "to enter the Middle Way treatise"[51]—namely, the *Treatise on the Middle Way*. This, in turn, should be taken to mean *Fundamental Wisdom*.[52] For instance, when *Fundamental Wisdom* is cited as an authority in the commentary on this text, Candrakīrti frequently writes "in the *Middle Way*." Therefore the term should not be taken to refer to some other treatise on the middle way or some other meaning of the term *middle way*. *Lamp of Wisdom* too, drawing on the etymology of the roots of the term *middle way*, explains that both a treatise on the Middle Way as well as Middle Way philosophy can be referred to as "the Middle Way."[53] So, although only "Middle Way" appears here in the title, it must be understood as referring to the *Treatise on the Middle Way*.

What, then, is the manner in which this treatise enters *Fundamental Wisdom*? Here some assert that in Nāgārjuna's treatise the natures of the conventional and the ultimate truths have not been expounded extensively, whereas here [in this text] these have been presented extensively, so this text "enters into" that treatise.

With respect to the varieties of reasoning for establishing suchness, however, *Fundamental Wisdom* is far more extensive than *Entering the Middle Way*. So I do not see this as a good explanation. As for our own position, this work enters *Fundamental Wisdom* in two ways—it enters from the perspective of the profound aspect of the path and from the perspective of the vast aspect. In relation to the first, the *Commentary* states:

"This tradition is unique," so must the learned ones ascertain.

And also:

Not realizing this, they abandon this profound teaching. Thus to present without error the truth of the treatise, I have composed this work *Entering the Middle Way*.[54]

Candrakīrti states that he composed his *Entering the Middle Way* to show that the meaning of the *Treatise on the Middle Way* as established by him is distinctive compared to other Middle Way proponents and to strengthen the conviction that the meaning of the treatise cannot be explained in conformity with the consciousness-only (*vijñaptimātra*) standpoint. In his *Clear Words* too, Candrakīrti says that, insofar as the nature of dependent designation is concerned, this should be understood from *Entering the Middle Way*.[55] [5] Furthermore, the refutation of the consciousness-only standpoint is not extensive in either *Fundamental Wisdom* or *Clear Words*, but it is entensive here. Therefore ascertaining excellently the meaning of *Fundamental Wisdom* and appreciating these two objectives [(1) providing a unique interpretation of Nāgārjuna's *Fundamental Wisdom* compared to other commentators and (2) offering an extensive refutation of the consciousness-only standpoint] on the basis of that treatise, [these two together] constitute one way in which this text enters the *Middle Way*.

Entering the *Middle Way* from the perspective of the vast aspect of the path is as follows. In accordance with the tradition of the noble Nāgārjuna, abiding in the two vehicles [of Hīnayāna and Mahayana] is not distinguished based on whether one possesses wisdom realizing the utterly profound truth of suchness. Furthermore, although no distinctive features of the vast path of Mahayana besides the dimension of the profound are presented in *Fundamental Wisdom*, that work was composed from the Mahayana standpoint within the division of Mahayana and Hīnayāna. This is because the extensive presentation of the selflessness of phenomena by a profuse variety of reasoning is done only in the Mahayana training, and this is how the presentation is made in *Fundamental Wisdom*. The *Commentary* makes this point very clearly:

> That it presents Mahayana is indeed correct, for it does so to elucidate the selflessness of phenomena. And the intention [of Nāgārjuna] is to explain such selflessness in an extensive manner. In the Śrāvaka Vehicle, the selflessness of phenomena is confined only to brief illustrations.[56]

I will explore this point further in another section below.

Thus the path presented in Nāgārjuna's text should ideally be complemented with the other dimensions of the Mahayana path as found in other instructions of the noble Nāgārjuna. For this reason Candrakīrti presents these supplements in his work: (1) the three factors of the ground of ordinary beings, (2) the ten grounds of the ārya bodhisattvas on the learner's stage, (3) the resultant ground, and (4) on the basis of explaining the sequence of the fifth and the sixth grounds, the cultivation of penetrative insight grounded in tranquil abiding, which is the essence of meditative absorption probing the suchness of the two selflessnesses. Therefore, when contemplating the meaning of *Fundamental Wisdom*, you must do so by bringing to mind these aforementioned points taught in *Entering the Middle Way*. Otherwise, the two aims of composing *Entering the Middle Way* will have been lost. The second manner of entering the *Middle Way* by way of this text, then, is entering the path of *Fundamental Wisdom* from the perspective of the vast aspect of the path.

The translator's homage

I pay homage to the gentle lord Mañjuśrī.

The meaning of these words is easy to understand. [6] Given that this text presents the ultimate Abhidharma and because it principally pertains to the training in wisdom, here the translator pays homage to Mañjuśrī in accord with a time-honored decree.[57]

The meaning of the treatise itself

This has four sections: (1) the salutation: a means of entering into the task of composing the treatise, (2) the actual body of the treatise, (3) the manner in which the treatise was composed, and (4) dedicating the merits of having composed the treatise.[58]

The salutation: A means of entering into the task of composing the treatise

This is twofold: (1) praising great compassion without differentiating its characteristics and (2) paying homage to great compassion by differentiating its characteristics.

Praising great compassion without differentiating its characteristics

The revered Candrakīrti, who for the purpose of entering the middle way wished to compose *Entering the Middle Way*, did not take as his object of salutation śrāvakas and pratyekabuddhas, who have been objects of salutation in other texts. And even in relation to the buddhas and bodhisattvas, it is great compassion—the first perfect cause of buddhahood, characterized by total rescuing of all sentient beings bereft of refuge and caught in the prison of cyclic existence, and the principal cause designated by the name of its effect, the Blessed Mother—that he wished to demonstrate is more worthy of praise.[59] To that end Candrakīrti wrote the two stanzas beginning with the line "Śrāvakas and middle-level buddhas . . ."[60]

This has two sections: (1) how compassion is the principal cause of bodhisattvas and (2) how compassion is also the root of the two other causes of bodhisattvas.

How compassion is the principal cause of bodhisattvas

This has three parts: (1) how śrāvakas and pratyekabuddhas are born from sovereign sages, (2) how buddhas are born from bodhisattvas, and (3) the three principal causes of bodhisattvas.

How *śrāvakas* and *pratyekabuddhas* are born from sovereign sages

Śrāvakas and middle-level buddhas arise from sovereign sages. 1.1a

They listen to perfect instructions from others and, as the fruit of their meditation once they have attained śrāvaka enlightenment, they then enable others to hear that truth; hence they are known as *śrāvakas* ["hearers"]. The manner in which they enable others to hear is found repeatedly in such scriptural statements as "Thus I have completed my task. I will know no lives beyond this one."[61] [7]

Although this etymology of the word *śrāvaka* does not apply to all śrāvakas, such as those in the formless realm, this is not a problem. For a term to be used as a noun in a practical context, it does not have to constitute the explanatory basis for the etymology of that term. For example, the term *lake-born* (*saroruha*) can refer to a lotus born on dry land. Alternatively, the etymology of the Sanskrit term *śrāvaka* can be taken to be "one who proclaims what was heard." By this explanation, śrāvakas are so called because, having heard from the buddhas the path to travel to the highest fruit of buddhahood, they then proclaim it to those who are inclined toward the Mahayana and seek that path. The *White Lotus of the Good Dharma* states:

> Savior, we heard and have become śrāvakas today!
> We will proclaim perfectly the sublime awakening;
> we will utter thoroughly too the word of awakening;
> so we are like those formidable śrāvakas![62]

These two grounds for calling someone a śrāvaka (hearer) constitute for bodhisattvas the basis for their resemblance to śrāvakas, while śrāvakas themselves actually fit the name "one who proclaims what was heard."

Some, because the word "sublime" is not mentioned explicitly in the third line of the above quote, say that the first "awakening" refers to that of the Mahayana while the second one refers to the awakening of the śrāvakas. The understanding of the *Commentary*, however, is to take the first "awakening" as referring to the awakening of the Great Vehicle and the second to the path leading to that awakening.

Some might wonder, "Bodhisattvas also hear the path to buddhahood from the buddhas and proclaim it to other trainees; do they also become śrāvaka disciples?" This is not a problem. Śrāvakas proclaim the [Mahayana] path but do not practice it themselves, not even a facsimile of it. This then is the meaning of this term *śrāvaka*.

With respect to the term *buddha* in **"middle-level buddhas,"** some explain this in accordance with the *Commentary*'s statement, "The suchness of a buddha applies to all three persons,"[63] whereby the term *tattva buddha* ("one who has realized suchness") is explained as applicable to all three categories of persons. This is excellent. As it is stated "*Tattva* refers to 'suchness,' while *buddha* means 'to realize within,'"[64] the realization of suchness is taken to be the meaning of the term *buddha*. In this interpretation, the term describes all three categories of persons. So although the intention here is to say that the term "one who has realized suchness" applies to pratyekabuddhas as well, the term has been rendered in Tibetan simply as "buddhas." But whereas the term *buddha* can be translated as the Completely Enlightened One in general, to do so in the present context would be inappropriate. In any case, since the term *buddha* can also refer to the blossoming of lotus petals or to waking up from sleep, one need not always translate the term as the Completely Enlightened One.

The meaning of "middle-level" is this: Pratyekabuddhas, [8] because of their distinction in having cultivated merit and wisdom for a hundred eons, are superior to the śrāvakas. Since they lack the dual collections of merit and wisdom, the great compassion that extends to all beings at all times, and the complete knowledge of all aspects of phenomena, however, they are inferior to the buddhas. They are thus of the middle level.[65]

Some say that the nature of their superiority to śrāvakas in terms of gnosis is explained in the line "Because they have overcome objective conceptualization."[66] This is incorrect. In this [Candrakīrti's] tradition, both śrāvakas and pratyekabuddhas are understood to possess the realization that all phenomena lack intrinsic existence. Furthermore, the one who makes the assertion above appears to himself uphold this very tenet of Candrakīrti![67] Therefore the *Commentary* describes pratyekabuddhas as superior in their advancement in wisdom, "superior" meaning their ever-enhancing progression on the path. They immerse themselves in the accumulation of merit and wisdom for one hundred eons; śrāvakas, on the other hand, are incapable of sustaining such a prolonged cultivation of the path.

Although the term *collection* may apply to merit and wisdom in general, the primary referent of "collection" here is as stated in the following in the *Clear Words* commentary:

They uphold great awakening by cultivating the perfect truth, and thus the collection is constituted by great compassion and so on.[68]

Here, "collection" applies to those factors that uphold the fruit—unsurpassed awakening—through methods that accomplish it without distortion. Hence the term refers to merit and wisdom that embody this meaning; those not encompassed by this meaning are only ordinary collections. This connotation of the term comes from the etymology of *sambhāra*, which is the Sanskrit word for "collection."

Now because the span of their merit and wisdom is far greater than that of the śrāvakas, even in the desire realm, pratyekabuddhas during their last existence can engender an arhat's gnosis without hearing teachings from a teacher. And given too that it is for their own sake that they become enlightened—that they attain or are attaining the arhat's state—they are called *pratyekabuddhas* ("self-enlightened ones") and also "self-arisen ones."

The term *sage* (*muni*) may generally apply to śrāvaka and pratyekabuddha arhats, but since they are not sovereign among the sages, only buddhas are referred to here by the expression "sovereign sages." Buddhas have attained the highest mastery of truth, which cannot be excelled by śrāvakas, pratyekabuddhas, or even bodhisattvas, and it is the buddhas' sacred words that enable the three persons to master the Dharma. The statement that **from these sovereign sages** the śrāvakas and pratyekabuddhas **are born** means that they are produced by the buddhas. [9]

One might ask, "In what way do sovereign sages produce śrāvakas and pratyekabuddhas?" When a buddha appears in the world, he teaches the profound truth of dependent origination without distortion. Śrāvakas and pratyekabuddhas listen to this, reflect upon the meaning of what they have heard, and meditate on the meaning of what they have reflected upon. Through this process śrāvakas and pratyekabuddhas realize their wishes in precise consonance with their aspirations. In that it's from such sovereign sages the two are born, they are produced by the sovereign sages.

One might wonder, "Many from the śrāvaka lineage realize enlightenment in the very life in which they hear teachings from a buddha, whereas those of pratyekabuddha lineage do not actualize enlightenment in the same lifetime. It must be incorrect to say that they realize their wish based on study, reflection, and meditation on the basis of being taught by a buddha."

This is not a problem. Some among the pratyekabuddha lineage, having gained expertise in the realization of the ultimate truth from listening to a buddha's revelation of dependent origination, may not attain the pratyeka-buddha nirvana in the same life in which they hear the teaching. Just as someone who has accrued a definite karma but does not experience its fruit in the very life in which it was accrued will definitely experience it in some later life, the seeker of the pratyekabuddha state to whom a buddha revealed dependent origination may not attain nirvana in that very life but will defi-nitely attain it in a subsequent life. So the earlier statement that that they realize their wishes on the basis of study, reflection, and meditation was not intended to mean within a single lifetime exclusively. As *Four Hundred Stanzas* states:

> He who knows suchness, even if
> he does not attain nirvana in this life,
> will definitely attain it without effort
> in other lives, just as in the case of karma.[69]

The *Treatise on the Middle Way* too states:

> When the fully awakened ones do not appear
> and the śrāvakas are no more,
> the gnosis of pratyekabuddhas
> spontaneously arises independently.[70]

With regard to the meaning of "If, some say . . ." in the *Commentary*,[71] some assert that this is a response to the following contention: "Since there appear to be some who do not attain the states of śrāvaka and pratyekabuddha even when dependent origination has been revealed to them, the states of śrāvaka and pratyekabuddha would not come to be fully realized through the teach-ing of dependent origination."[72] Others interpret this as a response to the objection "[If enlightenment is the fruit of a buddha's teaching, then] this fruit should come about the moment one has put into practice the meaning of the unborn nature of dependent origination, but this is not the case; [10] in the future too, it will not produce such a fruit."[73] These explanations stem from a failure to understand the context. The context here is how sovereign sages produce pratyekabuddhas, where there is the greater doubt, and it is this doubt that needs to be addressed with special emphasis. This these com-mentators have failed to do.

How buddhas are born from bodhisattvas

Buddhas are born from bodhisattvas. 1.1b

Now, if śrāvakas and pratyekabuddhas are born from sovereign sages from whom do these sovereign sages come about?

The fully awakened **buddhas are born from bodhisattvas.** One might object: "Are not bodhisattvas called 'the Conqueror's children' because they too come into being on the basis of what a buddha revealed to them? Since they are the Conqueror's children, how can it be that the buddhas are born from the bodhisattvas? The father of a son cannot be born to that same son!"

It is true, bodhisattvas are children of the conquerors. Nevertheless, bodhisattvas serve as a cause of buddhas on two grounds. First, bodhisattvas serve as a cause of buddhas through their states of being: *tathāgatahood is the fruit of bodhisattvahood.* In other words, all those who have attained the state of buddhahood have done so on the basis of having first attained the state of the bodhisattva while on the learner's path. Thus it is through being an indirect substantial cause—that of sharing a continuum with a buddha—that a bodhisattva is shown here to be a cause of a buddha.

Second, bodhisattvas serve as a cause of buddhas through enabling them to uphold the perfect truth. For example, one reads in the sutras about how the bodhisattva Mañjuśrī enabled our Teacher and other buddhas to first uphold the awakening mind. This establishes how, through serving as the cooperative condition for the buddhas with whom they do not share the same continuum—the buddhas whose states are objects of attainment of other bodhisattvas—bodhisattvas give birth to the buddhas.

[*Question:*] When the opponent objects, "Since bodhisattvas are the Conqueror's children, it would be correct to say that bodhisattvas are [11] born from conquerors, but to assert the opposite would be illogical," the author himself indicates that he admits [the premise], writing, "It is true, bodhisattvas are children of the conquerors." In that situation, one needs to give reasons why, despite accepting [the premise], there is no contradiction in saying buddhas are born from bodhisattvas. It is insufficient to simply provide reasons proving that buddhas are born from the bodhisattvas. For even if such proofs are presented, the doubt raised earlier would remain unresolved.[74]

[*Answer:*] Such a fault does not arise. The meaning of the root text's statement that buddhas are born from bodhisattvas is this. In the first reason— that on the basis of undertaking the practice of the path, the bodhisattva on the learner's stage attains the fruit of buddhahood—one understands that such a bodhisattva is not the child of the buddha he will become. So how can it be the case that the author is saying "Though this is true" to that. Furthermore, although the bodhisattva who is freshly born from our Teacher's sacred words is a child of the Buddha, it is not the case that the Buddha came to be born from such a bodhisattva. The objection thus trades upon not distinguishing these two different contexts to which the *Commentary* has responded [through differentiation]. So why, if one possesses some intelligence, does one not understand this on the basis of Candrakīrti's own *Commentary*? Be that as it may, it seems that numerous pointless explanations have emerged in response to this question.

Because bodhisattvas are a principal cause of buddhas, for this reason alone the buddhas eulogize the bodhisattvas. This is how one should read. There are four grounds for such eulogizing: (1) It is so because the perfect cause of buddhahood is most profound—it is extremely precious. (2) It is understood that, by offering salutation to the bodhisattva—the cause—one implicitly offers salutation to the resultant buddha as well. (3) Just as when one sees the young sprout, with its main stalk and so on, of a medicinal tree that could produce desired fruits, one nurtures the plant with special care during its sapling stage with its tender leaves, one must cherish with care and nurture with great effort a bodhisattva on the beginner's stage, who represents the sprout that could bring forth the tree of the buddha as a wellspring of relief for all beings. (4) Finally, it is to help sustain those who happen to be in the vicinity when extolments of the bodhisattva are being uttered and have already been placed among the three vehicles to definitely connect them to the Great Vehicle alone. [12]

It says, for example, in the *Heap of Jewels Sutra*:

> Kāśyapa, it is thus. For instance, one pays homage to the new moon but not to the full moon. Likewise, Kāśyapa, those who thoroughly revere me should pay homage to the bodhisattvas but not so to the tathāgatas. Why? It is from the bodhisattvas the tathāgatas emerge, and all the śrāvakas and pratyekabuddhas emerge from the tathāgatas.[75]

The above citation establishes by means of scriptural authority how the buddhas are born from the bodhisattvas, while the two reasons stated earlier establish it through reasoning.

Therefore, the reason no direct salutation is offered to śrāvakas, pratyeka-buddhas, buddhas, and bodhisattvas—famed as objects of salutation elsewhere—is because a salutation is offered here to their root cause. And the reason these four categories of persons are shown, in their respective sequence, in the two lines "Śrāvakas and middle-level buddhas . . ." as causes and effects is to help identify what constitutes their final root cause.

In this light, although it is on the basis of what is taught by the buddhas that the bodhisattvas are born, it is not necessary to explain the line "buddhas are born" in exactly the same manner as the birth of śrāvakas and pratyeka-buddhas. The significance of demonstrating how these two are born from sovereign sages is to show how, when traced to their source, even the roots of these two are connected to compassion. How the root of the bodhisattva connects to compassion is explained separately.

The three principal causes of bodhisattvas

> The compassionate mind and nondual cognition
> as well the awakening mind: these are causes of bodhisattvas. 1.1cd

Now, if śrāvakas and pratyekabuddhas are born from sovereign sages and the sages are born from bodhisattvas, what then are the causes of these bodhisattvas?

The compassionate mind, which will be explained below, the wisdom or **cognition** that realizes **nondual** truth or freedom from the dichotomy of extremes of thingness and no-thingness and so on, **as well as the awakening mind: these** three **are the** primary **causes of bodhisattvas** who are children of the conquerors.

The *Commentary* states that the awakening mind referred to here is as presented in a passage it cites from a sutra. The sutra reads:

> Having realized the suchness of one's own reality, [13] one gener-ates the mind with the thought, "I will help sentient beings real-ize this ultimate nature of things," and this is called *awakening mind*.[76]

This citation focuses on only one aspect of the objective of the awakening mind, and so what is presented here does not complete its definition. Also, one reads in the *Commentary*, "One should definitely generate the mind with the thought, 'I will rescue the entire world from suffering and definitely connect them to buddhahood.'"[77] Here too, because it does not mention awakening itself—the object of attainment—it is only a partial definition. Therefore the *Commentary* clearly states, when showing how the awakening mind arises in dependence on compassion, that such a mind focuses on the object of attainment, awakening itself. It says:

> [The awakening mind] aspires to perfectly attain this buddhahood alone, which is the cause from which emerges both the excellent taste of the ambrosia of sublime Dharma characterized by the cessation of all distorted conceptualizations and the one who embodies true friendship to all beings.[78]

In light of this, the following should be accepted as the full definition of the awakening mind: "It is the wish to attain unsurpassed enlightenment— the object of attainment—for the benefit of all sentient beings, its intended objective." This is how this mind is defined in the *Explanation of the Commentary*[79] as well, which is excellent. There is thus no divergence [with respect to defining the awakening mind] between Candrakīrti's tradition and the one presented in *Ornament of Realizations*.[80]

Understanding these three factors [compassion, nondual awareness, and awakening mind] as being the cause of the bodhisattvas is the tradition of *Precious Garland*, which states the following:

> If one aspires for oneself and for the world
> to attain the unexcelled enlightenment,
> the roots of this are an awakening mind
> as firm as Meru, king of mountains,
> compassion extending in all directions,
> and gnosis not rooted in duality.[81]

Although this citation presents these to be the roots of awakening and does not explicitly state these to be the roots of bodhisattvas, the word *root* has the connotation of being first, and furthermore since the context here is the presentation of the three principal causes of that first stage, from its context one can infer that these three are the principal causes of bodhisattvas. The demonstration of these three factors as being the cause of bodhisattvas [in *Entering the Middle Way*] takes place in the context of asking, if śrāvakas and pratyekabuddhas are born from the buddhas and the buddhas are born from the bodhisattvas, from where do bodhisattvas take birth? Given this, such causes cannot be understood in terms of the explanatory cause of the bodhisattva; rather, they must be understood as the bodhisattva's producing cause.

[*Question*:] Is the bodhisattva for whom these three factors are taken to be the causes at very least a bodhisattva who is on the initial stage of having entered the path? If so, then it is not correct to say the Mahayana awakening mind is his cause, [14] for the moment such a mind is attained, the person is already by definition a bodhisattva. Similarly, positing the gnosis that does not tend toward any of the two extremes as a cause of bodhisattvas is also untenable, because bodhisattvas first generate conventional awakening mind and subsequently engage in the practices of the six perfections. It is only when the bodhisattva is training in the perfection of wisdom that he or she trains in the gnosis not tending toward the two extremes. Now, if you do not take the reference to be the initial-stage bodhisattva, this contradicts the statements describing him as a new moon–like bodhisattva or a bodhisattva that resembles the sprout of a medicinal tree.

[*Reply*:] Since the exact faults you have leveled above will ensue, we do not accept the second option but subscribe to the first. Nonetheless, the fault you have cited earlier will not arise for us because the generation of the awakening mind prior to the bodhisattva stage is understood in terms of the meditative cultivation of the awakening mind; it does not refer to the actual generated mind that has arisen on the basis of such cultivation. For example, just as there is the experience of tasting the bark of the sugarcane and the experience of tasting what is inside the bark, in the same manner, the mere thought "I will attain buddhahood for the benefit of all beings" is only a reflection that follows after the words. This is similar to the tasting of the bark of sugarcane. Although it is called "generating the awakening mind," it is not the actual generated mind. In contrast, the extraordinary experience that has arisen on the basis of training in accordance with the instructions of cultivating awakening mind, an experience that can wonderfully bring about an effect in one's mind, is analogous to tasting the actual sugarcane inside the bark. It is therefore the genuine generation of the awakening mind. With this in mind, the *Invoking the Altruistic Resolve Sutra* states:

Just like the bark, it is but speech.
The real mind is the taste.[82]

As to how, given that the bodhisattvas of higher mental acumen seek the view of suchness first and then generate the awakening mind, the second fault does not arise, this will be explained below.[83]

"Nondual awareness" does not refer here to awareness of the absence of subject-object duality. In the *Commentary* it is explained in terms of wisdom free from the two extremes,[84] which can arise prior to being a bodhisattva, so there is no inconsistency here. Those who interpret this wisdom in terms of the ultimate awakening mind are entirely missing its proper context;[85] the "nondual awareness" here [in the salutation verse] has to be a wisdom that is the cause of the bodhisattva who has entered the initial stage of the path. [15]

How compassion is also the root of the two other causes of bodhisattvas

> As compassion alone is accepted to be
> the seed of the perfect harvest of buddhahood,
> the water that nourishes it, and the fruit that is long a source of
>   enjoyment,
> I will praise compassion at the start of all. 1.2

Since compassion is the root of the awakening mind and of nondual awareness as well, Candrakīrti wrote "As . . ." and so on with the intention of showing how compassion is primary among these three factors.

As compassion alone is crucially important in the beginning to help produce **the perfect harvest of buddhahood**, it is like **the seed**. To **nourish** [the plant] to ever higher states, in the middle, **it is** like **the water**; finally, **as a source of enjoyment** by the trainees for a **long** time, **it is** accepted as resembling **the** ripened **fruit**. Therefore **I**, Candrakīrti, **will praise compassion**, as opposed to śrāvakas, pratyekabuddhas, bodhisattvas, or the other two other causes, **at the start of** composing this treatise.

It is not that compassion is praised at some later point in the text; it is praised here itself by simply showing how it is important at the beginning as well as at the end and in the middle when it comes to producing the fruit of a conqueror. The exclusionary modifier "alone" indicates that, unlike in the analogy of an external crop—where what is crucial in the beginning, at the end, and in the middle are different—in the context here, compassion alone is crucial for the crop of a conqueror at the beginning and at the end, as well as in the middle.

Here is how, like the seed, compassion is crucial at the beginning. Those with great compassion feel pain at the suffering of other sentient beings, so to help protect all suffering-ridden sentient beings, they generate the mind directed toward their welfare and contemplate, "I will rescue all these sentient beings from suffering and definitely join them to the buddhahood." Seeing that this is dependent on attaining buddhahood themselves, they generate the mind focused on awakening with the thought "I will, by all possible means, attain buddhahood for the sake of these beings." Recognizing that such a pledge cannot be fulfilled if one forsakes the altruistic deeds, including nondual wisdom, perfection of generosity, and so on, they then definitely engage in the practice of all the deeds, including especially the cultivation of gnosis. Therefore great compassion is the seed of all the attributes of the buddha. With this understanding, the *Precious Garland* states: [16]

> In the scriptures of the Great Vehicle,
> in which are taught all the practices,
> stainless wisdom, and so on preceded by compassion,
> what sane person would deride such teachings?[86]

The stanza above states how all the essential points of the Mahayana are encompassed within the three practices—(1) the awakening mind preceded by compassion, (2) the bodhisattva deeds in general, which are brought forth by the awakening mind, (3) and, in particular, the practice of wisdom free from the stain of objectification in terms of two extremes.

Here is how, like water, compassion is also crucial in the middle. Even if the seed of compassion produces the sprout of awakening mind at the beginning, if it is not repeatedly moistened with the water of compassion later on, one will fail to gather the vast twofold collections that are the cause for the fruit of buddhahood. One will definitely actualize the nirvana of either a śrāvaka or a pratyekabuddha instead. If, however, it is repeatedly moistened with the water of compassion, one will not end up in that situation.

Here is how, like the ripened fruit, compassion is also crucial at the end. Even if one attains the conqueror's state, if one lacks the ripened fruit of compassion, one will not become a resource that sustains other sentient beings. The proliferation of the uninterrupted lineages of ārya śrāvakas, ārya pratyekabuddhas, and ārya bodhisattvas—one following another in a continuous lineage—will also not come about. If compassion is perpetually present on the resultant ground, only the contrary situation will come about.

Therefore, through explicating the meaning of these four lines [that begin] "As compassion alone is accepted to be," we should gain a firm conviction that these lines demonstrate the following: "If I aspire to follow the Great Vehicle, I must first become moved by the power of compassion, and on that basis, I must then generate the awakening mind from the depth of my heart. Having generated such a mind, I must, without doubt, engage in the bodhisattva deeds in general and, in particular, penetrate the depth of the profound view of emptiness. In this way, I must train in these."

Paying homage to great compassion by differentiating its characteristics

This has two parts: (1) paying homage to compassion that takes sentient beings as its object and (2) paying homage to compassion that takes phenomenal reality and takes no reference as its object.

Paying homage to compassion that takes sentient beings as its object

> First, with the thought "I am," they cling to a self;
> then, with the thought "mine," they become attached to things;
> like buckets on a waterwheel, they turn without control;
> I bow to the compassion that cares for such suffering beings. 1.3

[17] Since the identity view grasping at "I" gives rise to the identity view grasping at "mine," **first**—that is, prior to the identity view manifestly clinging to "mine"—the identity view grasping at "I," assuming **a self** that does not possess intrinsic existence as existing by virtue of an intrinsic nature, manifestly **clings to** the referent of **the thought "I am"** as real. **Then**, in relation **to things** other than the object of "I" grasping—body, eyes, and so on—**with the thought "mine," they become attached**, grasping in terms of "this is mine." Thus, **like buckets on a waterwheel** in motion or spinning in a circle, sentient beings turn in a cycle **without control**, and it is **to the compassion** that **cares for such suffering beings** that **I bow** here. This then is the meaning of paying homage to compassion that takes sentient beings as its object.

In what way do transmigrating beings resemble the perpetual motion

of a waterwheel? Here the two things—sentient beings and the perpetually moving waterwheel—are the basis of comparison: namely, the analogy and what resembles it. Here are six aspects to the analogy—being tied
by a rope and so on—that illustrate the features that are similar [to the
waterwheel]:

1. The first aspect is that this constrained world [of sentient beings]
   is bound very tightly by the ropes of karma and afflictions [like a
   waterwheel bound by ropes]. The pronoun "this" [in the phrase "this
   constrained world"] should be applied to the remaining five characteristics as well.

2. This [world of sentient beings] is propelled by consciousness, which is
   analogous to the operator who sets the waterwheel in motion.

3. It rotates from the depths of the great river of cyclic existence, from
   the peak of existence down to the hell of Avīci, with no interval at all.

4. It travels downward to the lower realms, on its own with no need for
   exertion, while it requires great effort to draw it upward to the higher
   realms.

5. There are three afflicted classes [within the twelve links of dependent
   origination]: (1) the *afflictions* of ignorance, craving, and appropriation, (2) *karma*—namely, volition and becoming—and (3) afflicted
   birth—namely, the seven remaining links. Yet there is no fixed
   sequence to their origination.

6. And, on a daily basis, this world is assailed by the suffering of suffering, the suffering of change, and the suffering of pervasive conditioning. Therefore, this world of transmigrating beings is nothing but a
   condition akin to a perpetually moving waterwheel.

The comparison by means of these six characteristics is drawn not simply
to engender an understanding of how sentient beings wander in cyclic existence. What is it for then? [18] Earlier it was shown that those who aspire to
enter the Great Vehicle must first generate great compassion; however, it was
not explained how compassion comes to be generated—that is, on the basis
of what kind of meditative cultivation? So here it is shown that great compassion is generated through contemplating the way sentient beings wander
without control in the cycle of existence.

"What factor makes us revolve in such perpetual cycle?" It is our utterly
uncalm and undisciplined mind alone that does it. "In what domain and
in what manner do we revolve?" In this domain, from the peak of exis-

tence down to the hell of Avīci, we revolve without any interval when we are not in motion. "Owing to what causes and conditions do we revolve?" It is through karma and the afflictions. Owing to demeritorious karma and its related afflictions we revolve in the lower realms, and due to meritorious and unwavering karma we revolve in the higher realms. We enter the first effortlessly, without needing to strive to take birth there. It is harder [to be born in] the latter, since their causes require cultivation with great effort. This is as mentioned in the *Basis of Discipline*, where the Buddha says that the number of those who migrate from the higher and lower realms on their way to the lower realms are like the number of particles of dust that exist on this great earth, while those migrating from these two realms on their way to the higher realms are like the number of dust particles collected between the tips of his fingers.[87]

Thus we should reflect on the following. During the period of [the activity of] any of the three afflictions [ignorance, craving, and appropriation] of a single cycle of dependent origination, the two other afflicted factors [karma and birth] pertaining to a different cycle of dependent origination can come to operate, and so the continuity never ceases. Furthermore, we are tormented by the three classes of suffering on a daily basis, not just once but constantly, like endless ripples of water.

Now, if someone experiences no effect whatsoever in his mind when he reflects initially on the way he himself wanders in the cycle of existence, there is no way that such a person would experience on the beginner's stage an unbearable concern for others when contemplating their suffering. Therefore, just as explained in *Commentary on the Four Hundred Stanzas*, one must first contemplate suffering in relation to one's own self.[88] Then one should contemplate in relation to other sentient beings.

We might ask, "Will merely having contemplated how other sentient beings are tormented by suffering and its origin in the cycle of existence induce great compassion? Or does it require some additional complementary factor?" The fact is, when we see an enemy suffering, far from any unbearable feeling, a sense of joy may even arise in its place. Similarly, when we encounter the suffering of someone who has neither benefited nor harmed us, most of the time, we are unmoved by their plight. This happens because we lack, on our part, a sense of holding them dear. In contrast, when we see the suffering of those we love, close kin, we find this unbearable. In fact, the more profoundly we hold someone dear, it seems, the more intense the feeling of unbearableness. Thus the essential point is how we need to generate a sense of endearment toward other sentient beings, a deep regard for them, cherishing them in our heart. [19]

Now, with respect to the method for generating this sense of endearment, there seem to be two approaches among the learned masters. The first is as explained by Candrakīrti in his *Commentary on the Four Hundred Stanzas*, where he speaks of how, once one has contemplated that all sentient beings have been one's kin—having been one's parents, for instance, since beginningless time—one will have the forbearance to plunge into cyclic existence to help free them.[89] This is also the method taught by the great being Candragomin as well as the learned Kamalaśīla.[90] The second approach is the tradition of glorious Śāntideva. This I have explained elsewhere, so please understand it from there.[91]

Thus those who strive in training in great compassion on the basis of two factors—deeply caring for sentient beings in one's heart and contemplating the manner in which they are tormented within cyclic existence—have made Candrakīrti's unique choice of compassion as the object of salutation serve its purpose. The explanation of one who fails to do this yet harbors the pretension of being versed in this text will resemble the recitation of a parrot. One should understand this point in other contexts of the text as well. As to how this [specific form of compassion] constitutes compassion that takes sentient beings as its object, that will be explained later.[92]

Paying homage to compassion that takes phenomenal reality and takes no reference as its object

> Beings are like reflections of the moon in rippling water;
> seeing them as fleeting and as devoid of intrinsic nature, 1.4ab

To elucidate compassion that takes phenomenal reality as its object and also compassion that takes no reference as its object by means of their distinct objects, the two lines beginning with the word "beings" are presented here. Reading these lines as "I will bow to the one who, **seeing beings** to be subject to moment-by-moment disintegration, **as fleeting like reflections of the moon in rippling water** stirred by wind, becomes compassionate toward them" is to pay homage to compassion that takes phenomenal reality as its object. Similarly, to read these lines as "I will bow down to the one who sees transmigrating beings, though appearing, **as devoid of intrinsic nature**, just like the reflection of moon in water, and becomes compassionate toward them" is to pay homage to compassion that takes no reference as its object.

In the *Commentary*, the word "transmigrating being" is dropped and reads, "I bow to that compassion which . . ." This is done because it is understood that "transmigrating beings" are implicit in the context of the two latter objects.[93]

Now, in an utterly clear pool shimmering with ripples caused by a breeze, reflections of the moon appear, and as one sees the rise and fall of these reflections together with its basis, the water, [20] as if seeing the moon itself in the water, the wise ones—that is, those who are versed in understanding this nature—will perceive, on a moment-by-moment basis, these reflections to be transient and devoid of the reality of being the moon that they appear to be. Just like this example, bodhisattvas under the power of compassion, when they see other sentient beings—beings who reside in the ocean of identity view, an ocean into which flow the vast blue lakes of ignorance replenishing it, an ocean that is being beaten up by the storms of false mental projections—when they see such beings before them, beings who appear like reflections of their own positive and negative karma and upon whom befalls the suffering of conditioned existence of moment-by-moment disintegration, and see these beings as devoid of intrinsic existence, great compassion for them arises [in the bodhisattvas]. As explained above, this also arises on the basis of a sense of endearment toward other sentient beings and from contemplating their plight of wandering in the cycle of existence. Although the identity view is a form of ignorance, ignorance is mentioned here separately [in the *Commentary*], and it refers to the ignorance of grasping at the self-existence of phenomena, which induces the identity view.[94]

The *Commentary* explains that the three types of compassion are to be distinguished not on the basis of their *cognitive aspects* but on the basis of their *focal objects*, for the aspect of all three is the wish for sentient beings to be free of suffering. As such the three are also similar in taking sentient beings as their object of focus. For instance, in the context of the first compassion, the *Commentary* states "having become compassionate for transmigrating beings," while in the contexts of the two latter compassions, it states "fleeting transmigrating beings." So they present the sentient beings to be their object of focus. Therefore compassion that takes phenomenal reality as its object does not merely take sentient beings as its object; it takes as its object sentient beings who are disintegrating on a moment-by-moment basis. Thus it focuses on sentient beings qualified by impermanence in the sense of their momentariness.

Within the awareness that ascertains sentient beings to be disintegrating moment by moment, the apprehension of sentient beings as permanent, unitary, and autonomous ceases. One is then able to ascertain the absence of sentient beings that possess a reality separate from their aggregates, to understand sentient beings to be designated upon the mere collection of aggregates, and to ascertain that sentient beings designated upon mere phenomenal reality like aggregates come to be the object of one's compassion. Thus it is referred to as "taking phenomenal reality as its object." The phrase "impermanent sentient beings" is only an illustration; taking "sentient beings devoid of self-sufficient substantial reality" as an object can also be referred to as "a compassion that takes the phenomenal reality as its object." So when the phrase "taking the phenomenal reality as its object" is used for taking sentient beings merely designated upon their phenomenal reality, [21] the modifier "mere" is left implicit.

Compassion that takes no reference as its object also does not focus merely on sentient beings; it focuses specifically on sentient beings devoid of intrinsic existence. "No reference" means no object of apprehension is clung to through the mind grasping at signs; thus it refers to absence of true existence. In this way, taking sentient beings qualified by lack of true existence as its object is referred to as "compassion that takes no reference as its object" or as "nonreferential compassion," with the modifier "mere" left implicit.

Many Tibetan commentators assert that the second compassion itself perceives sentient beings as disintegrating moment by moment and that the third compassion itself perceives beings as devoid of intrinsic existence. These pronouncements betray a lack of correct understanding of the *focal object* versus the cognitive *aspect* of these compassions. Both of these compassions must be accepted as having a cognitive aspect wishing sentient beings to be free of suffering. If, however, momentariness and absence of intrinsic existence were asserted to be objects of their cognitive aspects, a single instance of compassion would possess—insofar as its held objects are concerned—two dissimilar cognitive aspects. This said, it is the case that to take sentient beings qualified by these two characteristics as a focal object, the person who possesses these two types of compassion within his mental continuum must first ascertain sentient beings to be momentary and devoid of intrinsic existence and, on that basis, have the aspects of these two facts appear to his mind. It is not that the compassion itself needs to perceive the beings in those two terms.

In both the root text and the *Commentary*, the two latter compassions are described as being qualified by the two characteristics referred to above, while the first compassion is described as having sentient beings alone as its object, with no qualification by any of these characteristics. So the phrase "compassion that takes sentient beings as its object" too involves a truncation [of the word "alone"] for the sake of expressive concision.

In view of this, those who assert that the first compassion invariably takes as its object sentient beings characterized as permanent, unitary, and autonomous are saying something untenable. Even with respect to compassion that arises in the hearts of those who have not found the view of selflessness, on many occasions it can arise simply on the basis of merely taking sentient beings as its object [without qualifying it in any terms]. In the case of those who have found the common-level view of selflessness or suchness as well, one finds within their mindstreams many instances of compassion focused on sentient beings without qualifying them in either of the two ways mentioned above. For example, with respect to someone who has eliminated the object of clinging grasping at a vase as permanent and has thus realized it as impermanent, [22] there can still be many instances where he takes the vase as his focal object but does not qualify it as impermanent. And likewise, in the case of those who have not realized the vase to be impermanent, every time they take a vase as their focal object, they need not do so by qualifying it in terms of permanence. The same is true here as well.

These three types of compassion are all—regardless of which of the three focal objects they take—endowed with the cognitive aspect wishing to protect all sentient beings from all forms of suffering. In that sense, they are all very different from the compassion of śrāvakas and pratyekabuddhas. When such a type of compassion is produced, one comes to generate the awakening mind aspiring, "I will, by all means, attain buddhahood for the sake of all sentient beings."

As for the compassion that is the object of salutation here, although it is the initial-stage compassion that is primary, other instances of a bodhisattva's compassion are included within it as well. There is thus no contradiction for the *Commentary* describing in some contexts, such as here, the person who is generating the compassion to be a bodhisattva.[95]

Suppose one asks, "Are all three types of compassion present with respect to the compassion that is the cause of the bodhisattva who has first entered the path?" There are two possibilities. There are those of the Mahayana lineage who follow by way of understanding reality. They first seek the understanding of perfect suchness and then, following their successful establishment of the ultimate truth, generate great compassion for other sentient beings to induce the awakening mind. Then they train in the bodhisattva deeds, which constitute the conduct of a sage. In contrast, there are those of the Mahayana lineage who follow by way of faith. They are not able to realize suchness first. In the wake of generating the awakening mind, they then train in the deeds that include seeking the understanding of perfect truth. *Ornament of the Middle Way*, for instance, states:

> First searching for perfect understanding
> and ascertaining thoroughly the ultimate truth,
> they then generate [great] compassion
> for the world enveloped in destructive views
> and become heroic in working for others.
> These wise ones for whom the mind of awakening flourishes
> engage perfectly in the conduct of the sages,
> which is adorned with wisdom and compassion.
>
> Those who follow by way of perfect faith,
> first generating the mind for full awakening,
> they embrace the conduct of the sages
> and then seek perfect understanding.[96]

So, as stated above, one can identify cases where all three types of compassion are produced prior to entering the path. With someone who has found the view of suchness first too, not only is there no contradiction in his continuing to establish the truth of suchness and training in it even during the period of training in the bodhisattva deeds, that is in fact precisely how he must proceed. [23]

Having made salutation in the above manner, no explicit promise to compose the work follows [here in root text]; but this is not a flaw. It is not unlike Nāgārjuna's *Fundamental Verses on the Middle Way* or his *Sixty Stanzas of Reasoning*. Similarly, in other types of texts, such as the *Friendly Letter*, the promise to compose the text is found but there is no explicit salutation verse. Since it is with the intention to compose *Entering the Middle Way* that the salutation is made, the promise to compose the text is implicitly present as well.

With regard to the means to help others engage with a text, such as the text's purpose and connections,[97] the text's *subject matter* is the twofold profound and vast aspects of the path, and the text's distinctive *purpose* has already been explained.[98] As for its *goal*, the immediate ones include putting into practice what one has understood from the meaning of the treatise up to traversing the first four paths.[99] The ultimate goal of the text is the attainment of the resultant ground of buddhahood. The goal depends upon the purpose, the purpose depends, in turn, on the treatise, and this interrelationship is their *connections*.

Part I: The First Five Grounds

2. General Presentation of the Grounds

The actual body of the treatise

This is twofold: the causal grounds and the resultant ground.

The causal grounds

This has three parts: (1) how to practice the path according to this system in general, (2) practicing on the ordinary person's stage in particular, and (3) presenting the grounds of ārya bodhisattvas.

How to practice the path according to this system in general

"If, in this treatise, the profound and vast paths of the bodhisattva are established by following Nāgārjuna, the question arises as to what kind of stages of the path leading to buddhahood is upheld within the savior Nāgārjuna's system?"

The purpose of establishing the system of the second Buddha Nāgārjuna and so on by means of study and critical reflection is to ensure that we find a deep conviction in the method of practicing the perfect path so that we cannot be led astray by deceptive false paths. Those engaged in study and reflection who—however much they engage in the study of the treatises of the systems of the great charioteers—never find ascertainment with respect to their own personal practice are clearly not approaching their study and reflection in an effective manner. As such, even were they to strive hard in the Great Vehicle, they would fail to extract its value. Therefore, we must strive to understand how to traverse the stages of path. [24]

Although Nāgārjuna explains partial aspects of the path in numerous texts, three treatises present the overall body of the path, both the profound and vast aspects. As for how the *Precious Garland* presents the path, lines such as "the roots of this are an awakening mind" and "all the practices . . . preceded by compassion" were already cited above.[100] In the same work, it says:

> Here, to present in brief the qualities
> of the bodhisattva, they are:
> generosity, morality, forbearance, diligence,
> meditative absorption, wisdom, compassion, and so on.
>
> *Generosity* is the utter giving up of self-interest;
> *morality* refers to working for others' welfare;
> *forbearance* is to relinquish hostility;
> increasing positive deeds is *diligence*;
> *meditative absorption* is one-pointedness with no afflictions;
> *wisdom* is to establish the meaning of truth;
> *compassion* is an intelligence that cares
> for all beings equally as if they're all same.
>
> Generosity brings resources, morality happiness,
> forbearance luster, diligence majesty,
> meditative absorption brings tranquility, and wisdom release,
> and all aims are realized with a compassionate heart.
>
> Through simultaneous perfection of
> all seven of these, without exception,
> one attains lordship of world itself,
> the sphere of inconceivable gnosis.[101]

The text here identifies the six perfections and explains their benefits as well. It also outlines how to train in them with the complimentary factor of compassion. In this way, [Nāgārjuna] teaches us how the awakening mind—the basis of the bodhisattva deeds—comes first and how, through these deeds, we traverse the ten grounds of a bodhisattva.

In his *Praise to the Ultimate Expanse* too, Nāgārjuna speaks of generating the awakening mind on the basis of going for refuge, how the ten perfections enhance the natural sphere (*dhātu*), and he presents the ten bodhisattva grounds as well.[102] In elaborating on this rough summary of the body of the path, Nāgārjuna speaks in his *Compendium of Sutras* about how finding a life of leisure and opportunity as well as finding faith in the teaching are difficult, and how, compared to these, generating of the awakening mind is even more difficult to achieve.[103] He also provides extensive explanations of topics such as how attaining great compassion for sentient beings is difficult, and how, compared to all the things mentioned earlier, it is even more difficult to achieve the elimination of the karmic obscuration borne of injuring a bodhisattva, elimination of the thought disparaging them, elimination of the acts of Māra, and elimination of the deed of abandoning sublime Dharma.[104]

Compared to the first two texts by Nāgārjuna, this work [the *Compendium of Sutras*] is certainly more explicit. Nonetheless, for those stages of the path that remain difficult to comprehend, Śāntideva, the great upholder of master Nāgārjuna's tradition, presents them in both his *Compendium of Training* and *Guide to the Bodhisattva Way*. In particular, Śāntideva presents these elements of the path clearly and most extensively in his *Compendium of Training*, which is effectively a meaning commentary on Nāgārjuna's *Compendium of Sutras*. [25] The text explains, for example, that one first contemplates the benefits of making this human life meaningful on the basis of contemplating how this life of leisure and opportunity is of great value and most difficult to find. Next, by cultivating faith in general and a firm faith based on contemplating the qualities of the Mahayana in particular, one generates the aspirational awakening mind and then upholds the vows of the engaging awakening mind. Next, one gives away, protects, purifies, and enhances one's body, material resources, and the roots of virtue. It is on the basis of such a presentation that Nāgārjuna's *Compendium of Sutras* should be explained.[105]

Āryadeva's *Four Hundred Stanzas* also presents the overall body of the profound and vast aspects of the path. Furthermore, the presentations on the overall structure of the path in condensed formats found in Bhāviveka's *Essence of the Middle Way*, Śāntarakṣita's *Ornament of the Middle Way*, and Kamalaśīla's *Stages of the Meditation* on the middle way are all similar. Therefore, when it comes to the basic framework of the path, all the great upholders of the noble Nāgārjuna's tradition converge. As for a method that would easily bring forth ascertainment of these points, an approach that is most accessible for those on the beginner's stage, I have presented an approach to guiding others on the path that is extremely easy to understand in my *Stages of the Path to Enlightenment*,[106] representing the instruction of glorious Dīpaṃkara, most learned in the systems of the two great charioteers. Thus one can learn from there.

How to practice on the ordinary person's stage in particular

[*Question*:] If this treatise presents systematically both the profound and vast aspects of the bodhisattva path as well as their results—which constitute the object of attainment—then the stages of the path of the ordinary person, which are so important for the bodhisattvas, should have been presented immediately after the salutation. But this is not the case. Instead, the text begins directly with the presentation of the grounds of ārya beings. How could this be right?

[*Reply*:] The stages of the path of the ordinary person were actually presented already in the context of the salutation verse, so it is not explained at this point here. By presenting the three principal causes [compassion, awakening mind, and nondual awareness] on the basis of practicing which one becomes a bodhisattva, it was shown that those who wish to enter the Great Vehicle must first cultivate these three factors. Not only must these three be practiced at the outset, they must also be practiced even after one has become a bodhisattva. Furthermore, given that gnosis not tending to duality is the principal practice of a bodhisattva, we must understand that its inclusion illustrates the need to train in the other bodhisattva practices as well. The following passage from Nāgārjuna's *Compendium of Sutras* relates to this point:

> O bodhisattva, do not apply yourself to the profound nature of things divorced from skillful means. [26] For joining method and wisdom into a union is the perfect practice of bodhisattvas.[107]

You should thus train in the union of method and wisdom. Don't be content with a partial method or wisdom, nor place your confidence in a mere single-pointedness of mind that lacks any distinctive features of method and wisdom.

I notice that some people fail to demarcate what is to be negated using reasoning that probes the nature of suchness, and they end up negating everything. They conflate all forms of thought with grasping at true existence; they relegate the entire presentation of conventional reality to what exists only from another's perspective; they assert that on the resultant stage there is only *dharmakāya*, by which they mean mere suchness devoid of gnosis; and they say that the buddha's form body (*rūpakāya*) exists purely within the subjective experience of spiritual trainees.[108]

For those who make such assertions, all these facts—how, on the basis of scriptural authority and reasoning, śrāvakas and pratyekabuddhas are born from sovereign sages, buddhas are in turn born from bodhisattvas, and so on—will not constitute standpoints of *Entering the Middle Way*. Furthermore, the three factors to be cultivated would be posited merely from the standpoint of others and thus would not represent the Madhyamaka's own perspective. In so doing they would be denigrating all the paths that they themselves need to practice. Moreover, all the statements about how sentient beings, who lack intrinsic existence, revolve in cyclic existence through six factors that parallel features of a waterwheel will become nothing but a series of contradictions. Recognize, therefore, that such proponents are peddling a distorted exposition of the meaning of the treatise, starting right from its salutation verses.

Understanding that even with respect to the training in generosity and so on presented in the context of the grounds of the āryas, there are many deeds that need to be practiced from the start, right from the level of the ordinary person, we should strive to engage in their practice from this very moment.

Presenting the grounds of ārya bodhisattvas

This third outline has three parts: presenting the ten grounds collectively, presenting the individual grounds, and presenting the qualities of the ten grounds.

Presenting the ten grounds collectively

The explanation here of eleven grounds such as the Perfect Joy is based on the following passage in the *Precious Garland*, where a broad presentation of ten or eleven grounds is given:

> Just as eight śrāvaka grounds
> are taught in the Śrāvaka Vehicle,
> ten bodhisattva grounds
> are found in the Great Vehicle.[109] [27]

Candrakīrti also bases his presentation on the *Ten Grounds Sutra*. Here, the characterization of the ten grounds such as Perfect Joy as the "ten awakening minds" must be understood in terms of the ultimate awakening mind.

The *Commentary* characterizes the nature of the ten grounds as the ultimate awakening mind in the following:

> When the uncontaminated gnosis of bodhisattvas, which is sustained by compassion and so on, is divided in terms of its facets, it acquires the name *ground*, for it constitutes the locus of the qualities.[110]

In the above, the ground [i.e., uncontaminated gnosis] is explained through four factors—(1) its nature, (2) what sustains it thoroughly, (3) how it acquires the name *ground*, and (4) the etymology of its name.

Some explain the nature of uncontaminated gnosis using the definition found in the *Treasury of Abhidharma* in terms of "not suitable for enhancing contamination."[111] This suggests a lack of understanding of the unique meaning of what it means to be uncontaminated according to this system [of Candrakīrti]. Our own position is this: "What is contaminated is tainted either by ignorance grasping at true existence or by the imprints of such ignorance. The gnosis free of such a taint is uncontaminated." This is as stated in Candrakīrti's *Clear Words*:

> From the perspective of the nature that is the object of uncontaminated gnosis free of the obscuring cataract of ignorance, [things do not exist].[112]

Until the attainment of the buddha's ground, the only mental state not tainted by imprints of ignorance is the nonconceptual gnosis of an ārya in meditative equipoise. Such gnosis comes about only intermittently, for when āryas rise from their meditative equipoise, their mental states are once again tainted by the imprints of ignorance. The taint of ignorance exists up until the seventh ground. The stain of ignorance itself disappears for those on the eighth ground and up as well as for the two types of arhats, since the pollutant ignorance has ceased, but they still possess taints in the form of residual imprints of ignorance. Again, when the *Commentary* refers to the first ground as "that which bears the name of nondual wisdom,"[113] it's saying that the gnosis is free of dualistically perceiving subject and object as separate from each other. It is not referring merely to a gnosis free of the two extremes.[114]

This master, on numerous occasions in his writings, speaks of "wisdom and gnosis free of the cataract of ignorance." Therefore, when those who take ignorance and its imprints to be universal properties of awareness assert that when these two [ignorance and its imprints] cease, gnosis too becomes no more, and maintain that such is the standpoint of this master, they are in fact committing serious denigration [of the master]. For this is similar to the view of the non-Buddhist Mīmāṃsakas, who maintain that when the pollutants are exhausted, the mind too comes to cease. The claim that there is no gnosis during an ārya's meditative equipoise is also similar to that view. [28] In the *Precious Garland* too it states:

> Therefore one becomes free by seeing thus.
> "By what means does one see?"[115]
> Conventionally, I say "by the mind."[116]

Here, in response to the question "Through what kind of subjective act does one perceive suchness directly?" it is stated that the mind directly perceives suchness on the conventional level. Also the *Praise to the Ultimate Expanse* states:

> It is just as body armor is cleansed by fire,
> for when armor tainted by all kinds of stains
> is placed in a blazing fire,
> its stains are burned but not the armor.

> Likewise with this luminous mind
> ridden with stains born of desire—
> the fire of gnosis burns the stains
> but not the luminous mind itself.[117]

The above states that, just as when chain-mail armor is placed in a fire, the fire burns off the stains but not the armor itself, likewise, when the stains of the mind are burned off by the fire of wisdom, only the stains are burned; the luminous mind is not incinerated.

The gnosis of meditative equipoise of ārya bodhisattvas and the gnosis of meditative equipoise of ārya śrāvakas and pratyekabuddhas are equal when it comes to realizing the ultimate nature of things directly, without any taint from the imprints of ignorance. The reason one type of gnosis is defined as an ārya bodhisattva ground while the other is not is owing to whether one has come under the sway of great compassion and whether one is endowed with the power of the twelve hundred sets of qualities. Furthermore, as mentioned earlier, there is a tremendous difference between them in terms of whether, during the paths of accumulation and path of preparation, one has enhanced one's intelligence in relation to the truth of the two types of selflessness through employing limitless forms of reasoning.

The phrase [from the *Commentary* cited above] "when . . . divided in terms of its facets" means that it is one and the same uncontaminated gnosis—which is the whole—that is being differentiated in terms of stages, with earlier and latter parts becoming the individual facets. These are referred to as *grounds* because they serve as the locus, or basis, for the bodhisattva's qualities. They resemble the ground in this sense, and hence the epithet "ground." These statements indicate that all ten ultimate grounds are to be posited on the basis of nonconceptual gnosis alone.

Although they are all equal in being nonconceptual gnosis, the manner in which the grounds such as Perfect Joy are defined as distinct grounds is by means of the following four features:

1. The first distinctive feature arises on the basis of progressive increment in the number of qualities, such that there exists the set of twelve qualities in hundredfold on the first ground, the set of twelve in thousandfold on the second, and so on; these will be described below.

2. The second distinctive feature pertains to the ever-increasing enhancement of excellent power. Although some describe this in terms of the shaking of a hundred realms, a thousand realms, and so on, this ability is included in the increment of the number of qualities.[118] [29] It thus appears to pertain instead to the ever-increasing power of the individual grounds—their power to cleanse pollutants and traverse the path.

3. The third pertains to the feature of excellence with respect to the perfections—excellence in the perfection of generosity on the first ground, excellence in the perfection of morality on the second ground, and so on.

4. The fourth distinctive feature pertains to the ever-enhancing fruitional effects. This might mean, on the first ground, being born as a monarch that reigns over the earth; on the second ground, being born as a monarch that reigns over the four continents; and so on.

Thus, with respect to the nonconceptual gnosis of the individual grounds, given the great variety in their potency, such as in the number of qualities they possess, these grounds are defined as distinct. Nevertheless, since the qualities in the intervals between meditative equipoise of individual grounds must also be included as part of these respective grounds, these grounds should not be defined by their meditative equipoise alone. It is in this manner the individual grounds must be distinguished, even though these ultimate grounds do not differ whatsoever in their object or aspect of cognition. The *Ten Grounds Sutra* states:

> Just as wise men cannot speak of or see
> the traces of birds soaring across the sky,
> the same is true of the grounds of the Conqueror's children.
> And if one cannot speak of them, how can one hear of them?[119]

Although birds soar through the empty skies, the wise people of the world cannot describe in words the traces of these birds; nor can they perceive such traces with their mind. Likewise, although the ultimate grounds, analogous to the birds, soar across the space-like ultimate nature of things, āryas themselves cannot express how these grounds are traversed exactly the way they experience it, and so those who are listening to it certainly cannot hear it exactly as seen. This is stated in the sutra passage above.

3. The First Ground, Perfect Joy

Presenting the individual grounds

This has three parts: (1) explaining the first five grounds, Perfect Joy and so forth, (2) explaining the sixth ground, The Manifest, and (3) explaining the remaining four grounds, Gone Afar and so forth.

Explaining the first five grounds, Perfect Joy and so forth

The first is fivefold: (1) the first ground, Perfect Joy, (2) the second ground, The Stainless, (3) the third ground, The Luminous, (4) the fourth ground, The Radiant, and (5) the fifth ground, Hard to Conquer.

The first ground, Perfect Joy

This has three parts: (1) a brief definition of the ground, the basis, (2) an extensive presentation of the qualities, the attributes, and (3) a conclusion stating the qualities of the ground. [30]

A brief definition of the ground, the basis

> The bodhisattva's mind falls under compassion's sway,
> yearning to set free every transmigrating being. 1.4cd

> Through intense dedication with Samantabhadra's prayers,
> he abides in Perfect Joy; this is called the first ground. 1.5ab

The bodhisattva on the first ground has seen beings to be devoid of intrinsic existence and has taken this absence of intrinsic existence to qualify his object of compassion in the manner described earlier, and his **mind falls under** great **compassion's sway, yearning to set free every transmigrating**

being. On the ground that bears the name **Perfect Joy, he abides through intense dedication** of all his virtues **with** the bodhisattva **Samantabhadra's prayers.** This ultimate [awakening] mind of the bodhisattva who thoroughly abides in such nondual gnosis, which is illustrated by its fruits such as its number of qualities, **is known** as **the first** supramundane mind.

The countless hundreds of thousands of aspirational prayers made by the bodhisattva on the first ground, such as the ten great aspirational prayers mentioned in the *Ten Grounds Sutra*, are all encompassed in Samantabhadra's prayers. To indicate all aspirational prayers, the root text mentions "Samantabhadra's prayers," which refers to the *Vows of Good Conduct*.[120] In particular, the *Compendium of Training* describes the two stanzas that begin with the words "Just as the heroic Mañjuśrī" in this prayer as the unexcelled dedication.[121]

In the *Commentary*, one finds the following statement:

> Just as one does not assert that a śrāvaka on the path of preparation has entered the first fruit [of stream entry], similarly, even the greatest of the great stage that engages by means of imagination on the bodhisattva path [of preparation]—from where the first ground would imminently spring forth—this too is a ground where the bodhisattva's awakening mind is not yet generated.[122]

What the above citation means is that this is a stage where the ultimate awakening mind has not yet been generated. Generally speaking, however, as I explained above, it is accepted in this [Madhyamaka] tradition that even from a stage lower than this [path of preparation], the mind for unexcelled awakening has already been generated and there are bodhisattvas below this level. Śāntideva's *Compendium of Training*, too, establishes by means of numerous sutra citations the presence of the awakening mind in ordinary beings. So those who assert that such beings are not actual but only mere facsimiles of bodhisattvas are engaging in false explanations.

Here one might contend, "The *Compendium of Abhidharma* describes the stage of entry to the fruit of stream entry as the point when, on the śrāvaka path of preparation, a single sitting would lead to the attainment of the first fruition.[123] So the analogy you have cited above [about the śrāvaka path] does not hold."

Vasubandhu's *Treasury of Abhidharma* states that the stage of entry to stream entry is attained on the ārya level, whereas the *Compendium of*

Abhidharma presents it differently, as cited above. [31] Of these two divergent positions, this master [Candrakīrti] accords with the *Treasury of Abhidharma*. He also accords with what is described in the *Compendium of Sutras* as follows. Compared to someone offering, on a daily basis, heavenly nourishment endowed with hundredfold flavor and heavenly garments to trainees following by way of faith as numerous as the atoms in the entire universe, a person offering a single meal for a single day to a trainee following by way of reality generates incalculable and far greater merit. Again, compared to someone making similar offerings to trainees following by way of reality as numerous as the followers of faith in the preceding example, another person who offers a single meal for a single day to a person on the eighth stage generates incalculable and far greater merit.[124] These two types of trainees are clearly on the path of accumulation and path of preparation [and not on the ārya level].

An extensive presentation of the qualities, the attributes

This has three parts: (1) the qualities that beautify the bodhisattva's own mental continuum, (2) the qualities that outshine others' mental continua, and (3) the quality that comes to be superior on the first ground.

The qualities that beautify the bodhisattva's own mental continuum

This has two parts: (1) describing the individual qualities separately and (2) presenting the qualities together in a summary.

Describing the individual qualities separately

The first has three parts: (1) the quality of obtaining a meaningful title, (2) four qualities, such as being born in the lineage, and (3) three qualities, such as stepping on to the higher grounds.

The quality of obtaining a meaningful title

> From that point on, having attained this ground,
> he is hailed by the name *bodhisattva* alone. 1.5cd

From that point on, the bodhisattva **having entered this** first **ground** has attained the ultimate [awakening] mind. At this time when he has transcended the stage of ordinary person, **he is hailed by the name** *ultimate bodhisattva* **alone.** He should no longer be referred to by characterizations not consonant with this title, for he is, by then, an ārya bodhisattva.

The *Commentary* cites the *Cloud of Jewels Sutra* where it states that someone on the great stage of supreme mundane dharma on the path of preparation has not attained the ultimate bodhisattva ground,[125] so from this we can understand that the title *bodhisattva* being designated here is in the sense of a specific meaning. The *Perfection of Wisdom in Twenty-Five Thousand Lines* states:

> How does one understand this? Regarding things that have not yet come into being, those that have not perfectly come into being, and those that have ceased, [32] they relate to these not in a manner imputed by childish ordinary beings nor in a manner obtained by childish ordinary beings. Therefore they are called *bodhisattvas.*[126]

What the above conveys indirectly is that bodhisattvas find the suchness of these phenomena, just as in the manner found by the āryas. Here too the intended referent is ultimate bodhisattvas. This sutra passage is not suggesting there are no genuine bodhisattvas on the stages of ordinary beings.

Four qualities, such as being born in the lineage

> He is born into the lineage of the tathāgatas as well;
> he has utterly purged the three binding factors.
> Such a bodhisattva upholds the state of supreme joy
> and has the power to shake a hundred worlds. 1.6

Furthermore, this bodhisattva who abides on the first ground, because he has gone well beyond all the grounds of an ordinary person as well as those of śrāvakas and pratyekabuddhas, and because the path that is certain to lead to the ground of buddhahood has arisen within his mental continuum, **is born into the lineage of the tathāgatas as well.** No longer embarking on other paths, his lineage is confirmed within his own path. Since on the first ground he directly perceives the selflessness of persons—that the person lacks existence by virtue of its own characteristic—**he has utterly purged the three binding factors:** (1) the identity view, (2) the tendency (*anuśaya*) to doubt, and (3) the grasping at false views as supreme and at inferior discipline and conduct as superior; that is, that they will no longer arise for him. This indicates that their seeds have been relinquished and that the identity view [referred to here] is the acquired kind, which is an object of elimination on the path of seeing, and not the innate one.

One might ask, "Given that he has rid himself of other negative tendencies as well, tendencies that are objects of elimination by the path of seeing, why are only these three mentioned?"

[*Reply:*] There appear to be two opinions on the interpretation of the intent of this statement from the sutra. Of these two, the better one is the one presented in the *Treasury of Abhidharma* where it says:

> Not wanting to go, choosing a wrong path,
> and harboring doubts about the path—
> these obstruct the journey to liberation;
> therefore these three are stated.[127]

For someone who wishes to travel to another place, for example, there are three main obstacles—not wanting to go, choosing the wrong road, and harboring doubts about one's road. The journey to liberation, similarly, [33] has three principal obstacles. Due to the first [identity view], one comes to fear liberation and does not want to travel there. Due to the third [grasping at false views and false morality as superior], one relies on contrary paths and chooses the wrong path. Due to the second [afflicted doubt], one harbors doubt about one's path. Therefore these three were listed.

This bodhisattva on the first ground, having entered a confirmed lineage as described above, obtains the qualities that result from this and becomes free from the faults that are eliminated by this ground. As such, a unique joy arises within him. And because he experiences abundance of perfect joy, **such a bodhisattva upholds the state** that constitutes **supreme joy.** Possessing extraordinary perfect joy, this ground is known also as Perfect Joy. [On this ground] **he has the power to shake a hundred** different **worlds.**

Three qualities, such as stepping on to the higher grounds

> Stepping on from one ground to another, he travels perfectly to the
> higher ones.
> At that point the paths to all lower realms are blocked for him;
> at that point all the grounds of ordinary persons cease for him. 1.7abc

Rejoicing greatly in **stepping on from** the first ground to the second ground, the bodhisattva **travels perfectly to the higher grounds**. When the first ground is attained, **at that point**, for this bodhisattva, **the paths to all the lower realms are blocked** or have come to an end.

One might ask, "After attaining the *peak* stage of the path of preparation, isn't it impossible for someone to fall to the lower realms due to karma? If so, why is the ending of the path to the lower realms contingent upon attaining this ground?"

[*Reply*:] The fact that it is impossible to go to the lower realms after attaining the peak stage is not because the seeds that lead to them have been destroyed by their antidotes. Rather, it is because no adequate conditions can converge any more. Here on this first ground, in contrast, this is because their seeds have been destroyed by their antidotes. The *Compendium of Abhidharma* too describes the aggregates and elements of the lower realms as objects to be eliminated by the path of seeing.[128] **At the point** when the bodhisattva attains the first ground, **all the grounds** or states of **ordinary persons cease for him**.

Presenting the qualities together in a summary

His is described clearly in terms akin to the eighth ārya. 1.7d

In brief, **the eighth ārya** being [34]—eighth counting from the top down the four abiding in the fruits and the four entering the fruits—has entered the fruit of stream entry because he has attained the attributes of an ārya and enjoys the qualities of abandonment and realization commensurate with his stage. **Akin** [to this eighth ārya being], this bodhisattva too **is described clearly** as enjoying the qualities of abandonment and realization due to his having attained the first ground.

The qualities that outshine others' mental continua

This has three parts: (1) how, on this ground, śrāvakas and pratyekabuddhas are outshone by means of the bodhisattva's lineage, (2) how, on the seventh ground, śrāvakas and pratyekabuddhas are outshone by means of the bodhisattva's intelligence, and (3) the concluding implications of these statements.

How, on this ground, śrāvakas and pratyekabuddhas are outshone by means of the bodhisattva's lineage

> Even when abiding on the first ground of the mind for full awakening,
> he surpasses those born from the Sage's speech and the
>   pratyekabuddhas
> through the power of his merit, and his merit increases ever more.
>   1.8a–c

Let alone on the second and subsequent grounds of **the mind for full awakening, even when abiding on the first ground, through the power of his merit** of conventional awakening mind and compassion, he surpasses, that is to say outshines, śrāvakas who are **born from the sage's speech and the pratyekabuddhas. And his merit increases ever more,** unlike those two. This then is another distinctive quality of the bodhisattva beyond the qualities mentioned above. In relation to this, the *Liberating Story of Maitreya Sutra* states:

> Child of the lineage, it is like this. The son of a king born not long ago bears the name of royalty, and because of the greatness of his family lineage, he outshines the entire assembly of senior and chief ministers at court. Likewise, the bodhisattva on the beginner's stage who has generated awakening mind not so long ago has been born into the lineage of the sovereigns of Dharma, the tathāgatas. Because of his awakening mind and compassion, he outshines the śrāvakas and pratyekabuddhas who have practiced pure conduct over a long time.[129] [35]
>
> Child of the lineage, it is like this. The newborn offspring of a garuḍa, the king of birds, has qualities—strength of wings, total clarity of vision, and so on—that do not exist in mature birds of all other breeds. Likewise, a bodhisattva who has generated the first ground of the awakening mind and has thus perfectly penetrated the ongoing lineage of the great garuḍa-like tathāgatas has qualities—the powerful wings of his generation of awakening mind aspiring for the omniscient state, a power eclipsing others like the wings of a garuḍa offspring, and the clarity of his vision of utterly pure altruistic intention—that do not exist in śrāvakas

or in all the pratyekabuddhas that have definitely shunned cyclic existence for hundreds or for a thousand eons.[130]

Although the *Explanation of the Commentary* interprets the meaning of these two citations in terms of verbally derived awakening mind,[131] the phrases "on the beginner's stage" and "having generated the mind not long ago" are to be understood in terms of ultimate awakening mind. For instance, it was mentioned above that birth in the lineage of the tathāgatas is from the first ground. In these two sutra citations, apart from the two distinct metaphors, their reference is the same. Furthermore, the meaning of these three lines of the root text (1.8a–c) appears to summarize the content of that cited sutra. As for the "awakening mind of pure altruistic intention," many sources, including the *Ornament of the Mahayana Sutras*,[132] describe this as the awakening mind of the first ground.[133]

"If this is so," one might ask, "do you deny that the conventional awakening mind of a bodhisattva on the ordinary stage outshines śrāvakas and pratyekabuddhas?"

This is indeed not the meaning. For in that very sutra, it says:

> Child of the lineage, it is like this: Even a broken piece of diamond, the most precious stone, still outshines all the amazing ornaments of gold. It does not lose the title "the king of all precious stones," and it can totally relieve poverty. Likewise, O child of the lineage, the diamond that is the mind generated for the omniscient state, though it may lack power, still outshines all the golden ornaments that are the qualities of śrāvakas and pratyekabuddhas; [he who possesses] this does not lose the title of bodhisattva, and such a mind overcomes all the indigence of cyclic existence.[134]

In the *Compendium of Training* the above sutra is cited to substantiate the point that one should not disparage an awakening that is divorced from the bodhisattva deeds,[135] and that it is impossible for someone who has attained the bodhisattva grounds [36] to have an awakening mind divorced from the deeds.

How, on the seventh ground, śrāvakas and pratyekabuddhas are outshone by means of the bodhisattva's intelligence

When at Gone Afar, he will also surpass them by his intelligence. 1.8d

When this bodhisattva on the first ground arrives **at** the ground of **Gone Afar**, in addition to outshining śrāvakas and pratyekabuddhas through his conventional awakening mind, **he will also surpass them** especially **by** the power of **his intelligence**. This is as stated in the *Ten Grounds Sutra*:

> Children of the conquerors, it is like this: The son of a king born into the royal lineage and bearing the name of royalty, because of the king's majesty, outshines the entire assembly of ministers the instant he is born. He does not achieve this through his critical acumen, by the power of his intelligence. However, at the point he reaches maturity, by exercising the power of his intelligence, he totally exceeds the activities of all the ministers. Likewise, O children of conquerors, the bodhisattva, because of the greater power of his altruistic intention, outshines all śrāvakas and pratyekabuddhas the instant he generates the awakening mind. This is not achieved through his critical acumen, by the power of his intelligence. However, the bodhisattva on the seventh ground, since he abides with the greatness of his knowledge of the relevant object, totally exceeds all the works of the śrāvakas and pratyekabuddhas.[136]

Given that the phrase "the instant he generates the awakening mind" is being used here in the context of the first ground, it refers to the awakening mind of pure altruistic intention. So it is only from the ground of Gone Afar that the bodhisattva outshines śrāvakas and pratyekabuddhas through the power of his own intelligence as well. He does not outshine them through the power of his intelligence on the sixth ground and below. The phrase "exceeding all the activities of the śrāvakas and pratyekabuddhas" means the bodhisattva outshines these two categories of beings through his intelligence. That this is so can be understood on the basis of the *Commentary*'s summary statement.

In the explanation of what is meant by the power of intelligence, there is the phrase "he abides with the greatness of his knowledge of the relevant object." This is the greatness of the bodhisattva knowing his relevant object—cessation, [37] which is the perfect endpoint.[137] On this point, (1) some assert that although there is no difference between gnosis of those on the sixth ground and below and that of the seventh with respect to their natures, the former do not possess the capacity to eliminate the obscurations to knowledge, while gnosis of the seventh ground has that capacity. "This," they assert, "makes the difference between outshining and not outshining through intelligence." (2) Some maintain that this difference is because from the seventh ground the bodhisattva is able to enter into meditative concentration through a process of leaping over. (3) Still others claim that the bodhisattva outshines [śrāvakas and pratyekabuddhas] through his intelligence because the gnosis of the seventh ground is manifestly directed toward the irreversible eighth ground.

Of these, the first position is incorrect. For in this tradition [of Candrakīrti] it is maintained that all instances of grasping at self-existence of persons are forms of afflicted ignorance, and to eliminate this ignorance so that it cannot resurface, its seeds must be exhausted as well. Furthermore, since such elimination [of afflictions] is common with the two arhats as well, eliminating the seed of grasping at true existence does not constitute eliminating the obscurations to knowledge. As for obscurations that are in the form of residual imprints—which are distinct from seeds—identified here as "obscurations to knowledge," their elimination does not occur until the eighth ground. Therefore, Candrakīrti's system does not accept the presentation of those schools of thought that maintain that grasping at true existence is an obscuration to knowledge and, on that basis, elaborate nine classes of obscuration to knowledge in terms of their strength (weak, medium, and great), which are eliminated on the path of meditation—on the second ground and up. I will explain more about this point below.[138]

The second position is also incorrect. In lexicons of archaic Tibetan terms, the word for "leaping over" (*thod brgal*) is written also as "jumbled sequence" (*snrel zhi*), which refers to a conflation of sequence. There is no explanatory basis as to why entering into meditative concentrations through such a [leaping-over] process would not be found on the sixth ground and below but would be present only from the seventh ground onward.

The third position is incorrect as well, because the question of why bodhisattvas on the sixth ground and below do not outshine [śrāvakas and pratyekabuddhas] through their realization and why they can do so on the seventh ground is still left unresolved. So this third explanation amounts to citing the subject of an argument as its proof of demonstration!

The *Explanation of the Commentary* states that there is exertion on the seventh ground because there stills exists the thought "I will enter the path." Yet because the bodhisattva does not engage with signs, such as reading or listening to teachings such as the sutras, he has attained the path of signlessness. In contrast, those on the sixth ground and below as well as śrāvakas and pratyekabuddhas lack such signlessness. Thus the bodhisattva outshines [śrāvakas and pratyekabuddhas] through intelligence on the seventh ground.[139]

Be that as it may, I feel that this differentiation has to be associated with the realization of suchness. This too must be made in terms of entering into and rising out of suchness, the perfect endpoint. As will be explained below in the chapter on the seventh ground, it is on this ground and above that the bodhisattva is able to enter into and arise out of cessation, the perfect endpoint within each and every moment of cognition. [38] This is not possible on the lower grounds. This is what my precious teacher says, and it is an excellent explanation.[140] On the paths where one engages suchness by means of imagination, given that in such a meditative concentration on emptiness one's mind and suchness have not fused into a single taste, it is not difficult to enter and rise out of such meditative states within short moments. But on the ārya stage, where one's mind has fused with suchness like water poured into water, this mode of entering into and arising out of emptiness within a short moment is extremely difficult.

You might be wondering, "Why are we discussing how on the seventh ground śrāvakas and pratyekabuddhas are outshone through intelligence when the context here is a description of the qualities of the first ground?"

[*Reply:*] The fault of conflating contexts does not apply. The presentations in this text on the first ground and so on are based on the *Ten Grounds Sutra*, and that sutra clarifies that one abiding on the first ground outshines śrāvakas and pratyekabuddhas through his conventional awakening mind and not through his ultimate awakening mind. Then, to help dispel the qualm "Well then, from what ground does the bodhisattva outshine the others through his realization?" it explains that he would outshine the others through his realization starting from the seventh ground. This statement from the sutra is presented here in [Candrakīrti's] text as well, so you should know that the context is perfectly appropriate.

The concluding implications of these statements

This has three parts: (1) how the *Ten Grounds Sutra* demonstrates that śrā-vakas and pratyekabuddhas possess the realization of phenomena as lacking intrinsic existence, (2) the sources that substantiate this point, and (3) rebutting objections raised against this presentation.

How the Ten Grounds Sutra *demonstrates that śrāvakas and pratyekabuddhas possess the realization of phenomena as lacking intrinsic existence*

This is twofold: (1) explaining clearly the intent of the *Commentary* author and (2) how this is also the standpoint of *Guide to the Bodhisattva Way*.

Explaining clearly the intent of the Commentary *author*

On the basis of this citation from the *Ten Grounds Sutra*, where it states that on the sixth ground and below the bodhisattva cannot outshine śrāvakas and pratyekabuddhas through his realization, it can be clearly determined that śrāvakas and pratyekabuddhas also possess the knowledge that phenomena lack intrinsic existence. Without such wisdom then, like the seers who become free of attachment toward all levels [cyclic existence] except the peak of existence through the mundane path [viewing the realms of existence in terms] of gradations of refinement, śrāvaka and pratyekabuddha arhats too would be outshone through his realization, even by the bodhisattva who has generated the first ground of the ultimate awakening mind. [39] This would be so because śrāvakas and pratyekabuddhas would lack the knowledge that things lack intrinsic existence.

The [*Commentary's*] statement that "Otherwise, like non-Buddhist seers, śrāvakas and pratyekabuddhas would not have eliminated all the afflictions pertaining to the three realms along with their seeds"[141] indicates that if śrāvakas and pratyekabuddhas have not familiarized themselves with emptiness by perfectly realizing it, they will not have destroyed the seeds of afflictions, and their paths will resemble the mundane path that views the realms of existence in comparative terms of fine and coarse.

Furthermore, śrāvakas and pratyekabuddhas, by lacking the realization of suchness, would then objectify the aggregates of form and so on as real, and their minds would continue to be distorted. In that case, their realization of the selflessness of persons would be superficial and incomplete, for they would not have eradicated the mind that perceives the aggregates—the basis for conceiving self or personhood—as real. This suggests that if one has not eradicated the object of apprehension in relation to grasping at the aggregates—the designative bases—as real, one will also have not eradicated the object of apprehension in relation to grasping at the person—the designated attribute—as real. In that case, Candrakīrti's text shows, since one would have not realized the person to be empty of true existence, one then would have also not realized genuine selflessness of persons in its entirety.

The meaning of these points presented above seems especially difficult to comprehend; even those who typically rely on this tradition [of Candrakīrti] and Śāntideva's works appear to have struggled to explain them well. So, to critically examine this issue [of whether śrāvakas and pratyekabuddhas possess the realization of emptiness], I will present here (1) how the doubt arises in the first place and (2) how to resolve it.

[*Question*:] "It is certainly the case that one can and does establish by means of a valid cognition the sixteen characteristics of the four noble truths, such as impermanence and selflessness—the latter here understood in terms of the absence of a substantially existing self-sufficient person that is neither identical with nor separate from the aggregates.[142] When this happens, it will also emerge that the principal trainees of such a path will come to cultivate great familiarity with such understanding of selflessness. And if this can happen, then a direct realization of the selflessness of persons can be established through the reasoning that proves how yogic direct perception is possible.[143] If so, it will then follow that such a *path of seeing* realizing such selflessness can eliminate the acquired afflictions. When this is established, then the path of meditation, wherein the selflessness of persons that has already been directly seen is made familiar, becomes established as well. This means then that such a path can eliminate even the innate afflictions, thus establishing the possibility of the cessation of all contaminant afflictions. In that case, it would follow that even without realizing emptiness, one can eliminate all the afflictions of the three realms together with their seeds. This would be so because the eliminations effected by means of the two paths—the path of seeing and the path of meditation—would have taken place in the manner of, as described above, eliminating [afflictions] through supramundane path. Therefore, even with the path contemplating the sixteen characteristics such as impermanence, [40] all the afflictions can be eliminated."

[*Reply*:] Let me explain it like this. We do not say that, if one has not found the view of suchness, it would be impossible to establish the truth of sixteen characteristics such as impermanence by means of valid cognition, or that the principal trainees of these paths cannot meditate upon them with great effort and, on the basis of such meditation, directly perceive the coarse level of selflessness and achieve familiarity with what they have perceived.

[*Question*:] "What do you say then?"

[*Reply*:] We say the path described thus does not constitute a genuine comprehensive realization of the selflessness of persons. As such, this path is neither the supramundane path of seeing nor the supramundane path of meditation, and therefore it cannot eliminate the seeds of the objects of elimination by either the path of seeing or the path of meditation. Here the tradition [of Candrakīrti] would be to interpret such presentations—those statements about how such paths constitute the paths of seeing and meditation, how they eliminate the objects of relinquishment together with their seeds, how at the end of these two paths one attains the arhat's state, and so on—as provisional teachings. This is analogous to the following example.

One might allow that Cittamātra's negation of indivisible atoms and external objects composed through aggregation of such atoms, as well as its negation of a subject that possesses a substance different from its objects, can be established by means of valid cognition. Furthermore, one might allow that if a trainee tamed by such an approach were to cultivate familiarity with these truths he has perceived over a long period, he could come to have direct insight and that what was seen could be made familiar. However, the statements about how one can traverse the ten bodhisattva grounds as well as the three final stages of the path on that basis—these a Mādhyamika will interpret as provisional. The same is true of the example cited above.

Although one meditates on the sixteen characteristics such as impermanence, it is the realization of selflessness of persons as defined above that is asserted [by the other Buddhist schools] to be the actual path that frees one from the afflictions. The *Compendium of Abhidharma*, for example, explains how it is the focused mentation of selflessness that eliminates the afflictions, while the [fifteen] other characteristics are for helping to thoroughly purify the afflictions.[144] In line with this, the *Exposition of Valid Cognition* states:

> One is freed through the view of emptiness;
> the other contemplations support that.[145]

Misled by the phrase "the view of emptiness" here, even some Indian masters assert that this refers to the view realizing suchness.[146] This is decidedly not the meaning. Here it refers to the view realizing the person as empty of self-sufficient substantial reality. Such a path cannot eliminate the seeds of afflictions, but it can temporarily relieve manifest afflictions. For if we admit, as was stated above, that the path that compares realms of existence in terms of level of refinement—a path shared with non-Buddhists—*can* eliminate manifest afflictions below the peak of existence, then there is no question that the path referred to above can also temporarily relieve manifest afflictions. The afflictions here in the phrase "temporarily relieve manifest afflictions" [41] are the afflictions characterized by objects and aspects as defined in the two Abhidharma systems.[147] In regard to afflictions not mentioned in the Abhidharma systems—such as the grasping at true existence that, in Candrakīrti's tradition, is said to be a form of afflicted ignorance, as well as other afflictions defined from this standpoint consisting both of cognitive and noncognitive forms—even their manifest levels cannot be eliminated [by the path described above]. That said, there is indeed this difference. Although manifest afflictions present on the peak of existence cannot be eliminated by the mundane path that compares realms in terms of their refinement, they can be eliminated through cultivating familiarity with the realization of the coarse selflessness of persons as defined above [in the Abhidharma system].

With these, I have explained clearly the *Commentary*'s statements on how paths divorced from the realization of suchness that are yet claimed to be antidotes against the afflictions are similar to mundane paths that trace the levels of refinement of the realms of existence and how, like those of non-Buddhists, these paths cannot eliminate all the afflictions.[148]

How this is also the standpoint of Guide to the Bodhisattva Way

This standpoint is also maintained by the great bodhisattva Śāntideva. His *Guide to the Bodhisattva Way* poses the following question:

> It's through seeing the truths one is freed;
> what need is there then to see emptiness?[149]

[The questioner is arguing:] "One becomes free from the afflictions through the path seeing the four noble truths and their sixteen characteristics such as impermanence. Therefore it is not necessary to see emptiness in order to eliminate the afflictions." Responding to such an objection, Śāntideva writes:

> For the scriptures state
> that without this path there is no awakening.[150]

Śāntideva states here that, without this path of seeing the emptiness of intrinsic existence, there is no attaining any of the three types of enlightenment. How this is stated in the scriptures is explained by the great commentary on *Guide to the Bodhisattva Way*, which cites the mother [Perfection of Wisdom] sutras that speak of how there is no liberation for those who perceive real entities, and how from stream entry to pratyekabuddhahood past, present, and future, all of these states are attained through the perfection of wisdom alone.[151] So taking the word "awakening" in the second line in the above quote [as some do] to refer only to the unexcelled awakening [of a buddha] is not the meaning.

Then the four lines beginning "Since the true monk is the root of the Dharma"[152] also present how a path that involves a mind infected by objectification through grasping at true existence cannot lead to attainment of nirvana. Next, one reads:

> If one is freed through elimination of the afflictions,
> then it should happen immediately afterward.[153]

Here the line "If one is freed through elimination of the afflictions" presents the opponent's position. The meaning of this line should be explained in the same sense as the line "It's through seeing the truth one is freed"—in terms of the query "If one becomes free from the afflictions through the path seeing the four noble truths and their sixteen characteristics such as impermanence..." [42] This is because the context here is about whether freedom from the afflictions can be attained through the path of the sixteen characteristics such as impermanence alone. That this is so is clear also from the argument in the line "It's through seeing the truths..."[154]

In view of the above, it is definitely incorrect to explain these lines as an approach whereby, while accepting that the afflictions can be eliminated through the path of sixteen characteristics such as impermanence alone, one still maintains that this path cannot bring freedom from all suffering. The correct meaning intended here is this: When those afflictions defined in common with the two śrāvaka schools [Vaibhāṣika and Sautrāntika] temporarily cease to manifest for some practitioners because they generated the path of four noble truths and sixteen characteristics described above, if this were to truly constitute freedom from the afflictions, then such persons should attain total cessation of all contaminations immediately after such a temporary elimination of manifest afflictions. [Such is not the case, however.] This is how the opponent's position is refuted here. That such a consequence cannot be accepted is explained in the following:

> Though they possess no afflictions,
> one sees in them the potency of karma.[155]

Although such practitioners possess no manifest afflictions, because of their karma, a potency to propel future births can still be discerned.

Thus these lines [from *Guide to the Bodhisattva Way*] should be explained in the above way. Some Indian commentaries as well as some Tibetans interpret these lines as follows. Although Maudgalyāyana, the ārya Aṅgulimāla, and the like do not possess afflictions, one can see in them the results of karma accumulated by causing suffering when they were ordinary beings, and thus they do not attain freedom immediately. This interpretation is incorrect. Here, the potency to produce suffering within this lifetime is not the issue, it is the potency of karma to propel future births; there is no true freedom if this has not ceased. This is how the texts should be explained.

Again, one reads:

> Like the meditative attainment of no-perception,
> the mind divorced from emptiness,
> though ceased, will arise again.[156]

If one is divorced from the realization of emptiness, the mind ridden with afflictions may have ceased for a while through practicing other paths, but as they have not been permanently turned away, the afflictions will resurface in a manifest manner. As such the circling in cyclic existence under the power of karma would persist. The statement that there is a temporary stoppage of the afflicted mind is to be understood as explained above—as a temporary elimination of manifest afflictions.

Now, to present the opponent's response to the line, "One sees in them the potency of karma," the text reads:

If one asserts, "It is certain that they've
no craving that leads to appropriation,"[157]

"Since, by that path, the craving that appropriates future births is brought to
an end, it is certain that they do not take future births under the power of
karma." [43] In response to this, Śāntideva writes:

Though this craving may be unafflicted,
might it yet exist like ignorance?[158]

Śāntideva's response here is this: "Just as the opponent accepts there to
be two types of ignorance—one that is an affliction in the sense defined in
the Abhidharma and another type that is not—cannot he also accept, with
respect to craving, one type that is an affliction in the sense defined in the
Abhidharma and another type that is not?" The suggestion here is that there
is a form of craving that is not an affliction in the sense commonly assented
to both by the two śrāvaka schools and by the Mahayana. This does not
mean, however, that such a craving is not accepted to be an affliction in Śāntideva's own tradition. Therefore, the meaning is this: Such beings may have
temporarily eliminated the manifest craving brought about by grasping at a
self of persons as a self-sufficient substantial reality, but they may still possess a craving brought about by the identity view grasping at the person as
existing by way of its own essence. Thus, for those who have eliminated the
manifest levels in the manner described above, when it comes to this latter
identity view and craving, even their manifest levels persist.

Now, insofar as when the manifest afflictions are eliminated the roots
of these afflictions persist, it is the same for both of these two traditions
[Abhidharma and Candrakīrti's]. If no difference were found [between the
two systems] as to the presence or absence of the manifest levels, it would be
pointless to distinguish different types of craving.

Next, the text reads:

Craving is conditioned by feeling,
and feeling is present in them too.[159]

These lines explain why craving will not come to end for one who has eliminated manifest afflictions on the basis of other paths. Without the view
realizing suchness, he will not eliminate the ignorance grasping at the true

existence of feelings, not even to a small degree. In that case, when a pleasurable feeling has arisen in him, why would craving in the form of longing not to be separated from it not arise in him? And when an unpleasant feeling has arisen, why would craving that longs to be separated from it not arise for him? For it is certain that effects will ensue from a cause when all the favorable conditions have gathered and there are no obstacles.

The way we explain how craving in relation to feeling is brought to an end is as presented in *Guide to the Bodhisattva Way*:

> When there is no one who feels
> nor any feelings either,
> at that point, given this situation,
> why would craving not come to an end?[160]

These lines explain how, when one habitually sees that nothing—neither the one who feels nor the feelings themselves—has intrinsic existence, craving will come to an end. These lines also indicate that, if one lacks such a path, there is no reason why all craving would come to an end. The same meaning is conveyed in the *Sixty Stanzas of Reasoning*:

> In those whose mind possesses a locus,
> why would the grave poison of afflictions not arise?[161]

The earlier statement about there being craving because of the presence of feeling was criticized by [44] Chapa and Tsek Wangchuk Sengé. They asserted that this is a not a sound reasoning, for it involves inferring an effect on the basis of the presence of a cause. In this way they refute *Guide to the Bodhisattva Way*.[162] They engaged in such refutation for the following reasons. Between the two schools of thought on whether or not śrāvakas and pratyekabuddhas realize the selflessness of phenomena, the latter standpoint was more prevalent in Tibet, and as such people were more familiar with that tradition, and they have not engaged in a comprehensive study of the scriptural sources and the reasoning of the first school of thought. They have therefore failed to appreciate the finer points of the most profound style of philosophical reasoning [of Candrakīrti]. In this way, they naively attributed faults to those who are highly learned. This is a grave error. Similarly, some Tibetans apparently raised criticisms against Candrakīrti.[163] Here too, these are gratuitous objections leveled without a careful understanding of the opponent's position; they only betray the person's true nature, one that would be a source of deep embarrassment were it to be seen by the learned ones.

Understood thus, the *Explanation of the Commentary*'s assertion that the path of sixteen characteristics, such as impermanence, can eliminate the acquired afflictions but not the innate ones remains incorrect as well.[164] For insofar as temporary cessation of mere manifest afflictions acknowledged commonly by all three vehicles [of śrāvaka, pratyekabuddha, and bodhisattva] is concerned, this is the same for both the acquired as well as the innate. And as for not eliminating their seeds is concerned, this is also the same for both acquired and innate afflictions. The author of the *Explanation* seems to have failed to understand here how to demonstrate that the intentions of Candrakīrti and Śāntideva remain the same.

Now, if one has not realized the aggregates' lack of true existence, one will not realize the person's lack of true existence, in which case one would then not have realized the selflessness of persons. Just as the emptiness of true existence of the aggregates and so on is defined as the *selflessness of phenomena*, the emptiness of true existence of persons must be defined as the *selflessness of persons*. The reason is identical in both contexts. Understood thus, grasping at a true existence of persons must be defined as grasping at the self-existence of persons. Until this is extinguished, afflictions cannot be completely extinguished. And moreover, the grasping at the true existence of persons and phenomena must be characterized as forms of affliction. This exact standpoint must be attributed to the tradition of Śāntideva as well.

The sources that substantiate this point

This has two parts: (1) the sources in the Mahayana sutras and (2) the sources in the treatises and Hīnayāna sutras.

The sources in the Mahayana sutras

The *Discourse for Sthīrādhyāśa*, as cited in the *Clear Words*, says:

> "For example, when the musical spell of a magician is heard, some, seeing a woman conjured by the magician, [45] experience lustful thoughts. His mind driven by desire, he becomes self-conscious among his companions, and feeling embarrassed, he

leaves his seat and walks away. Having thus gone away, if he now engages in contemplating that woman as unattractive, transient, dissatisfying, and empty and devoid of selfhood, O child of the lineage, what would you think of this? Is this person proceeding in the right manner, or is he proceeding in a distorted way?"

"Blessed One, when there is no such woman, the striving of that person who engages in contemplating her as unattractive, transient, dissatisfying, and empty and devoid of selfhood is a distortion."

The Blessed One then responded: "Here too, O child of the lineage, you should view those monks and nuns as well as some male and female lay disciples who engage in contemplation of phenomena that are unborn and unoriginated as unattractive, as transient, as dissatisfying, and as empty and devoid of selfhood to be likewise. I do not say that these foolish people are practicing on the path, for they should be described as proceeding with distortion."[165]

Here, a parallel is drawn between someone grasping at an illusory woman as an actual woman and contemplating her impermanence and so on, on the one hand, and someone grasping at the aggregates to be real and contemplating their being impermanent and so on, on the other. To draw an analogy between the two requires instances where one takes real aggregates as one's object of focus and contemplates their impermanence and so on. Since this is a distorted state of mind, erroneous in relation to its apprehended object, its content is of course not established by valid cognition. However, within the mental continuum of a person who has not yet eradicated the apprehended object of grasping at true existence, there *can* still be numerous instances where he takes the aggregates as his object without qualifying them either as true or false and, on that basis, establishes their impermanence and so on by means of valid cognition, again without qualifying these as either true or false. When one meditates upon these facts as well, similarly, stages of the path [realizing impermanence, and so on] will arise in his mental continuum [unqualified] in a manner described above.

Again, the *Concealing the Concentrations Sutra*, as cited in the *Clear Words*, states:

> Mañjuśrī, as they do not see the noble truths perfectly as they are, sentient beings whose minds have become erroneous through

the four distortions will not transcend this imperfect cycle of existence.[166]

To this, Mañjuśrī responds with the appeal, "O Blessed One, pray reveal to us [46] what is it that if perceived prevents sentient beings from transcending cyclic existence."

Thus, in response to the Buddha's statement that it is through not understanding perfectly the four truths as they are that sentient beings fail to transcend cyclic existence, Mañjuśrī asks, "Do tell us what point and in what manner of perceiving it prevents sentient beings from transcending cyclic existence." The Buddha replies that if one meditates on impermanence and so on with the thoughts "*I* will transcend cyclic existence" and "*I* will attain nirvana," conceptualizing these in terms of clinging to them as real, then the thoughts "*I* have understood suffering," "*I* have eliminated its origins," "*I* have actualized the cessation," and "*I* have cultivated the path" will arise, and he will come to think, "*I* have become an arhat." So when he succeeds in temporarily eliminating manifest afflictions, as discussed earlier, the thought will arise in him that all contaminations have now ceased. However, at the time of his death, when he sees that he is going to take a rebirth after all, he will engender doubt toward the Buddha, and as a consequence of this damaging thought, the sutra states, he will be reborn in the great hells. This refers, of course, to only a few among those who are abiding on such a path; it does not apply to all of them.

Next, when Mañjuśrī inquires, "How does one realize the four noble truths?" he is following up on what was stated earlier—that one must realize the four truths perfectly as they are. In response, the sutra says:

> O Mañjuśrī, he who sees all mental formations as unborn thoroughly recognizes suffering. He who sees all things as not coming into being has eliminated all its origins. He who sees all phenomena as permanently transcending sorrow has actualized cessation. He who sees all phenomena as utterly unborn has cultivated the path.[167]

In this way, the sutra explains how, through this path, free of appropriation, one transcends sorrow. This presents very clearly how it is seeing the four truths as devoid of intrinsic existence that frees one from cyclic existence, and how the path undivorced from grasping at true existence cannot help transcend cyclic existence. It therefore demonstrates how the path of the four truths and their sixteen characteristics such as impermanence alone cannot eliminate the seeds of afflictions and how, to eliminate these, one must meditate on the truth of "the way things really are" on the basis of realizing it.

Now if one fails to distinguish these points properly, one might hold that śrāvakas possess merely the path meditating upon sixteen characteristics such as impermanence and assert that ārya śrāvakas and śrāvaka arhats [47] are not genuine āryas and genuine arhats. In this way, one might accumulate the grave negative karma of denigrating the āryas. And if the one who is uttering such things happens to possess the bodhisattva vow, he will accrue a root infraction as well. The *Compendium of Training*, for example, describes this act as a root infraction:

> "The vehicle of trainees does not
> eliminate attachment and so on": one holds
> and causes others to hold the same.[168]

The *Diamond Cutter Sutra* too clearly states this same point [about śrāvakas realizing emptiness]:

> Subhūti, what do you think of this? Does the stream enterer have the thought "*I* have attained the fruit of stream entry"?
>   Subhūti replied, "O Blessed One, he does not."
>   "Why is this so?"
>   "Blessed One, this is so because he does not enter anywhere. Hence he is called *stream enterer*."[169]

It also says:

> Blessed One, if this stream enterer were to harbor the thought "*I* have attained the fruit of stream entry," this in itself would constitute grasping at self, grasping at sentient being, grasping at life force, and grasping at person.[170]

Similar statements are found in relation to the remaining three abiding in the fruits as well.[171]

The statement "If one grasps at the one who has attained the stream enterer's ground as well as the attained fruit as real and engenders the thought 'I have attained stream entry,' this would constitute grasping at his self-existence" suggests that the grasping at the true existence of the two— the person as well as the fruit—are forms of grasping at self-existence. Of these, the first is a grasping at self-existence of person while the second constitutes a grasping at self-existence of phenomena. The statement that the stream enterer does not apprehend with the thought "I have attained the fruit" on the basis of grasping at true existence is made from the point of view that it is not the case that he has not eradicated the object of apprehension of grasping at true existence. This does not suggest, however, that such a person has no innate grasping at all.[172] On the basis of explanation offered here, one should understand similar statements related to the subsequent [fruits: once-returner, nonreturner, and arhat].

Although some Svātantrika Madhyamaka masters interpret the meaning of this *Diamond Cutter* citation differently, Prajñākaramati quotes this to substantiate the point that in order to journey to śrāvaka and pratyekabuddha enlightenment, one must realize emptiness. This is excellent.[173]

These scriptural citations clearly demonstrate how, if one is divorced from the view of suchness, one will not become free from cyclic existence, and how such a view is essential for gaining freedom from cyclic existence. That śrāvaka and pratyekabuddha arhats are not free from the bondage of cyclic existence is something no learned person would assert, nor is such a viewpoint tenable. Therefore these sutra citations clearly demonstrate that śrāvakas and pratyekabuddhas possess the realization that phenomena lack intrinsic existence. [48] There are many more scriptural sources, such as the great mother sutras and so on. However, fearing excessive length, I have not written about these here.

The sources in the treatises and the Hīnayāna sutras

The *Precious Garland* states:

> So long as there is grasping at the aggregates,
> there is grasping at "I."
> When there is "I"-grasping, there is karma,
> and from this in turn comes birth.

With three avenues, no beginning, end, and middle,
this round of cyclic existence resembles
a ring of fire; thus one causing the other,
beings revolve in this cycle of existence.

Since it is not to be found at all
in both self and others, even in the three times,
grasping at "I" will come to cease;
from this, action and birth [will cease] as well.[174]

The first two lines of this citation indicate how, so long as there is grasping at true existence of the aggregates, the identity view grasping "I am" will emerge from it. In so doing, these lines demonstrate how, for the identity view to cease entirely, grasping at true existence of the aggregates must cease. From this we can discern that even śrāvaka and pratyekabuddha arhats have completely eliminated the grasping at true existence of the aggregates. This being so, unless the object of apprehension of grasping at true existence is eradicated, the object of apprehension of the identity view will not be eradicated. Thus we come to recognize that the selflessness of persons that is accepted commonly by both Hīnayāna and other Mahayana schools negates only a coarse self-existence of persons and that such negation does not constitute the subtle selflessness of persons.

In view of the above, those who maintain that the master Candrakīrti's position on how śrāvakas and pratyekabuddhas realize the selflessness of persons is the same as other schools but assert that he differs from others on the question of whether śrāvakas and pratyekabuddhas realize selflessness of phenomena, they have failed to properly comprehend this master's position. For it is stated in the *Commentary* that there is no realization of selflessness of persons for someone who is divorced from the view of suchness.[175]

The next two lines [from *Precious Garland*] indicate how one accumulates karma because of the presence of the identity view, and how one takes birth in the cycle of existence owing to the force of karma. All of this is stated to address one who has yet to eradicate the object of apprehension of grasping at true existence in relation to the aggregates. The statement is not made from the more general perspective of the mere presence of the identity view in a person. For example, although the identity view persists up until the seventh ground, one no longer takes birth through the power of karma from the first ground onward.

Texts such as those cited above demonstrate how, if one is divorced from meditative cultivation of the view of suchness, one cannot bring about the cessation of the identity view. They thus show that if one possesses only the path of the sixteen characteristics such as impermanence, the afflictions cannot be eliminated. Therefore, to read Candrakīrti as presenting a unique understanding of the selflessness of persons [49] but then leave intact the presentations on the afflictions, including identifying what constitutes the identity view, based on the common-level view of the selflessness of persons, one would be committing a serious error. One would be failing to appreciate thoroughly the uniqueness of Candrakīrti's philosophical system. Now on these points, how can this master, who is sovereign among the learned ones, ever be mistaken? Those who fail to comprehend that Candrakīrti, in fact, establishes the standpoint that śrāvakas and pratyekabuddhas do possess the realization of the selflessness of phenomena, those for whom it does not even cross their mind to inquire whether there is a unique presentation on the afflictions—such supposed followers of Candrakīrti relate to this tradition with their devotion alone. What I have indicated here is only illustrative; there are numerous other points [of uniqueness to the system] that need careful investigation.

"The three avenues" here are the three thoroughly afflicted factors of (1) afflictions, (2) karma, and (3) birth. That there is no beginning, no end, and no middle to these three is because from the afflictions arise karma, from this arise the sufferings, and from the sufferings arise its own subsequent stages as well as further afflictions. Since each produces the other, there is no fixed sequence; in other words, they mutually serve as each other's cause and effect. This dependent origination does not come into being from self, other, or both, and moreover it does not obtain its arising through intrinsic nature in any of the three times, nor is such arising seen in any manner. And owing to this reason [of seeing emptiness of intrinsic arising], the identity view ceases, and in this way one's wandering in the cycle of existence comes to be overturned.

Having established that the aggregates, elements, and so on lack any intrinsic existence, the text explains in its conclusion how it is through having seen the truth of suchness that one transcends sorrow:

> Thus, with this perfect truth,
> knowing that beings lack essence,

like a fire starved of its fuel,
with no basis, nothing to appropriate, one transcends sorrow.[176]

If one contends that this seeing spoken of here describes the view of bodhisattvas alone, this is incorrect. That this is being stated in connection with śrāvakas and pratyekabuddhas is evident from the fact that, immediately following the phrase "one transcends sorrow," the text says:

> The bodhisattva too will see thus
> and definitely aspire for his awakening.
> However, because of his compassion,
> he will take births until his awakening.[177]

The texts of the *Precious Garland* cited in Candrakīrti's *Commentary* appear to be from an early translation that is not very good.

Also, in a sutra taught to śrāvakas to help eliminate their afflictive obscurations, [50] conditioned things are analyzed as lacking intrinsic existence by means of five similes:

> Form is like a mass of foam,
> feelings are like water bubbles,
> perceptions are like mirages,
> mental formations are like plantain trees,
> and consciousness is like an illusion.
> Thus taught Sūryamitra.[178]

Commentary on the Awakening Mind draws a distinction, stating that the Buddha taught śrāvakas the five aggregates while he taught bodhisattvas how forms and so on resemble the five similes such as a mass of foam.[179] The reference there is to those śrāvakas who, for the time being, remain unable to realize suchness. It is not meant to include all śrāvakas. For in this same text, it reads:

> Those who do not understand emptiness
> are not receptive vehicles for liberation;
> such ignorant beings will revolve
> in the prison of existence of the six classes of beings.[180]

When presenting how the absence of intrinsic existence of phenomena is taught in the Hīnayāna scriptures, the *Precious Garland* says:

> In the Great Vehicle nonorigination is taught,
> and in the other "exhaustion"—namely, emptiness.
> Since cessation and nonarising are the same,
> concede [that Mahayana scripture is authentic].[181]

Here, Nāgārjuna states that in the Mahayana sutras, "nonorigination through intrinsic nature" is taught to be emptiness, while when the other—Hīnayāna—sutras teach emptiness, they teach the exhaustion of conditioned things. Since the referents of these two presentations of emptiness are the same, Nāgārjuna is saying, one need not be intolerant of the teaching of emptiness in the Mahayana sutras.

On the matter of how the referents of these two presentations are identical, some explain this as follows. If the followers of the śrāvaka schools were to accept exhaustion with respect to conditioned things, given that exhaustion is not possible if things possess intrinsic existence, then one who accepts exhaustion must also accept, right from the start, the absence of intrinsic existence. Therefore these two are in actual fact identical.[182] This interpretation is totally incorrect. For one could apply the same argument to the Madhyamaka: since intrinsic existence is impossible if it exists, whatever phenomena such as sprouts and so on that Madhyamaka accepts will have to be accepted, right from the start, as empty of intrinsic existence. This could bring the absurd consequence that all phenomena such as sprouts would be identical to emptiness! Similarly, the statement in the *Precious Garland* commentary that "There is no actual difference whatsoever between nonorigination and momentariness"[183] also betrays a misunderstanding of the text's meaning.

In a Hīnayāna sutra cited in the *Commentary on the Sixty Stanzas of Reasoning*, one reads:

> That which is the total elimination of *this* suffering, a definite elimination, a purification, an exhaustion, freedom from attachment, a cessation, well pacified, a dissolution, where no additional suffering is led to, this nonorigination, and nonarising, is peace; this is excellence. It is thus. For *this* is the definite elimination of all the aggregates, it is the extinction of existence, [51] it

is freedom from attachment, it is cessation, and it is the transcendence of sorrow.[184]

In explaining the meaning of this citation, Candrakīrti says, given the usage of the demonstrative "this," the statement from "total elimination" up to "dissolution" is made from the point of view of our present suffering or aggregates alone, while from "no additional suffering is led to" up to "transcendence of sorrow" is made from the perspective of our future suffering.

The thought might occur to some that "*this* suffering or aggregate" here refer to the afflictions, which are specific instantiations of these two factors [suffering and the aggregates]. So a generic ["aggregate"] is being used here to refer to a particular. This explanation too is incorrect. Now, if a generic term cannot be explained in terms of a universal, it then needs to be interpreted in terms of a particular. Here, however, the word can be explained in the sense of a generic term.[185]

To summarize: according to the Buddhist essentialists, since one cannot explain the meaning of the word *exhaustion* in the manner the *Sublime Continuum* says that the afflictions are primordially exhausted[186]—which is that the aggregates are primordially exhausted because they are primordially devoid of arising through their intrinsic nature—one will have to explain *exhaustion* instead as "total elimination through actualizing the path." However, when what is actualized, nirvana, is present, the one who is actualizing it no longer will be; and conversely, when the one who is actualizing it is present, the aggregates will not have ceased, and so no nirvana will have been actualized. Thus one will be unable to explain the meaning of the sutra cited above.

According to us [Madhyamaka], however, *exhaustion* in that sutra is not an exhaustion secured through the application of an antidote. Rather, it can be explained in terms of the statement "It is called *exhaustion* because it is primordially exhausted."[187] Thus we are able to explain the meaning of this sutra well.

In light of the foregoing, the two things that the noble Nāgārjuna spoke of as being the same with respect to their referents are (1) *nirvana* that is the cessation of suffering as presented [in the Hīnayāna sutras] on the basis of defining what constitutes *exhaustion*, and (2) the *cessation* presented [in Mahayana sutras] in terms of the absence of intrinsic arising. This is a point that does not appear to have been understood, so I have explained it here in some detail.

In *Fundamental Wisdom* too it says:

> The Blessed One, who clearly knows
> entities and their absence, has denied
> in the *Advice to Katyāyana*
> both "it exists" and "it does not exist."[188]

This statement too indicates how the rejection of the two extremes has been taught in Hīnayāna sutras. This sutra appears to be in the *Connected Discourses*.[189]

These sources are only a few illustrative examples. There are, for example, numerous other lines in the *Precious Garland* not cited here, and one also finds numerous such statements in Nāgārjuna's *Sixty Stanzas of Reasoning* and in his collection of hymns. [52]

Rebutting objections raised against this presentation

This has two parts: rebutting objections mentioned in the commentary and rebutting objections not mentioned in the commentary.

Rebutting objections mentioned in the commentary

Here, in the *Commentary* it says:

> Some feel that if the selflessness of phenomena is taught in the
> Śrāvaka Vehicle, there would be no point teaching the Great
> Vehicle. I understand their standpoint to be contrary to reason
> and scripture, as revealed below.[190]

Here, the opponent being critiqued is Bhāviveka. For example, Buddha-pālita's commentary on the seventh chapter [of *Fundamental Wisdom*] explains the meaning of the statements in the Hīnayāna sutras about all phenomena being devoid of self-existence in terms of their lack of existence through an essence.[191] Bhāviveka objects to this in his *Lamp of Wisdom*, saying, if this so, it would be pointless to teach Mahayana (the Great Vehicle).[192]

One could ask Bhāviveka: "Are you saying that the Mahayana teaching in general would have no purpose? Or are you saying that the teaching of selflessness of phenomena in the Mahayana would have no purpose?" If it is the first, and if there is a logical entailment here, then the teaching of the Mahayana would be reduced to the teaching of the selflessness of phenomena. There is no such entailment, however, for the Great Vehicle also teaches the following: the bodhisattva grounds, the practice of the perfections such as generosity, aspirational prayers and expansive dedications, great compassion and so on, as well as the great waves of the dual accumulations of merit and wisdom and the most excellent powers of the bodhisattvas, phenomena that are inconceivable by ordinary beings as well as by śrāvakas and pratyekabuddhas. For example, the *Precious Garland* states:

> In the Vehicle of Śrāvakas,
> the bodhisattva's aspirational prayers,
> their deeds, and their dedications are not taught,
> so how can they become bodhisattvas?

> The essential points of the bodhisattva deeds
> are not taught in their sutras;
> they are taught in the Great Vehicle;
> this the learned ones should uphold.[193]

This was stated to dispel the misconception that one could travel to buddhahood on the basis of the path presented in the Hīnayāna baskets alone, that there is no need for another vehicle, the Mahayana. According to Bhāviveka, Nāgārjuna should have said here the following: Given that the selflessness of phenomena is taught in the Great Vehicle, what is taught in the Hīnayāna sutras must be inadequate. But Nāgārjuna instead explains how the Great Vehicle teaches the other dimension, the vast aspect of the path.

Now, if you, Bhāviveka, opt for the second alternative, [53] here too there is no logical entailment. For in the śrāvaka baskets the selflessness of phenomena is taught only briefly, while in the Mahayana the selflessness of phenomena is taught extensively through a multitude of avenues. This is indeed the view of the noble Nāgārjuna. He says, for example, in his *Hymn to the World Transcendent*:

> "Without realizing signlessness,
> there is no liberation," you've declared,

so you taught this signlessness
in its entirety in the Great Vehicle.[194]

The first two lines of this stanza show how, since it is impossible to exhaust the afflictions without realizing signlessness, it is thus impossible to attain liberation without it. The final two lines indicate that signlessness—the selflessness of phenomena—has been taught in its complete form or in its entirety in the Great Vehicle. From this, one discerns that the selflessness of phenomena is not taught in its entirety in the Hīnayāna teachings.

Now one might wonder, "How does the word 'so' [in the above quote] indicate that the selflessness of phenomena is taught in its entirety [in the Great Vehicle]?"

[*Reply:*] Without realizing signlessness one cannot attain liberation, the exhaustion of the afflictions. This means the selflessness of phenomena has to be taught even in the śrāvaka basket. Yet there also has to be a difference between Hīnayāna and Mahayana in this domain. And the line "so you taught this . . ." needs to be explained in terms of the reason-indicating word "so."

These analyses reveal how the objection raised by Bhāviveka in his critique as well as the contrary consequence it generates are flawed with no logical entailment. Therefore, these objections of Bhāviveka are contrary to reason. That they are contrary to scriptures has already been explained numerous times above.

"In that case," one might ask, "what then is the meaning of what this master Candrakīrti says on whether or not the selflessness of phenomena is taught in its entirety in the baskets of Mahayana and Hīnayāna, and on whether or not one meditates on the selflessness of phenomena in its entirety on the paths of both of these vehicles?"

[*Reply:*] Now the point is not at all that the realization that all phenomena lack intrinsic existence is present in the Mahayana practitioner but absent in śrāvakas and pratyekabuddhas, who possess only a partial realization, or that they realize only certain phenomena as devoid of intrinsic existence. For once one has established, by means of valid cognition, the selflessness of phenomena in relation to even a single basis, then when one examines other bases in terms of whether they possess true existence, drawing on the previous reasoning, one will be able to realize others as lacking true existence as well.

Some among those who claim to be proponents of Madhyamaka, while supposedly upholding the tradition wherein the true existence of entities has been negated, assert the emptiness of true existence itself to be truly established. Some others assert that the ultimate nature of things is an affirmative truth, independent, and truly established.[195] Of these two, the first suffers from the flaw of not properly identifying the criteria of true existence, thus negating only a rough approximation of it. The latter standpoint, though casting itself as having negated the true existence of conditioned things, does not appear to have done so through valid cognition; [54] it instead appears constitute a view that denigrates conditioned things. There isn't much left to say [about this view] beyond these points.

To conclude, even when a Mahayana practitioner is establishing the lack of true existence of even a single basis, he does so through limitless varieties of reasoning and proofs, like those found in *Fundamental Wisdom*. In this way, his intelligence comes to be greatly enhanced with respect to suchness. In contrast, the Hīnayāna practitioner establishes suchness by means of valid cognition only on the basis of limited reasoning. Since he does not proceed in a manner commensurate to the former, his enhancement of intelligence with respect to suchness is also not commensurate. Because of this, Candra-kīrti distinguishes between the two in the following: how one employs extensive forms of reasoning while the other a condensed form, and how one engages in a comprehensive meditative practice of selflessness while the other a less comprehensive and incomplete meditative practice of selflessness. Such differences exist because śrāvakas and pratyekabuddhas strive only to eliminate the afflictions, while Mahayana practitioners strive to eliminate the obscurations to knowledge. To achieve this latter objective, one's intelligence must be greatly enhanced by the blossoming of one's wisdom of suchness.

Rebutting objections not mentioned in the commentary

One might ask, "Be that as it may, how should one interpret the following lines from the *Ornament of Realizations*?:

> Because they've shunned concepts of held objects,
> because they've not shunned concepts of apprehending subjects,
> within these two is perfectly encompassed
> the path of the rhinoceros-like."[196]

This states that the pratyekabuddha path can eliminate conceptualizations clinging to true existence in relation to the objects but not in relation to the subject.

"Also, how does one interpret the following, where clinging to the true existence of objects is said to be an obscuration to knowledge?:

> Because they undermine, respectively, the three—
> afflictions, knowable, and the path—there are the purities:
> that of the śrāvaka, the rhinoceros, and the bodhisattva."[197]

[*Reply*:] There are only two senses in which [a pratyekabuddha's supposed] "elimination of clinging to the true existence of external objects" can be defined. One is that, while the existence of external objects is established through valid cognition, their true existence is negated through reasoning, and by meditating on this fact as set forth in Madhyamaka thought, one comes to eliminate clinging to their true existence. Alternatively, as in Cittamātra thought, one negates external objects through reasoning, and then by meditating on this fact, one eliminates grasping at the existence of external objects. Of these two, if it is to be understood in the first sense, this is untenable. For if, while capable of positing external reality in general, one has negated its true existence through a reasoning probing into the truth of its suchness, then on the basis of the force of the previous reasoning, one should be able, the instant one inquires, to realize that subjective cognition also lacks true existence. For example, Āryadeva states:

> He who sees the suchness of one thing
> sees the suchness of all things.[198]

Choosing to understand the meaning in the second sense represents, in fact, the standpoint of the commentarial tradition of masters like Haribhadra. For according to them, the absence of external reality is established by valid cognition. [55]

In general, once the absence of external objects has been established, anyone, no matter how inferior his mental faculty, will affirm quite easily the fact that the perceiving subject does not exist as a separate substance from such purported objects. So the statement [in *Ornament of Realizations*] that pratyekabuddhas have not eliminated clinging to the true existence of the subject should be understood to mean that they still hold consciousness to be truly existent. It is definitely not the case that, from within a set of substantially distinct object and subject, pratyekabuddhas have negated one half while holding the other half to be truly existent. Regarding those who amusedly remark that it is astonishing to see a similarity between the philosophical standpoints of pratyekabuddhas, who propound the true existence of subject, and that of Cittamātra, who propound ultimate reality of nondual consciousness: their laughter only reveals their own ignorance.[199]

Here the *Ornament of Realizations*, when describing the pratyekabuddha path as the Medium Vehicle, distinguishes whether one has eliminated clinging to true existence with respect to objects and subjects. By analyzing these two aspects, such a vehicle is described as superior to that of the śrāvakas and inferior to the Great Vehicle; hence it is the Medium Vehicle. In this view, the persons of the three vehicles—Lesser, Medium, and Great—are characterized respectively as of inferior, middling, and greater mental faculties, a hierarchy of mental faculties posited particularly in relation to realization of no-self. Therefore, the Madhyamaka view, which represents the highest, is correlated with the Great Vehicle; the Cittamātra view is correlated with the Medium Vehicle [of pratyekabuddhas]; and the Lesser Vehicle is correlated with the lowest view—namely, the common-level understanding of selflessness of persons. Though this is how they are defined [in that text], this is not invariably the case. Even from the position that accepts that the view of suchness is present in all three vehicles, it is no contradiction to say there are three levels of mental faculties defined on the basis of whether, for instance, one can penetrate the view of suchness in a swift manner.

Given that *Ornament of Realizations* differentiates the inferiority and superiority [of the pratyekabuddha and bodhisattva vehicles, respectively] on the basis of whether or not clinging to the true existence of the subject is eliminated, the view of selflessness taught in the *Ornament of Realizations* cannot be described as the Cittamātra view, as is the case with the *Ornament of the Mahayana Sutras* and the two *Differentiations*.[200] Even in India there were approaches to reading the *Ornament of Realizations* that interpreted it according to Madhyamaka as well as those interpreting it according to Cittamātra. There thus is a need to say a lot about the reasons for these different interpretations; fearing excessive length, however, I will not write about them here.

The *Ornament of Realizations* also has the following stanza, which indicates that even among śrāvakas and pratyekabuddhas, some possess the realization of the selflessness of phenomena:

Because no differentiations exist in the ultimate expanse,
distinctness of lineages cannot be sustained;
due to particularities of the supported attributes,
distinctions are spoken of in relation to it.[201]

With respect to the term *ultimate expanse* (*dharmadhātu*), *Light on the Perfection of Wisdom in Twenty-Five Thousand Lines* says:

> "Conceptualization" or "thorough conceptualization" refers to manifest clinging to entities and their signs. Since the ultimate expanse is devoid of such conceptualization, understand this to be the absence of attachment itself. This *nonexistence* itself is the *thatness* of all phenomena. Therefore it is stated here that because it is the ultimate expanse itself, which is the cause of the qualities of the āryas, [56] the *naturally abiding lineage* is the basis of meditative cultivation.[202]

Thus *ultimate expanse* is defined in terms of the emptiness of true existence, which is the nonexistence of entities and their signs as grasped at by the attachment clinging to true existence.

Following this explanation, an objection is entertained: "If ultimate expanse is the lineage, all sentient beings would abide in the lineage, for the ultimate expanse resides universally in all."[203] Here, abiding in the lineage is understood in terms of abiding in the lineage in the context of the path.

In response, Vimuktisena writes that, since we speak of *lineage* as that which, when taken as an object, serves as the cause for the qualities of āryas, no such absurd consequence ensues. So it is not the case that the mere presence of ultimate expanse entails abiding in the lineage on the level of the path. Rather the meaning is that, when the path takes suchness as its object and meditates upon it, and when it becomes thereby a special cause for the qualities of the āryas, it [suchness] is then posited to be a special kind of lineage. However, in response to the objection, "Since there is no differentiation in the ultimate expanse, distinctness of the lineages of the three vehicles cannot be sustained," it is explained that distinctness of lineages is spoken of on the basis of distinctness of the paths—the supported attributes—that take the lineage as their object.[204]

Here, "basis" refers to the object of focus and "supported" to that which focuses. Within that which focuses, the two vehicles of śrāvaka and pratyekabuddha are included as well. Now, to take suchness as its object, suchness must be present in the perspective of such cognition; and without negating true existence within the perspective of one's cognition, the emptiness of true existence simply cannot be established in that perspective. If this is not established, ultimate reality will not be established within one's cognition. This in turn needs to be ascertained first in relation to a given basis. And this [above stanza from the *Ornament of Realizations*] indicates how, even among śrāvakas and pratyekabuddhas, there are those who, on the basis of focusing on external and internal objects, perceive their ultimate reality— the absence of true existence. Understood thus, even some pratyekabuddhas have realized the truth of suchness. Therefore it is not the case that pratyeka-buddhas are uniformly incapable of eliminating clinging to true existence of consciousness. [Seen in this way] we also need to distinguish between two kinds of śrāvakas—those who have realized suchness and those who have not. So the *Ornament of Realizations* mentions two kinds of Hīnayāna practitioners. Therefore, when it comes to grasping at the true existence of subject and object as substantially distinct, we must [according to this text] identify two types: one that constitutes the subtle obscuration to knowledge and one that does not.

If one contends that the dispute here is not about the untenability of the distinctness of the lineages of the three vehicles but about the inappropriate-ness of the division into thirteen lineages,[205] this too is incorrect. For exam-ple, *Light on Perfection of Wisdom in Twenty-Five Thousand Lines* says:

> This is like this statement in the sutra: "So Mañjuśrī, if there is one ultimate expanse, one suchness, one perfect endpoint, how can such labels as *suitable receptacle* and *unsuitable receptacle* be applied to it?"[206]

[57] The sutra here raises the question of how one can determine, given there is no differentiation in the ultimate expanse, who is a receptacle of the Great Vehicle and who is not. This current argument is similar to the previous one. The debate is about the unsustainability of maintaining dis-tinct lineages of the Great and Lesser vehicles. For if it is interpreted in terms of the thirteen lineages, the objection about whether someone is a suitable or an unsuitable receptacle simply cannot be raised.[207] The great master Haribhadra too upholds a position consonant with that of Ārya Vimuktisena.

Likewise, the root text as well as the commentary of the *Sublime Continuum* also make many statements about how there are both śrāvakas and pratyekabuddhas who have realized the ultimate nature of things and those who have not. Fearing excessive length, I will not expand on these here.

The reason the *Ornament of Realizations* presents the *knowledge of the path* pertaining to the paths of śrāvaka and pratyekabuddha is to help sustain those who possess the lineages of śrāvaka and pratyekabuddha. Among Hīnayāna practitioners, there are those who are suitable receptacles for profound emptiness and those who are not. Since the latter is the majority, [*Ornament of Realizations*] mostly presents their paths [when presenting the Hīnayāna path].

Just as one finds among followers of the Great Vehicle those who will not discover the Madhyamaka view unless they are first led through the Cittamātra view, this is true also among pratyekabuddhas; and it appears to be true also among śrāvakas. Furthermore, in both *Light on Perfection of Wisdom in Twenty-Five Thousand Lines* as well as *Exposition on the Eight Thousand Line Perfection of Wisdom*, to substantiate the point that the ultimate expanse is defined as the lineage of all three vehicles, they cite the statement that all āryas are defined in terms of the unconditioned alone.[208] In the *Diamond Cutter Sutra* the line "Because ārya persons are defined in terms of the unconditioned alone"[209] is presented as a substantiation of the statement "Neither the attributes of the buddha exist nor all the teachings he has revealed." This means that all the āryas of Hīnayāna and Mahayana are defined on the basis of actualizing the unconditioned, the ultimate truth, which is the nonexistence of all phenomena on the ultimate level. Therefore [on this point of the presence of the knowledge of emptiness among śrāvakas and pratyekabuddhas,] there is no contradiction between this tradition of Candrakīrti and the *Ornament of Realizations*.[210] So, even according to the tradition of the commentators on the *Ornament* [such as Vimuktisena] mentioned above, we should understand there to be two types [among śrāvakas and pratyekabuddhas]. I could elaborate further.

The quality that comes to be superior on the first ground

This has four parts: (1) the generosity of one abiding on the first ground, (2) the generosity of the lower stations, (3) the generosity of bodhisattvas [58], and (4) the divisions of the perfection of generosity.

The generosity of one abiding on the first ground

At this point the first cause of full awakening,
the perfection of generosity, will become preeminent;
committed to giving away even his very flesh,
giving becomes a sign to infer his unseen qualities. 1.9

At this point when the ground of Perfect Joy is attained, it is **the perfection of generosity** alone among the ten perfections that **becomes preeminent** for that bodhisattva. It is not the case, however, that he does not possess the other perfections. This supramundane perfection of generosity is also the **first cause of full awakening**; this is, of course, to be understood in terms of the supramundane level of generosity.

Although generally the subsequent perfection is superior to the one that precedes it, generosity is described as superior here because the power to practice generosity on this ground excels to an extent that is not the case for morality and so on. On the first ground, the bodhisattva is capable of engaging in such acts of generosity as giving away his body and external belongings, without the slightest glimmer of the attachment or possessiveness that undermine the perfection of generosity. He is, however, not yet capable of engaging in the morality that never engages, even in dreams, in immoral acts, which are the forces contrary to discipline, a capacity he will attain on the second ground.

Furthermore, on this ground, realizations that remain imperceptible can be inferred through his generosity. For example, not only is the bodhisattva dedicated to giving away external belongings, he becomes **committed** ever more to generosity, **giving away even his very flesh.** So his **giving becomes a sign to infer** his inner realizations, such as his attainments, which remain **unseen** to many others. This is similar to inferring the presence of fire on the basis of smoke. This stanza describes how the bodhisattva is free of the taint of possessiveness in relation to giving away his body, life, and material resources. For even as he gives these away, his mental state remains steadfast, not wavering in any way.

The generosity of the lower stations

This is twofold: generosity brings the happiness of cyclic existence, and generosity brings the happiness of nirvana.

Generosity brings the happiness of cyclic existence

> All living beings eagerly yearn for happiness,
> yet for humans there is no happiness without resources.
> Material resources, in turn, come about from generosity;
> knowing this, the Buddha spoke on generosity first. 1.10

> [59] Those with weak compassion and ruthless minds,
> who seek their own welfare with enthusiasm,
> even for them, the wealth they desire will come
> from generosity, a cause that relieves suffering. 1.11

All of these **living beings eagerly yearn for happiness**, which helps rectify such sufferings as hunger, thirst, sickness, heat, and cold. **Yet for humans** and their like, **there is no happiness without** consuming the **resources** that are the objects of desire—food, drink, cures against sickness, clothes, and shelters. So, **knowing** that **these resources, in turn, come about from** the accumulation of merit born of **generosity** in the past, **the Buddha,** who perceives the minds of all beings, thus **spoke on generosity first.** Leading others to this way [of generosity] is easier as well.

One might wonder, "In order to obtain excellent material resources through the act of generosity, must the giver be perfectly aligned [with the criteria of authentic generosity]?"

This is not necessary. We should even respect a merchant who seeks greater wealth by giving away a small portion of his wealth, or someone who gives to a beggar in hopes of producing greater wealth. Such givers are unlike the bodhisattvas who, under compassion's sway, do not aspire for the fruits of giving but give celebrating the joy that is the wish to give. Now an ordinary giver may be not only **weak** in **compassion,** he may even possess a **ruthless mind** toward other sentient beings; he may **seek with enthusiasm his own welfare,** such as birth in the higher realms—that is to say, he may make his pursuit [of self-interest] his guiding principle. **Even for them,** it is **from generosity**—a generosity whose only positive quality, turning away from clinging to resources, is based on an expectation of the fruits of generosity—that wonderful and excellent **wealth they desire will come** about. In this way, such generosity can become **a cause that relieves** the **suffering** of hunger, thirst, and so on.[211]

Generosity brings the happiness of nirvana

> Indeed it is through the practice of generosity
> that he will swiftly, at some point, meet the āryas.
> He will then cut clean the continuum of cyclic existence,
> and as a result, he will journey to the state of peace. 1.12

[60] **Indeed** with respect to one who, while divorced of compassion, devotes himself to generosity to secure his own happiness and relieve his personal suffering, [the *Commentary*] states, "The sublime ones walk among those who give."[212] So **it is through the practice of generosity that he will swiftly, at some point, meet** with the fortune of encountering **the āryas**. Then, from having such a sublime being teach him the Dharma, he will come to perceive that the cycle of existence is bereft of beneficial qualities. **He will then**, actualizing the uncontaminated path of the āryas, come to eliminate ignorance and thus **cut clean the continuum of cyclic existence**—the continuity of birth and death since beginningless time. **And as a result** of meeting with a sublime one, **he will journey to the state of peace**: the attainment of a śrāvaka's nirvana or that of a pratyekabuddha.

The generosity of bodhisattvas

This has four parts: (1) the unique benefits of a bodhisattva's generosity, (2) how the discourse on generosity is primary for both types of practitioners, (3) the types of joy a bodhisattva obtains from engaging in generosity, and (4) whether the bodhisattva suffers when giving away the body.

The unique benefits of a bodhisattva's generosity

> Those who keep in mind their pledge to help sentient beings,
> without much delay, attain joy through their generosity. 1.13ab

Non-bodhisattvas do not invariably enjoy the happiness that is the fruit of their generosity immediately after the act—that is to say, simultaneous with the recipient being satisfied through that giving. Because they do not see the fruits of their giving directly, they may not continue to engage in generosity. In contrast, bodhisattvas **who keep in mind their pledge to help sentient**

beings in the long run and to bring about their happiness in the immediate term, seeing the feeling of satisfaction brought about in the recipients **through their generosity**, they will, **without much delay, attain** supreme **joy** as the fruit of their giving. And as they experience such fruits of generosity, they will continue to delight in giving at all times. [61]

How the discourse on generosity is primary for both types of practitioners

> Since it's for both the compassionate and the one who is not,
> this discourse on generosity is primary. 1.13cd

Since, as explained above, generosity brings forth all the happiness of birth in the higher realms as well as that of the *definite goodness* of all beings, of **both** the bodhisattva who is **compassionate and** [the ordinary person] **who is not** an embodiment of compassion, **this discourse on giving is primary** in that it is the most important. The *Friendly Letter* states:

> Knowing wealth to be fickle and devoid of essence,
> pray engage in giving perfectly to the monks,
> to the brahmans, to the hungry, and to your friends.
> There is no greater friend to your next life than generosity.[213]

The types of joy a bodhisattva obtains from engaging in generosity

> If simply hearing or thinking of the phrase "give me"
> brings such joy to the children of the Conqueror—
> joy not experienced even by the arhats who enter into peace—
> what need is there to speak of the joy when giving away everything?
>   1.14

One may ask, "What kind of extraordinary joy arises in the bodhisattva when recipients are satisfied through material resources, the very cause that underlies the bodhisattva's dedication to the act of generosity?"

If simply hearing or thinking about the meaning of **the phrase "give me" brings such joy to the children of the Conqueror,** giving rise to the thought "they are asking something from me"—such a **joy is not experienced even by the arhats who enter into** the state of **peace,** the expanse of nirvana. If this is so, **what need is there to speak of the joy when giving away everything,** both internal and external, and satisfying the recipient in such a manner that this engenders joy greater than that of the bliss of tranquility; there is no need at all.

When one's mind is attracted to the bliss of tranquility, one becomes diverted from others' welfare. In contrast, when one's mind is inspired by the bodhisattva's joys as described above, this would engender even greater enthusiasm for pursuing the welfare of others. There is a difference between these two [types of joy]. [62]

Whether the bodhisattva suffers when giving away the body

If asked, "Does a bodhisattva who gives away his outer and inner belongings—who has been described as engendering excellent bliss on the basis of giving—experience physical pain?"

Now, if the question relates to the great being that has attained one of the bodhisattva grounds, then, like the chopping up of inanimate objects, he experiences no physical pain. The *Questions of Gaganagañja Sutra*, for example, states the following:

> It is thus. Say there is a great forest of *sāla* trees, and some people appear and cut a *sāla* tree. The remaining *sāla* trees do not feel attachment or aversion, or conceptualization or thorough conceptualization, toward them with the thought "That tree has been cut; we haven't been cut yet." So too the bodhisattva's forbearance that resembles this, which is a thoroughly trained forbearance, is most excellent and is equal to space.[214]

The *Precious Garland* too says:

> He has no physical pain,
> so how would he have mental pain?
> Through compassion he feels the world's pain;
> because of this he long endures.[215]

This statement too is intended from the point of view of a bodhisattva that has attained the grounds.

Cutting his body and giving it away, he sees from his own pain
the pain of others, such as their birth in the hells,
as if he were undergoing these situations himself;
thus swiftly he strives to cut away all their pain. 1.15

Now, if the question posed above were from the point of view of one who
has not attained the ground of Perfect Joy—a ground totally free of attachment to one's body and material possessions—there would be physical pain,
since he would undoubtedly encounter conditions that tax his body. Nonetheless, even on such occasions, because of that suffering, he will abide in conditions that lead him to seek the welfare of other sentient beings even more.
For when the bodhisattva sees those who are trapped in the unbearable states
of existence as hell beings, as animals, as hungry ghosts, and so on, whose bodies are being consumed by intense suffering without interruption—suffering
that is a thousandfold more unbearable than the pain of slicing off a piece
of his own flesh—the bodhisattva will disregard his own suffering caused
by **cutting his body and giving it away. From his own pain**, disregarding it
[63] and **taking this experience of his own suffering** as the reason, **swiftly he
strives with effort to cut away the pain of others, such as their birth in the
hells.**[216] In Naktso Lotsāwa's translation this stanza appears in the following:

Through the pain of cutting his body and giving it away,
he views the sufferings of others, such as those of in the hells,
and on the basis of what he has experienced,
he strives with effort to cut away the pain of others.[217]

Thus, the explanation I have provided above is based on drawing from two
different versions of translation of this stanza.

So it is only when one possesses this kind of power of intention that one
can give away one's body. And since there is no contradiction in asserting the
presence of such intention even before the bodhisattva grounds are attained,
it is said that even bodhisattvas who have not yet attained the grounds give
away their body.

The divisions of the perfection of generosity

Generosity devoid of the gift, receiver, and giver
is called a supramundane perfection,

but when attachment for these three arises,
it is then said to be a mundane perfection. 1.16

Such **generosity**, the intention to give, when sustained by uncontaminated wisdom **devoid** of the perception of truly existent **gift, receiver, and giver, is called** by the great mother Perfection of Wisdom sutras a "**supramundane perfection.**"[218] Since the meditative equipoise of an ārya that does not objectify is supramundane, generosity sustained by this is characterized as supramundane perfection. In contrast, generosity that is not sustained by such nonobjectification is a mundane perfection. The clear distinction between these two cannot be ascertained directly by those who have not attained the ground of the ultimate awakening mind.

The term *beyond* (*pāra* in Sanskrit)[219] refers to the other shore or the other side of the ocean of cyclic existence, thus it refers here to buddhahood, the total elimination of two obscurations. "To reach beyond" (*pāramitā*) is to have gone beyond. In explaining this term, the *Commentary* writes:

> The grammatical rule "If there is a subsequent term, do not make it invisible" makes the accusative case visible, retaining its form. Alternatively, because it belongs to the group of the type *prīṣodara* and so on, it is left as a word possessing a suffix *ma*.[220]

Paṇḍita Jayānanda explains this *Commentary* passage as follows:

> In Sanskrit, "beyond" is *pāra* while "to go" is *itā*, and when these two words are combined, the accusative singular *am* is added onto *pāra*, while the particle *su* of nominative case is added after *itā* [thus deriving the compound] *pāraṃ itā*. When combined as *pāramitā*, although *am* and *su* should become invisible, [64] here, through the rule "If there is a subsequent term, do not make it invisible," the *su* from the root word is made invisible yet *am* is not. "Through this rule the accusative case . . ." refers [therefore] to the accusative singular *am*. As this particle is not made invisible, the term assumes the linguistic form *pāramitā*. Being in "*prīṣodara* and so on," the suffix *ma* is added to make the word *pārama*. Since it is to be read as *pārama* it is stated "do not make it invisible." Thus by erasing *a* of *am* and leaving *ma*

intact and giving it the vowel *i*, it becomes *mitā*. This is how it is explained.[221]

The nominative ending *su* given here seems to be incorrect, so check whether this should be *si* instead.[222]

Some Tibetans assert that from the Sanskrit word *pāraṃ itā*, the *anusvāra* atop *ra* is placed alongside on the same row,[223] which then results in *pārama itā*; and when the *saṃdhi* rule is applied to this, the vowel *i* is given to the letter *ma*, and when the vowel *a* is erased it assumes the form *mitā*. There seems to be many confused explanations such as this. However, the explanation offered by the paṇḍita cited above seems to be best.

The two lines beginning "Generosity devoid of the gift, receiver, and giver" take the wisdom realizing the three elements of giving to be imperceptible as a point of reference and indicates how generosity sustained by it is an instance of the perfection of generosity. Other instances of perfections such as generosity that are not sustained by this wisdom are still called "perfections" because they are similar to those perfections sustained by wisdom. For example, an instance of generosity may not be sustained by wisdom, but because it is sustained by dedication to great awakening, it is accepted as certain to go beyond. So it is suitable to be called the *perfection of giving*.

Thus, with respect to the etymological meaning of the word *perfection* (*pāramitā*), if it is read as "gone beyond to *that* state"—in terms of accusative case—the word refers to having arrived at the ground of the buddhahood. And if the word is read as "going beyond by means of *this*"—in terms of instrumental case—then perfections exist even on the learner's path.

This explanation I have offered here in relation to generosity should be understood in the context of other perfections as well, such as for the perfection of morality and so on. In other words, those other instances also contain both kinds—those sustained by the awakening mind and by dedication and those that are sustained by wisdom as well.

But when attachment or clinging to true existence **arises for these three** elements of giving—if one is fettered by clinging to true existence of the [gift, receiver, and giver]—this generosity **is then said** in the sutras **to be a mundane perfection.**

Here is how what has been explained above can be practiced right now from this very moment. To give away your body to others and generate extraordinary joy in doing so, train first by taking it as an object of imaginative cultivation. As for other forms of generosity, such as giving material things, cultivate these in relation to the fields of giving, both to those of elevated status and to the lowly, on a regular basis through such acts as offering even a simple thing like water. [65] On these occasions be sure you are sustained by the wisdom realizing the imperceptibility (emptiness) of the three elements of giving. Mentally, give away repeatedly your body, material resources, and the roots of virtue for the benefit of other sentient beings. And contemplate how, even if you do not give them away, they will perish nonetheless, and you will have to discard them anyway. Contemplate how, since you will have to give them up anyway, it would be better to mentally give them away beforehand. Proceed as described in *Guide to the Bodhisattva Way*:

> My body and my material resources,
> and roots of virtue of all three times—
> I will give these away without reserve
> to fulfill the wishes of all beings.[224]

And:

> By giving away everything one transcends sorrow,
> and my mind seeks this transcendence of sorrow.
> Since everything must be given up anyway,
> to give these to sentient beings is most excellent.[225]

A conclusion stating the qualities of the ground

Now to present briefly, as described earlier, the attributes of this ground of Perfect Joy as qualified by uncontaminated wisdom, the root text says:

> Abiding perfectly in the bodhisattva's mind
> and endowed with light beautifying the sublime ones,
> this ground of Perfect Joy is the water-crystal gem [the moon],
> which dispels all darkness and reigns victorious. 1.17

This ground of Perfect Joy is like **the water-crystal gem**—the disc of the moon. It resembles the moon in three ways. (1) It resides at a high point in that it **abides perfectly in the mind of the bodhisattva** on the first ground, who has attained the qualities of the ground described above. As such, it abides high up on the path, like the moon abides high up in the sky. Since the first ground is a facet of the mind of that bodhisattva, one speaks of abiding in it. This is like, for example, the eyes being located on the head. (2) Because the ultimate awakening mind of the first ground is **endowed with light** of gnosis in the mind of the **sublime** or excellent person, [66] thereby **beautifying him**, it is like the moon, which makes its space, the skies, beautiful through its bright illumination. (3) Also, because the first ground **reigns victorious** over the objects abandoned on the path of seeing, it resembles the moon that **dispels all** aspects of the thick or dense **darkness**.

This concludes exposition of the first ground of the ultimate awakening mind, from *Illuminating the Intent: An Exposition of Entering the Middle Way*.

4. The Second Ground, The Stainless

The second ground, The Stainless

[67] This has five sections: (1) how morality is completely purified on this ground, (2) the praises of morality, (3) the analogy for how the bodhisattva does not mix with forces opposing morality, (4) the divisions of the perfection of morality, and (5) a conclusion stating the qualities of the ground.

How morality is completely purified on this ground

This has four parts: (1) showing that morality is perfected on this ground, (2) showing that on this basis the qualities become completely purified, (3) how morality becomes superior compared to the first ground, and (4) other causes that purify morality.

Showing that morality is perfected on this ground

> He is endowed with perfect morality and purity;
> even in dreams, he shuns the stain of immorality. 2.1ab

The bodhisattva abiding on the second ground—because **he is endowed** with the **perfect morality** as well as the qualities of **purity**, not only during his waking period but **even in** his **dreams—shuns the stain of immorality**; that is, he remains untouched by it. This includes not just the immorality of root infractions and naturally reprehensible deeds; he also relinquishes the stains of the immorality of violating rule-based precepts.[226]

Because he does not inflame the afflictions that give rise to immorality, and because the nonvirtuous karma of transgressing prescribed rules does not occur for him, he has attained the coolness borne of having extinguished the fires of remorse from accruing the downfalls of violating prescribed rules. This is therefore called *morality*. The Sanskrit term for morality is *śila*, which is composed of the words *śīta*, referring to "coolness," and *lati*, meaning "to attain." Alternatively, it is called "morality" (*śīla*, literally meaning also "correct discipline") because, being the cause of happiness, it is something that is sought after by the sublime ones. These are explanations of the word *śīla* based on its etymology.

With regard to its actual nature, morality is defined in terms of the seven relinquishments, the abandoning of the seven immoral acts of body and speech. The underlying states of mind that give rise to these seven relinquishments are (1) nonattachment, which is the absence of covetousness, (2) nonaversion, which is the absence of harmful intent, and (3) right view, which opposes wrong view. By including these motivating factors, *morality* refers to the ten relinquishments, ten positive courses of action that overcome the ten negative courses of action. [68]

Showing that on this basis the qualities become completely purified

> Since all movements of his body, speech, and mind are pure,
> he accumulates the excellent virtue of all ten courses of action. 2.1cd

One might ask, "How do the qualities of this bodhisattva come to be purified because of his perfect morality?"

Since all his **movements**—the threefold activity of **his body, speech, and mind—are pure**, without even subtle downfalls throughout his waking and dream states, **he accumulates**, without omission, **the** sublime or **excellent virtue of all ten courses of action**. To accumulate all ten courses means to fulfill the first three courses of action, such as relinquishing killing, through his body, the four middle ones through his speech, and the three final courses through his mind.[227] In pursuing this, not only does the bodhisattva refrain from transgressing the bounds of proscribed acts, he also accomplishes all the positive prescriptions of the moral code.[228]

How morality becomes superior compared to the first ground

> Not only this path of virtue but in all ten deeds,
> he becomes most excellent and pure.
> Just as the radiant autumn moon [adorns the night sky],
> morality adorns him with peace and radiance. 2.2

One might ask, "Isn't it the case these ten courses of positive action are accumulated in their entirety by the bodhisattva on the first ground as well?"

[*Reply:*] Yes, they do accumulate them. However, to the extent that the second-ground bodhisattva excels in **not only this path of virtue** [in general] **but in all ten** [courses of positive] **deeds, he becomes most excellent and pure,** to an extent beyond the bodhisattva on the first ground. Because he already possesses optimally the superior generosity described in the discussion of the first ground, and since among the remaining nine perfections, he does not possess the excellence in the practices of forbearance and so on to the extent he has for morality, morality is described as superior here. It is not that the other perfections are not present. The reference to the ten deeds is but an illustration of the prescriptive morality intended, so we must include here all positive prescriptions of morality as well.

Just as the radiant autumn moon possesses the twin qualities of cooling the scorching pain of heat and being resplendent with a white halo of light, likewise the bodhisattva who always abides in utterly pure ethical discipline—the one who abides in such pure **morality**—is **adorned** beautifully **with** the **peace** of having guarded the doors of his senses [69] **and radiance** such that his body glows with light.

Other causes that purify morality

> Should he, though pure, see in terms of intrinsic nature,
> his morality will remain impure because of this.
> Thus with respect to all three elements of discipline,
> he always remains free of the flow of dualistic thoughts. 2.3

A fully ordained monk may be especially pure in his morality with respect to his pratimokṣa monastic vows, but **should he** not relinquish **seeing** phenomena as established through their **intrinsic nature**, this monk's **morality will remain impure because of this** reason. He will be like a moral degenerate who pretends to be endowed with moral discipline. The *Heap of Jewels Sutra* states:

> Kāśyapa, now here, some ordained monks who are endowed with moral discipline, who are restrained by pratimokṣa vows and abide in them, whose rites and sphere of conduct are perfect,

who view minute reprehensible acts with fear—having correctly taken the [precepts], they cultivate the bases of the training and become endowed with perfectly pure actions of body, speech, and mind. Because of these, their way of life is perfectly pure, but they still speak in terms of selfhood. Kāśyapa, this is the first example of a moral degenerate pretending to be endowed with moral discipline. . . .

    Kāśyapa, again here, some ordained monks embrace perfectly the twelve learned qualities, but they objectify them. Thus those who abide with grasping at "I" and grasping at "mine," O Kāśyapa, is the fourth example of a moral degenerate pretending to be endowed with moral discipline.[229]

"To speak of selfhood" is to objectify. This is indicated by "abiding with grasping at 'I' and grasping at 'mine.'" And its meaning should not be understood in terms of the commonly shared notion of identity view; rather, it should be understood as not relinquishing grasping at "I" and "mine" as existing through their intrinsic characteristics. Since the pronoun "he" cannot be related to what has immediately preceded [at the end of the previous verse], the following translation by Naktso seems to be better:

> If one sees his discipline to be pure intrinsically,
> by this he becomes morally degenerate.[230]

    Because one's morality does not become purified if one does not relinquish object-laden views, the bodhisattva on the second ground **always remains free of the flow of dualistic thoughts** grasping at intrinsic existence in terms of real versus unreal and so on **with respect to all three elements**— the beings in relation to *whom* immorality is to be relinquished, *what* antidote is applied to relinquish, and *who* relinquishes them. [70]

The praises of morality

This has five parts: (1) how enjoying the results of generosity in the higher realms depends upon morality, (2) how enjoying the results of generosity through successive lives depends upon morality, (3) showing that it is extremely difficult to escape the lower realms if one is divorced from morality, (4) the reason the discourse on morality comes after the discourse on generosity, and (5) proclaiming that morality is the cause both of higher rebirths and of definite goodness.

How enjoying the results of generosity in the higher realms depends upon morality

Having spoken of how the bodhisattva's morality is endowed with perfect factors, the following is presented to show how, in addition, the qualities of generosity are exceeded by those of perfect morality, which is the support for all perfect qualities:

> Wealth through generosity is found even in the lower realms;
> this occurs when one has fractured the legs of morality. 2.4ab

Generosity by a giver that, had it been endowed with morality, could have brought perfect enjoyment of extraordinary **wealth** in an existence as a celestial being or a human, may instead bring enjoyment of varieties of perfect **wealth in the lower realms**, such as when one takes birth in the occasional hells, as a bull, as a horse, as an elephant, as a monkey, as a *nāga* serpent, and so on, or as a hungry ghost with great supernatural powers. **This occurs when one has fractured the legs of morality**—that is to say, when one is divorced of morality.

This explains how, if one is divorced of morality, the material resources that are the effects of having practiced generosity, instead of coming into fruition during an existence in the higher realm, may be realized during an existence in the lower realms. Therefore the person who practices generosity and wishes the fruits of his generosity to ripen during existence in the higher realms, as referred to above, should guard moral discipline.

How enjoying results of generosity through successive lives depends upon morality

> When interest and capital itself are both exhausted,
> no prospects remain for one of any future wealth. 2.4cd

[71] If divorced of morality, the fruits of one's generosity will ripen during existence in the lower realms, and in this life too, one will experience merely the fruits of past acts of generosity. Owing to extreme foolishness [in the

lower realms], one does not cultivate generosity and the like anew, and in this way one **exhausts the interest and**, along with it, the **capital**, the root itself. Then once the fruits of all past generosity have been spent, **no prospects remain for one of any future wealth.**

Consider this analogy. A farmer plants a few seeds, obtains an abundant harvest, and then plants even more seeds to grow more crops. For such a man, there is no interruption [of the fruits of his labor], since crops multiply. On the other hand, the foolish one who consumes [his crops] without planting new seeds will experience no such continuous increase.

Showing that it is extremely difficult to escape the lower realms if one is divorced from morality

By breaking the legs of morality, one will not only find it hard to obtain continuous increase in the enjoyment of material resources, one will also fall into the lower realms. Once in the lower realms, one will find it extremely difficult to escape. This is presented in the following.

> If, when free and living with favorable conditions,
> we do not retain this status we enjoy,
> we will fall into the abyss and be at the mercy of others.
> What could enable us to rise up again from such a state? 2.5

When, like a heroic warrior who is **living with favorable conditions free** of bondage, we freely engage in whatever we wish without relying on others and live in the congenial celestial and human realms, **if we do not retain this status we enjoy** and protect ourselves from falling into the lower realms, then just like a [captive] heroic warrior who is bound and tossed from a high cliff, we **will fall into the abyss** of the lower realms **and be at the mercy of others**, and we will have no freedom. Once gone to the lower realms, **what could enable us to rise up again from such as state?** There is nothing that will help do such a thing.

In general, it is extremely rare that one would cultivate virtue while living in the lower realms. Furthermore, one will accumulate negative karma rapidly, so one will be compelled to pass birth after birth solely in the lower realms. Therefore, the sutras state, "Even if one is reborn among humans once in a hundred eons, two types of fruitions will occur."[231] Thus being reborn as a human is said to be difficult indeed. So starting now, we must prepare so that we do not fall to the lower realms. For this too, we need to strive in moral discipline. [72]

The reason the discourse on morality comes after the discourse on generosity

> Therefore, having engaged in the discourse on generosity,
> the Buddha proceeded to the discourse on morality;
> and when qualities spring up in the field of morality,
> enjoyment of their fruits will become continuous. 2.6

Immorality is a source of numerous flaws, such as being led to the lower realms. **Having engaged in the discourse on generosity, the Buddha**, who has defeated all negative karma, **proceeded to the discourse on morality** to ensure that qualities like generosity do not become wasted. That is to say, he conducted the discourse subsequent to generosity. The reason is that morality, as the foundation of all qualities, is the field. **When qualities** such as generosity and so on **spring up in this field of morality**, then acts of giving and so forth as well as the **enjoyment of their fruits**, such as excellent physical forms and wealth, will **become continuous.** In this way, the array of such excellent fruits will increase, and one will be able to enjoy these for a long time. Otherwise, one will not be able enjoy such continuous fruits.

The significance of the above lines is this: Those who give should consider not only the possibility of the perfect enjoyment of wealth, which is the fruit of generosity, but they should also consider what the perfect form of existence is for enjoying such material resources, and how one can enjoy such resources across successive lifetimes. For these too, one should understand that moral discipline is an extremely important means.

As for the bodhisattvas on the beginner's stage, they too must strive in acts of giving as explained above, and they must undertake this for the purpose of attaining buddhahood for the benefit of all sentient beings, the intended beneficiaries of such an aspiration. However, in the near term, the fruits of their generosity must ripen during their existence in the higher realms, and this must occur over successive lifetimes as well. As for such births, this depends on morality, and without such forms of favorable existence, the conditions for practicing the bodhisattva deeds will remain incomplete.

Proclaiming that morality is the cause of both higher rebirths and definite goodness

> Ordinary beings and the speech-born śrāvakas,
> those who are established for self-enlightenment,
> and the children of the conquerors—as to their definite goodness
> and birth in higher realms, the cause is none other than morality. 2.7

[73] Both the attainment of physical existence in the higher realms as well as lasting enjoyment of the fruits of generosity while living there depend upon morality, and morality is indispensable for attaining definite goodness as well.[232] In this manner, **the cause** of **birth in higher realms** for **ordinary beings** who have not yet entered the path and the cause of **definite goodness** for **śrāvakas**, who are **born from** the Sage's **speech**; for **those who are established for** the path of **self-enlightenment**; and for the bodhisattvas, who are **the children of the conquerors, is none other than morality.** The meaning here is not that morality is the sole cause and that other causes are somehow excluded, for there are numerous causes besides morality. The meaning rather is that to achieve an exceptional birth in the higher realms or to achieve definite goodness, all other conditions must be definitely connected to morality; if it is shunned, these fruits can never be achieved.

These lines actually summarize what is stated in the *Ten Grounds Sutra*.[233] There, each of the ten nonvirtues, such as taking a life, is divided into great, middling, and small degrees, which lead, respectively, to the hells, to the animal realm, and to the hungry ghost realm. Even if one is ultimately born among humans, having taken a life, for instance, brings forth two undesirable effects—brevity of life and abundance of illness—and likewise, each of the remaining nine acts also brings about two undesirable effects. In contrast, the ten virtues result in births as humans and celestial beings in the desire realm on up to the peak of existence [in the formless realm].

Above this, if the ten virtues are accompanied by an intermediate intention, one that focuses on securing one's own welfare and renouncing cyclic existence out of fear and without great compassion, and if this is thoroughly purified by means the wisdom that realizes selflessness by following another's words, one will definitely gain freedom through the Śrāvaka Vehicle. Above this, if in one's final life in cyclic existence one does not rely on another's power and focuses on the awakening of a pratyekabuddha, and if, without great compassion and skillful means, one comes to be purified by penetrating the truth of profound dependent origination, one will definitely gain freedom through the Pratyekabuddha Vehicle. Above this, if one has a loving heart that is vast and limitless, if one is endowed with compassion, if one's path encompasses the skillful means, if one makes great waves of aspirational prayers, if one does not forsake sentient beings, and if one comes to be purified by focusing on the expansive wisdom of the buddhas, one will totally purify the bodhisattva grounds and achieve the vast deeds of pure perfections.[234] It is these points from that sutra that Candrakīrti summarizes here.

The *Friendly Letter* too says:

> Pray cultivate morality that is undamaged, [74]
> not low in esteem, unadulterated, and untainted.
> Like the earth that supports everything both moving and
>   stationary,
> morality is taught to be the basis supporting all qualities.[235]

Thus training in morality has been stated to be most important.

These statements above have been made in the context of the second ground, but in terms of actual practice, even bodhisattvas on the beginner's stage need to engage in the practice [of morality]. One must, for instance, contemplate the crucial ethic of applying restraint against the ten nonvirtues, guarding even against motives that give rise to them, just as stated in the lines [above] "Wealth through generosity is found . . ." up to "the cause is none other than morality."[236] And every time one trains in morality, one must do so on the basis of being sustained by the wisdom that realizes things without objectifying them. In addition, mere intellectual understanding and familiarization on a few occasions will get one nowhere; one must contemplate these points on a sustained and regular basis. If one cultivates familiarity on a sustained and regular basis, then the time will come when one's mind engages these with a natural ease, even the practice of the bodhisattva deeds—which, when one first hears of or tries to engage in, may make one disheartened—and even those deeds that our Teacher, the Buddha, was not able to put into actual practice for a long time. The *Praise to the One with Infinite Qualities* states:

> Even just hearing about this causes beings great distress,
> those [deeds] that even you did not engage in for a long time,

through familiarity, in time, these deeds came to you naturally. Thus these qualities are hard to enhance without utter familiarity.[237]

An analogy for how the bodhisattva does not mix with forces opposing morality

> Just as the ocean and a corpse do not remain together,
> and just as good fortune and calamity do not keep company,
> likewise the great ones who are governed by morality
> do not wish for the company of immorality. 2.8

Just as the great **ocean**, because the obsessively clean nāga serpents live there, casts ashore by its tides all **the corpses** and **does not remain together** with the carcasses, **and just as** the perfect factors of **good fortune do not keep company with** Lady Black-Ear—**calamity**—**likewise the great ones** of the second ground who are **governed by** thoroughly pure **morality do not wish for the company of immorality.**

This above reference does not contradict the statement in *Commentary on the Four Hundred Stanzas* that "Where Lady Auspiciousness (Maṅgala) lives, without doubt, Lady Black-Eared (Kālakarṇa) can be as well."[238] [75] There the statement refers to two individuals bearing those names; here Lady Black-Eared is a term for misfortune.

The divisions of the perfection of morality

> *Who* relinquishes *what* and in relation to *whom*—
> when any of these three is objectified,
> such morality is described as mundane perfection;
> free of attachment to these three is supramundane. 2.9

When someone is incapable of ceasing the seed of **objectifying the three** as real—the person *who* **relinquishes,** *what* objects of abandonment he relinquishes, **and in relation to** *which* sentient beings he relinquishes—**such morality is described as mundane perfection.** If that very morality is **free of attachment to these three** spheres in the form of perceiving them as real— that is to say, if it is sustained by uncontaminated wisdom realizing them as not perceivable—it **is supramundane** perfection. Hence, by this distinction, morality is twofold.

A conclusion stating the qualities of the ground

> This bodhisattva born of the radiant moon of morality,
> who is not of cyclic existence yet is its glory,
> the stainless, who, like moonlight on an autumn night,
> removes the pain from the minds of sentient beings. 2.10

Just as **moonlight on an autumn night** is free of obscuring taints and helps relieve people's agony [of heat], likewise **this bodhisattva born of the radiant moon of morality**—the second ground, which is free of the stains of immorality—the one who bears its name, The Stainless, who is true to its meaning, he too **removes the pain** engendered by immorality **from the minds of sentient beings**. As this bodhisattva on the second ground does not belong to the class of those who revolve in the cycle of existence, **he is not of cyclic existence, yet** he **is its glory**. This is because all perfect qualities follow for such a bodhisattva and because he has attained, through the power of his aspirational prayers aimed for all sentient beings, [76] the excellent causes of becoming a universal ruler reigning over the four continents.

This concludes exposition of the second ground of the ultimate awakening mind, from *Illuminating the Intent: An Exposition of Entering the Middle Way.* [77]

5. The Third Ground, The Luminous

The third ground, The Luminous

This has four sections: (1) the etymology of the name of the ground, the basis, (2) the qualities of the ground, the attributes, (3) the distinctive characteristics of the first three perfections, and (4) a conclusion stating the qualities of the ground.

The etymology of the name of the ground, the basis

> Because the fire burning off the fuels of all phenomena
> produces light here, this third ground is called The Luminous.
> Here the child of the Tathāgata perceives
> a copper-colored glow like that of a sunrise. 3.1

The third ground of the bodhisattva **is called The Luminous.** If asked, "Why is it called The Luminous?" It is true to the meaning of this name. When the bodhisattva attains the third ground, **the fire** of gnosis **burning off all the fuels of phenomena**—a fire that has the capacity to pacify all dualistic elaborations within meditative equipoise—**produces light here. Here** at this point, **the child of the Tathāgata** who has generated the third ground of the awakening mind **perceives** the light of gnosis with **a copper-colored glow like** the glow **that** appears at **sunrise.** That is to say, during post-meditation periods on this ground, the bodhisattva experiences the dawning of pervasive red or orange lights. Thus the *Precious Garland* states:

> The third ground is The Luminous,
> for the pacifying light of gnosis dawns.
> Absorptions and clairvoyance have arisen,
> and attachment and aversion have utterly ceased,
> and as a fruitional effect of these [attainments],

he will engage especially in forbearance and diligence.
This great celestial being is most learned;
he has undone the attachment of the desire realm.[239]

The qualities of the ground, the attributes

This has four parts: (1) showing how forbearance is superior on this ground, (2) how to cultivate other types of forbearance, (3) the divisions of the perfection of forbearance, and (4) the other pure qualities that arise on this ground.

Showing how forbearance is superior on this ground

[78] The lines "Were a disturbed person . . ." and so on present the way the perfection of forbearance comes to be superior for this bodhisattva who has attained the light of gnosis:

> Were a disturbed person to slice flesh from the bones
> of the body of a bodhisattva though he be innocent,
> cutting it off ounce by ounce over a prolonged period,
> this will serve to increase his forbearance toward the torturer. 3.2

Since the bodhisattva already possesses optimal excellence in generosity and morality, as described above, here, from among the eight remaining perfections, forbearance comes to be superior for him. The way it comes to be superior is this: The bodhisattva achieves excellence in the practice of forbearance to an extent he does not for the other remaining seven perfections. The bodhisattva of the third ground is characterized here as being **innocent**—an inappropriate object for anger—because he guards others' minds, because he possesses pacifying gnosis as described in the lines ". . . the fire burning off all fuels of knowable objects,"[240] and because he does not exhibit with his body, speech, or thoughts such concerns as "He harmed me and my kin in the past," "He is causing harm now," or the suspicion that "He might do so in future," which fuel antipathy toward others.

Though this is so, **were a person** who is **disturbed** from within to not only **slice flesh** but to do so **from the bones of the body of a bodhisattva**— not in large slabs but **cutting it off ounce by ounce** [and this too] not in one go but **over a prolonged period**, pausing regularly so that the cutting is not completed quickly—the bodhisattva will not experience any vexation **toward the torturer**. In fact, **this will serve to increase his forbearance** toward that person, and the bodhisattva will direct his focus on the sufferings of the hells and so on that the person might undergo because of that negative karma, suffering that is graver than any other types of similar suffering. This is how the bodhisattva comes to excel in forbearance.

Now on the first two grounds such as Perfect Joy, there is no disturbance within his mental continuum in response to having his body cut, but it's said that he has not gained quite this level of mastery in forbearance. Therefore one should understand that it is from this ground onward that one comes to excel in forbearance.

> For a bodhisattva who sees selflessness,
> *who* cuts *what* at *what point* in time *in what manner*?
> He sees all phenomena as images in a mirror,
> and by seeing thus too, he will have such forbearance. 3.3

Not only does his forbearance come to excel on the basis of focusing on the extensive sufferings, such as those of the hells, **a bodhisattva** of the third ground **who sees selflessness and** directly perceives these three spheres—[79] the one *who cuts*, *what* is being cut, [the act of] cutting of the body at *what point in time*, and in *what manner*—in fact **sees all phenomena as images in a mirror**. Free of acquired conceptions of "I" and "mine" **too**, the bodhisattva **will have such forbearance** [when facing harm].

The *Commentary* says, "The grammatical particle 'too' indicates that this too is a cause of forbearance."[241] Not only does the bodhisattva remain undisturbed because of the reason given above, he also has great forbearance because of what has been just explained here. Also, just before this in the *Commentary,* the phrase "For this reason too"[242] should be read as "By seeing thus too."

How to cultivate other types of forbearance

This has two parts: the inappropriateness of becoming angry and the appropriateness of cultivating forbearance.

The inappropriateness of becoming angry

This is fourfold: (1) It is inappropriate to become angry because it is pointless and will have grave consequences. (2) It is contradictory to loathe future sufferings but retaliate against harm. (3) It is inappropriate to become angry because it destroys virtues accumulated in the past over a long period. (4) Rejecting anger on the basis of contemplating the numerous faults of intolerance.

It is inappropriate to become angry because it is pointless and will have grave consequences.

Not only does forbearance accord with the hearts of the bodhisattvas abiding on the grounds, it is also, for others not yet abiding on the grounds, the cause safeguarding all their qualities, ensuring they do not dissipate. The lines "If you respond with vengeance . . ." up to "cultivate swiftly and constantly the forbearance praised by the āryas" (verses 4–9 below) demonstrate to the intolerant how it is wiser to turn away from anger.

> If you respond with vengeance when someone harms you,
> does your bitterness reverse what was already done?
> Resentment serves no purpose here in this life,
> and it brings more conflicts in the world beyond too. 3.4

Now **if you respond with vengeance** or anger **when someone harms you**—namely, you react with anger toward the perpetrator of that harm—**does your bitterness** or rancor against the person help **reverse what was already done?** No, it does not. Therefore, **resentment** toward that person **serves no purpose here in this life.** *Rancor* is a fierce state of mind that is utterly harsh and has the same meaning as *hostility.* Not only is anger pointless, **it brings more conflicts** with one's own welfare **in the world beyond too.** By giving license to anger, one casts oneself into future undesirable effects that will ripen after death. [80]

It is contradictory to loathe future suffering but retaliate against harm.

While enduring miseries that are the fruits of his past misdeeds but being ignorant of this, he who harbors the thought "Others have harmed me" will feel anger toward the perpetrators of harm. By retaliating in return for injury, he actually obstructs what he himself wants—to no longer experience the sufferings caused by the harms. This is presented in the following:

> He who speaks of exhausting
> the fruits of nonvirtuous actions performed in the past,
> how can he bear to plant the seeds of future pain
> by inflicting harm on others and being angry at them? 3.5

Now with respect to those great sufferings inflicted by one's enemies and so on that injure one's body, for someone **who speaks of** his wish to **exhaust the fruits of nonvirtuous actions performed in the past** such as taking a life—the consequences of which are the severe fruitional effects of the three lower realms as well as encountering all the undesirable causally concordant effects—**how can he**, such a person, **bear** once again **to plant the seeds of future pain**? How can he, **by inflicting harm on others** in retaliation and by **being angry at them** with anger churning from his depths, lead himself to misery that is greater even than what he currently experiences? This would be illogical. Therefore, just as one endures pain inflicted by a physician, such as with a sharp needle, to help cure an illness, likewise, to avert limitless future sufferings, it is most appropriate to have forbearance toward immediate minor suffering.

It is inappropriate to become angry because it destroys virtues accumulated in the past over a long period.

This has two parts: the points related to the actual context and the points that emerge as side considerations.

The points related to the actual context

Not only is intolerance a cause casting unwelcome fruitional effects into the future, it will also cause the merits collected over a long period to diminish. This is presented in the following:

> Indeed anger felt toward the Conqueror's children
> destroys in an instant the virtue gathered

by generosity and morality over a hundred eons;
thus there is no evil similar to intolerance. 3.6

[81] **Indeed** for whatever reason—either not ascertaining the object to be a bodhisattva or, though ascertaining to be a bodhisattva, out of strong habituation to the afflictions—if a bodhisattva experiences an **anger felt even for an instant toward the Conqueror's children** who have generated the awakening mind, based on exaggerated projection of real or unreal faults, this alone **destroys** a collection of merit **gathered over a hundred eons**, such as **virtue** derived from habituation to the perfections of **generosity and morality** as described before. If this is so, what need is there to speak of a non-bodhisattva experiencing anger toward a bodhisattva? Therefore, just as the volume of water in the oceans cannot be measured with a scale, the extent of the fruitional effects of being angry toward a bodhisattva cannot be determined. Therefore, when it comes to propelling unwelcome consequences as its effects and when it comes to harming the virtues, **there is no evil similar to intolerance**—namely, anger. In *Explanation of the Commentary*, the phrase "exaggerated projection of real or unreal faults" is explained as exaggerating a minor fault as a great fault.[243]

With respect to the destruction of the roots of virtue, the *Manifestations of Mañjuśrī Sutra* says:

Mañjuśrī, what is called "anger, anger" is so named because it verily destroys virtues gathered over a hundred eons.[244]

Although it is not explicit in this sutra whether the object of the anger and the person who is angry here are both bodhisattvas, in Candrakīrti's *Commentary*, both the object and the agent are described as bodhisattvas.[245] The *Compendium of Sutras* too, just before citing the above passage from the *Manifestations of Mañjuśrī Sutra*, quotes the following from the *Maitreya's Lion Roar Sutra*:

If a bodhisattva were to berate, utter threats, and beat all ordinary sentient beings within this billionfold world system with a whip, a club, or with his fist, to that extent the bodhisattva would not suffer wounds or become injured by these. If, however, a bodhisattva were to engender a harmful intent, enmity, or a thought of hatred toward a single fellow bodhisattva, this alone would inflict wounds to that bodhisattva and injure him. Why is this so? Because if he had [by such an act] not already forsaken omniscience, such a bodhisattva would need to put on an armor for eons equal to the moments he engendered harmful intent, enmity, and thoughts of hatred to another bodhisattva.[246]

[82] Thus Candrakīrti's account of how both the object and the agent of the anger here are to be explained as bodhisattvas appears to be based upon this sutra passage.

If this is so, how does one understand master Āryaśūra and Śāntideva's statements, such as the following, about how anger destroys roots of virtue gathered over a thousand eons?

> Gathered over a thousand eons,
> through giving, venerating the sugatas, and so on,
> whatever good deeds there are,
> an instance of anger destroys all.[247]

Although some commentaries on *Guide to the Bodhisattva Way* state that a single instance of anger toward a sentient being destroys virtues gathered over many thousands of eons, this is hard to believe. In any case, although these two masters do not specify the object and the agent, the object of anger that destroys roots of virtue of a hundred or a thousand eons has to be a bodhisattva. As to the agent of such anger, the expression "great bodhisattva being" infers that it is a bodhisattva more advanced than the bodhisattva who is the object of such anger.

The agent of anger in this context is certain to be a bodhisattva on the ordinary stage, while the object can be either one who has attained the grounds or one who has not. So, the following three permutations are possible: (1) a more advanced bodhisattva being angry at a less advanced one, (2) a less advanced bodhisattva being angry at a more advanced one, and (3) both the object and the agent of the anger have equal attainment. In the first case, the virtues destroyed would be those of a hundred eons, and if a non-bodhisattva were to become angry at a bodhisattva, it seems the virtues destroyed would be that of a thousand eons. As to how extensively the roots of virtue are destroyed in the second and third cases, and how to understand the superiority and inferiority of the object in the context of the second example, these should be examined on the basis of scriptures.

The passages in the *Maitreya's Lion Roar Sutra* citation "within this billionfold world system" up to "not . . . injured by these"[248] explain how a bodhisattva who, on the basis of experiencing anger in his mind toward a non-bodhisattva, verbally berates him and physically hits him is different from one who wounds a bodhisattva and injures a bodhisattva. From this we can understand that it is not necessary in such a case to don the armor once again from the start. In contrast, regarding a bodhisattva who merely engenders anger toward another bodhisattva, even without any manifestation in body and speech, it is said that he needs to don armor for eons equaling the number of instants such a state of mind lasted. It seems that the object of such anger is a bodhisattva who has received the prophecy, while the agent is a bodhisattva who has not yet received the prophecy. The *Condensed Perfection of Wisdom* states:

> If a bodhisattva who has not yet received the prophecy [83]
> feels anger and initiates dispute with one who has received it,
> he must don the armor for as many eons as the moments of his
>   flawed mind of enmity.[249]

The need "to don the armor once again from the start" means the following. Say a bodhisattva is able to progress soon from the "great" stage of the path of *accumulation* to the path of *preparation*. Were he to become angry at a fellow bodhisattva who has received the prophecy, then equal to the number of instances he experienced such anger, for that many eons, he will not be able to advance to the path of preparation. He will instead need to train on the path once again. In this respect, the *Guide to the Bodhisattva Way* says:

> If, toward a bodhisattva who is a great benefactor,
> one were to engender thoughts of ill will,
> for eons equal to the instants such ill will arose
> he will reside in the hells, so the Sage said.[250]

Here, it is stated that equal to the instants of angry thoughts that one has engendered toward a bodhisattva, for that corresponding number of eons, one would remain in the hells. There is also the ill consequence of destroying the roots of virtue gathered over many eons. Now, if someone who has not received prophecy were to experience anger toward a bodhisattva who has received it, he will remain in the hells; this is just as mentioned in the immediately preceding passage. There is also an instance where the bodhisattva will have to don the armor for that number of eons. Thus there are two cases.

The *Gathering All Fragments Sutra* states that if one accrues the karma of abandoning the Dharma, one would have to declare and purify this defect three times every single day for up to seven years to purity its fruitional effects, but to obtain the forbearance level of the path of preparation would require ten eons, even it were swift.[251] As this states, purifying and cultivating resolve in all possible ways may not rectify the delaying of the path, but it will cleanse the fruitional effects of the karma; so we must strive in them.

The points that emerge as side considerations

There are instances where both the object and agent are not bodhisattvas, yet when anger is experienced it destroys the roots of virtue. This is, for example, as explained in the following text from the Sarvastivāda school cited in the *Compendium of Training*:

> "O monks, look at the monk who prostrates with his entire body to a reliquary containing hair and nails and purifies his thoughts. Monks, this is excellent. O monks, this monk will enjoy the kingdom of a universal monarch a thousandfold corresponding to the number of grains of sand that exist between the surface of the earth that his body covers down to the golden base that lies at a depth of eighty thousand *yojana* leagues . . ."
>
> Then, with his palms folded, Upāli approached where the Blessed One was and asked, "If the Blessed One speaks of how great the root of virtue of this monk is, [84] how does such a root of virtue come to be diminished, thoroughly purged, and completely exhausted?"
>
> "O Upāli," replied the Buddha, "I have seen nothing comparable to inflicting wounds on and causing injury to those who are engaged in the practice of pure conduct. Upāli, this will thin out, thoroughly purge, and completely exhaust that great root of virtue. Therefore, O Upāli, if one should not harbor malevolent thoughts even toward a log, what need is there to speak of harboring malevolent thoughts toward a body imbued with consciousness?"[252]

"Thinning out" refers, for example, to turning a root of virtue that was great when generated into a smaller one, what was long when generated into a shorter one, and so on. This is a weaker form of exhaustion, as it does not destroy the effects entirely. It appears that "purging" refers to a medium level of exhaustion, while "completely exhausting" refers to a great degree of exhaustion. In the *Moon Lamp Sutra* cited in the *Compendium of Sutras* one reads:

> He who acts toward those around him with harmful thoughts,
> he will not be protected by moral discipline and study,
> he will not be protected by meditation and solitude,
> nor will he be protected by giving and venerating the buddhas.[253]

Here "those around" refers to fellow monastics. That he cannot be protected by the six factors, such as moral discipline, means that for him the destruction of the roots of virtue by anger cannot be averted.

As to what specific roots of virtue come to be destroyed, this is not explicitly stated in the sutras cited above. However, the *Guide to the Bodhisattva Way* explains this to be those of generosity, venerating the sugatas, and so on, while *Entering the Middle Way* explains it as those of generosity and moral discipline. Since Candrakīrti's *Commentary* speaks of "the collection of merit," it seems that this does not refer to the roots of virtue consisting in the excellent realization of selflessness; do examine this question further, however.

The *Teachings of Akṣayamati Sutra*, as quoted in the *Compendium of Sutras*, cites the simile of a drop of water that falls into the great ocean. Just as that drop does not dry up until the dawn of the great eon, the roots of virtue dedicated to enlightenment do not expire until awakening is attained.[254] Similarly, the *Adornment of Trees Sutra* cites the simile of transforming a thousand ounces of base metal into gold with an ounce of mercury elixir known as "gold-appearing" without the base metal ever consuming the elixir. Like this, it is stated, the mercury elixir of the awakening mind cannot be consumed by all the base metals of afflictions.[255]

If one thinks, relying on such statements, that the awakening mind, the roots of virtue sustained by it, and those virtuous roots dedicated toward awakening cannot be destroyed by anger, one would be mistaken. For it has been stated that even the virtuous roots of the great bodhisattvas can be destroyed. [85] Thus the meaning of the first sutra cited above is that these roots of virtue are not exhausted because of their fruition; it does not mean that they cannot be eroded by anger. And the meaning of the second sutra is that the afflictions cannot totally annihilate the awakening mind in the way in which, on the basis of awakening mind, the afflictions can be eliminated.

Regarding the phrase "destroying the roots of virtue," some assert that it means the potency of the virtues to swiftly produce effects is destroyed—the production of their fruits is postponed, and the fruits of anger and the like are brought forth in its place. But it is not the case, they say, that their fruits cannot ripen later on if those roots of virtue meet the appropriate conditions. For if no mundane path can eliminate the seeds of their corresponding objects of relinquishment, how can an affliction eliminate the seeds of virtue? This would be impossible, they assert.

There is no logical entailment in this reasoning. Take the example of nonvirtues that have been purified by ordinary beings through applying the four powers in antidote practice. This does not eliminate the seeds, and yet it remains impossible for a karma thus purified to produce ripening effects, even if suitable conditions are later met. Similarly, one who attains the *peak* and *forbearance* stages of the path of preparation has not yet eliminated the seeds of wrong view or the causes for taking birth in the lower realms, and yet it remains impossible for wrong views to arise or for one to take birth in the lower realms, even if the bodhisattva were to meet the conditions in the future. So it has been stated.

Furthermore, a sutra cited in the *Commentary on the Treasury of Abhidharma* states:

> As for karma's fruitions, those heavier,
> those closer in time, those most habitual,
> and those committed earliest—
> among all karma these are reaped first.[256]

As stated here, whatever karma happens to be reaped first, virtuous or nonvirtuous, this blocks the space for other karmic fruits to be reaped. But this alone is not reason enough to say that it destroys virtues or nonvirtues; nowhere has this situation been explained in such terms. Had it been so, all the other powerful nonvirtuous karma should also have been described as "destroyers of virtuous roots." In any case, the autocommentary to the *Essence of the Middle Way* explains that in both of these two cases—cleansing of nonvirtues through application of the four powers and the destruction of the roots of virtue by wrong views and harmful intent—[the karma] are akin to damaged seeds from which no sprouts can emerge, even when suitable cooperative conditions are met; that is, they remain incapable of producing effects even if they later meet with conditions.[257]

The destruction of virtues by anger does not mean that the instant anger has arisen, virtues become nonexistent in the mental continuum of that person. Rather, it injures the virtues' capacity to produce their effects. Here too, since three degrees of annihilation—small, medium, and great—are described, to the extent [a root of virtue] has been injured, to that extent it is made incapable of bearing its fruits. Thus there are two ways [the arising of anger] can inflict an injury. One is the destruction of the power to swiftly give rise to new levels of paths, and the other is to harm the arising of fruits such as birth in the higher realms.

Being angry toward a bodhisattva, insulting them, and disparaging them out of negative motivation are described [86] in the *Compendium of Sutras* as limitless in terms of their ill consequences.[258] Furthermore, the consequences are the same regardless of whether one has recognized one's object to be a bodhisattva and whether one's grounds for being angry are valid. In view of this, we must strive with all our efforts to prevent anger in general and, in particular, anger directed toward those who are engaged in monastic life as well as toward bodhisattvas.

The *Ākāśagarbha Sutra* states that a root infraction will destroy virtues that have been generated in the past.[259] The *Compendium of Training* states that gazing at the householder's life while yearning for gifts and honor, swelling with manifest conceit, and forsaking the Dharma are all acts through which virtues generated in the past will be consumed and virtuous activities will fail to increase.[260] Therefore, recognizing the conditions that destroy roots of virtue, we must specially strive to relinquish them. What I have presented here is but a brief summary; one should definitely read the *Compendium of Sutras* and the *Compendium of Training*.

Rejecting anger on the basis of contemplating the numerous faults of intolerance

This impotence caused by intolerance may damage oneself alone; the potent force that is the absence of compassion, however, damages both self and others. This is as follows.

> Wrath disfigures your face and leads you to what is unwholesome;
> it robs your mind of the judgment of what is right and wrong;
> intolerance is swift to throw you to the lower realms. 3.7abc

The instant it arises, **wrath disfigures your face and leads you to what is unwholesome;** and **it robs your mind of the judgment** that helps evaluate **what is right** to do and **what is wrong** to do. This **intolerance,** anger, **is swift to throw you to the lower realms** after death. So contemplate these ill consequences, and with the thought "I will never give an opportunity to anger," prevent anger.

The appropriateness of cultivating forbearance

This is twofold: (1) contemplating the numerous qualities of forbearance and (2) a summary with advice to cultivate forbearance.

Contemplating the numerous qualities of forbearance

If the above are the faults of intolerance, what are the qualities of its opposite, forbearance?

> But forbearance brings qualities opposite to those just described: 3.7d
> forbearance makes you attractive and dear to the sublime ones,
> you become wise in knowing what is appropriate and what is not,
> afterward you gain birth as a deva or a human,
> and it secures the exhaustion of negative karma. 3.8

[87] **But** practicing **forbearance brings qualities opposite to those** faults of anger **just described.** For example, practicing **forbearance makes you attractive** in physical appearance, you become **dear to,** or cherished by, **the sublime ones,** and **you become wise in knowing what is appropriate** or correct and **what is not** appropriate or correct. **Afterward,** following your death, **you gain birth as a deva or a human,** and **it secures the exhaustion of** your **negative karma** gathered through anger and so on in the past. Contemplating these benefits, develop the power of forbearance.

A summary with advice to cultivate forbearance

> Knowing the faults and benefits of anger and forbearance,
> respectively, of ordinary beings and bodhisattvas,
> shun intolerance and cultivate swiftly and constantly
> the forbearance praised by the āryas. 3.9

As described above, **knowing the faults** or the ill consequences of **ordinary beings** experiencing anger **and the benefits of** a **bodhisattva's forbearance, shun intolerance and cultivate [swiftly and]**[261] **constantly**—that is, at all times—**the forbearance** that is **praised by the āryas.**

The divisions of the perfection of forbearance

> Forbearance, even dedicated toward perfect buddhahood,
> is mundane if objectified in terms of the three factors.
> If there is no such objectification, the Buddha said,
> this is a perfection that indeed transcends the world. 3.10

The division of the perfection of forbearance into two—mundane and supramundane—is presented in the four lines beginning "**Forbearance, even dedicated toward perfect buddhahood.**" This distinction can be understood on the basis of what has been already explained above [in relation to the first two perfections].

The other pure qualities that arise on this ground

> On this ground the bodhisattva attains absorptions and clairvoyance;
> here attachment and aversion come to exhaust completely. 3.11ab

[88] Just as **on this** third **ground the bodhisattva** attains purity of the perfection of forbearance, in the same way, he **attains** the purity of four **absorptions** (*dhyāna*), such as the first level of absorption. And, exemplified by this, he will attain the four formless attainments (infinite space, infinite consciousness, nothingness, and the peak of existence), the four immeasurables (loving kindness, compassion, sympathetic joy, and equanimity), and the five types of **clairvoyance** (supernatural feats, divine ears, knowledge of others' minds, recollection of previous lives, and divine eyes).

Although he may enter and exit these absorption states and formless states seeing that they help complete the causes of awakening, he will take birth through the power of aspiration prayers thinking especially of this. He will not take birth through the power of the mundane absorptions and formless attainments. He is able to do this starting from the first ground, but on this ground the bodhisattva attains a higher training in concentration that is far superior to previous grounds, and with that, he experiences greater temptation to take birth through such power. This is why this point is mentioned here. And **here**, on this ground, **attachment and aversion come to exhaust completely**, thus attaining their cessation.

The conjunction "and" (*dang*) carries the meaning of "also," and it is there to include what is not mentioned—namely, delusion.[262] The meaning of the word "exhaust" here should not be taken to be total exhaustion. For even the sutras state that all four fetters of desire, form, cyclic existence, and ignorance are thinned out.[263]

With respect to what is meant by these statements [about exhaustion of attachment, aversion, and delusion on this bodhisattva ground], Asaṅga's *Bodhisattva Grounds* explains that it is through the power of mundane meditative absorption and formless attainment that one becomes free from attachment toward the desire, form, and formless realms. This is the elimination of manifest level as spoken of earlier. This seems, therefore, why the word "thinned out" is used. The fetters [being thinned out] too seem to be the ones mentioned in the Abhidharma texts.

In connection with this matter at hand, there is the statement in the *Ten Grounds Sutra*, "His fetters in the form of views were already eliminated previously."[264] Some explain this sentence to mean that the last three of [five types of false] views are eliminated on the path of seeing. However, this should be taken to mean that the acquired dimension of the five views have been eliminated on the path of seeing. The *Bodhisattva Grounds*, however, reads this in the following way: "The fetters that are views are eliminated from the ground of engagement by imagination, because it is there that one first aspires to the suchness of the ultimate nature of things."[265]

Next in that same sutra, it states that false attachment, aversion, and delusions, which are not likely to recede for many hundred thousands of eons, are eliminated on this ground.[266] This should be understood as the elimination of their seeds, and that too in terms of the specific object of abandonment relinquished on this ground. Of the innate afflictions relinquished on the path of meditation, the first six—the three levels of great and the three levels of the medium—[89] are correlated with the second to the seventh bodhisattva grounds.[267]

The *Commentary*'s author [Candrakīrti] does not speak explicitly of the elimination of acquired afflictions from the first ground and of the elimination of the innate dimensions from the second ground onward. But Nāgārjuna's *Precious Garland* states that until the eighth ground is attained, there is no annihilation of the seeds of the afflictions; grasping at true existence must be considered an affliction; until grasping at true existence is annihilated, the identity view does not come to be annihilated; and on the first ground, the three binding factors are eliminated.[268] Therefore it is extremely clear that a differentiation between two classes [acquired versus innate] must be made within the afflictions in general and a twofold distinction needs to be made with regard to the identity view in particular.

Now, in this Candrakīrti tradition, which takes grasping at true existence as an affliction, when the afflictions are eliminated by the uncontaminated paths, the seeds of grasping at true existence are invariably eliminated as well. However, at this stage, one cannot permanently annihilate, even in part, the habitual propensities for dualistic perception, which are other than these seeds and are taken to be subtle obscurations to knowledge. So, since no subtle obscuration to knowledge can be eliminated until all afflictions are annihilated, the subtle obscurations to knowledge are eliminated during the three pure grounds [the eighth to tenth].

> Because of this he is at all times also able to destroy
> all the attachment associated with the desire realm. 3.11cd

The bodhisattva abiding on the third ground becomes almost like the celestial king Indra, the sovereign among the gods. He will **at all times** be **able to destroy all the attachment** of the world of the sentient beings **associated with the desire realm**. As such he will become a chief [of beings] and will be thus skilled in rescuing other sentient beings from the mires of desire. As for the conjunctive particle "also," what appears in Naktso's translation "Also at all times he will destroy attachments toward the desire realm"[269] seems to read better.

The distinctive characteristics of the first three perfections

Now [Candrakīrti] presents clearly the distinctive features of the practitioners of the first three perfections, the nature of their collection, and what fruits are achieved:

> The three practices of generosity and so on
> the Sugata lauded mostly for the householder.
> They also constitute what is known as the collection of merit,
> and they are the cause of the buddha's form body. 3.12

Although both lay and monastic bodhisattvas are practitioners of generosity, [morality, and forbearance], from the point of view of what is easier and what is more difficult to pursue, **the three practices of generosity and so on** are said to be easier **for the householder** bodhisattvas to pursue. So **the Sugata lauded** these three **mostly** for such practitioners. These three **also constitute what is known as the collection of merit** from among the twin collections [of merit and gnosis]. [90] This collection is **the cause of the buddha's form body**—that is, its principal cause. The *Precious Garland* too states:

> There, generosity and morality
> and the teaching on forbearance
> were taught especially for the laity.
> So constantly cultivate familiarity with these
> that take compassion as their essence.[270]

In the context of the three teachings that are easier for lay bodhisattvas to pursue, *generosity* refers to supplying material needs and fearlessness, *morality* is that of the laity, while *forbearance* is primarily the one derived from reflecting resolutely on the Dharma. In contrast, diligence, meditative absorption, and wisdom are easier to pursue for monastic bodhisattvas. It is not the case, however, that either of these two [lay and monastic bodhisattvas] do not possess the other remaining perfections. The "collection of gnosis" consists of meditation and wisdom, and these two are principally the cause of the buddha's dharmakāya. Diligence is a condition for both collections.

A conclusion stating the qualities of the ground

> This bodhisattva, who abides in the sun radiating light,
> having first dispelled perfectly the darkness within his own self,

wishes keenly to utterly destroy the darkness in other beings.
On this ground, though extremely piercing, no heat of anger remains.
3.13

**This bodhisattva who abides in the sun radiating light, having first dis-
pelled perfectly the darkness** residing **within his own self** that obstructs
the emergence of this ultimate ground, shows this to others and **wishes
keenly to utterly destroy the darkness in other beings** that obstructs
their [attainment of the] third ground. Since this bodhisattva destroys the
darkness of faults that undermine the higher qualities, **on this ground** he
becomes **extremely piercing**, like the sun. Nevertheless, **no heat of anger
remains** toward defective beings, for his habituation to forbearance has
become supreme and his mental continuum has become well polished by
compassion.

This concludes exposition of the third ground of the ultimate awakening
mind from *Illuminating the Intent: An Exposition of Entering the Middle
Way.* [91]

6. The Fourth Ground, The Radiant

The fourth ground, The Radiant

This has three parts: (1) showing that diligence is superior on this ground, (2) the etymology of the name of the ground, and (3) showing what is particularly relinquished.

Showing that diligence is superior on this ground

On this ground, more than the first three perfections, it is diligence that comes to be superior. As the text says:

> All higher qualities follow after diligence;
> it is the cause of merit and wisdom, the two collections.
> Where diligence comes to be set ablaze,
> that ground is the fourth, The Radiant. 4.1

No higher qualities come about for someone who does not take joy in virtue[271] because there is no engagement at all in generosity and so on. In contrast, for those who derive joy from having gathered or in gathering the qualities like generosity mentioned above, the qualities that he has already attained will be enhanced and those not yet attained will be achieved. Therefore, **all higher qualities,** without exception, **follow after diligence,** and **it is the cause of the two collections of merit and wisdom,** or gnosis. The ground **where** such **diligence comes to be** especially **set ablaze, that ground is the fourth, The Radiant.** Since on the third ground the bodhisattva has attained higher training in concentration far more excellent than that of the first two grounds, from this he has achieved a unique pliancy that permanently dispels laziness. So on this ground, the perfection of diligence comes to be superior.

The etymology of the name of the ground

Here the Sugata's children come to have,
through their special practice of the factors of enlightenment,
the light of gnosis far brighter than the glow of shining copper. 4.2a–c

"Why is this ground called The Radiant?" one might ask. Here, on this fourth ground, **the Sugata's children come to have, through their special practice of the** thirty-seven **factors of enlightenment** to a level far **superior** compared to before, **a light of gnosis** similar to but **far brighter than the glow of shining copper** mentioned in the context of the third ground. [92] Because this light of the fire of perfect gnosis comes to be far superior on this ground, this bodhisattva ground is called The Radiant. These very features are as stated below in the *Precious Garland*, features cited also in *Entering the Middle Way*:

The fourth is called The Radiant
for the light of perfect gnosis has emerged,
for he has cultivated especially
all the factors of enlightenment.

As a fruitional effect of this,
he will be a king of Conflict-Free (Yāma) gods;
he will be skilled in utterly destroying
the identity view and its derivatives.[272]

The thirty-seven factors of enlightenment refer to the seven sets, such as the four establishings of mindfulness.

The *four establishings of mindfulness* are the establishing of mindfulness of (1) the body, (2) feelings, (3) mind, and (4) mental objects.

The *four perfect endeavors* are (1) generating the virtuous factors that have not yet arisen, (2) increasing those that have already arisen, (3) not generating the nonvirtuous factors that have not yet arisen, and (4) perfectly relinquishing those that have already arisen.

The *four limbs of supernatural feats* are those of (1) aspiration, (2) diligence, (3) mind, and (4) analysis in the form of concentration.

The *five faculties* are the faculties of (1) faith, (2) diligence, (3) mindfulness, (4) concentration, and (5) wisdom.

The *five powers* are the powers of faith and so on.

The *seven limbs of enlightenment* are the limbs of enlightenment of perfect (1) mindfulness, (2) clear discrimination of the character of phenomena, (3) diligence, (4) joy, (5) pliancy, (6) concentration, and (7) equanimity.

The *eightfold ārya path* consists of the ārya paths of right (1) view, (2) intention, (3) speech, (4) action, (5) livelihood, (6) diligence, (7) mindfulness, and (8) concentration.

Now, the first ground is the basis for training. As far as the actual training goes, the higher training in morality correlates to the second ground, the higher training in the mind [or concentration] correlates to the third ground, while the higher training in wisdom correlates to the fourth, fifth, and sixth grounds. So here on this ground, the bodhisattva becomes especially endowed with the training in wisdom that is highly versed in the coarse and subtle aspects of the thirty-seven factors of enlightenment. [93]

Showing what is particularly relinquished

Thoughts associated with identity view totally cease. 4.2d

[Here on this ground] **thoughts** that are **associated with identity view**—namely, the subtle identity view and thoughts that precede it, such as grasping at coarse levels of "I" and "mine" in terms of holding on to a self, to a sentient being, and so on as substantially existent, as well as grasping at the self-existence of phenomena in terms of clinging to the aggregates, elements, sense bases, and so on as truly existent—these **will totally cease**. The meaning of the word *cessation* here is that the bodhisattva eliminates those seeds of the twofold self-grasping that are the specific objects of abandonment to be relinquished by this ground; it is not the case that the entirety of self-grasping is annihilated. The sutra itself also indicates the presence of innate identity view [in such bodhisattvas].[273]

This concludes exposition of the fourth ground of the ultimate awakening mind from *Illuminating the Intent: An Exposition of Entering the Middle Way*. [94]

7. The Fifth Ground, Hard to Conquer

The fifth ground, Hard to Conquer

This has two parts: (1) the etymology of the name of the fifth ground and (2) becoming superior in meditative absorption and mastering the truths.

The etymology of the name of the fifth ground

> This great one on the ground of Hard to Conquer
> cannot be defeated even by the entire host of māras. 5.1ab

The great one abiding **on** the fifth **ground of Hard to Conquer,** if he **cannot be defeated even by the entire host of māras** such as Devaputra residing throughout the world systems,[274] what need is there to speak of others such as the servants of Māra under his command? Therefore this ground is named Hard to Conquer. The *Precious Garland* says:

> The fifth is Hard to Conquer
> because it's so hard for all the māras to subdue it.
> Here mastery in understanding arises
> on the subtle points of the ārya truths and so on.
>
> As for its ripening effect,
> he will be a king of the Tuṣita gods.
> He undoes the contents of the afflicted views
> crafted by all proponents of extremes.[275]

Becoming superior in meditative absorption and mastering the truths

> Excelling in meditative absorption and in the truths of the wise,
> he gains mastery in refined understanding as well. 5.1cd

On this fifth ground, among the ten perfections, it is the perfection of **med-itative absorption** that one comes to **excel in**. Seeing as the bodhisattva had previously become superior in the first four perfections—generosity up to diligence—it is easily understood that the point of reference here must come from among the remaining six perfections. This is to say, the bodhisattva has attained on this ground a level of absorption that can never be trodden upon by such opposing forces as distraction, and this extent of mastery is lacking for the perfection of wisdom and the rest. Not only does the bodhisattva become superior in meditative absorption, **he** also **gains mastery in refined understanding** of the nature or essence of **the truths of the wise**—namely, the āryas—understanding that requires comprehension through refined intellect. Therefore here he becomes endowed with superior wisdom versed in the coarse and subtle aspects of the truths.

The *Ten Grounds Sutra*[276] says that the fifth-ground bodhisattva comes to be versed in the four noble truths of suffering,[95] its origin, cessation, and path, and separately it also says that he comes to be versed in the conventional and ultimate truths. This raises the question of how there can be four truths distinct from the two truths when it is clearly stated in the *Meeting of Father and Son Sutra*[277] as well as in Nāgārjuna's *Fundamental Wisdom* that the number of truths is exhausted within the division of two truths.

To respond to this question, Candrakīrti's *Commentary* confirms that there is no truth not encompassed within the two truths. The four truths, he explains, were taught to demonstrate that what is to be relinquished (the class of afflicted phenomena) includes their origin (the cause) and suffering (the effect), and what is to be affirmed (the class of enlightened phenomena) includes the path (the cause) and cessation (the effect). Of these, the *Commentary* states that truths of suffering, its origin, and the path belong to the conventional truth, while the truth of cessation belongs to the ultimate truth.[278]

In his *Commentary to Sixty Stanzas of Reasoning* too, Candrakīrti explains nirvana to be the ultimate truth and the other three truths [out of the four] as conventional truths,[279] and *nirvana* here refers to the truth of cessation. Furthermore, in this commentary to *Sixty Stanzas of Reasoning*, Candrakīrti points out how the Buddha accepts the possibility of direct knowledge of the truth of cessation, and how this would be untenable for the Buddhist essentialists who assert direct valid cognitions to possess as their object things endowed with intrinsic characteristics. In his own tradition, Candrakīrti establishes the understanding of how cessation is directly known in terms of the realization of suchness by the uncontaminated gnosis of meditative equipoise. So, if cessation were conventional truth, such presentations would become utterly untenable. Furthermore, Candrakīrti repeatedly endeavors to establish the necessity of direct realization of the truth of suchness when nirvana is actualized. Therefore to speak of the truth of cessation as a conventional truth would indicate an incomplete analysis.[280]

Now, although the negation of true existence—the object of negation—on a given basis is defined as the ultimate truth, this does not entail that the object of negation of whatever constitutes ultimate truth is necessarily nonexistent. For example, the *Praise to the Ultimate Expanse* states:

> That which if not known
> makes one revolve in the three worlds,
> that which definitely abides in all beings—
> to that ultimate expanse I bow and pay homage.
>
> That which is the cause of samsara,
> from purifying this very thing comes
> the purity that is nirvana;
> dharmakāya too is this.[281]

This states that when the ultimate nature of things tainted with stains is purified, that constitutes nirvana and dharmakāya. Similarly, there are numerous instances [in the texts] where the object of negation in the context of pristine ultimate reality is described as a "stain." Now, if it were impossible for the ultimate nature of things to become free of stains, endeavor would then be pointless. [96] If, on the other hand, it is possible, then this implies that its object of negation does have an existence and is knowable. This is analogous to the following example. The rabbit's horn, which is the object of negation in the context of the phrase "the nonexistence of rabbit's horn," does not exist as a knowable, yet one can still posit the absence of a vase—whose object of negation [i.e., a vase] does exist [in general] as a knowable—as an instance of that nonexistence of a rabbit's horn.[282]

So, from the point of view of the ultimate nature of things that pervades all phenomena, both pure and impure, this is indeed defined in terms of the negation of the two kinds of self, where what is negated has no existence in reality at all. However, as a given basis becomes progressively more purified of stains, its ultimate nature too becomes progressively more purified. Therefore, for certain special types of bases, it is inadequate to leave its purity only one-sided. Its purity must also include the purification of the relevant adventitious stains, and it is this [such ultimate nature] that is called "the truth of cessation."[283]

Many terms mentioned in the *Ten Grounds Sutra* contain the word *truth* in them, such as "being versed in the truth of defining characteristics" on this ground, and among these, there is none that is not encompassed within the two truths.

This concludes exposition of the fifth ground of the ultimate awakening mind from *Illuminating the Intent: An Exposition of Entering the Middle Way*. [97]

Part II : The Sixth Ground, The Manifest

8. Introducing the Sixth Ground

Explaining the sixth ground, The Manifest

This has four parts: (1) the etymology of the name of the ground and its superiority in wisdom, (2) praise of the perfection of wisdom, (3) explaining reality in terms of seeing profound dependent origination, and (4) a conclusion stating the qualities of the ground.

The etymology of the name of the ground and its superiority in wisdom

> On Directly Facing[284] he abides in the mind of meditative equipoise
> and turns to the attributes of perfect buddhahood.
> This bodhisattva, who sees the truth of dependent origination,
> attains true cessation by dwelling in wisdom. 6.1

Having attained on the fifth ground a thoroughly pure perfection of meditative absorption, the bodhisattva **abides in** the most excellent **mind of meditative equipoise** of the sixth ground—namely, **Directly Facing**, or The Manifest. Thus **this bodhisattva** on the sixth ground, **who** on this basis **sees the** profound **truth of dependent origination** of *mere conditionedness*, **attains true cessation** because of his **dwelling in** the most excellent perfection of **wisdom**. Prior to this, such as on the fifth ground, the bodhisattva did not attain such cessation, for he has not reached superiority in the excellent perfection of wisdom. One cannot attain the cessation through excellence in the first five perfections alone. This ground is called The Manifest (1) because here, on the basis of superiority in wisdom, the reflection-like ultimate nature of things becomes manifest, (2) because on the fifth ground the bodhisattva took the true paths as his object, and (3) because the bodhisattva now **turns to the attributes of perfect buddhahood**.

The *Explanation of the Commentary* interprets the second reason here in terms of the path by which the nonperception of cognition and its object becomes manifest.[285] However, the description of how "on the fifth ground the bodhisattva took the true path as his object" simply refers to the last of the four truths. The meaning, in other words, is that the bodhisattva on the fifth ground became versed in the coarse and subtle aspects of the four noble truths, and on the sixth ground, the wisdom versed in the four truths comes to full realization.

The first reason indicates how the wisdom versed in the sequential and reverse order of [the twelve links of] dependent origination comes to full realization here on this sixth ground. Thus the meaning here is that, on the basis of full realization of these two trainings in wisdom, the four noble truths and dependent origination have come to be manifestly known by the bodhisattva. Since the three trainings in wisdom [illusion-like reality, the four noble truths, and the twelve links of dependent origination] are fully realized on this ground; [98] given that the more distinctly superior one's tranquility the more distinctly superior will be one's insight; and given how on the fifth ground the bodhisattva attained the most excellent perfection of meditative absorption, so here on the sixth ground, the perfection of wisdom comes to be most excellent. Therefore it is from this ground onward that the special form of absorption into cessation is attained. The *Precious Garland* states:

> The sixth is called Directly Facing
> for it directly faces the buddha's attributes.
> Through familiarity with tranquility and insight,
> one flourishes with the attainment of cessation.
>
> As for its fruitional effect,
> one will be the king of the Pranirmāṇa gods.
> Since he is not outshone by śrāvakas,
> he pacifies those with inflated pride.[286]

Pranirmāṇa refers to Nirmāṇarati.[287]

Praise of the perfection of wisdom

To demonstrate that the collections other than the perfection of wisdom, such as of generosity, depend upon the perfection of wisdom to traverse to the resultant ground, the following is stated:

Just as a single man with eyes can easily lead
a group of blind men to their desired destination,
here too intelligence leads the sightless virtues
and guides them to the Conqueror's state. 6.2

Just as, for example, **a single man with eyes can easily lead a group of blind men to their desired destination**, likewise **here too**, in the context of the path, **intelligence**—namely, the perfection of wisdom—**leads** or thoroughly sustains **the virtues** such as generosity that are **sightless** in relation to suchness. **And** in this way, wisdom **guides them to the** resultant **Conqueror's state.** For it is through the perfection of wisdom that one sees without distortion what is a right path and what is not. The *Condensed Perfection of Wisdom* too states:

Millions and billions of blind people bereft of sight,
ignorant of the roads, how can they reach the towns?
Without wisdom these five perfections,
lacking sight, cannot touch awakening.[288]

The *Diamond Cutter* too says:

A person with sight who steps into the dark will not see anything. So too view the bodhisattva who has fallen into grasping at real entities while engaging thoroughly in generosity. O Subhūti, it is thus. When day breaks and the sun shines, the person with eyes will see all the varied forms. [99] So too view the bodhisattva who has not fallen into grasping at real entities while engaging thoroughly in generosity.[289]

The same applies to morality and so on.

Explaining suchness in terms of seeing profound dependent origination

This has five parts: (1) promising to explain the profound truth, (2) identifying those who are vessels for explaining the profound truth, (3) the way higher qualities ensue if suchness is explained, (4) urging those who are suitable vessels to listen, and (5) the way the suchness of dependent origination is expounded.

Promising to explain the profound truth

One might ask, "How is it, as stated above, that when the bodhisattva on the sixth ground sees dependent origination, he sees the suchness of dependence origination in terms merely of *this* emerging from *that*?" To respond to this, the *Commentary* says:

> The nature of this is something that does not fall within the purview of those like us whose eyes of intelligence are entirely covered by the dense cataracts of ignorance. It does fall, however, within the purview of those abiding on the advanced grounds, such as the sixth ground. Therefore, this is not something to be asked of someone like us. One should pose this question to the buddhas and the bodhisattvas who are free of the cataracts of ignorance, whose eyes of intelligence are anointed with the salve that is the excellent vision of emptiness, which destroys the cataracts of ignorance.[290]

The application of an eye ointment makes one's vision clearer but does not remove the eyes. Likewise, applying the ointment that is the vision of emptiness makes one's eyes of intelligence clearer, but it does not remove one's eyes of gnosis. If one understands this point, one will not be tainted by the pitiful disparaging view that there exists no gnosis in the meditative equipoise of āryas.[291]

Now one might ask, "Don't sutras such as the *Mother* [*Perfection of Wisdom*] and the *Ten Grounds* teach that bodhisattvas who engage in the perfection of wisdom see the suchness of dependent origination? So why don't you follow the scriptures when you expound it?"

[Candrakīrti responds that] ascertaining the purport of the scriptures is also difficult, so someone like us cannot reveal suchness even by citing the scriptures.

This statement is made from the perspective of teaching suchness independently by oneself. However, to indicate that treatises have been composed by authentic masters who can expound the scriptures without distortion, and how, on the basis of these, one *can* ascertain the purport of the scriptures, the text says: [100]

> One who has realized the utterly profound truth
> through scripture and through reasoning as well
> was the noble Nāgārjuna. So I will expound here
> his tradition as it appears in his treatises. 6.3

Like the bodhisattvas on the sixth ground, **one who has realized the utterly profound truth** of emptiness **was the noble Nāgārjuna.** Having understood the scriptures without distortion, he presented the suchness of all phenomena in extremely clear manner in his *Treatise on the Middle Way* **through scripture and through reasoning as well.** Therefore, just as the treatises of the noble Nāgārjuna present suchness, I, Candrakīrti, [too] **will expound here his tradition as it appears in his treatises.**

One might ask, "How did the noble Nāgārjuna ascertain the meaning of the definitive scriptures?"

This we know on the authority of the scriptures. The *Descent into Laṅkā Sutra* states:

> In the south in the land of coconuts,
> there will come a monk known as the Glorious
> who will be called by the name Nāga.
> He'll crush standpoints of existence and nonexistence;
> he'll expound in the world my vehicle,
> this unsurpassed Great Vehicle.
> Accomplishing the ground of Perfect Joy,
> he'll depart to [the pure land] Sukhāvatī.[292]

Thus it was stated that Nāgārjuna will expound the definite vehicle, which is the freedom from the two extremes of existence and nonexistence. This prophecy refers to the Licchavi youth Lokapriyadarśanā, a contemporary of the Buddha mentioned in the *Sublime Golden Light Sutra*[293] who would later take birth [as Nāgārjuna]. The *Great Clouds Sutra* states:

> When it has been four hundred years after my death, this youth
> will become a monk known by the name of Nāga and will
> propagate my teaching. Finally, he will become a king called

Jñānākaraprabha in the realm known as Utterly Transparent Light.[294]

These citations establish with certainty, therefore, that there exists in the definitive scriptures an undistorted prophecy of Nāgārjuna.

The *Mañjuśrī's Root Realizations Tantra* also gives the time of Nāgārjuna's coming and his name as found in the preceding sutra. There it is stated that he will live six hundred years.[295] In the *Great Drum Sutra* it is stated that this Licchavi youth Lokapriyadarśanā will be a monk bearing the name of a teacher and will propagate the teaching when it comes to decline eighty years after the Buddha's death. He will pass away after a hundred years [101] and will take birth in Sukhāvatī.[296] This too is accepted by the elder Bodhibhadra and the great Atiśa to be a prophecy of the master[297] and is premised on the account of Licchavi Priyadarśanā sharing the same mental continuum with Nāgārjuna. In the *Great Drum Sutra*, the monk is stated to be of the seventh ground.[298] However, this statement and those cited above cannot be taken as contradicting each other. For example, some scriptures describe some of the Guardian Kings as stream-enterers, while others describe them as buddhas, so one finds a lot of variations in the scriptures.

Identifying those who are vessels for explaining the profound truth

As for the definitive treatises, they should also be taught to not just anyone but to those who, because of past habituation, have planted the seed for realizing emptiness. Others, even if they listen to treatises that present emptiness, will suffer grave injurious consequences because they are plagued with distorted understandings regarding emptiness. Such grave injurious consequences will transpire like this: some, being unlearned, will forsake emptiness and will depart to the lower realms; some will apprehend the meaning of emptiness of intrinsic existence in a distorted way as "All of these phenomena are nonexistent; they do not exist at all." They will thus apprehend it mistakenly, and the wrong view disparaging all the phenomena of causes of effects will be first engendered and, held on to, will come to increase further and further. In relation to this issue, Candrakīrti comments on the following stanza:

Emptiness viewed mistakenly
dooms those of weak intelligence,

like a snake wrongly held
or a spell wrongly incanted.²⁹⁹

He says that, to not fall to the extreme of disparaging conventional truth, one must not slight the reflection-like karma and its effects; and to not fall to the extreme of reifying ultimate truth, one must see karma and its effects only in things with no intrinsic existence.³⁰⁰ To be contrary to these two is described as falling to the extremes of eternalism and nihilism. Thus Candrakīrti has stated that were one to conceive conditioned things as nonexistent, this would constitute a wrong view. Now there may be a linguistic level of difference between *nonexistent* and *not being existent*; but insofar as conveying the sense of nonexistence is concerned, no matter how carefully one might analyze, no difference whatsoever can be found between these two words.

Also, in commenting on the following lines from *Four Hundred Stanzas*—

One goes to the lower realms alone;
those not ordinary go to peace alone³⁰¹

—Candrakīrti explains that some who are not sublime and listen to the teaching of selflessness only end up going to the lower realms because of a tendency to either (1) dismiss emptiness or (2) gain distorted understanding of it.³⁰² Thus both these responses are described as leading to the lower realms. [102] "To gain a distorted understanding" is to apprehend the meaning of emptiness in nihilistic terms as nonexistence.

Thus, regarding individuals who lack the power of intelligence to appreciate the extremely subtle points yet possess evident conceit of having such ability, if they engage with fervor in their false determinations of the mere words related to the profound truth that lies clearly beyond their capacity, this will bring grave injurious consequences. Therefore we need to be especially careful with matters such as these.

One may ask, "It seems to be difficult therefore to determine who is appropriate to teach emptiness to and who is not appropriate to teach. So how does one make such a determination?" To indicate that this can be made on the basis of external signs, the text says:

Even ordinary persons when hearing about emptiness,
sheer joy surges again and again within their heart,

tears born of such joy fill their eyes,
and their hair stands up in their follicles. 6.4

Such people have the seed of perfect buddhahood.
They are the perfect vessels for this teaching;
to them you should teach the sublime ultimate truth. 6.5a–c

Even ordinary persons on the beginner's stage, **when hearing** an undistorted discourse **about emptiness, sheer joy surges again and again within their heart** because of hearing such a discourse. **Tears born of such joy fills their eyes, and their hair stands up in their follicles.** Such people have what is called **the seed** of realizing emptiness, the seed of the nonconceptual gnosis of **perfect buddhahood.** It is people such as these who **are the perfect vessels for this teaching** by a well-versed master. So **to them you should teach the sublime ultimate truth,** the truth whose characteristics will be explained below.

The point here is that if one sees these physical signs emerge on the basis of two convergent facts—that the person hears the discourse on emptiness and that he understands what is being heard—then such signs indicate unmistakenly that the person is a suitable vessel. In contrast, if the person does not understand the meaning, or even if he does, if the signs do not arise, one cannot determine for the time being that he is a suitable vessel for the profound truth. Even so, if he adheres to the dictates of his sublime teachers, such a person may in the future become a suitable vessel to deposit numerous new potencies for realizing emptiness. [103]

The way higher qualities ensue if suchness is expounded

For them the ensuing qualities will come to birth. 6.5d

Adopting perfect morality, they will always abide by it;
they will practice generosity and cultivate compassion;
they will practice forbearance and will dedicate thoroughly
their virtue to freedom for all beings. 6.6

They will revere those who aspire to perfect awakening. 6.7a

Teaching emptiness to the vessels described above will not be fruitless. Why?

Not only will such listeners not be saddled with the injurious consequences of distorted apprehension of emptiness, **for them the ensuing qualities** that result from listening to the view of emptiness **will come to birth**. How do these come about? These suitable vessels will relate to hearing the view of emptiness like finding a treasure; and so that this view does not degenerate in other lives, **adopting perfect morality, they will always abide by it.** They will do so by reflecting, "If, due to moral degeneration, I were to fall into the lower realms, the continuity of the view of emptiness will be broken." Thus they will adopt moral discipline and guard it without degeneration. Becoming morally degenerate does not require first adopting a moral code; even committing those acts that are naturally reprehensible, which are contrary to virtue, constitutes moral degeneration.

They will further reflect, "Even if, because of observing morality, I am born in the higher realms, I may become poor and bereft of the conditions for sustenance, such as food, drink, medicine, and clothing, and devoted to seeking these, the continuity of my hearing the view of emptiness and meditating on its meaning will be broken." Thus, as explained before, **they will practice generosity** in relation to the higher and lower fields.[303] Reflecting "It is the view of emptiness sustained by great compassion that will lead to buddhahood and not otherwise," they will **cultivate** the habit of great **compassion**, which is the root. Reflecting, "Through anger one goes to the lower realms, destroys one's virtues, and acquires an extremely unappealing countenance, and because of these the āryas will not be pleased," **they will practice forbearance**. Given that morality and so on that are not dedicated repeatedly to a buddha's omniscience do not become causes for buddhahood, and that uninterrupted continuity of their fruits in the form of embodiments and material resources will fail to emerge, [104] they **will dedicate thoroughly their virtue** of morality and so on **to freedom** from cyclic existence **for all beings**. And seeing that others like śrāvakas and pratyekabuddhas cannot teach the profound dependent origination like bodhisattvas, **they will** come to tremendously **revere** the bodhisattvas **who aspire to perfect awakening**.

For those of the Great Vehicle whose understanding of the view of emptiness has penetrated the essential point, a perfect understanding as described above will arise, and they will become reverential toward cultivating the vast aspects of the path. Such people would certainly be objects worthy of the highest acclaim. The *Commentary on the Awakening Mind* states:

Those who understand this emptiness of phenomena
and also conform to the law of karma and its results:
that is more amazing than amazing!
That is more wondrous than wondrous![304]

Such things will come to pass for those who have the following two characteristics: (1) They have shunned the two faults, which are forsaking emptiness by being either of the two kinds of unsuitable vessels—one that lacks admiration for the teaching and the other that seems to admire it but concludes that reason negates the entire world of cause and effect—and (2) they have come to realize that, on the basis of the view of emptiness as the absence of intrinsic existence, all presentations [such as causality] are all the more tenable.

Otherwise, when one allegedly engages from the standpoint of someone who has found the view, the entire presentation of karma and its effects, such as morality, risks being reduced to something akin to counting the ridges of a rabbit's horn. One might come to hold the view that "All such presentations [of morality and so on] are for the benefit of those who have not understood the definitive meaning but are irrelevant for someone who has understood the definitive meaning. They are nothing but conceptual fabrications, and all thinking constitutes grasping at signs in the form of clinging to true existence." Thus, like the Chinese monk Heshang Moheyan, one will come to undermine all the virtues. Some might say that for now, one does need to observe the ethical norms [at least] from the standpoint of delusory perception. Now, if one does distinguish two kinds of thinking—one that grasps at true existence and one that does not—then the assertion that reason negating intrinsic existence negates everything becomes meaningless chatter. If one recognizes no such differentiation of two types of thoughts, then the two categories of realization—those pertaining to the view of emptiness and those pertaining to the aspect of altruistic conduct—will each come to undermine the other, just like heat and cold. Furthermore, it will become impossible to define (1) the delusory perspective the *standpoint from which* [*things are posited*], (2) *that which posits*, and (3) *what are being posited*. So to speak in such terms [that things are posited purely from a delusory perspective] amounts to nothing but a conjuration in the dark.[305] Such protagonists in fact uphold the very standpoint critiqued by the treatises referred to above. [105]

Urging those who are suitable vessels to listen

> Gaining mastery of ways profound and vast,
> * such persons will gradually attain the ground of Perfect Joy.
> So all those who thus aspire, pray listen to this path. 6.7b–d

Such people, while **gaining mastery of ways profound and vast** as described above on the ordinary ground, will definitely gather the collections of virtues of both profound and vast aspects for a long time without interruption. Because of this, **such persons will gradually attain the ground of Perfect Joy. So all those who thus aspire** to attain the ground of Perfect Joy, **pray listen to this** profound **path** that will be presented below. In this way they are being urged here.

The *Commentary on the Four Hundred Stanzas* says:

> If he grows to esteem the discourse on emptiness of intrinsic existence, then by cultivating conditions conducive to it, his behavior will help increase his admiration for emptiness. His compassion will be great, he will repay the kindness of the Blessed Tathāgata, and he will have the wish to completely relinquish the causes that obstruct the sublime Dharma—namely, the causes of the great abyss. He will consider the destitute and will give away even those things that are hard to give. He will gather others as well through the four means of attraction. So, with all your efforts, certainly reveal this sublime teaching to those who are the vessels of sublime Dharma.[306]

So, as the above teaches, one should reveal this discourse with great effort. This is, of course, to those who are free of the two faults of being an unsuitable vessel. Even to those who have admiration but do not understand it exactly as it is, one should explain this teaching skillfully so that it does not undermine their conviction in dependent origination. For a speaker who is most learned, to teach his listeners, including those at least minimally qualified as suitable vessels, is a deed of great merit. For example, the *Compendium of Sutras* states:

> He who aspires for the profound teaching collects all the merit,
> for he will, until buddhahood is attained, accomplish all the

mundane and supramundane perfect factors. This is spoken in the *Gift of Youth Ratna Sutra*: "O Mañjuśrī, compared to a bodhisattva bereft of skillful means who engages in the six perfections for a hundred or thousand eons, someone who listens to this class of teaching [on emptiness] even with doubts [106] will generate far more merit. If this is so, what need is there to speak of listening to it without doubt. What need is there too to speak of someone who writes it out in words and transmits it through reading, upholds it, and teaches it extensively to others as well?"[307]

In the *Diamond Cutter* too it says:

The Blessed One stated, "Subhūti, what do you think? Say, for example, there were banks of the river Ganges equal in number to the number of grains of sand that exist on the banks of the Ganges, will this be a great number of grains of sand?"

"If the grains of sand on the banks of the Ganges are so numerous, what need is there to speak of the grains of sands of that many banks of the Ganges?" replied Subhūti.

To this the Blessed One said, "O Subhūti, I will share this with you. Understand thus. Say a man or a woman fills worlds equal in number to the grains of sand on the banks of the river Ganges with seven types of precious materials and offers these to the tathāgatas. Will that man or woman generate, on that basis, a vast amount of merit?"

"O Blessed One," replied Subhūti, "yes, this will be a vast amount. O Tathāgata, this will indeed be a vast amount."

Then the Blessed One said, "One who upholds even a stanza of four lines of this class of teaching and reveals it to others as well will generate even greater merit.[308]

In the *Treasury of Tathāgatas Sutra* too, after enumerating the ten great nonvirtues, it states that if someone who possesses these were to enter the teaching of selflessness with faith and aspiration to understand all phenomena as being primordially pure, such a sentient being will not go to the lower realms.[309] Also the *Chapter on Defeating the Māras* says:

A monk who understands all phenomena to be utterly tamed understands even the initial thresholds of misdeeds to be devoid of intrinsic existence and dispels the remorse borne of the occurrence of misdeeds and thus does not consolidate it. Because of this, if this act subdues even the heinous deeds, what need is there to speak of the minor deeds—erroneous practices of the rites and moral discipline?[310]

In the *Ajātaśatru Sutra* it says:

If someone who has committed a heinous act hears this teaching and engages with it and aspires for it, I do not speak of his karmic deed as a karmic obscuration.[311]

Such are the benefits of teaching and listening to the profound truth; these are also the benefits of aspiring for and contemplating it on other occasions. [107]

Now, to optimize the benefits received from expounding [the profound truth], two conditions must be present: one's motivation must be pure through not seeking gifts, honor, or fame, and one must not misconstrue the meaning of the teaching one is expounding but explain it without distortion. For it has been said that if one expounds on the basis of both or either of these two faults, this will impede the gathering of great stores of merit. For example, the master Vasubandhu says:

Therefore, those who expound the Dharma inaccurately, and expound it with afflicted mind yearning for gifts, honor, and fame, they will undermine their own great store of merit.[312]

The same is true here as well. Since the listener too must have a pure motivation and not misconstrue the meaning, both teacher and student should ensure that at least a minimum of qualifications is present when teaching and listening.

9. Identifying the Object of Negation

The way the suchness of dependent origination is expounded

This has three sections: (1) how this is presented in the perfect scriptures, (2) how the meaning of the scriptures is established by reason, and (3) enumerations of emptiness: the established conclusion.

How this is presented in the perfect scriptures

The first has two parts: (1) citations showing how it was taught in the scriptures and (2) identifying the forces opposing the understanding of suchness.

Citations showing how it was taught in the scriptures

Here in the *Ten Grounds Sutra* it states:

> When the bodhisattva on the fifth ground enters the sixth ground, he does so by means of ten perfect equanimities with respect to phenomena. What are these ten?
>
> They are (1) the perfect equanimity of all phenomena in their absence of signs; (2) the perfect equanimity of all phenomena in their absence of defining characteristics, likewise (3) in their absence of birth, (4) in being unborn, (5) in being void, (6) in their primordial purity, and (7) in their freedom from elaborations; (8) the perfect equanimity in their absence of affirmation and rejection; (9) the perfect equanimity of all phenomena in their resemblance to illusions, to dreams, to mirages, to echoes, to reflections of the moon in water, to mirror images, and to conjurations; and (10) the perfect equanimity of all phenomena in their absence of the duality of real and unreal.
>
> When he realizes the nature of all phenomena in such terms,

because of his sharp and apposite forbearance, [108] he will attain the sixth ground—namely, The Manifest.[313]

"Likewise" indicates that the phrase "[the perfect equanimity of] all phenomena" must be extended up to "in their absence of affirmation and rejection." These two [the absence of affirmation and rejection] are a single perfect equanimity. The equanimities in terms of phenomena's resemblance to the seven similes such as illusions should be taken as one perfect equanimity. And the last two [of real and unreal] should also be considered as a single perfect equanimity. There seems to be some variance in the identity of the ten perfect equanimities even between the *Commentary on the Ten Grounds Sutra* and the *Bodhisattva Grounds*.[314] Since those two texts differ in their interpretation of emptiness from this tradition, the ten perfect equanimities are here explained in a manner distinct from them.

Of these [ten perfect equanimities], the first is that all phenomena are equal insofar as all these appearances of diverse signs do not exist from the perspective of the ārya's meditative equipoise. The second is the equanimity of all phenomena insofar as they are all devoid of existence by virtue of their intrinsic characteristics. These two represent a general presentation.

The remaining eight present particular variations of the very truth thus explained in general. For instance, the "absence of birth" is from the perspective of the future, and "unborn" is from that of another temporal standpoint. That all phenomena are equanimous or equal must be understood in the context of other [remaining statements] as well. "Being void" refers to being devoid of "what is to be born" and "what is already born." These, in turn, must be understood in the sense of being "absent" of existence qualified by intrinsic characteristics, as stated in context of the second perfect equanimity. This fact too [of being devoid of existence through intrinsic characteristics] is not something constructed by scripture or reason; rather, they remain so as primordially pure. This is the sixth.

The seventh, the absence of dualistic elaboration, should be correlated to the first equanimity, while the freedom of elaboration of language and conceptualization should be correlated to the second equanimity.[315] The same [second] equanimity statement should be applied to the eighth as well. The ninth consists of numerous analogies that help ascertain the truth as explained above. The tenth refers to the fact that whatever the phenomenon, all are the same in lacking intrinsic existence in terms of the duality of real versus unreal. "Sharp" refers to swift intelligence, while "apposite" refers to forbearance toward the unborn nature commensurate with that of the eighth ground.[316] There appears to be various types of apposite forbearance depending upon the context.

Although many scriptures teach the suchness of phenomena, the context here is the explanation of how the wisdom of the sixth ground realizes suchness. Thus the citation here is from the scripture that states how the bodhisattva enters the sixth ground by means of ten perfect equanimities.

Identifying the forces opposing the understanding of suchness

In setting forth all phenomena as devoid of true existence, if one does not understand well what constitutes *true existence* and what constitutes *grasping at true existence*, one's view of emptiness will certainly go astray. Here, *Guide to the Bodhisattva Way* states [109]:

> Without touching upon the imputed entity,
> the absence of its reality cannot be grasped.[317]

Thus if the imputed entity—namely, the generic concept of "what is to be negated"—does not appear clearly to one's mind, it is said that one will not be able to pinpoint the absence of that object of negation. Therefore, if a clear sense of what is the purported true existence—that which is said not to exist—as well as what phenomena are understood to be empty of—the object to be negated—does not arise in one's mind, it would be impossible to ascertain clearly the nature of the absence of true existence as well as the nature of emptiness. It is not enough to have identified true existence as postulated by proponents of philosophical tenets or their corresponding apprehensions of true existence. It is most essential, therefore, to have identified well the *innate grasping at true existence*—which persists since beginningless time and is present both in those whose minds are tempered by philosophical tenets and in those whose minds are not thus tempered—as well as the purported *true existence* grasped at by such an innate mind. Without identifying these, one might engage in eliminating the object of negation through reasoning, but this would not undermine whatsoever the clinging to true existence that persists since beginningless time, and thus miss the entire purpose at hand. Now to do this, we must first identify the grasping at true existence that lies within our own mind and understand how the various Madhyamaka reasonings function directly and indirectly to eradicate its object. Negation and affirmation that are directed solely outward will have scant benefit.

On a related note, if one can understand the identification of what is to be negated according to the Prāsaṅgika Madhyamaka and Svātantrika Madhyamaka, one will be able to appreciate the fine differences in their views. Hence, this presentation has two parts: identifying grasping at true existence according to the Svātantrika Madhyamaka standpoint and identifying grasping at true existence according to the Prāsaṅgika Madhyamaka standpoint.

Identifying grasping at true existence according to the Svātantrika Madhyamaka standpoint

This has three parts: (1) identifying *true existence* and *grasping at true existence*, (2) presenting truth and falsity within the context of worldly convention through the analogy of magical illusion, and (3) explaining the analogy by relating it to the actual referent.

Identifying true existence *and* grasping at true existence

Other reliable treatises of Svātantrika make no clear identification of the object of negation, but Kamalaśīla's *Light of the Middle Way* presents a criterion for conventional existence, the contrary of which can be recognized as constituting the criterion of ultimate or true existence. Here is what the text says:

> Though things do not possess essence in reality, the erroneous mind reifies them contrary to their nature. This [erroneous mind] is called the *conventional* [*saṃvṛti*, literally, "concealer"] because, as it were, it obscures suchness or, through it, suchness is covered over. As such the sutra states:
>
>> The arising of things is on the conventional (*saṃvṛti*);
>> on the ultimate there is no intrinsic nature. [110]
>> That which is mistaken toward no intrinsic nature
>> is held to be a concealer (*saṃvṛti*) of the perfect truth.[318]
>
> Because it [perception of things] originates from this [erroneous mind], what it reveals—namely, all the false things being

perceived—are stated to be conventional only. This [erroneous mind], in turn, comes about from the ripening of a habitual propensity to err that exists since beginningless time. That [mind] reveals entities to all sentient beings as if they were real in nature, and this they all come to perceive. Therefore all things that are false in their nature and [are posited] by virtue of the power of the minds [of sentient beings] are said to exist only conventionally.[319]

Up to "This [erroneous mind] is" [in the first part of the citation] indicates how beings mistakenly ascribe ultimate existence to what are ultimately devoid of intrinsic nature. From "conventional" up to "covered over"[320] presents the meaning of the phrase "concealer of final truth"; here "conventional" is taken to be the concealer in that it conceals the final truth. Because it originates from grasping at true existence, that which sees what that grasping reveals as truly existent is a thought, not a sensory cognition. The commentary to the *Two Truths* states that true existence, which is the object of negation, does not appear to sensory perceptions,[321] and this remains true here as well. From "This [erroneous mind], in turn," up to "beginningless time" presents this grasping at true existence to be innate. Thus "to all living beings" is mentioned. As for the minds of these living beings, this is not only conceptual thoughts; it also includes the nonconceptual cognitions. Things come to be posited by virtue of these two [classes of consciousness]. That things do not exist on the ultimate level and that these false entities exist only on the conventional level is the meaning of the line "The arising of things is conventional." The meaning here, however, is not that they exist as the concealer—as the grasping at true existence. Understood thus, *an existence through its own objective mode of being and not posited in dependence on being perceived by cognitions or posited by virtue of the power of cognitions* constitutes true, ultimate, and final existence.[322] And grasping at this is the innate grasping at true existence.

One might ask, "If this is so, how do you explain this statement in the *Light of the Middle Way*: 'To say that ultimately there is no arising is to say that they [arising, disintegration, and so on] are not established as such by perfect cognition'?[323] For, through implication, this defines *ultimate existence* and [*ultimate*] *arising* in terms of being established as arising and as existence by a rational cognition of suchness?"

[*Reply:*] Yes, this is true. But you must understand that, with respect to the proviso "ultimately," there are two senses of the term *ultimate*. One is where rational cognition [of emptiness] in the form of the threefold wisdom of hearing, reflection, and meditation are characterized as "ultimate"; phenomena are not established by such cognitions in the manner defined above. The other sense of *ultimate* is where *existence through a thing's own objective mode of being and not by virtue of the power of cognitions* is defined as "ultimate existence." [111]

Of these two, the first *ultimate* and something established from its perspective do exist, while it is impossible for the second *ultimate* and something established from its perspective to exist. Therefore, while existing ultimately in the second sense does imply existing ultimately in the first sense, grasping in terms of the first sense of ultimate existence does not constitute innate grasping at true existence. For innate grasping at true existence requires grasping at things in the second sense of ultimate existence.

Failing to draw this distinction, many appeared who considered "that which is capable of withstanding reasoned analysis" or "an entity capable of withstanding such analysis" to be the measure of the object of negation. Numerous errors have apparently been made because of this. For instance, some assert that ultimate truth is not a knowable phenomenon; others view it as truly existent.[324] In contrast, if one appreciates well the above distinction [between the two senses of "ultimate"], one will come to appreciate such crucial points as there being no contradiction between the statements "things do not exist through their own essential mode of being or ultimately" and yet "the ultimate nature of things does exist" and to speak of this as constituting the *essential mode of being* and the *ultimate*.[325]

Presenting truth and falsity within the context of worldly convention through the analogy of magical illusion

The analogy of magical illusion has been hailed as a way of making one understand how something exists by virtue of being posited by the power of the mind and how something exists without being posited in such a manner. When the magician conjures a horse or an elephant from pebbles, sticks, and so on, three types of people are present—the magician himself, the spectators whose eyes are affected, and the spectators whose eyes are unaffected. In the first case, the horse or elephant is perceived but not apprehended; in the second case, it is both perceived and apprehended; while in the third case, there is neither perception nor apprehension of a horse or an elephant. Now, when the basis for conjuring the illusion is perceived as a horse or an elephant—unlike in mistaking a rope for a snake, where one can say that the rope is a snake for that perception but not in general—one cannot say that the basis for conjuring the illusion appears as a horse or an elephant merely to an erroneous cognition but that, in general, there is no such appearance. For even without such qualification, one has to accept that [the pebbles or the sticks] are being perceived as a horse or an elephant. Were this not so, then no perceptual error in relation to appearance would be possible. Therefore one can posit that the basis for conjuring an illusion does appear as a horse or an elephant.

Now, for the magician, the illusory elephant or horse is posited from the point of view of how it appears to an erroneous perception. It is not posited, however, from the point of view of the basis for conjuring the illusion. From the perspective of the spectators, however, the appearance of a horse or an elephant does not seem to be posited through the power of the mind; rather, they apprehend a real horse or elephant fully occupying space on the very spot where it is being perceived. This is how, on the basis of the analogy, one apprehends something to be posited through the power of the mind or not posited through it. So when an appearance is perceived in relation to a given basis, there are two possibilities—one where what appears constitutes its mode of existence as perceived and [112] another where it does not.

By comprehending this point well, one will be able to avoid the confusion that arises from the thought "Since objects are established by valid cognitions, and since valid cognitions are themselves cognitive states, their establishment of the objects would constitute the objects being posited through the power of the cognitions. In that case, true existence will be negated even in the system of the Buddhist essentialists." One will thus be able to disentangle the conflation of these two senses. For the sense in which objects are said to be defined by valid cognition refers to the two classes of objects being cognized by valid cognition. So this sense is very different from the previous sense [of the objects being posited by virtue of the power of cognitions].

According to Yogācāra-Madhyamaka, the appearance of the illusion is established by reflexive awareness. According to Svātantrika Madhyamaka, which accepts external reality, it is established by sensory perception that apprehends either the basis, such as the environs, or the empty space. That it does not exist in the way it is perceived is established through such reasoning as "If it did exist in such a manner, this would be seen by unaffected eyes as well, but that is not the case." When, through negation such as this, there is the convergence of *its appearance as such* and *it being empty of such*, then, from the perspective of ordinary conventional cognition that is not seeped in philosophical standpoints, such an illusion is established to be a falsehood. This [cognition of falsehood] and the cognition that establishes a mirror image to be empty of what it appears to be, therefore, do not constitute either coarse or subtle levels of rational cognition [pertaining to suchness]. Even with respect to true existence from the perspective of ordinary conventional cognition generally, when there is the appearance of a thing as being something, then it being empty of such a thing simply does not occur. Similarly, when it is found to be empty of being such a thing, its appearance as such just does not occur. Where there is indeed the convergence of the two [e.g., mirror image], such things are false even from the perspective of ordinary conventional cognition.

Explaining the analogy by relating it to the actual referent

Just like those spectators whose eyes have been affected, when outer and inner phenomena appear as truly existent, sentient beings grasp at these phenomena not as posited by virtue of the power of the mind but as existing in their own right. This is the innate grasping at true existence that has persisted since beginningless time.

Compared to the mind grasping at the object of negation as defined by Prāsaṅgika Madhyamaka, this presentation of Svātantrika Madhyamaka is very coarse and therefore does not constitute the subtle innate grasping at true existence. Nevertheless, when true existence as conceived by such grasping has been negated through reasoning, then just like the magician, one will no longer apprehend outer and inner phenomena as possessing a mode of existence not posited by cognitions; one will come to understand them as existing merely as established by virtue of the power of cognitions. And it is those things established by virtue of the power of cognitions and not invalidated by [other] valid cognitions that are accepted to possess conventional existence. It's not the case that whatever the mind posits is accepted to have conventional existence. [113]

Suppose our cognition posits the arising of a sprout from its seed; this does not contradict the sprouts arising from their seeds on their own part as well. Similarly, things that are the basis for conjuring an illusion do appear, on their part too, as a horse or elephant. By this one should understand the way all phenomena exist on the conventional level. Since even the ultimate nature is established by virtue of its appearance to the cognition that perceives it, it does not stand as a counterexample to the entailment of [whatever is established by virtue of the power of cognitions necessarily being] conventional existence. Therefore the following is definitely not the sense in which the analogy of illusion is to be understood: "Just as an illusion appears as a horse or an elephant but is empty of them, all things, such as a vase, appear as a vase and so on but are devoid of vases and so on." For if that were so, there could be nothing that could be said to be itself. Furthermore, the parallels being drawn between the analogy and its referent here would be in terms of their appearance as such but not in terms of their actuality.[326]

Now, at the point when the nonconceptual gnosis of meditative equipoise has arisen, within that perspective all dualistic appearances are pacified. This is analogous to those spectators who, because their eyes are unaffected, have neither the perception nor the apprehension of the illusion.

Given that there will be no presentation of the unique style of negation through reasoning by Svātantrika Madhyamaka in the subsequent sections, I will briefly explain here, in a manner easy to comprehend, how phenomena would come to be perceived as illusion-like according to that tradition.

Determining that all knowables are subsumed by the twofold classification into the conditioned and the unconditioned, conditioned things are further differentiated into material and not material. Based on this, one then refutes the notion that matter is composed of particles that are partless in the sense of having no directional parts, such as east and so on, and the notion that mental phenomena are composed of a series of indivisible points devoid of temporal parts, such as preceding and subsequent moments. These refutations one should understand as explained elsewhere.[327] One establishes in this way the logical entailment that all conditioned things are composed of parts. Next, if the parts and the bearer of the parts are distinct entities, they will then become unrelated, which is rejected; thus they are shown to be a single entity. Now at this point, however much one directs one's thought to a given thing, it becomes undeniable that parts and their bearer, though being a single entity, appear as if they are distinct. Like a magician's illusion, the convergence of two facts is established: the *appearance* of things as something and their *emptiness* of it.

This is not a problem for a false mode of existence posited through our cognition. But such a convergence becomes untenable if we are speaking of an objective mode of existence not posited by virtue of its perception in cognition. For if something were to possess true existence as defined earlier, there could be no disparity between *the way the thing actually is* and *the way it appears.* For if something is truly existent, it must remain so invariably, shunning any aspect of falsehood. Furthermore, the cognition that perceives the parts and their bearer as distinct entities would have to be veridical, which would invalidate their being one entity.

Once this absence of true existence of conditioned things is established, one can also negate, with the very same reasoning, [114] the true existence of the unconditioned. For example, one must admit that even unconditioned space pervades some material objects, and thus there must be parts that pervade the east and parts that extend in other directions. Likewise, suchness too has numerous directional parts in terms of its extension as well as [conceptually] distinct parts, those realized by distinct preceding and subsequent moments of cognition. The same is also true of other unconditioned phenomena. Now, since parts and their bearer cannot be of different entities, they are of one entity. Furthermore, a disparity between appearance and reality is permissible in something that is false but not in something that is truly existent. So when one engages in the foregoing refutations, one will establish that all phenomena lack true existence. This is the approach of Śāntarakṣita and his spiritual heir Kamalaśīla. Those who confine their analysis of parts and wholes to conditioned things alone suffer from a weak intellect.

Now there is indeed a sense of falsehood that is well known even to a mind not informed by philosophical thinking, but this is not the same sense of falsehood being proposed here by the Madhyamaka. Therefore, although things can be posited by such a [nonphilosophical] mind, this is only in the sense acknowledged within such a perspective. This would not be accepted by the Madhyamaka to exhaust the meaning of "being posited by the mind." In view of this, although there is no mode of existence that is not posited by virtue of being perceived by the mind, it is not a contradiction in this tradition [of Svātantrika Madhyamaka] for there to be a mode of existence that is posited by virtue of being perceived by the mind yet is not a mere nominal designation. Given this, a great deal of difference can be perceived by the mind between the objects of negation of the two Madhyamaka schools.

I have offered these explanations here seeing that the eyes of people today will come to be excellently opened to the view if they are first well led through the identification of what constitutes *true existence* and what constitutes *grasping at true existence* according to this system [of Svātantrika Madhyamaka], including a brief introduction to their reasoning negating them, and are then presented with the Prāsaṅgika Madhyamaka system.

Identifying grasping at true existence according to the Prāsaṅgika Madhyamaka standpoint

If one understands how, according to this system, phenomena are posited through mere conceptualization, one can then easily recognize how its opposite would constitute grasping at true existence.

This presentation has two parts: (1) how phenomena are posited through conceptualization and (2) presenting grasping at true existence, the contrary apprehension.

How phenomena are posited through conceptualization

The *Questions of Upāli* states:

> The flowers with their open petals that delight so many minds,
> the supreme gold mansions resplendent and attractive—
> none of these has a creator; [115]
> they're posited through the power of conception.
> Through conceptualization the world is imputed.[328]

Thus phenomena are taught to be posited through the power of conceptualization. On many other occasions phenomena are described as mere imputations of thought and as posited by virtue of the power of conceptualization. In *Sixty Stanzas of Reasoning* it says:

> The buddhas have stated
> that the world is conditioned by ignorance,
> so why would it be unreasonable to say
> this world is [a product of] conceptualization?[329]

The commentary explains this verse to mean that the world is a mere conceptual imputation and does not exist in its own right.[330] *Four Hundred Stanzas* also says:

> If without conceptualization
> attachment and so on do not exist at all,
> what intelligent person would grasp
> something as perfectly real and as conception?[331]

In its commentary too one reads:

> Those things that exist only because of the presence of concep-
> tualization and have no existence when there is no conception
> are without doubt like the snake conceived upon a coiled rope—
> definitely not established in their own right.[332]

"Perfectly real" means something existing in its own right, and "conceptualization" arises in relation to it. The statement in this commentary about how
attachment and so on are like the imputation of a snake upon a rope merely
presents them as examples. The statement in fact shows how all phenomena
are posited by conceptualization just like a snake conceived on the basis of
a rope.

For instance, when a rope that looks like a snake because of its multicolored pattern and the manner in which it is coiled is encountered in a
poorly lit area, the thought "This is a snake" may arise. At that moment, there
is not the slightest objective basis on the part of the rope—either in aggregate or in its parts—that can be identified as an instance of a snake. Therefore this snake is a mere conceptual imputation. Similarly, when the thought
"I am" arises in dependence upon the aggregates, there is not even the slightest basis on the part of the aggregates—whether as a collection of earlier
and latter continua or as collection of simultaneous factors and parts—that
can be posited as an instance of this "I." This will be explained more extensively below. For this reason and because there is not even a slightest entity
that is distinct from the aggregates—whether in terms of their parts or their
bearer—that can be taken to be the basis [of this "I"], so this "I" is posited
through mere conception in dependence upon the aggregates; it has no existence in its own right. This is stated in the *Precious Garland* as well:

> The individual is not the earth or the water;
> he is not the fire, not wind, nor space;
> he is not the consciousness; so if he is not all these,
> where then is the individual apart from these?[333]

Here "individual" is the person, the sentient being, the "I," or the self. "Not
the earth" and so on up to "not the consciousness" refutes the postulation
of the six elements of the sentient being, which are its parts, as constituting
the person, while "not all these" [116] negates postulating the sum of these

elements as the person. The final line refutes postulating something that is a different entity from these elements as the person. Nevertheless, it is not the case that one does not accept the existence of the person at all; nor does one accept foundation consciousness and so on as the person. Therefore the noble Nāgārjuna too accepts [the nature and existence of the person] exactly as explained by the *Commentary*'s author.

If one understands how the person is posited through conception like this, one will understand how all other phenomena are posited through conceptualization in exactly the same way. The *King of Meditations Sutra* says:

> What you've discerned with respect to the self,
> you must extend that thought to everything.[334]

And in the noble *Condensed Perfection of Wisdom* it says:

> Just as with the self, understand all sentient beings;
> just as with sentient beings, understand all phenomena.[335]

The *Precious Garland* too says this clearly in the following:

> Since the person is a composite of six elements,
> it has no absolute existence. And likewise,
> since each of the elements is in turn
> a composite, they too have no absolute existence.[336]

The point of the first line is to state the reason "Because the person is designated in dependence on the collection of the six elements." The point of the third and the fourth lines is to state that, since it is impossible for something not to consist of parts and a bearer of the parts, each element is, in turn, designated in dependence on the collection of many constitutive parts. Therefore they do not exist on the level of absolute reality or by virtue of their own essence. Furthermore, if they are designated in dependence on the collection of their constitutive parts, neither the parts nor the bearer of the parts can be the thing itself, yet something of different entity from these cannot be the thing either.

Now, insofar as the way vase and so on are conceptually posited, they are, in that respect at least, exactly similar to a snake imputed on the basis of a rope. However, between the vase and so on on the one hand and the rope-snake on the other, the two cases are entirely different when it comes to whether they exist, whether they are capable of effective functions, and so on. This is because there is a clear distinction between the two in whether their conventions remain essential for everyday transaction and whether the usage of such conventions is susceptible to invalidation. That everyday transactions remain tenable in this world posited through conceptualization represents, among the commentators of the words and meaning of the Madhyamaka treatises, a unique tradition of interpreting the noble Nāgārjuna and his son by the three masters—Buddhapālita, Śāntideva, and this master Candrakīrti. This issue [of how everyday translations remain possible in a world posited through conception] is indeed the most difficult point of the final view of the Middle Way.

Understood thus, then as the *Precious Garland* states, nothing whatsoever, not even the mere names, exist on the ultimate level, and on the conventional level too, nothing exists other than what are posited as mere designations through conventions such as names:

> Because material things are mere names, [117]
> the space too is a mere name;
> how can there be matter with no elements?
> Therefore mere names too do not exist.

> Feelings, discriminations, mental formations,
> and consciousness—contemplate these
> just like the elements or the self.
> Therefore the six elements have no selfhood.[337]

And

> Apart from being designated by conventions,
> how could there be a world in reality
> as either existent or nonexistent?[338]

If one understands these well, one will soundly comprehend (1) how phenomena are necessarily posited through dependence, (2) how, by the very virtue of their being dependently designated and having arisen through dependence, they have no existence in their own right, (3) how they do not possess an independent nature, something not posited through the power of some other conventions, and (4) no matter the phenomenon, when it is posited as existent, it is done so without analysis—without seeking a true referent behind the designation.

Grasping at true existence, the contrary apprehension

Grasping at things as existent as described above—not posited by the power of conventions such as name alone—constitutes innate grasping at things as (1) "true," (2) "ultimate," or (3) "absolute existence," (4) "existence by virtue of an essential nature," (5) "existence through intrinsic characteristic," or (6) "intrinsic existence." And the object grasped at by such a mind is, hypothetically speaking, the *measure* of true existence.

It is the case here as well that one needs to be cognizant of there being two senses of the term *ultimate* when qualifying the object of negation with the proviso "ultimately."[339] Although the proponents of Svātantrika Madhyamaka maintain existence in terms of the first three—true existence and so on—to be impossible, they nonetheless accept, on the conventional level, the remaining other three—"existing by virtue of an essential nature" and so on.[340] Personally, I see this Svātantrika standpoint to be an example of great skillful means to help guide those who are, for the time being, not capable of easily realizing the extremely subtle view of suchness.

Thus "the purported reality of phenomena, not dependent upon some other factor (namely, the convention-making conceptualizing subject)—an intrinsic nature supposedly not posited through such conceptualization"— is what is called *self-existence*, and this is the object of negation. And the absence of this in relation to a person has been stated to be the *selflessness of persons*, while its absence upon phenomena such as eyes and so on has been stated to be the *selflessness of phenomena*. From this we can implicitly understand that grasping at such an intrinsic nature on the basis of the person and on the basis of phenomena are the two forms of self-grasping. This is as declared in *Commentary on the Four Hundred Stanzas*:

> Here what is referred to as "self" is that intrinsic nature— namely, the nature of things conceived of as not dependent upon others—[118] and the absence of this is *selflessness*. Because of the twofold distinction of persons and phenomena, this selflessness is understood in terms of two kinds—the selflessness of phenomena and the selflessness of persons.[341]

Here too, in the following, Candrakīrti explains that the two forms of self-lessness are distinguished not from the viewpoint of what is to be negated but from the viewpoint of their basis:

> The Buddha taught no-self in twofold terms, that of phenomena
> and that of persons. (6.179b)

With regard to the innate identity-view of grasping at self-existence, since the root text [of *Entering the Middle Way*] rejects the aggregates as its object of focus, and furthermore, in the *Commentary*, the self that is dependently designated is said to be its object of focus, we should take the mere "I" or the mere person that is the focal object giving rise to the thought "I am" to be the object of the identity view. As for its aspect, the *Commentary* says:

> The thought "I am" imputes a self that does not exist, conceives
> such self to exist, and manifestly clings to it as real.[342]

So, as stated here, the identity view grasps the "I" as truly existent. Furthermore, the *Commentary* states:

> The identity view is an afflicted intelligence that operates by way
> of "I" and "mine."[343]

Therefore, as described here, for something to be the focal object of the innate identity-view, it must spontaneously give rise to the thought "I am." Thus, although the innate grasping at persons with separate continua as existing through their own intrinsic characteristics does constitute grasping at the self-existence of persons, it is not the innate identity-view. The phrase "operating by way of 'I' and 'mine'" does not indicate that mere "I" and mere "mine" are the held objects of apprehension [of this innate identity-view]; what is indicated is that such an innate identity view possesses the aspect of apprehending these two, "I" and "mine," as existing through their intrinsic characteristics. Furthermore, it is "mine" itself that is the focal object of the innate identity-view grasping at "mine;" we should not understand the eyes and so on to be its focal object. As for its apprehending aspect, it grasps at "mine" as existing through intrinsic characteristics, on the basis of taking "mine" it as its focus.[344]

[*Question*:] If this is so, how is it that in the *Commentary*, in the part pertaining to the line "then, with the thought 'mine'" (1.3b),[345] Candrakīrti writes, "Thinking 'this is mine,' they manifestly cling to all the things that are other than the object of grasping at 'I'"[346] and thus states that clinging to "this is mine" on the basis of focusing on bases such as the eyes is a form of grasping at "mine"?

[*Reply*:] The meaning here is this. On the basis of having perceived the eyes and so on as "mine," we tend to manifestly cling to a "truly existing mine." It is not the case, however, that eyes and so on—which are instances of "mine"—are themselves the objects of focus. For this would bring the consequence that being an instance of identity view and a grasping at the self-existence of phenomena would not be mutually exclusive. [119]

As for the focal object of the innate grasping at the self-existence of phenomena, this includes grasping at the aggregates of form and so on, at the eyes, ears, and so on of both self and others, as well as at the external environment that is not part of our inner world. As for the aspect apprehended by this grasping at the self-existence of phenomena, it is the same as explained above [in the context of grasping at self-existence of persons].[347]

Now it is these forms of grasping at self-existence, of persons and phenomena, that constitute the ignorance binding us to the cycle of existence. For example, *Seventy Stanzas on Emptiness* says:

> Things arisen from causes and conditions:
> that which conceives these to be real
> the Buddha taught to be ignorance;
> from this emerge the twelve links.[348]

Thus taking the things and phenomena as one's objects and grasping at them as existing with final reality is said to be the ignorance that is the root of cyclic existence. And since such grasping at the self-existence of phenomena brings ignorance grasping at the self-existence of persons, it is taught that the twelve links of dependent origination come into being from such grasping. For this ignorance to cease, one must see how nothing exists in the way such ignorance apprehends it and how the self-existence it conceives has no bearing on reality. *Seventy Stanzas on Emptiness* states:

> But when one realizes things are empty,
> one sees the truth and is confused no more.

Ignorance comes to cease;
from this the twelve links cease.[349]

Praise to the Ultimate Expanse says:

Grasping at "self" and "mine,"
long does one conceptualize the "external."
When one sees the two selflessnesses,
the seed of cyclic existence ceases.[350]

And:

That which supremely purifies the mind
is the teaching of no intrinsic existence.[351]

Four Hundred Stanzas too says:

When one sees no-self in the objects,
the seed of cyclic existence will cease.[352]

And:

Therefore all afflictions will be destroyed as well
through the destruction of delusion.
When this truth of dependent origination
is seen, delusion will emerge no more.

Therefore, with all your efforts,
engage this discourse alone.[353]

Since the context in this passage is that of identifying delusion from among the three poisons, the delusion referred to here is afflicted ignorance. And for that ignorance to cease, it is said that one needs to realize the profound truth of dependent origination, whereby the meaning of emptiness arises in terms of dependent origination.

The *Commentary*'s author too writes "Yogis engage in the negation of selfhood" (6.120d) and states how it is necessary to realize selflessness through eradicating the object of self-grasping. Therefore, if one simply withdraws the mind from pursuing its object, without eradicating the object of self-grasping, [120] this cannot be taken as engaging with no-self. The reason is this: When the mind engages an object, it does so in one of three modes: (1) apprehending that object as truly existent, (2) apprehending it as not truly existent, and (3) apprehending it without qualifying in either of these two terms. It is not invariably the case that because one does not apprehend something as lacking true existence one apprehends it as truly existent. Likewise, just because one does not engage with either of the two forms of selfhood does not necessarily mean that one is engaging with either of the two forms of selflessness. There are countless instances where the perspective of the mind remains in a third option.

When it comes to the two forms of self-grasping as well, we should identify them in our own mental continuum. Looking there, we need to establish, on the basis of the very thing we are deluded about, how it does not exist in the manner we ourselves are apprehending it. Otherwise, if our refutation [of self-existence] and affirmation [of emptiness] are directed only outwardly, then our pursuit becomes like a person searching for the footprints of a thief in the meadow while the robber has in fact fled into the woods. Such a pursuit will have no impact at all.

So when we have thus identified well what constitutes grasping at true existence, we come to recognize numerous instances of thought that do not constitute either of the two forms of grasping at self-existence. This will, therefore, help prevent all the misconceptions pertaining to the view that reasoning inquiring into suchness negates all objects apprehended by conceptual thoughts, no matter what. There are so many issues arising from questions such as this that require more discussion. Some of these have already been addressed on numerous occasions elsewhere, and some will be addressed below as well. So I will not elaborate further here.[354]

10. Refuting Arising from Self and Other

How the meaning of the scriptures is established by reason

This has two parts: establishing the selflessness of phenomena through reasoning and establishing the selflessness of persons through reasoning.

Establishing the selflessness of phenomena through reasoning

This has four parts: (1) refuting arising from the four extremes on both levels of truth, (2) rebutting objections against refuting intrinsic arising, (3) how arising through dependent origination prevents distortions of adhering to extreme views, and (4) the fruits of having engaged in analysis with reasoning.

Refuting arising from the four extremes on both levels of truth

This has three parts: (1) stating the proposition that there is no arising through intrinsic nature, (2) the logical proofs that establish this through reasoning, and (3) the conclusion of having negated arising from the four extremes.

Stating the proposition that there is no arising through intrinsic nature

Understanding that, out of the ten perfect equanimities, the other perfect equanimities can be easily indicated by presenting through reasoning the perfect equanimity of the absence of arising through intrinsic nature alone, [121] the noble Nāgārjuna states the following at the beginning of his *Treatise on the Middle Way*:

Not from itself, not from other,
not from both, nor from no cause—
nothing anywhere
ever possesses arising at all.[355]

"Ever" is synonymous with "on any occasion," while the word "anywhere," which is synonymous with "in any place," is a locative. And these terms, which present the basis where there is no arising, indicate place, time, and philosophical standpoints. The word "nothing" refers to things of inner and outer that do not arise in any of these three terms. Thus the meaning of this stanza that begins "Not from itself" is as follows.

"It is never possible for anything of the outer and inner worlds to arise from itself at any place, at any time, and through any philosophical standpoint." This is how one should apply the three terms and explain. Similarly, one should extend this application [of the three terms] to the other three propositions as well: "It is never possible for anything to arise from other, from both self and other, and from no cause." Although in the Tibetan version of *Clear Words*, this phrase is translated as "from itself nothing whatsoever" the translation [suggested] here reads better.[356]

The phrase "at any place, at any time" negates the possibility of interpreting along the lines akin to the situation where grapes do not grow in some areas (due to place) and crops do not grow during some seasons (due to time). Thus the inclusion of the word "never" is not meaningless. Similarly, the phrase "through any philosophical standpoint" rejects the thought that although intrinsic arising may not exist from the standpoint of Madhyamaka, it could exist due to the philosophical standpoint of an essentialist school. This is not to state, however, that things do not arise according to the essentialist schools.

The *Commentary* says:

Here the term "not" should be associated with arising from itself [and so on]—the proof of existence—and not with existence per se. For the negation of that [existence itself] is effected by way of implication.[357]

What this states is that [Nāgārjuna's stanza] should not be read by dividing the stanzas into two parts, with the last two lines presenting the thesis and the first two lines presenting the argument. Rather, it should be read as

"There is no arising from itself [ever or at any time]" and extend this same predication to the other three theses as well. The point is simply this: Were there arising through intrinsic nature, one would have to accept arising from any of the four possibilities as its evidence. Hence Candrakīrti refers to arising from four extremes as the "proof of existence." Now when arising from the four extremes is negated, then by implication, arising through intrinsic nature is also negated, hence there is no fault of not being able to establish the absence of intrinsic arising by formulating the argument in this way. This then is the meaning of the last word "implication" [in the above *Commentary* passage.] I am not saying that it is incorrect to take the negation of arising from the four extremes as the logical reason to establish the absence of intrinsic arising, as it is done in *Light of the Middle Way*.[358] [122] What I am saying is that dividing Nāgārjuna's stanza into separate parts, in the manner described above, is not what the text itself intends.

"Things do not arise from other at any place, at any time, or because of any philosophical tenet" is how the three terms should be applied. Similarly, the following appears in *Clear Words*:

> We accept conventional truth to be established by mere conditionedness, not on the basis of adhering to any of the four positions. To do so entails the consequence of speaking of things as endowed with intrinsic nature.[359]

So *arising from other* is not a convention of the scriptures; it is a convention of philosophical schools. Furthermore, when arising from other is proposed, it is done so on the assumption that the *other* is something that exists by way of intrinsic characteristics. Therefore, if one accepts such arising, one naturally subscribes to the notion that things are endowed with an intrinsic nature. In this Candrakīrti tradition, however, *arising from other* does not exist even on the conventional level. We accept cause and effect to be distinct entities on the conventional level, but this alone does not meet the criteria of what constitutes *arising from other*. This is analogous to the following: as is stated [in 6.23a], given that each and every phenomenon bears dual natures on the conventional level, nature is something that does exist, but such a nature is not accepted in terms of intrinsic arising.

Clear Words states that the thesis that things are devoid of arising from themselves is a nonimplicative negation, and this is true also of the other three propositions. Therefore, when establishing the absence of intrinsic

existence, the thesis to be established must be a nonimplicative negation—
that is, the simple elimination of what is being negated. This is stated by
Clear Words when it says:

> Since statements such as "Whatever sounds there are in the
> world, / they are all unreal" and "nothing exists" are found, the
> intention is to express the negation without implication. So the
> meaning of "unreality" here is absence of intrinsic existence.[360]

Also, the *Commentary* says:

> Having stated the four theses, now to establish these through rea-
> soning, I will explain . . .[361]

Later on, using the negation of arising from the four extremes as the reason,
things are spoken of as being free of intrinsic arising. Furthermore, at the
end of negating arising from the four extremes, *Clear Words* states, "Thus
this establishes that there is no arising."[362] It is not the case therefore that
Candrakīrti does not wish to establish that things are devoid of intrinsic
arising.[363]

The statement in *Clear Words* that "The inferences have as their effect
only the negation of what others propose"[364] refers to the fact that propositions are there only to refute intrinsic existence adhered to by the other; the
sense here is that, apart from this, they do not establish anything else. The
statement does not, however, reject the establishment of that simple negation. Likewise, there is the following statement:

> As for us, [123] we do not establish this to be either nonexistent
> or existent; rather, we refute what others impute to be existent
> and nonexistent. This is because our wish is to clear away the two
> extremes and establish the path of the middle way.[365]

The meaning of this statement too is that one merely eliminates the two
extremes of existence and nonexistence as adhered to by the other, and apart
from this, nothing else is to be established. It is not the case, however, that
the simple negation of the two extremes is not being established; for it states
that the wish is to clear away the two extremes and establish the path of the
middle way. If things are not established as devoid of intrinsic existence,

then since there is no third possibility, this would entail that things have intrinsic existence. This is clearly stated in *Averting the Objections*:

> For if what is devoid of intrinsic nature
> negates the absence of intrinsic nature,
> then with the reversal of absence of intrinsic existence,
> things will have intrinsic existence.[366]

As for the reasons why, although one accepts the thesis and proofs such as these, one does not become a Svātantrika Mādhyamika, I have explained these extensively elsewhere.[367] So I will not elaborate further here.

How then are the two forms of negation defined? In general, negation is cognized by the mind on the basis of explicit elimination of the relevant object of negation. So the determination of something as not being that which is not itself [e.g., a vase not being a non-vase] is not in itself a negation. On the other hand, we find terms like *ultimate nature* and *ultimate truth*, which do not explicitly negate any opposites on the linguistic level, yet when their referents appear to the mind, they do so in the aspect of eliminating conceptual elaborations. Such terms are therefore terms of negation.

Negation is of two kinds.[368] Of the two, *nonimplicative negation* does not imply or affirm any other fact following the explicit elimination of its object of negation. For example, when asked, "Are brahmans allowed to drink alcohol?" the response "They do not drink alcohol" is a simple rejection of the drinking of alcohol. The statement does not affirm in any way that they do or do not drink other beverages. Conversely, an *implicative negation* implies or affirms other facts following the mind's elimination of its object of negation. For example, when wishing to demonstrate that one of two individuals belongs to the commoner's caste, if one utters the statement "He is not a brahman," this does not merely negate the person being a brahman. While a negative statement, it also affirms that the person belongs to a caste other than that of the brahmans—namely, a commoner's caste.

There are three ways such other facts may be implied [by a negative statement]—through direct implication, indirect implication, and contextual implication. First is like the statement "No-self exists," whereby the elimination of the object of negation and affirmation of other facts are both effected with a single declaration. The second is like the statement "Stout Dharmadatta does not eat during the day," where another fact is implied indirectly. These two, respectively, give specific examples of implying another fact directly or indirectly. [124] An example where [a fact] is implied both directly and indirectly is the statement "Dharmadatta, who does not eat during the day, is not skinny." The third type is like the statement "He is not a brahman" when stated in a context where it has not yet been determined whether the person is of the royal or brahman caste. Here the statement [what caste he is] is not explicitly made. A text cited in *Explanation of the Commentary on the Lamp of Wisdom* says:

> Negation that reveals by implication,
> that which affirms by means of one word,
> and that which does both but does not express the word itself—
> these are implicative [negation]; others are different.[369]

Some assert that when a negation term is combined with a term that is affirmative, it is not a nonimplicative negation. This is incorrect. Just because the term *brahman* is affirmative does not preclude the fact that the statement "Brahmans do not drink alcohol" represents a simple elimination of its object of negation. This is analogous to the fact that just because sound itself is an evident fact does not preclude sound's impermanence being a concealed fact. Some others say that when a negation is paired with the subject of the proposition [e.g., "Brahmans do not drink"], some other fact is implied. This too is incorrect. "Brahman," for example, is the basis upon which one considers whether some other fact is being implied; it certainly cannot be the other fact that is being implied.

Thus, to present the noble Nāgārjuna's four propositions, [Candrakīrti writes]:

> Not originating from itself, and how from something other?
> Not from both, and how from no cause? 6.8ab

Not originating from itself—namely, from its own essence—**how** can the effect originate **from something other**—causes that exist as other through intrinsic characteristics? It cannot. It does **not** originate **from both** self and other, **and how from no cause?** It does not. Now were there things that possess intrinsic existence, this would entail that they arise by way of one of the four possibilities. Within the notion of intrinsic arising, there are only two possibilities: from a cause or from no cause. And within the possibility of arising from a cause, there are only three possibilities—arising from itself, from other, or from the combination of both self and other. Therefore these four positions are exhaustive.

The logical proofs that establish this [absence of intrinsic arising] through reasoning

This has four parts: (1) refuting self-arising, (2) refuting arising from other, [125] (3) refuting arising from both self and other, and (4) refuting arising from no cause.

Refuting self-arising

This has two parts: refuting self-arising through the *Commentary* author's reasoning and refuting self-arising through *Fundamental Wisdom*'s reasoning.

Refuting self-arising through the Commentary *author's reasoning*

This has three parts: (1) refuting the views of the philosophers who claimed to have realized suchness, (2) demonstrating how there is no self-arising even on the conventional level from a perspective unaffected by philosophical views, and (3) summarizing the essential points of these refutations.

Refuting the views of the philosophers who claimed to have realized suchness

This has two parts: (1) refuting arising from a cause that is identical in nature with its effects and (2) refuting that cause and effect are identical in nature.

Refuting arising from a cause that is identical in nature with its effects

The first has three parts: (1) If an effect arises from a cause that is identical to it in nature, its arising will be pointless. (2) If an effect arises from a cause that is identical to it in nature, it's contrary to reason. (3) Rejecting the defenses aimed at averting these flaws.

If an effect arises from a cause that is identical to it in nature, its arising will be pointless.

If things originate from themselves, nothing is gained. 6.8c

[*Question*:] On the basis of what reasons can one ascertain that things do not arise from themselves?

[*Response*:] **If** things—a sprout, for example, which is the agent in the context of something coming to arise—**originate from themselves, nothing** additional **is gained** by coming into being in such a manner. The reality of the sprout, which is its existence, has already been obtained before, at the time of its cause.

Here Sāṃkhyas maintain there is no denying that diverse causes and conditions bring forth a single common effect. For this to be possible, they assert that a single primal substance must pervade them all, a shared single nature of these causes and conditions. Therefore whatever is the nature of the cause—a barley seed, for example—is the same nature as that of the conditions, the water, fertilizer, and so on. Likewise, the nature of the sprout and the nature of its causes and conditions are also the same. This they assert to be the nature of all manifestations of phenomenal reality.[370]

Now since they do accept that the seed and the sprout are distinct, they do not say that the sprout arises from the sprout itself. Nevertheless, when they assert that the sprout arises from its seed and from its own nature, given that according to them the two natures are identical, it must arise from its own nature and an unmanifest sprout must exist at the time of its cause. This is, in fact, how they uphold the notion of self-arising. Although some elements of Sāṃkhya do not speak in terms of "arising" but assert that what was unmanifest [at the time of cause] becomes manifest from the cause, the meaning remains the same.

This is also the manner in which Sāṃkhyas accept the universal and its particulars to be identical in nature, which is utterly different from the Buddhist view that holds, say, *functional thing* and *vase* as sharing the same nature. Now if the entire reality or nature [126] of the sprout were to exist at the time of the seed, given that it is impossible for there to be a manifest sprout that is different from the sprout's reality, then the sprout itself will have to be present at the time of its cause, not just the sprout's nature or its reality. In that case, having already come into being, it would be pointless for it to arise again.

If an effect arises from a cause that is identical to it in nature, it's contrary to reason.

> Furthermore, something already born cannot repeat its birth. 6.8d

Furthermore, something that is **already born cannot repeat its birth** again, arising in a redundant manner having already arisen. The conjunctive "furthermore" indicates that this is a fault that ensues in addition to the point about how arising becomes pointless if something arises from its own nature.

Even if one upholds the thesis of manifest [versus unmanifest effects, we could refute by saying that] if the manifest effect is already present at the time of the cause, this contradicts one's own premise. And if it is not present, we could refute the thesis by analyzing whether the manifest effect and its nature are identical or different.

Since the mere statement "Self-arising is contrary to reason" is only a proposition, the following is stated to present the reason that refutes self-arising:

> If you conceive that what is once arisen can arise again,
> the growth of sprouts and so on will never happen in this world;
> and seeds will reproduce themselves until the end of time. 6.9a–c

Now **if you conceive**—that is, assert—**that what is once arisen**, such as a seed, **can arise again**, repeating its birth, on what grounds will you assert that this repeated arising of the seed will end and the sprout will appear? What condition is there to prevent the seed arising again? There is none. In that case, **the growth of sprouts and so on**—the stalk, the sprouting blades—**will never happen** here **in this world**. Another fault that ensues is that **seeds will reproduce themselves** perpetually, without interruption, **until the end of time**; for what has already arisen must arise again [and again].

This objection reveals two flaws—effects within a shared continuum will never arise, and causes within a shared continuum will arise perpetually with no interruption—and states self-arising to be contrary to reason.

Rejecting the defenses aimed at averting these flaws

> For how can the sprout ever bring about the seed's cessation? 6.9d

Suppose they maintain that the conditions beneficial for the arising of the sprout—water, the spring season, and so on—help transform the seed into something resembling a moist grain and, in this way, produce the sprout. Furthermore, since it is contrary for the sprout to be present at the same time as the seed, the sprout causes the seed to cease and allow itself to come into being. So we are not vulnerable to these two flaws of being contrary to reason. [127] And since the seed and the sprout are not of different nature or reality, it is also not the case that things do not arise from themselves.

This response too is untenable. Given that the two natures—the nature of the seed and that of the sprout—are identical in all possible respects, **how can the sprout ever bring about the seed's cessation?** This is not possible, just as the sprout cannot bring about the cessation of the sprout. So Candra-kīrti understands.

Even if they foresee these sorts of possible objections, the reason they cannot avert them is this: They rebuff the objection with the thought that since the sprout's destruction of the seed is on the manifest level, this is not similar to something destroying itself. But to argue in this way is actually quite foolish. For if all the realities and natures are identical to each other, distinct manifestations cannot be established. So the objections cannot be avoided.

Refuting that cause and effect are identical in nature

This has three parts: (1) refuting using the consequence that the seed and the sprout will not have distinct shapes and so on, (2) refuting the responses aimed at rebutting the objections, and (3) refuting using the consequence that in both situations, its perceptibility or lack thereof would be the same.

Refuting using the consequence that the seed and the sprout will not have distinct shapes and so on

> For you then, there cannot exist a sprout distinct from the seed that
>   causes it,
>   in shape, color, taste, potency, and ripened effects. 6.10ab

There are other flaws as well. **For you** [Sāṃkhya] **then, there cannot exist a sprout distinct from the seed that causes it, in shape** such as long and short, **color** like green, yellow, and so on, **taste** like sweet, sour, and so on, **potency, and ripened effects**. This is because you make no distinction at all between the reality or the nature of the seed and that of the sprout.

Given all these undesired consequences, and furthermore, given that we do not perceive them as being not distinct, the realities of these two [a sprout and its seed] cannot be identical in all respects. In this way Candra-kīrti throws [to his Sāṃkhya opponent] the reverse of the consequence. There is, however, a great difference between throwing the reverse of the consequence and throwing a reverse of a consequence that contains an autonomous syllogism.[371]

"Potency" here refers to such properties as that of medicine against hem-orrhoids, which clears away the ailment the moment it comes into contact with the body, and that of some medicinal essences that permeate the sur-roundings when hung in the air. "Ripened effects" are the changes effected in results owing to variable conditions. For example, when Indian goose-berry and long pepper trees[372] and their like are nourished with milk, their fruits acquire a sweet taste. [128]

Refuting the responses aimed at rebutting the objections

> If it is through shunning its prior reality that a thing turns
> into another thing, how then can the two be identical? 6.10cd

You might assert, "By abandoning the seed stage, it changes into a dif-ferent state—namely, that of the sprout. The seed and the sprout are merely different stages. The seed itself becomes the sprout."

[*Response:*] Now, **if it is through shunning its prior** stage, the stage of the **reality** of the seed, it **turns into** a stage that is **another thing**, the reality of the sprout, in that case, **how then can** it **be** correct to assert that **the two are identical**, such that the nature of that seed is also the very nature of the sprout? For, according to you, the reality at that stage *is* the reality of that thing itself, and apart from that reality, there is no other thing that is sepa-rate. Therefore the [thesis that] the reality of the seed and the sprout are not distinct at all in any respect is undermined.

If the thought occurs, "Although the shapes and so forth of the seed and sprout are distinct, they are not distinct with respect to their substance, so there is no contradiction [in the thesis of self-arising]," this too would be untenable. For without apprehending the shapes and so on, one cannot apprehend the seed and sprout even in terms of their substance.

Refuting using the consequence that in both situations, its perceptibility or lack thereof would be the same

> If for you the seed is not different from the sprout before us,
> then just like the seed, what you call the sprout would be invisible;
> or, being identical, just like the sprout, the seed too should be
>   perceived.
> Thus you should not uphold this thesis [of identity of cause and effect].
>   6.11

There are other faults as well. With regard to the realities of the seed and sprout, **if for you the seed is not different from the sprout before us, then just like the seed** cannot be perceived at the time of the sprout, likewise **what you call the sprout would** also **be invisible.** The term "or" indicates that alternately, **being identical** in all respects, **just like the sprout, the seed too should be perceived** by the senses at the time of the sprout. [129] Since this is not so, **you** who wish to avert these two faults **should not uphold this thesis** that there is no distinction between the realities of the seed and sprout.

If one understands these forms of reasoning well, all misconceptions—such as the view that while all phenomena are distinct realities with relation to each other, the ultimate natures of all are mutually inclusive of each other and are in fact one, the view that the ultimate nature of a thing's earlier state *is* itself the ultimate nature of its later state, and so on[373]—will be avoided.

Demonstrating that there is no self-arising even on the conventional level from a perspective unaffected by philosophical views

Having thus refuted the self-arising postulated by the Sāṃkhya system, which claims to contemplate the ultimate nature of reality—a system at odds with the Buddhist way—the following is now stated to show that, even from the perspective of worldly convention not trained in any philosophical tradition, it is incorrect to conceive of such self-arising:

> Because the effect can be seen when the cause is no more,
> even ordinary people do not accept that the two are one. 6.12ab

Because the effect can be seen when the cause, the seed, **is no more, even**

ordinary people do not accept that the two, the seed and the sprout, **are one.**

Summarizing the essential points of these refutations

> Thus the postulation that things originate from themselves
> is untenable in reality as well as in everyday experience. 6.12cd

Since self-arising is contrary to reason both on the ultimate level and on the level of worldly conventional truth, **this postulation** that outer and inner **things originate from themselves is untenable in reality**—ultimate truth—**as well as in everyday experience** of the world. Because of this, when the noble Nāgārjuna refutes self-arising, he does not qualify it in terms of "ultimately" or "conventionally"; he refutes it in general, using the phrase "not from itself." So when master Bhāviveka [130] applies the proviso "ultimately" in [his syllogism] "that things do not arise from themselves ultimately because they are existents, like, for example, sentient beings,"[374] we should understand that such a qualification is in fact pointless.

Refuting self-arising through Fundamental Wisdom*'s reasoning*

> If you assert self-arising, the produced and that which produces,
> as well as the act and the agent, will become identical.
> Since these are not the same, we reject self-arising,
> for it entails the unwanted consequences explained at length. 6.13

There are other faults as well. **If you assert self-arising** for effects, **the produced** (the effect) **and that which produces** (the cause) **as well as the act** being done **and the agent** that does the act **will become identical. Since they are not the same, we should reject self-arising. For** to assert it would **entail** many of **the unwanted consequences explained at length** in this text as well as in *Fundamental Wisdom*. For example, with respect to the first fault, *Fundamental Wisdom* states:

> That the cause and effect are one,
> this can never be tenable,
> for if the cause and effect are one,
> the produced and the producer would be one.[375]

So if the cause and the effect have identical natures, this is saying, then the father and the son or the eye and its consciousness will also become one.

With respect to the second fault, *Fundamental Wisdom* says:

> If the fuel were identical with the fire,
> agent and act would be one.[376]

When refuted thus, the opponent might respond by saying, "If the consequence leveled is 'Are the father and his son and the agent and the act identical in their natures,' the answer is 'Yes, I agree.' But if the consequence leveled is 'Are they identical in general?' the answer then would be 'No, there is no such entailment.'" Nonetheless, because of the reasoning that forces the consequence that "if two things are identical in nature, as asserted in the manner characterized above, their manifestations would also be identical," the opponent cannot avoid the above-stated faults. Therefore, because of the pitfalls exposed thus far, those who wish to realize the two truths without distortion must not subscribe to the notion of self-arising, so we are advised. Furthermore, [logically speaking,] *existence* and *nonexistence* of self-arising are direct opposites observing the law of the excluded middle. That is to say, when one is eliminated through negative determination, then if its opposite is not affirmed through positive determination, such an opposite has no existence.[377] As such, one must accept the truth that there is no self-arising. [131]

Refuting arising from other

This has two parts: stating the opponent's standpoint and refuting that standpoint.

Stating the opponent's standpoint

The Buddhist essentialist schools assert the following: "Since arising from self would be pointless, self-arising is untenable; and since that does not exist, arising from a combination of both self and other is also untenable. As for arising from no cause, this is utterly deplorable and deserves to be rejected. However, arising from other cannot be rejected, as done so in the line "How from something other?" (6.8a). And furthermore, because the scriptures state that the four conditions, intrinsically distinct from their effects, are the causes that produce things, one has no choice but to accept arising from other."

As to what these four conditions are, some schools assert the following. The term *causal condition* refers to five out of the six causes, excluding active cause, as stated in the line from the *Treasury of Abhidharma* that "What is called *cause* refers to the five causes."[378] The *objective condition* is as found in the line "Objective conditions include all phenomena"[379]—that is, all phenomena that are objects of six consciousnesses. The *antecedent condition* is as found in the lines "The minds and derived factors that have arisen, / their final instance, not of the same kind, is the immediately preceding,"[380] meaning all the minds and mental factors that have arisen prior to entering the nirvana without residue. The *dominant condition* is the active causes, as stated in the line "What is called *active cause* is the dominant conditions."[381] So the six causes are, as the *Treasury of Abhidharma* says:

> Active cause and the simultaneous,
> the homogeneous and the concomitant,
> the pervasive and the ripening cause—
> these are the six causes, they assert.[382]

Some schools, based on the statement "That which creates something is its cause," assert the following. That which abides in the state of its producing seed is its *causal condition*. And, just as in the example of an old man standing up, the objects that serve like walking canes for the mind and mental factors that are in the process of arising are their *objective conditions*. The final moment of the cessation of the cause is the *antecedent condition* of the effect that is arising. For example, the final moment of cessation of the seed is the condition immediately preceding the origination of the sprout.[383]

The *Commentary* says, "For example, the final moment of cessation of the seed is the antecedent concomitant condition of the sprout."[384] In *Clear Words* too, his refutation of intrinsically real antecedent conditions is done in relation to the antecedent concomitant condition of the sprout.[385] Buddhapālita upholds a similar position. So theirs is a tradition in which an antecedent concomitant condition is accepted even for material things.

The dominant condition is that which, when present, the other (the effect) comes into being. *Clear Words* states that such a condition includes what has arisen before, [132] that which is arising concomitantly, and that which will arise subsequently.[386] The *Commentary* too describes the latter two the same way.[387] This is identical in meaning to the statement in the *Lamp of Wisdom* that reads, "The conditions as postulated by the other schools, such as the immediate condition that is in front of us, the existing condition, and the no longer existing condition . . . ,"[388] where the translation of the terms seem in fact better. As for the meaning of this passage [from Bhāviveka's *Lamp of Wisdom*, Avalokitavrata's] explanatory commentary says the following:

> The *immediate condition that is in front of us*, as postulated by Sthavira, refers to the objective condition that has arisen directly before our senses. The *existing condition* refers to the causal and dominant conditions, while the *no longer existing condition* refers to the antecedent condition, so they assert.[389]

So were we to examine their characteristics, despite some slight variance in their names, all the conditions can be subsumed into the four conditions. Since Īśvara and so on are not conditions, there is no fifth condition. This must be definitely upheld, for it is as stated in the *Treasury of Abhidharma*:

> Four conditions generate the mind and mental factors,
> three produce both meditative attainments,
> and the others arise from both [causal and dominant
>   conditions].
> Not from Īśvara and so on, for things arise in sequence.[390]

This is how they accept [the notion of the four conditions].

Refuting that standpoint

This is twofold: (1) refuting, in general, the standpoint that asserts arising from other and (2) refuting, in particular, the Cittamātra standpoint.

Refuting, in general, the standpoint that asserts arising from other

This has five parts: (1) the actual refutation of arising from other, (2) rebutting objections to this refutation from the worldly perspective, (3) the merits of refuting arising from other, (4) how intrinsic arising does not exist in any manner, and (5) the benefits of negating intrinsic arising on both levels of the two truths.

The actual refutation of arising from other

The first has three parts: (1) a general refutation of arising from other, (2) a specific refutation of arising from other, and (3) a refutation of arising from other by examining the four possibilities with respect to effects.

A general refutation of arising from other

The first has two parts: (1) refuting by revealing absurd consequences and (2) rejecting the response aimed at avoiding these faults.

Refuting by revealing absurd consequences

The first has two parts: the actual absurd consequences and a decisive analysis of these points. [133]

The actual absurd consequences

This arising from other cannot be posited, for it is contrary to reason and scripture. With respect to the latter, the thesis of arising from other contradicts many scriptural sources, such as the statement in the *Rice Seedling Sutra*, "And that sprout of name-and-form was not created by itself nor by something other."[391] To explain that arising from other is contrary to reason, the following is stated:

> If something can originate from something other,
> then pitch darkness can originate from burning flames.
> In fact, everything could arise from everything,
> for after all, being other equally pertains to all nonproducing things.
>   6.14

If, in dependence upon a cause that is intrinsically **other, something**—an intrinsically different effect—**can originate, then pitch darkness can originate from burning flames,** which are actually what is dispelled and that which dispels. **In fact, everything,** regardless of whether it is an effect,

could arise from everything, whether it is its cause or not. Why? Because **all nonproducing things,** insofar as **being** something intrinsically **"other"** with respect to the effect, **are** exactly **equal** to those things that are accepted as the cause of that effect. Thus these two extreme absurd consequences ensue from the opponent's own accepted reasoning.

Let me explain these two consequences. Just as, according to the opponent, a rice seed that produces the rice sprout is, by virtue of its intrinsic characteristic, "other" than its effect, the rice sprout, in the same way, those things that do not produce rice sprouts—fire, charcoal, barley seeds, and so on—are also, by virtue of their intrinsic characters, "other" than the rice sprout. This is the way in which those who propound other-arising assert their position. Now, if these two cases of being "other" are admitted as equal, then just as from a rice seed—which is "other"—a rice sprout grows, then by extension, a rice sprout should arise from fire, charcoal, and so on as well. Similarly, just as a rice sprout—which is "other"—grows from a rice seed, things like a vase, cloth, and so on too must also come from a rice seed. Like this, parallels are drawn [between the two types of "other"]. This reasoning revealing such an extreme consequence is presented in the following in *Fundamental Wisdom*:

> That cause and effect are different
> is [a thesis that is] not tenable . . .
> for if cause and effect are different,
> cause and non-cause will become equal.[392]

In the case of both of these consequence-revealing arguments, *Commentary* states that they throw their reversals.[393]

A decisive analysis of these points

This has two parts: (1) why extreme consequences ensue for arising from other [134] and (2) demonstrating that it is not a contradiction to accept the reverse of the consequences.

Why extreme consequences ensue for arising from other

Here, some Tibetans assert that absurd consequences ensue for subscribing to the thesis of arising from other because cause and effect are, in temporal terms, necessarily sequential while *otherness* requires simultaneity. This is totally incorrect. For in that case, all the faults one has leveled against the opponent to refute arising from other will equally apply to one's own position. Now if one responds to this by saying, "We have no position," then one's effort to seek the reason [to refute arising from other in the first place] becomes pointless.

Now, many Tibetans assert[394] the following. When logicians establish an entailment, for example, between fire and smoke on the basis of a specific instance of a smoke, or between being impermanent and being a product, they do so by establishing invariability across all places and all times. This is done first on the basis of a specific instance, such as in relation to a kitchen [in the case of fire and smoke] or a vase [in the case of being impermanent and being a product], and their aim then is to establish invariability [between the two members of the entailment] by drawing similarity across other times and places. So what Candrakīrti is doing here, these Tibetans assert, is to throw an absurd consequence against them by using the argument that "insofar as being 'other' is concerned, all things are equal." They say that this type of argument topples the opponent's position with a kind of domino effect.[395]

This too is an expression of someone who has not understood the meaning of the text and has failed to comprehend how logical reasoning works. Now when invariability is established between fire and smoke or being a product and being impermanent in general terms, without specifying a particular smoke or the product in a specific time and place, one can certainly remove the doubt that perhaps there are instances where although fire and being impermanent are negated, the two examples cited as reasoning proofs [smoke and being a product] are not negated. In contrast, there are many instances where the two things can be negated as being cause and effect but may still exist as mere others. So how can these cases be similar? In fact, the very expression "toppling with a domino effect" reveals that theirs is an argument betraying ignorance of the way of reasoning. That this is so I have discussed extensively elsewhere.[396]

In view of the above, how is this [statement of no position] to be understood? Here, *Clear Words* states:

> We accept the establishment of conventional truth in terms of
> mere conditionedness, not on the basis of adhering to any of the
> four positions [self-arising, arising from other, from both, and

from no cause]. Otherwise there is the consequence that things possess intrinsic nature, which is untenable. If one accepts this mere conditionedness, cause and effect will then be mutually contingent and thus will not exist by virtue of an essence. As a result, one will then not speak of things as being endowed with intrinsic nature.[397]

In this manner, Candrakīrti explains the distinction between the kind of arising he does accept and the kind he does not. Fundamentally, he states that if one accepts arising in terms of the four theses, [135] one then has to speak of things being endowed with intrinsic natures. Therefore, if one accepts arising from other, one subscribes to the notion of intrinsic arising necessarily; and in contrast, if one accepts arising by way of mere dependent origination, one need not accept intrinsic arising. Therefore *other* in the context of "arising from other" does not refer to just "otherness"; it is an intrinsically established other. As such, extreme absurd consequences are revealed to those who accept this thesis. Such consequences are not leveled against accepting mere otherness.

This [consequential] argument is similar in logical style to the one found later in the text, where it reads:

> Things different from each other through intrinsic
>   characteristics
> could not logically be part of a single continuum. (6.61cd)

There, against the assertion that although the earlier and later temporal stages of a thing are distinct, they share the same continuum, the objection is raised that if the two things are distinct by virtue of their intrinsic characteristics, they cannot belong to the same continuum. For if they [the two relata] are *other* from each other by virtue of their intrinsic characteristics, any contingent relationship between the two would become untenable; yet if they are totally unrelated, then absurd consequences will ensue. That is, when a particular effect arises from its cause, it should do so from all others, even those that are non-causes; and when a particular cause produces its effect, it should produce all others that are not its effects as well.

The reason some people do not understand this type of reasoning, as explained above, is because they fail to clearly differentiate what exactly is to be negated in delineating the object of negation, on the one hand, from what minimal standpoints are to be accepted in the presentation of dependent origination. So when engaged in refuting the object of negation, recall what was said above concerning the criterion of what is to be negated.[398]

Demonstrating that it is not a contradiction to accept the reverse of the consequences

One might wonder, "If one accepts the reverse propositions of those two consequential arguments presented above, how would one then interpret the following statements in *Clear Words*:

> The reverse propositions of consequential arguments are relevant only to the opponent, not for us, as we have no thesis.[399]

And:

> When the proponent of no intrinsic existence presents a consequential argument to those who propound intrinsic existence, how can it follow that the proponent [himself] has to accept the reverse propositions of these consequences?[400]

Also:

> Therefore the statement in a consequential argument merely refutes the opponent's thesis; there is no [affirmation of] the reverse proposition of such consequences.[401]

This is not a problem. These statements are relevant only in the context of refuting self-arising, not with respect to all consequential arguments presented by the Mādhyamika. These statements apply to the two *reductio ad absurdum* arguments refuting the thesis of self-arising. [136] The *reductio* consequences being drawn out in those two arguments are not simply that "arising will become pointless" and that "it will be endless"; the consequences being drawn out are that "re-arising will be pointless" and "there will be an infinite regress of arising." The reversal of these consequences—that "there is a point in such re-arising" and that "the process of such re-arising is finite"—are positions the Sāṃkhya opponent alone upholds. And because we Mādhyamikas do not have such a thesis [of self-arising], we are not implicated by contradictions ensuing from adhering to such a tenet. This then is the meaning of the first citation [from *Clear Words*].

Buddhapālita too speaks of "there being no point in arising again," mentioning the word "again"[402] just as *Clear Words* uses the word "again." The present text too reads, "If you conceive that what is once arisen can arise again . . ." (6.9a). So it is *existence* and *re-arising* that are incompatible, not existence and arising per se. Similarly, it is *existence* and *finitude of re-arising* that are incompatible, not existence and finitude of arising; the latter two are not mutually exclusive.

The meaning of the second citation [from *Clear Words*] is this: When the Mādhyamika—the proponent of no intrinsic existence—presents the two *reductio* arguments against the Sāṃkhya, as outlined above, he himself has no wish to subscribe to the reverse propositions of those consequences. It is also not the case that, despite having no intention to subscribe to them, he is somehow compelled to do so against his will. Therefore the citation states that we Mādhyamikas do not subscribe to the reverse propositions of those two *reductio* arguments.

The meaning of the third citation is as follows. Although the reverse propositions of the two *reductio* arguments—that there is a point to arising again and that such arising is infinite—do not operate as logical proofs to establish the absence of self-arising, this does not mean they serve no purpose whatsoever. Through demonstrating that arising would be pointless and that there will be an infinite regression to arising—something the Sāṃkhya does not accept—these *reductio* arguments serve merely to negate self-arising, which the Sāṃkhya does adhere to. In contrast, in the case of the two *reductio* arguments [in the context of refuting arising from other], we Mādhyamikas do accept the reverse of the two consequential arguments.[403] We should therefore understand that there are two kinds of reverse propositions of consequentialist arguments: ones we accept and ones we do not.

Rejecting the response aimed at avoiding these faults

This has two parts: (1) the response aimed at avoiding these faults and (2) rejecting that response.

The response aimed at avoiding these faults

> [*Opponent*:] That which is capable of being produced is called, there-
>   fore, the *effect*,
> and that which is capable of producing it, though other, is the *cause*.
> Sharing the same continuum, the effect arises from its producer.
> Hence rice sprouts cannot come from something like barley seeds. 6.15

Here the opponent states the following. Cause and effect are other from one another by virtue of their intrinsic characters, [137] but this does not mean that anything can arise from anything, for one can see that cause and effect, in their own ways, have a determinate correlation with one another. This is so because **that** very thing that **is capable of being produced** by another thing **is called** or deemed, **therefore, the *effect*** of that [other thing]. The presence of the word "therefore" is at variance with the *Commentary*.[404] And a specific cause **that is capable of producing it** [the effect], **though** it is intrinsically **other, is the *cause*** and hence is determined to be the cause. Therefore, so they assert, it is only by means of a special type of otherness that cause and effect are posited, not on the basis of mere otherness in general.

Furthermore, **rice sprouts** come from rice seeds **sharing the same continuum**; they **cannot come from something like barley seeds**, which do not share the same continuum, in the way that barley sprouts grow from barley seeds. Even in cases where they share the same continuum, only **from** those that are **its producer** can **the effect arise**. For example, subsequent instances do not produce preceding instances—it is only the preceding instances within the same continuum that produce subsequent instances. Hence, [the opponent] might assert, not just anything can arise from anything.

Rejecting that response

To those who speak of the cause and effect as existing by virtue of their own essences, we ask the following: "What accounts for the determinate correlation between a rice seed and a rice sprout?" If the opponent answers, "We can see such a determinate correlation," we might then ask, "Why is it that you see such fixed correlation?" When probed in this way, the opponent is reduced to simply stating, "Because such a determinate correlation can be observed, we see such a determinate correlation." In doing so, the opponent in fact presents no reason for the existence of such a determinate unique causal connection. Therefore he cannot avoid all the objections outlined above, not in the slightest. Thus Candrakīrti argues.[405]

The meaning of the [above paragraph] is this: The opponent has failed to demonstrate any reason why there is no contradiction in asserting a determinate correlation between [cause and effect] even though the two are distinct by virtue of intrinsic characteristics. So his rebuttal does not remove the fault.

Furthermore, to underline the fact that this otherness through intrinsic characteristics would equally apply to everything—whether or not they are related to each other as cause and effect—and that the opponent's heralded claim would in fact undermine his own standpoint, the text says the following:

> [*Objection*:] You do not think of barley, lotus pistils, *kiṃśuka* flowers,
>   and so on
> as producing rice sprouts; indeed they have no power to do so.
> They do not belong to the same continuum; they share no likeness.
> Likewise, rice seeds, also being other, differ from their sprouts as well.
>   6.16

Just as, for example, **you do not think of barley, pistils** (*kesara*) **of lotus, *kiṃśuka* flowers**, [138] **and so on**, on account of just being "other," (1) **as producing rice sprouts**, (2) [you admit that] **indeed they have no power to do so**, (3) **they do not belong to the same continuum**, and (4) **they share no** preceding instances of **likeness** [as rice sprouts]. **Likewise, rice seeds, also being other**, would not possess those four characteristics with respect to the rice sprout, for they too **differ from their sprouts** by virtue of their own intrinsic characteristics **as well**. This type of argument demonstrates how the notion of the presence or absence of these four characteristics cannot be postulated even in relation to things that are separate and unrelated.

A specific refutation of arising from other

This has two parts: (1) refuting arising from other where cause and effect are regarded as sequential and (2) refuting arising from other where cause and effect are regarded as simultaneous.

Refuting arising from other where cause and effect are regarded as sequential

The first has two parts: the actual refutation and rejecting objections raised against the refutation.

The actual refutation

Up to now, for the sake of argument, we have engaged in refutation based on taking the *otherness* established by intrinsic characteristic as known to the opponent as if it were to exist. Now the following is stated to demonstrate that intrinsic otherness is in fact impossible with respect to cause and effect:

> A sprout does not exist at the same time as the seed,
> so without its correlate, how can seed be "other"?
> As it is not established that the sprout arises from the seed,
> you should discard the view that things arise from other. 6.17

For example, in the case of examples of already existing Maitreya and Upagupta, it is only on the basis of their contrast with each other that we perceive one to be different from the other. In contrast, **a sprout does not exist at the same time as the seed**, for without the transformation of the seed's form, there is no sprout at all. There is, in the seed, no otherness from the sprout that exists by virtue of its own essence, and **without its correlate, how can the seed be** truly **"other"** from the sprout? It cannot. Since there is no intrinsically real otherness, **it is not established that the sprout arises** through its own essence **from the seed**. So **you**, the opponent, **should discard the view that things arise from other**.

This demonstrates that, if the seed's separateness from the sprout were to exist by virtue of its intrinsic nature, given that what possesses intrinsic existence can never cease to exist, then even at the time of the seed it would exist as a substance separate from the sprout. [139] And in that case [given that the seed's existence as a separate substance presupposes the existence of its point of contrast—namely, the sprout], then the two would become temporally simultaneous. Since this cannot be so, this demonstrates that these two things have no intrinsically existing otherness. This argument does not reject the view that cause and effect are different entities on the conventional level.

It is critical to understand that this argument touches upon the object of negation [i.e., the purported intrinsic otherness of cause and effect].

Rejecting objections raised against the refutation

> You may say that, like the up and down of two sides of a scale,
> which cannot but be seen to take place at the same time,
> the arising and ceasing of the produced and producer occur together.
> Even if they are simultaneous, there is no simultaneity [of seed and
> sprout] here. 6.18

[*Opponent*:] **You may say that** our statement that the sprout does not exist simultaneously to the seed is incorrect. For example, **like the up and down of two sides of a scale, which cannot but be seen to take place at the same time, the** twin acts of **arising and ceasing** of, respectively, **the producer**— the seed—**and the produced**—the sprout—**occur together** in temporal terms. Therefore the seed and sprout too can be said to be simultaneous.

[*Response*:] It is inappropriate to employ the analogy of a scale to conceive the simultaneity of the ceasing of the seed and the arising of the sprout. For **even if** the ascending and descending movements of the two sides of the scale **are simultaneous, there is no simultaneity here** between the seed and sprout, the referents of that analogy. So the analogy does not hold. The following is stated to show how this analogy does not hold:

> For as you contend, that which is arising is *about to arise*, so does not
> yet exist,
> while that which is ceasing, though existent, is *about to disintegrate*.
> If this is so, how can such a case be likened to a scale?
> It makes no sense to speak of an arising when there is no producer. 6.19

For as you contend, that which is called *arising*, because it **is about to arise** and exists as a future sprout, **does not yet exist** in the present. [140] **While that which is** *ceasing*, **though existent, is about to disintegrate**, so it does exist in the present. **If this is so** in that, at the moment when the sprout is about to arise, the seed is present but the sprout is future, **how can such a case**—the temporal status of the seed and sprout—**be likened to** the ascending and descending sides of **a scale?** They cannot be. Because when the twin movements of the two sides of a scale are present, the ascending and descending of the scale also exist simultaneously. In contrast, there is no simultaneity between the seed and the sprout.

These passages show that citing the example of the two sides of a scale—one ascending and the other descending—is inappropriate for demonstrating how the seed and sprout are simultaneous because their two acts [ceasing and arising] happen to occur simultaneously. They do not demonstrate, however, that if two acts happen to occur at the same time, this necessarily means that the two things [whose acts we are speaking of] should themselves exist simultaneously in that very moment.

Now, if the opponent were to think, "Although there is no simultaneity between something like a seed its sprout, there is simultaneity between the acts of these two," this too is untenable. These opponents did not assert actions to be objectively distinct from the things themselves.[406] Furthermore, the context here is the refutation of the intrinsic existence of the twin acts.

There is another fault as well. The sprout—which in relation to its act of arising is the agent—is of the future in the moment of its arising, so the sprout does not yet exist at that time. Without its existence, however, **it makes no sense to speak of an arising**, which is the dependent activity, **when there is no** sprout, the **producer**. Therefore, since the sprout is not concurrent with the [process of] ceasing, the claim that the two processes are simultaneous is untenable.

[*Opponent*:] "Does not this passage in the noble *Rice Seedling Sutra*, 'The instant the seed ceases, the sprout arises, in the manner of the ascending and descending of sides of a scale,'"[407] present this very analogy of a scale? Therefore it is incorrect to refute the view that the seed and sprout resemble the ascending and descending sides of a scale."

[*Response*:] "It is true that this analogy is cited in that sutra. However, this does not demonstrate arising from other; nor does it illustrate arising by virtue of intrinsic characteristic,"[408] states Candrakīrti. Therefore the arising that is negated in the context of the line "Such arising is . . ."[409] is the arising that exists by virtue of the thing's own essence. The simple arising of a sprout from its seed is not being negated at all.

One might ask, "If that sutra is not showing the simultaneity of the seed and sprout by way of the ascending and descending sides of a scale, then what kind of simultaneity is being illustrated by that analogy?"

The *Commentary* states that this analogy is employed to thoroughly illustrate the illusion-like mutually dependent originations, which come about simultaneously and are established within an unanalyzed perspective.[410] The phrase "dependent originations, which come about simultaneously" [141] needs to be related to the simultaneous presence of the two processes. Furthermore, in that sutra the analogy of the ascending and descending sides of a scale is supposed to illustrate [two things] that are simultaneous, but this cannot be related to the simultaneity of seed and sprout. Therefore, the rejection of the simultaneity of two acts here is that of two acts said to exist by virtue of their intrinsic nature; temporal coexistence of two acts in general is not being rejected. For, as long as one accepts arising, the cessation of the cause and the approach of the effect to the point of arising would have to be taken to be simultaneous.

Thus there is nothing wrong with accepting arising per se and arising on the conventional level. The contradiction only comes into play for ultimate arising or arising by virtue of intrinsic characteristics. In the first case [on the conventional level], even if the processes of cause and effect, ceasing and arising, are simultaneous, the cause and its effect themselves need not coexist in time. In the latter case [on the ultimate level], however, if the processes are simultaneous, the cause and effect themselves must necessarily coexist in time as well.

Here is the point. When it comes to the activity of an effect's arising, it is in relation to an agent, such as the sprout, that one can say such things as "This arises." So there is a mutual relationship of the "support" (agent) and the "supported" (its activity). Now if the two, the support and the supported, were to possess ultimate existence, then it would be illogical for the two to change their natures into something else. This would mean that the activity [of arising] would exist at all times as the supported, with the consequence that even when the sprout and the like are in the arising phase, the sprout must exist as the support for the arising process. Since such a standpoint is vulnerable to objections, such as that cause and effect would be simultaneous, it is untenable. In the conventional sense of arising, however, even if [two things] are once the support and the supported, they need not remain so at all times. So the situation differs between these two cases.

[To summarize,] the act of a sprout's arising—which temporarily coexists with seed—is the process of the sprout approaching the moment of arising. Such a process and the sprout are the supported and the support, yet at the time of this process, although the sprout does not exist, its process can exist, and there is no contradiction in maintaining this. This is analogous to the following example. Generally speaking, if a thing that is in relation does not exist, the other relatum will also not exist. Furthermore, the seed is the thing that is in relation, while the sprout is the other relatum. Nevertheless, one can say, without contradiction, that at the time of sprout, the seed is no more but the sprout is present.

If one understands how to posit the flawless Madhyamaka standpoint on the basis of understanding well how to refute the opponent through these types of reasoning and how our arguments do not revert to our own side, one is then a true Mādhyamika. If, in contrast, we encounter those who utter all sorts of fallacious arguments when engaged in refutation but, when these arguments are upended, seek haven in duplicitous bluster, we should relate to them as Candrakīrti says in his *Clear Words*, "I will not debate with those who blatantly deny what is obvious."[411] [142]

Refuting arising from other where cause and effect are regarded as simultaneous

> If, for visual cognition, what exists at the same time as itself—
> eyes and so forth, as well as concomitant discrimination, and so on—
>   are its producer,
> what need is there for it to arise, since it already exists?
> If you say it does not yet exist, we have already shown the faults of this.
>   6.20

The opponent here asserts the following. Now arising from other may be untenable for seed and sprout, which have no intrinsic otherness owing to their lack of temporal simultaneity. However, arising from other could exist when causes and effects are simultaneous, since they possess real otherness. Take, for example, eye consciousness and its concurrent factors of feeling and so on. Just as eye consciousness arises through the mere coming together of the eyes, form, and so on, as well as feelings and so on, in the same manner, the eyes and so on as well as the minds that are concomitant serve as conditions of feelings and so on. So some opponents might assert.

[*Response*:] Say that, **if, for visual cognition**, eye consciousness, **what exists at the same time as itself**—such as **eyes and so forth, as well as** other **concomitant** factors like **discrimination and so on**—**are** conceived to be **its producing** conditions. In that case, even if one were to allow that such an eye consciousness were to be distinct from discrimination and so on, still, **since** something that **already exists** at the time of its cause will come into being again, **what need is there for it** [visual cognition] **to arise?** None whatsoever. Wishing to avoid the fault of nonarising, you, the opponent, may **say** the effect **does not yet exist** at the time of the cause. In that case, **the faults of this**—how there can be no intrinsic otherness to things that are sequential—**we have already shown** above.

In sum, this argument demonstrates how with respect to what are asserted to be cause and effect, even if otherness *per se* exists, intrinsic arising remains impossible. In this way, the argument shows the impossibility of arising from other. The previous argument (6.17–19) demonstrated how, though arising is possible in relation to cause and effect, intrinsic otherness is not possible for them, and how because of this, arising from other is impossible. Therefore the statement "there is arising from other" has long become empty of content, reduced to a mere sound proclaiming such a thing. [143]

A refutation of arising from other by examining the four possibilities with respect to effects

> If the cause is a producer that produces something other,
> "Is what it produces existent, nonexistent, both, or neither?"
> If existent, what need is there for a producer? If nonexistent, what can
>   a producer do?
> If both, again, what use is it? If neither, what use does a producer serve?
> 6.21

If the cause is a producer that produces something other, we will examine by asking, "**Is what** that cause **produces** intrinsically **existent, nonexistent, both,** or something **neither** existent nor nonexistent?" Now **if,** for now, the effect is intrinsically **existent, what need is there** then **for** it to have a condition as its **producer?** For if something that has intrinsic existence can come to arise, then what has already arisen will arise again, and this we have already demonstrated to be untenable. For a **nonexistent** effect, too, **what can** its **producer,** the conditions, **do?** Like the horns of a rabbit, it is nonexistent! As for the combination of **both** existent and nonexistent, **again what use is** a producer, the conditions? Such a combination of the two is impossible. Also, with regard to that which is **neither** existent nor nonexistent, **what use does the producer,** the conditions, **serve?** For that which is neither of the two is impossible.[412]

11. The Two Truths

Rebutting objections to this refutation from the worldly perspective

This has two parts: (1) repelling objections from the worldly perspective assuming that arising from other is accepted in worldly convention and (2) repelling objections from the worldly perspective on the basis that arising from other does not exist even in worldly convention.

Repelling objections from the worldly perspective assuming that arising from other is accepted in worldly convention

The first has two parts: (1) the opponent's objection that such refutation is invalidated by worldly convention and (2) the response that worldly convention does not invalidate the refutation.

The opponent's objection that such refutation is invalidated by worldly convention

[*Opponent*:] "You may claim that the arguments we have put forth to prove arising from other have all been burned up by the fire of your intelligence like dry logs soaked in melted butter. So go ahead and stir these logs with the blazing fire of your wisdom; it is pointless now to add more fuel. Now you might ask, 'Isn't it the case that arising from other cannot be established without reasoning?' To this we would say no. There is nothing any reasoning can do about what is established by the world. [144] For what is perceived by the world possesses great power." This point is rendered in the following:

> [*Opponent*:] Worldly perspective, grounded in its own views, is
> authoritative;
> that things come from what is other than themselves is perceived by
> people.

So what use is reasoning here in this context?
Thus *other-arising* is established; what need have we of reasoning? 6.22

Given that the world's population, **grounded in its own views** alone, asserts that the **worldly perspective is authoritative**, this [perspective] possesses great power. And **that things**, effects that are other, do **come from** causes that are intrinsically **other than themselves is perceived by people** of the world. Furthermore, when presenting logical proofs of the two kinds of facts—those that are evident and those that are not—reason is relevant only in the latter case. Since the first is established by direct valid perception, proof through reasoning is unnecessary. **So here in this context** of other-arising, **what use is** any other type of logical **reasoning?** It is pointless. **Thus, as other-arising is established** without recourse to any other proof, **what need have we of reasoning?** None; it is established by direct perception. So the opponent might assert.

The response that worldly convention does not invalidate this refutation

Those who do not understand without distortion the meaning of the scriptures, those who are bereft of the means—repeated study of the nature of no-intrinsic existence—that helps one part from the long-acquainted friend, the manifest clinging to the true existence of things stemming from the ripening of the habitual propensities for grasping at true existence imprinted within during the beginningless cycle of existence, such people might appeal to mere worldly convention, the arbitrary terms of the world. Now this objection from arbitrary worldly conventions cannot be averted easily; it requires a lot of explanation about how the conventions of the world came to be. For one, one needs to demonstrate how the perspective of the world can invalidate in the case of certain phenomena, identifying the specific characteristics of such a category of facts, and demonstrate how the worldly perspective cannot invalidate in the case of another category of facts. [145]

To do this, one must first present the differentiation of the two truths. This has five parts: (1) general presentation of the two truths, (2) relating this presentation to the actual context, (3) the nature of each of the two truths, (4) objections to the assertion that worldly perspectives invalidate the refutation [of arising from other], and (5) the contexts and the manner in which worldly perspectives can invalidate.

General presentation of the two truths

This has four parts: (1) how phenomena, differentiated in terms of the two truths, have dual natures, (2) further presentation of the two truths, (3) distinctions within conventional truth from the perspective of the world, (4) how the apprehended object of that which is deluded with respect to its object of apprehension does not exist even on the conventional level.

How phenomena, differentiated in terms of the two truths, have dual natures

The first is as follows.

> [*Response:*] All entities bear dual natures
> as obtained by correct or false views [of them].
> What is seen by perfect vision is the ultimate truth,
> and what is seen by false vision is conventional truth, it is taught. 6.23

The buddhas, who realize without distortion the individual natures of the two truths, have shown that **all entities**—both inner, such as motivational factors like intention and so on, and outer, such as sprouts and so on—**bear dual natures**. What are these two? It is their nature in terms of conventional truth and their nature in terms of ultimate truth. This indicates that, when differentiated, there are two natures even in the case of a single entity such as a sprout—a conventional one and an ultimate one. It certainly does not indicate that one and the same entity—the single sprout, for example—is one truth or the other depending on whether the point of view is that of ordinary persons or āryas.

This understood, it is furthermore impossible for a phenomenon to have no nature at all. So insofar as something is an established base, it must be either identical in nature or different in nature from other things. Furthermore, it is not inconsistent to accept things to possess a nature yet reject that they possess intrinsic nature. Here, the ultimate nature of entities such as sprouts is the nature of the thing **obtained** as the object of a specific gnosis **by** those who possess **correct view** and directly perceive the perfect truth. Such a truth is not established, however, through its own essence. This then is one of the two natures referred to above. "Specific gnosis" indicates that it is not obtained by just any gnosis of an ārya person; rather it must be a specific or particular type of gnosis. That is to say, it is obtained by the gnosis that realizes the way things really are.

Now, in presenting this as obtained or established by that gnosis, one might wonder whether something established by that [gnosis] must be truly existent. To help avert this, Candrakīrti writes, "It is not established by virtue of its own essence, however."[413] [146] Given this statement, some assert that if the meditative equipoise of āryas were to realize the ultimate truth, it would become truly existent; hence ultimate truth is not an object of knowledge in the tradition of this master [Candrakīrti]. Such people have not understood at all the significance of this tradition's statement that just because something is obtained by meditative equipoise does not mean it has true existence. By making such an assertion, they allow the tradition of the learned ones to be defiled.

The conventional nature, which is other than the ultimate, is that nature obtained by ordinary beings, whose eyes of cognition are utterly obscured by the cataracts of ignorance through the force of their **false views**. This reality, perceived within the field of the vision of the childish [ignorant ones] as possessing existence by virtue of intrinsic characteristics, does not exist in the manner in which it is perceived. This, then, is [the second] one of the dual natures.

One needs to understand the statement that it is āryas who obtain ultimate truth in the sense of their being primary. The statement does not imply that Candrakīrti holds that ordinary beings who have gained the Middle Way view cannot obtain it. Similarly, the statement that it is the ordinary common person who obtains conventional reality should be understood in the sense that perceptions of outer and inner phenomena, which are the instances of conventional reality, occur primarily through the power of ignorance. It is not the case that Candrakīrti says these phenomena cannot be obtained by the valid conventional cognitions of the āryas.

Although individual examples of conventional truth, such as vase and so on, can be obtained even by those who have not found the Middle Way view, to ascertain a particular phenomenon as a conventional truth by means of a valid cognition, one must first gain the Middle Way view. Because if a given phenomenon had been established as a conventional truth, this would mean that it would be established as false; and to establish something explicitly as false, one first has to negate true existence with respect to that phenomenon by means of valid cognition. Therefore, although as suggested by the phrase "through the force of false views," ordinary common people perceive false realities, this does not imply that they establish these phenomena *as* false. For example, when the spectators at a magic show see conjured horses and elephants, they *do* see false things, but they do not necessarily establish these perceptions to be false. Therefore the fact obtained through seeing false reality, which defines something to be a conventional truth, refers to that which is obtained by valid conventional cognition perceiving false and deceptive objects of cognition.

Of these two natures or realities described above, **what is seen by perfect vision**—the object obtained by rational cognition realizing that perfect truth—**is** suchness, **the ultimate truth.** This will be explained below in the section pertaining to the lines "Through the force of an eye disease, one perceives / such false things as floating hairs" (6.29). [147] That object of knowledge—namely, **what is seen by false vision** and obtained by conventional valid cognition—**is taught** by the Buddha to be **conventional truth.** The two domains in relation to which the ultimate and conventional truths are defined have been described as distinct; there are not two different modes of obtaining one and the same thing.

Further presentation of the two truths

There seem to be a variety of views when it comes to the basis for differentiating the two truths. Here, however, we take as that basis the object of knowledge. The *Meeting of Father and Son Sutra* says, as cited in *Compendium of Training*:

> Thus the Tathāgata comprehends the two truths, the conventional and the ultimate. What is to be known by conventional and ultimate truth is also exhaustive. Furthermore, because the Blessed One clearly *saw* them, clearly *understood* them, and excellently *actualized* them within emptiness, he is referred to as the Omniscient.[414]

The expression "what is to be known" identifies objects of knowledge to be the basis for differentiating [the two truths], while "is also exhaustive" indicates that the division into the two truths encompasses everything, and so because the Tathāgata comprehends both truths, he is described as the Omniscient. Therefore the exposition of those who propound that the standpoint of *Guide to the Bodhisattva Way* is that ultimate truth is not an object of knowledge and that it is not realized by any cognition is a distorted one.[415]

The division into two—conventional truth and ultimate truth—constitutes the actual differentiation. On the question of what exactly the meaning [or nature] of such a differentiation is, here too there seem to be many diverse opinions. I will explain this, however, as follows. Both of these two truths possess natures, and it is impossible for two members to be neither identical nor different in nature. Now if things happen to be different in nature from their emptiness of true existence, they will then come to possess true existence. Therefore, just like being a *product* and being *impermanent*, the two [the conventional truth, such as a vase, and its ultimate truth, its emptiness of true existence] are identical in nature but have distinct conceptual identities. *Commentary on the Awakening Mind* says:

> Independent of the conventional,
> no ultimate truth can be found.
> The conventional is taught to be emptiness;
> emptiness itself is the conventional;
> one does not occur without the other,
> just as being produced and impermanent.[416]

The meaning of the first four lines is this: The suchness of the conventional is not of a different nature, because conventional truths are themselves empty of true existence, and furthermore, the emptiness of true existence is itself posited as the basis of the conventional. The last two lines state that such being the case the two observe an invariable relationship whereby one does not come into being without the other. And since theirs is a relationship of identical nature, the two are shown to be like "being produced" and "being impermanent," which are also identical in nature.

As for the character of the individual members of this division, [148] this is as mentioned above, when the individual truths were defined as what is obtained by the two types of valid cognitions (6.23).

Now if what is presented here is to be harmonized with Śāntideva's *Guide to the Bodhisattva Way*, how would one explain the following in that text?

> The conventional and the ultimate—
> these are accepted to be the two truths.

The ultimate is not an object of intellect;
the intellect is said to be conventional.[417]

The first two lines here present the division into the two truths. Then, when identifying the individual members of that division, ultimate truth is identified in one line, "The ultimate . . . ," while conventional truth is identified in another line, "The intellect is . . . conventional." The assertion that what has been presented as the thesis in the preceding line—that the ultimate is not an object of intellect—is being established by the subsequent line ["the intellect is said to be conventional"] does not appear to be the intent of the text at all. In fact, the identification of the two truths found here in *Guide to the Bodhisattva Way* appears to be a restatement of the following passage from the *Meeting of Father and Son Sutra*, as quoted in Śāntideva's own *Compendium of Training*:

> Of these two, the Tathāgata sees the conventional to be the purview of the world. That which is the ultimate is ineffable: it is not an object of knowledge, it is not an object of detailed knowledge, it is not an object of thorough knowledge, it is not shown. . . .[418]

The meaning of the statement that the ultimate truth is not knowable is that it is not an object of cognition in the manner that I will explain below when interpreting a passage from *Entering the Two Truths Sutra*.[419] Otherwise, if the ultimate truth is not an object of any cognition at all, this will contradict the statement [found in that same *Meeting of Father and Son Sutra*] that because the Buddha has directly actualized both conventional truth and ultimate truth—namely, emptiness—he is defined as the Omniscient. I will touch upon this point [about the buddha's cognition of the two truths] more extensively in a section below as well.[420]

As for the identification of conventional truth [in *Guide to the Bodhisattva Way*], it is not that intellect alone should be taken as such; the intended referent is the *object* of the intellect. Just as the sutra states this to be "the purview of the world," here too it refers to facts obtained from within the sphere of experience or from the purview of the worldly or conventional consciousness, which perceives false realities. This is how one should understand the sense in which the object of the intellect constitutes the conventional truth.

The division of objects of knowledge into two truths underlines the point that all objects of knowledge are exhausted within this twofold division. For a scriptural citation on this point, there is the passage from the *Meeting of Father and Son Sutra* quoted above, and this is also stated explicitly in the *Meditation on the Definite Revelation of Suchness*:

> There is the conventional and likewise the ultimate;
> there is never such a thing as a third truth.[421]

The *Commentary* too says: [149]

> Likewise, whatever other truths there may be, all of these should also be ascertained as encompassed by either of the two truths.[422]

In this way, the *Commentary* explains how the numerous enumerations bearing the word "truth" found in the *Ten Grounds Sutra* are encompassed within the two truths. There, the truth to be understood by means of differentiation is identified as referring to the presentations of the aggregates, elements, and sources, so this master [Candrakīrti] too accepts the division of truth into two as exhaustive.

Here is the reasoning: *When something is determined to be false and deceptive, then its being nondeceptive and true must necessarily be negated.* This is because being deceptive and being nondeceptive are direct opposites, mutually excluding each other. Given this, [the two truths] must pervade the entire class of knowables, and as such they exclude any third possibility that is both or neither. This is as stated, for example, in *Light of the Middle Way*, where it says:

> Those that have the characters of mutually excluding each other are such that, when one is eliminated through negative determination, if its opposite is not affirmed through positive determination, then its opposite has no existence. To conceive of something that is neither of the two is illogical.[423]

Also:

> Those two things—of which one does not exist if it is not established through positive determination when its opposite is eliminated through negative determination—mutually exclude each other. Those characterized by such mutual exclusion are perva-

sive with respect to everything. And that which pervades everything eliminates any other possibilities. Take, for example, the
case of an embodied being and a non-embodied being.[424]

This point should be understood in the context of all other examples of
direct opposites.

Now if an example of direct opposites that excludes the possibility of
a third term cannot be shown, there will then be no facility to engage in
refutations based on critical analysis where the possibilities are confined to
binary terms, enquiring "whether something *does* or *does not exist*," "whether
it is *one* or *many*," and so on. But if there do exist [such examples of direct
opposites], then when one of the two terms within that direct opposition is negated, if the other is not established, then the other term has no
existence. Therefore, to say that there are no direct opposites according to
Prāsaṅgika Madhyamaka suggests a failure to become versed in the ways of
refutation and affirmation. Insofar as when one term in a direct opposition
is eliminated the other comes to be established, and when one is negated the
other is affirmed, there is no difference between Prāsaṅgika and Svātantrika
Madhyamaka.[425] [150]

Distinctions within conventional truth from the perspective of the world

Of the two, objects and subjects within conventional truth, to state that the
class of subjects includes, from the perspectives of worldly cognition, both
those that are veridical and those that are distorted, the text says:

> False vision is also said to be of two kinds:
> that of clear senses and that of impaired senses.
> Cognitions deriving from impaired senses are
> held to be distorted compared with those of the unimpaired. 6.24

Not only is the class of knowables differentiated into two truths, **false
vision** in the case of subjective mind **is also said to be of two kinds**—those
that are veridical and those that are distorted. They are **that of clear senses**,
untainted by temporary conditions of illusion and cognitions based upon
them, **and that of impaired senses**, subjects tainted by temporary conditions
of illusion. Of these, **cognitions deriving from tainted senses are held to be**

distorted compared with those of the unimpaired, cognitions untainted by temporary conditions of illusion. The former [cognitions of clear senses] are accepted to apprehend the objects without distortion. This distinction between the two is drawn not from the Madhyamaka's own standpoint but from the perspective of the everyday world.

Just as the class of subjective cognition is differentiated in terms of distorted and undistorted, this is true for the class of objects as well. That this is so is stated in the following:

> Everything the six unimpaired senses grasp
> and perceive within everyday experience of the world
> is true from the perspective of the world;
> the rest the world itself defines as false. 6.25

Everything the six unimpaired senses grasp, senses unimpaired by temporary conditions of illusion, **and perceive within everyday experience of the world**—this **is true** or veridical within the framework of or **from the perspective of the world**. These objects are not posited as being true or veridical from the perspective of the āryas. Here the two phrases "from the perspective of the āryas" and "from the Madhyamaka standpoint" share the same meaning. **The rest**, such as mirror images and so on, which are perceived as objects when the senses are impaired, **the world itself defines as false**. The term "itself" here suggests that, to establish these cognitions as deluded, valid conventional cognition alone is adequate. There is no need to seek recourse in rational cognition [inquiring into suchness]. [151]

The conditions that impair the senses from within refer to cataracts, having yellowish vision, eating *datura* fruit, and so on.[426] Datura is a resin plant, and when its fruit is consumed, everything appears golden. The phrase "and so on" includes disease epidemics among other things. The conditions that impair the senses from without are mirrors, cave acoustics, bright colored sand when struck by the spring sun, and so on. In these cases, even though the conditions distorting the senses do not reside within the person, they still become the cause for apprehending mirror images, echoes, and mirages grasped as water. One should also understand this class of external conditions [of illusion] to include the spells and relevant substances prepared by magicians.

The conditions that impair mental cognition include, in addition to such spells and relevant substances, distorted philosophical views, false arguments, impairment by sleep, and so on. Since sleep is described here as a factor that impairs our mental faculty from among the six senses, those who claim that master Candrakīrti accepts sensory perceptions to be present in sleep represent a great distortion.

This being so, the causes of impairment in the particular context here should not be held to be the impairment caused by the contamination of ignorance, such as of the two forms of grasping at self-existence ingrained in us since beginningless time. Here, as explained above, the causes of impairment are the conditions of illusion that impair our senses temporarily. And the distinction drawn here—how conventional facts apprehended by the unimpaired six consciousnesses are veridical and how those that are contrary are distorted—remains solely within the context of the world's perspective. The analysis is on the basis of whether something perceived to exist within such a perspective is invalidated by everyday cognitions of the world. From the perspective of the āryas, however, no such distinction between veridical and distorted conventional truths can be made. Just as reflections and the like do not exist in reality as they appear, blue and so on perceived by those who possess ignorance do not exist by virtue of their intrinsic characteristics as they are perceived to. Thus no distinction can be made between these two types of cognitions with respect to whether or not they are mistaken.

[*Question*:] Now, with respect to such instances—the perception of false objects due to one's sense organs being impaired by immediate conditions, perception of people and so on in a dream due to impairment of mental consciousness by conditions such as sleep, perception of magical horses and elephants and mirages grasped as water and so on that occur in waking states—it may well be true that even ordinary worldly cognition can realize that such perceptions are distorted. [152] However, what is apprehended falsely by the mind impaired by inferior philosophical tenets cannot be cognized as distorted by ordinary worldly cognition. How then are such things posited as distorted solely from the perspective of the world?

[*Reply*:] The impairment here in the context of examining whether a perception is impaired is not the impairment from grasping at things distortedly due to our innate ignorance. In any case, the postulations of inferior philosophical tenets refer to notions such as *primal substance* and so on, which are conceived falsely because one's mind has been conditioned by philosophical views. True, ordinary worldly cognitions would not realize that such notions are distorted. Nonetheless, if the valid conventional cognitions of those whose minds may have not been directly informed by an understanding of suchness realize they are distorted, this constitutes their being realized as false by worldly cognition.[427] As for other categories, such as the referents conceived by the two types of grasping at self-existence, these belong to the class of what are referred to as "objects apprehended by unimpaired senses." Such things are thus veridical or true from the perspective of ordinary worldly understanding; nonetheless, they have no existence even on the conventional level.

One might ask: "You may not distinguish veridical from false conventional truths because you do not accept the possibility of a *veridical conventional* as such. But why would you not posit the subject, cognitions tainted by ignorance, and its objects as distorted conventional truths?"

[*Reply:*] This is because the positing of conventional truth by valid conventional cognition, if one posits distorted conventional truth, must be done from the perspective of such cognition. However, valid conventional cognition cannot establish the distortion induced by the habitual propensity toward ignorance to be an error.

How the apprehended object of that which is deluded with respect to its conceived object does not exist even on the conventional level

Now to relate what has already been explained in general—how an impaired mind distorts its conceived object—to a specific context by way of an analogy, the text says:

> Overcome as they are by ignorance's sleep,
> tīrthikas postulate a "self."
> As with things imagined as real owing to illusion, mirage, and the like,
> this has no existence even according to the world. 6.26

Tīrthikas are overcome by ignorance's sleep. Their minds suffer from impairment by inferior philosophical tenets and false logic, and because they wish to engage with suchness, they do not uphold accurate [notions of] arising or disintegration that even the philosophically untrained like the cowherders, [unlearned] women, and so on acknowledge. [153] Instead, out of their desire to surpass ordinary people of the worldly perspective, they are like someone climbing a tree who lets go of the lower branch before grabbing on to the next; they will suffer a great fall into an abyss of inferior philosophical views. Because they are divorced from the perfect vision of the two truths, they will not obtain the resultant liberation. Therefore the **"self" postulated** by these upholders of extreme views as found in their individual treatises, characterized by three attributes [eternal, unitary, and indivisible], does not exist even on the level of worldly conventional truth. This statement clearly refutes the assertion that, in this tradition [of Candra-kīrti], existence on the conventional level is defined purely in terms of an existence from the perspective of a deluded cognition. Similarly, **as with all things imagined as real owing to illusion, mirage,** mirror images, **and the like**—as real horses, real elephants, and real faces, for example—**this has no existence even according to the world**: namely, conventional truth. There-fore, for something to exist on the conventional level, it must be established by valid cognition. Now although such conceived objects [of deluded per-ceptions] do not exist even on the conventional level, Candrakīrti does not hold the situation to be the same when it comes to their appearing objects.[428]

The perception of the five sense objects of forms, sounds, and so on as existing by virtue of their own characteristics, which we experience right now with our sensory cognitions, is due to the contamination of ignorance. Therefore, insofar as their being deluded with respect to their appearing objects is concerned, the only difference between our everyday perceptions tainted by ignorance, on the one hand, and the delusory perceptions of mirror images, echoes, and so forth on the other is the degree of subtlety. Furthermore, although the intrinsic existence of blue and so on as well as reflections being the real face remain impossible, just as the reflection itself exists, likewise, blue and so on exist, despite their lack of intrinsic existence. Moreover, Candrakīrti accepts reflections to be visible forms just like other external objects. Later in the text, in fact, he speaks of how mirror images produce sensory perceptions. This mode of understanding should be extended also to the example of magical illusions, in which the eyes perceive horses and elephants, as well as to echoes and so on. And this presentation is unique to the excellent system [of Candrakīrti].[429]

Relating this presentation to the actual context

> Just as what is perceived by an eye afflicted with disease
> cannot invalidate the perception of those free of such defect, [154]
> likewise the mind deprived of stainless wisdom
> cannot invalidate a pure, untainted mind. 6.27

Given that the truth of suchness is not established by conventional cognition, arising from other cannot be refuted if one remains only within the ordinary worldly perspective. It is negated on the ultimate level by accepting the vision of the āryas. Hence the refutation of arising from other takes place with the proviso "ultimately." In view of this, **just as what is perceived by an eye afflicted by disease,** such as the vision of floating hairs and so on, **cannot invalidate the perception of those free of such defect** and thus do not experience such false vision, **likewise the mind** of ordinary persons tainted by ignorance and **deprived of** or divorced from the **stainless** or uncontaminated **wisdom cannot invalidate a pure mind** that is **untainted,** not polluted by ignorance. Hence, this negation of arising from other on the ultimate level cannot be invalidated [by a worldly cognition], even if one were to allow other-arising to exist, for the sake of argument, from the perspective of worldly cognition. Therefore the opponent is justifiably a source of amusement for the learned sublime ones.

The nature of each of the two truths

This has two parts: conventional truth and ultimate truth.

Conventional truth

The first has three parts: (1) the perspective from which the conventional is true or untrue, (2) how the mere conventional appears or does not appear to the three individuals, and (3) how the ultimate and conventional become as such from the perspectives of ordinary beings and āryas.

The perspective from which the conventional is true or untrue

The first has two parts: the actual point and a unique presentation of the afflictions.

The actual point

> Because delusion obscures the true nature, it is a *concealer*;
> that which is contrived by it and appears to be real
> the Buddha spoke of as *true for a concealer*;
> and fabricated entities are merely *conventional*. 6.28

Because it **obscures** sentient beings from viewing **the true nature**—the way things really are—it is called **delusion**. This ignorance that reifies the reality of things, attributing intrinsic existence to them when there is no such intrinsic existence, and that has the characteristic of obscuring vision of the true mode of being **is a** *concealer*. This line identifies what is the *concealer* (*saṃvṛti*) [155] in relation to the word *truth* in the context of the term *conventional truth* (*saṃvṛtisat*), where one is speaking of the concealer from the perspective of which [things are conceived to be true]. This line does not define what conventional [truth] is in general.

This identification [of what "conventional" means] parallels the following stanza from the *Descent into Laṅkā Sutra*, where cognition that mistakes what is essentially devoid of ultimate intrinsic existence as possessing such existence is stated to be the "concealer":

> The arising of things is on the conventional (*saṃvṛti*);
> on the ultimate there is no intrinsic nature.
> That which is mistaken toward no intrinsic nature
> is held to be a concealer (*saṃvṛti*) of the perfect truth.[430]

The Sanskrit term for "conventional," *saṃvṛti*, can also connote something that conceals, so *saṃvṛti* is referred to here as a "concealer." What does it conceal? As the phrase "concealer of the perfect truth" suggests, it conceals the meaning of the perfect truth; so it is asserted to be "conventional" (*saṃvṛti*) or a "concealer." This phrase "concealer of the perfect truth" is not referring to veridical conventional truth within the distinction of veridical and distorted conventional truths. Thus the *saṃvṛti* in the first line and the *saṃvṛti* in the last two lines [of the sutra quote] should not be understood to have the same meaning. The first refers to "conventional" in the sense of a framework within which one accepts that things possess [attributes like] arising and so on. The latter usage [of *saṃvṛti*] is in the sense of a "concealer" that grasps at true existence, which is the perspective that holds all things to be true.

Through the force of that "concealer" grasping at true existence, phenomena such as blue and so on, which are in fact contrived and fabricated, appear to sentient beings as possessing intrinsic existence despite being devoid of such status. These phenomena **that are contrived by it and appear to be real**—since they are true [only] from the perspective of distorted conventions of the world—**the Buddha spoke of as true for a con-**

cealer. How it was taught is as found thus in the sutra cited above.[431] Those **entities fabricated** by conceptualization, which remain untrue from the perspectives of any of the three individuals [śrāvaka and pratyekabuddha arhats and bodhisattvas who have attained the purified grounds] because they remain untrue from their perspectives, **are** referred to as "**merely conventional.**" The following passage, which I will explain, appears here in the *Commentary*:

> A few examples of dependent origination, such as reflections in a mirror, echoes, and so on, do appear as false to those ridden with ignorance; yet some examples, such as the blue color of material forms, the mind, feelings, and so on, appear to them as real. The true nature that is the mode of being of all phenomena never appears to those ridden with ignorance. Therefore such intrinsic nature and those things that are false even on the conventional level are not conventional truths.[432]

The phrase "a few examples" is translated as "some" in Naktso's version, which reads better. "Reflections in a mirror, echoes, and so on do appear as false" refers to these perceptions being erroneous. This is a falsehood in the sense of something appearing as a face but at the same time being devoid of being such. So emptiness of true existence in that context refers to its lack of being the real face it appears to be; [156] it does not mean the reflection's emptiness of true existence in the sense of its lack of existing by way of intrinsic characteristics. Therefore, even when the reflection is established as the absence of being the real face, there is no contradiction at all in deeming it to be real from the perspective of the "concealer," the mind that grasps it to exist through its intrinsic characteristic. So a mirror reflection *is* indeed a conventional reality.

The statement here [in the *Commentary* cited above] that mirror reflections are not conventional truths should be understood as follows. From the perspective of the worldly conventions of those versed in language, something like a mirror image is false in that it is not a real face, and in that sense it is not a conventional truth. It cannot be the case that a mirror image is not accepted to be a conventional truth as defined in the line "and what is seen by false vision is conventional truth, it is taught" (6.23d).

If, in contrast, it were contradictory for something to be a conventional truth because it lacks true existence on the conventional level, this would violate many presentations: such as the statement that there is no existence by virtue of intrinsic characteristics even on the conventional level, or that negating true existence and establishing the absence of true existence are all undertaken on the conventional level, and so on. Therefore the assertion that such things as mirror images, recognized as erroneous even by ordinary everyday cognition, are not conventional truths but are "mere conventionalities" reflects an apparent failure to properly understand the following points: the exhaustive nature of the twofold division of truth, and the distinction between the differentiation of truth and falsity from the perspective of the world and the Madhyamaka's differentiation of truth and falsity.

The statement "The true nature that is the mode of being of all phenomena never appears to those ridden with ignorance" also needs to be understood in terms of cognitions tainted by ignorance. For it is maintained that āryas who have not yet fully abandoned ignorance do realize suchness through direct perception. Now, although post-equipoise states of the gnosis of āryas on the learner's stages and the views of ordinary beings realizing suchness, since they are tainted by ignorance and its habitual propensities, do not perceive ultimate truth directly, it is not the case that they do not perceive it at all.

Understood thus, Candrakīrti's statement "Therefore conventional truth is defined on the basis of afflicted ignorance, which is one of the factors connected with cyclic existence"[433] indicates that the ignorance that grasps at phenomena as truly existent—known as grasping at the self-existence of persons and of phenomena—is understood to be the link of ignorance within the twelve links of dependent origination. It is thus not held to be an obscuration to knowledge. The statement that conventional truth is defined on the basis of such ignorance grasping at true existence indicates how such conventional facts are characterized as true from the point of view of a specific perspective. [157] It does not suggest that conventional realities like vases, bolts of cloth, and so on are established by this ignorance grasping at true existence. Because what is posited by such grasping at true existence is something that Candrakīrti does not accept even on the conventional level. Since the "conventional" in "conventional truth"—which refers to the perspective from which things are posited as being true—and the "conventional" in the conception of a vase and so on as "conventionally existent" are the same term, it appears there have been many who conflated these two senses of the term. It is therefore critical that we differentiate these different senses correctly.

[*Question*:] Are these phenomena like vases and so on true from the perspective of the conventions of all beings who are not fully enlightened, or are there some individuals from the perspective of whose conventions these are not true?

[*Reply*:] Phenomena like forms, sounds, and so on, which are defined as conventional truths, says Candrakīrti:

> These, in fact, possess the nature of being contrived for śrāvakas, pratyekabuddhas, and bodhisattvas who have abandoned the affliction of ignorance and perceive the conditioned world to be like mirror images. These phenomena are not true for them because these beings have no pretensions of them being true.[434]

As to the meaning of this statement, there are three kinds of persons for whom such phenomena are not true—śrāvakas, pratyekabuddhas, and bodhisattvas. Here too, it is not just any śrāvaka or any pratyekabuddha or bodhisattva; it is those with specific characteristics. One such feature is the direct realization that all conditioned things are just like reflections in that although devoid of intrinsic existence, they appear as such. To exclude bodhisattvas below the seventh ground and śrāvakas and pratyekabuddhas on the learner's stage, who also have this realization, the three individuals are also described [in the *Commentary*] as having "eliminated the affliction of ignorance." Thus we must understand these persons to include bodhisattvas on the purified grounds and śrāvaka and pratyekabuddha arhats. It is from the perspectives of these three that phenomena remain untrue.

That which is untrue includes, as the phrase "these, in fact"[435] suggests, outer and inner phenomena. The reason they are untrue [for these beings] is because these beings have no inclination for apprehending true existence given that ignorance grasping at true existence has ceased for them. Therefore these [passages from the *Commentary*] establish how the outer and inner phenomena remain untrue from the perspective of the convention (*saṃvṛti*) of these three kinds of persons. So since the *Commentary* in no way establishes these phenomena to be not conventional truths [for these beings] other than demonstrating them to be untrue [for them], those who read these passages as demonstrating these phenomena are not conventional truths [for the three persons] expose a great crudeness in their intellectual engagement. This is therefore an inferior standpoint whereby the intention of the master Candrakīrti is soiled by the stains of their own [feeble] intellect.

It is not that these phenomena are being demonstrated as untrue to the three kinds of persons for their benefit; it is for people like ourselves that these phenomena are demonstrated to be untrue from the perspectives of those three kinds of person. [158] As for beings who are other than the three classes and below them, they all possess innate grasping at true existence, and so nothing can be demonstrated to be devoid of true existence from the perspectives of any of their conventions (*saṃvṛti*).

Now if the meaning is not as explained above, and that it *is* the case that these phenomena are being shown to not be conventional truths for these individuals, then the rationale presented would become totally irrelevant.[436] For to establish via an instance of cognition that a particular thing is a conventional truth, that thing needs to be established as false, and so to cite the absence of clinging to true existence as the reason in that case would be laughable. The reason why a fact needs to be established as false to be established as a conventional truth by an instance of cognition is this: When the meaning of *truth* is understood in the context of the conventional truth of, for example, vases and so on, we need to bear in mind two senses of the term *truth*—one from the perspective of the subject (for the cognition) and the other in the objective sense. When one sees that their truth is not posited in the objective sense but posited as true merely from the perspective of grasping at true existence, a concealer (*saṃvṛti*), one comes to recognize that without such qualification, such phenomena do not possess true existence and are instead seen to be false. This is the critical point to understand.

A unique presentation of the afflictions

I feel it is crucial to recognize that this tradition has an identification of the afflictions that is distinct from the Upper and Lower Abhidharma systems. In general, grasping at the true existence of things is twofold—grasping at the true existence of persons and grasping at the true existence of phenomena. It was already mentioned above that Candrakīrti also considers these two to be the two types of grasping at self-existence. Candrakīrti describes such grasping at true existence as afflicted ignorance both in his commentary on *Entering the Middle Way* and in his commentary on *Four Hundred Stanzas*.[437] He states furthermore that such ignorance has been eliminated by śrāvaka and pratyekabuddha arhats, and in his *Commentary on the Four Hundred Stanzas*, he states that bodhisattvas that have obtained forbearance toward the unborn nature have also eliminated such ignorance.[438]

Therefore this afflicted ignorance is the force opposing the knowledge of suchness—namely, no-self. The opposite of such knowledge, in turn, should not be understood as a mere absence of knowledge or some such. It should be understood as a direct opposite, for it reifies the person and phenomena as intrinsically existent. Understood thus, the reification of self-existence of phenomena is considered afflicted ignorance, and the twin grasping at the intrinsic existence of "I" and "mine" constitute the identity view. So in this respect [on how identity view is defined], this Candrakīrti tradition diverges from that of the Abhidharma.

The Abhidharma tradition, as found in the ninth chapter of Vasubandhu's *Treasury of Abhidharma* autocommentary, on the other hand, identifies grasping at persons as self-sufficient, substantial realities as the identity view that grasps at "I," and the identity view that grasps at "mine" [159] it identifies to be viewing things conceived as "mine" belonging to such a person. So the way identity view is defined is very different. Now although the grasping at persons as self-sufficient, substantial realities is found in those whose minds are not tempered by philosophical thinking, grasping at persons as entities separate from the aggregates with distinct characteristics does not exist in those whose minds are not conditioned by philosophy. So even with respect to views grasping at extremes, there are two types.[439]

"If this is so," one might ask, "how would you prove to those who maintain persons and phenomena to exist through their intrinsic characteristics that grasping as such constitutes afflicted ignorance and represents the twofold grasping at self-existence?"

[*Reply*:] Now insofar as intrinsic existence of persons and phenomena is concerned, this will be negated by those reasonings that refute it; and when this happens, apprehending things in such terms as true existence will come to be established as erroneous with respect to its apprehended object. When this is established, then grasping at the true existence of persons and phenomena will come to be confirmed as constituting the twofold grasping at self-existence. Once these facts are confirmed, then grasping at true existence will come to be affirmed as the force directly opposing the knowledge of suchness, and as such, it will be understood to be a form of ignorance. Since it can be shown that as long as such ignorance [grasping intrinsic existence] does not cease, identity view too will not come to an end, this leads to the conclusion that such ignorance *is indeed* an afflicted ignorance. Thus it is critical to understand how to define [Candrakīrti's] unique presentation of the afflictions.

The way other afflictions such as attachment operate on the basis of the delusion grasping at true existence is explained in *Four Hundred Stanzas* and its commentary as follows:

> Just like body faculty in the entire body,
> delusion resides in all [afflictions].[440]

Candrakīrti's commentary on these lines says:

> "Delusion" refers to ignorance, for it apprehends things as real; as such, it operates by way of exaggeration superimposing truly existent natures upon things. Attachment and so on also operate by thoroughly attributing qualities of attractiveness or unattractiveness upon the nature of things imputed by delusion, and as such, they do not operate independently of delusion. Furthermore, they are contingent on delusion in that delusion is the primary factor.[441]

Up to the end of the first sentence shows that delusion here refers to grasping at true existence. The statement that attachment and so on do not operate independently of delusion indicates that they function in association with delusion, not divorced of it. The reason for this is presented in the passage that reads "Attachment and so on" up to "imputed by delusion." Since attractive and unattractive qualities are superimposed [160] by incorrect mentation, which is in fact a cause of attachment and aversion, the passage here does not identify the mode of apprehension of attachment and aversion themselves. Therefore the phrase "upon the nature of things imputed by delusion" is to be understood to mean that attachment and aversion operate on the basis of superimposing intrinsically existing qualities of attractiveness and unattractiveness. The passage is not saying that it is only the true existence superimposed by delusion that constitutes the focal object of attachment and so on—that is, in the differentiation between the focus and aspect [of these emotions]. This is because, between the two facets of the object of the two innate self-graspings—their focal object and their object in terms of apprehending aspect—their focal objects do exist as established bases. And since afflictions such as attachment are concomitant with delusion, their focal object is the same as that of the delusion. This means attachment and aversion are defined by their aspects of attraction toward an object and repulsion from an object induced by the two types of incorrect mentation. So states of mind with aspects of wanting or not wanting induced by grasping at persons as self-sufficient, substantial realities alone is not defined here as attachment and aversion. Therefore the way in which attachment and aversion are defined is also quite different here.

"Furthermore, they are contingent on delusion" means that it is through the initial delusion of grasping at things as existing by way of their characteristics that attachment and aversion are brought forth. The analogy of body faculty and its connection to the body illustrates that, just as there is no support for the other four sense faculties that is discrete from the body, similarly all the afflictions operate with delusion as their support and not divorced from delusion. Because of this, all the afflictions will become undone if delusion is destroyed. Thus, Āryadeva says, we should revere the discourse on dependent origination in terms of the emptiness of intrinsic existence, which is its antidote.[442]

This grasping at true existence of things is described in *Seventy Stanzas on Emptiness* as the ignorance that is the root of cyclic existence; and *Sixty Verses of Reasoning* also says:

> Having found a locus, one is caught
> by the twisting snake of the afflictions.
> Those whose minds have no locus
> will not be snared [by such a snake].[443]

Thus it says that if one finds any locus as the focus of objectification for grasping at true existence, one will then be snared by the snake of the afflictions. Immediately after this stanza, it says:

> In those whose minds have a locus,
> why would the grave poison of afflictions not arise?[444]

This then is the excellent standpoint of the noble Nāgārjuna.

In a comment linking these last two lines [to the preceding ones], one reads in Candrakīrti's commentary [on *Sixty Stanzas*] the following: [161]

> To demonstrate that it is impossible for those who objectify forms and so on to relinquish the afflictions, though they might aspire to, Nāgārjuna states the following. . . ."[445]

And in subsequent comments too it says:

> Now if one objectifies things as real entities, then myriad afflic-
> tions like attachment will emerge inexorably. Why? Because in
> the event something appeals to one's mind, it would be difficult
> to avert attachment toward it. In the event one's mind finds it
> unappealing, however, it would then be difficult to avert aversion
> and hostility toward it.[446]

Even if the object happens to be something that is neither appealing nor
unappealing, the commentary states, ignorance will still arise in relation
to it.[447] Therefore, while the apprehension of things as existing by way of
their own characteristics remains present within in one's mind, it is maintained that either attachment or aversion will arise; and even if these two are
absent, instances of delusion will continue to arise. The *Guide to the Bodhisattva Way* too says:

> The mind that takes focal objects
> will get stuck on one or another;
> and the mind divorced of emptiness
> when ceased will arise again,
> just as in the meditative attainment of nondiscrimination.[448]

In this regard, there is no difference between these two masters [Candrakīrti
and Śāntideva] and Buddhapālita when it comes to the interpretation of the
intention of the noble Nāgārjuna.

An implication of this important point is this: The presentation that
one could attain nirvana through only the path of the sixteen characteristics [of the four noble truths] such as impermanence becomes provisional,
and the identification of the afflictions based on such a presentation of the
path remains incomplete as well. One can, from this discussion, also understand other afflictions such as conceit. With respect to ignorance, identity
view, and the view grasping at extremes as defined in this unique way too,
one should understand that each consists of two levels: the acquired and
the innate. Fearing excessive length here, I will not spell out these issues in
greater detail.

Similarly, there is the presentation where the conceptualization of grasping at things as true existence is characterized as what is to be relinquished on

the path of meditation, differentiating it into nine levels of small, medium, and great, and correlating these to their corresponding antidotes—namely, the nine stages of the path of meditation. This too should be understood as being provisional, a teaching presented for the benefit of those who, for the time being, are not capable of fully realizing both the coarse and subtle levels of selflessness of phenomena. This is analogous to the [Yogācāra] teaching where the conceptualization grasping at *subject-object duality* is differentiated into nine levels in terms of lesser, medium, and greater degrees, each correlated with its relevant antidotes vis-à-vis the nine stages of the path of meditation, which too remains provisional.

How the merely conventional appears or does not appear to the three individuals

Entities, though not possessing intrinsic existence, appear to childish ordinary beings to do so, and through this they deceive such beings. [162] In contrast, for the three classes of persons referred to above, who are different from these ordinary childish beings, things remain contrived entities that are dependently originated; for them they exist as *mere conventionalities*, not truly existent. And these [merely conventional] entities appear to the āryas abiding in the stages subsequent to meditative equipoise—stages where one remains within the sphere of perceptual experience tainted by ignorance and its habitual propensities. This is because they possess a form of ignorance that is not afflicted but is characterized as an obscuration to knowledge. In contrast, the entities do not appear at all to āryas who are abiding in meditative equipoise, for they are devoid of [dualistic] perceptions.[449]

"How does one define the obscuration to knowledge according to this Candrakīrti tradition then?" In this regard, the *Commentary* says:

> Now, the habitual propensity toward ignorance constitutes the obstacle to thorough comprehension of the object of knowledge. And that habitual propensities toward attachment, aversion, and so on exist is indicated by their corresponding physical and verbal actions, which are also their causes. These habitual propensities toward ignorance, attachment, and so on cease for the omniscient and the buddhas alone, not for others.[450]

"The physical and verbal actions" here refer to such behaviors as those present even in an arhat, such as jumping about like a monkey or calling someone a "lowly commoner," physical and verbal deportment proscribed by the Buddha that they still have not curtailed. "Also" indicates that the habitual propensities toward attachment and so on are obstacles to fully comprehending objects of knowledge as well. Thus the habitual propensities of afflictions are obscurations to knowledge, and included within this class of obscurations are all the facets of deluded dualistic perceptions as well, which are the effects of those habitual propensities. Of the two types of habitual propensities toward afflictions—one in the form of a seed of the afflictions and the other not in the form of such a seed—it is the latter that is understood to constitute the obscuration to knowledge. As such [with respect to the three classes of persons cited above], because all the seeds of the afflictions have ceased for them, grasping at true existence no longer arises in them. Nonetheless, since they remain tainted by the habitual propensity toward ignorance, cognitions deluded with respect to their appearing objects still arise in them.

Since āryas who have yet to attain buddhahood have still not eliminated ignorance belonging to the class of obscurations to knowledge, the two states—post-equipoise states characterized by dualistic conceptual thoughts and meditative equipoise devoid of [dualistic] perceptions—will occur intermittently. In contrast, given that the buddhas have thoroughly comprehended or directly realized the aspects of both the ultimate and conventional truths of all phenomena, for them all turnings of conceptualizing mind and mental factors have come to cease permanently.[451] Buddhas, therefore, have no intermittent meditative equipoise and post-equipoise states involving conceptual thoughts characterized by [dualistic] perceptions. The term "permanently" indicates that the ceasing [of dualistic perceptions] for the other āryas during their meditative equipoise is only intermittent. [163] Because of this, meditative equipoise and post-equipoise states occur sequentially for them. The rationale "because they experience ignorance that belongs to the class of obscurations to knowledge"[452] is not a reason to demonstrate that [the āryas] possess [dualistic] perceptions; it is an explanation to substantiate the point that for them the absence and presence of dualistic perceptions alternate in line with periods of equipoise and post-equipoise. The "turnings of mind and mental factors" is to be understood in terms of conceptualizing thoughts. For example, *Clear Words* says:

Conceptualizing processes constitute the turnings of the mind. Because suchness is devoid of this, it is absent of conceptualization. It says in a sutra, for example, "What is the ultimate truth? That for which if there are no turnings of the mind; what need is there at all then to speak of the words?"[453]

How the ultimate and conventional become as such from the perspectives of ordinary beings and āryas

The *Commentary* says:

> That which is the ultimate for ordinary beings is merely conventional for those āryas who [still] possess the sphere of experience within which dualistic perceptions remain. Emptiness, the nature of these [merely conventional entities], is the ultimate truth for them.[454]

The meaning of the first part is this: Phenomena such as vases, which ordinary beings grasp as possessing ultimate existence, remain merely conventional for the three classes of āryas referred to above, who experience dualistic perceptions in post-equipoise states after arising from meditative equipoise. Thus Candrakīrti's statement negates such phenomena to be true for these beings. It does not negate these to be conventional truths for them, and it also does not suggest that the conceived objects of ordinary beings who grasp vases and so on as having ultimate existence becomes conventional for the āryas. Such conceived objects have no existence at all.

As for the latter part of the citation, it states that the ultimate nature of things, which is the nature of the dependently originated conventional truths, is the ultimate for the āryas. So to assert that one and the same thing—a vase, for example—is *itself* a conventional truth for ordinary beings and an ultimate truth for the āryas contravenes the meaning of the text. Such an utterance reveals an ignorance of the fact that to establish something as a conventional truth entails that it is negated [first] as true within the perspective of that cognition.

Next, the *Commentary* reads,

> What is ultimate for the buddhas is true nature alone. Because

it never deceives, it is the ultimate truth, and it is known by buddhas alone.[455]

The word "alone" in "it is true nature alone" is a term of exclusion; it excludes in that it demonstrates how [the ultimate of the buddhas] is unlike the shifting characteristics of the other āryas for whom the ultimate truth is posited as absent of dualistic perceptions during meditative equipoise but characterized by dualistic perceptions in post-equipoise. Thus it suggests that what is ultimate for buddhas constitutes [164] the ultimate nature of things, which is the true nature upon which buddhas remain equipoised at all times. The purpose of the statement "Because it never deceives . . ." is to define the meaning of the truth as "that which abides as undeceiving from the perspective of seeing suchness," so as to demonstrate how such ultimate truth does not constitute true existence.

Ultimate truth

This has two parts: explaining the meaning of the lines of the root text and rejecting objections against this explanation.

Explaining the meaning of the lines of the root text

The first is as follows:

> Through the force of an eye disease, one perceives
> false things such as floating hairs and so on;
> those with clear vision see what is actually so.
> Understand suchness to be like this as well. 6.29

[Here the *Commentary* says:]

> Now I wish to present ultimate truth. Because ultimate truth cannot be expressed by words, because it is not an object of cognition that follows from the words, it cannot be presented directly. To help elucidate its nature, I will give those who wish to listen an analogy drawn from the ordinary person's experience.[456]

The meaning of the statement that ultimate truth is not an object of cognition is as indicated by the phrase "it cannot be presented directly." In Naktso's translation, this phrase appears as "cannot be shown in a direct demonstration." As to the meaning of this point, there is the following from *Clear Words*, when Candrakīrti comments on Nāgārjuna's statement that suchness cannot be known from others:

> When someone with myodesopsia sees false realities such as floating hairs, even though the person who free of the eye malady may show him [that there are no such floating hairs], the other person remains incapable of perceiving the fact as it is—he is incapable of perceiving the absence of floating hairs in the way in which the person without myodesopsia does.[457]

The person who has no myodesopsia, Candrakīrti says, might point to the one who has it and say, "There are no floating hairs here," but that does not mean the other person will then perceive the absence of floating hair in the same way as the person without myodesopsia. The point is that the listener does not perceive the absence of floating hairs the way [the one without the eye malady does]. This does not mean, however, that the other person does not understand the absence of floating hair whatsoever. Taking this as an analogy, when suchness is presented, Candrakīrti maintains, although the listener does not realize it in the way those who are free of ignorance's taint perceive it, this does not mean that, in general, they do not realize suchness at all. Therefore it is not the case at all that ultimate truth [165] cannot be taught in the definitive scriptures about the profound truth, that it cannot be expressed by the speech that reveals it, or that it cannot be realized by cognitions that arise from such statements. This understanding should be applied in all contexts where suchness is characterized as not being the object of cognition and words.

Through the force of the eyes being affected by **an eye disease**, someone afflicted with such a malady **perceives false things as such as floating hairs** in a dinner bowl—one made from rhinoceros horn perhaps—held in the hands. The phrase **"and so on"** indicates things like flies. To remove them, the person may try and shake the bowl again and again. Someone **with clear vision**, on seeing this, might approach that person who sees hair and so on, who might direct his attention there. But not only will he not perceive hair and such, he will also have no conceptions of any properties predicated on such hair. And when the person with myodesopsia shares his thoughts with the one who is free of disease, saying, "I see floating hairs," the one free of myodesopsia, wanting to dispel the false thoughts of the one affected by the disease, may for the benefit of the other utter words to negate this, saying, "There are no floating hairs." Nevertheless, in so saying, such a speaker is by no means denigrating the phenomenon of floating hair. In fact, it is only the one who is free of myodesopsia, not the one with the disease, who sees **what is actually so** pertaining to the supposed floating hairs seen by the one with myodesopsia. And as with these two examples [of one afflicted by myodesopsia and other not], **understand suchness to be like this as well**, which is the referent of the analogy.

Understand this as follows.[458] The reality of the aggregates, elements, sense bases and so on perceived by those who do not see suchness and those whose mind is tainted or adversely affected by the eye malady of ignorance is the conventional nature of the aggregates and so on, analogous to the perception of floating hairs by someone with myodesopsia. That very reality of the aggregates and so on that are perceived by those who do not see their suchness is in fact perceived by the buddhas—who are free of the obscuration to knowledge in the form of habitual propensities toward ignorance—in a manner similar to those whose vision is unaffected by eye malady and thus do not perceive floating hairs and so on, and *this* nature of the aggregates and so on is the ultimate truth for the buddhas.

Rejecting objections against this explanation

[*Question*:] Just as eyes unaffected by myodesopsia do not see even the appearance of floating hairs, if the buddhas do not perceive conventional realities like aggregates and so on—which appear to a mind adversely affected by ignorance [166]—wouldn't these things then become nonexistent? For if they do exist, the buddhas would necessarily see them. Furthermore, if conventional realities like aggregates and so on do not exist, there will then be no attainment of buddhahood as well, because the being who first generated the awakening mind had to be someone who was affected by ignorance.

[*Reply*:] Let me explain how this fault does not follow. To begin with, there are two modes by which a buddha's gnosis perceives objects of knowledge: (1) the way in which all that is knowable within the sphere of ultimate truth is known and (2) the way in which all that is knowable within the sphere of conventional truth is known. Of these, the first is the knowing of suchness *in a manner of not seeing* the diverse appearances of the conventional truth. As for the second, since an indirect knowing—knowing but not directly perceiving it—cannot be posited in relation to a buddha, conventional realities must be known by a buddha on the basis of directly perceiving them. So within the perspective of a buddha's gnosis perceiving things in their diversity, the buddha perceives conventional realities in a manner where the subject and its object do appear as distinct.

Now it is not that a buddha's knowledge of things in their diversity perceives aggregates and so on because it is affected by habitual propensities of ignorance. Nevertheless, a buddha must perceive the appearances experienced by other beings whose cognitions are tainted by ignorance. There is no denying that such appearances do exist, and if such conventional truths exist, it must be perceived by buddha's gnosis pertaining to things in their diversity. In the case of the analogy, however, though there is no appearance of floating hairs and such for the visual perception of someone free of myodesopsia, this does not entail that such an appearance does not exist at all. In this respect it is different from the case of the buddha.

Until the habitual propensities toward erroneous dualistic appearances cease, one is not capable of generating direct realization of things in their diversity and the way things really are within a singular instance of knowing. Until then one cognizes the two in alternation, one during meditative equipoise and the other during post-equipoise states. Thus the knowing of the two [things in their diversity and the way things really are] within a single instance of wisdom does not occur. Once all habitual propensities toward error are eliminated, the two aspects of the buddha's gnosis arise uninterruptedly as a singular instance of knowing within each and every individual moment. As such there is no need for a temporal sequence for the direct realization of the two objects of knowledge. Therefore the following statement contains no contradiction:

> Even with a single instance of knowing,
> he pervades the entire field of knowledge.[459]

This feature—that the two dimensions of gnosis, which are identical in nature, have not the slightest contradiction in knowing the two objects simultaneously—appears to be a characteristic unique to the buddhas. There are some who appear to take the mode of knowing ultimate truth alone to be the buddha's mode of knowing and denigrate the buddha's knowing of things in their diversity, asserting that such knowing is absent in the buddha's own mind and exists only within the mental continuum of trainees. [167] Some appear to claim that even the gnosis knowing the way things really are is absent in the buddha's mind, thus denigrating both aspects of the buddha's gnosis. I will address some of the remaining related points below in the section on the resultant ground.[460]

[*Question*:] Isn't it the case that such nature, which is constituted by the dissolution of all dualistic appearances, is not seeable? So how it is that the buddhas see such ultimate truth?

[*Reply*:] Since all dualistic appearances have ceased within the perspective of seeing suchness, it is true that suchness is not seen in a dualistic manner. Nonetheless, we do speak of seeing suchness *in a manner of nonseeing*.[461]

Here is how the statement above suitably responds to the objection raised: it states that the buddha's gnosis that directly knows the way things really are does see the *suchness* of aggregates and so on; the fact that the aggregates and so on are not established from the perspective of that seeing is itself the suchness of these phenomena; and that such gnosis therefore sees the suchness of the aggregates and so on in a manner of not seeing. Thus the *Commentary* states:

> He directly perceives the true nature alone without touching the produced entities themselves. Having fully realized this nature, he is called an awakened one.[462]

Here Candrakīrti is saying that a buddha's gnosis that knows ultimate truth actualizes the ultimate nature of things alone without touching their bases. This has the same meaning as the statement that the buddha's gnosis sees the suchness of the aggregates and so on in a manner of not seeing the aggregates and so on themselves. As for the meaning of the citation "No seeing is the sublime seeing,"[463] it is not suggesting that one accepts not seeing anything at all as a form of seeing. Rather, as explained above, not seeing conceptual elaborations is defined as seeing the absence of elaborations. Therefore, *seeing* and *not seeing* are not being defined in relation to one single thing.[464] This said, the *Condensed Perfection of Wisdom* states:

> He sees no form, nor does he see feelings as well;
> he sees no discriminations, nor does he see volitions;

he sees no consciousness, nor mind and mentality,
this is seeing reality, so taught the Tathāgata.

People utter words like "I see space."
"How do they see space?" This we will examine here.
Seeing reality is shown to be likewise by the Tathāgata;
such seeing cannot be conveyed by any other analogy.[465]

Here, what is not seen is stated to be the five aggregates while what is seen is referred to as "reality," which means suchness. This is similar to the statement "He who sees dependent origination sees reality."[466]

Space, given here as an analogy, is defined in terms of the mere absence of obstructive property, and so seeing or perceiving it entails not seeing what is to be negated—namely, a space-obstructing property that if it existed would have to be perceivable. [168] Here, what is seen is space while what is not seen is the property of obstructing space. Just as in this analogy, *not seeing* should be understood in terms of not seeing suchness in a manner similar to seeing a blue color, a manner of seeing negated in the final line of the citation.

To substantiate the assertion that the buddha's gnosis sees suchness in a manner of not seeing, Candrakīrti cites the *Entering the Two Truths Sutra*:

> O celestial child, if the ultimate truth, on the ultimate level, takes on the nature of being an object of body, speech, and mind, it would then not belong to what is called *ultimate truth*. It would become a conventional truth only. Instead, O celestial child, on the ultimate level, ultimate truth transcends all conventions. It has no differentiation; it's unborn, unceasing, free of what is uttered as well as of utterances, and free of what is known and knowing.[467]

The meaning of the first part of the sutra citation is this: If ultimate truth, from the perspective of seeing the ultimate truth, is not seen in a manner of not seeing conventional truths such as the aggregates but instead becomes an object within the field of experience of body, speech, and mind, like the aggregates and so on, then such a seen truth would not be ultimate truth. It would become a conventional truth, a conceptual elaboration. Understood thus, this first part of the sutra citation becomes a reason explaining how a buddha's gnosis sees the ultimate truth in a manner of not seeing.

The second part of the sutra citation has the meaning that, from the perspective that directly sees ultimate truth, there can be no differentiation—varied instantiations—within ultimate truth. The next three attributes [being unborn, unceasing, and beyond conventions] are easy to comprehend. The phrase about the ultimate truth being, from such a perspective, free of the activity of speech is easily understood as well. Although one can posit the gnosis directly perceiving the ultimate truth as the *knower* and ultimate truth as the *known object*, there is no contradiction in maintaining that, from the perspective of such gnosis, there is no such act and its agent. This is because the distinction between the two—an act and its agent—is posited from the standpoint of cognitions related to conventional truth alone. It is like the case where, although one can posit an inferential rational cognition of emptiness as the *subject* and ultimate truth as its *object*, the distinction of the two as subject and object is not posited from within the perspective of that rational cognition.

Next, the *Commentary* goes on to cite:

> O celestial child, this ultimate truth, which is endowed with all supreme qualities, transcends being an object [of cognitions] up through a buddha's omniscient gnosis . . . It does not exist in the manner expressed in the statement "*This* is ultimate truth." All phenomena are false in that they are deceptive realities.[468]

The meaning of this citation is as follows. Up to the phrase "up through a buddha's omniscient gnosis" indicates how ultimate truth transcends being the object of the omniscient gnosis. [169] As to the sense in which ultimate truth transcends [such gnosis], this is indicated by the next part that reads, "It does not exist in the manner expressed . . ." up to the end, where it reads "deceptive realities." As an example, when someone says, "*This* is ultimate truth," the subject and object appear as two distinct entities to the thought that follows after that utterance. For the buddha's omniscient gnosis perceiving the way things really are, however, ultimate truth lies beyond the sphere of knowing it in such a dualistic manner. All phenomena within dualistic perception are false and deceptive, and as such, they do not exist from the perspective that perceives only the undeceiving truth of suchness.

All of these authoritative sources substantiate the point that, within the perspective of direct seeing of suchness, conventional realities like aggregates and so on are not perceived. For within the perspective of direct seeing of suchness, all dualistic elaborations like "things and nonthings" remain impossible because these conceptual elaborations cannot be found within such a perspective. Thus when contemplating suchness, only āryas are valid with respect to suchness in a manner that is direct; non-āryas are not valid in such direct manner. In view of this, the rejection of arising from other is done from the perspective of āryas; it cannot be invalidated by perspectives stemming from the everyday world.

Objections to the assertion that worldly perception invalidates the refutation [of arising from other]

> If ordinary perception constitutes valid knowledge,
> suchness will be seen by common folk.
> What need for the āryas then? And what need for ārya paths?
> Yet it's wrong to take the foolish mind as valid as well. 6.30

> Since ordinary perception has no validity in every respect,
> no worldly perspective can invalidate in the context of suchness. 6.31ab

Now the opponent might wish to raise objections from [the perspective of] the everyday world to the refutation of arising from other on the ultimate level. Had we here admitted that perceptions of the everyday world were authoritative in the sphere of inquiring into the nature of suchness, such objections might be appropriate. For **if ordinary perception constitutes valid knowledge** with respect to suchness, **suchness will** then **be seen** or directly realized **by common** worldly **folk.** And given that this situation would have to have been true since beginningless time, one would then have to admit that common people have eliminated ignorance. In that case, **what need** is there **for the āryas then,** who are others, for direct realization of suchness? [170] And **what need** is there then **for** seeking **the ārya paths?** There will be no point in doing so. **Yet it is wrong to take the foolish mind** of ordinary people **as valid** with respect to suchness **as well. Since ordinary perception has no validity in every respect** in the context of inquiring into suchness, **no worldly perspective can invalidate in the context of suchness.**

Some, taking the phrase "Since ordinary perception has no validity in every respect" as a rejection of any notion of valid cognition, criticize this system [of Candrakīrti] as an inferior tradition. Others, citing the same reason, extol it as an excellent system. Both interpretations make assertions without properly understanding the standpoint of this master, thus revealing their own true selves. This is because both parties apparently take the statement that worldly perspectives are never authoritative in every respect when it comes to suchness to mean that valid cognition cannot be accepted in any context. Insofar as valid cognition and its object are concerned, these must be understood [in Candrakīrti's system] as they are explained in *Clear Words*, where valid cognitions and their objects are negated as existing by virtue of an essence and are presented instead as mutually defined. I will expound more on this below.[469]

The contexts and manner in which worldly perspectives can invalidate

> If everyday facts are rejected from a perspective of worldly consensus,
> then this will be invalidated on the authority of everyday experience.
> 6.31cd

"In that case," one might ask, "what is the manner in which the worldly perspective might invalidate?" Now, **if everyday facts** acknowledged and established by the world **are rejected from the perspective of worldly consensus, then** [the standpoint of] **this** person **will be invalidated on the authority of everyday experience.**

Say a person states that "Someone stole a substance of mine!" Another person asks him, "What kind of substance?" to which he replies, "A vase." Now if, in response, the other person retorts, "A vase is not substance because it is a cognizable object, like the vase in a dream," it is the content of this kind of refutation that is undermined by the perspectives of the world. In contrast, when it comes to the presentation of suchness, which is done on the basis of taking one who is learned in ultimate truth as authoritative, taking into account the āryas' perspective on the ultimate truth, in such a context, there can be no invalidation stemming from the perspectives of the everyday world.[470]

The *Commentary* states that "The learned ones should analyze other [similar] questions on that basis as well."[471] [171] This demonstrates how refutations like the following, which some today consider exemplars of great Madhyamaka reasoning, are open to invalidation from the perspectives of the world. These include such refutations as "I am not the owner of the vase, and Devadatta is not the one who stole it, because [Devadatta and I lack intrinsic existence].” Similarly, when someone says, “It grew at my farm,” and another asks, “What is grown?” to which he replies, “A sprout.” Say then that the other person counters, “A sprout is devoid of arising because it is a cognizable object” and “just like a dream person or a dream sprout.”[472]

Repelling objections from the worldly perspective on the basis that arising from other does not exist even in worldly convention

So far we have rejected there being any problem refuting arising from other from the perspective of the world, even if one were to allow [for the sake of argument] arising from other from the standpoint of worldly convention. We will now explain how, given that arising from other does not exist even within the perceptions of the world, there can be no invalidation coming from the world, even for someone who wishes to negate arising from other while remaining within the worldly view. This is stated by the following:

> In everyday experience, a man who simply left the seed
> claims “I fathered this son!” or thinks “I planted this tree.”
> So arising from other doesn’t exist
> even from the perspective of the everyday world. 6.32

Why is it that, **in everyday experience, a man** points to another person with male characteristics and **claims “I fathered this son?”** Though he may claim this, the father has not extracted from his body a person with full male features and somehow implanted him into the womb of the mother. What is it then? He has **simply left** or placed **the** mere **seed** of the son, an impure substance, inside the mother’s womb. So the father, having placed the cause of the son, points to someone to be his son. This clearly proves that within the everyday experience of the world, people do not conceive the seed and the son to be intrinsically different. **So, even from the perspective of the everyday world**, grasping at the impure seed and the son as well as the barley seed and its sprout as **arising from other doesn’t exist**. For were these conceived as different by virtue of their own essences, the father would not point to his son and claim “I produced him” any more than a different person would in relation to that son. Similarly, when someone plants the mere seed of a tree and a tree grows from this, [172] he **thinks “I planted this tree.”** [In relation to this example too], one should reflect, as above, “there is no arising from other within the perspectives of everyday world” and so on.

Although the two seeds planted are not the tree and the son, when a tree or a son is born as a result of having planted either of these two seeds, one can point to one or the other and claim legitimately, "I planted this." Analogously, although a hand that is injured and healed is not actually the person, one can legitimately say the person has been injured and healed when his hand was injured and healed.

Thus arising from other does not exist within the conventions of the everyday world. But that does not mean that the existence of arising from other can be negated through everyday-world perceptions. This is because one must probe the nature of suchness to negate cause and effect being different entities by virtue of their intrinsic natures. Therefore the sense of arising from other asserted by proponents of other philosophical schools is this: *arising from something that is other by virtue of its intrinsic characteristic*; it is not something established simply as other. It is also not the case that this sort of mere otherness is not established from the everyday-world perspective.

Now the statement "So other-arising doesn't exist / even from the perspective of the everyday world" should not be confined to mean solely that ordinary people of the world do not grasp a substantial cause and its effect—a seed and the sprout, for example—to be different by virtue of their intrinsic characteristics. These lines also demonstrate how arising from other does not exist even on the conventional level. For example, the *Commentary* says in the section on the refutation of arising from both:

> So, just as it has been shown how arising from self and arising from other are untenable on the level of worldly convention as well as on the level of ultimate truth, likewise, to those who speak of arising from both too, the arguments stated above demonstrate it to be impossible.[473]

Thus the nonexistence of arising from other even on the conventional level has been stated explicitly.

In *Clear Words* too, in response to the question "If there is no arising of things from themselves, from other, from both, and from no cause, how is it that the Buddha taught 'Conditioned by ignorance, there is volition'?" Candrakīrti writes, "Let me explain this. This is on the conventional level; not on the level of suchness."[474] Thus he explains how the engendering of volition by ignorance and so on is on the conventional level and not on the ultimate level. Then, in response to the question "What kind of presentation of conventional truth you are speaking of?" Candrakīrti replies, "We accept the establishment of conventional truth in terms of mere conditionedness; not on the basis of adhering to any of the four positions."[475] Thus he clearly explains how, in accepting the arising of *this* from *that* condition on the conventional level, he does not adhere to arising from one of the four possibilities. [173] So the assertion some make that "This tradition [of Candrakīrti] does not reject arising from other on the conventional level" is a statement that does not understand this system properly.

12. The Merits of Negation

The merits of refuting arising from other

A system that, as explained above, propounds the absence of real entity in the form of intrinsic existence has the merit of not falling into the extremes of eternalism and nihilism because it affirms dependent origination that is free of eternalism and annihilationism. To demonstrate this:

> Because the sprout is no other than the seed,
> there is no extinction of the seed at the time of the sprout;
> and because the sprout and seed are not identical,
> it cannot be said that seed exists when the sprout is there. 6.33

If the sprout were intrinsically other than the seed, the seed and the sprout could not be a cause and its effect. In that event, the seed's continuum would certainly cease once the sprout exists. The seed and the sprout would be totally unrelated, and so even if the sprout were present, this would not in any way preserve the lineage of the seed. To illustrate, the presence of a cow-like beast in no way ensures the non-cessation of a cow's lineage after death. Likewise, the presence of ordinary beings in no way ensures āryas do not sever the continuum of their own cyclic existence.[476]

Because there is no contradiction for the seed and the sprout to be cause and effect even when **the sprout is not** intrinsically **other than the seed, there is no extinction** of the lineage **of the seed at the time of the sprout.** In this way, one avoids the extreme of annihilationism. It has on numerous occasions been explained that the seed comes to cease at the time of the sprout, and the meaning of seed's *extinction* has been explained in the *Commentary* as the termination of its continuity.[477] Furthermore, the nondisintegration of the seed is rejected as well. Therefore the phrase "cessation of the seed's continuum"[478] here has to be understood in terms of the cessation of its lineage.

And because the two, **the sprout and the seed, do not exist as identical,** and also because the seed did not transpose itself onto the sprout, the non-disintegration of seed at the time of the sprout has been rejected. So **it cannot be said that seed exists when the sprout is there;** hence the extreme of eternalism is prevented as well. These statements convey the intent of the following lines from the *Play in Full Sutra*:

> If the seed exists, the sprout would be the same.
> What is the seed? It is not the sprout;
> it is not something other nor is it identical with it;
> thus it's neither eternal nor annihilated. Such is their truth.[479]
> [174]

The meaning of these lines is as follows. Were the seed to exist, the sprout, which is caused by the seed, would come into being in the same manner as the seed. Now when the sprout comes into being, it cannot do so from something other than the seed, and so one might think that the seed and the sprout are identical in nature. [The sutra states] that although the sprout does not come into being from something different from the seed, it is not that the seed comes to transpose itself onto the sprout. Why? Because the sprout is neither intrinsically other from the seed nor is it intrinsically identical with it in nature. When both of these possibilities are rejected, the true nature of the sprout is revealed to be a reality that is free of the extremes of eternalism and nihilism. The same sutra states this point in the following:

> The volitions are conditioned by ignorance;
> such volitions do not exist in ultimate reality.
> Both volition and ignorance are empty,
> for they lack intrinsically real movement.[480]

The first line presents the logical reason—that volitions originate in dependence upon ignorance. The second line presents the thesis, which is that the volitions do not exist in ultimate reality. The third line presents how both the cause and effect are empty. And the fourth line presents the manner in which they are empty. "Movement" here refers to [volition's] activity of conditioning, and the lack of this indicates how volition is empty of volition. This too is stated with the proviso "they lack intrinsically real movement," indicating how what is being negated is qualified. This qualification has the same meaning as the phrase "do not exist in ultimate reality." In *Fundamental Verses on the Middle Way* too, the meaning of this sutra citation is presented as the following:

> That which originates in dependence on something
> is not, on the one hand, identical with that other,
> but neither is it different from it.
> It is therefore neither eternal nor annihilated.[481]

How intrinsic arising does not exist in any manner

This has two parts: (1) refuting the view that asserts existence by virtue of intrinsic characteristics and (2) rejecting objections raised against such a refutation.

Refuting the view that asserts existence by virtue of intrinsic characteristics

This has three parts: (1) the consequence that an ārya's meditative equipoise would become the cause for the destruction of things, (2) the consequence that conventional truths would withstand reasoned analysis, and (3) the consequence that ultimate arising would not be negated.[482]

The consequence that an ārya's meditative equipoise would become the cause for the destruction of things

> If the intrinsic characteristics of things were to arise dependently,
> things would come to be destroyed by denying it; [175]
> emptiness would then be a cause for the destruction of things.
> But this is illogical, so no real entities exist. 6.34

Candrakīrti states, "One must accept without doubt the statement 'There is no intrinsic arising with respect to any phenomenon.'"[483] So, logically, this is a point we must definitely accept. We should not assert the contrary, saying, "It is not appropriate in this tradition [of Candrakīrti] to posit a standpoint."

Now, in contrast, **if the intrinsic characteristic of a thing** such as form or feelings **were to arise in dependence** upon causes and conditions, through its own essence, this would imply that a yogi directly perceiving the emptiness of intrinsic existence of all phenomena would realize emptiness **by denying** such a nature of things. Meditative equipoise does not actually perceive form and so on, but if they were to exist through their intrinsic characteristics, then meditative equipoise would necessarily perceive them. It does not. And if this were so, these **things would** then become nonexistent. If they do become nonexistent, it would then be the case that what was existent prior to the meditative equipoise would subsequently **come to be destroyed** or ceased. The meditative equipoise would become the cause for their destruction. So just as hammers and the like are causes for the destruction of vases and the like, seeing **emptiness** too **would then be a cause for the destruction of** the nature of **things**, thus denigrating them. **But this is illogical, so no real entities** exist—that is, say, by virtue of their intrinsic characteristics—and we must never uphold such a notion of intrinsic arising.

Now, those Mādhyamikas who accept arising by virtue of intrinsic characteristics do maintain that even though things exist through their intrinsic characteristics, this does not constitute [an admission of] true existence. They assert that if phenomena such as forms exist through their intrinsic characteristics, this does not necessarily entail that they are perceived within the direct vision of suchness.[484] They may claim such things, but that this degree [of objectivity] does in fact constitute true existence has already been explained above.[485] I will elaborate on this point further below as well. So the opponent cannot avoid the flaws revealed in this argument above.

Here as well in the *Commentary*, Candrakīrti cites the following passage from the *Heap of Jewels Sutra*:

> Kāśyapa, furthermore, the middle path perfectly discerning reality does not make phenomena to be empty. Phenomena are themselves empty...[486]

Candrakīrti cites similar statements in that sutra in relation to signlessness, wishlessness, and the absence of conditioning, as well as to being unborn and unoriginated.[487] [176]

Now, if phenomena were to possess natures that exist through their intrinsic characteristics, then these phenomena would not be empty. And then the sutra's statement that "phenomena are themselves empty" would become incorrect.[488] Since existence in its own right by virtue of an essence is not then negated, things will have to be shown to be empty of something else. This of course will contradict the sutra's statement that "emptiness does not cause phenomena to become empty." All of this shows how the middle path, by examining the individual characteristics of phenomena, reveals how all phenomena are empty of existing in their own right—that is, existing by virtue of their own essence.

This sutra also rejects the assertion of the Cittamātra school that the dependent nature is not empty of existence by virtue of intrinsic characteristic but is empty in the sense of being devoid of a substantial duality of subject and object. It says in *Four Hundred Stanzas*:

> It's not what is not empty is seen as empty;
> if one harbors the thought "May nirvana be mine,"
> one cannot attain nirvana
> through such a false view. So taught the Tathāgata.[489]

Fundamental Wisdom as well presents the meaning of the sutra cited above:

> The Conqueror has stated
> that emptiness eliminates all [metaphysical] views.
> So he who views emptiness [as real],
> this the Buddha called incurable.[490]

This then is also the intended meaning of the statement that all phenomena are empty of their own essence. Therefore it is totally incorrect to assert that a vase being empty of true existence but not being empty of itself constitutes *extrinsic emptiness* and that the vase being empty of the vase itself constitutes *intrinsic emptiness*.[491] For if the vase were empty of itself, the vase would not exist in a vase. And if something, say a vase, does not exist in itself, since it cannot exist in any other thing either, this implies that the vase does not exist at all. This will be equally true of all other things as well, and so the person uttering such statements would also not exist. This renders the entire discourse about emptiness—something being empty of *this* but not of *that*—totally impossible.

Now some people assert this form of emptiness [a thing being empty of itself] to be a perfect view while others hold it to be a nihilistic emptiness. Both of these remain, however, outside the true understanding of dependent origination free from the extremes of eternalism and nihilism, which has been established by the conqueror [Nāgārjuna] and his spiritual heir [Āryadeva], not just once but repeatedly. In particular, those who assert that the entire reality of conventional truths must be established as empty of themselves and assert this form of emptiness to constitute a nihilistic emptiness are utterly incorrect. There is none among the four Buddhist philosophical schools that recognizes a particular view to be nihilistic yet cultivates it within their own mind.[492]

The notion of emptiness generally entails that a given entity, the basis of negation, is demonstrated to not exist in a manner that is being negated or is shown to be empty of what is to be negated. This much is the same for all forms of emptiness. It is, however, the emptiness of phenomena in the sense of being devoid of existing by virtue of intrinsic characteristic that constitutes the true meaning of things being empty of their own essence. [177] All other forms of emptiness do not constitute the emptiness of things' own essence. Here is the reason. As long as the impact of having established emptiness of the first type [intrinsic emptiness] by means of a valid cognition remains undiminished, there is no possibility at all during such a period for any reification of that basis to arise through grasping at true existence owing to any kind of philosophical reflection. With respect to those other types of emptiness, however, though one may have established them through valid cognition and their impact remains undiminished, there is nothing to preclude, during the same period, reifying things as truly existent or as real due to philosophical speculation.[493]

The consequence that conventional truths would withstand reasoned analysis

[The *Commentary* says:]

> Here, some assert the following: "It is logical that, since there is no arising on the ultimate level, arising from self and other are negated. Nonetheless, insofar as the natures of form, feeling, and so on perceived by the two kinds of valid cognition are concerned, these will arise without doubt from [something that is] other. For if one does not accept this, how can one speak of the two truths? There will be only one truth. Therefore," they say, "arising from other does exist."[494]

Those who argue in the above manner, given that they appear to accept the absence of arising on the ultimate level but assert arising from other on the conventional level, are certain Svātantrika-Mādhyamikas. Their assertion, "If arising from other in terms of intrinsic arising does not exist on the conventional level, there will then be only one truth," is intended to suggest that if there is no arising by virtue of intrinsic characteristic on the conventional level, conventional truth will have no reality. Since conventional truth would be untenable, there would be only the ultimate truth.

In response, the *Commentary* says:

> You are right. From the point of view of ultimate truth, there are not two truths. For we find statements such as the following: "O monks, this truth, the ultimate, is only one: it is nirvana, a reality that is nondeceptive. All conditioned things are false and deceptive."[495]

The meaning of these statements is this: Given that "nondeceptiveness" is what is meant by *truth*, a view Candrakīrti himself upholds, it is true that ultimate truth alone is true in the sense of being nondeceptive. So Candrakīrti responds, "You are right." The phrase "From the point of view of ultimate truth . . ." indicates that, within the perspective of seeing suchness, there is no duality of conventional and ultimate truth. [178] Within such a perspective, the Buddha has spoken of only the ultimate truth. The *truth* that is *ultimate* is to the ultimate truth. That within such a perspective there exists no conventional truth can be understood by the statement that "conditioned things are false and deceptive."

To summarize the meaning [of the above *Commentary* passage]: Were phenomena to exist by virtue of their intrinsic characteristics, conditioned things would not be established as false and deceptive. And without conventional truth, there would be no two truths. In contrast, when there is no existence by virtue of intrinsic characteristic, both conventional truth and ultimate truth become possible.

Based on the sutra citation above that states that nirvana alone is true while other conditioned phenomena are false, the thought might arise that although conditioned phenomena do not exist by virtue of their intrinsic characteristics, nirvana—the ultimate truth—must exist by virtue of its own intrinsic characteristic. But the sutra itself defines the truth being referred to here in terms of nondeceptiveness, not in terms of existing by virtue of intrinsic characteristic. Furthermore, from the statement that "All conditioned things are false and deceptive" too, we can infer that the meaning of *truth* in the sutra citation is that of nondeceptiveness. In his *Commentary on Sixty Stanzas* too, Candrakīrti explains how, unlike conditioned phenomena, which deceive childish beings through appearing in false manner, nirvana does not deceive beings by appearing thus. Hence, he explains, nirvana is said to be true while others remain untrue.[496] The distinction between truth and untruth here must therefore be drawn in the sense of being "nondeceptive" and "deceptive."

Candrakīrti's *Commentary on Sixty Stanzas* elsewhere makes a statement to the effect that nirvana is true on the conventional level.[497] There the meaning is that nirvana's status as an ultimate truth is to be posited from the perspective of conventional truth. It is not that Candrakīrti accepts nirvana to be a conventional truth. Since conventional truth is the means by which one enters ultimate truth, then just as one entertains conventions in the everyday world without probing into whether things arise from self or another, the Mādhyamika accepts [conventional truths] in the same [unanalyzed] manner.

[To proceed with the root text:]

> Thus, when such phenomena are analyzed,
> nothing is found as their nature apart from suchness.
> So the conventional truth of the everyday world
> should not be subjected to thorough analysis. 6.35

Thus, when such phenomena as form, feelings, and so on **are analyzed** thoroughly, in terms such as "Does it arise from itself or does it arise from other?" beyond the fact they do not arise or cease on the ultimate level—that is, **apart from suchness as their nature—nothing** else **is found**, no other or extra dimension such as arising and so on. **So the conventional truth of the everyday world should not be subjected to thorough analysis** in terms such as "from itself, from other," and so on. [179] We should just accept the facts of worldly perception, captured in statements such as "If this exists, that follows." We should do this on the basis of participating in the conventions that are dependent on others—those of the world. For example, Āryadeva says:

> Just as a barbarian cannot be sustained
> through a language other than his own,

likewise worldly people cannot be sustained
except through the conventions of the world.[498]

Fundamental Wisdom too says:

> Without relying on conventions,
> ultimate truth cannot be realized.
> Without realizing ultimate truth,
> nirvana cannot be attained.[499]

And, *Averting the Objections* says:

> Without accepting conventions,
> we will not engage in exposition.[500]

Here "analysis" and "nonanalysis" refer to analysis or nonanalysis pertaining to suchness. And in this regard, it is critical to understand what mode of analysis constitutes an analysis into suchness, so I will explain this point a little.

In the Prāsaṅgika system, if one is unsatisfied with conventional designations, and in relation to statements such as "the sprout arises," one analyzes what exactly is the referent of that phrase—does the sprout arise from itself, from another, and so on. From that point on, the analysis becomes an inquiry into suchness. This is entirely different from everyday inquiries based on worldly conventions, such as "Where have you come from?" "Where are you going?" "Where is it, outside or inside?"

Svātantrika Madhyamaka, on the other hand, does not consider the above degree of analysis to constitute probing into suchness. For them, an analysis becomes an inquiry into suchness when someone analyzes whether something exists by virtue of the power of being perceived by a cognition as defined above,[501] or whether it exists objectively as not posited by virtue of being perceived by a cognition. Thus, because of their two different ways of identifying the object of negation, two different boundaries of what constitutes an analysis into suchness emerge for them as well.

Failing to comprehend [what exactly constitutes an analysis into suchness], some define the distinction in the following manner. Say Devadatta has not arrived at a specific place. Initially, one mistakenly thinks that he had arrived but subsequently, when one examines whether he has arrived, comes to realize that he has not. In this way, they characterize all unanalyzed perspectives to be erroneous and all analyzed presentations to be veridical. But such an approach is neither that of the Madhyamaka system nor that of Buddhist epistemological (*pramāṇa*) schools. For one finds in both of these two traditions numerous facts established by valid cognition within the unanalyzed perspective. I have addressed this question extensively elsewhere, so I will not elaborate further here.[502] In brief, we should understand that if one analyzes the facts of conventional truth through critical reasoning inquiring into suchness, all conventions of the everyday world will come to be undermined. [180]

The consequence that ultimate arising would not be negated

> In the context of suchness, certain reasoning disallows arising
> from self or from something other, and that same reasoning
> disallows them on the conventional level too.
> So by what means then is your arising established? 6.36

[Here, the *Commentary* states the following:]

> Why is it that when all [the ropes of] clinging to things as true existence are cut, one clings terrified to conventional truth as real? If you say, "We must ensure that some things do arise with a reality established by intrinsic characteristics or by virtue of substance, for they constitute the causes of bondage and freedom by being part of the afflicted class or the enlightened class," to this I would say, "Now what remains for you are merely the words."[503]

Why? **In the context of** an analysis into **suchness** or the ultimate truth, **certain reasoning** presented above **disallows** the **arising** of phenomena such as form **from self or from something other.** Likewise, **on the conventional level too, that same reasoning disallows them**—the arising of form and so on through intrinsic characteristics. **So by what means** of valid cognition **then is your** intrinsic **arising established?** It is not.

"Therefore," Candrakīrti states, "arising by virtue of intrinsic characteristic does not exist on either level of truth. You may not like this, but you should undeniably admit it nonetheless."[504]

As for the *arising* negated through an analysis into suchness even on the conventional level, the *Commentary* characterizes this—in his commentary preceding the relevant root text—as an arising possessing a reality borne of substance. The [subsequent] summary statement explains it as well in the same manner. Therefore it refers only to [a form of arising] whereby what is to be negated is qualified in terms such as "arising by virtue of intrinsic characteristic." It in no way refers to arising *per se*. For Candrakīrti states on countless occasions that it is inappropriate to apply ultimate analysis to the facts of conventional truth.

Why does Candrakīrti maintain that if the reasoning probing into suchness does not negate arising by virtue of intrinsic characteristic on the conventional level, it would mean that ultimately established arising remains not negated as well? It is because the moment something is characterized as existing by virtue of its intrinsic characteristic, this in itself constitutes true existence. In that case, Candrakīrti maintains, it makes no difference whether one applies the qualifier "on the conventional level."

Now there are countless instances in the sutras, in the writings of Nāgārjuna father and son, and in those of this master [Candrakīrti] where the object of negation is qualified in terms such as "by virtue of intrinsic characteristic," "through intrinsic nature," "by virtue of an essence," and so on. Furthermore, as we saw above, Candrakīrti even takes some fellow Mādhyamikas to be the object of critique when he is engaged in such negation. [181] In his *Clear Words* too, Candrakīrti writes:

> Indisputably, it must be accepted exactly in this way. Otherwise conventional truth will come to possess objective evidence, would it not? In that case, it would then become suchness itself, not conventional.[505]

Thus, when refuting the approach whereby, being unsatisfied with mere designations on the conventional level, one posits the facts of conventional truth on the basis of analyzing the referents of their designations, Candrakīrti objects that the facts in that case will become ultimately existent and that form and so on would then not be facts of conventional truth. These consequences are being thrown against someone who rejects the ultimate existence of form and so on and takes them to be conventional. Since this cannot be said of the proponents of real entities, it is very clear that the opponent here is Svātantrika Madhyamaka.

Master Candrakīrti also states in the *Commentary* that "Some assert that the refutation of arising by the noble Nāgārjuna in the treatise, in lines such as 'Not from itself, not from other,' refers to the rejection of arising in relation to the imputed nature whereby subject and object are conceived as being substantially different; it does not refer to the negation of the true existence of dependent nature. Since they cannot establish this [claim] without evidence, those who interpret thus deserve only to be disputed and examined."[506] Some early Tibetan scholars claim that the opponent here is Sthiramati, but such statements are not readily found in his works. Dharmapāla, in his commentary on *Four Hundred Stanzas*, reputedly interprets the view of the *Four Hundred* to be Cittamātra; so it is more appropriate to relate this critique to Dharmapāla.[507]

The question now is: "How do those who interpret the meaning of the profound sutras in Cittamātra terms explain the intent of the treatises of the noble Nāgārjuna?" The works of great ones such as the master Vasubandhu contain no explicit statements about how they would interpret the meaning of Nāgārjuna's treatises. In works such as *Rules of Exposition*, basing himself on the *Unraveling the Intent Sutra*, Vasubandhu appears to characterize the Perfection of Wisdom sutras as provisional. Thus we could assume he would explain [Nāgārjuna's treatises] similarly. It seems inconceivable that [Vasubandhu] would refute the noble Nāgārjuna's treatises; but at the same time, if he were to explain them according to their literal meaning, then what reason would he have not to do the same for the Perfection of Wisdom sutras? Now if he were to interpret [Nāgārjuna's works] in nonliteral, interpretable terms,[508] he would clearly do so from the Cittamātra standpoint.

This said, since those statements that present all phenomena as lacking ultimate existence and as not existing by virtue of their intrinsic characteristics are established to be literally true by means of reasoning, there is no effective objection to their literal meaning. Hence these treatises cannot be explained as provisional, requiring further interpretation. It is with this point in mind that Candrakīrti says, "They deserve only to be disputed and examined."[509] [182] The point of giving effective objections against a nonliteral reading and presenting countless proofs to support a straightforward reading is to establish that the meaning of Nāgārjuna's treatises cannot be interpreted in some alternative manner. Candrakīrti addresses this point [about differentiation of definitive and provisional sutras] only briefly here.

Rejecting objections raised against such a refutation

[*Objection*:] If arising by virtue of intrinsic characteristic does not exist on the level of both truths, form and so on would become nonexistent. In that case, the perception of the reality of form and so on by cognitions—by that of the eyes and so on—would be impossible in the world. Otherwise, [nonexisting things like] rabbit's horns could be perceived by cognitions such as those of the eyes and so on. The reason is exactly the same in both cases.

To respond to this, it reads:

> Empty things dependent on convergences,
> such as reflections and so on, are not unknown.
> And just as from an empty thing like a reflection
> a perception can arise that bears its form, 6.37
> likewise although all things are empty,
> they do arise from emptiness in a robust way. 6.38ab

Empty things such as reflections and so on, including echoes and the like, arise **dependent on convergences** of causes and conditions—the meeting of mirror and face, of a cave and the issuing of sound, and so forth: such things **are not unknown** to the world; they are well known. **And just as from** something known to the world, **an empty** or false **thing like a reflection**, a **perception** such as that of the eyes **can arise that bears its form**, that of a reflection and the like. In other words, from a false thing like a mirror image arises a perception bearing that false aspect. **Likewise although all things are empty** of existence through their intrinsic characteristics, **from** causes that are **empty** of such an existence, effects that are empty of such an existence **do arise in a robust way**.

Here Candrakīrti speaks of the arising of a visual perception on the basis of a mirror image. Now a mirror image is a conditioned thing, and since it is different in nature from cognition, it is an external reality. [183] Furthermore, since it is the objective condition of visual perception, Candrakīrti takes it to be a visible form. We should also discern from this the status of phenomena such as a double moon, the appearance of floating hairs, a mirage, and so on, as well as echoes and similar examples.

The existence of things by virtue of intrinsic characteristics—which is being perceived by cognitions of any of the five unimpaired senses—is analogous to phenomena such as a face's reflection, a double moon, floaters, and so on, which appear to distorted sensory perceptions. That existence by virtue of intrinsic characteristic is perceived despite being impossible is analogous to the existence of reflection as a face and so on being impossible and yet still being perceived as such. Form, sound, and so on are analogous to phenomena like mirror images, echoes, and the like. So, just as we would not take the intrinsic existence of the five sensory objects such as form to be external realities yet would posit the form and so on that are perceived as such to be external realities, likewise, although one would not regard the reflection of a face to be an externally real face, one can still characterize phenomena themselves, mirror images and so on, as external realities. So when it comes to characterizing what is and is not an external reality, the situation is equal for both [form and so on, on the one hand, and mirror images and so on, on the other].

The false nature of a reflection—in the sense of it lacking the reality of a face—is something that can be established by all reasonable, literate people of the world whose minds are not informed by scripture or reasoning presenting emptiness. So it is entirely wrong to say that the realization of this level of falsehood represents some kind of a coarse rational cognition [of emptiness].

"In that case," one might ask, "when one comes to establish the false nature of a reflection along the lines familiar [to the world], does this not establish falsehood as defined by Madhyamaka? If not, how does the former [a mirror image] serves as an analogy for the latter [Madhyamaka emptiness]?"

Here, the use of phenomena such as a mirror image as an analogy involves citing [a level of falsehood] already established by the world from everyday experience. It is not the sense of falsehood as defined by Madhyamaka that the person has already established that is being cited as an analogy.

With a reflection perceived as a face, no differentiation whatsoever can be made on the level of appearance itself, saying, "This part of the reflection appears as the face and that part does not." It is the entirety of the reflection that appears as the face. So citing this analogy of how, though the entirety of the perception of a face [in a mirror image] does not exist as it appears, there is no contradiction in maintaining that such a reflection arises in dependence upon its causes. In the same way, when a blue [object] appears as existing by virtue of its intrinsic characteristic, no differentiation whatsoever can be made as to which part does and which part does not appear as existing through intrinsic characteristics. Furthermore, what is perceived does not exist as perceived in its entirety. Nonetheless, it can be established that there is no contradiction with the fact that the blue thing is produced from its own causes and that it can produce its own effects. Now if one can maintain the standpoint whereby, while there is nothing in the mirror image that exists as a face as perceived, [184] this does not lead to the mirror image becoming nonexistent, it would then become possible to uphold the standpoint whereby, although nothing within the entire field of perception of a blue object exists by virtue of intrinsic characteristic as it appears to, one can definitely still posit the existence of the blue object. This kind of clear differentiation employing refined intellect as to how, in relation to form and so on, one distinguishes between the two—"*This* is to be negated" and "*This* is not to be negated"—on the basis of the analogy of a mirror image, is an indispensable aid to finding the Middle Way view. So we should not be easily contented [with our understanding of the role of such an analogy].

In view of these, the *Commentary* says:

> While understanding the fact of causes and effects even in relation to a mirror image that has no intrinsic existence, what learned person would, simply on the basis of perceiving form, feelings, and so on that are not outside the realm of causes and effects, determine these to be endowed with intrinsic nature? Therefore, although learned ones perceive these as existing, they have no intrinsic arising.[510]

Candrakīrti thus draws a distinction here between mere existence and intrinsic existence. Furthermore, Candrakīrti demonstrated above that things do arise, and here he demonstrates that there is no intrinsic arising, so he makes a clear distinction between *arising* and *intrinsic arising*. Without such distinctions, then existing things would exist in their own right, and things that do not exist in their own right would then become nonexistent. In this way, one would fail to transcend the two extremes of reification and denigration. In his *Commentary on the Four Hundred Stanzas*, for example, Candrakīrti says:

> Those who propound the existence of real entities consider things to be existent only so long as they are thought to possess essence. The moment things are understood to lack an essence, they come to be [for them] utterly nonexistent. For them such things then become as nonexistent as the horn of a donkey. They

are thus compelled to speak in such dichotomous terms, so it is difficult for them to satisfy all their expectations.[511]

Therefore, being free from all extremes of existence—through understanding that nothing exists by virtue of its own essence—and being free of all the extremes of nonexistence in that one can posit everything from cause and effect to the very facts of the world as possessing no intrinsic existence appears to be a distinctive interpretation of the noble Nāgārjuna's thought by the master Buddhapālita and the revered Candrakīrti. So distinguishing two types of existence and two types of nonexistence is crucially important.

That emptiness should be presented by the analogy of reflection is found in the following from the *Meeting of Father and Son Sutra*:

> Just as a reflection of a form
> with no intrinsic existence
> appears in a clear mirror,
> so understand phenomena such as trees.[512]

That is, one should understand the other analogies of falsehood—how these analogies and their referents are to be correlated—along the same lines as this example [of the mirror image]. [185]

The merits of negating intrinsic arising on both levels of the two truths

This has two parts: (1) the merit of more readily avoiding the views of eternalism and nihilism and (2) the merit of how cause and effect become most tenable.

The merit of more readily avoiding the views of eternalism and nihilism

> Since no intrinsic nature exists in either of the two truths,
> phenomena are neither eternal nor annihilated. 6.38cd

Like reflections, all things are empty of intrinsic existence, and **since no intrinsic nature exists** equally **in either of the two truths**—that of the ultimate and that of the conventional—**phenomena** such as form do not intrinsically exist; they **are neither eternal nor annihilated**. "Annihilation" here refers to the sense explained in the line "So at the time of the sprout, there is no extinction of the seed."[513] In *Fundamental Wisdom* it says:

> As they assert what existed before is now no more,
> they fall therefore into annihilationism.[514]

Nāgārjuna is stating here that if, having asserted intrinsic existence of things, one accepts that something that existed previously later becomes nonexistent or is impermanent in the sense of having disintegrated, this would constitute an annihilationist view. For if one holds that things exist intrinsically, Nāgārjuna says, then whether one asserts a thing to be permanent or impermanent, this would constitute either an eternalist or a nihilist view.

At this point in the *Commentary*, Candrakīrti cites the passages from *Fundamental Wisdom* where Nāgārjuna states that the agent and the acts done are like when the Buddha manifests one emanation who in turn manifests another emanation.[515] "Thus," Candrakīrti writes, "Nāgārjuna has shown how things with no intrinsic existence do arise from no intrinsic existence."[516] Candrakīrti's point is that when every function is posited in a context of no intrinsic existence, there is no [danger of falling into] nihilism.

In brief, if one fails to negate existence by virtue of intrinsic characteristic on the conventional level, one will fail to realize the extremely subtle level of selflessness. It would also become difficult to ensure that the subtlest degrees of eternalist and nihilist views do not arise within one's mind. Therefore the benefit that comes from eliminating that object of negation on the conventional level is the relinquishing of all eternalist and nihilist views, with no residue. If such an existence is negated on the conventional level, one will not only avoid falling into eternalist and nihilist views with respect to the ultimate truth, one will escape being soiled by the stains of eternalist and nihilist views with respect to conventional truth as well. It thus has the merit of easily abandoning the views of eternalism and nihilism. [186]

The merit of how cause and effect become most tenable

This has three parts: (1) someone who does not assert intrinsic existence need not accept foundation consciousness, (2) illustrating by analogy how effects come into being from cessation of actions, and (3) rejecting objections to this presentation.

Someone who does not assert intrinsic existence need not accept foundation consciousness.

The first has three parts: (1) explaining the *Commentary*'s transitional passage, (2) explaining the meaning of the words of the root text, and (3) discussing related issues arising from this.

Explaining the Commentary's transitional passage

[The *Commentary* states:]

> In this way, because things do not have intrinsic existence on the level of both truths, one casts views of eternalism and nihilism far away. Not only that, it becomes tenable to maintain that karmic acts—even if committed long before—remain connected to their effects without conceiving such notions as *foundation consciousness, mental continuum, noncorrosion*, or *obtainment*.[517]

Here Candrakīrti states that for the standpoint with no intrinsic existence, not only is there the merit of casting eternalist and nihilist views far away, there is also the merit of the complete tenability of connecting karma and its effects without having to resort to notions like the foundation consciousness and so on.

From the traditions of interpreting the treatises of the noble Nāgārjuna comes this unique interpretation, whereby one can still posit all effective transactions [of the world] even though not even the tiniest particle of intrinsic reality exists. Based on this approach, many perfect tenets emerge that are unique compared to other commentators. What are these tenets? For now here are the principal ones:

1. Rejecting a foundation consciousness that is separate from the sixfold classes of consciousness
2. A unique method of refuting reflexive awareness (self-cognition)
3. Rejecting the use of autonomous syllogism to engender of the view of suchness in others; thus three rejections.

4. Accepting external reality's existence to the same extent as one accepts the existence of consciousness

5. Accepting that even śrāvakas and pratyekabuddhas realize the selflessness of phenomena

6. Accepting that grasping at the self-existence of phenomena is a form of affliction

7. Accepting that the disintegration [of things] is a conditioned thing

8. Because of this reason, accepting a unique way of defining the three times.[518]

Of these, the first is presented in the present section of the root text. How rejecting reflexive awareness is related to nonacceptance of intrinsic existence [187] will be explained later. I have already explained extensively elsewhere how disavowing autonomous syllogism is related to the rejection of intrinsic existence,[519] and a brief explanation will be presented here as well. How acceptance of external reality also derives from such rejection will be explained later.

How the fifth tenet is due also to this rejection [of intrinsic existence] is as follows. Just as Buddhapālita defines the self-existence that is negated in the śrāvaka scriptures—such as in the statement "All phenomena are devoid of self-existence"—to be that of existence by virtue of an essence, this approach is accepted here as well. The sense here is that of a comprehensive understanding of selflessness. The meaning of a comprehensive understanding of the selflessness of persons is to be understood as the absence of a person existing by virtue of its own essence. The point is that realizing such selflessness of persons correctly requires correctly realizing the selflessness of phenomena as well. Given this, one must definitely admit grasping at the self-existence of phenomena to be a form of affliction. This in turn gives rise to numerous distinctions [between this system and that of Svātantrika Madhyamaka], such as two different ways of defining the afflictions, one subtler and the other coarser; two different opinions on the question of whether the path of the sixteen characteristics [of the four noble truths] such as impermanence can itself lead to freedom; and different opinions on what specific stage of the path one begins to eliminate the obscurations to knowledge, and so forth.

[*Question:*] Both Madhyamaka schools accept that there are some who, having entered the Mahayana path first, established well the view of suchness but later fell into the śrāvaka or pratyekabuddha path. In that case, one must accept, he would gain insight into such truth through meditation on the selflessness of phenomena in a direct manner, and he will have gained deeper familiarity with what he has seen. If so, one must also admit that through such a path, he will have eliminated, on the path of seeing, the acquired levels of grasping at self-existence of phenomena, and he will have eliminated, on the path of meditation, innate self-grasping. This being so, the question becomes, within the standpoint of the Madhyamaka tradition that accepts things to exist through intrinsic characteristics [that is, the Svātantrika Madhyamaka], should one accept two types of grasping at the self-existence of phenomena—one that belongs to the class of afflictions and one that does not?

[*Reply:*] No clear statements on this point appear [in the Indian sources themselves]. These Svātantrika Mādhyamikas do have to maintain that such śrāvakas or pratyekabuddhas may attain temporary elimination of the manifest levels of grasping at the self-existence of phenomena through their meditative cultivation of the path. Nonetheless, without the complementary factor of the limitless collection of merit, it remains impossible to eliminate the seed of either of the two levels [acquired and innate] of grasping at the self-existence of phenomena. So such Mādhyamikas would have to say that although some śrāvakas and pratyekabuddhas may be able to temporarily eliminate the manifest levels of the obscuration to knowledge, the elimination of their seeds remain impossible. In the view of our master Candrakīrti, in contrast, grasping at the self-existence of phenomena belongs to the class of afflictive obscurations, so to eliminate its seed does not require the complementary factor of the limitless collection of merit. [188] Such a complementary factor is only necessary, he maintains, to purify the habitual propensities toward delusory dualistic perceptions, which belong to the class of obscurations to knowledge. Since gaining some understanding of these points just addressed seems to make a great deal of difference, I have discussed them here.

Explaining the meaning of the words of the root text

What then is the account from the standpoint that asserts no intrinsic existence for how the connection between karma and its effects is maintained without accepting foundation consciousness or the like?

Now all Buddhist schools, both higher and lower, agree that even when a long period has elapsed between karma and its effects, from virtuous and nonvirtuous karma will emerge effects in the form of happiness and suffering.

This said, for the karmic act to remain present up to the point immediately before issuing its effect, it would have to be permanent. Since something permanent cannot be causally efficient, the causal relation that allows effects to originate from such an act would become impossible. If, on the other hand, the karmic act were to disintegrate in the subsequent moment—that is, in the moment immediately following the execution of the act—this would mean that from that point on up to the moment before the effect is issued, the karmic act would not be present. And yet the disintegration of a karmic act cannot be a conditioned thing; so how then can effects arise from these karmic acts?

To respond to this problem of how the karmic act—which comes to cease in the second moment—deposits its potential immediately prior to ceasing, (1) some postulate a *foundation consciousness* (*ālayavijñāna*). (2) Others assert something called *noncorrosion* (*avipraṇāśa*), resembling a guarantee or a promissory note in relation to a loan, that belongs to the category of nonassociated mental formations and is allegedly separate from either of the two karmic acts. (3) Some others postulate what is known as *obtainment* (*prāpti*), something different in nature from the karmic act and belonging to the class of nonassociated mental formations. (4) Others postulate a *mental continuum* (*cittasaṃtāna*) that has been imbued with the habitual propensities of the karmic acts. Thus they all maintain that there is no contradiction for a karmic act that has ceased to bring forth its effects in the future long afterward.[520]

Since the karmic act deposits its imprint upon foundation consciousness, such imprinted potential is the effect of the karmic act, and it is through the continuity of successive series of such an imprint that eventually effects come into being. This is how, they say, effects of the initial karmic act come into being through a continuous series of effects. We should understand the other three positions along these same lines as well.

Of these, the first is the standpoint of certain Cittamātras. As for the second, [189] Avalokitavrata attributes it to the Vaibhāṣika school;[521] however, it is a school other than the Kashmiri Vaibhāṣika. The third is also a subdivision of the Vaibhāṣika school. As for the fourth, although no explicit identification of it is found, this position looks like the view of the Sautrāntika and Kashmiri Vaibhāṣika if one correlates it to the ninth chapter of Vasubandhu's *Commentary on the Treasury of Abhidharma*.[522] However, although it is true that Kashmiri Vaibhāṣika accepts a notion of obtainment, they do not assert that obtainment is a product of the two karmic acts, the thing being obtained. Here [the third position] appears to refer to someone who does accept this. This is the significance of the phrase [in the *Commentary*] "According to you . . ."523

[To proceed, the root text says:]

> Since actions do not cease in an intrinsic manner,
> they remain potent even in the absence of a foundation consciousness.
> Indeed in some cases, the acts themselves may have long ceased,
> yet their effects will come about without fail; this you should know.
>   6.39

For the Prāsaṅgika Mādhyamika, according to whom the karmic act did not arise of its own being, **since** karmic **actions do not cease in an intrinsic manner,** there is no contradiction for an effect to originate from something that has not ceased intrinsically. So, **even** though one does not subscribe to **a foundation consciousness, in** its **absence** one can maintain that **they,** the karmic acts, **remain potent** in bringing forth their effects. **Indeed in some cases, the** two karmic **acts** [virtuous and nonvirtuous] committed **themselves may have long ceased** in the mental continuum of the sentient being such that many eons have past, **yet** once committed, **their effects will come about without fail. This,** that effects inviolably follow from their causes, is something **you should know.** This being so, the causal connection between karma and its effects remains entirely tenable according to this standpoint.

The point of these lines is that each of the four positions responding to the above debate adhere to the view that a karmic act possesses arising and ceasing by virtue of its intrinsic characteristic, and that it ceases in an intrinsic sense in the aftermath of the act itself. Candrakīrti refutes these standpoints by stating that it is incorrect to respond by saying that although the karmic act ceases in an intrinsic sense, there is no problem because we accept foundation consciousness or the like. And he refutes them with the argument "because there is no intrinsically established arising and ceasing of karmic acts."

To demonstrate that this is the way in which Nāgārjuna would respond, Candrakīrti cites the following:

> Why has karma no arising?
> Because it lacks intrinsic nature.

And since it is unarisen,
it does not corrode.[524]

The meaning here is this: Because there is no intrinsically existing karmic act, there is no arising through its own being. Therefore, since it is not possible for the karmic act to cease intrinsically, it is incorrect to hold that cessation of the karmic act following its commission to have intrinsic existence and then think of it as constituting noncorrosion. Although this reasoning is presented in [*Fundamental Wisdom*] in the context of refuting *noncorrosion*, this can be applied equally to refute the other three positions as well, for the reasoning is exactly the same in all respects.

Furthermore, Candrakīrti cites the following from the sutra:

Human lifespan is a hundred years;
one might say humans live up to that; [190]
but there is no real piling up of years.
What is established too is like that.

Whether one speaks of *no exhaustion*
or one speaks of the *exhaustion* of karma,
in emptiness there is no exhaustion;
exhaustion is taught in conventional terms.[525]

This is a scriptural source to demonstrate that there is no intrinsically existing exhaustion or cessation and that these two are posited from the standpoint of conventions. In Naktso's translation, we find the following rendering:

Just as a heaping together of years
does not exist, so should you view,
ultimately, this collection as well.

These statements qualify what is being negated—namely, that things "do not cease by virtue of an intrinsic nature."

Discussing related issues arising from this

This has two parts: (1) why the absence of intrinsic existence in something that has ceased is a reason to reject foundation consciousness and (2) how a basis for habitual propensities is posited despite the rejection of foundation consciousness.

Why the absence of intrinsic existence in something that has ceased is a reason to reject foundation consciousness

[*Question:*] There may be no intrinsic ceasing according to your own standpoint, but there are still statements like "Indeed in some cases, the acts themselves may have long ceased" (6.39c), "actions ceased and lacking intrinsic existence" (6.40c), and "exhaustion is taught in conventional terms."[526] So you have to admit that following its execution, the karmic act has ceased to exist. Since *being ceased* does not exist as conditioned thing and you do not accept foundation consciousness or the like as the ground for the relationship between a karmic act and its effects, then the objection still stands that it is untenable for effects to emerge when much time has elapsed following the cessation of the karmic act. So your responses remain inadequate.

[*Reply:*] There is no such problem. The very reason stated in the lines "Since actions do not cease in an intrinsic manner . . ." (6.39a) establishes that from the disintegration of karmic acts, which consists in the fact of the karmic acts having ceased, the subsequent effects originate. Because of this, Candrakīrti did not present any specific separate solution. The key point here is this: For all the standpoints asserting things to exist through their intrinsic nature, *being disintegrated* cannot be a conditioned thing. For the Madhyamaka, however, which upholds no intrinsic existence, being disintegrated is established as a conditioned thing.

According to the first standpoint [that asserts intrinsic existence], when a conditioned thing such as a sprout has disintegrated, all conditioned factors that are part of the sprout have become undone, and no other entity—say, a vase—is obtained either [in the aftermath of disintegration]. They maintain, therefore, that this fact of being disintegrated is in no way a conditioned thing. This is because no aspect of the specific conditioned thing can be identified with its disintegration, whether it is an individual sense base, such as blue color, or a composite thing like a vase, which is made up of its parts. [191] Therefore, in their mind, disintegration cannot be a conditioned thing.

According to the second standpoint [that of Madhyamaka], take for example [someone named] Upagupta. None of the five aggregates of Upagupta—whether individually, collectively, or of a different nature from these—can be said to constitute Upagupta, and neither can Upagupta himself be identified with any of these three. Yet there is no contradiction in saying that what is imputed as Upagupta, on the basis of his aggregates, is a conditioned thing. In the same manner, in the case of disintegration too, nothing within the conditioned thing that has disintegrated or any other conditioned thing that shares the same nature can be identified with it. Yet, because disintegration occurs in dependence upon the conditioned thing that has disintegrated, it *is* a conditioned thing.

In *Clear Words* Candrakīrti presents both scriptural citations and reasoned arguments to prove this. The first refers to the statement in the *Ten Grounds Sutra* that "Conditioned by birth, aging and death come about."[527] "Death" refers to the disintegration of a sentient being, and this, the sutra states, is produced in dependence on birth. The same sutra also says:

> Dying consists of two activities: it involves disintegration of karmic activity, and it brings forth the cause that ensures uninterrupted continuity of ignorance.[528]

The sutra states that dying performs two functions: it makes death a caused event, and it perpetuates ignorance. Disintegration is produced by a cause, and disintegration thereby also has the capacity to produce effects. Although the *disintegration* referred to here is that of a continuum, the same is also true of momentary disintegration, where the first moment disintegrates at the time of the second moment. So this [sutra citation] also indicates how the first moment is the cause of its own disintegration in the second moment. Therefore, whether it is between a sentient being's birth and death or between a momentary phenomenon's *not persisting* at the time of its second moment and *not having persisted* at the time of its second moment, they are entirely equal in whether they can be considered conditioned things and whether they are produced by their causes. In view of this, *Fundamental Wisdom* says:

> Things and nonthings are both conditioned phenomena.[529]

And *Sixty Stanzas of Reasoning* states:

> The pacification derived from extinction of cause
> is understood to be exhaustion.[530]

Thus, in the above, things such as sprouts as well as their nonexistence are both described as conditioned phenomena, and the extinction of the cause, like the exhaustion of oil in a lamp, is said to be the cause for the extinction of the effect, such as the lamp flame. We must therefore accept this without doubt to be the intention of the noble Nāgārjuna.

Now, since the disintegration of the first moment at the time of the second moment is something that must be cognized by means of an explicit elimination of its object of negation, it is a form of negation; and, furthermore, since it is not a nonimplicative negation, it is an implicative negation. This is because it has not simply eliminated a thing that has become disintegrated; it also implies, in the course of its negation, some other conditioned thing. As for more details on the remaining parts of the reasoning proving [disintegration to be a conditioned thing], you could learn these from my commentary on *Fundamental Wisdom*.[531] This reasoning [on disintegration] represents a form of reasoning that is most subtle and an important feature of Candrakīrti's tradition. [192]

How a basis for habitual propensities is posited despite the rejection of foundation consciousness

[*Question*:] One may not accept foundation consciousness, but one must nevertheless acknowledge that the propensities of virtuous and nonvirtuous karma can be imprinted and that, through maturation of these propensities, effects do come into being. For in *Commentary on Entering the Middle Way* it says that "Beings cling to things as real owing to thorough maturation of the propensities toward real entities deposited through the beginningless cycle of existence."[532] Many similar statements can be found as well. Since habitual propensities will be untenable if there is no basis for depositing them, the question arises, "What is this basis?"

[*Reply*:] Just as those who assert foundation consciousness take such a consciousness—which they conceive to be the objective support for the afflicted mind generating the thought "I am"—to be the basis on which the propensities are imprinted, in the same manner, this tradition [of Candrakīrti] holds the very object of the innate mind that takes the form of the thought "I am" to be the basis on which the propensities are imbued.

In that case, one might ask, "What is the meaning of the statement in the *Commentary on Entering the Middle Way* that the mental continuum is the basis of habitual propensities?"[533] [*Reply*:] Since the mere "I" is a continuum imputed upon the mind or consciousness, it is referred to as the "mental continuum" as well. And if we take the mind's own successive states as being referred to as the *continuum* here, in the sense of the type continuity,[534] this too constitutes an intermittent basis for imbuing the habitual propensities. As for the nature of ignorance's habitual propensities, *Commentary on Entering the Middle Way* says:

> That which percolates the mental continuum, imbues it, and makes it follow is a *habitual propensity*. The "final base" of the afflictions, their "habit," their "root," and their "habitual propensities"—these are synonyms. Even śrāvakas and pratyeka-buddhas who have already eliminated the afflictions through their uncontaminated path do not eliminate them. They are like, for example, when one has already removed the sesame oil or the fragrant flowers, one can still sense their subtle traces in the vase or the piece of cloth that came into contact with them.[535]

One should extend this point about how there are these two types of bases[536] to other habitual propensities as well, such as those of virtue and nonvirtue.

"In that case," one might wonder, "at the time of the *uninterrupted* phase of the path of seeing, although it is true that the object eliminated by the path of seeing is no more, the latent dispositions of the object eliminated by the path of meditation still persists. Nonetheless, the mental consciousness in that phase remains uncontaminated, unsoiled by habitual propensities toward delusory dualistic perceptions. Thus it would be incorrect to maintain that latent dispositions reside within such a mind. Sensory consciousness cannot serve as the basis for these propensities, nor can the physical body be such a basis. Since you do not accept foundation consciousness, [193] there is then no basis for these dispositions."

[*Reply:*] There is no such problem. At that time, the mere "I" serves as the basis for the latent dispositions of the factors to be eliminated by the path of meditation. One should extend this understanding to other objects of elimination and their corresponding antidotes as well.

If one understands the unique way this system [of Candrakīrti] defines the nature of person, arguments such as the following pose no problems. These include "When uncontaminated states of mind manifest in the mental continua of āryas born in the first three formless states—infinite space, infinite consciousness, and nothingness—their very status as persons would come to an end because no mundane levels of mind are present." "Similarly," one might object, "when within the mental continuum of an ārya born in the [highest] formless state *peak of existence* arise uncontaminated states of mind belonging to the [second-highest] formless state *nonthingness*, the beings of both peak of existence as well as nothingness would come to cease. Their uncontaminated mind cannot serve as the basis for the identities of the two beings as well as serve as the basis for the identity of the person who has attained nirvana."

The reason [such arguments pose no threat to Candrakīrti's view] is because, according to Candrakīrti, one can legitimately define a person even without positing either of the two—contaminated or uncontaminated mind—to constitute the person's identity. The opponent's standpoint, on the other hand, assumes that the nature of the person, those who have not yet entered a path and those on the learner's stage [i.e., the first four of the five paths], belongs to the class of phenomena that is neutral and nondefiling.[537]

As for the responses offered above, how can someone like me speak independently on matters related to these great systems of thought? I have spoken on these issues, however, on the basis of the traditions of the great charioteers who knew how to present the thought of the savior Nāgārjuna exactly as it is and in its entirety. Judging from these responses, it appears that the remaining arguments aiming to prove the existence of foundation consciousness would also pose no problem to this system of Candrakīrti. Anyway, those whose intelligence is great, refined, and sharp should inquire further.

Illustrating by analogy how effects come into being from the cessation of actions

To illustrate the point above about how effects originate from disintegrated actions, it reads:

> Having experienced certain things in a dream,
> a fool may continue to lust for them even when awake.
> Likewise, even from actions ceased and lacking intrinsic existence,
> effects will come to be. 6.40

Having perceived certain things such as beautiful women **in a dream,** [194] **a fool may continue to lust for them**, things now ceased, **even when** he is awake—that is, even after having woken up. **Likewise, even from** karmic **actions ceased and** also **lacking intrinsic existence, effects will come to be.** This illustrates how effects can arise from karma following its disintegration.

To substantiate the point of this analogy, Candrakīrti cites the *Transferring to Another Existence Sutra*:

"O great king, it is thus. A man experiences a dream wherein he is making love to a beautiful woman. Were he to continue to think of that beautiful woman after waking from that dream, O great king, what would you think of this? Is this person who, having dreamed of making love to a beautiful woman, continues to think of that beautiful woman even after waking from sleep someone who has the character of a learned one?"

"Blessed One," replied the king, "this is not so. O Blessed One, if the beautiful woman of his dream does not exist, and if she cannot be observed, what possibility is there to experience her? Such a man will be someone who is depraved and desperate."[538]

Up to this, the sutra presents the analogy. The following presents how the analogy should be applied to its referent:

O great king, likewise, childish beings on the ordinary stage who are not endowed with learning, having seen forms with their eyes, manifestly cling to forms that inspire pleasure in their mind. And having clung to them, they engender attachment toward them. Being attached, they engage in acts with their body, speech, and mind stemming from attachment, from aversion, and from delusion. Having executed the karmic acts, the acts come to cease. When these karmic acts have ceased, they do not reside in the east with a support. . . . They do not reside in the intermediate directions.[539]

"Not endowed with learning" here refers to not having the realization of suchness on the basis of having heard the teaching on suchness; "manifest clinging" is clinging to self-existence. As for the three karmic acts [of body, speech, and mind] stemming from attachment, these include both virtuous and nonvirtuous karmic acts. Karmic acts stemming from aversion are nonvirtuous, while karmic acts stemming from delusion can accumulate both [virtuous and nonvirtuous] karma. The statement that karmic acts cease immediately after their execution is on the conventional level, while the remainder of the sutra citation rejects such cessation to exist by virtue of an essence.

Next the sutra says:

> Then, at another time, when the person nears the time of death, and as the lifespan propelled by a karma that is commensurate with it becomes exhausted and the last moment of consciousness ceases, [195] then like the mind of a person waking up from sleep turning to the beautiful woman he dreamed of, the person's mind will turn toward that karma.[540]

Having exhausted a karma that is commensurate—namely, the karma that helps sustain the continuity in this life of the aggregates of the same kind—and when the last moment of consciousness of this present life comes to cease, then like the lustful man who, after waking, instantly thinks of the beautiful woman of his dream and turns his attention to her, the dying person's mind at the point of death turns toward the karma whose potency has been reactivated and is therefore likely to mature in the next life. This, however, is not an instance of remembering.

Candrakīrti then goes on to cite the following:

> In this way, as the last moment of consciousness ceases and the first moment of consciousness that is part of the next birth arises—and if one is going to be reborn among the celestial beings . . . Alternatively, if one is going to be reborn among the hungry ghosts . . .[541]

The cessation of the last moment [of consciousness] refers to that of this life. The emergence of the first moment of consciousness that is part of the next birth is indicated with the phrase "among the celestial beings" and so on. Since the intermediate state does not represent any of the six realms of existence, [the first moment of] consciousness referred to here is that of the new birth. Although an intermediate state exists between death and the next birth, [the scriptures] often do not mention it [when speaking of karma and its effects]. This is because the primary aim is to establish the causal connection between karma and its effects from the perspective of birth and death.

Candrakīrti then cites the following from the same sutra:

> The instant the first moment of consciousness ceases, the con-
> tinuity of the mind will emerge commensurate with the frui-
> tional effect that one will come to experience. O great king, no
> phenomenon whatsoever is transferred from this world to the
> next; yet there is the transition of death and what manifests as
> a rebirth. O great king, here the cessation of the final moment
> of consciousness is what is called the *transition of death*; and the
> emergence of the first moment of consciousness is what is called
> *birth*. O great king, when the final moment of consciousness
> ceases, it does not go anywhere. When the consciousness that
> is part of the rebirth emerges, it does not come from anywhere.
> Why is this so? It is because they lack intrinsic existence. O great
> king, the final moment of consciousness is empty of the final
> moment of consciousness. Death and transmigration are empty
> of death and transmigration; karma is empty of karma; the first
> moment of consciousness is empty of the first moment of con-
> sciousness. Birth is empty of birth, yet one observes that karmic
> acts do not corrode.[542]

So, the sutra states, prior to connecting with existence via rebirth, one experiences happiness or suffering as a result of past karma. From the continuity
of that consciousness that experiences these, birth emerges in the form of the
first moment of the consciousness of rebirth. The sutra also states how the
two—the transition of death and birth—exist on the conventional level and
not on the ultimate level. [196] And the reason stated for this is "because
they lack intrinsic existence," where what is being negated is qualified, a
qualification that must be applied to the statements about how consciousness and so forth are empty of themselves. Now when such statements are
made, given that there is the risk that people might consider karma and its
effects to be nonexistent, the sutra states that karmic acts do not corrode.

Rejecting objections to this presentation

This has two parts: (1) rejecting the objection that karmic acts will give forth
infinite fruitional effects and (2) rejecting the objection that we are contradicting with scriptures that present a foundation consciousness.

Rejecting the objection that karmic acts will give forth infinite fruitional effects

> While nonexistent objects are equal in their unreality,
> those with eye disease perceive floating hairs,
> not the forms of just any nonexistent thing.
> Know likewise that ripened acts do not bear fruit again. 6.41

[*Question*:] You assert that fruitional effects emerge from karmic acts, which have no intrinsic exhaustion because they are not born by means of an intrinsic nature. If so, then fruitional effects should similarly emerge from those [karmic acts] for which fruitional effects have already ripened. There will therefore be the fault of endless process.

[*Reply*:] **While nonexistent objects are equal in their unreality, those with eye disease**, for example, **perceive** with their eyes nonexistent forms such as **floating hairs** and do **not** see **the forms of just any nonexistent thing**, such as the horns of a donkey or the son of a barren woman. **Know likewise that**, while they are equal in having no existence through intrinsic nature, fruition takes place from [karmic acts] that have not yet ripened and that already **ripened acts do not bear fruit again.**

To indicate that this analogy establishes not only that effects certainly emerge from karmic acts but also that virtuous and nonvirtuous acts are individually correlated to desirable or undesirable effects, the root text reads:

> As such, unwholesome effects come from dark acts,
> while wholesome effects are seen to come from virtuous acts,
> and the wise, for whom there is no virtuous or nonvirtuous, become
> free.
> Thus speculation on karma and effects has been discouraged. 6.42

There is a reason those with eye disease see floating hairs and not donkey horns. **As such**, wholesome fruitional effects do not emerge from nonvirtuous karma, and undesirable fruitional effects do not emerge from virtuous karma. [197] One can see that it is **from dark** karmic **acts** that **unwholesome** or undesirable fruitional **effects come**, and it is **from virtuous acts** that **wholesome** or desirable fruitional **effects come**. As for **the wise, for whom there is no virtuous or nonvirtuous** karma—that is, those who realize [karma and its effects] cannot be objectified in term of intrinsic existence—they **become free** from the cycle of existence. Therefore, thinking that ordinary people—those who strive to determine through evidential reasoning why this or that specific feature of the effect emerges from such and such specific karma—may come to denigrate karma and its effects, thus destroying conventional truth, the Conqueror stated that the fruitional effects of karma remain inconceivable. **Thus speculation on**, or analysis of, **karma and effects has been discouraged** by the Buddha.

Fearing the danger of losing conviction in the law of karma, this treatise strives to engender conviction in karma through numerous avenues such as those presented above. This point needs to be appreciated. We should make our view of emptiness a complementary factor that strengthens this conviction [in the law of karma], and on that basis, we should strive to ensure that this one time we do not return empty-handed from our visit to the island of precious gems.

Rejecting the objection that we are contradicting with scriptures that present a foundation consciousness

This has three parts: (1) the actual meaning of the words that eliminate contradiction with the scriptures, (2) the question of whether a foundation consciousness separate from mental consciousness has been taught [in the scriptures], and (3) examples of scriptures that were taught with specific intentions.

The actual meaning of the words that eliminate contradiction with the scriptures

[*Question:*] If one can posit a causal relation between karma and its effects without foundation consciousness, does that mean what has been stated in the *Descent into Laṅkā* "and so on," which refers to the *Unraveling the Intent Sutra* as well as in the *Mahayana Abhidharma Sutra*—namely, "foundation consciousness" characterized as the repository for the potentials of all entities, as containing all the seeds, and as the cause of all outer and inner entities, which emerge like waves from the ocean—should not be presented at all as something taught in the scriptures?

[*Reply:*] This is not the case. For the benefit of those who can be tamed through teaching the existence of foundation consciousness, it was indeed taught to exist. [198] This response indicates how the existence of foundation consciousness was accepted for a specific purpose from the perspective of trainees. Thus, according to Madhyamaka's own standpoint, when such a statement is being shown to be a teaching with specific intent, it is done like this: the basis of the intention—what is in fact intended—is emptiness in the sense of a lack of intrinsic existence, and it is referred to here by the term *foundation consciousness (ālayavijñāna)*; the reason emptiness is being called the *foundation of all (ālaya)* is because this nature pervades all entities.

Furthermore, not only did the Buddha teach foundation consciousness for a specific purpose, he taught the substantial reality of persons as well. This is because by teaching that persons possess substantial reality, the Buddha can sustain those individuals who can be tamed through such a teaching. This refers to, for example, the statement, "O monks, the five aggregates are the burden; that which carries this burden is the person."[543] Here, in response to questions from those who conceive the person to be substantially real, instead of teaching that this does not exist, the Buddha taught that the person who is the carrier of the burden does exist. Although the word "substantial" is not explicit [in the quote], the reference is to a substantially real person.

Again for the benefit of some other trainees, the Buddha taught mere aggregates with no substantially real person, such as in the following:

> Whether one calls it "mind," "mental faculty," or "consciousness,"
> it is this that is thoroughly imbued over a long period of time
> with faith, moral discipline, and so on, and when it advances fur
> ther, one will go to the higher realms in the next life.[544]

Thus, for the benefit of those who, because of grasping at the true existence of the way to the higher realms and to the freedom of enlightenment, wonder what degree of reality they should accept, the Buddha taught that aggregates alone exist, without refuting the object of their clinging to true existence. So by implication, the Buddha is teaching here that the aggregates have true existence. All of these were taught by the Buddha due to specific underlying intentions.

"For what kind of trainees, then, did the Buddha teach foundation consciousness?" one might ask. In response, the root text reads:

> "Foundation consciousness exists," "Persons exist,"
> "These aggregates alone exist":

such teachings were given for those
who cannot understand the most profound truth. 6.43

In regard to teachings such as "**Foundation consciousness exists,**" "**Persons exist**" as a substantial reality, and "**These aggregates alone exist**" in that they possess true existence, **such teachings were**, as explained above, **given for** the sake of **those** trainees **who,** for the time being, **cannot understand** or realize the meaning of **the most profound truth.** Some trainees have been habituated to extreme views over long periods and remain incapable of engaging the profound reality. For example, the *Precious Garland* says:

> "I do not exist!" "I will not be!"
> "*Mine* do not exist!" "*They* will not be!"
> Thus the childish come to be terrified.[545]

So when the ultimate nature is first taught, [199] some may become terrified and regard the Buddha's teaching as akin to an abyss. In doing so, they will turn away from the teaching and will not enter it; the teaching will then serve no great purpose. On the other hand, by not teaching the profound final truth right at the beginning but teaching foundation consciousness, true existence of the aggregates, and so forth, the teaching instead cleanses trainees of their heterodox standpoints and leads them toward greater objectives. In the future, they will come to comprehend the meaning of the scriptures excellently and will relinquish their belief in the existence of foundation consciousness and the like. Therefore there can be only merit for teaching such things, and for the Buddha to teach these is not a fault. Understanding this to be the proper sequence of teaching, *Four Hundred Stanzas* says:

> In whatever teaching one delights in,
> one should partake in this first.
> He who might come to be damaged
> is in no way a vessel of that teaching.[546]

Now, those who need to be taught that there is a foundation consciousness that is separate from the sixfold collection of consciousness must also be taught to reject external reality. They are therefore suitable vessels for teaching suchness only in terms of the emptiness of a substantial subject-object duality. Since they do not know how to posit a causal relation between karma and its effects without embracing a consciousness characterized in the above terms, they are referred to as "those who cannot understand the most profound truth" (6.43d).

The question of whether a foundation consciousness separate from mental consciousness has been taught

Many scriptures, such as the *Hundred Thousand Lines on the Perfection of Wisdom*, mention a sixfold collection of consciousness when listing classes of consciousness; thus many sutras do not speak of more than this sixfold collection. So there are two categories of scriptures—those that posit foundation consciousness and those that do not. In the same vein, when the revered Maitreya expounds the meaning of these scriptures in his *Differentiation of the Middle and the Extremes*, *Ornament of the Mahayana Sutras*, and *Differentiation of Phenomena and Their Ultimate Nature*, he presents the standpoint that accepts foundation consciousness and the absence of external reality. In contrast, in his *Ornament of Realizations* and *Sublime Continuum*, Maitreya presents the standpoint that does not posit foundation consciousness and does not reject external reality. The great master Asaṅga too did not interpret the intention of the *Sublime Continuum* from the Cittamātra standpoint at all; rather, he expounded the text from the Madhyamaka perspective. Furthermore, in his commentary on the *Sublime Continuum*, Asaṅga explains in the following manner the very scriptural proof cited from the Abhidharma in his *Summary of the Great Vehicle* to establish the existence of foundation consciousness:

> The Buddha said that although the Tathāgata element that constitutes an essence is present in sentient beings, they do not recognize it. For example, it says in the sutra:

> > This element since beginningless time
> > is the locus of all phenomena;
> > due to its presence, all migrations
> > as well as nirvana are attained.[547] [200]

This verse is cited as a scriptural authority to establish the presence in all sentient beings of the ultimate reality that is buddha nature. Such an approach accords with our master Candrakīrti, who explains emptiness to be the underlying intended meaning of the teaching of foundation consciousness. So Asaṅga too understands that a foundation consciousness separate from the sixfold collection of consciousness is something taught by the Buddha for the sake of certain trainees and for a specific purpose.

[*Question:*] "In that case," one might ask, "how does one interpret the following in *Commentary on the Awakening Mind*, where it says that foundation consciousness sustains existence?"

> When close to a lodestone,
> an iron object swiftly moves forward;
> it possesses no mind of its own
> yet appears as if it does.
>
> Likewise foundation consciousness too
> appears to be real though it is false;
> it moves to and fro in this way
> and sustains [the three realms of] existence.
>
> Just as the ocean and the trees
> move about though they possess no mind,
> likewise foundational consciousness
> moves about in dependence upon the body.[548]

[*Reply:*] It is shown [earlier in *Commentary on the Awakening Mind*] how the teaching of mind only—according to which, following the rejection of an external reality independent from the mind, the mind alone is left, without negating its intrinsic existence—was taught to help the childish overcome their terror toward the teaching that everything is empty, and therefore it does not constitute the definitive truth. Furthermore, the text refutes the Yogācāra view that a pure state of mind possessing intrinsic existence and attained through the *transformation of the base* exists as the sphere of experience of the reflexive gnosis [of āryas]. When this is refuted, there remains the salient question, "If the mind has no true existence, how can processes such as a sentient being entering this world from the previous one and departing to the next one from this present world function?" In response to such a qualm, the text states how the iron object and tree do not have minds of their own and yet they move about as if they do. In the same manner, the text says, foundation consciousness has no true existence and yet it is perceived with activities like leaving and entering as if it does possess true existence. So this text does not indicate that the author accepts intrinsically real foundation consciousness, as described in other treatises.

One might think, "Although this text [*Commentary on the Awakening Mind*] might not accept a foundation consciousness that exists by virtue of its intrinsic characteristic, it does accept an illusion-like consciousness that is separate from the six classes of consciousness—a form of consciousness endowed with all the seeds of afflicted phenomena and all those of the enlightened class of phenomena."

[*Reply:*] Were the text to accept this kind of foundation consciousness, it would also have to reject external reality, since [on that view] forms, sounds, and so on are claimed to appear merely from the maturing of propensities contained in foundation consciousness. In that case, how would one understand the following from the same text?

> The cognizer perceives the cognizable;
> without the cognizable there is no cognition.
> Therefore why do you not admit
> that neither object nor subject exists [at all]?[549] [201]

This says that, insofar as their existence or nonexistence is concerned, both the outer object of knowledge and the inner cognition are equal. If one does not exist, neither will the other, the text states. This standpoint is no different from the statement here in our work [*Entering the Middle Way*], where Candrakīrti says that objects and their cognitions are exactly equal with respect to their existence or lack thereof. As such, it is wrong to discriminate between the two in terms of their existence or nonexistence on the level of either of the two truths. Therefore the existence of a consciousness with no parallel external reality is not a position of the master Nāgārjuna.

Since there is no foundation consciousness separate from mental consciousness according to Nāgārjuna, what is called "foundation [consciousness]" [in his *Commentary on the Awakening Mind*] refers, in general, to the mind characterized by mere awareness and luminosity and, more specifically, to mental consciousness. The reasons are that the context here is a response that demonstrates (1) that causal efficacy remains tenable despite the mind's general lack of intrinsic existence, (2) that it is mental consciousness that assumes birth in cyclic existence, and (3) that it is mental consciousness that is the basis of all classes of phenomena, both afflicted and enlightened.

The literal truth of [the teaching of] foundation consciousness is rejected in [Bhāviveka's] *Essence of the Middle Way* too. Similarly, given that he accepts external reality, the master Jñānagarbha does not accept foundation consciousness. There also seems to be two camps within the Cittamātra, which rejects external reality—one that asserts foundation consciousness and another that does not. Even the master Kamalaśīla, who does not accept external reality, writes, "Mental consciousness alone is endowed with the potency to connect with another life."[550] He then goes on to cite the following from Vasubandhu's *Treasury of Abhidharma*:

> Severing, reconnecting, being freed from attachment,
> degenerating, transitioning through death, being born—
> these we maintain to be mental consciousness alone.[551]

It is clear from the above that the great master Śāntarakṣita also does not accept foundation consciousness. The same is true also of master Abhayākaragupta.

Other Mahayana scriptures too do mention the term *foundation consciousness*, but they do not specify clearly what the term actually refers to. However, if one examines their meaning, there is never any apparent acceptance of something distinct from the six classes of consciousness. So, to conclude, this tradition [of *Commentary on the Awakening Mind*] appears, in fact, to belong to the standpoint that accepts external reality; and it is mental consciousness that is being designated by the term *foundation consciousness*. These issues require extensive treatment, but fearing excessive length, I will not write about them more here.

Examples of scriptures taught with specific intentions

> Even though the Buddha was free of identity view,
> he did speak in terms of "I" and "mine." [202]
> Likewise, though things are devoid of intrinsic existence,
> he spoke of their existence in a provisional sense. 6.44

It is not only foundation consciousness that has been taught to help trainees initially engage [with the teaching]. For example, **even though the Buddha,** being **free of identity view** and its habitual imprints, totally eliminated all conceptualizations grasping in terms of "I" and "mine," **he did** still **speak in terms of "I" and "mine."** This is a skillful means to help the world comprehend the truth of his teachings. **Likewise, though things are devoid of intrinsic existence,** the Buddha **spoke, in a provisional sense** alone, **of their existence** as though they possessed intrinsic nature. This is a skillful means to help the world to gradually comprehend suchness.

In brief, the meaning is this: It appears as though the Buddha possesses conceptions of I and mine as judged by his utterance of "I" and "mine," yet the Buddha's lack of conceptualization remains the definitive truth. In the same way, when the Buddha taught as though phenomena possess intrinsic existence, this appears to reflect his intention. Nonetheless, the definitive truth remains that phenomena do not exist in such terms.

The way the Buddha engaged with conventional truths in consonance with the world is as extensively presented in the following stanzas from a sutra belonging to the [early Buddhist] Pūrvaśaila sect:

> If the saviors of the world
> do not engage in accord with the world,
> no one will know the nature of the Buddha
> and what is buddhahood.

> Maintaining that aggregates, elements,
> and sense bases are one in their natures,
> [yet] he speaks of the world of three realms.
> This is to accord with the world.

> The realities that have no name
> are inconceivable, yet through names
> he speaks of these to sentient beings.
> This is to accord with the world.

> Revealing clearly the absence of entity
> and abiding in the buddha's nature,
> "There is no absence of entity at all," he teaches.
> This is to accord with the world.

Not seeing truth or the absence of truth,
yet he speaks of cessation and sublime truth;
he utters such excellent speech.
This is to accord with the world.

There is no disintegration or birth,
and though things are equal within the ultimate expanse,
he speaks of the eon-ending conflagration.
This is to accord with the world.

Whether past, present, or future, the nature
of sentient beings cannot be observed,
yet he speaks of sentient beings' natures.
This is to accord with the world.[552] [203]

Of these, the last stanza presents the selflessness of persons in terms of sentient beings lacking intrinsic existence, while the remaining stanzas present, by reference to "entity" and "absence of entity," the selflessness of phenomena. In the *Blaze of Reasoning*, the Pūrvaśaila sect is described as having emerged as a branching off from the Mahāsāṃgika.[553] Thus it appears that at least one sutra in the śrāvaka scriptural collection clearly teaches phenomena to be devoid of intrinsic existence.

13. Refuting the Cittamātra Standpoint

Refuting, in particular, the Cittamātra standpoint

This has three parts: (1) refuting intrinsic existence of consciousness with no external reality, (2) refuting the proof for intrinsic existence of dependent nature, and (3) how the word "only" in the statement about mind only does not reject external reality.

Refuting intrinsic existence of consciousness with no external reality

This has two parts: presenting the opponent's standpoint and refuting that standpoint.

Presenting the opponent's standpoint

The proponents of consciousness (Vijñānavāda), who are unable to bear the Madhyamaka standpoint presented thus far, go about establishing the meaning of the scriptures by propounding a standpoint that does not reflect the [Buddha's] intention but is instead created out of their own preconceptions. To state this standpoint clearly as outlined in their own texts, first the opponent's position is presented:

> [*Cittamātra:*] "Apprehending no objects, he perceives no subject,
> and understanding the triple world to be mere consciousness,
> the bodhisattva who abides in the perfection of wisdom
> realizes suchness in terms of consciousness only. 6.45

The bodhisattva on the sixth level **who abides** or resides **in the** superior **perfection of wisdom** and meditates on suchness, using the very reasoning that led him to cognize ultimate reality without distortion and to see without superimposition of a subject-object duality, **realizes suchness in terms of consciousness only.** [204] This is how Cittamātra interprets.

This bodhisattva also realizes that mind and mental factors, given there is no external reality, are mere dependently originated entities with no correspondence to an external reality. This is therefore referred to as "realizing suchness in terms of mere consciousness." When asked, "How does such a bodhisattva realize suchness?" they respond as follows.

This bodhisattva has established, through reasoning to be presented below, that phenomena such as forms emerge from the maturation of inner habitual propensities. He **is apprehending no objects** separate from the mind, and without them **he perceives no** apprehending **subject** separate from such objects. **Thus thoroughly understanding the triple world to be mere consciousness,** he cultivates familiarity with this suchness of nonduality, and through such familiarity, he sees this suchness of nonduality directly with his own reflexive awareness. Having pursued such gradual familiarization in the past, the bodhisattva on the sixth level realizes suchness in terms of consciousness only.

If asked, "If all this is consciousness only and there is no external reality, how does mere mind possessing the aspect of such external reality come to arise?"

> "Just as in the ocean whipped by windstorm,
> waves rise high one after another,
> so from the seed of all, foundation consciousness,
> mere consciousness arises through its own potential. 6.46

[*Response:*] **Just as in the** great **ocean,** source of waves, for example, when it is **whipped** and beaten hard **by windstorm,** what previously seemed calm as if sleeping gives way to **waves that rise high one after another,** as if competing with each other. **So** like that, this imperfect dependent world that is **mere consciousness arises from foundation consciousness, the seed of all** outer and inner phenomena, **through** the maturing of its **potentials** commensurate with their own class. These potentials were deposited upon foundation consciousness through the ceasing of afflictions such as attachment and virtues such as faith. The childish conceive the world in dualistic terms of subject and object, dividing it into the inner and the outer. Yet no object exists, not even the slightest, that is substantially separate from consciousness. [205]

This above statement indicates that in much the same manner as those who assert God (Īśvara) and so on to be the creator of the world of beings, the proponents of foundation consciousness speak of it as the bearer of all the seeds, since it is the basis of all the entities that are perceived as objects of consciousness. For example, one reads:

> A spider is the cause of a spider web,
>   water stone that of water,
> and just as the tree trunk is the cause of its branches,
>   it [God] is the cause of all beings.[554]

The difference is that while God is eternal, foundation consciousness is impermanent. It is through teaching foundation consciousness, therefore, that the Buddha tames many who have been habituated to heterodox views over many lifetimes.

[*Question:*] When presenting the view of the Cittamātra, the *Commentary* often speaks of there being "no external reality." It also says things like "Objects separate from consciousness do not exist in the slightest," which qualifies the nonexistence of objects such as form in terms of [not existing as] "separate from consciousness . . ." And on the line "is what is conceived as the physical eye organ" (6.62d), Candrakīrti writes in the commentary, "There is no eye organ that is separate from consciousness." So in relation to Cittamātra, should one qualify what is being negated in the context of the rejection of external reality in the above terms, or should one accept, without any qualification, that the five sense objects such as visible form and the five sense organs do not exist at all?

[*Response:*] Yes, in the *Commentary* both instances are found—namely, with the qualification applied and without it. That said, just as repeated instances of qualification in the context of negating arising must be extended to all instances where it is not found, the same must be done here as well. For example, *Summary of the Great Vehicle*, an authoritative text representing the opponent's standpoint, says:

> Why is it called the *appropriating consciousness*? Because it is the
> cause of all physical sense organs, and it is the basis upon which
> all physical bodies are appropriated. Therefore, so long as one's
> lifespan endures, it sustains the five physical sense organs without
> disintegration.[555]

And:

> The "common ones" are all the seeds of the container world; the "uncommon ones" are all the seeds of an individual being's sense bases. The common ones are seeds from which insentient things emerge.[556]

Thus the seeds for the container world residing in the foundation consciousness are described as the seeds of all the entities that are insentient; and the same statement is found in the *Summary [of the Explanations of the Levels of Yogic Practice]* as well.[557] In *Commentary on the Dependent Origination Sutra* also, it says that name-and-form come into being through being conditioned by foundation consciousness, where it identifies *name* as the remaining four aggregates and *form* as material forms composed of elements and their derivatives.[558] Further, it speaks of how such a form does not exist in the formless realm but does exist in the other two realms. Thus there appear to be many instances where the Cittamātra school does seem to accept material form.

If this is not the case, then when it comes to all the contexts where [206] one speaks in terms of form, sound, and so on—which are defined on the basis of the form aggregate—it would not be viable for the Cittamātra to engage in everyday transactions using such conventions, unless some entirely new system of convention were created. As far as I can tell, there is no one among the Buddhists of the noble land of India who, despite seeing that conventions such as [form, sound, and so on] cannot be maintained within their system, still maintains that theirs is an excellent standpoint. As for the meaning of the phrase "those who propound objects of knowledge to be internal," "objects of knowledge" refers to form, sound, and so on, and these are not asserted to be external but are propounded to be inner realities.

[*Question:*] Now if the Cittamātra school accepts form, sound, and so on, then their rejection of external reality will amount to a merely semantic point. For it is those very things like form and the rest that are perceived as external that others posit to constitute external reality.

[*Response:*] This would be like saying to the Madhyamaka that its argument rejecting the intrinsic existence of form and so on yet maintaining their existence is raising a merely semantic point, because they still acknowledge the existence of form and so on whose very intrinsic existence they deny. In any case, this touches upon a point that seems to be most difficult for both schools. Not only is it a challenge for the Madhyamaka standpoint [to posit form and so on in the aftermath of negating their intrinsic existence], there is the similar challenge for the Cittamātra too. For if external reality is negated, form and so on become nonexistent, and if form and so on are posited, then external reality may need to be admitted as well. These are certainly thorny questions, but fearing length, I have not written more about these matters here.

[To continue, the root text reads:]

> "Therefore dependent nature, which is the cause
> of imputed things, has intrinsic existence:
> (1) it emerges in the absence of external objects,
> (2) it actually exists, and (3) it is beyond the realm of concepts."[559] 6.47

[*Cittamātra:*] Given that the settled meaning of the scriptures is known to be as we have explained above, one should accept without hesitation, **therefore**, that **dependent nature has intrinsic existence**. This is because we maintain it to be **the cause of** the entire network of conceptualization, such as the apprehension of the **things** of the subject-and-object world as **imputed**—as existing as substantially distinct from each other.

Now the illusion of a snake that is based on seeing a coiled rope does not arise where no rope is present, and similarly the false perception of objects such as a vase does not occur just in the sky, without some physical locus. In the same manner, there is the question of what is the basis or the cause of the illusion that conceives things such as a blue patch as external since there is no external reality? Therefore, one must accept without doubt the existence of an imperfect dependent nature that is perceived in dualistic terms of substantially distinct subject and object, which is the cause for the illusion of external reality. And this basis of perception [namely, dependent nature] constitutes the cause of both the bondage to afflicted existence and the freedom of enlightenment. [207]

In either of the two systems, whether Madhyamaka or Cittamātra, if there is a presentation of emptiness whereby the very thing that constitutes the basis of clinging—the thing that ordinary sentient beings perceive and grasp as truly existing in the manner they perceive it to—is shown to be empty of that mode of existence, then the realization of such an emptiness constitutes the path [to liberation]. If one does not take the negation of that conceived object of ordinary sentient beings' clinging to true existence to be the realization of emptiness but establishes some extraneous emptiness to be the truth instead, this will not be an antidote to any levels of the clinging to true existence, coarse or subtle, that has been ingrained in us since beginningless time. One's efforts will then be fruitless.

Understood thus, one will come to recognize correctly that, just as the *dependent nature* that appears in dualistic terms is perceived in the dichotomous terms of substantially distinct subjects and objects, the absence of such an *imputed nature* that one grasps to be real constitutes the emptiness of that object of negation. And what is left behind—the *basis of emptiness* and the *emptiness itself*—possesses true existence according to this [Cittamātra] system. Knowing this perfectly, one will comprehend excellently the meaning of emptiness as well.[560]

The opponent's thesis presented here is the standpoint encapsulated in the phrase "the absence of this in that . . ." found in *Bodhisattva Grounds* as well as in *Commentary on the Differentiation of the Middle and Extremes*, the meaning of which is as explained above.[561] The *Commentary on Sublime Continuum*, however, contains an explanation of a similar phrase "that which is absent in that . . ."[562] This latter case presents a way of explaining the phrase according to the Madhyamaka standpoint that is totally different from the first two texts. Again, fearing excessive length, I have not written about this point here.

This dependent nature **emerges** from its own habitual propensities alone **in the absence of external objects; it actually exists** intrinsically; and it exists as something that is, as understood in this [Cittamātra] system, ultimately **beyond the realm of concepts**—namely, of language and thought. Cittamātra consider the linguistic terms associated with the outer [world of objects] and the inner [world of experience] to represent the unanalyzed perspective.

In brief, the dependent nature has three characteristics: (1) it comes into being in the absence of external reality, (2) it exists intrinsically, and (3) it is not an object of conceptual elaborations in the ultimate sense as understood in this tradition. Since being "the cause of the imputed nature of things" is included within the characteristic of "being an intrinsically real entity," it is not a separate attribute from the three. The statement that "the dependent nature exists" does not refer to its mere existence; it refers to a special kind of existence. The master Sthiramati says this in the following:

When the text states, "The conceptualization of that which is not the real exists," the word "intrinsically" is implied.[563]

Recognizing this qualification becomes critical later on. [208]

Refuting that standpoint

This has two parts: the extensive refutation and a summary that concludes the refutation.

The extensive refutation

The first has three parts: (1) refuting the analogy for the intrinsic existence of consciousness and the absence of external reality, (2) refuting the arising of consciousness devoid of external reality through the potency of propensities, and (3) how such refutation is not inconsistent with meditation on foulness.

Refuting the analogy for the intrinsic existence of consciousness and the absence of external reality

This has two parts: refuting the dream analogy and refuting the analogy of seeing floating hairs.

Refuting the dream analogy

The first has three parts: (1) how the dream analogy does not establish intrinsic existence of consciousness, (2) how the dream analogy does not establish nonexistence of external reality, and (3) how the dream analogy establishes all entities to be false.

How the dream analogy does not establish intrinsic existence of consciousness

> Where is your analogy for this mind with no external reality?
> If you say, "Like a dream, for example," let's examine this.
> Since such a mind does not exist for me even in a dream,
> this analogy of yours has no validity. 6.48

If you, Cittamātra, assert that there is **no external reality** but there is a **mind** that exists through its intrinsic characteristic, **where is your analogy for this**—something you could cite and say, "**for example**"?

To this Cittamātra responds: "Say one is sleeping inside a tiny room and, due to illusion caused by sleep, one dreams of an entire herd of mad elephants. Could those elephants be inside that room? They could not. **Like this dream**, I accept with certainty that while there are no external objects, an intrinsically real consciousness does exist.[564]

To demonstrate that such a response is pointless, Candrakīrti says: "**Let's examine**—that is to say, analyze—**this** example here." What is it that needs to be analyzed? It is this: Just as elephants in a dream have no existence, **this mind that dreams** of a herd of mad elephants, a mind that [supposedly] exists by virtue of its intrinsic characteristic, **has no existence for us** either. [209] This is because it is unborn. And if there is no consciousness that exists by virtue of its intrinsic characteristic, then **this analogy of yours has no validity**, for it would not be established for both parties. Therefore there can be no consciousness without external reality.

What is not being demonstrated here is that, just as elephants in a dream do not exist, neither does consciousness. One must understand that this statement indicates the nonexistence of intrinsically real consciousness. For the dependent nature devoid of external reality asserted by Cittamātra is said to possess intrinsic reality. In the *Commentary* too, when commenting on the concluding summary "Just as there is no cognizable object, understand that there is no cognizing mind either" (6.71cd), one finds the following explicit qualification: "Know that the cognizing mind that takes on the aspects of the objects of knowledge too is unborn *by virtue of its own essence.*"[565] Furthermore, both the root text and its relevant commentary contain numerous instances where, when refuting concepts such as this, the object of negation is qualified. Moreover, what Candrakīrti states in the following line about how ignorance gives rise to volition and how volition gives rise to consciousness has to be from the perspective of his own standpoint:

Why then would the Great One proclaim in the same sutra
that the mind was born from delusion and karma? (6.88cd)

In light of this statement, how could any thinking person attribute to Candrakīrti the view that consciousness has no existence? Therefore, with respect to all such instances where parity is being drawn between the cognizer and cognized insofar as their existence or nonexistence is concerned, we should understand these to be from the perspective where what is being negated is qualified.

Now, the opponent might entertain the thought "If no deluded consciousness exists in dreams, it would be impossible to recall the dream experiences after waking up." This kind of objection arises from an assumption that if consciousness does not exist by virtue of its own essence, it has no existence at all. This objection is illogical, the text says:

> If you say that the mind must exist because we remember our dream
> when we wake up, the same must be true of external objects.
> For just as you can recall in terms of "I dreamed this,"
> similar recollection exists for external objects as well. 6.49

If you say that the intrinsically real dreaming **mind must exist because we remember our dream when we wake up, the same must be true for** the **objects** of that dream, such as the elephants being perceived as **external**; they too would similarly exist. Why is this so? Because, **just as** you assert that mental consciousness exists because, when awakened, **you can recall in terms of "I dreamed this"** when I was dreaming, [210] **similar recollection exists for external objects** that one has dreamed **as well**, in terms of "I saw this and that in my dream." Thus you are compelled to admit either that external objects exist as well or that even consciousness has no existence.

[*Question:*] Since recollections of both the experience of a dream and the objects in it do exist even from our own standpoint, how does one understand their existence or nonexistence?

[*Reply:*] The *Commentary* mentions two aspects of recollection—remembering the experience of dreaming itself and remembering experiencing the objects of the dream. So in the context of seeing elephants and so on in a dream, just as when one sees a reflection of a face in a mirror, the eye consciousness does not experience the face, but it still experiences an object—namely, the face's reflection—in the same manner, even though there is no actual experience of an object in the sense of seeing a real elephant at the time of the dream, there is still an experience in the form of the perception of an elephant. So although one might speak of "remembering the object," what one actually remembers is the experience of perceiving such an object. Differentiating between *perceiving* and *experiencing* as having distinct senses may be necessary in some specific contexts, but in numerous contexts such as the present one, there is no need for such distinction.[566]

So the assertion that dependent nature devoid of external reality exists by virtue of its intrinsic characteristic cannot be sustained. This is because no possible analogy could directly illustrate this; nor could there be analogies similar to those used in the proof of past and future lives—where although no direct example exists, illustrations can be made on the basis of providing a proof through a different syllogistic formulation.[567] [In view of all the above,] one should understand that the arguments entailed in the refutation of Cittamātra are extremely powerful.

How the dream analogy does not establish nonexistence of external reality

> You may say, "Since there is no visual cognition in sleep,
> no external object is seen, and thus mental cognition alone exists;
> it's the aspects of the mind that are grasped as external.
> So as in dreams, it's the same with waking life." 6.50

You may say, "If the body of an elephant and so on were to exist during dreams, then visual cognitions perceiving them would also be present while dreaming. This, however, is not correct. Since there is no visual cognition present in dreams for the person who remains afflicted by sleep, no external object, such as the body of an elephant perceptible to visual cognition, is seen during dreams. And thus in that state mental cognition alone exists. Therefore no external reality such as a visible form exists at all, and it's only the forms of external objects appearing as aspects of the mind that are ineluctably grasped as external. [211] So as in dreams, it's the same with waking life, wherein mere cognitions emerge with no external objects at all."

To argue thus is to assert that, even if one grants that the dream analogy offered previously does not work, the dream example still establishes the existence of consciousness devoid of external reality. Here the *Commentary* states, "This is incorrect because it is impossible for mental cognitions to emerge in dreams."[568] The meaning of this statement is that even if we grant the absence of visible forms in a dream, a mental cognition existing by virtue of its intrinsic characteristic yet devoid of such content would be impossible even in a dream. Candrakīrti is saying that the Cittamātra [analogy of a dream] marries two things—the nonexistence of external reality and the intrinsic existence of mental cognitions—and therefore it cannot be a viable analogy.

> Just as for you no external realities are born in a dream,
> no mental cognitions are born either;
> so all three factors of perception—the eyes, their object,
> and the mind engendered by them—are fictitious. 6.51
> For the ears and the rest too, these three factors lack birth. 6.52a

Just as for you no external objects or facts **are born in a dream, no mental cognitions are** intrinsically **born either.** Thus, just as during the waking state when one perceives a form three things converge—the eyes, the visible form, and mental faculty—in the same manner, when one registers an object in a dream, it is through the convergence of three things that a cognition would perceive that object. Also, just as **the eyes** as well as **their object,** the visible form, are not present in a dream state, the **mind engendered by these** two factors—namely, visual consciousness—also does not exist. So **all three factors of perception**—the eyes (organ), the visible forms (object), and the mental faculty (antecedent condition)—**are fictitious.** Just as for the eyes, **these three factors lack** intrinsically real **birth for the ears and the rest too.**

The *Commentary* says "the words 'and the rest' include from sound and auditory consciousness up to mental element and dharma element, as well as up to mental consciousness."[569] So the four remaining physical sense organs (from the ears up to the body organ), the four remaining sense objects (from sound to texture), and the four remaining cognitions such as auditory consciousness—all of these remain fictitious. Even though they have no existence in the dream states, they appear as if they do, hence they are all false. The three factors of mental cognition do exist during the dream state, but they still remain false, for they appear to possess intrinsic reality when they do not.

Those who take the presence of sensory consciousness in a dream state as representing master Candrakīrti's position and then go about refuting it reveal excessive crudeness in the use of their intellect. This is exactly like the saying "Letting the sun of refutation rise before the daybreak of opponent's standpoint has arrived."[570] So cast this kind of activity far away. Some Tibetans, while harboring pretensions of being great scholars, fail to comprehend even the rough outline of the positions of the great bodhisattvas [212] who are most learned in philosophical matters such as these. They thus relate to these masters as objects of continual accumulation of demerits and lead many others to such demerits. So please be mindful.

Bhāviveka responds to Cittamātra's positing of its own standpoint, as outlined in the lines "Since there is no visual cognition in sleep . . ." (6.50), by demonstrating how the opponent's analogy remains unestablished. He writes how in a dream state there do exist forms belonging to the class of mental objects, forms that are perceivable by mental consciousness, hence no instance of consciousness exists that has no object.[571]

In critiquing this [passage of Bhāviveka], Candrakīrti writes:

> This too is incorrect because the existence of all three factors remains utterly impossible in the dream state. If you accept these [three factors in the dream state] for the sake of refuting the opponent's standpoint, the dream analogy would in that case become meaningless. If the dream has content that is not fictitious, then it cannot illustrate that the actual referent, the things, have the character of being false.[572]

The meaning of the above statement is this: The intrinsic existence of objects, sense organs, and consciousnesses is totally impossible even in a dream state. It is therefore illogical to say that in a dream state there exists a mental-object form that is an entity distinct from consciousness. This is how one should [correctly] respond [to the Cittamātra proposition].

Now the existence of such a form is something that one must also accept; there is no contradiction in maintaining that such form exists in the dream state. So what becomes clear from the above exchange is that Bhāviveka accepts such a form [in dream state] to possess an intrinsic existence, while Candrakīrti's passage argues against such existence. If the intrinsic existence of a mental-object form were to be accepted because doing so could help refute Cittamātra's dream analogy that purports to demonstrate consciousness without external reality, this would then make the Madhyamaka's own use of the dream analogy to illustrate the absence of true existence of things meaningless. For [according to Bhāviveka] dream would then have content that is not fictitious and would itself exist by virtue of its intrinsic characteristic. This would then make it impossible to use the analogy of a dream to help establish the falsehood of the things that are the actual referents of such an analogy. For as long as one does not reject intrinsic existence, it is impossible to relate the reason as well as the predicate to be proven to the example cited.[573] In view of all of these, [compared to what Bhāviveka has suggested] the response we have presented above—that everything perceived in a dream lacks intrinsic existence—is far more excellent. [213]

[*Question:*] According to our own system, are those forms that are perceived vividly in dreams accepted as mental-object forms or not?

[*Reply:*] Since there is no sensory consciousness in a dream state, what appear as five sense objects are in fact being perceived only by mental consciousness. So although one cannot posit the presence of the five sense objects such as visible form, the objects of dreams are mental-object forms. This is analogous to recognizing the vivid perceptions of skeletons in mental consciousness [in meditative states] as being mental-object forms. Out of the five types of mental objects, dream objects belong to the category of imputed forms.[574] Through this analysis we should understand the status of many other similar facts.

How the dream analogy establishes all entities to be false

Having established that dreams have no reality on the grounds that what appear as the three factors in a dream—object, sense organ, and consciousness—are all unreal, Candrakīrti, to demonstrate the unreality of all the other phenomena that have yet to be established as lacking true existence, states that even during the waking state, all phenomena are proven to lack intrinsic existence. He writes:

> And as in dreams, here too in the waking state,
> phenomena are false and mind has no existence;
> there are no objects of experience and no senses either. 6.52b–d

Just as the three factors—object, sense faculty, and consciousness—are false **in dreams, phenomena are false here too in the waking state.** Therefore **the mind** [perceiving these phenomena] **has no** intrinsic **existence.** Likewise, **there are no objects of experience** of the senses, such as form and so on, **and no** intrinsically arising **senses either.**

[The *Commentary* says:]

Thus it is stated in the sutra:

> Just as one perceives magically conjured animals,
> things though appearing do not exist in reality;
> they resemble illusions and are like dreams.
> This truth has been shown by the Tathāgata.

Also:

> The beings of cyclic existence are dream-like:
> there is no birth nor death for anyone,
> and no "sentient," "human," or "life" can be found.
> All these phenomena are like foam or a banana tree.

Statements such as these then become truly well-uttered insights.[575]

The phrase "no birth for anyone" and so on should be understood just as in the case above, where the negation is expressed with the phrase "do not exist in reality." [214] These sutra passages demonstrating all phenomena as lacking existence in actual reality fit well with the Madhyamaka standpoint but not with that of Cittamātra. This is why Candrakīrti states that these [sutra citations] become truly well-uttered insights.

[To continue, the root text reads:]

> So here, just as with the waking state,
> the three factors of dream exist until woken up—
> upon rousing, the three become no more.
> So it is for those awakened from the sleep of delusion. 6.53

So here, with respect to people in the world, there are some who, though caught in ignorance's sleep, are free from ordinary sleep in the sense of being awake. Nothing arises for them through its own essence, but within the dream-like perspective of ignorance's sleep, all three factors [object, sense organ, and cognition] do exist [intrinsically for them]. **Just as with the waking state,** for someone who is asleep, as long as they remain in that state and **until woken up, the three factors**—objects, senses, and cognitions—**of dream** continue to **exist.** Yet, **upon rousing** from sleep, **the three** things of his dream **become no more. So it is** for the buddhas who, having **awakened from**, or eradicated, **the sleep of delusion** in its entirety, have actualized the ultimate expanse of reality; for them all three factors no longer exist at all.

So consciousness in the absence of external reality [as postulated by Cittamātra] has no existence at all. This said, it is from within the perspective of a buddha's seeing the way things really are (emptiness) that the three factors are not perceived. As for his seeing things in their diversity (conventional truth), although no perception arises from the buddha's mind being infected by the propensities of ignorance, it does know these three factors through perceiving what appears to sentient beings whose minds are thus afflicted.

Refuting the analogy of seeing floating hairs

If Cittamātra asserts, "Those with myodesopsia perceive floating hairs and so on that do not actually exist. Similarly, even though no external reality exists, consciousness does exist by virtue of its intrinsic nature."[576] This too is untenable. Why is this so? Candrakīrti writes:

> The cognition of one suffering from defective sight
> perceives floating hair because of his malady.
> For such cognition, both floating hair and its perception are true;
> for those who have clear sight, both these things are false. 6.54

> If cognition exists without the cognized,
> one should see floating hair even without the malady
> that makes the eyes see such things.
> This is not the case, and so no such cognition exists. 6.55

The cognition of one suffering from defective eyesight perceives floating hair because of his malady. Now **for such cognition** of the person, **both** visual **perception** and its object, the **floating hair, are true**. Yet from the perspective of **those who have clear sight**—those whose vision has not been affected by such a malady—[215] **both these things**, what appear as floating hair as well as the cognition that perceives it, **are false**; both are unborn. For without an object, even a merely appearing one, it would be difficult to posit the existence of cognition. However, this is exactly what [the opponent] will have to admit.

If one does not admit [the above consequence] and asserts that even **without the cognized** floating hair, intrinsically real **cognition** perceiving floating hair does **exist** for someone affected with myodesopsia, in that case, **one should see floating hair even without the malady**—the defect **that**

makes the eyes see such things as floating hair. For they are both exactly equal insofar as nonexistence of their objects are concerned.

This argument is similar to the one where it's demonstrated that if something arises from an intrinsically real other, it must then do so from everything else that is other. Here too, if something arises from an intrinsically real consciousness, the nonexistence of floating hair being equal, one cannot maintain that someone with an eye malady sees floating hair while the perception of floating hair does not arise in someone free of such a malady. This is because, with the implication that such a cognition [seeing floating hair] does not depend on the presence of the eye malady, we can force the consequence that these two will be totally unrelated to each other. So since it **is not the case** that cognition of floating hair arises without such an eye malady, **no such** intrinsically real **cognition** in the absence of external reality **exists** at all.

Refuting the referent, the arising of consciousness devoid of external reality through the potency of the propensities[577]

This has three parts: (1) refuting the view that cognitions of external reality arise or do not from maturation or its lack, (2) refuting the opponent's restatement that consciousness without external reality exists, and (3) how refuting the Cittamātra standpoint does not contradict the scriptures.

Refuting the view that cognitions of external reality arise or do not from maturation or its lack

The first has two parts: stating the opponent's position and refuting that position.

Stating the opponent's position

> Now if [you assert] that such perceptions do not occur
> in those who have clear sight because the potentiality has not matured,
> it's not merely that the cognizable objects do not exist. 6.56a–c

[*Cittamātra:*] "Granted, if the presence of objects such as the appearance of floating hair were the condition for the arising of the cognitions, such floating hair should appear to someone with no eye malady as well. This, however, is not the case."

If asked, "What is it then?" "It is the maturation or the lack of maturation of the potencies, the propensities imprinted on one's consciousness in the past, that causes the arising or nonarising of such cognitions. Thus the only person who will perceive floating hair is someone whose propensities imprinted by past perceptions of floating hair have come to mature." [216]

Now if [you assert] that such perceptions as that of floating hair do not occur in those who have clear sight and have no eye malady because the potentiality or the propensity for perceiving floating hairs has not matured in such persons, then it's not merely that such cognitions do not arise because the cognizable objects, the floating hairs, do not exist.

Refuting that position

This has three parts: (1) refuting the intrinsic existence of potentiality in present cognition, (2) refuting the intrinsic existence of potentiality in future cognition, and (3) refuting the intrinsic existence of potentiality in past cognition.

Refuting the intrinsic existence of potentiality in present cognition

> But such potential does not exist, so this cognition is not established.
> 6.56d

> Potentiality cannot exist for what is *already arisen*;
> for what is *not yet arisen* too, there can be no potentiality. 6.57ab

If there were an intrinsically existent potentiality, one might allow for the possibility of the occurrence or nonoccurrence of cognitions on the basis of the maturation or the absence of maturation of such a potentiality. But such inherently established potential does not exist, so this cognition [you assert to be intrinsically real] is not established.

"How is it that it is not established?" you might ask.

When you conceive of such potentiality, is it associated with the present cognition? Alternatively, is it connected with past cognition or future cognition? Now for what is *already arisen*—that is, present cognition—

no such intrinsically real **potentiality** is possible; such a thing **cannot exist. For what is** *not yet arisen*, the future, **too, there can be no** such **potentiality.**

For instance, when one asserts potentiality in present cognition, the cognition and the potentiality would exist simultaneously. In that case, if the relationship between the potentiality and its bearer is represented by the sixth genitive case as the "cognition's potency," the two cannot be separate entities. Yet the potent cognition cannot be the same as the potentiality itself, for if it were, then the effect would have no cause distinct from the effect itself.[578] Furthermore, even when the sprout is born, the seed would persist without disintegrating. If, however, the relationship between the potentiality and its bearer is represented by the fifth ablative case as "cognition from potentiality," it would be incorrect to assert that cognition *already arisen* emerges from a potentiality that is contemporaneous to it. For there would be the consequence that the effect would already exist at the time of the cause. So the so-called potentiality, the purported cause of the cognition, does not exist in the present cognition. [217]

Refuting the intrinsic existence of potentiality in future cognition

> Without the qualifier there can be no qualified,
> otherwise even a barren woman's son could have such potential. 6.57cd

> If you speak of potentiality because consciousness will emerge,
> there will be no cognition since there is now no potential.
> "Things that exist through mutual dependence
> have no true existence." So the sublime ones have taught. 6.58

Now if [you contend that] the potentiality exists in the *not yet arisen* cognition, there is the following analysis. When we relate the two terms in the phrase "potentiality of cognition," *potentiality* is the qualified and *cognition* the qualifier. However, when it comes to the future or not yet arisen cognition, one cannot characterize it in positive terms as "cognition," nor can it be characterized in negative terms as "noncognition" in the sense of something with intrinsic existence. Furthermore, since future cognition does not exist in the present as cognition, how can one qualify such potentiality in terms of "*this* potentiality is of *this* cognition"? This is not possible. So **without the qualifier**, the "cognition," **there can be no qualified**, the "potentiality."

Otherwise, there would be the consequence that **even a barren woman's son could have such potential!**

Thinking of a specific cognition that may emerge from its potentiality, [the opponent] might assert: "When we say, '*This* is the potentiality of *this* cognition, and it's from this potentiality that this cognition will emerge,' the two become qualifier and qualified. For example, in worldly convention, one uses imperatives like 'Cook the rice' and 'Weave a cloth from this thread' on the basis of imagining the cooked rice or woven cloth. In the *Treasury of Abhidharma* too, when the author writes, 'The womb-born is threefold: the universal monarch and the two self-arisen ones,'[579] he is speaking of someone entering the womb who *will* [in the future] become a universal monarch. So here, too, we are **speaking of potentiality** of cognition **because** we are thinking of the **consciousness** that **will emerge.**"

[*Response:*] This rejoinder too is pointless. If something does have existence on occasion, then at some point in time, such an effect will come into being. In contrast, things that will never come into being—the son of a barren woman or unconditioned space, for example—will come into being neither in the present nor at any subsequent point in time. So although one might accept the occurrence of cognition if intrinsically real potencies do exist, [218] given that no such intrinsically real future cognition exists at any time, the potentiality that produces such cognition does not exist at all. Therefore, just like the son of a barren woman, **since there is now no** intrinsically real **potential** producing cognition, **there will be no** occurrence of intrinsically real **cognition.**

In numerous instances of Madhyamaka's refutation of the sprout arising by virtue of its own characteristic, consequences like the following are leveled [at the opponent]: "If the sprout can arise even though it does not exist at the time of its seed, then such things as the horn of a rabbit too could come into being." The significance of hurling such extreme absurd consequences is this: An intrinsically existing sprout, if it lacks existence at any particular point of time, would have no existence at all at any time. Such a sprout would thus be indistinguishable from something with no existence whatsoever. This is the point. It's patently not the case that, in general, if the sprout can arise even though it is not present at the time of its cause, then the horn of a rabbit can also come into being. Through this reasoning, such examples as the cooked rice are explained. For if things do come into being through their intrinsic natures then potential things such as cooked rice would become totally nonexistent.

Furthermore, perhaps [you the opponent say that] "It's in relation to the potential emerging cognition that its potentiality is posited, and similarly, it is in relation to such potentiality that cognition is posited. Hence the two **things exist through mutual dependence.**"

[*Reply*:] This is exactly why **the sublime ones taught that** cognitions **have no** intrinsic or **true existence.** In the *Commentary*, Candrakīrti states that relational existents like "long and short," "here and there," and so on exist as imputed constructs and that they lack existence through intrinsic nature.[580] Therefore one should understand that it is not existence in general that is being negated in relation to these things; rather it is their intrinsic existence that is being rejected. This distinction must be understood.

Now if you [Cittamātra] speak in such terms [of relationality], you are then actually following our discourse.[581] In short, such potentiality does not exist even in the future cognition.

Refuting the intrinsic existence of potentiality in past cognition

Now to explain how such potentiality does not exist in past cognition as well, it reads:

> If consciousness arises from the maturing of potentiality already past,
> it will have then emerged from a potential extraneous to itself.
> And since the moments of this continuum would be alien to each
>   other,
> anything and everything could emerge from anything. 6.59

[219] **If it is from the maturing of potentiality already past**—such as a specific potentiality imprinted on foundation consciousness by cognition as it was ceasing, a potentiality for the production of a commensurate effect— that future **consciousness arises, then** an intrinsically distinct effect **will have emerged from a potential** that is an intrinsically **extraneous** cause. Why is this so? **Since the moments of this continuum** emerge in a sequence, the preceding and subsequent members in the continuum **would** for you **be alien to each other** by virtue of their own intrinsic natures.

The root for the Sanskrit word for a continuum is *tan*, and it is stated "*continuum* refers to 'extend,'"[582] and by applying an affix to this verbal root, there emerges the sense of "transmitting," hence "continuum" (*tantra*). So through the formation of a continuum, causes and effects operate in a related sequence like the flow of a stream, and the continuity of birth and death remains without any intervals of disruption. It is just such a momentary phenomenon, composed of three temporal stages and persisting from past to future, that is called *continuum*.[583] Since the individual moments are its constitutive parts, the continuum itself is a whole, the bearer of the parts, and not merely the absence of interruption between the preceding and subsequent moments. Furthermore, since the continuum encompasses all its parts, the individual moments within the continuum are referred to as "moments of the continuum." Similarly, because the constituents or the parts of the continuum belong to the continuum, the continuum is referred to also as the "appropriator of these members." A "vase," for example, is the appropriator of the lip, neck, and so on of that vase.

According to the opponent, such preceding and subsequent moments [in a continuum] are distinct from each other, and their distinctness exists by virtue of their intrinsic natures. This means that from a potentiality that is intrinsically distinct can emerge something that is intrinsically separate from it. Now if you, the opponent, were to think: "Since I do accept this consequence, there is no fault here," [we would say] then **anything and everything** other than itself **could emerge from anything**.

> You may say that though these moments are distinct,
> they have no separate continua, so therefore
> the objection does not apply. But this thesis is unproven.
> For such a single shared continuum is untenable. 6.60

> Attributes of Maitreya and Upagupta,
> who are distinct, cannot belong to a single continuum.
> Things different from each other through intrinsic characteristics
> could not logically be part of a single continuum. 6.61

You may say that though these individual **moments** in a continuum—in which the successive moments function in a temporal sequence—are **distinct** from each other by virtue of their intrinsic nature, these sequential moments **have no separate continua.** They all share a single continuum. **So therefore the objection** that everything can originate from everything else **does not apply.** This assertion that the successive moments share a single continuum is also the core of the opponent's rebuttal against Madhyamaka refutation of arising from other.[584]

[*Reply:*] It may be that if a single shared continuum can be established for two temporally sequential moments that exist as intrinsically separate entities, [220] the fault charged might not hold. **But** since existence of such a shared single continuum has not been established, **this thesis is unproven.** How is this so? **For such a single shared continuum is untenable** for preceding and subsequent moments of **things** that are **different from each other through intrinsic characteristics.** For example, when one speaks of the **attributes of Maitreya and Upagupta, who are distinct** persons, they **cannot belong to a single** shared **continuum.** Similarly, intrinsically separate temporally sequential moments **could not logically be part of a single** shared **continuum.**

When understood thus, we can see that the essential point here is how the opponent's defense—that a rice seed and its sprout share the same continuum but not a rice seed and a barley sprout so the absurd consequence that "everything can originate from everything else" will not ensue—fails to rebuff our objections precisely because the opponent asserts intrinsic separateness of things. It's crystal clear that the objection is not against mere otherness. So some who use the approach of knocking over the first domino,[585] failing to understand that what is being negated is being qualified in terms of the phrase "intrinsically existing other," they leave aside Candrakīrti's own explanation of how the opponent cannot rebuff our objection and conjure their own fantasy explanation, something Candrakīrti hasn't stated at all. To do this is to sully Candrakīrti's perfect philosophical system.

Refuting the opponent's restatement that consciousness without external reality exists

This has two parts: stating the opponent's position and refuting that position.

Stating the opponent's position

Having presented [their standpoints] thus far, with the view of still achieving their aim, the Cittamātra may once again assert their own standpoint:

[*Cittamātra:*] "The arising of visual perception takes place
from its own potentiality wholly and at once.

This potentiality, which is the basis of such consciousness,
is what is termed 'the physical eye organ.'" 6.62

The arising of visual perception or consciousness **takes place** on the basis of **its own potentiality**, which exists in the form of an imprint placed on the foundation consciousness, a potentiality that has been imprinted by another consciousness, **wholly and at once**, while it is ceasing. [221] It is from the maturing of such potentiality that an eye consciousness that resembles a previous visual cognition later arises. And **this** uninterrupted continuum of **potentiality, which is the basis of such** eye **consciousness, is what is termed** by worldly people because of their ignorance as **"the physical eye organ."**[586] In actuality, no eye organ exists that is distinct from consciousness. One can extend this point to the other physical sense organs as well.

In this view, the propensity that is the cause for the arising of eye consciousness is its *causal condition*, while the eye faculty is its *dominant condition*. The statement made here of the eye faculty being an immediate cause of visual cognition should be understood in relation not to just any eye faculty but to those where the propensities for the arising of visual cognition have matured. In connection with this, *Differentiation of the Middle and Extremes* says:

> Perceptions of objects, of sentience, and of self—
> cognitions perceiving these do arise,
> yet no external objects exist.[587]

The statement that perceptions of objects (form and so on) and sentience (the five sense faculties) do arise is a reference to foundation consciousness. The master Sthiramati, in commenting on this passage, also explains the physical sense organs as objects of foundation consciousness.[588] So according to the Cittamātra school, which accepts foundation consciousness, what appears as physical sense faculties to foundation consciousness is the eye organ and so on.

Having thus shown how there exist no faculties of the eyes and so on separate from consciousness, Cittamātra states the following to demonstrate that even material forms do not exist as separate from consciousness:

> You say, "Not knowing that perceptions emerging from the senses—
> such as the simple perception of blue—

come from their own seeds with nothing outer to grasp,
people speak of apprehending external objects. 6.63

"In dreams, where no external forms are present,
mind assuming their aspects arises from their ripened potentiality.
So just as in dreams, in waking states too,
the mind exists with no external reality." 6.64

You say that **perceptions emerging from the five senses—such as the simple perception of blue—come from** the maturing of **their own seeds** imprinted on foundation consciousness, **with nothing outer**, like a blue object, **to grasp. Not knowing** this, however, worldly **people speak of apprehending external objects** in place of consciousness and accordingly cling to them as such. But no external reality exists apart from consciousness.

Alternatively, **in dreams, where no external forms are present, mind assuming their aspects** such as of forms, sounds, and so on **arises from their ripened** imprints or **potentiality. So just as in dreams, in waking states too, the mind exists with no external reality.** [222]

Refuting that position

If the opponent argues in the above terms, their position would be untenable. To state this, the text says:

[*Refutation:*] Since without sight, mental cognitions
that perceive blue and so on occur in a dream,
why would such a perception not arise from its ripened potential
for a blind person without eyes? 6.65

Since without sight, mental cognitions that perceive blue and so on occur in a dream, why would such a perception not arise from its ripened potential for an awake **blind person without eyes?** Why wouldn't it arise exactly as it would in someone with unimpaired sight? For insofar as the eye organ is absent, both the dream state [of a sighted person] and the waking state of a blind person are exactly the same. The force of the argument stems from the fact that if intrinsically real cognitions can arise without any external reality such as visible form, then there should be no difference at all between dream and waking states.

The opponent might respond: The reason why mental cognition perceiving forms and so forth with clarity does not arise for a blind person—along the lines experienced in a dream [by the sighted]—is not due to the absence of eyes. If asked, "What then is the reason," the opponent would say it is because the potential for the occurrence of such mental cognition has not · yet matured. Therefore, for someone in whom such a potential has matured, associated mental cognition emerges. Here too, due to the condition of sleep, such mental cognition exists only in dreams, not in the waking state.

This too is untenable. [The root text says:]

If, according to you, there is the ripening of potentiality
for the sixth consciousness in dreams but not in an awake blind person,
then just as there is no ripening of potentiality of the sixth for the
     blind,
why can't one say that it does not exist in dreams either? 6.66

For **if, according to you, there is the ripening of potentiality for the sixth consciousness in dreams but not in an awake blind person, then just as there is no ripening of potentiality of the sixth** consciousness—such as those to which forms and so on appear clearly—**for the blind, why can't one say that it does not exist in dreams either?** Not to do so would be logical.

Here too, the argument trades upon [the opponent's assumption of intrinsic existence], which is the object to be negated. Now if you [the opponent] are going to engage in discourse by relying on mere words with no supporting reasons, we too can be content by leaving it at what we have already stated so far. Furthermore, just like with the blind person, there is no active functioning of the sense organ—the basis of cognition—in the case of seeing experienced during a dream. So the cognition in that dream state cannot be a mental cognition that has emerged from the maturation of a potentiality associated with the perceptual pattern of visual cognition that, in turn, arose in dependence on a potentiality called the eye organ. [223]

[To continue, the root text says:]

So just as eyelessness is not a cause for such ripening,
in dreams too, sleep is not the cause [for such activation].
So you must concede that even in a dream,
the dream sight and its objects are causes for false subjects. 6.67

So just as eyelessness is not a cause in an awake blind person **for such ripening** of the propensity for perceiving external objects, **in dreams too, sleep is not the cause** for the maturation of the propensities for perceiving external objects in dreams. For if intrinsically real cognition can arise without external reality, such cognition would not depend upon the maturing of propensities at all. **So,** since it is from unreal propensities that unreal cognitions perceiving dream objects arise, **you,** the opponent, **must concede that even in a dream,** just as is the case with waking states, **dream sight and its objects,** such as forms and so on, **are causes for false subjects.**

The *Commentary* states in this context, "When an object is experienced in a dream, it is perceived in terms of the convergence of three factors."[589] Again he declares that in a dream state no sense objects or eye faculty, or any visual cognition produced by these two, exists.[590] These statements indicate that, for Candrakīrti, all three factors—sense organ, object, and mental faculty—associated with the five sense perceptions such as visual perception are perceived within the perspective of the person who is actually dreaming. So [these statements] indicate that Candrakīrti does accept the existence of dream eyes, dream eye perception, and dream objects. This is not to say that he admits they exist as eyes and so forth in actuality. This is analogous to the case where even though one might accept the presence of magically conjured horses, elephants, and humans, doing so in no way entails admitting that such things are actually horses, elephants, and humans.

> Whatever responses they may present
> can be viewed as akin to their thesis.
> Therefore this contention is brought to an end. 6.68a–c

In view of these, in brief, **whatever responses** Cittamātra **may present** to the Madhyamaka, they **can be viewed as akin to their thesis**—something yet to be proven. **Therefore this contention**—the assertion of consciousness-only—**is brought to an end** or rebuffed.

Let me illustrate these rebuttals by way of few examples. For instance, Madhyamaka presents the following argument:

> (*Subject*) The three factors (object, sense faculty, and consciousness) of the waking state
> (*Probandum*) are empty of intrinsic existence

(*Reason*) because they are perceived,
(*Exemplification*) like, for example, a dream.

In response, Cittamātra presents the following:

1. Cognition of waking state
   is devoid of external reality
   because it is a cognition,
   like, for example, dream consciousness.

2. The objects perceived during the waking state
   are false
   because they are objects,
   like, for example, dream objects.

3. Likewise, if there exists no dependent nature—which is
   the basis for the afflicted and the enlightened classes of
   phenomena—then phenomena of both the afflicted and
   enlightened classes will have no existence. This is because
   they will have no basis, like a cloak made of turtle hair.

"Likewise, we will also explain this by means of the analogy of eyes infected
with myodesopsia."[591] Their rejoinders are of this sort.

As for the first two syllogisms [of Cittamātra], since their exemplifica-
tions remain unestablished, the reasons they offer remain the same as their
theses. [224] This is because in a dream state, there do exist mental object-
forms that are of a different nature from mental consciousness. With respect
to the third argument, the [opponent's] intention is to prove the existence
of an intrinsically real basis for the afflicted and unafflicted classes of phenomena. If the assertion is that no such basis will exist, the reason will be
unestablished. If, however, the intended basis is something with intrinsic
reality, then there will be no entailment.

How refuting the Cittamātra standpoint does not contradict the scriptures

The buddhas never taught that real entities exist. 6.68d

Not only is refuting the Cittamātra standpoint unharmed by reason, it's not possible for this refutation to be invalidated by the scriptures either. This is because, insofar as their own standpoint is concerned, **the fully awakened buddhas never taught** in any of the scriptures **that real entities exist**. In fact, the *Descent into Laṅkā Sutra* states:

> The three worlds are mere imputations;
> no entities exist by virtue of their essence.
> What are in fact imputed things,
> these logicians conceive to be real.
>
> There is no matter (*rūpa*), no consciousness;
> there is foundation consciousness, no entity.
> It's the logicians, the uncouth childish,
> the zombie-like who construct such things.[592]

The first line states that the three worlds exist as mere imputations of the mind, with the second line explaining what this means. Since the explanation is offered in terms of the absence of entities existing by virtue of their own essences, the scripture is not stating that nothing exists at all. Rather it is the entities established through their essence that have no existence, and it is the logicians who have failed to find suchness who assert what are mere imputations of the mind have existence by virtue of their essence. This is explained in the last two lines that contain the word "construct." In this way, the absence of entities existing by virtue of their essences is presented in general. To present this point in specific terms, the Sanskrit term *rūpa* refers to both "matter" as well as to "intrinsic nature," and here it should be understood to mean "matter." This is because it is meant to contrast with the word paired with it, "consciousness." The word "entity" in the phrase "no entity" refers to "essence" [not to things], for the absence of things such as cognitions and material objects was already stated. It refers to the "essence" that is rejected in contexts such as the negation of the true existence of things and other similar negations. [Logicians] are zombie-like in that they lack a mind capable of probing suchness. In brief, this scriptural citation refutes the view that dependent phenomena of the three realms possess intrinsic existence. [225]

The opponent might respond: "These scriptural citations present how one, the *dependent*, is essentially empty of the other, the *imputed*—namely, the substantive duality of subject and object. So these citations do not undermine [our Cittamātra standpoint]."

[*Reply:*] Such an emptiness is not suited to be the perfect emptiness. The *Descent into Laṅkā*, for example, says:

> O Mahāmati, the emptiness of one being absent in another is the most inferior among all forms of emptiness.[593]

The *Commentary* explains:

> The assertion that because an ox is empty of being a horse, it has no existence as such is illogical; for the ox still exists by virtue of its own essence for you. We would respond to you in terms such as this.[594]

In place of the phrase "exists by virtue of its own essence" Naktso translates "has its own essence," which reads better.

Here is how this emptiness of "one being absent in the other" is captured by the above analogy. The Buddha taught emptiness in terms of the absence of intrinsic existence to help extinguish sentient beings' beginningless clinging to entities such as form as possessing true existence. And for this it is necessary to demonstrate how *dependent phenomena*—perceived in terms of form and so on—do not have true existence. So when, instead of showing this, Cittamātra asserts that the *dependent* does not exist in terms of subject-object duality, this is like giving the ox's nonexistence as a horse as proof of its nonexistence!

Therefore there is no difference at all between Madhyamaka and Cittamātra when it comes to identifying what is the basis for clinging by sentient beings. It is those very phenomena that are perceived as external or internal. The same is true of the purpose of demonstrating that these phenomena are empty—to help extinguish clinging to those bases. Where they diverge is on what constitutes such clinging. For Cittamātra clinging consists of grasping at subject-object duality, the perception that the dichotomy of *outer* versus *inner* represents a real separation. The antidote, says Cittamātra, is to take the perceived dependent phenomenon itself as the basis and to negate its existence in terms of a substantial subject-object duality. In that case, the *basis of negation* [say a blue object] is negated as being [substantially distinct from its perception] the *object of* negation, in the sense of one being the other.

For Madhyamaka, in contrast, clinging consists of grasping at the apparent world as having true existence rather than as something posited by conventional cognition. So, for its antidote, the apparent world itself is taken as the basis and is revealed to not possess true existence. This too is a case where the *basis of negation* is negated as the *object of negation* in the sense of one being the other. For when sentient beings cling, they do so by grasping at the thing itself in terms of what is to be negated, not in terms of the negation of the presence of some extraneous fact over and above the thing. With emptiness too, what needs to be demonstrated is this: that things are *empty of that very mode of existence* as conceived by the sentient beings. [226]

Some, viewing the emptiness of true existence of everyday perceived objects as a kind of annihilationism, forsake it and take something else as the basis, and then instead of demonstrating how that thing is not being what is to be negated, they seek to show how the thing is devoid of some extraneous thing. This is not the approach of either Madhyamaka or Cittamātra. By searching within yourself, you should examine whether such a manner of grasping exists in the beginningless clinging of sentient beings. It appears that we are in an era when what the glorious Dharmakīrti said has come true, something discerning individuals should remain cognizant of:

> For this Buddha's way too, there are some who object.
> So the darkness of evil pervades everywhere.[595]

In the *Meeting of Father and Son Sutra*, which is cited in the *Commentary* to present the absence of intrinsic existence of the twenty-two faculties, it states:

> They are thus merely imputed as labels. On the ultimate level, no eye faculty is found. . . . Likewise, all phenomena are imperceptible in terms of their essence.[596]

Thus the scriptures state that phenomena are nominal designations alone and, ultimately, there are no eyes and no faculties. [The above citation] indicates how, when qualifying what is to be negated, these two ["ultimately" and "in terms of their essence"] are equivalents, and also how all of our own positions need to be posited from the standpoint of mere nominal designations. Furthermore, Candrakīrti makes the statement that "If the objects of lovemaking in dreams cannot be found by the person even within the dream state itself, what need is there to speak of not finding them while awake." There are many such similar statements [of Candrakīrti]. Therefore those who assert that, for Candrakīrti, there is no difference at all between a dream person and an awake person in both being an actual person are totally wrong. For Candrakīrti has stated that even in the dream state itself, the individuals that one dreams of making love to cannot be found as actual persons. Nonetheless, one must admit that they can be found as actual persons in the waking state. Therefore those who claim that the existence of sensory cognitions such as visual perceptions during the dream state is the standpoint of this tradition [of Candrakīrti] are in grave error.

In view of all the above, the endeavor of the Cittamātras to lead people to their tenets, despite lacking the competence of intellect to realize the ultimate and definitive truth, is something that deserves only to be discarded. [227]

How such a refutation is not inconsistent with the meditation on foulness

> The yogis who, on the basis of their guru's instruction,
> see the ground as filled with skeletons,
> here too, all three factors must be seen as devoid of arising.
> This is thus described as [meditation] attending to a fictitious object.
> 6.69

> If these objects of foulness meditation are,
> for you, just like your objects of sense perception,
> then when other persons direct their mind to it,
> they too should cognize it; this means they are not fictitious. 6.70

> The same is true of someone with an eye disease;
> so too is a preta's perception of a river as a stream of pus. 6.71ab

The opponent might entertain the following thought: If no intrinsically real cognition perceiving form, sound, and so forth exists in the absence of external reality, then how is it possible for **the yogis who, on the basis of their guru's instruction, see the ground** around themselves **as filled with skeletons?** Therefore, although such skeletons do not exist, intrinsically real cognition [perceiving them] must have existence.

Even in this case of a yogi who meditates on foulness of his body in accordance with his master's instruction and sees the ground around himself as filled with skeletons, **here too, all three factors**—the object, the sense faculty, and the cognition—**must be seen as devoid of** intrinsic **arising. This** meditative concentration **is thus described** in the sutras **as attending to a fictitious object**, something that is unreal.

However, if the cognition that perceives skeletons were to exist intrinsically, what it perceives too would similarly possess intrinsic existence. In that case, such cognition would be engaging with what is actually true in reality. This is something you, the opponent, would be compelled to admit. If such were the case, this consequence would follow: **Just as** when one person watches a performance such as a play, and sense perception bearing the aspect of the performance arises from directing his eyes to that object, **the** same **objects of sense perception** would be perceived by other spectators as well. In the same manner, **for you**, just as the yogi sees **objects of foulness meditation, when other persons** who are not yogis **direct their mind to** the object, the perceived skeletons, with the wish to see such objects, **they too should cognize** the skeletons. This would be just like the perception of blue and so on they experience.

When we consult the *Commentary*, it appears that we may need a different translation [of the verse], something like the following:

> Just like objects you attend to with your senses,
> likewise, with respect to the mentation on foulness:
> perception [of skeletons] will arise, and it won't be false,
> for those others who direct their mind to it as well.

Furthermore, **this means** this foulness meditation is **not** attending to **fictitious objects.** [228] The point of drawing equivalence between yogis and non-yogis is this: if cognition existed intrinsically, one could then negate its dependence on the meditation that accords with the instruction [on cultivating the perception of] skeletons.

We should also know how to respond in a similar manner to the citation of other examples, such as an illusion, the reflection of a face in a mirror, and so on, [recognizing how] **the same is true of someone with an eye disease.** In the case of **a preta's perception of a river as a stream of pus**, too, we should understand this phenomenon similarly.

Now, with respect to the five mental-object forms, these are not metaphysical constructs of the Buddhist essentialists;[597] they are mentioned in the sutras, and Candrakīrti accepts them within his own system as well. So this vivid appearance of skeletons being perceived even though none exists must be considered a kind of a form like a mirror image. Since it is perceived only by mental cognition, however, it cannot be a visible form like the reflection of a face in a mirror. It also cannot be any of the remaining nine material forms [sound, smell, taste, and texture, plus the five sense organs]. Hence the occurrence of its name "imputed mental-object form." The appearance of floating hairs being perceived by visual cognition, however, is a visible form just like the reflection of a face in a mirror. As for a hungry ghost's perception of a flowing stream as pus and blood, it too must be accepted to be a visible form since it is perceived by their eye consciousness. *Summary of the Great Vehicle*, too, says:

> For hungry ghosts, animals, humans, and gods,
> commensurate with their own stations,
> a single thing engenders different cognitions;
> so we assert the nonexistence of external reality.[598]

Summary of the Great Vehicle does not clarify what that "single thing" is and how it is perceived differently. Asvabhāva, however, gives the following explanation in his *Interspersed Explanation* [*of the Summary of the Great Vehicle*]:

> In relation to that thing, a flowing stream, hungry ghosts, owing to the fruitional effects of their karma, see it as full of pus and blood. In relation to the same thing, animals like fish live in it, perceiving it as their habitat, while humans, considering it to be a sweet, clear, and cool water, clean themselves with it, drink it, and immerse themselves in it. Celestial beings abiding in the meditative attainment of Infinite Space perceive it as space, for they have dismantled all perceptions of materiality.[599]

Here, one might raise the following question: "The perceptions of these sentient beings are valid conventional cognitions. Yet if contradictory [perceptions] of a single thing can all exist as valid cognitions, then what is made of pus and blood would not be mutually exclusive with what is not of pus and blood. [229] There would then be no reliability at all to what is established by valid cognition."

[*Reply*:] Now if the question raised is this: "To understand the meaning of the text in the above terms would clearly render valid cognitions to be unreliable. Since this is unacceptable, how should one understand the meaning of the text?" If this is indeed the question, it is that of a discerning mind. If, on the other hand, one takes the above understanding to be the actual meaning of the text and one goes on to assert that valid cognitions cannot be established with any reliability, this would be utterly untenable. Such a person will not be able to posit a single thing and say, "I know this." He will thus be denigrating all instances of valid cognitions.

"How then should we understand the text?" one might ask. To explain this, let me start with an analogy. Say a person who has mastered the mantra spell for not being burned when touching a burning red metal ball picks up such a metal ball with his bare hands. When he does so, his tactile sense does perceive the texture of that metal ball, but that texture is not experienced as extremely hot and burning. This is because his hand has been washed with water enchanted by mantra spells and other such conditions. To those who do not possess the mantra spells, the texture of that metal ball will be extremely hot and burning. Now both the burning and the non-burning textures will have to be accepted as textures of that single metal ball. It is also not the case that what is perceived by one type of tactile sensation is being affirmed by the other as well. So even though both sensations are accepted as valid, it is not that what is perceived by one is negated by the other.

Likewise, one dimension of that stream at the site where a river flows exists as pus and blood to the hungry ghosts owing to the power of their karma, while the stream arises for humans, owing to their karma, not as pus and blood but as water for drinking or washing. Now both [the pus and blood as well as the water] are dimensions of one and the same stream; at the same time, the facts affirmed by the perceptions of hungry ghosts and human beings are two distinct things. It is also not the case that what is established by one is somehow being affirmed by the other as something wholly different.

Similarly, the *Friendly Letter* states:

> For hungry ghosts, the moon is hot in the fall,
> and in winter, even the sun is cold.[600]

So due to the power of their past karma, hungry ghosts experience the light of the moon in the fall as extremely hot, while in the winter even the temperature of the sun manifests as freezing. Yet there is no contradiction in human beings experiencing sensations of coolness and heat in relation, respectively, to the rays of the moon and sun. It is also not the case that *one and the same sensation* perceived as cold by one instance of valid cognition is perceived as heat by another instance of valid cognition. However, since both of these temperatures reflect the sensory experience of one and the same sun or moon, [230] the expression "one thing" is used. So, without finely analyzing the intended meaning of the text, do not become complacent with a premature conclusion when some rough understanding happens to arise in you.

A summary that concludes the refutation

> In brief, this is the point: just as there is no cognizable object,
> understand that there is no cognizing mind either. 6.71cd

To summarize the points explained extensively above, **in brief, this is the point: just as there is** [for you, Cittamātra] **no** intrinsically real **cognizable object**, likewise **understand that there is no cognizing mind** arisen through its essential nature **either** bearing the appearances of such objects.

Here Candrakīrti demonstrates that, when it comes to their lack of intrinsic existence, there can be no difference between the cognizing mind and its object of cognition. In light of this, statements such as "Since there is no floating hair, there is no cognition that perceives it" and "Since there is no apprehended object of the mind that perceives magically manifested horses and elephants, the mind that apprehends such things does not exist either" cannot be the position of the master Candrakīrti at all. In *Hymn to the World Transcendent* too it states:

> Without being known, it's not an object of knowledge;
> and without that there is no consciousness either.
> Therefore the knower and the known
> possess no intrinsic reality, you've taught.[601]

And:

> That consciousness is like an illusion,
> this the Sun-Like Friend has taught.

> Its object too is similar—
> certainly it resembles an illusion.[602]

So as stated in these lines, if something cannot be said to be known by a cognition, it cannot be characterized as an object of knowledge. Similarly, if a cognizing mind cannot be shown to know some kind of object, it cannot be characterized even as a form of cognition. Without the cognized, there can be no consciousness. Given that cognition and the cognized are defined mutually, Nāgārjuna states that you, the Buddha, taught that both lack intrinsic existence. This indicates that the position of the noble Nāgārjuna is to not differentiate between these two—cognition and cognized—on either level of the two truths when it comes to their existence or nonexistence. *Commentary on the Awakening Mind* states:

> The cognizer perceives the cognizable;
> without the cognizable there is no cognition;[603]

This passage is similar to the citation from the hymn above, so it too represents an authoritative source for the parity between external reality and consciousness when it comes to their existence or nonexistence. [231]

14. Refuting the Proof of Intrinsic Existence of Dependent Nature

Refuting the proof for intrinsic existence of dependent nature

This has four parts: (1) refuting reflexive awareness as the proof of dependent nature, (2) how the Cittamātra standpoint falls short on both levels of the two truths, (3) therefore it is logical to follow Nāgārjuna alone, and (4) how negating dependent nature is not similar to rejecting worldly convention.

Refuting reflexive awareness as the proof of dependent nature

The first has four parts: (1) asking for the proof of dependent nature and showing how it is unsound, (2) rejecting the opponent's response that reflexive awareness is indeed tenable, (3) demonstrating through other arguments how reflexive awareness remains untenable, and (4) stating that intrinsically existing dependent nature is akin to the son of a barren woman.

Asking for the proof of dependent nature and showing how it is unsound

Having demonstrated how consciousness without external reality is impossible, the following refutes intrinsic existence of the entity, the dependent nature itself, without qualifying it in terms of the absence of an external reality:

> Now if this entity *dependent nature*—
> free of duality and devoid of object and of subject—exists,
> by what means is its existence known?[604]
> Without observing it, you cannot say it exists. 6.72
>
> Cognition that is aware of itself is not established. 6.73a

If, as you Cittamātra assert, **this entity** *dependent nature*—which is **free of duality and** is **devoid of** external reality as an **object and** devoid of a **subject** that is distinct from such **object—exists,** we will then ask, "**By what means** of knowing **is** the **existence** of this dependent nature **known?**"

To assert that one and the same cognition apprehends itself would be untenable. For it would be a contradiction to speak of something acting upon itself. Here are some analogies: The blade of a sword cannot cut itself; the tip of one's nail cannot touch itself; no matter how expertly trained and flexible, an acrobat cannot sit astride his own shoulders; fire does not burn itself; and the eyes do not look at themselves. I will later discuss a unique explanation according to another source as to why cognition cannot apprehend itself.[605] [232]

According to the opponent, cognition cannot be perceived by a separate cognition that is essentially distinct from it, for this would contradict their own Cittamātra tenet. For example, the following point is expressed in the treatises of Cittamātra:

> If, when a transformation of the base into a resultant stage has
> not yet been achieved, a consciousness with a separate reality can
> be the appearing object of another consciousness, then the asser-
> tion of consciousness-only will be undermined.[606]

So for Cittamātra, there can be no such mode of apprehension whatsoever. Thus when Madhyamaka utters the challenge "**Without observing it** by cognition, **you cannot say it exists**," Cittamātra might respond: "Yes, it is true that consciousness is not apprehended by a cognition that has a different reality; but there is self-cognition. And it is this reflexive awareness alone that apprehends dependent nature; so dependent nature does exist."

Now if the opponent offers this defense, [the Mādhyamika would respond]: **Cognition that is aware of itself is not established.**

To present briefly sources for the opponent's thesis—namely, the Cittamātra view on reflexive awareness—*Blaze of Reasoning* says that Cittamātra asserts that consciousness appears as twofold: self-perceiving and object-perceiving. The dimension of consciousness perceiving objects assumes aspects of external reality and becomes an object of the cognition perceiving itself. Responding to this [thesis], Bhāviveka writes:

> What kind of mind is perceived
> apart from the perceiving of objects?[607]

Thus Bhāviveka says that he sees no cognition [supposedly] perceiving itself that is separate from cognitions perceiving objects.

Thus Cittamātra asserts an inward-directed cognition that is free of all dualistic perceptions and maintains this to be a *reflexive awareness* in that it is self-cognizing. This said, they maintain that there is no dualistic perception of *knower* and the *known* vis-à-vis such cognition. In *Commentary on the Differentiation of the Two Truths*, when refuting reflexive awareness, Jñānagarbha writes:

> Cognition emerges as awareness that is itself empty of duality and cognizes that absence [of duality]. It cannot [cognize the absence of duality], however, if it is not [itself empty of duality].[608]

When Cittamātra establishes the dependent nature to be devoid of the imputed nature (a substantial duality of subject and object), if cognition (the dependent nature) is first affirmed by a reflexive awareness free of dualistic perceptions, then such a basis could be realized in terms of the absence of subject-object duality. If, on the other hand, such a basis is not first established by reflexive awareness, then one cannot take it as the basis and establish it as empty of the imputed nature. This is what Cittamātra says. Hence Jñānagarbha presents the argument that, according to you Cittamātra, the dependent nature must be established by its evidence, which is the nondual reflexive awareness. [233] However, this [reflexive awareness] remains unestablished.

Some claim that in refuting this kind of reflexive awareness, Jñānagarbha is dismissing yogic reflexive gnosis wherein suchness is perceived within each unique individual experience, and that he is also rejecting reflexivity in the conventional sense indicated when a person utters statements such as "I am aware of myself." These are simply foolish talk.

Rejecting the opponent's response that reflexive awareness is indeed tenable

This has two parts: presenting the opponent's position and refuting that position.

Presenting the opponent's position

Subscribing to the Sautrāntika view, some—that is, Cittamātra—present the following to prove reflexive awareness. The instant a flame appears, it simultaneously illuminates both itself as well as objects such as a vase; it does not illuminate these sequentially. Similarly, when one utters the word "vase," it engenders [awareness of] both the sound of the word and the vase that is the referent of that word. Consciousness too, when it arises, is aware of both itself as well as its object; it does not become aware of the two in sequence. Therefore reflexive awareness is something that definitely exists. So they claim.

Furthermore, they assert, even those who do not yet accept reflexive awareness will have no choice but to admit its existence. For if one does not accept it, there can be no subsequent recollection of an object in terms of "I have seen *this*" or recollection of the subjective experience of seeing that object in terms of "*I* have seen this." Why is this so? It is impossible to have a recollection of something that has not been experienced. Remembering is thus a subjective experience that has as its object something that was previously experienced. According to you who deny reflexive awareness, they say, since the previous cognition such as the perception of a blue object was never experienced in its own time, there can be no subsequent recollection of it.

This argument seeks to prove the existence of a prior experience of perceiving a blue object by using its subsequent recollection as the logical reason. Otherwise, if the argument were formulated as "There exists for the previous perception of a blue object a reflexive awareness that experienced it," no suitable example could be found that could be established for the other party [in the debate]. So they don't formulate the proof statement that way. Once it's established that there is a subjective experience of perceiving a blue object, then such an experience can be determined to be either self-cognition or cognition by other. The first alternative is not acceptable to you [who reject self-cognition], while the second is something that our standpoint has ruled out. In this way, the generality "being experienced" comes to be untenable for you, which means, for you, even experience itself would become impossible. This is how Cittamātra argues against [their opponent]. In fact, this is their best argument to prove reflexive awareness.

[To continue,] now it is incorrect to assert that the previous perception of a blue object is experienced by some separate cognition. [234] If such were the case, two problematic consequences would follow. First, there would be the problem of infinite regress. For if the cognition explicitly perceiving a blue object is established by another subsequent cognition, the question arises: Does that cognition require another separate cognition as its cognizer? If it does not, then the previous cognition too should not require this [subsequent cognizer]. And if it does require another separate cognition, it too would require another one and so on, ad infinitum. Such an endless chain incurs the flaw that there will be no experience of the first instance of perception of a blue object.

The second consequence is that cognition will not positively determine[609] other objects. If the preceding cognition were to be perceived by the subsequent cognition, the latter would then not perceive other objects such as form, sound, and so on, for the subsequent cognition would not direct [its focus] to other objects. This is because the entire continuum of cognition—all the moments within a stream—will have their preceding moments as their objects. There is no problem of the logical entailment not holding here. For if the preceding cognitions are perceived by the subsequent cognitions, it is on the basis of taking the preceding cognition as an appearing object that subsequent cognition has to arise. In that case, it will not let go of the inner objective condition, which is more proximal, to take on an external object, which is more distant.

Now you might offer the following rejoinder: the *subsequent* blue-perceiving cognition that cognizes the *preceding* blue-perceiving cognition arises simultaneously with another instance of cognition perceiving a blue object, so there is thus no problem of cognition not moving to other [external] objects. If you assert this, you will incur the consequence of two separate continua of eye consciousness belonging to the same class of consciousness arising simultaneously in one and the same person. If you admit this, you would be contradicting the scriptural statement: "Sentient beings possess singular or separate individual continua for [each class of] consciousness."[610]

The *Commentary* says on this point:

> Just as a hundred petals of a blue lotus are pierced [by a single shot of an arrow], consciousnesses arise serially even though it seems as if they engage simultaneously.[611]

Jayānanda's *Explanation of the Commentary* takes this to be a response to a point being raised about whether all five sensory cognitions—perceiving all five sense objects, the dancer's faces, their songs, and so on—can arise simultaneously. And the response, according to the *Explanation*, is that although the different classes of consciousness arise in a sequence, given the speed of their engagement, it feels as if they all arise at the same time.[612] This is totally wrong. Those who argue for reflexive awareness—Sautrāntika and Cittamātra, for instance—understand the meaning of the sutra statement that "sentient beings possess singular continua for [each class of] consciousness" in terms of how no two continua of consciousness of the same class can arise simultaneously in a single person. This is as stated in the following in [Dharmakīrti's] *Exposition of Valid Cognition*:

> Potencies [of consciousness] are determined
> in terms of their similar classes.[613]

[235] It's definitely not the case that they [Sautrāntika and Cittamātra] understand the sutra statement to suggest that consciousnesses belonging to different classes cannot arise simultaneously in a single person.

Some Tibetans assert that when asked, "When you look at a colorful brocade, do the numerous cognitions perceiving different colors—white, red, and so on—arise simultaneously?" one should respond: "Although these distinct cognitions arise sequentially, they appear to arise at the same time." Those who say this fail to comprehend that the sutra statement about "the continuum of consciousness being singular" is intended to mean [the nonoccurrence of multiple streams of] primary consciousness belonging to the same class. By displaying their ignorance of the simple fact that visual cognition perceives multiple colors [simultaneously], they appear to be unable even to comprehend visual perception of multicolored object.

In light of these considerations, it seems we need to interpret [Candrakīrti's passage together with his analogy] as a response to the objection pertaining to the simultaneous arising of [multiple streams of] consciousness belonging to the same class—with his response being that "although they arise serially, consciousnesses appear as if they are simultaneous because of their speed." This said, as stated in *Exposition of Valid Cognition*,[614] the two schools [Sautrāntika and Cittamātra] that argue for reflexive awareness actually reject the fast speed of cognitive engagement as being a cause for the illusion of simultaneity. It is therefore difficult to state this as being the position of those two schools. Perhaps the problem here stems from some corruption in the Indian text [of Candrakīrti's *Commentary*]. Whatever the case, this is a matter requiring further investigation by those of discerning intellect.

In brief, [Cittamātra concludes that] since one must avoid the above two flaws—that of infinite regress and that of [subsequent cognition] not perceiving other objects—others will have no choice but to accept reflexive awareness without any reservation. It is thus on the basis of subsequent recollection of both the object and its subjective experience that Cittamātra adduces the experiencing of both the object and subject in the very moment one perceives a blue object. Now once they succeed in establishing such self-cognizing reflexive awareness, they believe, then the existence of their *dependent nature* will be affirmed by such reflexive awareness. This is why, when the Mādhyamika asks the question "By what means is its existence known?" (6.72c), Cittamātra presents this [proof of reflexive awareness] as their response.

Refuting that position

This has three parts: (1) the actual refutation, (2) how recollection arises in the absence of reflexive awareness according to our system, and (3) rebutting objections raised against our refutation.

The actual refutation

> If you say this reflexive awareness is proven by later recollection,
> this is not so. For the evidence you cite remains itself unproven,
> and what is not established cannot be a valid proof. 6.73b–d

[236] If you, Cittamātra, claim, on the assumption of there being intrinsic characteristics, that **by** the occurrence of **later recollection,** prior cognition that is being recalled is established as self-cognized, **this is not so. For the evidence you cite** to prove reflexive awareness to the other party for whom it **remains unproven**—the purported intrinsically existing recollection—**cannot be a valid proof** of reflexive awareness. This would be like citing as proof for sound being impermanent that it is a visible thing!

If, however, your assertion is within the context of worldly convention, in that case, there is no such recollection that is the effect of reflexive awareness. Why is that so, you may ask. Just as, if there is fire, smoke can be perceived as its effect, similarly, if reflexive awareness does exist, one can then establish its causal relations, such as the occurrence of subsequent recollection. In which case, one can ascertain self-cognizing awareness on the basis of subsequent recollection. However, since such reflexive awareness remains still unestablished for the other party, how can there be recollection—the supposed effect of self-cognition—which is thought to emerge through a necessary causal relation with reflexive awareness? That there can be no proof in the absence of a necessary causal relation is illustrated by the way one cannot infer the presence of the jewel water crystal from the mere presence of a body of water, and the way one cannot infer the presence of a magnifying glass from the presence of fire. For a body of water can appear from rain and so on, and similarly, fire can appear from the rubbing of dry sticks. I will explain later, how, likewise, recollections can occur according to our own system without the existence of such reflexive awareness.[615]

To this refutation, Cittamātra might respond as follows. We do not infer reflexive awareness on the premise of establishing a causal connection between subsequent recollection and reflexive awareness in the manner of [inferring] fire from smoke. Rather, as stated before, we first infer the existence of the experiencing of the prior cognition on the basis of its subsequent recollection. Furthermore, we demonstrate how such an experience must be either self-cognized or other-cognized, for there is no third possibility. In this way, a conclusion is drawn that cognitions are self-experienced.

This is what the opponent might contend, but being experienced by cognition need not in fact be limited to these two modes as defined by Sautrāntika and Cittamātra. For example, although the light of an oil lamp does not illuminate itself, this does not negate it being an illumination. Similarly, although cognition does not experience itself in the manner defined by the opponent, this does not negate its experience per se. If you, Cittamātra, say that the light of an oil lamp illuminates itself, in that case darkness must conceal itself. And if you admit this too, then just as a vase is concealed by darkness, then according to you, darkness would be obscured by darkness too. For instance, *Fundamental Wisdom* says:

> For if the oil lamp
> illuminates itself and others,
> darkness too should, no doubt,
> conceal itself and others.[616]

Candrakīrti then states:

> Even if reflexive awareness were allowed [for the sake of argument],
> it would still be illogical for memory to recall [prior cognition];
> the two being different, it would be like the recollection of someone
>   with no prior knowledge.
> This reasoning destroys all other aspects [of the purported proof] as
>   well. 6.74

Even if [for the sake of argument] we were to let go of our critical examination and **allow reflexive awareness** and its awareness of objects as well, [237] for you, **it would still be illogical for memory to recall** [both] object and its subjective experience. This is because you maintain subsequent recollection and prior cognition of objects to be distinct by virtue of their intrinsic natures. Upagupta's mind, for example, does not remember Maitreya's reflexive awareness or his experience of perceiving objects for the simple reason that he has no knowledge of these. Such recollection cannot occur in someone who does not possess [associated] prior cognition. This **would be like the recollection of someone with no prior knowledge** or experience. **The two being** intrinsically **different**, it means that even the subsequent cognitions within the same mental continuum would not have experienced prior cognition and its object; so there cannot be their recollection. If you, Cittamātra, think, "Recollection does exist because those that belong to a single continuum exist as cause and effects," this too would be untenable. For **this reasoning**, "Because they exist intrinsically as other," **destroys as well all other aspects** [of the purported proof], such as belonging to shared single continuum, being cause and effect, and so on. This is something that has already been explained extensively above in the context of the line "Qualities of Maitreya and Upagupta" (6.61a).

How recollection arises in the absence of reflexive awareness according to our system

This has two parts: the approach presented in this text and the approach presented in other texts.

The approach presented in this text

> Apart from the recollection of the experience of the object,
> for us, there is no recollection that is extraneous;
> therefore the memory "I saw that" can occur.
> This too is within the norms of worldly convention. 6.75

[*Question*:] According to you who do not accept reflexive awareness, how does recollection occur then?

[*Response*:] We already explained above how, in our system, **there is no** such **recollection that is** intrinsically **extraneous to the** prior **experience of the object.** I have also already stated (6.32) how in ordinary people there does not exist grasping at intrinsic separateness of things that are causes and effects within a single shared material continuum, like a seed and a sprout. Therefore even here, with respect to the prior cognition of an object and its subsequent recollection too—which are cause and effect—there is no grasping at intrinsically established separateness of the two insofar as the innate perception of worldly people is concerned. Not only is there no such grasping at separateness, but when recollection occurs of what was seen by visual perception of a blue object, he would use conventions like "*This* I have seen before as well." This clearly shows that there is no conception of one's prior experience and subsequent recollection as well as their respective two objects [238] as being somehow distinct by virtue of their intrinsic characteristics, when it comes to the perception of ordinary people of the world. If this is not the case [and cognition and its subsequent recollection are distinct from each other by virtue of their intrinsic characteristics], then a person could recall an experience belonging to someone else's mental continuum! Since what the prior cognition has experienced and determined are not something that the subsequent recollection did not experience or determine, **so the memory "I saw that** before as well" **can occur. This too is** something to be accepted **within the norms of worldly convention.** It should not be posited by means of critical analysis, whereby, not content with mere designation, one searches for objective referents over and above the constructs. For were we to search for the objective referents of the designations, nothing can be found, indicating that they are fictitious and [mere] conventions of the world.

In the *Commentary*, after refuting substantially real reflexive awareness and recollection existing by virtue of their intrinsic characteristics, Candra-kīrti writes:

> If [the assertion] is from the perspective of worldly convention, even then there cannot be a recollection that is caused by reflex-ive awareness.[617]

Thus, reflexive awareness is rejected not only on the ultimate level but even on the conventional level. He then goes on to say, "I will show how recollec-tion can emerge in the absence of reflexive awareness below."[618]

Now [those who propose reflexive awareness] think that the thought "*I have seen it*" is a recollection of a subjective experience, while "I saw *this* thing" in relation to, say, a blue object is a recollection of an object. There is then the thought "I remember what I myself saw before," which is a special case of recollection. When this kind of recollection occurs, it is clear that the prior cognition—say, an experience of seeing Maitreya—had experience itself. For recollection follows the exact pattern of one's prior experience.

In our view, we accept that ordinary people experience recollections, but we do not say that these occur because the prior cognition experiencing the object has cognized itself. Such recollection occurs because the very object perceived by the prior cognition is determined by the subsequent recollec-tion as well—that is, they share the same object. This is why subsequent recall takes the form "I have seen this person Maitreya before as well." So we ourselves do accept conventions such as "I remember what I myself saw before." Yet our acceptance of such conventions is very different from [the account according to the alleged] reflexive awareness.

The Cittamātra opponent posits the prior experience and its subsequent recollection as well as their respective objects as being distinct from each other by virtue of their intrinsic characteristics. And so, even though they may assert the prior cognition and its subsequent recollection as having the same object and also claim that they belong to a shared single continuum, these remain untenable for them. This has been explained numerous times above. [239]

So even though one [loosely] speaks of "*this* Maitreya," it is not a locus and time-specific Maitreya, such as the one coinciding with the utterance of this very sentence or the Maitreya one remembers having seen in a specific place. Rather, what is being remembered is just Maitreya in a general sense. That this is so can be discerned by observing one's own mind.

The approach presented in other texts

Of the two major schools of thought on how recollection can arise in the absence of reflexive awareness, the views of the illustrious Śāntideva are presented in his *Guide to the Bodhisattva Way*, such as in the following lines:

> If there is no reflexive awareness,
> how is consciousness remembered?[619]

The opponent's standpoint cited here [in these lines] is the same one that has been discussed already quite extensively above. To the opponent's proof statement [no reflexive awareness → no recollection], Śāntideva responds by pointing out that no entailment holds both for the consequence thrown as well as its reverse syllogism.[620] The question then remains, "How then can recollection occur in the absence of reflexive awareness?"

When cognition of an object rather than that of a subjective experience takes place, it is from that cognition experiencing the object that recollection of the subjective conscious experience occurs.

[*Opponent:*] It is illogical to assert that recollection of a subjective experience occurs owing to the experience of some other object, for this will lead to absurd consequences.

[*Response:*] No such fault exists. For when subjective experience is recalled on the basis of having experienced an object, it is not independent of [remembering that] cognition; rather recollection takes form through a blending of the object and its subjective experience, such as in the thought "*I* saw *this* thing before." That is to say, the two are remembered in a fused manner.

Here is an analogy. When [an animal is] bitten by a shrew in the winter, even though poison enters the animal's body at that time, it's the bite that is experienced and not the infection with the shrew's poison. Later, however, on hearing the sound of thunder [and rising from hibernation], the animal comes to remember that poison entered its body when it was bitten, even though it did not experience being infected the moment of the bite. Being bitten by the shrew is analogous to the cognition experiencing its object by perceiving a blue thing; poison entering the body at the time of the bite is analogous to the subjective experience present when the blue object is experienced; that the subjective experience does not experience itself is analogous to the absence of perceiving the poison when the animal is bitten;

and subsequent recollection of being infected is analogous to remembering the experience of the blue object. The recollection of the experience of the object itself led to remembering the prior experience, even though such a subjective experience did not experience itself at the time, and this is analogous to remembering being poisoned even though this was not perceived before but arose only through the force of recalling the experience of having been bitten.

This seems to be a most excellent [analogical] argument developed by a learned master on how recollection occurs in the absence of reflexive awareness. However, those who have commented on Śāntideva's *Guide to the Bodhisattva Way* appear not to have explained this [argument] satisfactorily. So to the syllogism "No recollection by subsequent cognition is possible because the prior cognition did not experience itself," this tradition [of Śāntideva] responds by stating, "There is no logical entailment." In view of this, those who claim that it is not the intention of *Guide to the Bodhisattva Way* to reject reflexive awareness on the conventional level definitely do not represent the great bodhisattva's view. [240]

Rebutting objections against our refutation

This has two parts: (1) rebutting objections concerning other direct perceptions and inferential cognition and (2) rebutting objections concerning other mental cognitions.

Rebutting objections concerning other direct perceptions and inferential cognition

[A Mādhyamika might ask:] We do have to accept in our own system that cognitions such as the perception of blue do exist. And if that is true, wouldn't the same objection we have raised against the opponent in the lines "By what means is its existence known? Without observing it, you cannot say it exists" (6.72) apply to us as well? For if that perception of blue is known through itself, we will have to admit reflexive awareness, and yet that it is known by some separate cognition remains untenable.

[*Reply:*] This raises an extremely challenging point, so let me explain. It might be easier to understand if I explain by citing the example of how we remember objects and our subjective experience of them. It's owing to the simple fact of remembering the object that we recall its subjective experience as well; no separate independent recollection of the subjective experience is necessary. Likewise, the simple fact of establishing the object of a perception of blue, for example, affirms the cognizing subject that perceives that blue thing as well. Thus, apart from the means by which [the object] blue is established, no separate means is needed to establish the cognizing subject perceiving that blue thing.

That it's the appearance of an aspect, a likeness, projected onto the perception by the blue object, that establishes the existence of this blue thing, on this point, our view is no different from those of other [Buddhist] schools. Here is where the difference lies. The other schools maintain that the cognition perceiving blue is established by means of reflexive awareness—a bare subjective aspect devoid of dualistic perception—something they assert is true for all other cognitive states as well. We, on the other hand, agree with Bhāviveka's *Essence of the Middle Way* and with Jñānagarbha's *Two Truths* and its autocommentary, where it says that such a bare subjective aspect is impossible. So [cognition] is not established by a self-cognizing reflexive awareness; rather the establishment of the blue object in itself establishes the perception of blue [at the same time]. It's through remembering the object that its subjective experience is remembered as well; such recollection is not induced by the prior subject having experienced itself in the manner asserted by other schools.

That this is how we should proceed is stated clearly in Candrakīrti's *Clear Words*:

> The classification of valid cognition is due to the objects of cognition. And it is through finding their own characters, through simply assuming the aspects of their objects of cognition, that valid cognitions are defined.[621]

The meaning of these sentences is this: The classification of valid cognition into two [perception and inference] is determined by the fact that objects of cognition are determined to be twofold. And it is on the basis of how the aspect of an object appears to valid cognition that a valid cognizer comes to be defined as possessing its own character. The significance of the exclusion term "simply" is to reject the following assertion of Sautrāntika and Cittamātra: [241] Valid cognition resembles and assumes the aspect of the object, and the object comes to be established through this, while valid cognition itself is established by a separate cognition—a bare subjective aspect that is free of dualistic perception with respect to the valid cognition itself; that is to say, it is established by reflexive awareness. This is what the exclusion term "simply" precludes. In other words, [cognition] is established through the mere establishment of its object.

This is also the intention of the noble Nāgārjuna himself:

> If valid cognition is established by itself,
> then for you, the means of valid cognition will be established
> independently of the objects of valid cognition;
> for self-established does not depend on others.[622]

If the simple establishing of the object is not adequate to establish the valid cognition, and if valid cognition is established by itself, as claimed by the opponent, then a valid cognition can exist without depending on its object of cognition. Were this admitted, things could exist without needing to depend on other causes and conditions. This is how Nāgārjuna refutes [self-establishment], and by way of implication, he also reveals how the mere establishing of the object of cognition establishes the valid cognition as well. In brief, Nāgārjuna presents how the blue-perceiving cognition is not established by itself through reflexive awareness, as asserted in others' system. Rather, as he demonstrates, it's established by valid sensory perception, for its presence is known simply through the blue-perceiving cognition establishing its own object. Therefore all valid cognitions are established simply through the establishment of their objects.

Rebutting objections concerning other mental cognitions

In this [Candrakīrti] system, things like mirror images and echoes are, as explained above, accepted as visible forms, sounds, and so on. Furthermore, *Clear Words* says:

> As for a double moon and so on, such things are not direct perceptions from the perspective of cognitions not affected by an eye disease. However, from the perspective of someone whose sight is infected, they are direct perception alone.[623]

So this school of thought applies the term *direct perception* (*pratyakṣa*) to objects such as forms and sounds in actual terms and figuratively to the subject that apprehends such objects. In so doing, Candrakīrti explains how, although a distinction may be made from the perspective of ordinary worldly people as to whether things like the appearances of a double moon are objects of direct perception, in our system, however, even the appearance of a double moon is an evident object of direct perception. Therefore, regardless of whether such sensory cognitions are deluded by the standards of ordinary worldly convention, the subject [cognition] is established simply through the existence of its object.

[*Objection:*] Those of you who do not accept reflexive awareness will not be able to establish the instances of mental consciousness of the ordinary ground that are deluded in relation to their objects of perception and conception. This is because there can be no establishing of the subject merely through the cognizing of their objects.

[*Reply:*] Let me respond to this. [242] Since this system [of Candrakīrti] accepts no additional consciousness outside the six classes of consciousness, only two types of valid cognition are possible—valid cognition contingent upon physical sense faculties and valid cognition based on the mental faculty alone. Also, when it comes to valid cognitions, *Clear Words* mentions four kinds—direct perception, inference, valid testimonial knowledge, and valid analogical knowledge. This is based on [Nāgārjuna's] *Averting the Objections* and its autocommentary. That the last two valid cognitions are encompassed within inferential cognition is stated in the following in Candrakīrti's *Commentary on Four Hundred Stanzas*:

> Not all things can be known through direct experience; some must be cognized through inference.[624]

Within the class of perceptual valid cognitions, of the four types asserted by other schools, Candrakīrti rejects reflexive direct perception. He also does not agree with how mental direct perception is defined in the [Buddhist] epistemological texts. In his *Commentary on Four Hundred Stanzas*, for example, in explaining the meaning of the statement in the Abhidharma scriptures that each of the five sense objects such as form are to be known by the senses and mental consciousness, he states the following:

> It is not that one object is known by two types of consciousness. Rather, that which arises first [sensory consciousness] directly

determines the object; the subsequent cognition does not perceive the object in a manner of direct engagement. It arises and apprehends its object through the force of [the preceding] sense consciousness. And when this happens, we designate the latter too as having consciousness of that object.[625]

So Candrakīrti says that it's the sense consciousness that cognizes things such as form directly first, and mental consciousness apprehends them through the force of the sensory perception. It does not cognize [the object] directly like sense perception does; in fact, he says that [mental cognition] is a form of recollection.

Furthermore, *Commentary on Four Hundred Stanzas* says:

> It [mental cognition] does not experience [its object] along the lines of a *feeling* and so on; nor does it positively determine form, sound, and so on by means of the *senses*.[626]

Candrakīrti thus speaks of two modes of cognizing in the manner of direct experience—the manner in which sensory perceptions cognize their objects such as form, and the manner of positively determining through inner experience, such as through feelings of pleasure and pain. Of these two, the second must be accepted even on the ordinary level. Yet, as he does not speak of any form of direct perception apart from the four types mentioned [in the texts], and since such feelings cannot be considered yogic direct perception or reflexive awareness, they must be understood to be a type of direct mental cognition. So although Candrakīrti differs from the Buddhist epistemologists as to how mental perception is defined, it is not that he does not accept valid mental perception at all. [243]

Since "to feel" is an expression associated with activity by an agent, it has three aspects: "*This person* feels," "It is being felt *by this means*," and "*This* is what is being felt." Of these, the second is a valid cognition—the mental factor of feeling—while the third is the object: the sensations of pleasure, pain, and neutrality. We are speaking here, of course, in relation to *mental* consciousness. As for the three categories of feeling belonging to *sensory* experiences, they engage in positive determination of sense objects like form, sound, and so on, and the manner in which they are established is as explained above [that is, the same as the sensory cognitions].

[*Question:*] If the feeling within mental cognition directly determines pleasure, pain, and neutral feeling, does this not constitute reflexive awareness?

[*Response:*] There is no such fault. Reflexive awareness that has been refuted refers to a bare subjectivity alleged to be present in all mental states, which is inward oriented and for which the knower-known duality has dissolved. Here, however, we are speaking of a unique class of subjective experience characterized in the sutras as feeling. In everyday conventions of the world too, one speaks of *experiencing* pleasure and pain. So what is being experienced and the experiencer [mental cognition] can be perceived as distinct, hence what we are speaking of here is not the same as the reflexive awareness postulated by the opponent. Therefore the existence of feeling too comes to be established simply through experiencing pleasure and so on.

When mental-object forms arise in mental cognitions—such as when a mental cognition perceives a vivid image of skeleton—they are established through their images appearing to the mind. How is it that the perceiving mental cognitions too come to be established in this way? It is exactly the same [as in the example of sense perceptions]. Such objects are, however, distinct from the mental cognitions themselves.

On the question of how mental cognitions like the two self-graspings are established, we should discern this in accordance with the following passage in Candrakīrti's *Clear Words*:

> All objects characterized as well as characteristics, be they individual characteristics or universals—insofar as they exist in the world—must be directly observable and not remain obscure. Therefore, together with the cognitions that have them as objects, all of these are established as direct perceptions alone.[627]

The Sanskrit word for *objects characterized* (*lakṣya*) is the same as the one for *definiendum* ["what is to be defined"], so some translators render the word as "object characterized" (*mtshan gzhi*) while others translate it as "definiendum" (*mtshon bya*). Since Candrakīrti's statement that the defining characteristics (the *means by which* something is defined) as well as the objects characterized (*that upon which* something is defined) are directly observable appears in the context of identifying what direct valid cognition is within the fourfold division of valid cognition, he is not speaking here of how an omniscient mind directly observes things. [244] Nor is he suggesting that all instances of individual characteristics and universals are evident facts and [that there exist] no obscure facts at all. For immediately after the previously cited passage, he writes:

> An inference is a cognition that has arisen through the use of a faultless sign in the context of establishing an obscure fact.[628]

Nonetheless, whether it is the perception of individual characteristics or universals, there does emerge in each of these cases the perception [of that thing], and what is perceived is the direct object of that cognition. In this way, what is perceived and its subjective experience, the cognition, are characterized as being direct perceptions. Thus Candrakīrti understands the term *direct perception* (*pratyakṣa*) to apply factually to the object and only derivatively to the subject, cognition.

If all the appearances directly perceived by a given cognition are direct objects of that cognition, then in that case, those appearances would be evident to such cognition. Furthermore, if that cognition is nondeceptive with respect to what is being perceived, it could be an instance of valid cognition; for in everyday convention of the world, nondeceptive cognitions are referred to as "valid cognition." As for the fact that when the cognition's perception of the object is established, the subject becomes established as well, this is exactly the same as before. This being so, even in the case of such mental states as the two self-graspings, they experience direct perceptions of the appearance of the two forms of selfhood; furthermore, insofar as subjective experience establishes the evident fact of the perceiving of their objects, this is again exactly the same here as before. In this way we should also understand other [cognitions that are] erroneous with respect to their object of apprehension.

In brief, although all mental states are equal insofar as their appearing objects—the perceived objects—are found to be evident, there is nonetheless a great difference in their validity with respect to their objects [of apprehension], such as between the two forms of [conceived] selfhood versus the two types of selflessness, and between permanence versus impermanence of forms and so forth. Thus the distinction between valid and nonvalid cognitions can still be maintained. In addition, these mental cognitions described as being valid with respect to their appearing objects, having eliminated all other possibilities, must be recognized as valid direct mental perceptions in relation these objects. Such mental cognitions cannot be direct perception in the form of reflexive awareness, since there exists a dualistic perception with respect to their object.

Although dualistic perceptions have ceased for the uncontaminated mind of meditative equipoise, such a meditative state and the ultimate nature of things can still be spoken of, respectively, as the *knower* and the *known*. This is totally different from [the alleged reflexive awareness], an inward-oriented subject supposedly present in all cognitions for which dualistic perceptions have ceased and yet still characterized in terms of knower and known. For in the second case, except for a philosophical postulation of a subject-object relation, no matter how much one directs their mind, no image of two things—a known and a knower—can be conceived. In the first case, however, if one directs one's mind to it and speaks of it to others, distinct aspects of the subject, the mental state, and its object, suchness, can definitely be conceived. Now, when nonconceptual gnosis of meditative equipoise establishes its object, suchness, it also comes to establish through the force of this the subject, gnosis, [245] for which the dualistic perception of knower and known has dissolved. As to how this is not the same as the opponent's claim of a bare subjective aspect—an inward-oriented subjectivity present in all cognitions for which dualistic perceptions have ceased yet can still be described in terms of the known and knower—this will be explained below in the section on the resultant ground.[629]

These kinds of nuanced distinctions may not be essential to those who, when the opponent turns back the objection we [the Madhyamaka] have raised against them with the line "By what means is this known?" and so on, fail to comprehend the subtleties of the particular philosophical standpoints of the great beings and are unable to ground their own positions in the meaning of definitive scriptures or in extremely complex and subtle paths of reason. Thus in response, such people may reply with statements like "Since we have no position of our own, we are not vulnerable to such faults." In this way, they seek haven only in duplicitous bluster. However, thinking of the learned people who are wise and gifted with refined intellect—those who are not convinced until and unless they have seen the path that distinguishes what is flawed from what is excellent on the basis of subtle points of reasoning—I have offered my presentation here, in the manner of simply opening the door to reveal how this excellent system [of Candrakīrti] can be understood as flawless.

[*Question*:] Now the "I" in the context of remembering "*I* saw blue" refers to the person, and since person and cognition apprehending blue are not identical, how can such remembering of the person be a recollection of that blue-apprehending cognition?

[*Response:*] It is true that visual cognition apprehending blue and the person who is seeing the blue are not the same. Nonetheless, just as there is no contradiction in accepting the statement "I saw it" because the visual cognition saw the blue object, likewise, why should there be any contradiction in taking the recollection of the person—occurring in terms of "I saw this before"—to constitute the recollection of the visual perception's cognition of the blue object?

Demonstrating through other arguments how reflexive awareness remains untenable

This is as follows.

> Therefore, since no reflexive awareness exists,
> what is it that cognizes your *dependent nature*?
> Since agent, object, and action cannot be identical,
> the claim that cognition apprehends itself is untenable. 6.76

Therefore, as stated before, **since no reflexive awareness exists, what is it that cognizes your,** Cittamātra's, ***dependent nature*? Since** the three—the **agent** that cuts the tree, the tree that is the **object** of the act, **and the action** of cutting—**cannot be identical, the claim that** cognition **apprehends itself is untenable.**

How this objection applies can be understood from [Jñānagarbha's] autocommentary on the *Two Truths*: [246]

> With respect to cognition itself, neither atoms nor nondual [cognition] appear as things, and conventions do not apply to anything that cannot appear.[630]

So in critiquing the notion of pure subjective experience—an inward-directed awareness devoid of dualistic perception—which is posited, in the manner explained above, as both as the known as well as the knower, Jñānagarbha raises the following objection. If one posits a knower-known distinction for something that, no matter how much one applies their mind, no appearance of distinction of knower and known can be conceived, absurd consequences follow, including that the agent, the object of the act, and the act itself all collapse into one. So the master Jñānagarbha regards the Cittamātra's reflexive awareness as having exactly the same status as the Śrāvaka school's notion of indivisible atom insofar as its existence or nonexistence is concerned. Even for [the purported] indivisible atom, [so long as it's material] it will have to occupy a spatial locus, and when its form appears [to the mind], there is no other way for it to be perceived than as composed of parts. Therefore these two concepts of the two schools—the [nondual] knower and known and the indivisible atom—remain mere philosophical postulations.

Jñānagarbha even rejects the idea that these two things appear [to the mind] but are not ascertained. For in his autocommentary on the *Two Truths* he writes:

> If you assert that while they do appear [to the mind], they cannot be ascertained, then what exactly are they? There can be no terms for such things. Since we cannot rely on your statement that it does appear, you are asking us to simply take your word for it.[631]

Thus Jñānagarbha says that the only proof [the opponent has] for his claim that it does appear [to the mind] is his swearing it to be so.

Also, through the reasoning found in the *Descent into Laṅkā Sutra*, reflexive awareness becomes untenable:

> Just as the blade of a sword
> does not cut itself, and just as
> the tip of a nail does not touch itself,
> the self-cognition of mind is the same.[632]

Stating that intrinsically existing dependent nature is akin to the son of a barren woman

This is as follows.

> If this entity that is your *dependent nature*,
> which has no arising and is uncognized, can still exist,

> why would something not fit to be existent,
> such as the son of a barren woman, offend you? 6.77

That the dependent nature does not arise from itself or from something other has already been explained. Also I have just shown how reflexive awareness establishing [such dependent nature] does not exist as well. So **if this entity that is your** *dependent nature*—**which has no** intrinsic **arising and is uncognized** by valid cognition—**can still exist** by virtue of its essence, then **why would something not fit to be existent, such as the son of a barren woman, offend you**, Cittamātra? In other words, why do you not accept its existence? You should. [247] So you, the Cittamātra, should go ahead and assert that there exists something called the son of a barren woman that transcends all conceptual elaborations, that is ineffable by its very nature, and that remains only within the sphere of experience of ārya's gnosis![633]

How the Cittamātra standpoint falls short on both levels of the two truths

This is as follows.

> Now if dependent nature does not exist in the slightest manner,
> what then can be the cause for conventional realities?
> Because you remain attached to something substantially real,
> you demolish all facts of worldly convention. 6.78

If dependent nature does exist through its intrinsic nature, what is stated in the lines "which is the cause of imputed things" (6.47b) and so on may be okay. **Now if dependent nature** possessing intrinsic reality **does not exist in the slightest manner, what then can be the cause** or the substantially real basis for the deluded **conventional realities**? Nothing at all. This [argument] demonstrates that because they assert the dependent nature to exist on the ultimate level, they [Cittamātra] fall short of the level of ultimate truth.

So it will turn out for the Cittamātra that whatever causes of worldly convention there may be, none exist by virtue of their essential natures. Alas, you, **because** you Cittamātra lack the competence of wisdom discriminating the final definitive truth, **you remain attached to** real existence of mental states alone as **substantially real** dependent nature. Yet without hardening the clay pot of dependent nature in a kiln, you have poured water-like inappropriate philosophical analysis into it. Thus through inferiority of your intellect and inappropriate reasoning, **you demolish** or destroy **all facts of worldly convention** that are established purely within the framework of everyday transaction, such as "Sit down," "Go there," "Do this," and so on. Similarly, you defy or undermine all such facts as the arising of feeling on the basis of perceiving external forms and external objects. Therefore, misfortune awaits you, Cittamātra; you will not attain the higher or excellent state of existence.

The argument that if external reality is rejected, [conventions] such as "Go there" become untenable indicates how these conventions are related to external reality. So this argument demonstrates how Cittamātra falls short on the level of the conventional truth. [248]

Therefore it is logical to follow Nāgārjuna's system alone

Those who remain outside the master Nāgārjuna's way,
they have no means for attaining true peace.
They have strayed from the truths of convention and of suchness,
and because of this failure, they will not achieve liberation. 6.79

The conventional truth is the means,
while the ultimate truth is its end.
Those who fail to know the distinction between the two
will enter wrong paths through false conceptualization. 6.80

Regarding **those who**—exposed to teachers who expound as definitive what is in fact provisional or false—have entered a system that has been constructed through someone's own conceptualization and fail to arrive at the Buddha's intention, they **remain outside the way** initiated by the noble **master Nāgārjuna.** For those who thus remain outside, **they have no** principal **means for attaining** the **true peace** of nirvana. Why? Because those who remain outside in such a manner **have** definitely **strayed from the truths of convention and of suchness**—that is, the ultimate truth. Once they fall short on the two truths, **they will not achieve liberation because of this failure** so long as this condition is not relinquished.

"Why is it," one might ask, "that falling short on the two truths means liberation is out of reach?" **Because** flawless positing of **conventional truth is the means** for realizing the ultimate truth as it is, **while** the realization of **ultimate truth is the end** resulting from these means. So **those who fail to know the distinction between the two** truths **will enter the wrong** or corrupt **paths through false conceptualization.** This [stanza] shows how until one has established a faultless system of the conventional truth, there is no realization of ultimate truth as it is. We should hence follow only the tradition initiated by Nāgārjuna.

To substantiate this point by reference to scripture, let me cite the *Meditative Absorption Definitely Revealing Suchness*:

> Not hearing it from another, the Knower of the World
> taught these two truths by himself.
> They are conventional truth and ultimate truth;
> nowhere does a third truth exist.[634]

This presents how the Buddha independently taught the two truths and how all objects of knowledge are encompassed within the category of the two truths. Then the sutra states:

> For the sake of engendering faith in bliss [249]
> in those beings journeying to the state of a sugata,
> the Conqueror has revealed the conventional truth;
> this is for the sake of helping people of the world.[635]

This stanza declares the [Buddha's] purpose in teaching the conventional truth. Next, the same sutra says:

> The six classes of beings revealed among sentient beings—
> hell beings, animals, and hungry ghosts,
> those of the demigod class, humans, and gods—
> the Lion among Humans labels these conventional truths.

> "Lower castes" and likewise "higher castes,"
> "wealthy households" and "poor households,"
> "laborer's class" and that of "servants,"
> the classes of "women," "men," and "neuters,"

whatever classification of beings there might be,
you, the Peerless One, have revealed them to be transient.
Having comprehended [their truth], you who are versed in
    conventions,
Knower of the World, you taught this [truth] to others.[636]

These lines indicate the way conventional truth was taught. Next, the sutra says:

Beings who delight in this [surface level of truth]
revolve in cyclic existence with eight worldly concerns:
gain and loss, pleasing and unpleasing,
praise and disparagement, pleasure and pain.

When they gain something, attachment for it arises;
when they do not gain, this too causes distress;
those not spoken of here should be known likewise.
Through these eight diseases, their minds are harmed.[637]

These lines show how clinging to this everyday conventional truth as real and delighting in it involves acting with eight worldly concerns and how, tormented by these, beings revolve in the cycle of existence. By presenting the first two worldly concerns, the sutra states how we should understand the remaining ones as well, those that are not mentioned explicitly.

Those who speak of this conventional truth as being the
    ultimate,
recognize them as having a flawed intellect.[638]

These lines explain how those who assert conventional truth, the six classes of beings, and so forth as being the ultimate—that is to say, as having true existence—we should recognize as having a distorted understanding. So these lines indicate how Buddhist schools that assert this have flawed philosophies.

Who speak of unattractive as attractive,
pain as joy, what is not self as self,
and what is impermanent as permanent—

who delight thus in these and grasp at signs,
should they ever hear the Sugata's words,
terrified, they will not comprehend and will shun them.

Having forsaken the Sugata's words,
they will experience relentless sufferings in the hells.
They seek happiness but inappropriately,
and so the childish will endure the eight types of suffering.[639]

These lines explain how those who are habituated to the four distortions, [250] as well as non-Buddhists tainted by doctrinal tenets affirming such distortions, would turn away were they to hear the Buddha's words. Because of this they will depart to the hell realms. Though they may search for the bliss of liberation, since it is through incorrect means, not only will they not attain liberation, they will instead be tormented by vast amounts of suffering.

Whosoever understands with undistorted mind
the teaching of the Benefactor of the World
will transcend all births, attaining true peace,
just like a snake that shuns its old skin.

All of these phenomena are devoid of intrinsic nature;
he who hears these words and experiences joy—
"emptiness," "signlessness," or the "ultimate"—
will attain the unexcelled enlightenment.

Conqueror, you saw the aggregates to be empty;
you saw the elements and sense bases to be likewise.
That our sense towns are devoid of signs,
O Sage, all of this you have seen as it is.[640]

Having stated how if one understands the meaning of the profound truth in an undistorted manner one will attain freedom from the cycle of existence, the sutra responds to the question "How does one gain such understanding?" by explaining that one will do so if one experiences joy when one hears that all phenomena are devoid of intrinsic nature and so on and then comprehends this truth. In brief, conventional truth was presented in the prior set of stanzas, and ultimate truth is presented here [in this set].

"Elements" refers to earth and so on; "sense bases" refers to [sensory objects such as] form, sound, and so on.

So how can there be liberation for those who lack the knowledge of conventional truths as mere designations and ultimate truth in terms of the absence of intrinsic existence?[641] Therefore those who propound consciousness only have entered only an erroneous path.

The presentation of conventional truth is the means; this is as stated in the *King of Meditation Sutra*:

> Reality, which is devoid of letters,
> who listens to it? Who teaches it?
> By superimposing onto what is unchanging,
> still some listen and some teach it.[642]

The first two lines of this stanza present how things do not exist on the ultimate level. So it is in relation to things devoid of letters on the ultimate level that through superimposition—that is, through conceptual designation—one comes to listen as well as teach about it. The Sanskrit term for "letter" is *akṣara*, which refers both to "letter" and to "unchanging." Here, however, it is more appropriate to render the phrase as "devoid of letters." Although the term *superimpose* often refers to exaggerating what *does not exist* as *existent* and what *is not* as *is*, we should not confine the meaning of the word to this alone. The term can also refer in a general sense to something posited on the basis of being imputed by conceptual thought. So it is by abiding in the conventional truth alone that the ultimate truth is revealed, and when one comprehends the ultimate truth on this basis, [251] then one attains the ultimate truth of nirvana. *Fundamental Wisdom* says:

> Without relying on the conventional,
> the ultimate truth cannot be taught;
> and without realizing the ultimate truth,
> nirvana cannot be attained.[643]

How refuting dependent nature is not similar to refuting worldly convention

[*Objection*:][644] If you Mādhyamikas say such inconsiderate things to us, we will not tolerate it. The only skill you display is in eliminating others' positions, and if in employing such skill, you eliminate the intrinsic existence of dependent nature on the ground that evidence does not support it, we too will eliminate conventions known to you by simply stating that they are untenable and employ the proofs used for refuting self-arising, arising from other, and so on.

[*Reply*:] Imagine someone robs you of wealth you accumulated since beginningless time through inconceivable hardship. If another person, pretending to be a friend to this robber, were to give him a poisonous meal and take back your stolen wealth for you, you would be happy. Like this, we are actually helping you by taking away the object of your grasping, the true existence of dependent nature. If in response you derive joy from harming us, this would be fine by us. On our part, we will take it as a compliment and as a good thing.

> The manner in which you assert your dependent nature
> we do not accept even on the conventional level.
> And yet to gain results for the sake of the world,
> we speak of things' existence even though they do not exist. 6.81

As to **the manner in which you**, Cittamātra, **assert your dependent nature** as something real and existing by virtue of its essence, such as is found in the line in *Thirty Verses* that says "For when one is not seen, the other isn't"[645]—[252] which you accept in your own system as autonomous and cognized by ārya's gnosis—**we**, for one, **do not accept** such intrinsic reality **even on a conventional level**. "What *do* you accept then?" you might ask. For me, **even though things** such as aggregates **do not exist** intrinsically, they are acknowledged within the framework of the everyday world alone. So it's **for the sake of the world** alone that **we speak of things' existence**.

There are two modes in which the aggregates and so on are posited from the perspective of worldly convention. One is the Madhyamaka's own positing of things on the conventional level, which is done so on the basis of acknowledging them from the perspective of valid conventional cognition but not done from the perspective of rational cognition [inquiring into the ultimate nature of things]. On some occasions, however, aggregates and so on *are* posited [in the scriptures] as intrinsic existents for specific purposes. But such assertions are not accepted as representing our own standpoint; they are acknowledged purely from the perspective of others. So refutation does not apply equally to these two [distinct] cases. Acknowledging things in such manner from the perspective of others is done **to gain results** or for a purpose. It is a skillful means to turn spiritual aspirants away from inferior philosophical views and to help gradually lead them to the realization of suchness.

The intention of this passage [of *Entering the Middle Way*] is certainly not to assert that every presentation is made from the perspective of others or to assert that we do not maintain any views in our system. That this cannot be the case can be discerned from the scripture Candrakīrti cites to substantiate here, the *Presenting the Three Vows Sutra*:

> It is the world that disputes with me; I do not dispute with the world. What is accepted in the world to exist, I too agree that it exists. What is accepted in the world to be nonexistent, I too agree that it does not exist.[646]

This is in fact the meaning of the following lines of the *Seventy Stanzas on Emptiness*, where Nāgārjuna states how all presentations, existence, nonexistence, and so on are posited from the point of view of conventions known to the world:

> Enduring, arising, and disintegration, existence and
>   nonexistence,
> inferiority, equality, and superiority—these the Buddha spoke
> in accordance with the conventions of the world
> and not according to final reality.[647]

[The root text then says:]

> Just as things do not exist for those arhats
> who have shunned the aggregates and abide in peace,
> if something does not exist from the perspective of the world,
> then even in terms of the everyday world, we do not say that it exists.
>   6.82

Just as all things of this conventional truth **do not exist for those arhats who have shunned the aggregates and abide in** the expanse of the **peace of** nirvana without residue, in the same manner, **if something does not exist from the perspective of the world**, then in that case, just as in the case of nirvana without residue, **we do not say that it exists even in terms of**, or from the perspective of, **the everyday world**. It is therefore only in dependence on worldly conventions that I accept the conventional truth; I do not assert it independently without being contingent on worldly conventions. [253]

First, it's the world alone that accepts this [conventional truth]. It is therefore on the basis of what has been accepted alone that [inappropriate claims] can be eliminated, and it would be legitimate as well to engage in such elimination. Such rejection cannot be from the Madhyamaka standpoint.[648] This is expressed in the following:

> If you think that the everyday world does not invalidate you,
> then, using [conventions of] the world, refute this [conventional
>   truth].
> You should thus enter into a dispute with the world,
> and we will follow whoever prevails from this. 6.83

On our part, given the tremendous hardship required to bring about the cessation of deluded perceptions pertaining to conventional truth in our own mental continuum, we will abide in the cultivation of the path. However, **if you think that the everyday world does not invalidate you**, then go ahead and **refute this conventional truth using [conventions of] the world** itself. And if you do succeed through your reasoning in refuting this, we too will side with you and be your ally. This said, since you will almost certainly be wounded by the world, we will not assist but remain neutral. **You should thus enter into a dispute with the world, and** in its aftermath, **we will follow whoever prevails from this**. If you win—and this is something we wish for—we will then follow you. If, however, the world defeats you, we will trust the world that possesses such great power. In view of all this, since the nonexistence of external reality is controverted by valid conventional cognition, you Cittamātra can never succeed in proving that there is no external reality.

[*Question*:] Does this mean that the Cittamātra reasoning, refuting external reality composed of indivisible atoms on the ground that such atoms do not exist, does not negate external reality composed of dimensionless particles?

[*Reply*:] I do not say that such a thing is not negated by valid cognition. Even though that kind of external reality is negated, this does not mean there is no external reality at all. We should understand in the same way how although temporally indivisible moments of consciousness and mental continua comprised of such moments are negated, this does not negate cognition itself.

In the opponent's view, when external reality composed of indivisible matter is negated, then sensory cognitions undeceived with respect to their perceptions are also negated. And since deluded sensory cognitions cannot posit facts, so the thinking goes, external reality itself comes to be negated. However, here in our system, we maintain that although deluded sensory cognition cannot posit a real object, such deluded cognition can in fact be a complementary factor for positing an unreal object. This is what Candrakīrti felt. This point is accepted by Āryadeva as well. In *Four Hundred Stanzas*, for instance, he states:

> "One exists" and "the other does not":
> this is neither in reality nor according to the world.[649]

He thus explains how a differentiation between external reality and consciousness with respect to their existence and nonexistence cannot be accepted according to the standpoint of either of the two truths. Making such discrimination is therefore not the view of the master Nāgārjuna either. [254]

15. How to Read the Sutras

How the word "only" in the statement about mind only does not reject external reality

This has three parts: (1) the intention of the mind-only statement in the *Ten Grounds Sutra*, (2) how external reality and the internal mind are equal with respect to existence or nonexistence, and (3) the intention of the mind-only statement in the *Descent into Laṅkā Sutra*.

The intention of the mind-only statement in the Ten Grounds Sutra

This has three parts: (1) establishing that the word "only" does not reject external reality by citing the *Ten Grounds Sutra*, (2) establishing this point also through other scriptures, and (3) establishing that the word "only" shows the primacy of mind.

Establishing that the word "only" does not reject external reality by citing the Ten Grounds Sutra

[*Opponent*:] You, Madhyamaka, remain divorced of actual proof or reasoning probing suchness, but because you fear being wounded by the world if you accept conventional truth, you have no choice but to accept the mind-only as well out of fear of being harmed by scripture. The *Ten Grounds Sutra* states, for example:

> He will think thus: "This world of three realms is mind only."[650]

[*Reply*:] To this we reply as follows. Say the Conqueror's words are like a field of precious lapis lazuli. Failing to recognize it as lapis lazuli, you who speak of consciousness as a real entity mistake it for water. So in your desire to fetch some water of real consciousness, you plunge into it the earthen pot of your intellect not yet hardened in a kiln. When as a result your intellect pot crumbles into a hundred pieces, you become an object of ridicule for those who recognize this fact. The meaning of the sutra, therefore, is not as it appears to your mind. What then, you may ask, is the meaning of the sutra? To explain this, we say:

> "The bodhisattva who is directly facing The Manifest
> realizes the threefold world to be merely consciousness";
> this statement is made to reject an eternal self or creator
> and to understand that mind alone is the creator. 6.84

This statement, "The bodhisattva on the sixth ground, **The Manifest—** who contemplates the omniscient gnosis and is **directly facing** the ultimate expanse—**realizes the threefold world to be merely consciousness,"** is made **to reject an eternal self or creator and to understand that mind alone,** a conventional reality, **is the creator.** Thus the bodhisattva understands the mind alone to be the creator of the world. [255] This point is expressed extensively in the *Ten Grounds Sutra* itself, such as in the following:

> The bodhisattva will thoroughly contemplate dependent origination in its sequential order. He will have the thought, "The suffering aggregates, this tree of suffering, these come into being merely with no creator or experiencer at all." He will then contemplate, "Because of clinging to an agent [a self], karmic acts come into being. Where there is no such agent, ultimately no karma will exist either." He will think thus, "This world of three realms is mind only. All of these twelve links of cyclic existence, which have been clearly distinguished and taught by the Tathāgata, are also dependent on this one thing, the mind.[651]

This sutra thus explains how such things exist as mere this or that with no creator and, when the meaning of "mind only" is explained, speaks of how the twelve links of dependent origination are dependent on the mind. Hence, the word "only" as found in this sutra does not negate external reality but rejects an agent that is other than the mind.

As for the opponent's thesis [being refuted here by Candrakīrti], it is the one found in the *Summary of the Great Vehicle*, where Asaṅga writes:

Here, the scripture is this. In the *Ten Grounds* the Blessed One states, "It is thus: this world of three realms is mind only."[652]

In presenting both scripture and reasoning to prove consciousness only, Asaṅga takes this [sutra passage] as his scriptural source. Similarly, in his autocommentary on the *Twenty Verses* too, Vasubandhu cites this same sutra and explains how the term "mind" must be understood to include the concomitant mental factors and how the word "only" rejects external reality.[653] Historically, it was Bhāviveka who first refuted [the Cittamātra reading of the scriptural statement] in the above manner; Candrakīrti undertook a similar refutation later.

Establishing this point also through other scriptures

Having explained how the word "only" in the mind-only statement rejects some other creator to be the meaning of the *Ten Grounds Sutra*, the text indicates how this very point is demonstrated by other scriptures as well:

> Therefore, to enhance the minds of the wise,
> the Omniscient One spoke in the *Descent into Laṅkā* sutra
> diamond-like words crushing the tīrthikas' lofty peaks;
> this was done to help get to the true intent. 6.85

[256] Since rejection of some other agent is what is meant by the word "only" in the *Ten Grounds Sutra*, **to enhance the minds of the wise** capable of realizing suchness, **in the *Descent into Laṅkā Sutra*** we find **diamond-like words** from **the Omniscient One crushing** the towering **lofty peaks** of inferior views present in the minds **of the tīrthikas**—views that assert self, primal substance, and so on as the agent creating the world. These words **were spoken** by the Buddha **to help get to the true intent** behind the mind-only statements found in other sutras as well. The "diamond-like [words]" refer to the following lines from the *Descent into Laṅkā Sutra*:

> "Person," "continuum," and "aggregates,"
> likewise "condition" and "atoms,"
> "primal substance" and "Īśvara, the creator"—
> these I have explained to be mind only.[654]

Thus the sutra states that none of these creators proposed by others, from the person to the creator Īśvara, is the agent; mind alone is the creator. To explain the meaning of this sutra, the text says:

> Based on their own treatises, the tīrthikas
> postulate such things as the person and so on.
> Seeing none of these to be the agent, the Buddha said
> that mind alone is the creator of the world. 6.86

So, of the various **things postulated by the tīrthikas** based on their doctrinal viewpoints presented in **their own treatises—the "person" and so on,** including the "continuum," the "aggregates," and so forth—**seeing none of these to be the agent, the Buddha said that mind alone is the creator of the world.**

The reference to "tīrthikas" in the root text should be understood in broad terms; even some followers of the Buddha postulate the "continuum" or the "aggregates" as being the [creator] agent. Alternately, one could say anyone who conceives such things as a "person" to be the agent does not qualify as a Buddhist. For, just like the tīrthikas, they have a distorted understanding of the Buddha's teaching. So the term *tīrthika* is a general, broad term. The *Precious Garland* too states:

> Those who assert "person" and "aggregates,"
> the Sāṃkhyas and the Aulūkyas,[655]
> and the Digambaras—ask if they speak
> of transcendence of existence and nonexistence.

> Therefore what the buddhas have taught,
> that which is immortal and profound
> and transcends existence and nonexistence—
> know this to be unique to his teaching.[656]

Thus Nāgārjuna says that among those who assert person and aggregates as possessing substantial reality, if any appear to speak of something that transcends the extremes of existence and nonexistence, ask them what it is. They will have nothing to say about it. Therefore, Nāgārjuna says, we should know that the teaching that transcends the extremes of existence and nonexistence is unique to the sublime Dharma, a distinctive feature that cannot be found in others' teachings.

[Here the *Commentary* writes:]

> As this cycle of existence has no beginning, why would inferior notions not have emerged in the past? In the future too, why would they not emerge? [257] Even in the present, some such as the white-clad renunciates appear to present aggregates and so on to be substantially existent.[657]

In some versions of Candrakīrti's text [in Tibetan], there is a difference in spelling.[658] In the Tibetan translation of Jayānanda's *Explanation of the Commentary*, however, one finds the phrase "the light-color-robed monk and so on,"[659] and he explains its meaning as referring to the monks of the Jaina school. In general, *renunciate* is an epithet of a meditator, so the phrase [in the *Commentary*] refers to the proponent of a Buddhist school known as the White-Clad Meditators, a school that asserts that substantially real aggregates are the agent.

Establishing that the word "only" shows the primacy of mind

Having shown how the rejection of an agent other than mind is the purpose of the word "only," it has been demonstrated that the word "only" does not negate external reality, the object of knowledge. Now the text presents a different explanation, based on stating the primacy of mind, of how it is impossible that external reality is being rejected [by the word "only"]:

> Just as the word *buddha* refers to
> "one who has blossomed into suchness," so the sutras
> speak of "mind only" because the mind is primary in the world.
> The meaning of such sutras is not that matter has no existence. 6.87

> For if the Buddha knew the world to be mind only
> and, on that basis, did engage in the rejection of matter,
> why then would the Great One proclaim in the same sutra
> that the mind was born from delusion and karma? 6.88

When **the word *buddha*** ("awakened and blossomed one") **refers to "the one who has blossomed into suchness,"** although first part of the name "awakened" is left implicit, the convention "buddha" is still used [as an epithet for such a person].[660] **Just so,** we should recognize that it is only **because the mind is primary** between the matter and mind **in the world** that the **sutras speak of** the world of three realms as being **"mind only,"** leaving implicit the second part of the phrase, which is "primary." In other words, this statement of "mind only" precludes form and so on as being primary in constituting the three realms. [258] **The meaning of such sutras is not** to state that mind alone exists intrinsically and to reject external reality and assert that **matter has no existence.**

So the meaning of the *Ten Grounds Sutra* must be accepted, without reservation, exactly according to how we have explained it. **For if,** in accord with your position, it were the case that **the Buddha knew the world** of the three realms to be intrinsically existent **mind only and, on that basis, did engage in the rejection of matter** in the *Ten Grounds Sutra*, in that case **why then would the Great One proclaim** in the **same** *Ten Grounds Sutra* **that the mind** or consciousness **was born from karma and delusion,** or ignorance? For he stated, "Conditioned by ignorance, volition arises; and conditioned by volition, consciousness arises." Such statements will become untenable.

So the Buddha stated in the *Ten Grounds Sutra* that consciousness is an effect of ignorance and volition; he did not say it has intrinsic existence. Even if [in general] the Buddha had taught [elsewhere] that consciousness is both dependently originated and intrinsically existent, given that it is inconceivable for a faultless speaker to adopt both of these positions as his own, we would have to recognize that he adopted such statements for others' sake, to help lead other spiritual trainees. Here is the reason why both positions cannot be the Buddha's own standpoint. Were consciousness to exist by virtue of its own essence, it would not be dependent upon ignorance and volition. The fact is, consciousness *is* dependent upon such factors, and as such, it has no existence by virtue of its own essence. It is certain, therefore, that in no possible manner does consciousness possess intrinsic existence. So just like floating hairs being perceived by someone with an eye disorder, we should understand that [an intrinsically real consciousness] is something that exists when the conditions are present for such distortion and does not exist when such conditions for distortion are absent. This, then, is the understanding.

That the sequential presentation of dependent origination shows how, when there is ignorance, the condition for distortion, consciousness, comes to exist, and how, when there is no ignorance, consciousness will come to cease, is stated through presenting the reverse order of dependent origination. Having thus presented, the sutra makes extensive statements, such as the following:

> Thus volition possesses faults of multiple ill consequences, and when it is discerned with discriminative awareness as devoid of essence, as unborn, and unceasing . . .[661]

So what sane person would, after seeing these statements in this sutra, conceive of consciousness as substantially existent? No one would. To do so would be because of philosophical biases grasping at true existence. The *Sixty Stanzas of Reasoning* also states:

> Since the Buddha has stated
> that the world is conditioned by ignorance,
> why is it not reasonable [to assert]
> that this world is [a result of] conceptualization?
>
> Since it comes to an end
> when ignorance ceases, [259]
> why does it not become clear then
> that it was conjured by ignorance?[662]

The point being made here is that if something were to exist by virtue of its own essence, it would exist as a true mode of being. That is, when delusory perception ceases, it should become clearer and clearer rather than becoming undone altogether.

To make the point that the mind is primary, the text says:

> It is the mind that constructed the vast diversity
> of both the domain of sentient beings and their universe as well.
> The Buddha said that all beings are born of karma;
> there is no karma without the mind. 6.89
>
> Even though matter does exist,
> it has no status of a creator like the mind,

so what is being denied is a creator other than the mind;
it is not that matter is being negated. 6.90

The domain of sentient beings obtains its reality through karma and afflictions accumulated by individual beings themselves, while **the vast diversity of their universe,** their container [the environment], is **constructed** or produced by the collective karma gathered by **the mind** of the sentient beings. This latter, container world spans from the wind-mandala base up to [the highest heavenly realm of] Akaniṣṭha.[663] As for the remarkable diversity of features, such as the brilliance of a peacock's feathers, these arise as products of the unique karma of these sentient beings alone. In contrast, the diversity of petal shapes and colors that exist among lotuses are produced by collective karma of the sentient beings. We should extend this same understanding to other cases [of diversity] as well. It is stated:

> It's owing to the power of sentient beings
> that volcanoes erupted in their time;
> so likewise weapons and jewel trees are found
> in the hells and in the higher realms.[664]

That these two domains [the universe and sentient beings] are produced by two types of karma—collective and not collective—is explained in the Cittamātra texts as well. So even according to Cittamātra, it is not the case that there is no container world.

Thus **the Buddha said that all beings are born of karma**; and furthermore, **there is no karma without the mind,** for it is only with mind that karma is accrued. So karma too is contingent upon the mind.

Thus, through statements with phrases such as "no agent," "no experiencer," the *Ten Grounds Sutra* shows how the word "only" rejects some other agent; and with statements of how all twelve links are dependent on one factor, the mind, the sutra demonstrates how the term "only" indicates the mind to be primary. The first explanation is from a negative standpoint, and the second from an affirmative perspective. In brief, it is the mind that is the primary cause of the activity of sentient beings, and factors other than the mind are not principal. Therefore the mind, not matter, is posited in the sutras as primary. Therefore, **even though matter does exist** and is indeed accepted, **it has no status of a creator** of beings **like the mind. So what is** being denied or negated is a creator other than the mind; it is not that external matter is being negated.

Some schools, such as the Sāṃkhya, [260] assert primal substance to be the creator, while some Buddhists assert the mind to be such an agent. In that matter is not the agent, there is no dispute. So, when examining things such as primal substance that others suspect or conceive to be the agent, the mind alone, which is observed to have the characteristics of an agent in the conventional sense, is spoken of as the agent to eliminate things such as primal substance, which actually do not possess the characteristics of being an agent. When the mind is thus spoken of as the agent, primal substance and the like are eliminated. So one could say that primal substance and so on have been expelled and that the disputed territory has been conquered. Say two kings are competing to rule the same region. If one loses and is expelled but happens to find his own land [to rule elsewhere], then because they both found what they need, ordinary people will not suffer harm. Similarly, here too, since both [matter and mind] are needed, and furthermore since there is no harm in accepting matter, we should conclude that matter too does exist.

How external reality and the internal mind are equal with respect to existence or nonexistence

> While remaining within the truth of the everyday world,
> all five aggregates known to the world do exist.
> When we speak of the arising of the gnosis of suchness,
> then, for the yogi, these five aggregates will be no more. 6.91
>
> So if there is no matter, do not hold that there is mind,
> and if there *is* mind, do not hold that there is no matter. 6.92ab

Thus, just as explained above, while remaining within the truth of the everyday world, external realities such as the aggregates are known to the world; thus all five aggregates do exist. However, when we speak of the arising of the gnosis directly perceiving suchness, then, for the yogi who is in such meditative equipoise, within his own perspective, these five aggregates such as form will be no more. Given this, if one asserts there is no matter, then do not hold that there is mind, and if, on the other hand, one indeed asserts there *is* mind, the internal, then do not hold that there is no matter, the external. In other words, if you conceive external matter to be nonexistent because it is found to be so when probed by reasoning searching for the true referent of designations, [261] then in that case, you will have to realize that the inner, the mind, also lacks existence because the existence of both outer and inner lack such logical evidence. Also, given that both are acknowledged by the world, if you [Cittamātra] conceive the mind to be existent, you must in that case admit matter as well.

The matter being referred to here, in relation to "nonexistence of matter" in the context of Cittamātra's differentiation between matter and mind with respect to their existence and nonexistence, is indeed matter of external reality. One reads, for example, the lines "[perceptions] such as the simple perception of blue / come from their own seeds with nothing outer to grasp" (6.63). In the relevant commentary too, Candrakīrti writes, "With no existence of external matter such as blue . . ."[665] Thus the negation of matter is qualified with the term "external." Again, in the *Commentary* one reads:

> Having stated how the term "only" cannot reject the object of knowledge, now to present how it is impossible to negate external objects on the grounds of other explanations as well . . .[666]

So in demonstrating how a rejection of matter is not the intent of the sutra, Candrakīrti defines the matter that is being denied [by Cittamātra] as external reality. Also, if one reads literally Candrakīrti's phrase "Having stated how the term 'only' cannot negate the object of knowledge," one would also have to say that he sees Cittamātra as asserting that the word "only" in "mind only" negates the object of knowledge itself.

Furthermore, in presenting the arguments for foundation consciousness, *Summary of the Great Vehicle* says:

> With respect to the appropriation of physical organs by [fetus] when the fluids have already merged, it is incorrect to assert that there exists no fruitional effect consciousness that is separate from that [fetus].

And:

> The emergence of consciousness and name-and-form, which function in a mutually supporting manner, like a beam and the

house, would not be possible if there were no fruitional effect consciousness.[667]

To assert that Cittamātra does not accept material phenomena at all would directly contradict these above statements. For those who assert so appear to maintain that if one accepts material phenomena, one must admit external reality as well. So please do not speak contrary to what is in fact their statement—namely, "Although we accept the arising of name-and-form conditioned by consciousness, we do not accept external reality." In any case, when it comes to the presentation of the unique tenets of Cittamātra, there appear to be many people who speak in such contradictory terms.

With respect to scriptures too, we should understand in the following manner how both external objects and internal cognitions are treated equally insofar as their existence or nonexistence is concerned. The root text reads:

> In the wisdom sutras the Buddha rejects them equally,
> but in the Abhidharma he speaks of the existence of both. 6.92cd

> Even after you have undone the structure of the two truths,
> the substantial reality you assert remains unproven.
> Thus you should know that from their very outset,
> phenomena are unborn in reality but born in terms of the world. 6.93

With respect to all five aggregates such as form, [262] **the Buddha in the wisdom sutras rejects them equally**—that is, he negates the intrinsic existence of all five aggregates. One reads, for example, "Subhūti, form is empty of intrinsic existence . . . consciousness is empty of intrinsic existence."[668] **But in the Abhidharma**, on the other hand, **he speaks of the existence of** all five aggregates equally in terms of their unique and common characteristics and so on. Therefore, since it has been established through scripture and reasoning that both external reality and inner experience are equally nonexistent on the ultimate level and equally existent on the conventional level, the opponent [Cittamātra] will have torn down **the structure of the two truths. Even after you have undone** [the two truths] in such manner, Cittamātra, **the substantial reality you assert**—namely, the *dependent nature*—**remains unproven.** Why is this so? Since substantially real dependent nature has been refuted many times before, your effort will be pointless. To avoid undermining the system of the two truths, you need to accept that [dependent nature] does not exist on the ultimate level but on the conventional level. Thus, Candrakīrti states in accordance with the stages of explanations offered above, **you should know that phenomena are, from their very outset, unborn in reality but born in terms of** everyday conventions of **the world.** This [passage] indicates how the nonarising of things is accepted on the ultimate level while their arising is maintained on the conventional level. Therefore it is essential to qualify what is being negated.

The intention of the mind-only statement in the Descent into Laṅkā Sutra

This has two parts: (1) how the statement about mind only with no external reality is provisional and (2) how to recognize the provisional and definitive meanings of the sutras.

How the statement about mind only with no external reality is provisional

This has two parts: (1) showing through scripture how such a statement is provisional and (2) showing through reason how such statement is provisional.

Showing through scripture how such a statement is provisional

This has two parts: (1) the actual point and (2) demonstrating that other similar sutras are also provisional.

The actual point

[*Opponent:*] You may explain the meaning of the *Ten Grounds Sutra* in the above terms, but there exist other scriptures, such as the *Descent into Laṅkā Sutra*:

> What appears as external does not exist;
> it is mind that is perceived as diverse things.
> What seem to be a "body," "resources," and "habitat"
> I have stated to be mind only.[669] [263]

Here, "body" refers to sense bases such as the eyes, which are physical; "resources" are the five sense objects such as form, sound, and so on; "habitat" refers to the container world. Since nothing external that is separate from the mind exists, when the mind alone appears as body, resources, and habitat, they are perceived as objects and things such as body and so on— something external and separate from consciousness. Therefore the three realms of existence are mind only.

[*Reply:*] To state that this sutra too is a figurative teaching, the text says:

> The sutras that state what are perceived as external do not exist,
> and it is the mind that is perceived in diverse forms.
> Such statements are intended for those extremely attached to forms,
> to help such people turn away from matter; so it is only provisional.
>   6.94

The intention of **the sutras that state** that **what are perceived as external do not exist** and that **it is the mind that is perceived in diverse forms** is this: **Such statements are intended for those** beings who, because they are **extremely attached to** material **forms**, act [in the world] with lust for things, with anger, with conceit, and so on, and who have thus lost their freedom and whose forceful clinging inclines them toward grave negative deeds and makes them fall short in accumulating merit and wisdom. So just like [meditation on] skeletons taught to help the lustful counter their attachment to external forms, likewise, **to help such people to turn away from afflictions** conditioned by attachment to **matter**, even though it is not the actual truth, the Buddha spoke of "mind only." This is how we should understand.

One might ask "On what basis do we understand this scripture to be provisional and not definitive?" [To respond, the text says:]

> The Buddha himself stated this to be only provisional,
> and reasoning too proves it to be only provisional. 6.95ab

As for the statement that "There is no external reality and it is mind only," **the Buddha himself stated this to be provisional** in meaning, **and reasoning too proves it to be only provisional.**

So with regard to the word "only" in the context of "mind only" in the [*Laṅkā Sutra*] lines "What appears as external does not exist" and so on, this master [Candrakīrti] does not interpret it the same way he did the *Ten*

Grounds Sutra—that is, that the word "only" does not reject external reality but an agent other than the mind. Instead, Candrakīrti acknowledges that here [in the *Laṅkā Sutra*] the word does reject external reality, but he says the statement is provisional in meaning.

The great master Bhāviveka, however, interprets even this *Laṅkā Sutra* statement as indicating how the mind arises assuming the likeness of body, resources, and habitat as if colored by their shadow-like forms. He understands the phrase "What appears as external does not exist" as negating the view that cognition perceives [objects] without an aspect [or mental image].[670] Thus Bhāviveka maintains that the term "only" does not reject external reality [even in this *Laṅkā Sutra* passage].[671] [264]

Demonstrating that other similar sutras are also provisional

> As for other sutras that may be of same type,
> they too are indicated by this scripture to be provisional. 6.95cd

Not only is the statement about the existence of mind only and the nonexistence of external reality in the lines "What appears as external does not exist . . ." provisional in meaning, **as for other sutras that may be of same type** as the one already mentioned and held by Cittamātra as definitive, **they too are indicated by this scripture** cited below **to be provisional** in meaning.[672] Here the *Commentary* states:

> What are those sutras of same kind? They are the statements found in *Unraveling the Intent Sutra*, where in presenting the three forms of identitylessness, it speaks of the nonexistence of imputed nature and the existence of dependent nature. Likewise, there are statements such as:
>
> > The appropriating consciousness is deep and subtle;
> > all seeds spring forth from it like a flowing river;
> > to conceive it as self would be inappropriate;
> > so I have not taught this to the childish.[673]

(1) In that sutra, a differentiation is made between the imputed nature devoid of existence by virtue of intrinsic characteristic and the dependent nature existing by virtue of such intrinsic characteristic. In that

Cittamātra system, existence by virtue of intrinsic characteristic remains impossible for such imputations as the two selfhoods superimposed on persons and phenomena based on their identity and attributes, but many of the imputations pertaining to identity and properties of things do exist [on the relative level]. In the sutra itself, although both dependent nature and perfected nature are stated to possess existence by virtue of intrinsic characteristic, the reason why only dependent nature is mentioned in the *Commentary* [in the passage cited above] is because dependent nature is the primary object of dispute between Madhyamaka and Cittamātra when it comes to the question of true existence or its lack. This is because the dependent nature is the designative basis for the imputed nature, while the perfected nature is necessarily defined on the basis of dependent nature as well. Candrakīrti's tradition maintains that this kind of differentiation [made in *Unraveling the Intent Sutra*] is only provisional in meaning.

(2) Further, there is in that sutra the presentation of eight classes of consciousness, where it speaks of foundation consciousness that is separate from the six classes of engaging consciousness, as in the passage that begins "The appropriating consciousness." This statement too is to be interpreted as provisional in meaning. And if there is no foundation consciousness, there cannot be [the seventh], the afflicted mental consciousness, either.[674] The words "and so on" [in the *Commentary* on this verse] indicate the following two: (3) the rejection of external reality in that sutra, and (4) statements about the ultimacy of all three vehicles. [265] Thus, altogether, there are four types of statements [in *Unraveling the Intent Sutra*] that need to be interpreted here as provisional in their meaning.

If we fail to cultivate a decisive understanding of this issue [of how to interpret certain scriptural statements as provisional], we will comprehend neither Madhyamaka nor Cittamātra thought in general, and more specifically, we will fail to appreciate the unique standpoints of this tradition [of Candrakīrti]. Seeing this, I have explained these in detail in *Differentiating the Provisional and Definitive Meanings*.[675]

The following specific phrases in *Unraveling the Intent Sutra*, as cited in Asaṅga's *Summary of the Great Vehicle*, are the ones that state the nonexistence of external reality:

> "O Blessed One, is the image that is the object of concentration different from the mind or not?"

The Blessed One replied: "Maitreya, it is not different."

"Why is it not different?"

"Because consciousness is defined purely in terms of cognition of its object, so I have stated."[676]

This tradition [of Candrakīrti] interprets all four types of sutra passages mentioned above as provisional; it does not differentiate among them, as some do,[677] interpreting some as provisional and accepting others as definitive.

As for the teaching about there being three ultimate vehicles, given that Nāgārjuna himself established the finality of only one vehicle in his *Compendium of Sutras*,[678] thinking that this can be understood from there, Candrakīrti did not address it here in his *Commentary*. With respect to the remaining three [types of sutra passages] that establish mind only to possess intrinsic existence and deny external reality, the following passage from the *Descent into Laṅkā Sutra* is the scriptural source revealing them to be provisional in meaning:

> Just as to a patient suffering from illness,
> a physician administers medicine,
> likewise for the sake of sentient beings,
> the Buddha taught mind only.[679]

Medicine cannot be administered to specific patients according the personal inclination of the physician; it must conform to the nature of the illness of the patients. In the same way, it is explained, the Buddha's teaching on mind only is also not given in accordance with the Buddha's own personal viewpoint; it is given in accordance with the mental dispositions of the spiritual trainees. In this way, we recognize the former scriptural statement [about mind only] to be provisional.

Following the passage "Just as to a patient suffering from illness . . ." cited in the *Commentary*, Candrakīrti writes, "Likewise, the Blessed One states in the sutra . . ." and cites [extensively] from the *Descent into Laṅkā Sutra* up to "How then can one attain full awakening?"[680] These passages are the scriptural sources that indicate how foundation consciousness, which Cittamātra hold to be definitive, is in fact provisional.

In his *Explanation of the Commentary*, Jayānanda says that the phrase "Likewise . . ."[681] has the following meaning. Just as the [Buddha's] statements about permanent enduring essence is provisional, likewise the

[Buddha's] teaching of mind only is shown to be provisional.[682] This is a distorted explanation. [266] For the *Commentary* itself makes it clear that the meaning must be understood in terms of how the teaching of mind only is provisional."[683] So just as the [*Laṅkā Sutra*] lines "Just as to a patient suffering from illness . . ." explain the teaching of mind only to be provisional, in the same manner, the statement about the provisionality of [the teaching of] permanent enduring essence proves that the teaching of foundation consciousness in the *Unraveling the Intent Sutra* is not literal. For this, however, one must first recognize that the teaching of an eternal immutable essence is not literal. Here, the *Descent into Laṅkā Sutra* states:

> The sutra that is taught [purely] in conformity with the mental dispositions of sentient beings is erroneous with respect to its content; it's not a discourse on suchness. For example, not being water, a mirage deceives those animals that take it for water. In the same manner, the teaching thus taught will please only the childish; it is not a discourse that will delight the gnosis of āryas. You should therefore follow after the truth and not be attached to words.[684]

And the same sutra raises the following question:

> Mahāmati asks: "In the sutras you spoke of a tathāgata essence that is naturally luminous, primordially pure, and endowed with the thirty-two exemplary marks of an ārya existing within the bodies of all sentient beings. You say that, like a precious jewel wrapped in a dirty rag, it is covered by the rags of aggregates, elements, and sense bases and has thus become tainted. If you speak of such an essence that is eternal, enduring, and immutable, how is this any different from the tīrthika's proposed self?"[685]

In responding to this, [the Buddha] points out that, since such a teaching is not literal, it is not at all similar to the tīrthika's self. The Buddha explains that the *intended purport*[686]—what was actually intended when such [an essence] was taught—is the selflessness of phenomena in terms of emptiness, signlessness, and wishlessness. The *purpose* for teaching the existence of such an eternal, enduring, and immutable essence is to help gradually lead the following classes of people to suchness: (1) the childish who shun selflessness out of fear, (2) the tīrthikas who are attached to propositions of self, and (3) those who were habituated to such views in past [lives]. So, the sutra states, present and future bodhisattvas must not cling to it as a self. Since to espouse such a view literally would be no different from clinging to the tīrthika's self, the intended meaning [of the sutra] is not to grasp at its literal meaning. The *explicit objection* against the literal reading of the sutra is this: to espouse it literally would be no different from espousing the tīrthika's self. As I have already explained these points extensively elsewhere, I will not elaborate further here.[687] [267]

In the *Commentary*:

> Again in that sutra it states, "Mahāmati, this [truth] contained within the scriptures of all the buddhas has the character of emptiness, nonarising, nonduality, and absence of intrinsic existence."[688]

After citing this, Candrakīrti says:

> Having therefore clearly elucidated, on the basis of this scripture, how all such similar sutras accepted as definitive by Cittamātra are in fact provisional in their meaning...[689]

"Such similar sutras" does not refer to the two passages of the *Descent into Laṅkā Sutra* that have been just cited. Both of those segments are not accepted by Cittamātra as definitive. Furthermore, the *Commentary* already explicitly explained these ["similar sutras" to be passages] from the *Unraveling the Intent Sutra*. As to what is being referred to in "on the basis of this scripture," Jayānanda's *Explanation* identifies it with a section in the *Ten Grounds Sutra* pertaining to the contemplation of dependent origination that negates an agent [other than mind].[690] This is totally incorrect. The rejection of such an agent is presented as the reason explaining how the term "only" in the statement "mind only" in the *Ten Grounds Sutra* does not negate external reality; it is not a reason explaining that the negation of external reality is provisional.

Thus three scriptural citations are indicated in the root text in the line "They too are indicated by this scripture to be provisional" (6.95d). Of these, the four-line [passage of the *Laṅkā Sutra*] "Just as to a patient suffering from illness" and so on demonstrates the provisional nature of mind only with its rejection of external reality; the scripture that reveals the provisionality of permanent enduring essence is the one that demonstrates the provisional nature of foundation consciousness. How does the provisionality of permanent enduring essence establish foundation consciousness to be provisional? The *Densely Arrayed Sutra* states:

> The various realms are foundation consciousness;
> the excellent tathāgata essence is this as well;
> the tathāgatas indicate this essence
> with the words "foundation consciousness."
> That this essence is expressed as foundation consciousness,
> this the feeble-minded does not even know.[691]

In the *Descent into Laṅkā Sutra* too we read: "The tathāgata essence, which is expressed as foundation consciousness, together with seven classes of consciousness . . ."[692] Thus these two are said on numerous occasions to be synonymous. This said, given that one is characterized as permanent and the other as impermanent, it cannot be the literal senses of the two terms that are being shown to be equivalent. Nevertheless, since foundation consciousness was taught on the basis of exactly the same intended purport underlying the teaching of essence, so from the perspective of their intended meaning, the two are synonymous and share the same reference. Therefore, by demonstrating the first [passage here] to be provisional, the latter too is established as provisional. The *Commentary* states:

> Because it leads [beings to enter] the nature of all entities, [268]
> we should understand that the words "foundation conscious-
> ness" refer to emptiness alone.[693]

Thus it is by conveying well with [the scriptural citations] how the teaching of permanent enduring essence is provisional that we comprehend how that same scriptural citation [from the *Laṅkā Sutra*] reveals foundation consciousness to be provisional too.

Immediately following the passage "Mahāmati, this [truth] contained within the scriptures of all the buddhas . . . character of emptiness . . ."[694] it reads in that same sutra, "Whatever sutra it may be, comprehend this meaning alone to be contained in it."[695] This is the scriptural citation that demonstrates the provisional nature of the teaching that differentiates between the first two natures with respect to their existence or nonexistence by virtue of intrinsic character.

Showing through reason how such a statement is provisional

To elucidate through reasoning how the statement about "mind only" is provisional, the text says:

> Once cognizable objects are shown to be no more
> then negation of cognition is easily obtained, the buddhas said.
> Thus if there is no object, cognition is easily negated as a consequence;
> so the buddhas first negated the objects of cognition. 6.96

As a skillful means to help lead them to [the truth of] suchness, [the buddhas] first expose those with good stores of merit to discourses on the practice of generosity and the like. In the same manner, with respect to those trainees who do not have the capacity to realize the full meaning of the profound truth right from start, the buddhas lead them toward the realization of no intrinsic existence gradually. To such [trainees], **once cognizable objects,** external reality, **are first shown to be no more, then negation of** intrinsically existing **cognition is easily obtained,** so **the buddhas** have **said.** This being so, the absence of the cognizable—in other words, negating external reality from the outset—is a means to help induce full realization of selflessness. **So the buddhas first** taught the **negation of** external **objects of cognition** alone; for **if there is no object**—that is, if the selflessness of external reality has been understood—**cognition is easily negated as a consequence;** that is to say, the selflessness of consciousness will be easily established.

Among those who have awareness of no intrinsic existence of external reality, some will realize no intrinsic existence of cognition on their own, while others will realize this on the basis of a brief explanation by another. That the statement about the nonexistence of external reality and the intrinsic existence of cognition are provisional is clearly stated in the *Commentary on the Awakening Mind* as well:

> "All of this is but one's mind":
> that which was stated by the Able One [269]
> is to alleviate the fear of the childish;
> it is not [a statement] of final truth.[696]

Āryadeva states this explicitly in his *Compendium of the Heart of Gnosis* as well.[697]

How to recognize the provisional and definitive meanings of the sutras

Those with intelligence should present other provisional scriptures, which do not explicitly teach suchness in its entirety, along these same lines. To state this, the text says:

> Thus having understood this account of the scriptures,
> understand those sutras that present what is not true suchness
> as provisional and interpret them accordingly,
> and know those that bear on emptiness are definitive. 6.97

Thus having understood this account of the provisional and definitive status of the **scriptures** in terms explained above, you should **understand** all **those sutras that present** or have as their content or subject matter **what is not true suchness**—those that teach provisional truths and do not explicitly elucidate dependent origination characterized in terms of no arising and so on—**as provisional and interpret them accordingly.** Recognize [such teachings] as being similar to those that serve as conditions for later entering the realization of the emptiness of intrinsic existence.

Hymn to the World Transcendent states, for example:

> The great elements are not perceived by the eye,
> so how can their derivatives be perceived by the eye?
> Speaking of material form in this manner,
> you clearly prevent grasping at form.[698]

The sutras also state that "the meaning of impermanence is nonexistence."[699]

The way in which the first citation presents logical reason is this: The Buddha taught in the Abhidharma that the four elements are tactile phenomena and are thus not visible objects of the eyes, while their derivative, the visible form, *is* a visible object. While one must accept both of these points, when it comes to presenting their suchness, one recognizes that were these phenomena to exist by virtue of their own essence, there would be this consequence: either one has to admit that the four elements are perceivable by the eye [just as the derived object is] or that the object, the visible form, is not perceivable by the eye [just as its constitutive subtle elements are not]. When one comes to appreciate this problem, one will then understand that the earlier [Abhidharma] statements do not present true suchness. In this way, one will realize their suchness anew and understand the earlier [Abhidharma] statements to be a means of leading to that suchness.

The second citation [on the meaning of impermanence being nonexistence] shows how the arising and disintegrating of things indicate the absence of intrinsic existence. Regarding those sutras that contain the truth of emptiness of intrinsic existence of persons and phenomena—that is, **those that bear on emptiness** and explicitly present this truth as their subject matter—**know** that those **are definitive** in their meaning. [270]

For instance, the *King of Meditations Sutra* states:

> Through emptiness as taught by the Tathāgata,
> the specificity of the definitive sutras will be known.
> Where "sentience," "person," and "individual" are mentioned,
> these are known to be provisional in meaning.[700]

"The specificity of sutras" indicates their distinction from the provisional sutras. The reference to "person" and so on are only examples; it also indicates those [scriptures that speak of] the existence of an agent, the object of an action, as well as the acts. This [citation from *King of Meditations Sutra*] is then a scriptural source for differentiating sutras into the two classes of provisional and definitive meaning.

Again the same sutra states:

> In the thousandfold world systems,
> all the teachings I have taught
> consist of different words but one meaning,
> but this [one truth] cannot be uttered.
>
> When you contemplate this one thing,
> you will be meditating on all [other teachings].
> So the numerous teachings of all the buddhas,
> all those that have been taught,
> are about the selflessness of all phenomena.
> If a person versed in meaning

trains in this essential point,
it won't be hard to find the Buddha's attributes.[701]

The first four lines, beginning with "In the thousandfold world systems," indicate that of all those sutras that have been taught, those that explicitly elucidate ultimate truth directly engage with true suchness; and those that do not present ultimate truth—the provisional ones—even they engage with suchness indirectly. So they have the same meaning with respect to engaging with the ultimate truth. And given that those training on the path at the beginner's level can never discover all the scriptures that exist throughout the universe, they should inquire into true suchness on the basis of whatever sutra is at hand. This is how we should read the passage. This can be discerned from the fact that this passage is cited to substantiate the point that even those sutras that do not explicitly teach suchness should be explained as conditions for approaching true suchness.

The two lines beginning "When you contemplate this one thing" indicate that if, on the basis of excellent understanding, one meditates upon the suchness of one subject, this is like meditating upon the suchness of all other phenomena. Thus it is not necessary to meditate individually upon the suchness of each and every specific phenomenon. As to how when one meditates upon [the suchness of] one entity, this constitutes meditating upon [the suchness of] all entities, this is explained by the three lines beginning "So the numerous teachings of all the buddhas." The fact that the sutra identifies selflessness of phenomena to be that one entity should not be understood as saying that only one single practice is adequate when it comes to the domain of vast practices [as well].

Candrakīrti says that, just as the *Candraprabha Sutra*[702] presents the method of defining the provisional and definitive nature of the scriptures, we should also appreciate the extensive presentations found in sutras such as *Teachings of Akṣayamati.* I have already explained these points exhaustively in my *Differentiating the Provisional and Definitive Meanings.*[703] The *Commentary*'s statement "One point I will explain though"[704] [271] indicates that he will explain briefly how to respond to the following question: "If you interpret the explanation of the three natures found in *Unraveling the Intent Sutra* as provisional, how do you define these three natures within your own system?"

[Candrakīrti continues:]

For example, the snake is a false construct in relation to a coiled rope because there is no such snake in that rope. In relation to an actual snake, however, it is established as real because it's not an imputation of something that is not there. Likewise, intrinsic or true nature too remains a construct—an imputation of something that does not exist—in relation to the conditioned dependent phenomena. For as *Fundamental Wisdom* says:

> Intrinsic nature is not fabricated;
> it's not dependent on others.[705]

Thus the true nature cannot be something produced. This intrinsic nature, which is imputed in relation to the reflection-like causally produced world of dependent origination—the things we can perceive and observe right here and now—within the sphere of the buddha's gnosis seeing the way things really are, represents actual reality, the true nature. There, it is not an imputation of something that is not there. This is because the buddha directly perceives the true nature alone without touching the causally produced things themselves. Having fully realized this nature, he is called an awakened one.[706]

As to how [such a gnosis] does not touch [the causally produced entities themselves], this will be analyzed later.

Candrakīrti then writes, "Having thus understood the presentation of the three natures, one should explain the intended meaning of the scriptures."[707] So, through such mode of exposition, we should discern the intention behind the presentation of three natures as found in the "Questions of Maitreya" chapter as well.[708] We should, on this [same] basis, also understand how the stated meaning underlying the presentation of three natures in the *Unraveling the Intent Sutra* is provisional in meaning. In fact, what Cittamātra takes to be the imputed nature—the subject-object duality imputed with dependent nature as its basis—needs to be critically examined. For the two factors, subject and object, are in fact dependent phenomena, and apart from these two, no other [third class of] dependent phenomena exists. As for the presentation of three natures in the "Questions of Maitreya" chapter as well as the presentation of three natures according to the *Unraveling the Intent Sutra*, I have explained these exhaustively in my *Differentiating the Provisional and Definitive Meanings.*[709] [272]

16. Refuting Arising from Both and from No Cause

Refuting arising from both self and other

The Jainas propound arising from both poles—self-arising and arising from other. So when a clay pot emerges from factors such as a lump of clay, a kneading stick, a spinning wheel, threads, water, and the potter, Jainas think that since the clay pot comes into being only in the nature of clay, it arises from itself. And given that factors other than clay, such as the activity of the potter, are engendering causes of the clay pot, it arises from something other than itself too. And just as with external things, inner experiences also arise from both self and other.

Jainas present nine categories of reality: (1) *life force*, referred to as "person" or "self"; (2) *faculties* and so on that are other than the life force; (3) *dharma* that helps attain higher rebirth and definite goodness [liberation]; (4) *opposite of dharma*, which leads to bondage; (5) *pollutant afflictions*; (6) *vows* that prevent immorality; "and so on,"[710] which include (7) *happiness*, (8) *suffering*, and (9) *cohering force*, which both arises from cognition and serves as the cause of cognition.

Jainas assert that a person—called, say, Maitreya—has taken birth in this life because he existed in past lives endowed with life force, and hence he is self-arisen, for Maitreya and his life force are not different. Life force possesses mobility, moving from one birth to another, they say; it travels into such transmigrations as those of the celestial realms. However, since Maitreya arises also from other factors—from his parents, from the wholesome and unwholesome factors, from the pollutants, and so on—Maitreya arises from something other as well. "Therefore," they claim, "we do not assert arising from self or from something other individually, so the specific refutations of self-arising and arising from other presented above will not affect us."

[To refute this, the text says:]

> Arising from both [self and other] is also not logical,
> for it is vulnerable to the objections already raised. 6.98ab

Just as arising from each is illogical, **arising from** the combination of *both* self and other **is also not logical.** **For** this standpoint of arising from both **is vulnerable to the objections already raised** to each of the two standpoints. [273] For example, if the opponent asserts that Maitreya is self-arising from the point of view of his life force, this would be refuted through arguments such as the pointlessness of its arising.[711] And if, from the point of view of his parents, they assert Maitreya as arising from something other, this would be refuted through [demonstrations of] extreme absurd consequences.

So, just as we have shown above how arising from self and from other are illogical, in both the sense of everyday conventional truth as well in the ultimate sense, here too, we say in the form of a summary that arising from both is impossible:

> This is neither found in the world nor accepted in terms of suchness,
> for *arising* is untenable in terms of either pole of self or other. 6.98cd

This arising from both self and other **is neither found in the world nor accepted in terms of suchness** or ultimate reality. **For** *arising* **is untenable in terms of either** the **pole of self or** the pole other, so arising from both remains illogical as well.

Refuting arising from no cause

The Cārvākas who propound the theory of *natural origination* assert the following. If arising is due to causes, then from the point of view of the effect, arising would be either from itself, from something other, or from both, so one will be susceptible to the objections. [274] However, since we do not accept arising from causes, we are not vulnerable to the faults leveled against those three positions. For example, when it comes to the rough texture of lotus stems and the softness of lotus petals, we do not observe anyone creating these. Nor do we witness anyone crafting the varied shapes and colors of the petals, pistils, and the stamens of the lotuses. This is true also of such varied things like breadfruit (Skt. *panasa*) and apples. And just as with these external things, so also with those that possess inner experiences, such as peacocks, partridges (*titiri*), roosters—we do not see someone diligently sculpting their shapes and painting their colors. Therefore the arising of things is such that they originate naturally on their own.

[To refute this, the text says:]

> If there can be arising from no cause at all,
> then anything could come always from anything. 6.99ab

If there can be arising of things **from no cause at all, then anything could come always from anything,** even from those that are not their causes; for everything will be equal in being not a cause. Furthermore, the ripening of mangoes, for example, is contingent upon the seasons and is seen only at a specific time of year. But something like this would exist at all times, for it would not depend on time. Likewise, crows would have peacock feathers, and peacocks would possess parrot's feathers, even during the gestation period! For these things would not be contingent upon their causes.

Having thus explained how such a standpoint contradicts reason, to present how it even conflicts with what we observe, we say:

> There would then be none of the manifold efforts of people,
> such as sowing seeds for the sake of raising a crop. 6.99cd

> If sentient beings had no causes at all,
> they would be ungraspable, like blue lotuses in the sky.
> Yet we do perceive the world in all its color and brilliance.
> So, like our own cognition, know that beings come from causes. 6.100

If you are right, **there would then be none of the manifold efforts of** ordinary people, **such as sowing seeds for the sake of raising a crop,** which they pursue so that they may reap the fruits of their labors, such as enjoying bountiful harvests come fall. Yet they do engage in such activity, so arising does not occur by itself. Furthermore, there is the following fault. **If sentient beings had no cause at all**—that is to say, they came into being with no cause at all—**they would be ungraspable, like** the scent and color of **blue lotuses in the sky.** Yet the fact is, **we do perceive the world in all its color and brilliance. So, like our own cognition** bearing the aspect of blue arises from a blue object, you, Cārvāka, too should **know that beings** or the entire world **come from** their own **causes** alone. [275]

According to Cārvāka, four elements serve as the cause of the entire diverse world of sentient beings, what are referred to as "earth," "water," "fire," and "wind." Through the maturation of these four elements, evidence can be found for the diversity we observe—lotuses and apples as well as peacocks, roosters, and so on. In fact, cognition itself, which cognizes the diverse realities, also arises from this same [maturation of the four elements] alone. So just as from the specific interaction of the elements in alcohol arises the potency of the intoxicant that causes drunkenness and loss of consciousness in living creatures, consciousness arises from the specific interaction of the great elements during gestation—at the time of the *kalala* embryo and so on. These then evolve up to the point when they can positively determine all sorts of things. Therefore, whether it is external things or internal experiences, all things come into being only from the causes of this world alone. There is no such thing as an afterlife, with fruition of past-lives karma ripening in this life and the fruits of karma created in this life being realized in some other world. So they think.[712]

They say:

> Enjoy women and eat like a glutton;
> your wonderful body once gone you'll not find;
> the body is merely a collection [of elements];
> what is lost can never return.[713]

This is a statement uttered by someone with a lustful desire to copulate with his own daughter, intending to convince her that there is no world beyond. Naktso translates the last line as "No dangers of the past will come to pass."

To this standpoint, we ask the following. "This certainty of yours that there is no world beyond, from what reason does it stem?" If the thought is that we do not presently see any life beyond, then is this nonperception of an afterlife an instance of direct perception or not? If you say that it is a direct perception, you would be asserting that what is in fact the opposite of a direct perception is an instance of direct seeing. In that case, it would not be contradictory to assert that a nonentity is an instance of direct perception, which means, according to you, something that is not an entity could also be an entity. This is because, for you, the absence of an afterlife would be an actual object of direct perception, just as an actual thing is an object of direct perception. This would mean that since there would be no *nonentity* at all, *entity* too would not exist, because there would be no contrasting point of reference for it. And if these two [entity and nonentity] do not exist, there cannot be the four elements. In which case, your thesis that an afterlife does not exist will be undone as well.

If, on the other hand, [your certainty] is not based on a direct perception, then it would not be an evident fact. [276] For if it is not apprehended by direct valid cognition, how is nonexistence of an afterlife established for you? Now if you assert that it is apprehended through inference, it is true in general that individuals can attain their goals not only through direct perception but also through inference, but you Cārvāka do not actually acknowledge inferential cognition! For instance, you assert:

> The person's cognition is limited
> to whatever is in the sphere of the senses.
> Noble lady, what is said by the learned
> is [deceptive] like the tracks of a wolf.[714]

Thus you assert that valid cognitions by means of which people realize their aims is limited to what is perceived within the sphere of their senses, such as their eyes.

[To continue, the root text says:]

> The elements do not have that nature by means of which
> you say that they become objects of cognition.
> How can you, whose mind is so thickly covered by darkness,
> ever correctly understand facts about the world beyond? 6.101

> You should know that when you negate the world beyond,
> you're viewing the nature of things in a distorted manner.
> You'll thus possess a body that supports such a denigratory view,
> just as when one asserts self-existence of the elements. 6.102

The four elements such as earth **do not have that nature by means of which you say** in your treatises **that they become objects of cognition.** Now if they do not exist in such a manner, then **how can you, whose mind is so thickly covered by darkness** with respect to what are very coarse facts, **ever correctly understand** very subtle **facts about** the existence or nonexistence of **the world beyond?** This is not possible. There is also a further fault. For **when you negate the world beyond,** you Cārvāka **should know that you are viewing the nature of things in a distorted manner.**

You will thus possess a body or a frame that resembles or is equivalent to a condition **that supports a denigratory view** pertaining to the world beyond. This is, for example, **just as when one asserts self** or true-existence **of the elements.**

The opponent may think, "When one cognizes the elements to possess true existence, one sees things in an undistorted manner, so the example you cite has no bearing on the predicated thesis." This response is untenable. For conceiving the elements—which are intrinsically unborn and nonexistent— as intrinsically existent and arising establishes that you Cārvākas are viewing reality in a distorted manner. [Candrakīrti's response] indicates that, in the case of our own valid proof statements, the example must have a bearing on the predicated thesis. [Candrakīrti also] explained above how "being a visible object of eye cognition" is an instance of an "unestablished proof" when cited as a logical reason to demonstrate that sound is impermanent. All of this reveals that all three modes of a sound proof are required to establish a thesis by means of valid reasoning.[715]

If you [Cārvāka] say that this fact of the elements being intrinsically unborn needs to be proven, we say this:

> That these elements do not exist in such a manner has already been
>   shown.
> In that arising from self, something other, and both
> as well as from no cause have all been refuted above,
> the elements cannot exist in terms not already covered. 6.103

That these elements do not exist in such a manner—namely, by virtue of their intrinsic nature—**has already been shown.** For example, earlier when **arising from self,** from **something other, and** from **both as well as from no cause** [277] were refuted, we **already refuted** intrinsic arising of the elements together or in a general sense. As such **the elements cannot exist in terms not already covered** or negated in this general sense. So our argument still holds.

Likewise, when refuting the views that denigrate [the existence of] omniscience and other views, such as the essentialist tenets of those who assert intrinsic existence, we could extend [the same objection that] they are conceiving reality in a distorted manner. We could, for example, rephrase the verse in the following manner:

You should know that when you deny buddhahood,
you're viewing the nature of things in a distorted manner.
You'll thus possess a body that supports such [denigratory] view,
just as when one asserts self-existence of the elements.[716]

We could do this because we wish to refute all standpoints that view things in terms of existence and nonexistence.

If the opponent thinks, "This same consequence applies to you [Madhya-maka] as well," we will respond, "This is not the case; there are no examples that help establish our view to be distorted." We could in fact say the following:

You should know that when you recognize there is an afterlife,
you're viewing the nature of things in an excellent manner.
You'll thus possess a body that supports such [correct] view,
just as when one asserts the realization of selflessness.

Likewise, [we could say]:

You should know that when you recognize there is omniscience,
you're viewing the nature of things in an excellent manner . . .

The [last two lines presenting the] reasoning sign and the example would remain the same [as the previous examples]. "We should extend this same rephrasing to the knowledge of all things as well."[717]

Therefore it is in such terms that the four theses proposed in the following lines have been thoroughly established:

Not originating from itself, and how from something other?
Not from both, and how from no cause? (6.8ab)

Given what Candrakīrti states here, we should not say such things as "We refute others' standpoints but do not establish any of our own."

The conclusion of having negated arising from the four extremes

[278] One might ask, "If things do not arise from themselves, from something other, from both, or from no cause, how then do they arise?" Here

I will say this: If things possessed some sort of intrinsic nature, no doubt things would have to arise or exist from themselves, from something other, from both, or from no cause because no other conception of arising is possible. Even for those who assert arising of things from Īśvara and so forth, Īśvara and so forth will have to be either self, something other, or both. Therefore, those who propose Īśvara and so forth as the cause, even they cannot escape the objections leveled [against arising from the four extremes]. No fifth possibility can be conceived of as the cause. Given that there is no such alternative, and since arising from the four conceived possibilities has been refuted, it has been demonstrated that things have no arising in any intrinsic sense. This is stated in the following:

> In that there is no arising from self, other, or both,
> or independent of a cause, entities are devoid of intrinsic existence.
>   6.104ab

In that there is no arising from self, from other, or from both, or independent of a cause, entities are devoid of intrinsic existence. This is what is being stated.

This [two-line passage] shows how, although arising from four extremes has been negated through consequence-driven logical arguments, in the end it's on the basis of a reasoning sign that inferential cognition arises. Here, "no arising from the four extremes" is the logical reason, "entities" refers to the subject, and being "devoid of intrinsic existence" is the thesis.

Rebutting objections against refuting intrinsic arising

This has two parts: (1) the actual point and (2) presenting that point by way of a summary. [279]

The actual point

One might ask, "If things have no arising through their intrinsic nature, how can such unborn things, like blue, be apprehended?" Now, whatever might be the essential nature of a phenomenon like a blue thing, it cannot be an object perceptible by someone deluded by ignorance. Therefore everyday cognitions like eye consciousness cannot apprehend the essential nature of such things as blue. "In that case," one might ask, "what is it that is seen again and again in the form of an object right in front of us?" This is perceived out of our delusion, so it cannot be the essential nature [of things]. For it is only through the pollution of ignorance that things are perceived in such terms. To indicate this, we say:[718]

> However, since dense ignorance enshrouds the world like thick clouds,
> phenomena are misperceived in distorted ways. 6.104cd

Since, or for the reason that, **dense ignorance enshrouds the world** of sentient beings **like thick clouds**, obscuring the essential nature from being seen, the childish have no vision of the essential nature of blue and so on. In fact, the natures of **phenomena are misperceived in distorted ways** by the childish who grasp at true existence of things.

"Even if one allows," one might ask, "that [the childish] do not see suchness because of being obscured by delusion, how is it that they come to see it in a distorted manner?" To demonstrate by means of an analogy how it is owing to the power of delusion [that the childish] perceive what has no intrinsic existence as having such existence, we say:

> Just as through a malady of the eyes some falsely perceive
> floating hair, double moon, peacock feathers, swarms of flies, and so on,
> likewise, through the power of delusion those who are unwise
> perceive all sorts of conditioned things with their cognitions. 6.105

> "Karma comes from delusion and not when delusion is absent":
> such statements are doubtless for the understanding of unwise alone.
> The wise, who have dispelled the thick darkness of ignorance
> with the sun of excellent intellect, realize emptiness and become free.
> 6.106

Through the power of their senses being infected with **a malady of the eyes, some** individuals who have such an eye disease **falsely perceive**, or see, such things as **floating hair, double moon, peacock feathers, swarms of flies, and so on**—even though there are no such things. **Likewise, through the power of delusion those who are unwise**, the ordinary beings, [280] **perceive**, or see, **all sorts of conditioned things**, such as blue, **with their cognitions**. The Buddha states in the *Dependent Origination Sutra*, for example, "Conditioned by ignorance volitions arises . . ." Likewise, he states,

"A person driven by ignorance will create merit, create demerit, and create unwavering karma," and "From the cessation of ignorance, volition will cease..."[719]

Such statements as "Karma comes from delusion and not when delusion is absent" are doubtless for the understanding of unwise alone— namely, they are from the point of view of ordinary beings alone. As for **the wise,** when they see statements such as "Conditioned by ignorance, volition arises," they **realize** volition's **emptiness** of intrinsic existence, and **with the sun of excellent intellect** realizing the truth of dependent origination, they will totally **dispel the thick darkness of ignorance.** Having eliminated ignorance, the cause for appropriating karmic acts, they will thus not appropriate karmic acts. In this way, they will definitely **become free** from the cycle of existence. The *Condensed Perfection of Wisdom* states:

> Just like a cloud-free sun dispels all darkness with its rays,
> the bodhisattva who understands through his wisdom
> that dependent originations have no arising or cessation
> will destroy the darkness of ignorance and attain freedom.[720]

[The text continues by raising an opponent's objection:]

> If entities do not exist in ultimate reality,
> then like a barren woman's son, they will have no existence
> even on the conventional level; so therefore
> things do exist through their intrinsic nature. 6.107

[*Question*:] **If entities** such as form **do not exist in ultimate reality**—that is, they do not possess any kind of nature in the ultimate sense—**then like a barren woman's son,** things like blue **will have no existence** or essence **even on the conventional level.** However, since **things** such as form do exist on the conventional level, they **do exist through their intrinsic nature** or in the ultimate sense.

[*Response*:] To this we say:

> You should first argue with those with an eye disease
> who see such unarisen things as floating hair; ask them,
> "Why is it you see such things but not the son of a barren woman?"
> Then you can refute those afflicted by the ills of ignorance. 6.108

You should first argue with those with an eye disease, whose eyes are impaired by myodesopsia and so on and **who see** as objects of their perception **such unarisen things as floating hair**; and **ask them, "Why is it that you see such** nonexistent **things** as floating hair **but not the son of a barren woman?"** [281] Then, afterward, **you can refute those who are afflicted by the ills of ignorance** and whose eyes of intelligence are obscured and ask: "Why is it that, despite both being equally unarisen, you can see forms and so on but not the son of a barren woman?"

As for us, this is not a matter of dispute or argument. We, for one, accept what is stated in the scriptures that the yogis see all things in such a manner [as devoid of intrinsic existence], and that those who aspire to attain a yogi's gnosis too should develop deep conviction in the statement that all phenomena are devoid of intrinsic existence. So, precisely according to scripture, we explain the absence of intrinsic existence of all things as comprehended by yogi's gnosis. We do not explain the nature of things from the point of view of our own [ordinary everyday] cognition. For our eyes of intelligence remain obscured by the cataracts of ignorance.[721] This is as stated in a sutra:

> Aggregates are devoid of intrinsic nature and empty;
> enlightenment is devoid of intrinsic nature and empty;
> the one who partakes in them is devoid of intrinsic nature and
>   empty;
> this is known by those with pristine gnosis, not by the childish.
>
> They will know the nature of gnosis itself to be empty,
> and having known the nature of knowables to be empty,
> when they understand the known to be same as the knower,
> I say, "They are traversing the path of enlightenment."[722]

Therefore this [question about the absence of intrinsic existence of things] is not something to be disputed and argued with the yogis. As for the yogis, they do not see, even on the conventional level, any intrinsic nature established by virtue of an essence in relation to any phenomena. And on the ultimate level, they see nothing at all.

So you [proponent of intrinsic arising] should forget about looking at those with an eye disorder as someone to dispute and argue with. For now, instead, you need to dispute and argue with your own self. So we say:

If indeed such unarisen things as dream objects, gandharva cities,
mirage water, magical illusions, mirror reflections, and so on can be
    seen,
given they too are nonexistent [just like the son of a barren woman],
how is it you see these but not the other? 6.109

So although things do not arise in ultimate reality,
unlike the son of a barren woman, they do serve
as objects perceived in the context of the everyday world.
Therefore your argument remains inconclusive. 6.110

You should ask yourself this: "**If indeed such unarisen things as dream
objects** like dream houses, **gandharva cities, mirage water,** a man and
woman conjured through **magical illusions, mirror reflections** of faces,
and so on—which includes echoes, magical emanations, and the like—**can
be seen, how is it** that **you see these but not the other,** the son of a child-
less woman, **given they too are** equally **nonexistent?**" This is illogical. You
should argue with yourself in this way, and afterward you can then come
and argue with me. **So although things** such as forms **do not arise in** terms
of **ultimate reality, unlike the son of a barren woman, they do serve as
objects perceived in the context of the everyday world.** [282] **Therefore
your argument**—"If things do not exist on the ultimate level, they would
then be unseeable even on the conventional level, just like the son of a barren
woman"—**remains** an **inconclusive** or flawed reasoning. The Buddha too
says:

Beings are spoken of as dream-like;
they're not posited in terms of reality.
While no entities exist in a dream,
someone with a distorted mind clings to them.

In whatever way one might perceive a gandharva city,
no such city exists in the ten directions or elsewhere;
this city remains in name only.
The Tathāgata sees sentient beings like this.

Though someone thinking of water might see it,
there is no water in a mirage.

Likewise someone stirred up by fantasies
sees what is not beautiful as beautiful.

Just as on the surface of a clear mirror,
a reflection appears as a face
that is devoid of intrinsic reality,
so, Druma, understand all phenomena to be likewise.[723]

So as shown in these scriptural quotations, form and so on, while intrinsically unarisen, do become objects of perception in the everyday world, which is not the case with the son of a barren woman. So this [dispute] remains unresolved only for you. As for us, there is no dispute about this matter. We do not assert intrinsic arising in relation to form and so on on the conventional level and then negate it on the ultimate level.

Presenting that point by way of a summary

In itself, the son of a barren woman has no arising,
either in reality or in the context of the everyday world.
Likewise, all things do not arise in and of themselves,
either through their essence or in terms of the everyday world. 6.111

Therefore the Buddha declared that all phenomena are
primordially tranquil and devoid of arising
and that they transcend the bounds of sorrow.
Thus things have no arising at any time. 6.112

[*Question*:] Why in your system do you not [first] perceive form and so forth as arising by virtue of intrinsic nature on the conventional level and then negate it on the ultimate level?

[*Reply*:] Just as **in itself the son of a barren woman has no arising, either in reality or in the context of** conventions **of the everyday world, likewise, all things**—form and so on—**do not arise in and of themselves, either through their essence or in terms of the everyday world.** [283]

Given what is stated here, it is not at all the case that Madhyamaka defines conventional existence as existence from an erroneous perspective that apprehends things as arising through their essences.[724] We should also note that what is to be negated is explicitly qualified here with the proviso "arising through their essence." It is from this perspective that the Buddha states that all phenomena are primordially tranquil, free of intrinsic arising, and naturally transcend sorrow. Therefore throughout all times no intrinsic arising exists whatsoever.

This is stated, for example, in the *Cloud of Jewels Sutra*:

> When the wheel of Dharma was turned,
> you, O Protector, revealed the truths that
> phenomena are primordially tranquil,
> unborn, and naturally transcendent of sorrow.[725]

The suchness of all phenomena is "tranquil" because it is the object of gnosis that has been calmed. The reason that it's [the object of such gnosis] is because it is intrinsically "unborn." And the reason for this in turn is that, were something to exist by virtue of intrinsic nature or an essence, it would then possess arising, but since no such intrinsic nature exists, what can arise? Therefore [the nature of things] is beyond sorrow; it is utterly pure. "Primordially" indicates that these phenomena are unborn not only on the stage of a yogi's gnosis. Prior to this [stage], even in the context of worldly conventions, these phenomena are unarisen through their own essence. This is what "primordial" indicates; it is a synonym for the word "first."

[To continue, the root text reads:]

> Things such as vases do not exist in ultimate reality,
> yet they exist as well-known entities of the world.
> Since all entities are likewise the same,
> the consequence that they are like a barren woman's son is not entailed.
>   6.113

Buddhist [essentialist] schools do not argue that "if something does not exist on the ultimate level, it would not exist even on the conventional level." Why is this so? This is because for them **things such as vases do not exist in ultimate reality; yet they exist as well-known entities of the world**— that is, they exist on the conventional level. **Since all entities are likewise the same**—they share the same status—**the consequence that** if they do not exist on the ultimate level **they are like a barren woman's son is not entailed.**

This is similar to what is stated in the *Treasury of Abhidharma*:

If the conception [of something] no longer applies
once it has been destroyed or mentally dissected,
then it exists conventionally, like a vase or like water.
Ultimate existence is the opposite.[726]

The *Commentary on the Treasury of Abhidharma* explains this in the following:

That thing whose conception no longer applies when it's dismantled into its parts has conventional existence. Take a vase, for example; when it is smashed into pieces, the conception of "a vase" no longer remains. Things whose conceptions no longer apply when they are mentally dissected also exist on the conventional level. Take water, for example; [284] when the mind reduces it to other properties—materiality and so on—the thought "water" no longer applies.

That which retains its conception even when destroyed as well as those that retain their conception even when reduced to other phenomena, these are ultimately existent. Take matter, for example. Here, whether reduced to atoms or when other properties such as taste are removed, the conception that it is in the nature of matter still applies. Extend this perspective similarly to [the aggregates of] feeling and the rest.[727]

Candrakīrti is saying that it would be illogical for these schools to assert that if something does not exist on the ultimate level, it would not exist on the conventional level either. He is not showing that what these schools identify as the two truths is in accord with the two that he himself presents. For what these schools define as "conventionally existent" invariably involves what the Mādhyamaka understands as grasping at ultimate existence.

[*Opponent:*] Now if the four elements, which are the designative basis of "vase" and so on, have substantial reality, it would then be logical to use terms like "vase" and so on, for there will be a cause or basis for such designations. However, since according to you Mādhyamikas, all phenomena are mere designations, there is no designative basis that is substantially existent. So the consequence that phenomena would be akin to the son of a barren woman cannot be avoided.

[*Reply:*] This [assertion] too is untenable. For you cannot prove that the basis of designation has to be substantially real. For example, in dependence on the coming together of nominally existent things like face and so on, a mere construct, the mirror image is perceived. Similarly, in dependence on nominally existent pillars and so on "house" is designated, and on the basis of trees "forest" is imputed. So, just as in a dream one perceives the arising of sprouts that are in actuality unborn by nature, it is perfectly logical for the designative bases themselves to exist only nominally when it comes to all things that are themselves nominally existent. [285]

How arising through dependent origination prevents distortions of adhering to extreme views

[*Question*:] Since you, Madhyamaka, have rejected arising from self, from something other, from both, and from no cause on the level of both truths, how then should one ascertain arising in the conventional sense, such as that of volition and consciousness from ignorance, that of a sprout from seeds, and so on?

[*Reply*:] To this we say:

> Because entities do not arise
> from no cause, from causes such as Īśvara,
> from self, from other, or from both;
> they arise entirely through dependence. 6.114

Because entities do not arise in the manners described above, by themselves **from no cause, from causes such as Īśvara** "and so on," indicating from time, from indivisible atoms, from primal substance, from being, or from Nārāyaṇa,[728] nor do they arise **from self, from** something **other, or from both**, *this* or *that* effect **arises entirely through dependence** on *this* and *that* cause and condition. The simple fact is, rejection of arising from the four extremes does not undercut everyday convention of cause and effect. The Buddha states, for example:

> Here are the terms that refer to phenomena. It is thus: if *this* exists, *that* comes about; *this* having arisen, *that* arises. Conditioned by ignorance volition arises . . .[729]

Precious Garland states:

An example for *this* exists, *that* comes into being:
if there is long there can be short.
An example for *this* arising because *that* has arisen:
the presence of light because of the lamp.[730]

Also *Fundamental Wisdom* says:

An agent depends upon the object of the act;
an object too originates only in dependence
upon the agent. Other than this, no cause
of establishing [the two] can be observed.

We should likewise understand appropriation,
for it is revealed to consist of objects and agents.
Through [this analysis of] object and agent,
understand all remaining entities as well.[731]

Only this much is stated and nothing about arising from any of the four extremes.

So just as the Buddha taught arising of mere conditionedness, the noble Nāgārjuna did the same. In particular, since Nāgārjuna upholds the view of dependent origination in terms of mutual dependence—the agent being dependent on the object of the act and so on—he used the phrase "other than this," thus distinguishing his own from others' views of arising. He states that this understanding should be extended to all entities that could possibly exist. This master, therefore, spoke of the need to posit arising in general, and how since arising from four extremes remains untenable, this implies that things arise through dependence. Nāgārjuna establishes this point through numerous strategies. [286] So those who assert, contrary to the standpoint of these traditions, "If things do not arise from any of the four extremes, there is no arising at all" are doing a good job of defiling through the stench of their false conceptualization the unexcelled tradition in which the meaning of profound dependent origination—the unrivaled proof to help realize emptiness—emerges in terms of the meaning of emptiness. This is what we should know.

Thus, when the dependent origination of mere conditionedness is propounded, not only does arising from the four possibilities such as no cause become impossible, it also reveals the impossibility of the objects conceived in terms such as the *eternalist view* that reifies intrinsic existence, the *nihilist view* that makes everyday operations [of cause and effect] untenable, *permanence* in the sense of something that existed at an earlier temporal stage persisting at subsequent temporal stages, *impermanence* in the sense of momentariness with intrinsically existent preceding and subsequent instances, and the essential existence of the *absence* of entities and nonentities. To present this, we say:

> In that things originate entirely through dependence,
> such concepts [as self-arising] cannot withstand analysis,
> so this reasoning of dependent origination
> rips to shreds the entire matrix of false views. 6.115

In that on the basis of this reasoning alone—"**things originate entirely through dependence**; from *this* cause *that effect* arises"—that conventional realities obtain their status as existence and not through some other means. **Such concepts** as arising from self, other, and so on **cannot withstand analysis. So this reasoning of dependent origination** through mere conditionedness **rips to shreds the entire matrix of false views**, such as those that view things in terms of arising from self, from other, and so on as defined above.

The Madhyamaka, which posits mere conditionedness as the meaning of dependent origination, does not assert intrinsic existence in relation to anything. *Sixty Stanzas of Reasoning* says:

> That which has originated due to *this* and *that*
> has not done so through its own essence.
> And how can that which has not arisen
> through its own essence be called "arisen"?[732]

As Nāgārjuna explains, that which has arisen through dependence has not arisen through its own essence, and so, he asks, "How can one say that a sprout and so on has arisen through its essence?" In *Fundamental Wisdom* too, Nāgārjuna explains that things are empty of intrinsic existence for the very reason that they are dependently originated:

> That which is dependently originated,
> this has been declared emptiness.

This too is designated as caused,
and this is the middle way.[733]

In a sutra too it says:

Whatever has arisen from conditions is unborn;
it does not have the nature of arising.
That which depends on conditions, I declare empty.
One who understands emptiness is at ease.[734] [287]

"Having arisen from conditions" is the logical proof; the meaning of "unborn," which is the thesis, is presented by the second line. The sense here is "not being born by virtue of an intrinsic nature," so it is not the case that no qualification is applied to what is being negated. This is clear from the *Descent into Laṅkā Sutra*, as cited in *Clear Words*, where the Buddha himself explains his intention:

Mahāmati, with the intention that they did not arise intrinsically,
I have taught that all phenomena are unborn.[735]

With his heart enthralled by the Buddha's teaching—that it's through this very reasoning of dependent origination, sovereign among all reasoning, that intrinsic existence is to be negated—Nāgārjuna in his numerous works, such as *Fundamental Wisdom* and *Sixty Stanzas of Reasoning*, praised the Buddha for having taught dependent origination. So no intelligent person would utter any foolishness such as "Because things arose through dependence, they are not produced."

So long as one does not accept intrinsic existence of entities, how could something devoid of intrinsic existence arise from itself, from something other, and so on? On the other hand, were there something that exists by virtue of intrinsic nature, its arising must be naturally in a spontaneous manner, from itself, from something other, or from Īśvara and so on. It would also be possible to conceive such a thing in terms of *permanence* in the sense of nondisintegration of what has arisen and *annihilation* in the sense of [real] disintegration. Such possibilities do not exist for the opposite [the Madhyamaka standpoint that rejects intrinsic existence]. To indicate these, we say:

> Such concepts would be in order if real entities did exist;
> that no such entity exists has already been analyzed.
> Without such an entity, those concepts would not come to be;
> for example, without fuel there can be no fire. 6.116

Such concepts grasping in terms of extremes **would be in order if** one apprehended intrinsically **real entities. That no such entity exists has already been analyzed** on the basis of reasoning outlined above. So, **without** grasping at **such an entity, those concepts** tending to extremes **would not come to be. For example, without fuel,** the cause, **there can be no fire,** the effect. Thus by gaining familiarity with the truth of suchness as set forth [by the Buddha], a yogi who has attained the ārya path and sees suchness in terms of not seeing any appearances of conceptual elaboration, in him conceptualizations clinging to true existence of phenomena habituated to since beginningless time will come to an end. For example, through application of eye ointment, someone affected with myodesopsia could experience the effect—namely, the disappearance of the perception of floating hair. [288] It is not that the floating hair and so on he had previously experienced somehow transformed into something that now has a different nature.

The fruits of having engaged in analysis with reasoning

> Ordinary beings are chained by conceptualization;
> yogis, who do not conceptualize, become free.
> The wise have said that the very cessation of conceptualization
> is the fruit of refined analysis. 6.117

Ordinary beings, who have no knowledge of this ultimate nature of things as explained above, **are chained** primarily **by conceptualization** grasping at extremes. In contrast, **yogis,** because of their comprehension of this ultimate reality, **do not conceptualize** in a distorted manner; they **become free.** Therefore **the wise have said** that **the very cessation of conceptualization** grasping at extremes through negating all their objects of apprehension **is the fruit of refined analysis** presented by the noble Nāgārjuna in his treatise on the Middle Way.

[Four] Hundred Stanzas too says:

> If things exist intrinsically,
> what benefits exists for seeing emptiness?
> Seeing through conceptualization is bondage;
> and this is what is being negated here.[736]

Āryadeva states here that were phenomena to exist intrinsically, this would then be their true character. In that case, it would be better to recognize that fact; no benefit would come from seeing the emptiness of intrinsic existence. However, since one is chained by seeing things via conceptualization—that is to say, via grasping at intrinsic existence—it's the object that is clung to [by such conceptualization] that is being negated here in [Nāgārjuna's] *Treatise on the Middle Way*.

In the commentary [on Āryadeva's stanza by Candrakīrti] too, it reads, "'Conceptualization' refers to superimposing a sense of essential nature onto things that does not accord with reality."[737] So Candrakīrti explains it in terms of projecting what does not exist in reality as having such an existence in reality. [289] So the "conceptualization" referred to here should not be understood as just any kind of conceptual cognition. It should be understood as the conceptualization of true existence and as conceptual thoughts grasping at the extremes.

With respect to conceptualization grasping at an extreme too, the term *extreme* can connote many things. The meaning here, however, is the sense of being free from extremes presented in [Kamalaśīla's] *Light of the Middle Way*:

> If, for Madhyamaka, the mind were to exist in any way as an ulti-
> mate entity with its own nature, then since it would have such
> a nature, how could clinging to it in terms of permanence or
> impermanence be an extreme? How could a correct mentation
> corresponding to the way things really are constitute a pitfall?
> This is illogical.[738]

So the object that exists as apprehended does not constitute an extreme, and the cognition [that apprehends it], being an instance of correct mentation, cannot be a grasping at an extreme either. The "extreme" in the context here refers to an edge one can fall off, just as in ordinary language one speaks of a precipice as an "extreme" [edge] and falling off it as a falling off an edge. Here too we can speak of "falling to an extreme" where the apprehension of a position leads to the person's downfall.[739] Since existence in terms of ultimate reality remains impossible even on the conventional level, the absence of existence in ultimate reality exists conventionally. So to hold everything as nonexistent on the ultimate level does not constitute grasping at the extreme of nihilism; and to repudiate it by saying "things do not exist in such a manner" does not constitute an elimination of the extreme of nihilism. However, if one grasps at the absence—the negation of intrinsic existence—as existing in ultimate reality, this would be falling into the extreme of nihilism. As such the elimination of such a standpoint would constitute elimination of the extreme of nihilism.

The fact that phenomena such as karma and its effects do exist on the conventional level cannot be undermined by any valid cognition. So to conceive them as having no existence or being nonexistent—both the object conceived as well the subject that grasps as such—are, respectively, the extreme of nihilism and grasping at the extreme of nihilism. To say that the Buddha has no faults is not an extreme of nonexistence, nor is the mind apprehending it as such nihilistic. Now the [denial of karma and its effects] is a nihilistic extreme through *denigration*, while the former [grasping at intrinsic existence of emptiness] is a nihilistic extreme through *reification*. Therefore, apart from the negations just referred to, in general the "extreme of existence" and "grasping at the extreme of existence" refer, respectively, to the object and the subject associated with grasping at phenomena as ultimately existent or as existing through intrinsic nature. To say that the Buddha has wisdom and compassion is not an extreme of existence, and to apprehend this does not constitute grasping at such an extreme. There are, however, some contexts in Madhyamaka treatises where ultimate existence is characterized as constituting the extreme of existence with respect to all phenomena.[740]

> Analysis in the treatise is not out of fondness for debate;
> it expounds suchness because it's aimed at freedom.
> If other philosophical systems are undone
> in the course of expounding suchness, however, this is not a fault. 6.118

In view of these, the noble Nāgārjuna engaged in such extensive **analysis** through varieties of reasoning **in his treatise** on the Middle Way **not out of fondness for debate** or to outdo others. [290] This is something we should understand. When his *Treatise on the Middle Way* **expounds suchness** when engaging in critical analysis through reasoning, **it's aimed at** helping people attain **freedom** with the thought "How I wish sentient beings would realize this suchness without error and attain liberation."

[*Question*:] Is it not the case you, Madhyamaka, have cited all the arguments and analyses of those who propound existence of real entities and have refuted them in your treatise? Therefore the activity of the treatise is indeed to engage in disputation; how can you state that the cessation of conceptualizations alone is the fruit [of such analysis]?"

[*Reply*:] Truly this analysis was not undertaken for the sake of disputation. This said, when suchness is carefully presented, given the weakness of the opponents' positions, the tenets of the opponents are unable to stand their own ground. So, just like darkness coming into contact with light, the opponents' positions are undermined. This, however, is not our fault. So, **if** the postulations of **other philosophical systems are undone in the course of expounding suchness, this is not a fault.** Also *Four Hundred Stanzas* says:

> This Dharma was not taught by the Tathāgata
> for the sake of engaging in disputation;
> however, just as fire burns its fuel,
> it does burn clean the opponent's challenges.[741]

For example, the goal of making a fire to boil water for drinking is not to produce ash or charcoal. These come about as a byproduct. Āryadeva thus explains it with this analogy.

[To continue, the root text says:]

> Attachment to one's own view and likewise
> aversion for others' views: all of this is just thoughts.
> Therefore it is by eliminating attachment and aversion
> and engaging in analysis that one swiftly gains freedom. 6.119

If, however, one were to give teachings out of attachment to disputation, then one will undeniably feel hostility toward others' flawed positions and attachment toward one's own logically sound standpoint. There will be no end to thought processes involving anger and attachment. Why? Because **attachment to one's own view and likewise** the feeling of **aversion to others' views** become **just thoughts** that chain oneself and prevent turning away from such anger and attachment, thus increasing them further. In this way, one will remain trapped in bondage and never become free. Given that this teaching [on emptiness] was not taught for the sake of disputation, **it is by eliminating attachment** to one's own standpoint **and aversion** toward positions **and engaging in refined analysis** through reasoning **that one swiftly gains freedom.** The *Sixty Verses of Reasoning* also states:

> For these great beings beyond dispute,
> they have no thesis at all; [291]
> and for those who have no thesis,
> how can there be a counter-thesis?[742]

And *Four Hundred Stanzas* says:

> If you're attached to your own position
> and dislike others' standpoints,
> you'll not travel to *nirvana,*
> and dissolution of duality will not be.[743]

The *King of Meditations Sutra* too states:

> He who experiences attachment upon hearing this teaching
> and engenders anger upon hearing what is contrary to it,
> crushed by pride and self-satisfaction, will be led astray;
> because of his pride, he will meet with suffering.[744]

It states that how, if we do not analyze with an objective mind forsaking biases born of attachment and hostility to our own positions and those of others, analytic contemplation of philosophical tenets could itself become the basis for chaining ourselves ever more tightly to the cycle of existence. We should view this as extraordinary advice given to us from a compassionate heart.

Candrakīrti states that the text has, from the section on the refutation of self-arising up to this point, presented the selflessness of phenomena.[745] What he means by this is that the selflessness of conditioned phenomena has of course been explained in many different contexts and that the selflessness of unconditioned phenomena has also been presented here and there in the text. [292]

17. The Selflessness of Persons

Establishing the selflessness of persons through reasoning

This has three parts: (1) showing how the seeker of liberation must first negate intrinsic existence of the self, (2) negating intrinsic existence of "I" and "mine," and (3) extending the analysis of self and chariot to others.

Showing how the seeker of liberation must first negate intrinsic existence of the self

Having thus presented, through scriptures and reasoning, the selflessness of phenomena, to present selflessness of persons, the text says:

> Seeing with their wisdom that all afflictions and all faults
> stem from the identity view grasping at the perishable collection,
> and knowing that *self* is the focus of this identity view,
> the yogi engages in the negation of selfhood. 6.120

A yogi seeking to enter suchness and eliminate all the faults of afflictions will contemplate, "What lies at the root of this wandering in cycle of existence?" When he examines in this manner, and **seeing with** his **wisdom that all afflictions**, such as attachment, **and faults**—birth, aging, sickness, death, and so on—**stem from the identity view grasping at the perishable collection**: an afflicted intelligence that apprehends in terms of intrinsically existent "I" and "mine." All of these [afflictions], without exception, are in fact effects of the identity view grasping at the perishable collection. When one sees this, the wish to eliminate this identity view will emerge. A person with sharp intelligence will at this point come to recognize that elimination of [the identity view] requires seeing how the self as conceived by this identity view has no objective existence, just as stated in the passages quoted above from *Praise to the Ultimate Expanse* and *Four Hundred Stanzas*.[746]

And when he examines what is the focus of clinging of this identity view, he will **know that** *self* or "I" in the thought "I am" **is the focus of this identity view**. This is because self is the object of "I"-grasping. This means the person who wishes to eliminate all the woes and faults needs to eliminate the identity view, which can be done by comprehending that the self—the focus of the identity view—has no self-existence or essential reality. Therefore the yogi will examine first, "Does this self, the object of my grasping at selfhood, have essential existence or not?" **The yogi** then **engages in negation of** such inherently real **selfhood**.

Since it's through eliminating identity view that all the afflictions come to cease, this kind of critical inquiry into the nature of self is a means to attain true liberation. The *Compendium of Training* states:

> The emptiness of persons is thus thoroughly established. Since the root has been cut off, none of the afflictions will ever reemerge. This is as explained in the *Secrets of the Tathāgata Sutra*:
>
>> Śāntimati, it is thus. When a tree is felled from its roots, all its limbs and leaves as well as all the tiny branches come to dry up. So too, Śāntimati, when the identity view is extinguished, all the afflictions and their derivatives come to be extinguished.[747]

[293] On this statement [that identity view is the root of all afflictions], all the learned masters agree. We should recognize, therefore, that whether according to Mahayana or Hīnayāna, we must proceed as follows. First, we must comprehend well the defects of cyclic existence and contemplate them. We must then identify what is the root of this [cyclic existence], and when the wish to relinquish it has arisen, we must find the view of selflessness— the negation of the object conceived by that root [identity view]—flawlessly and cultivate familiarity with this truth.

[*Question*:] *Precious Garland* says:

> So long as there is grasping at the aggregates,
> there remains grasping at an "I."
> If there is "I" grasping, there'll be karmic acts,
> and from karmic acts, birth comes to be.[748]

So if the text states that grasping at true existence of the aggregates—grasping at the selfhood of phenomena—is the root of cyclic existence, and here [in *Entering the Middle Way*], however, it says that the identity view grasping at the perishable collection is the root of cyclic existence, these two statements are contradictory, for it is illogical for there to be two different roots of cyclic existence.

[*Reply:*] There is no such fault. This system [of Candrakīrti] distinguishes the two forms of self-grasping on the basis of their distinct focal objects, but they do not have two different cognitive aspects with regard to their mode of apprehension. Both forms of self-grasping share the same cognitive aspect with regard to their apprehension—they both grasp [their objects] to exist by virtue of intrinsic characteristics. The illogicality of there being two roots of cyclic existence refers to any assertion that involves positing two roots of cyclic existence with two distinct modes of apprehending their objects. Therefore, when grasping at the selfhood of phenomena is shown to be the cause of identity view, then two subclasses within ignorance are being described as a cause and effect. And when both are portrayed as being the roots of afflictions, they are shown to be at the root of all the afflictions that have modes of apprehension distinct from each other. This characteristic is possessed by both [kinds of ignorance]; there is thus no contradiction [in maintaining that they are both roots of cyclic existence]. This is analogous to the fact it is not contradictory for the preceding and subsequent instances of ignorance to be roots of cyclic existence.

Negating intrinsic existence of "I" and "mine"

This has two parts: negating intrinsic existence of "I" and negating intrinsic existence of "mine."

Negating intrinsic existence of "I"

This has six parts: (1) negating a self that is different from the aggregates, as postulated by non-Buddhist schools, (2) negating aggregates as self, as postulated by fellow Buddhist schools, (3) negating the three remaining positions: the support, the supported, and so forth, (4) refuting a substantially real person that is neither identical to nor different from the aggregates, and (5) explaining with analogy how the self is a mere dependent designation, and (6) how positing self as mere designation leads to the benefit of easily abandoning conceptualizations grasping at extremes. [294]

Negating a self that is different from the aggregates, as postulated by non-Buddhist schools

This has two parts: (1) presenting the opponent's position and (2) refuting that position.

Presenting the opponent's position

If asked, "What is this *self* that is the object of focus of our identity view? Show me for I do not know what it is?" the response to this [from the non-Buddhist schools] has two parts: (1) the Sāṃkhya position and (2) the positions of the Vaiśeṣikas and others.

The Sāṃkhya position

> That self is the consumer, a permanent entity, and a non-creator;
> it is devoid of the qualities and inert. This is what the tīrthikas
>   postulate. 6.121ab

The self is the consumer in that it is the experiencer of happiness, suffering, and so on; it is **a permanent entity, and** it is **a non-creator** with respect to the manifestations; **it is devoid of the qualities** of activity (*rajas*), darkness (*tamas*), and purity (*sattva*), **and** because it is omnipresent, it **is inert.** The Sāṃkhya states the following:

> The primal substance is not a manifestation;
> seven, the great [intellect] and so on, are both;
> the sixteen [five organs and so on] are manifestations;
> the person is neither substance nor manifestation.[749]

The "primal substance" (*prakṛti*) is so called because it creates the effects. When does it create them? It does so when it perceives the desire of the person (*puruṣa*). For instance, when the desire arises to enjoy sense objects such as sound, the primal substance sees the person's desire and connects with the person. From this connection, sound and its like are brought forth by the primal substance. The process by which this occurs is the following. From primal substance the great [intellect (*buddhi*)] appears, from this the I-maker (*ahaṃkāra*), from this the sixteen—eleven faculties and five sense objects—arise; and from the sixteen the five elements appear, in that from the five objects of sound and so on emerge the five elements. This then is the process by which they come into being. The phrase "is not a manifestation" indicates that primal substance is a creator of the effects alone; it is not itself a manifestation, like the great elements and so on. As for the seven such as the great elements, they are both creators as well as manifestations. These seven are substances (*pradhāna*) with respect to their own manifestations, while they remain manifestations in relation to the primal substance. The sixteen such as the intellect are manifestations alone. The person, on the other hand, is neither a creator [295] nor a manifestation.

It's through being influenced by thoughts that the five senses such as the ears perceive objects such as sound, which are then latched on to by the intellect. It's these objects latched on to by the intellect that come into the awareness of the person (*puruṣa*). In this way, those with desire to experience the objects partake in their experience. With lesser attachment and through reducing attachment by recognizing the defects of sense objects, one becomes free from attachment. At that point the individual will cultivate the meditative absorptions in their proper sequence and, on this basis, attain superior knowledge of divine vision. When he looks at the primal substance with such divine eyes, the primal substance will become embarrassed, like the bashful wife of another man. Because of this, primal substance will not associate with the self (*puruṣa*)[750] and will part from it. All the manifestations too will totally dissolve into primal substance progressively in exactly the reverse sequence of their origination. When at this point all manifestations have disappeared, person (*puruṣa*) alone would remain. This, then, is known as true release. Such a self (*puruṣa*), because it remains utterly alone at all times, it is referred to as being "permanent."

One might ask, of the twenty-five categories of reality, which ones are agents and which ones are not? Activity, darkness, and purity are the three qualities. *Activity* has the nature of mobility and activity, *darkness* the nature of heaviness and blanketing, and *purity* has the nature of lightness and illumination. *Pleasure*, *pain*, and *indifference* are synonyms for these [three qualities]. The state of their equilibrium is known as *primal substance*, for in that state the qualities remain dominant, and there is total peace. So the stage where these qualities are not exhibited in manifestations is the primal substance. From this primal substance appears "the great," with the word "great" being a synonym for *intellect*, which is something to which both external objects and internal representations appear. From the great intellect appears the *I-maker*, which has three kinds—that which is manifest, that of activity, and that of darkness. It's from the *manifest* I-maker the five "that alone"—the five sense objects of form, sound, smell, taste, and tactility—come into being. From these sense objects emerge the elements—the earth, water, fire, wind, and space elements. From the I-maker of *activity* emerge the five action faculties, which are speech, hands, legs, anus, and genitals, and the five mental faculties, which are the faculties of eyes, ears, nose, tongue, and tactile sense, as well the faculty of mind, which shares the nature of being both [action faculty and bodily faculty]. [296] Altogether, there are eleven that emerge from this [I-maker of activity]. The *darkness* I-maker serves as the basis of activity of the other two I-makers. Of these categories, the seven—the great intellect, the I-maker, and the five sense objects—are both substances and manifestations; the ten faculties, mental organ, and the five elements are manifestations alone; while the primal substance is substance alone. This is their basic tenet.

The positions of the Vaiśeṣikas and others

> On the basis of slight and minor variations,
> the tīrthikas diverge into different positions. 6.121cd

Just as Sāṃkhya accepts [the existence of] self, likewise, **on the basis of slight and minor variations** [in their conception] of self, **the** systems of **tīrthikas diverge into different positions.** For example, the Vaiśeṣikas speak of nine attributes of the self—(1) intellect, (2) pleasure, (3) pain, (4) desire, (5) aversion, (6) effort, (7) merit, (8) demerit, and (9) inhering force. Of these, *intellect* apprehends objects; *pleasure* experiences objects that are desirable, while *pain* is its opposite; *desire* is the yearning for the objects one desires; *aversion* is the turning away from objects that are undesirable; *effort* refers to the mind's skillfulness in accomplishing its aims; *merit* is that which gives rise to higher rebirth and the definite goodness [of liberation], while *demerit* is its opposite; *inhering force* refers to that which arises from cognition and also serves as the cause of cognition. So long as these nine qualities of self come together in the self and remain present, one will revolve in the cycle of existence pursuing virtuous and nonvirtuous karmic actions produced by these qualities of the self. When, through an awareness perfectly realizing [the nature of] the person (*puruṣa*), one is able to terminate these qualities such as intellect and so on from their roots, one will abide in one's own true nature and attain freedom. Such a self is [according to Vaiśeṣika] *permanent, creator* of the effects, the *consumer* that experiences the fruits [of karma], and endowed *with qualities*. Because the self is omnipresent, they speak of it as being devoid of activity as well. Some Vaiśeṣikas do accept that such a self exhibits the activities of expansion and contraction.

Proponents of the Vedānta school assert that, just as the space in all the separate pots are one, in the same manner, because of the multiplicity of its supports—namely, the bodies [of beings]—one single self (*atman*) appears as diverse. Because the *Commentary* states, "On the basis of slight and minor differentiations in [their conceptions of] the self, the systems of the tīrthikas diverge into different positions,"[751] some [commentators] explain that, according to this tradition [of Candrakīrti], the non-Buddhist schools evolved into different schools as subdivisions of the Sāṃkhya school. [297] This represents a failure to understand the meaning of the text.

Refuting that position

> Like a barren woman's child, it's devoid of arising,
> so such a self simply does not exist.
> It also cannot be the basis for grasping at an "I."
> It cannot be claimed to exist even on the conventional level. 6.122

Such a self described in diverse ways in each one of those texts of the non-Buddhist schools **simply does not exist** the way they postulate. For **it is devoid of arising**—that is to say, it is unborn—which is a logical reason or inference the non-Buddhist schools themselves accept as valid. The example is **like a barren woman's son**. In this syllogism, the logical reason actually negates the explicitly stated subject, but this does not lead to a problem because, crucially, both the logical reason and the probandum are mere negations.[752] This self postulated by others **also cannot be the basis for** innate **grasping at an "I"**; the logical reason and example for this are the same as before.

The phrase "the basis of innate I-grasping" indicates that, with respect to the two aspects [of the grasping mind]—the focal object and the apprehended aspect—this [permanent] self cannot be the focus of innate

I-grasping. The *focal object* [of that innate grasping] is the mere "I," the person, and so on, and since we accept these to be conditioned entities, it would be contradictory to assert them as being unborn. The *apprehended aspect* [of that grasping], however, is the selfhood of person, which does not exist even on the conventional level, so there is no contradiction in asserting this as unborn. In view of these points, those who insist that in this system [of Candrakīrti] the self of persons does exist on the conventional level do so without discerning the central tenets of this school and fail to differentiate the focal object from the apprehending aspect of the identity view. Such talk is just whimsy. So negating the existence of self and rejecting it being the object of apprehension of I-grasping must be undertaken on the basis of qualifying what is to be negated. Not only this, we should also understand that these two [self and the apprehended object of self-grasping] are rejected **even on the conventional level**. The phrase **"the self does not exist"** in this context must be understood as the nonexistence of a substantially real self. [298]

Not only do these two, the logical reason [of being unborn] and the example [son of a barren woman], negate these two objects of negation, they also indicate how all the attributes of the self postulated by the non-Buddhists do not exist either.

> Since all the various attributes of such a self as proposed
> in one treatise after another by the tīrthikas are undone
> by this logical proof that "it is unarisen," which they accept,
> none of the attributes of their self remain tenable. 6.123

> Thus no self separate from the aggregates exists,
> for there is no apprehension of self apart from the aggregates. 6.124ab

This is because **this logical proof that "it is unarisen," which** the non-Buddhists themselves **accept, has undone all the various attributes of such a self as proposed in one treatise after another by the tīrthikas**—Sāṃkhya, Vaiśeṣika, and others. So **none of the attributes of their self**, asserted by Sāṃkhya and Vaiśeṣika as described above, **remain tenable**. They should be refuted in this way. When it comes to dealing with all the proponents of self (*atman*), this reason "being arisen" and the example "son of a barren woman" help eliminate the nature and attributes of the self conceived by these schools.[753]

Thus no self separate from the aggregates exists, for there is no apprehension of self alone by itself **apart from** grasping at **the aggregates**. The point here is this: If the self were a different entity from the aggregates, it would then have no relation with the aggregates, since neither form of logical relation would be possible.[754] In that case, just as one can apprehend a piece of cloth on its own without apprehending a vase, self too should be graspable by itself, yet this has never been observed. As *Fundamental Wisdom* says:

> It's illogical for the self to be different
> from the appropriated [aggregates],
> for if it's different, it should be graspable
> without the appropriated; this is not so.[755]

And:

> If it's different from the aggregates,
> it will lack the attributes of the aggregates.[756]

The phrase "the appropriated" refers here to the aggregates.

There is also the following further objection [against the non-Buddhist views of self]:

> It's also unacceptable to be the basis for beings' "I"-clinging,
> for the identity view is present even in those unaware of such self.
>   6.124cd

It is also unacceptable for this self that is said to be different from the aggregates **to be the basis** or focus **for beings' "I"-clinging** since beginningless time. **For even in those** sentient beings **unaware of such self** as conceived by the non-Buddhist schools—that is to say, without grasping at self in such terms—**the identity view is present**. Through their tendencies toward clinging, they do experience [the world] in terms of "I" and "mine." This objection is not a repetition of the previous one in the line "It also cannot be the basis for grasping at an 'I'" (6.122c). Previously, it was the *substantially real self* that was negated as the focus of the identity view. Here, however, it is *[a self that is] a separate entity from the aggregates* that is being rejected as the focus of the identity view.

One might think that even beings ignorant about the self characterized by permanence, unarising, and so on [299] will still grasp such [an eternal] self in terms of an "I" because of their past habituation.

[*Reply:*] This cannot be so. For it is only those whose minds have been influenced by inferior philosophical tenets who grasp at a self that is distinct from the aggregates, who take this as the basis of their "I"-clinging. [So the root text says:]

> Those who have spent many eons in the animal realm and so on
> do not perceive this unborn permanent entity,
> yet one sees that "I"-clinging operates in those beings as well.
> There is thus no self that is separate from the aggregates. 6.125

We can observe the presence of "I"-grasping even in sentient beings with no habituation to inferior philosophical tenets. For example, **those** sentient beings **who have spent many eons in the animal realm and so on** in the past and have not turned away from birth in the animal states **do not perceive this unborn permanent entity** postulated by the non-Buddhist schools. **One sees that "I"-clinging operates in those beings as well.** Having recognized this fact, what discerning person would cling to the self postulated by the non-Buddhists as the basis of "I"-grasping? **There is thus no self that is separate from the aggregates**, none at all. The "and so on" includes beings born in the hells and other such realms.

Negating aggregates as self, as postulated by fellow Buddhist schools

This has five parts: (1) objections against asserting the aggregates as self, (2) the reasoning showing such a view is incorrect, (3) further objections against proposing that the aggregates constitute the self, (4) the intention of statements about the aggregates being the self, and (5) showing that the opponent's position leads to irrelevance.

Objections against asserting the aggregates as self

The first has two parts: the actual point and refuting the opponent's rejoinders.

The actual point

The first has two parts: the opponent's position and refuting that position.

The opponent's position

> A self that is separate from the aggregates does not exist;
> the object of the identity view is thus the aggregates alone.
> Some assert the basis of this identity view to be
> all five aggregates, others the mind alone. 6.126

The fellow Buddhist schools assert the following. Since no self that is a different entity from the aggregates exists, the aggregates are the focal object, as opposed to the apprehension aspect, of the identity view grasping at the perishable collection. There are two possible candidates that can be determined to be such a focal object—something distinct from the aggregates or something internal, namely the aggregates themselves—and of these the first is unsuitable. [300] Therefore, they claim, the self is nothing but one's own aggregates. This is the position of the Saṃmatīya school, which includes such subschools as the Vātsīputrīya and others. Among them, **some Saṃmatīyas assert all five aggregates to be the basis** or the focus **of the identity view** and say that clinging to self arises on the basis the five aggregates as well. This is as stated by the Buddha in the following:

> O monks, be it a renunciant or a brahman, whosoever views with
> the thought of "I am" views so only in terms of these five appro-
> priated aggregates.[757]

They say that in order to point out to the non-Buddhists that their view [of self] pertains to a collection that is perishable and not to a [fixed] "self" or "mine," the Buddha characterized the views that take the forms of "I" and "mine" as the "view of perishable collection." So on the basis of the Buddha's statement that one views [self] in term of the five appropriated aggregates, these Buddhist schools assert all five aggregates to be the focal object of the identity view.

Some **other** Saṃmatīyas hold **the mind alone** to be the self. They assert this on the basis of passages like this one below, where the mind is referred to by the term "self":

> You are your own savior;
> who else can be your savior?
> Through taming his self well,
> the wise person attains the higher realms.[758]

On what basis do we know this? Because there is no self apart from the aggregates and because another sutra declares the disciplining of mind:

> A disciplined mind is excellent;
> a disciplined mind leads to happiness.[759]

So they assert that the mind, which is basis of "I"-grasping, constitutes the self. In *Blaze of Reasoning* too it says:

> So we too, on the conventional level, actually apply the term *self* to consciousness. In that it is consciousness that appropriates rebirth, it is the self. It [self] is thus designated on the body and the collection of faculties.[760]

So some sutras state that a disciplined *mind* leads to happiness, while others state that one attains higher rebirth by disciplining the *self*. They point to these as scriptural sources for positing mind as the self. For their logical reason, they argue that it's the self that appropriates the aggregates and consciousness that takes rebirth, hence consciousness is posited to be the self. Since this master [Bhāviveka] does not accept foundation consciousness, the consciousness that appropriates bodily existence has to be the mental consciousness. [301] This is the same for others who do not accept foundation consciousness. Those who accept foundation consciousness assert this foundation consciousness alone to define the person. Although these [Buddhists schools] do accept that śrāvakas and pratyekabuddhas realize the person to be devoid of substantial reality, they do not admit that the two realize the two types of consciousness to have no substantial reality. So, for them, the proposition that the person does not exist as substantially real is from the point of view of person itself; it is not asserted from the perspective of the consciousness that is defined as the person.

Refuting that position

> Now if the aggregates are the self,
> then since they are multiple, the self would be multiple.
> The self would also be substantial; viewing it would not be an error
> because doing so would pertain to a substantial reality. 6.127
>
> The self would definitely terminate at the moment of nirvana,
> and prior to nirvana, the self would rise and vanish every instant.
> With no agent, none of its effects could be,
> and acts done by one would bear fruits reaped by others. 6.128

Now if the position that one's five **aggregates are the self** is true, **then since they,** the aggregates, **are multiple,** even in the case of a single person, **the self would be multiple.** If one's view is that consciousness alone is the self, since there are multiple classes of consciousness, such as eye consciousness and so on, and numerous instances of consciousness arise and cease in every moment, the self too will become numerous as well. Here, in the *Commentary,* Candrakīrti levels this consequence of multiple selves ostensibly against the first of these two positions [all five aggregates constitute the self]. But since the fault extends to both positions, [the objection] can be applied in either case.[761]

Such a consequence cannot be raised against someone who accepts mere multiplicity and sameness in nature; the objection is leveled against a view that holds self and aggregates to be identical, with no separateness whatsoever. The opponent, however, does not assert this from the outset. Being one in nature yet conceptually distinct is not a problem within a framework that recognizes these to be unreal. But for the standpoint that accepts self and aggregates to have true existence, two things that have identical natures must be indivisibly identical in all respects. Once this consequence has been forced, one can level the consequence that either there must be multiple selves or the aggregates must be singular. However, the opponent does not actually accept the self to be many, given the scriptural statement, "When a sentient being is born, a person alone is born."[762]

For you, **the self would also be substantial,** or real. What you refer to as the *aggregates* are diverse, such as form, and have evolved into different entities on the basis of their past [and present] substances. [302] So because you refer to these [aggregates] alone as the *self,* self will be substantially existent in your view.[763] However, given the following statements, the opponent does not assert [self to be substantially existent]:

> O monks, these five, for instance, are mere name, mere conventions, and mere designations: "past," "future," "space," "nirvana," and "person."[764]

Similarly:

> Just as one speaks of a "chariot"
> in dependence upon a collection of parts,
> we speak conventionally of a "sentient being"
> in dependence upon the aggregates.[765]

Furthermore, [if aggregates are the self,] **viewing** the self in terms of the aggregates by the view grasping the perishable collection **would pertain to a substantial reality** in that it would take something substantially real as its object. In that case, [this identity view] would **be not an error**, for it would be just like perceptions of blue and yellow. This means when the identity view is eliminated, it will not be in a way that ceases all subsequent moments in a continuous process. Rather, it will be eliminated only through relinquishing the attachment that is drawn to the identity view, just as [one would abandon attraction to] perceptions of blue and yellow.[766]

Furthermore, if one's own aggregates are the self, according to you [Buddhist essentialists], **the self would** also **definitely terminate at** the **moment of** attaining **nirvana** without residue, when all five aggregates come to cease. Your view will therefore become a nihilistic view grasping at an extreme. For you maintain that to apprehend what is held to be the self as eternal or as having an end is to view it in terms of an extreme. Furthermore, during the moments **prior to** attaining **nirvana**, just as the aggregates arise and disintegrate moment by moment, the **self too would rise and vanish every instant**, with each instant essentially distinct from every other. Just as when one recalls a past life, one does not do so with the thought "This body of mine existed in the past," the Buddha too would not make statements such as "On that occasion and at that time I was the king known as Māndhātṛ."[767] This is because the self of that time no longer existed in the present, for just like the body, the self too had ceased. You, however, have accepted that a self that is intrinsically different from that past self has arisen in this life. *Fundamental Wisdom* too says:

> The self is not the appropriated [aggregates],
> which come into being and disintegrate.
> Otherwise, just like the appropriated [aggregates],
> the appropriator [self] would do so as well.[768]

And:

> If the self were the aggregates,
> it would arise and disintegrate.[769]

Now, if prior and subsequent moments [of self] are distinct by virtue of their essences, in that case, **with no** [continuous] self as an **agent**, karma too would not exist, since it would lack any basis to support its perpetuation. This would mean **none of its effects could be**, and karma would have no relation to its effects. [303] You might think there is no problem because the effects of karma created in preceding moments are experienced in the subsequent moments. In that case, since the fruitional effects of karma acquired by one will be experienced by a different person, **acts done by one would bear fruits reaped by others**. In other words, the fruits gathered by someone with one mental continuum would be consumed by a person of a different mental continuum. This would mean that a karmic deed already performed will be wasted and that one would experience the effects of karmic deeds done by another.[770] In *Fundamental Wisdom* too it says:

> For if [the present self] were indeed different from the past,
> then it would exist even if the past self [did not exist].
> Likewise the past self would continue to persist,
> or, without it having died, the present self would be born.
>
> There would be annihilation [of the past self],
> karmic acts would become wasted, and the fruits of action
> done by one person would be reaped by another.
> This and similar consequences would follow.[771]

So if the prior and the subsequent instances [of self] are intrinsically distinct, it would be illogical for [a later instance] to be contingent upon an earlier instance. As such, [the later instance] could come into being even without its preceding instance having taken place. And since the prior moment of self would remain just as it is, this would mean that one could take birth in this life even without the death of that earlier self.

Refuting the opponent's rejoinders

> You may say, "There is no fault because the instants share same
>   continuity,"
> but we have already shown through analysis the defects of such
>   continua.
> Therefore the aggregates and the mind cannot be the self. 6.129a–c

You, the opponent, may say that although the preceding and subsequent instances are distinct from each other, in reality they share the same continuity, so there is no fault. This too is untenable. We have already shown above through analysis the defects of such continua, which are premised on [the notion of a] shared single continuum of things that are intrinsically distinct from each other. This was in the context of the line "Attributes of Maitreya and Upagupta" (6.61a). *Fundamental Wisdom* too says:

> If the god is different from the human [of this life],
> [the self] will then become an impermanent thing.
> Furthermore, if the god and the human are different,
> there cannot be [a shared] continuum.[772]

Since a single shared continuum is untenable for things that are intrinsically distinct, the following consequences cannot be avoided: (1) a person will encounter [the effects of] karmic acts not done by himself, and (2) karmic deeds done will come to be wasted. Therefore the aggregates and the mind cannot be the self. [304]

The reasoning showing such a view is incorrect

> "The world is finite" and so on have not been declared. 6.129d

Not only is the self, as demonstrated by the reasoning just presented, not the aggregates or the mind as demonstrated by the reasoning just presented, it is also inappropriate for the aggregates to be the self given that all Buddhist schools accept that views such as **"The world is finite" and so on** pertain to unanswered questions. "And so on" includes these views: "The world is not finite," "It is both," and "It is neither"; "The world is eternal," "It is impermanent," "It is both," and "It is neither"; and "The Tathāgata exists after his death," "He does not exist," "Both," and "Neither." On top of these twelve are the two views "What is body *is* life force" and "Body is one thing and life force is something different." All Buddhist schools enumerate these as views to which answers **have not been declared.**[773]

If the term "world" refers to the aggregates, the Buddha should have answered that the world is impermanent, since your own position maintains that the aggregates arise and disintegrate. Furthermore, since, according to you, the aggregates do not exist in the aftermath of nirvana, the Buddha should have answered that the world is finite and also that the Tathāgata exists after his death. Since the Buddha refused to answer questions like "Is the world finite?" it is therefore inappropriate to assert that the aggregates are the self.

Here "life force" is a synonym for "self," and the question about the world [being finite or infinite] is asked from the perspective of self. If the question were asked to discover whether there is an inner self that is the agent, since such a thing does not exist, no answers could be given about its attributes. If, on the other hand, the Buddha were to answer the question from the point of view of self as a mere designation, those posing the questions would have no means to realize selflessness. So the question is left unanswered. [305]

Further objections against proposing that the aggregates constitute the self

> Furthermore, when the yogi sees the truth of no-self,
> for you, he would definitely see phenomena to be nonexistent.
> If you say it is eternal self that has been negated, then,
> for you, the aggregates or mind cannot constitute the self. 6.130

There are further objections. **When the yogi sees** directly **the truth of no-self** in relation to seeing the truth of suffering in terms of its aspect of no-self with the thought "All phenomena are devoid of selfhood," at that point, in seeing no-self, **for you, he would definitely see phenomena,** the aggregates, **to be nonexistent** as well. This is because for you the aggregates or the mind *is* the self. This consequence is something you do not accept, so the aggregates cannot be the self.

[*Opponent*:] Even according to the system that does not assert the aggregates to be the self, when [the yogi] directly perceives selflessness of person, he will have to see everything that is identified as the person to be nonexistent as well. So the same objection would apply to you as well.

[*Reply*:] It would be difficult to respond effectively here if one fails to appreciate the subtleties of reasoning. So let me explain. When the opponent asserts the aggregates and the mind to be the self, they do so on the basis of searching for the true referents of the terms without understanding that *self* and *person* are posited merely by virtue of the power of conventions. Because of this, the assertion that the aggregates or the mind is the self implies that they exist as the self in some essential manner. So when the yogi directly perceives there to be no self, given that he realizes such a self to be utterly nonexistent in any manner, the opponent is vulnerable to the charge that the yogi will perceive the nonexistence of everything alleged to be the self—the aggregates as well as the mind. However, for the system according to which everything is posited in nominal terms of mere designation, where one does not posit things on the basis of searching for the true referents of the terms, this problem [of yogis seeing the nonexistence of the aggregates] does not arise at all.

[*Opponent*:] Now, when the term *self* is used in the context of relating karma and its effects, since a self distinct from the aggregates is impossible, this term refers only to the aggregates. However, when the yogi perceives the absence of self, [306] the term [*self*] in that context refers only to the self as an inner agent as postulated by the non-Buddhists. Therefore, when the yogi sees the self to be nonexistent, he perceives the absence of such an inner agent and sees only mental formations. So there is no fault of the yogi seeing the nonexistence of entities such as the aggregates.

[*Reply*:] **If you say** that when the yogi sees no-self, **it is the eternal self** as an inner agent **that has been negated**, given that you maintain a particular view, you cannot use the term *self* to refer to something else in other contexts. Therefore, **then, for you, the aggregates or mind cannot constitute the self**, and this means your standpoint is undermined.

Now perhaps you insist that in the context of relating karma and its effects, it is not the case that the term *self* refers to the way it is defined by non-Buddhist schools, so there is no danger of undermining your own standpoint. This too is untenable. There is no rationale for you to act so capriciously, saying things like "Here the self is the inner agent" and "In the context of karma and its effects, it is the aggregates." If you say [further] that in the context of karma and its effects, an inner-agent self that is the agent of karmic acts and the experiencer of their effects is impossible, I have already explained before how the term *self* cannot be applied to the aggregates.

So if you maintain that in the context of the statement "All phenomena are devoid of selfhood" the term *self* does not refer to the aggregates, then you must admit that it does not refer to the aggregates in the context of karma and its effects either. On the other hand, if you maintain that in the context of karma and its effects if the term *self* does refer to the aggregates, then you will have to acknowledge that the term *self* refers to the aggregates in the context of the statement that "All phenomena are devoid of selfhood" too.

There are further problems as well:

> This means, according to you, that the yogi who sees no-self
> has not realized the suchness of form and so on,
> and so he would engage with form through objectification,
> giving rise to attachment and so on. He knows not form's true nature.
> 6.131

According to you, the yogi who sees no-self directly **has not realized the suchness of form and so on**; this is because he would have perceived merely the absence of an eternal self as conceived by the non-Buddhists. **And so he would** continue to **engage with form** and so on **through objectification** of their true existence, **giving rise to attachment and so on** in relation to form and so forth. For, according to you, **he knows not form** and so forth's **true nature** or suchness.

For example, simply saying "A bird is [feeding] on the flower stamen" without actually experiencing the sweetness of the stamen oneself, one does not perceive its sweet taste. [307] Similarly, the yogi may see the aggregates to be devoid of a permanent self, but there is nothing about the true nature of form and so on that the yogi comes to realize subsequently that he had not known already. Also, just because there is no bird feeding does not mean that the person enjoying the sweet taste of the stamen does not perceive that taste or that he lacks the apprehension of that taste being indeed sweet. Similarly, in someone who perceives true existence of form and so on yet sees the absence of a permanent self, what cause is there for such a person to relinquish attachment and so on toward form and so on? There would be none. As for the person who seeks to eliminate attachment to form and so on through seeing the absence of a permanent self too, he does not seek the objects that lead to happiness with the thought that this [permanent] inner agent person is real; nor does he shun encountering undesirable objects out of a fear that this inner permanent [self] might come to suffer. So such a person would have no means to eliminate attachment and so forth, and he will not gain freedom from the cycle of existence. Therefore [the yogi you speak of] will be similar to the non-Buddhists. This, then, is the import of Candrakīrti's argument here.[774]

The intention of statements about aggregates being the self

This has five parts: (1) explaining the meaning of the statement that all viewing of self is viewing the aggregates, (2) explaining, on the basis of other sutras, that the collection of aggregates is not the self, (3) negating the configuration of the collected aggregates as the self, (4) further objections against the assertion that the mere collection of aggregates is the self, and (5) the Sage taught that self is designated in dependence on the six elements and so forth.

Explaining the meaning of the statement that all viewing of self is viewing the aggregates

This has three parts: (1) demonstrating that the intention of the scripture is from the negative perspective of eliminating what is to be excluded, (2) even if one allows this statement to be from the affirmative perspective, it still does not indicate the aggregates to be the self, and (3) rejecting the opponent's objections against these points.

Demonstrating that the intention of the scriptures is from the negative perspective of eliminating what is to be excluded

> You assert the aggregates to be the self
> because the Buddha has said the aggregates are the self.
> But this statement rejects a self that is separate from the aggregates;
> also he said in other sutras that form is not self and so on. 6.132

In that it has been stated in other such sutras
that form and feelings are not self, and discrimination too is not,
mental formations are not self, and consciousness too is not,
the Buddha does not accept the statement that the aggregates are the
  self. 6.133

[308] The opponent might assert that they are upholding the validity of the
scriptures, which show the aggregates to be the self, and so are not vulnerable to the reasoning of the logicians. For example, the Buddha has stated:

O monks, be it a renunciant or a brahman, whosoever views with
the thought of "I am" views so only in terms of these five appropriated aggregates.[775]

So **because the Buddha has said the aggregates are the self, you assert
the aggregates to be the self. But this statement** does not present the aggregates to be the self. What does it do then? The intention of the Buddha here
is to **reject a self that is separate from the aggregates** as the focus of the
identity view, and this is done by using the modifier, the excluding particle
"only." So this [statement] is made to refute the tenets of the non-Buddhist
schools from the point of view of the conventional truth and to present the
conventionally existent self in an undistorted manner.

"On what grounds can we understand that this [statement of the Buddha]
rejects a self that is different from the aggregates?" one might ask.

[*Reply*:] Because **in other sutras he**, the Buddha, **said form is not self and
so on**, so he spoke about his rejection of form and so on as being the self.
You may ask, "How do these other sutras present such a rejection?" **In that
it has been stated in other sutras that form** is not self, **and feelings are not
self, discrimination too is not, mental formations are not self, and consciousness too is not** self as well, so **the** sutra **statement** "Whosoever views
with the thought of 'I am' views so only in terms of these five appropriated
aggregates" **does not** indicate that **the Buddha accepts that the aggregates
are the self**. It is definitely the assertion of a self that is separate from the
aggregates that is rejected by the modifier "only."

[*Question*:] It may be that the words "views only" in that sutra rejects a
self that possesses separate reality. Nevertheless, the aggregates are presented
clearly to be the object of focus of the identity view with the phrase "views
only in terms of these aggregates," since the sutra states that one views all five

aggregates. So it *is* the intention of that sutra to declare that the aggregates are the focus of identity view.

[*Reply:*] If this is so, it will contradict the other sutras that state that the five aggregates are not the self. Because within the two dimensions of that identity view—its focal object and apprehended aspect—anything that is the focus of the identity view must necessarily be [conceived as] a self. Therefore the meaning of what is stated in the second [group of] sutras is not vulnerable to any logical objection. As for the opposite thesis, objections have already been leveled against it, and more will be presented below. Therefore it is not the case that the first sutra shows the aggregates to be the focal object of identity view. It is clear, therefore, the Buddha's statement "one views the aggregates" indicates the focal object is a self conceived in dependence upon the aggregates. [309] [Both options]—something that is different from the aggregates and the aggregates themselves—have been negated as the focus of our grasping at self.

Furthermore, on the basis of the sutras that reject "aggregates such as form" as being the self and that demonstrate how it's a dependently designated self that is the focus of the identity view that appropriates the aggregates, we should understand that an intrinsically existent appropriator of the aggregates has also been negated. For the statement that form is not self and so on must be understood as having been made in the context of contemplating suchness of things. Thus if there is no intrinsically existent appropriator, then the aggregates—things to be appropriated by that self—cannot possess intrinsic existence either. In this way it becomes logical for someone to become freed from the attachment grasping at the true existence of phenomena such as form and so on.

So, through carefully comparing the sutras, we should reject that something different from the aggregates or the aggregates themselves are the focal object of grasping at self. On this basis, we should appreciate the unique presentation of the selflessness of persons, with self [or person] defined purely in terms of everyday linguistic conventions in dependence upon the aggregates alone. This understanding, which has been extracted through undistorted scriptural sources as well as logical reasoning, represents the perfect intention of the sutras. This is something that, despite their best efforts, many learned masters of lower or higher schools within our own fold who have interpreted the sutras have failed to elucidate. On the basis of this understanding [of the selflessness of persons], the selflessness of phenomena, whereby other phenomena are also posited as lacking a self, is elucidated in exactly the same manner. In these ways, [Candrakīrti] lays bare the extremely subtle intentions of the blessed Buddha. We should therefore strive to appreciate well all of the uncommon understandings of this most learned master.

Even if one allows this statement to be from the affirmative perspective, it still does not indicate the aggregates to be the self

> When it's stated that the aggregates are the self,
> this refers to the collection, not to the individual aggregates.
> And yet the collection cannot be the savior, the tamed, or the witness;
> the collection cannot be the self because it does not exist. 6.134

[*Opponent*:] Although this statement that "one views the five aggregates alone" indicates the aggregates to be the self from an affirmative perspective, it does not state each and every aggregate to be individually the self. If asked, "What is it then?" we would say **when it's stated** [in the sutra] **that the aggregates are the self, this refers to the collection, not the individual aggregates** [310]—that is to say, not each and every single aggregate is presented to be the self. For example, when one says, "The trees are the forest," the sentence does not express each and every single tree to be the forest, otherwise every single tree would be a forest!

In this way, the opponent cites an analogy that is established for the other party in the debate. Thus it is the [aggregates as a] collection that is the self, they say.

[*Reply*:] The Buddha has stated the self to be the "savior," the "tamed," and the "witness," and for you, **the** mere **collection cannot be the savior, the tamed, or the witness.** Furthermore, **the collection** itself **cannot be the self because it does not exist** as a substantial reality.

The Buddha spoke of the self to be the savior and so on in the following:

> You are your own savior;
> you are your own enemy too.
> When doing good or evil,
> you are your own witness.[776]

In this stanza [the self] is spoken of as the savior and as the witness. He also states:

Through taming his self well,
the wise person attains the higher realms.[777]

Rejecting the opponent's objections against these points

Were the collection the self, since a chariot and the self are alike,
the mere collection of chariot parts would constitute the chariot. 6.135ab

[*Opponent*:] Since the collection does not exist as a different entity from the components of that collection, the effects of being the savior and so on can be seen to belong [in actual fact] to the components of the collection. So it is tenable for [the collection of aggregates] to be the savior, the tamed, and the witness.

[*Reply*:] As to your applying the term *self*, sometimes to the collection of the aggregates and sometimes to the aggregates that are the components of the collection, I have already raised objections above against your capricious application of the word *self* to different things.[778] Still further problems arise. **Were the collection** of aggregates **the self**, there is the problem that **the mere collection of chariot parts** lying together unassembled **would constitute the chariot**. Insofar as they are posited in terms of a collection of their parts, **a chariot and the self are alike**. This similarity is presented in the following sutra:

What is called "self" is Māra's thought,
and this would be your view.
This formation of aggregates is empty;
in this, there is no sentient being.

Just as one speaks of a "chariot"
in dependence upon a collection of parts,
we speak conventionally of a "sentient being"
in dependence upon the aggregates.[779] [311]

Explaining, on the basis of other sutras, that just the collection of aggregates is not the self

The sutra states that the sentient is dependent upon the aggregates,
thus their mere convergence cannot be the self. 6.135cd

As explained above, since **the sutra states that the sentient** being **is** designated in **dependence upon the** collection of **aggregates**, the **mere convergence** or the collection of aggregates **cannot be the self.** To elucidate this by means of a syllogism: "That which is designated in dependence upon a collection cannot be the mere collection of the parts, which are the appropriated, because it's dependently designated, like the derivatives of elements." For example, derivative entities like blue color and so on and the eyes and so on are designated through taking the elements as the basis, yet these two [types of entities] are not the mere convergence of the [constitutive] elements. Similarly, that which has the nature of being designated by taking the aggregates as the basis cannot be the mere collection of the aggregates. This would be illogical.

[*Opponent*:] Granted, if the sutra had stated "in dependence upon the collection aggregates," the collection could not be the self. However, the sutra only says "in dependence upon the aggregates," so this sutra cannot be an authoritative source to posit the collection of aggregates to be the basis of the [term] *person.*

[*Response*:] This is incorrect. The context of the analogy includes the line "in dependence upon the collection of parts," which explains how a chariot is posited on the basis of the collection of its parts. So when an analogy is drawn with a chariot, although the word *collection* is not explicitly mentioned in the line "in dependence upon the aggregates," it is patently clear that it needs to be brought out [in the meaning]. This is how learned masters [like Candrakīrti] bring out the force of every single word of the sutras, and were we able to understand [the meaning of the sutras] in such a refined manner, it would fill our mind with joy.

If the opponent says, "There is no entailment [to your reasoning], for there are counterexamples, such as a vase," we would say that no such counterexamples in fact exist. Even such things as a vase do not exist as mere collections of form and so on. They too are equally subject to critical analysis, just like the self. This demonstrates that just as the self cannot be identified with the collection of its parts, vases and so on too cannot be identified merely in terms of the collection of their parts, and that the two cases are analogous. [312]

Negating the configuration of the collected aggregates as the self

If their shape is the self, since that is a property of physical things,
the body alone would be the self for you then.

The collection of mind and so on could not be the self,
for they possess no shape configuration at all. 6.136

[*Opponent*:] The mere collection of wheels and so on are not the chariot. So what is? Wheels and so on acquire the name "chariot" when they come together and acquire a special configuration. Similarly, **the self is** simply **the** configuration, the **shape**, of the aggregates that belong to the continuum of the sentient being, its body and so on.

[*Reply*:] **Since** such a shape **is a property** only **of physical things**, this would mean, **for you then**, it is **the body alone** that **would be the self. The self could not be identified with the collection of mind and so on**, the "and so on" indicating the mental factors. **For they**—the mind and its derivative mental factors—**possess no shape configuration at all** because they are not physical. So the argument goes.

Further objections against the assertion that the mere collection of aggregates is the self

That the *appropriator* and the *appropriated* are one is illogical,
for this would mean the object of an act and the agent are the same.
If you think, "the agent doesn't exist, but the object of the act does,"
this is incorrect for there is no act done without a doer. 6.137

There are other problems as well. *That* which appropriates a self is defined as **the** *appropriator*, and *that* which is appropriated—the five aggregates—are defined as **the** *appropriated*. In that **it is illogical** for these two things **to be one**, the collection [of aggregates] cannot be posited as the self. If, on the other hand, the collection of aggregates such as form *is* the self, **this would mean the object of an act and the agent** of the act **are the same.** This, however, cannot be accepted. Otherwise the two classes of matter—the elements and their derivatives—as well as the pot and the potter will become one as well. *Fundamental Wisdom* too says:

If the fuel is the fire, then the agent
and the object of an act would become one.[780]

And:

Through this example of fire and fuel,
everything should be thoroughly explained:
the self and all cases of appropriation
together with "vase," "cloth," and so on.[781]

[313] So, just as one cannot accept that a fire and its fuel are one, one also cannot assert that the self and the appropriated [aggregates] are one. These two cases have been stated to be the same.

If you think, "The agent that appropriates the collected aggregates **doesn't exist, but the object of the act**—namely, the mere collection of the aggregates, the appropriated—**does,"** this too **is incorrect. For without a doer,** the cause, **there is no act done.** *Fundamental Wisdom* says:

Likewise understand appropriation
through the elimination of object and agent.
Through [this analysis of] agent and object,
comprehend all remaining entities.[782]

We should understand that the intrinsic existence of the appropriated and appropriator are eliminated through the reasoning negating intrinsic existence of the object and agent of an action.

In commenting on "remaining entities," *Clear Words* says:

The produced and producer, going and goer, viewed and viewer, characteristic and the characterized, that which will come into being and that which brings it about, the parts and the whole, qualities and the bearer of these qualities, valid cognition and the object of cognition—all such entities without exception are negated as having intrinsic existence. Those with discerning mind should understand that they are established through mutual dependence alone.[783]

So [Candrakīrti] accepts act and agent in general, and the act and agency associated with valid cognition and the object of cognition in particular, to be devoid of intrinsic existence and to have [only] contingent reality. We should understand that [this Candrakīrti system] has a unique way of defining contingency in terms of mutual dependence.

As for the term "the appropriated" (*upādāna*) here, when the *lūṭa* affix is applied to the root word for an entity *upaṭra,* it gives the form the "appropriated" because it appropriates. Since the entities do not come into being without the factors that bring them about, so both the act of appropriating as well as that which appropriates are posited as "appropriated." If you say, "Since the *lūṭa* affix expresses only the act of appropriating, how does it express the object of the act of appropriation?" As it is stated in the Sanskrit treatises that "*krita* and *lūṭa* applies in most instances," it is true in most cases. However, when a *lūṭa* affix is used, it is not a contradiction for it to express an object of the act as well.[784]

Fundamental Wisdom states:

> Thus [self] is not different from the appropriated,
> and neither is it the appropriated themselves;
> the self does not exist without the appropriated;
> it's not ascertained as a nonexistent either.[785] [314]

Thus Nāgārjuna explains how the self is not different from the aggregates; how it is not the appropriated [aggregates] themselves; how it's also not the case that the self is not dependent on apprehending the appropriated [aggregates]; and how self is not nonexistent as well. Therefore the object of the act too cannot exist without an agent.

There is, however, the following statement in *Ultimate Emptiness Sutra*:

> An agent is not observed, yet karmic acts exist, and so do fruitional effects.[786]

Here too, we should understand that what the sutra negates is an intrinsically existent agent; we should not understand that it is rejecting [the agent] that is part of everyday convention and designated through dependence. That this is so has been extensively stated [by the Buddha], such as in the following:

> This person who follows the pattern of ignorance will engage
> through volition in the creation of merits as well . . .[787]

In *Rules of Exposition,* [Vasubandhu] says that the first cited sutra is not compatible with the proponents of identitylessness but is compatible with the Cittamātra standpoint.[788] This said, according to the method for defining the person by this supreme tradition [of Candrakīrti], even on the conventional level no agent exists separate from the aggregates. Yet when karmic cause and effect is accepted on the conventional level, given that one accepts the agent of a karmic act as presented in the second sutra citation, such an agent is not defined by identifying something from among the appropriated aggregates to be such an agent. This indeed is a most excellent approach.

The Sage taught that self is designated in dependence on the six elements and so forth

> Thus the Buddha said the self is dependent upon
> these six of earth, water, fire, wind, consciousness, and space,
> and also on the six sense faculties of the eyes and so on,
> which are in turn the bases for contact. 6.138

> He also said the self is conceived on the basis of
> the mind and mental factors. Therefore self is neither
> identical to any of these factors, nor is it their mere collection.
> Thus the thought "I am" does not grasp any of these. 6.139

There are further problems with asserting that the mere collection of aggregates is the self. Thus in the *Meeting of Father and Son Sutra* the Buddha said the self is dependent upon these six elements: earth, water, fire, wind, consciousness, and space, like the space in the nostrils; and also on the six sense faculties of the eyes and so on, which are in turn the bases for contact. [315] "And so on" indicates the inclusion [of the faculties] up to the mental faculty giving rise to contact. He also said definitely, which means "explicitly," that the self is conceived on the basis of the mind and other phenomena such as the mental factors as its bases of designation. Therefore self is neither identical to any of these factors, such as the earth element—that is to say, none of these can individually be the self—nor is it the case that their mere collection is the self. Thus the thought "I am"—ingrained in us since beginningless time—does not grasp any of these, neither the individual phenomena nor their collection. Here is how this point is stated in the sutra:

> O Great King, the individual, the person, consists of the six elements, the six sense bases of contact, and the eighteen turnings of mind.[789]

In Naktso's translation, it reads, "[the person is] a convergence of six elements, with six bases of contact, and is with eighteen spheres of experience of the mind," which seems better.

In general, *individual* and *person* are synonyms. The three—"convergence of six elements," "having six bases," and "with eighteen [spheres of experience]"—these are attributes one is endowed with, while *person* is the basis of these attributes. So these are characterized as being the basis in dependence on which *person* is imputed. "Eighteen turnings of the mind" refers to the six turnings of feeling pleasure in relation to six desirable objects, six turnings of feeling pain in relation to six undesirable objects, and six turnings of feeling neither pleasure nor pain in relation to six neutral objects. Since it is due to feelings of pleasure, pain, and neutrality that the mind repeatedly turns to form, sound, and so on, these feelings are referred to as "turnings of the mind."

Therefore the aggregates are not the focal object of innate "I"-grasping—the focal object as opposed to the apprehended aspect—and neither can something different from the aggregates be observed as its focus. And so when the yogi sees the lack of an intrinsically existent self, he also understands that "mine" too is essenceless, with no intrinsic existence. Through cutting the bonds to all aspects of conditioned cyclic existence, the yogi takes no subsequent rebirth and thus definitely attains the liberation of nirvana.

In view of all foregoing, here are some unique features of Candrakīrti's refined analysis [concerning the selflessness of persons]: Neither the aggregates, individually or collectively, nor something separate from the aggregates is posited to be the focal object of the identity view, and even so, one is able to correctly identify the object of identity view [316] and then define the emptiness of intrinsic existence of person on that basis. Such analysis is indeed most beautiful for those seekers of liberation who are of extremely sharp aptitude. Nothing in other philosophies can steal our heart as this tradition does.

Showing that the opponent's position leads to irrelevance

When searching for the true referent of the thought "I am," some identify it with all five aggregates while others assert it to be mind alone. According to these positions, then, so long as the aggregates come into being, the grasping at the self of persons will also persist. The reason is that as long as one defines [the person] on the basis of searching for the true referent behind the designation, what is found must be the basis or the apprehended object of the grasping at the self of persons. This is stated in the following:

> You say that it's eternal self that is negated when no-self is realized,
> yet you do not consider that to be the basis of "I"-grasping.
> So your claim that the knowledge of no-self definitely eradicates
> the view of self is most astounding indeed! 6.140

You say that when no-self is directly **realized** [by the yogi], **it's eternal self that is negated. Yet you do not consider that** eternal self **to be the basis** or the object **of "I"-grasping** by the innate identity view, either as its focal object or its apprehended aspect. **So your claim that** it is through habituation to the **knowledge of no-self** that one **definitely eradicates the view of self** ingrained in us since beginningless time, **is**, alas, **most astounding indeed!**

To illustrate, using an everyday analogy, that there is no connection between seeing the absence of a permanent self and the essential point about the elimination of beginningless self-grasping, we say:

> This is like a man who, seeing a snake in the cracks of his walls,
> seeks to clear the doubt about whether there is an elephant in the
>   room,
> hoping thereby to remove his fear of the snake.
> Alas! He will be an object of ridicule by others. 6.141

Say **a** foolish **man sees a snake** living **in the cracks of his walls** [317] and is living with fear. Another person tells him, "Be not afraid, **there is no elephant here**," and thus **clearing any doubt** about the presence of an elephant. Say then that the man, in addition to dispelling his fear of an elephant with this knowledge of the elephant's absence, were to **hope thereby to remove his fear of a snake** as well. **Alas! He would be an object of ridicule** or laughter **by other** more intelligent people.

So, even though the condition that caused the fear of a snake remains nearby, if owing to some foolish person's words, a person were to fail to see the danger of the snake and give up his efforts to remove that threat—letting down his guard with the knowledge that there were no elephants around—he might then be seized by that snake. Likewise regarding those who, believing through familiarity with the absence of an elephant-like permanent self that the danger posed by self-grasping ingrained since beginningless time has been averted, let down their guard, they will not be able to remove the identity view that [according to the Buddhist essentialist schools] has the aggregates as its object. Therefore [such an insight] will definitely fail to disrupt the person's cycle of existence.

This [above argument of Candrakīrti] reveals that the proponents of many schools, fellow Buddhists as well as non-Buddhists, who seek to establish suchness fail to understand how to eradicate the object grasped at by our innate self-grasping. Because of this, they forsake true suchness and seek to present other forms of suchness. The text shows here how all such presentations are pointless endeavors. To appreciate this point is critical.

Negating the three remaining positions: the support, the supported, and so forth

This has two parts: (1) negating the support, the supported, and inherence and (2) summarizing the essential points of what have been negated.

Negating the support, the supported, and inherence

Thus having demonstrated how the self is neither intrinsically identical to nor separate from the aggregates, [318] to indicate that the self and the aggregates do not intrinsically exist in a mutual relationship of support and the supported, we say:

> The self does not exist in the aggregates;
> nor do the aggregates exist in the self.
> If they were separate, such notions might be plausible.
> Since they are not different, these notions are mere concepts. 6.142

The self does not exist in the aggregates as intrinsically supported, **nor do the aggregates exist in self** as intrinsically supporting. The reason is that **if they**, the aggregates and the self, **were** to exist as inherently **separate**, then **such notions** as intrinsically existent *support* and *supported* **might be plausible**. However, **since they are not different**, intrinsically separate entities, **these notions** of the two being inherently established support and the supported **are mere** distorted **concepts**. In the everyday world, for example, we do observe a relationship of support and supported between two essentially different things, such as a bowl and the yogurt inside it. We do not see this in the case of the aggregates and the self. Therefore the two do not exist intrinsically as support and supported.

To show how the self does not exist intrinsically in the aggregates even in terms of an ownership, we say:

> Self cannot be said to own the aggregate of form;
> since self does not exist, such ownership is meaningless.
> One owns a cow through difference or a body through inherence,
> but self is neither identical to nor different from the body. 6.143

The **self cannot be said to own the aggregates of form**, for we have already rejected the self being either identical to or different from the aggregates. **Since self does not exist** as such, self's **ownership** of the aggregates **is meaningless** in terms of intrinsic existence. The relation of ownership either can take the form "Devadatta **owns a cow**," which is **through difference, or** can take the form "Devadatta **has a body**," in which case ownership is not through difference but **through inherence. But** since **self is not** one with or **identical to the body** and **neither** is it **different** or separate **from** it, the self's ownership of the body through an intrinsic nature remains impossible. One should understand that these arguments also reject an intrinsically existent self that owns the four remaining aggregates as well.

Summarizing the essential points of what has been negated

[319] Now, through bringing together all the positions that have been negated above, we will enumerate the ways in which the identity view assumes its form by focusing on distorted [objects]:

> The body *is* not self, nor does the self *possess* the body;
> self does not exist *in* the body, nor does the body exist *in* the self;
> in these four terms understand all the remaining aggregates.
> These are considered the twenty views of self. 6.144

(1) **The body *is* not self** yet one views it as such; (2) **the self does not** inherently *possess* **the body** yet one views it as doing so; (3) **the self does not** intrinsically **exist *in* the body,** (4) **nor does the body intrinsically exist**

in the self yet one views it in such terms. There are thus four views. Just as explained here in relation to the aggregate of form [the body], we should understand in these four terms how the identity view relates to all the remaining four aggregates, such as feeling. These then are considered the twenty views of self that grasp at the perishable collection.[790]

[*Question*:] It would be more appropriate to add the viewing of self and aggregates as different and have a fivefold analysis in relation to each of the aggregates. Does not *Fundamental Wisdom* state the following as well?

> Neither identical to nor different from the aggregates,
> the Tathāgata is not in the aggregates, nor the aggregates in him;
> the Tathāgata does not possess the aggregates;
> so what then is the Tathāgata?[791]

Thus the aspects [of identity view] should number twenty-five, so why do you speak of twenty?

[*Reply*:] The sutras present these twenty aspects of the identity view because the identity view cannot cling to a self without first grasping at the aggregates. So it is in these four terms [possible identity relationship] that one engages with self on the basis of focusing on the aggregates. Since the fifth basis of clinging to self as something separate from the aggregates is something that is found only among the proponents of the non-Buddhist schools and not others, this fifth aspect of identity view is not listed [in the sutra]. *Fundamental Wisdom* lists the fifth aspect to refute the standpoint of the non-Buddhist schools. This is how we should understand.

[To continue, the root text says:]

> When the scepter of wisdom realizing no-self crushes
> the mountain of self view, these twenty high peaks
> belonging to the mighty range of identity view
> will all be demolished together as well. 6.145

In the scriptures, it says:

> The fruit of stream entry is realized through demolishing the
> twenty towering peaks of identity view with the scepter of
> gnosis.[792]

When the scepter of an ārya's gnosis has not descended, the mountain of identity view, grasping at intrinsic existence on the basis of focusing on an "I," sends down boulders of afflictions day after day. This mountain has existed since the beginningless cycle of existence; its slopes pervade every direction and surface, and its peaks, the highest in the three realms, emerged from the ground of fundamental ignorance. However, **when the scepter of wisdom** directly **realizing no-self crushes the mountain of self view,** [320] **these twenty high peaks belonging to the mighty range of** the basic **identity view** just described **will all be demolished together** with it **as well.** These twenty are the ones described above in terms of four in relation to each of the five aggregates.

In the translation of the *Commentary*, although it reads, "One should understand that those that will be demolished together with the towering peak are peaks [too]," we should understand this, as found in the translation of the root text, as referring to those that emerge together with the basic identity view.

Given that the innate identity view is none of the twenty views described above, in the line "Belonging to the mighty mountain range of identity view," [Candrakīrti] explains these twenty peaks of identity view as being located within the basic identity view. Thus the twenty views relinquished by the stream enterer together with [basic identity view] are also acquired [views] as well. Such views are therefore not to be identified just with grasping at intrinsic existence of "I" in general; rather they are forms of grasping arising through inferior philosophical tenets that reinforce the validity of the mode of apprehension of such grasping at intrinsic existence. And it is the seed of such [acquired] grasping that is relinquished by the stream enterer.

Refuting a substantially real person that is neither identical to nor different from the aggregates

This has two parts: presenting the opponent's position and refuting that position.

Presenting the opponent's position

Now to dispel the assertion of the person as a substantial reality as postulated by the noble Saṃmatīya school, the text says:

Some assert a substantially real person that is inexpressible
as one or different [from the aggregates], as permanent, impermanent,
    and so on.
It is claimed to be knowable by six classes of consciousness;
and this is held to be the basis for "I"-grasping as well. 6.146

Some fellow Buddhists, the Saṃmatīya school, **assert** that because of the argument "for there is no apprehension of self apart from the aggregates" (6.124b), the person is not different from the aggregates; but neither is it something that has the nature of the aggregates, for if it were, the self would have arising and disintegration. Therefore the self or person **is inexpressible as one** with **or different [from the aggregates]**. Likewise, they assert the person to be inexpressible **as permanent, impermanent, and so on.** Nonetheless, they assert such a **person** to be **substantially real** for they describe it to be the agent of the two karmic deeds [virtuous and nonvirtuous] as well to be the "consumer" of the happiness and suffering that are the effects of these two karmic deeds. [321] It is also, according to them, what is imprisoned in the cycle of existence and liberated or released at the time of attaining nirvana. Such a self **is** also **claimed to be knowable by six classes of consciousness** and **is held to be the basis** or focus **for "I"-grasping as well.**

Refuting that position

To explain that this assertion of a substantially real person is untenable, the text says:

Just as you do not take mind's distinctness from body to be
    inexpressible,
you cannot conceive substantial realities to be inexpressible.
For if self exists in some manner as a real entity,
then, like the mind, it too will be real and not inexpressible. 6.147

Just as for the very reason that **you do not take** or assert **mind's** identity or **distinctness from body to be inexpressible, you cannot conceive** the entities or **substantial realities to be inexpressible** in terms of their identity or distinctness. **For if self** does **exist in some manner as a real entity** or substantial reality, **then, just like the mind, it too will be real and not**

inexpressible with respect to these two modes [as identical to or different from the body].

Having thus explained, in this preceding stanza, how it is impossible for something that is inexplicable to be substantially existent, to show the person to be a nominal reality the text says:

> For you, given that a vase is not a substantial reality,
> it thus remains ineffable apart from its form and other features;
> likewise, self too would be ineffable apart from the aggregates.
> Therefore consider not the self to exist in its own right. 6.148

For you, given that a vase is not a self-sufficient **substantial reality, it thus remains ineffable apart from its** attributes like **form and other features** in terms of being identical to or different from those attributes. **Likewise**, what you identify as **self too would be** a nominal reality and **ineffable apart from the aggregates** in terms of being identical to or different from them. **Therefore consider** or hold **not the self to exist in its own right**.

In these two stanzas we have refuted the substantial reality of the person and have demonstrated how the person is found to be a nominal reality. [322] We will now, by explaining how identity and difference are the basis for [conceiving something as] an entity, refute the substantial reality of self because it is devoid of such bases. Thus we say:

> You do not take consciousness to be different from itself
> but think it to be different from form and other aggregates.
> In all things these two aspects [of identity and difference] can be seen,
> and because the self lacks these reality attributes, it does not exist.
>   6.149

Just as **you do not take consciousness to be different from itself**, likewise you should assert that the person is definitely not different from itself but one with itself. Similarly, just as you **think** consciousness **to be different from form and other aggregates**, likewise you have to admit that the person is definitely an entity distinct from the aggregates. **These two aspects** of identity and difference **can be seen in all things, and because the self lacks these reality attributes** of identity and difference, **it does not exist** as a substantial reality.

Explaining with analogy how the self is a mere dependent designation

This has four parts: (1) how although self does not exist in any of the seven ways, like a chariot, it's a dependent designation, (2) explaining in depth the two remaining positions not addressed thus far, (3) rejecting objections against this explanation, and (4) how the referents of other terms of everyday convention are established.

How although self does not exist in any of the seven ways, like a chariot, it's a dependent designation

> Therefore the basis of "I"-grasping is not a real entity;
> self is not something different from the aggregates, nor is it the aggregates themselves;
> the aggregates are not its support, nor does the self possess them;
> this proves that the self exists in dependence on the aggregates. 6.150

Thus, when analyzed in the manner described above, the substantial reality of a person becomes untenable. **Therefore the basis** or focus **of "I"-grasping is not a real** or an intrinsically established **entity.** For when analyzed, the **self is not different** in nature **from the aggregates, nor is it the aggregates themselves**—either in terms of their collection or individually; the self is **not** the support of **the aggregates,** nor do the aggregates exist as **the support** for the self;[793] and such a **self does not possess the aggregates** in an essential manner. [323] So whether it is the fellow Buddhist schools that assert the self to be a nominal reality or those that state it to be devoid of ultimate existence, it's inappropriate to maintain any notion of self characterized in the above terms [of identity and difference]. So we say, **this proves that self exists in dependence on the aggregates.**

When one accepts the simple fact "conditioned by that, this comes into being," so that the framework of conventional truth is not annihilated, one does not do so on the basis of admitting arising through any of the four extremes such as no cause. Likewise, in the context of self, when we assert it to be designated in dependence upon the aggregates, this eliminates the opponent's flawed standpoint just described. Yet to abide by the conventions of the world, we assert [the self to be] designated in dependence upon the aggregates. This much we do accept. That conventional designation of self exists is something we observe incontrovertibly.

An analogy from the external world elucidates the points just explained so that self is established as a mere designation:

> A chariot cannot be said to be different from its parts;
> it is not identical with the parts, nor does it possess the parts;
> it is not in the parts, nor do the parts exist in it;
> it is not the mere collection, nor is it the shape. 6.151

A chariot cannot be said to be *different* from its parts; it is not *identical* or one with the parts, nor does it *possess* the parts; it is not *in* the parts as supported by them, **nor do the parts exist *in* it** as the supported in an intrinsic manner; **it is not the mere *collection*** of the parts, **nor is it the *shape*** of the parts. We should understand self and the aggregates in the same way.

Explaining in depth the two remaining positions not addressed thus far

This has two parts: the actual point and extending this reasoning to others.

The actual point

This has two parts: rejecting the assertion that the collection is the chariot and rejecting the assertion that the mere shape is the chariot.

Rejecting the assertion that the collection is the chariot

The opponent's standpoint has already been presented above. The following establishes the refutation of the [last] two possibilities [324]—the collection of parts and the shape—as being the chariot:

> For if the mere collection constitutes the chariot,
> the chariot would exist even when the parts are not assembled;
> since there can be no parts without the bearer of the parts,
> that shape alone is the chariot is illogical as well. 6.152

If the mere collection of the chariot's parts **constitutes the chariot**, then **the chariot would exist even** amid the collection of parts of a dismantled chariot, **when the parts are not assembled.** Although the rejection of the collection of parts as being the whole has already been explained above, this is stated here [again] to reveal a further objection different from the one presented above. The further objection is that **since there can be no parts without** the existence of **the bearer of the parts**, the parts would have no existence for these Buddhists. For they maintain that the chariot cannot have a bearer of parts [that takes the chariot as its part].[794]

[*Question*:] These Buddhist schools assert the collection of parts to be the bearer of parts and the parts to be its constitutive elements. They hold these two to be the *parts-bearer* and the *parts*. So it is not the case that these Buddhist schools deny the existence of the bearer of parts.

[*Reply*:] This is not a problem. In our own [Madhyamaka] system, since both the individual aggregates as well as the collection of aggregates are the *appropriated*, we do not assert these to be the *appropriator*. Likewise, we hold both individual parts of the chariot as well as their collection as *constitutive elements* and not as the *whole*. These fellow Buddhist schools, however, do not accept the existence of a whole that is not the collection, and it is this [view] that is being rejected as well. The adverbial phrase "as well" signifies the inclusion of collection, which is not explicitly mentioned. It is included to help us understand not only **that** saying the **shape** of the parts **alone is the chariot is illogical** but also for the mere collection [to be the chariot] is untenable **as well.**

Rejecting the assertion that the mere shape is the chariot

> For you, just as shapes exist previously in each of the parts,
> if these very shapes were to persist when the chariot is formed,
> then, just as there is no chariot in the unassembled parts,
> in the assembled parts too, there could be no chariot. 6.153

> If within the chariot that is right here and now,
> the wheels and so on have acquired different shapes,
> this fact would be perceived; but is not the case.
> Hence shape alone cannot be the chariot. 6.154

Furthermore, if you assert that the shape alone is the chariot, we would ask:

Is this shape that of the individual parts or is it that of the collection? If it is the former, [325] is it that of the parts prior to being assembled, before they have shed their individual characters? Or is it the shape of the parts after they have relinquished this earlier character? If you assert it to be the former, this too is illogical. Why?

For you, just as shapes exist in each of the individual chariot **parts** such as the wheels **previously,** before being assembled, **if these very shapes** that previously existed **were to persist** later **when the chariot is** perceived or **formed, then, just as there is no chariot in the unassembled parts, in the assembled parts too, there could be no chariot.** This is because you define the mere shapes of the individual parts to constitute the chariot, and insofar as their shapes are concerned, there is no difference between those of the earlier and later temporal stages.

Suppose you assert the second option—that the chariot is the subsequent shape that is different from the shapes of [the parts] prior [to the assembled] stage. In that case, **if within the chariot that is right here and now, the wheels and so on**, which includes the axle, bolts, and so on, **have acquired different shapes**, such as being square, oblong, circular, and so on, shapes that are different from those present previously when these parts were not assembled, **this fact** of the different shapes **would be perceived** with our eyes. This is not the case. **Hence the shape** of the parts **alone cannot the chariot.**

If the thought is that the chariot is the unique shape of the collection of its parts such as wheels when they are assembled, this too is illogical:

> Given that collection has no reality for you,
> the shape you mean cannot be that of the collection.
> For how can a be shape defined
> on the basis of something utterly unreal? 6.155

If there exists something called "collection," a real entity with substantial reality, one could then conceive of a shape on the basis of such a thing. However, there is not even the slightest degree of something called "collection of parts" that possesses substantial reality. **Given that, for you, collection has no reality**—that is, it has no substantial reality—**the shape you mean cannot be** conceived **of** by taking the **collection** of parts as its designative base. For you uphold the tenet that nominal realities such as [shape and the like] must have substantial realities as their designative bases, and you assert the collection of parts to be a nominal reality. Thus in this discussion of a chariot, **how can**, in the context of defining a chariot, **a shape** that is said to be the chariot **be defined on the basis of something utterly unreal**, with no substantial reality, as its designative basis? This cannot be so.

Here the opponent accepts that nominally real entities are [326] each conceived as dependent on a substantial real entity as its designative basis; they also maintain that both collection and shape are nominally real entities. Although a contradiction arises here only if the opponent asserts the collection to be the designative basis of shape, we should understand [the argument] along the following lines: Just as it would be illogical to posit that a person's color is the person, it would be illogical to posit the chariot's color and shape to be the chariot. This is because both things are among what is appropriated by [the designation] the "chariot."

Extending this reasoning to others

> Just as you admit here in the case of a chariot,
> know that effects that are unreal can come to be
> in dependence upon unreal causes;
> you should understand the same in all instances. 6.156

> This also reveals the untenable nature of the claim
> that perceptions like that of a vase come from real form and so on.
> With no arising, form and so on have no existence as well.
> For this reason too, things cannot subsist in shapes. 6.157

Say the opponent asserts that even if one grants that a collection, which is unreal, is a nominal entity, one can still conceive in dependence on it a shape that is unreal and is a nominal reality. In that case, **just as you now admit here in the case of a chariot** the positing of a nominally existent shape in dependence upon a nominally existent collection, you should **know that in dependence on unreal causes**, such as ignorance and seeds, that varied **effects** like karmic acts and sprouts, which **are unreal** in character or in their nature, **can come to be. You should** likewise **understand the same in all** other **instances** how it is from unreal causes and that unreal effects arise. So what point is there in clinging to what is false as real, to these [imagined] real entities that resemble shadow animals whose meat cannot be consumed no matter how one strives with hundredfold effort?

Now many fellow Buddhist schools claim that the collection, wherein the eight atomic constituents of the vase—its **form** atom **and so on**—exist in a cohered manner is what constitutes the vase. And it's from such an entity that **perceptions like that of a vase** occurs. Given that **this** chariot analogy **also reveals the untenable nature of** such a **claim**, the assertion remains incorrect. Furthermore, **with no** intrinsic **arising** as already explained above, **form and so on have no** intrinsic **existence as well. For this reason too**, the assertion that "vase" and so on appropriate substantially real entities remains untenable. [327] Therefore **things** like vases **cannot subsist in** specific **shapes** of forms.

Rejecting objections against this explanation

[*Opponent*:] We will say this: Were one to search for the referent of the term *chariot* through the seven-point analysis outlined above (6.151), there would be no chariot. And since the chariot would become nonexistent, our everyday conventions about the chariot would be undermined. This would be incorrect, for we see that everyday conventions such as "Fetch the chariot," "Buy the chariot," "Repair the chariot," and so on are necessary. Therefore, as they are known to the world, things like chariots do have an existence.

[*Response*:] Between the two of us, this fault applies to you alone; I should charge this against you. How so? You posit the reality of a chariot on the basis of analysis, searching for the true referent of the term *chariot*. You do not accept any alternative method of positing existence other than searching for the true referent of the designated term. And when the referent of the term is searched for through the sevenfold analysis, how can everyday conventions like "Fetch the chariot" remain established for you?

This is how the author of the treatise [Candrakīrti] responds to the above argument. Today's Tibetans who claim to be Prāsaṅgika, however, say that this argument—if the chariot cannot be found when searched for through sevenfold analysis, its existence cannot be posited—represents the Madhyamaka standpoint. In so doing, they tediously pollute a perfect system with the dirty water of inferior philosophical thinking.

For us [Madhyamaka], however, the fault raised in the argument made above does not apply. So we say:

> Although the chariot does not exist in any of the seven terms,
> both in ultimate reality and in terms of the world;

> we here impute the chariot in dependence on its parts,
> without analysis and through everyday convention alone. 6.158

Yes, **although the chariot does not exist** when searched for **in any of the seven terms, both in** suchness or **ultimate reality and in terms of** everyday conventions of **the world,** even then, **without analysis** that seeks the referent behind the term and **through everyday convention alone,** just like "blue color," "feelings," and so on, **here** too, [328] **we impute the chariot in dependence on its parts** like wheels and so on. Therefore, just as we accept the dependent origination of sprouts from seeds in terms of mere conditionedness, we assert that the chariot too is conceived in dependence upon its parts. "So for us," writes Candrakīrti, "everyday conventions like 'Fetch the chariot' do not become untenable. And this the opponent too should accept."[795] Given this statement, we should indicate that in this Madhyamaka system, where one does not posit a chariot on the basis of searching for the referent of the term, one accepts everyday conventions of the world and maintains that even the opponent should accept such everyday conventions. We should not say things such as "I have no position" when the opponent turns the objections leveled against him back on us and we are unable to respond.

How the referents of other terms of everyday convention are established

> It is the *bearer of the parts* and the *constituted*;
> the chariot itself is referred to as the *agent* of going;
> for people it is established as the *appropriator*.
> Undermine not the known conventions of the world. 6.159

Not only is it clearly established that in this Madhyamaka system the term *chariot* is designated on the basis of everyday conventions of the world, the other terms associated with the chariot are also accepted not through searching for their true referents but within the framework of what is known to the everyday world. For example, in relation to its parts like the wheels and so on, **the chariot is the *bearer of the parts*, and** in relation to its constituents like the wheel, it is **the *constituted*.** From the point of view of the act of appropriating what is to be appropriated, such as the wheels, **it is referred to** as the *agent* of going, and **for people it is established** also **as the *appropriator*** in relation to its object of appropriation, such as its body.

Some, understanding the meaning of the scriptures in a distorted way, assert that only the collection of [individual] parts exists and there is no bearer of the parts at all other than collection [of individual constituents], since nothing separate from such collections can be observed. They extend this [line of thinking] and assert that only the collection of constituents, of actions, and of the appropriated [aggregates] exist. [329] Other than these [individual elements], they claim, no such thing as the *constituted*, *agent*, and *appropriator* exists at all, for nothing different from these [individual elements] is perceived. According to those who speak about everyday established conventions of the world in such distorted terms, the very reasoning they have just presented about the nonexistence of a bearer of parts would make collection of [individual] parts to be nonexistent as well. So **undermine not**—that is to say, do not destroy—**the known** everyday **conventions of the world** such as chariots. This [dismantling of known conventions of the world] deserves only to be rejected.

Now the reason other fellow Buddhist schools, both higher and lower schools of tenets, assert the collection of parts and so on to be the bearer of the parts and so on is this: If these are not posited as the bearer of the parts, since no [bearer of parts] that is different from these [collections] is perceived, they remain incapable of positing a bearer of parts and so on that is capable of effective function. This is why they make such assertions. They do not know how to posit something if the true referent of its term is not found when sought. Therefore, since they do not accept chariots and so on to be mere designations of terms, they accept them as existing through intrinsic characteristics. Because of this, the *Commentary* speaks of them as "understanding the meaning of the scriptures in a distorted way." In this excellent system [of Candrakīrti], however, even though nothing whatsoever—the mere collection of parts, the individual parts themselves, and so on—is identified as the thing, one can still accord effective functions to the bearer of parts within nominal framework of mere designation. And this is explained to be the meaning of the scriptures, the unique intention of the Buddha. So those with discerning intelligence should learn this way of interpreting the intention of the scriptures.

How positing self as mere designation leads to the benefit of easily abandoning conceptualizations grasping at extremes

This has five parts: (1) the actual point, (2) rejecting objections against this explanation, (3) correlating "chariot" and "self" as analogy and referent, (4) other benefits of accepting a dependently designated self, and (5) identifying the self that is the basis of bondage and freedom for the ignorant and the learned. [330]

The actual point

> How can that which does not exist in any of the seven terms
> be said to exist at all? Yogis find no such existence.
> As such they also enter ultimate reality with ease,
> so we should accept a thing's existence as shown here. 6.160

This conventional truth of the world will not be found to exist when analyzed, as outlined above, through seeking true referents of the terms. Yet it does exist in terms of unanalyzed worldly convention. Therefore, when the yogi analyzes self and chariot in the manner outlined above, he will swiftly penetrate the truth of their suchness.

How is this so? For if the chariot does exist intrinsically, it should be findable among one of the seven options when sought through the sevenfold analysis; yet **yogis find no such existence** of a chariot. This being the case, **how can that which does not exist in any of the seven terms be said to exist** through intrinsic nature **at all?** It does not. Therefore a certainty will arise in the yogi that this so-called intrinsically existent chariot is something purely imagined by someone whose eyes of awareness are infected by cataracts of ignorance and it has no intrinsic existence. **As such they**, the yogis, **also enter ultimate reality with ease.** The term "also" implies how the yogis do not undermine the presentations of conventional truth. **So** here in the context of the Madhyamaka system, **we should accept a thing's existence**, such as that of the chariot, **as shown here** in terms of unanalyzed existence.

Candrakīrti states that those learned in the Madhyamaka tradition "should recognize that the position outlined above is free of faults and possesses great merit and should definitively be embraced."[796] Therefore we should accept this flawless position to be our own standpoint; we should not slander it by saying we have no positions at all.

Rejecting objections against this explanation

[*Opponent:*] It may be true that yogis do not observe the chariot when analyzed in the above manner. [331] However, the mere collection of parts that is observed does possess intrinsic existence.

[*Response:*] You seek yarn fibers in the ashes of a scorched woolen cloth, which is indeed laughable.

> If there is no chariot, then there could be
> no parts-bearer and hence no parts either. 6.161ab

If there is no intrinsically existing **chariot, then there could be no bearer of the parts** in its own right, **and hence** there could be **no parts** that exist in their own right **either.**

[*Question:*] Isn't it the case that even when the chariot is disassembled into individual parts, the collection of parts like wheels is still observed? So why do you say that without the bearer of parts, the parts themselves will have no existence?

[*Response:*] It is not like this. The reason why we grasp the dismantled individual parts like wheels and so on as chariot parts is because of our prior perception of their association with the chariot. It's on such a basis alone that we think of things like wheels and so on as parts of a chariot. Someone with no such prior perception will not hold them [to be chariot parts]. Such a person will perceive the wheels and so on to be wholes in themselves in relation to their own constitutive elements. Within the perception of such a person, the wheels and so on are far removed from association with a chariot, and as such they are not cognized as chariot parts.

Furthermore, this fact of how if the chariot has no intrinsic existence, its parts too cannot have intrinsic existence can also be understood from the following analogy.

> Just as when the chariot has burned no parts remain,
> when the fire of wisdom burns the bearer, parts are burned too. 6.161cd

Just as when, for example, **the chariot,** which is the whole, **has burned no parts remain,** as they have been burned as well, likewise, from the striking of dry sticks of analysis, **when the fire of wisdom** realizing objectlessness **burns** without trace **the bearer**—namely, the inherently existing chariot—**parts,**

which are akin to firewood for such wisdom fire, **are burned too**, for they are incapable of standing firm with intrinsic existence.

Correlating "chariot" and "self" as analogy and referent

> Similarly, through being known to the world,
> and in dependence on the aggregates, elements, and six sense bases,
> self too is considered the appropriator.
> The appropriated are the *object* and self is the *agent*. 6.162

So that conventional truth is not annihilated and so that the yogi easily engages with suchness, the chariot is posited as a dependent designation on the basis of contemplating the manner in which its existence is analyzed. [332] **Similarly, through being known to the world, and in dependence on the** appropriated **aggregates,** the six **elements, and six sense bases,** just like the chariot, **self too is considered the appropriator,** for it is designated on the basis of these factors. Likewise, we posit that **the appropriated** aggregates **are the** *object* [of the act] **and self is the** *agent* as well.

Other benefits of accepting a dependently designated self

When the self is posited as something dependently designated, it then does not become the basis for views tending to extremes in terms of it being immutable, mutable, and so on. Because of this, it becomes easier to cease conceptualizations such as [the self] being impermanent and so on in an intrinsic sense.

To state this, we say:

> Self does not exist as a real entity, so it is not immutable;
> nor is it not mutable; it does not arise or disintegrate;
> it possesses no attributes like permanence and so on;
> it has no existence in terms of identity or difference. 6.163

This **self,** which is designated in dependence upon the aggregates, **does not exist as a real entity, so it is not** in any intrinsic manner **immutable; nor is it mutable.** For if self did exist as something mutable in its own right, given that self and the appropriated aggregates cannot be different entities, the appropriated aggregates themselves would constitute the self. In that case, such a self will undergo inherent arising and disintegration during its discrete temporal moments, with the preceding and the subsequent instances [of self] becoming unrelated to each other. There will also be the consequence that what is appropriated would become the appropriator. So this [option that self exists intrinsically as something mutable] remains untenable. Similarly, the option that self is immutable or permanent is also untenable. For if it is permanent, the very same self that existed in a past life will be the self that came into being in this life; and since the appropriated aggregates associated with self of the past life and this life are different, the self cannot be one. For there is no self that is separate from the appropriated aggregates. *Fundamental Wisdom* states:

> If the self were the aggregates,
> it would arise and disintegrate.[797]

Candrakīrti says that from this above we can discern that citing the two attributes as in the line "**it does not arise or disintegrate**" accords with the master Nāgārjuna's intention. The arising and disintegrating referred to here are those that are [conceived to be] established in their own right. Such a self **possesses none** of the four **attributes like permanence and so on**.[798] This is similar to what *Fundamental Wisdom* explains in the following when contemplating the examination of the Tathāgata [333]:

> The four of permanence, impermanence, and so on,
> how can their pacification exist in it?[799]

This self **has no** intrinsic **existence in terms of identity or difference**. The reason for these is that an intrinsically real entity called *self* simply does not exist. A sutra states:

> Four types of inexhaustible facts
> were revealed by the world's savior:
> sentient beings, space, and awakening mind,
> and the qualities of the buddha as well.
>
> Were they to possess substantial reality,
> would they then not become exhaustible?

That which does exist has no exhaustion;
therefore they are described as inexhaustible.[800]

This statement, that sentient beings are inexhaustible because they do not exist as substantial realities, is an authoritative source here.

Identifying the self that is the basis of bondage and freedom for the ignorant and the learned

On the basis of this the thought grasping at an "I"
arises constantly in beings, and associated with this
thoughts grasping at "mine" arise—such a self exists
as a convention unanalyzed due to delusion. 6.164

Self is such that when its true referent is sought through the sevenfold analysis, [attributes like] permanence and impermanence remain impossible. However, those who fail to see that self is devoid of intrinsic existence cling in ignorance to its intrinsic existence. These beings that cling to self as intrinsically existent with an identity view wander in the cycle of existence.

Now when one comes to search for such a self and sees through one's analysis that it would be illogical for the aggregates themselves to be the self, non-Buddhist tīrthikas, who are mistaken with respect to the nature of the self, apprehend it to be an entity that is separate from the aggregates. Our fellow Buddhist schools, sensing that there cannot be a self that is different from the aggregates, mistakenly assert the aggregates alone to constitute the self. Both assume that one has to adopt one of these two options. Those who interpret the meaning of the scriptures without distortion recognize that self does not exist in either of these two ways. They understand that it is **on the basis of this** that **the thought grasping at an "I" arises constantly in** all **beings** residing in the realms of humans, hungry ghosts, animals, and so on. And with respect to the internal factors of the eyes and so on that are the causal basis for imputing self—upon which such a self exerts control and which are somehow **associated with this** self—[334] as well as external factors owned by that self, **thoughts grasping at "mine" arise. Such a self exists as a convention unanalyzed due to delusion** or ignorance; it does not exist in its own right.

Such a self does not exist intrinsically, but it is construed as such an existent because of delusion or ignorance. Nevertheless yogis never perceive such a self. And when the yogi does not perceive such an intrinsically existent self, he also does not perceive [the intrinsic existence of] the eyes and so on that are appropriated by such a self. Thus yogis do not perceive anything that is the causal basis of "self" and "mine" as possessing inherent existence. He will therefore attain freedom from the cycle of existence. *Fundamental Wisdom* says:

> With respect to inner and outer things,
> when the thought of "I" and "mine" ceases,
> appropriation will come to an end,
> and with cessation of this, birth ceases.[801]

Negating intrinsic existence of "mine"

> When there is no agent, the object of action is no more,
> so "mine" cannot be if there is no "I."
> Thus viewing the "I" and mine to be empty,
> yogis will attain total freedom. 6.165

One might ask, "How is it that if self has no intrinsic existence, 'mine' too would have no intrinsic existence either?"

[*Reply:*] Just as, **when there is no** potter, the **agent, the object of** his **action, the clay pot, is no more, so** intrinsically real **"mine" too cannot be if there is no** intrinsically real **"I." Thus viewing the "I" and mine to be** empty and becoming familiar with such a fact, **yogis will attain total freedom** from cyclic existence.

When one does not view form and so on as intrinsically existent, afflictions like attachment that conceive form and so on as possessing intrinsic existence will cease. So śrāvakas and pratyekabuddhas no longer take rebirth and transcend to nirvana. As for bodhisattvas, though they may have already seen the absence of such a self, [335] swayed by the force of their compassion, they continue to assume births in the continuum of cyclic existence until their enlightenment. Hence selflessness really is the most essential point of the path of both for Mahayana and Hīnayāna. Learned ones should therefore thoroughly investigate no-self as explained herein.

18. Extending the Analysis

Extending the analysis of self and chariot to others

This has three parts: (1) extending this to things like vases and woolen cloth, (2) extending this to things like causes and effects, and (3) rejecting objections against this analysis.

Extending this to things like vases and woolen cloth

Just as the constructs of self and its appropriated aggregates are [revealed] through analysis to be similar to a chariot, the same analysis is true also of other entities. To state this, the text says:

> Vases, woolen cloth, shields, armies, forests, garlands, trees,
> houses, carts, rest houses, and all such things
> that people designate based on their bases, know these likewise.
> The Buddha, for one, did not quarrel with the world. 6.166

> The parts, qualities, attachment, defining characteristics, fuel and so on,
> the whole, quality-bearer, object of attachment, the characterized, fire
>   and so on,
> none of these exist when subjected to sevenfold chariot analysis.
> Yet they exist in another way, through everyday conventions of the
>   world. 6.167

When things like **vases, woolen cloth, shields, armies, forests, garlands, trees, houses, carts, rest houses, and all such things** are **subjected to sevenfold chariot analysis** searching for the referents behind their terms, **none of these exist** in any of the seven terms. **Yet they exist in another way—** unanalyzed and **through everyday conventions of the world.**[802]

With respect to a "cart,"[803] some Tibetan teachers say that [the Sanskrit term] *śakaṭa*, which literally means "with wheels," refers to a mini-chariot capable of carrying about three tea crates and consists of a cabin with wheels and a partition as well. Likewise, we should recognize too all similar conventions **that people designate on their bases** [336] as existing only on the level of unexamined everyday convention. For this reason it is said [in the sutra] that **the Buddha, for one, did not quarrel with the world.** The *Presenting the Three Vows Sutra* in the Heap of Jewels collection states, "It is the world that disputes with me; I do not dispute with the world."[804] Thus the Buddha states that he too accepts what are posited as existents through unimpaired conventions of the world. Therefore one must not undermine the agreed-on conventions of the world.

How do the people of the world construct conventions and by what means? Just as the vase is **the whole** and its fired clay and so on are its **parts**, and just as the vase is the **quality-bearer** and its dark hue and so on caused by flames are the **qualities**, the basis of attachment for a sentient being or person who is attached to an attractive object is the **object of attachment**, while excessive craving fixated on an attractive contaminated object is the **attachment**. Similarly, the vase is the **characterized** thing, while "having a bulbous body with an open extended lip and long neck and so on" are its **defining characteristics**; **fire** is that which burns, while **fuel** is that which is being burned, **and so on.** Thus it is in dependence upon constituents that a "whole" is conceived, and it is in dependence upon a whole that "parts" are designated. The same is true likewise of all the examples up to fire and fuel, all of which are designated by means of mutual dependence. Although the referents for such terms do not exist when sought through the sevenfold analysis, one *can* posit their existence through everyday conventions of the world; they are not amenable to ultimate analysis probing their true suchness.

Extending this to things like causes and effects

Not only do constituents and so on exist through mutual dependence, causes and effects also exist through mutual dependence. To state this, the text says:

> If a thing produces an effect, it is indeed a cause on that account;
> if no effect is produced, with this absence, there can be no cause.
> Yet effects too come to arise when there is the cause.
> So tell me what comes from what, and what precedes what? 6.168

If, for example, a thing produces an effect, it is indeed a cause on that account; if no effect is produced, with this absence of an effect, there can be no cause for such an effect. Yet effects too come to arise when there is the cause, so the two, cause and effect, exist through mutual dependence and not through intrinsic existence. If, in contrast, cause and effect are conceived as having intrinsic existence, how then do cause and effect relate to each other and in what manner? Do tell me, between the two—cause and effect—what comes from what, and what precedes what, the cause or the effect? With respect to intrinsic existence, it would be illogical for the cause to be temporally prior, since its correlate, the effect—in relation to which it is defined as cause—must exist [at the time of the cause] as well. It would also be illogical for the effect to be temporally prior, for this would mean that the effect would have no cause. Therefore one should understand that what are conceived as causes and effects are established only through mutual dependence, just as in the case of a chariot; they have no intrinsic existence.

Furthermore, if the cause were to produce its effect intrinsically, would it do so on the basis of coming into contact with the effect?

If you say that a cause produces the effect through contacting it, [337]
cause and effect will be not distinct since they will share the same
    potency.
If they are indeed distinct, then a cause will not differ from non-causes.
Yet apart from these two, there is no other conception [of causal rela-
    tion]. 6.169

Since your cause produces no effects, there cannot be what you call
    "effects";
also a cause devoid of an effect would have no reason to be called a
    "cause."
In that both cause and effect are like illusions for us, we are not vulner-
    able to these objections.
And yet the things of the everyday world would still have existence.
    6.170

If you say that a cause produces the effect through contacting it, in that case, they, cause and effect, will share the same potency, like, for example, the waters of a river and ocean coming into contact with each other. Now if the potency of [cause and effect] does exist as one, one would then not be able to distinguish them and say, "This is the cause" and "This is the effect." And since what is a producer, the **cause, and** the **effect will not be distinct,** the question remains as to what produces what? **If,** in contrast, **they are indeed distinct** and the cause produces its effect without contacting, **then** what is asserted to be **a cause** of an effect will **not differ from** other **non-causes.** This is because things that are intrinsically distinct from each other would become random others, with no relation. **Yet** for those who speak of cause and effect as possessing intrinsic existence, **apart from these two** possibilities—the producer and the produced coming into contact with each other or not—**there is no other** third **conception** or possibility of causal relation. [338] It is definitely the case, therefore, that an intrinsically existent cause does not produce effects.

Since your cause, which you claim exists through intrinsic nature, **produces no effects, there cannot be what you call "effects"** that possess intrinsic existence. The basis on which a cause is defined as a cause is the arising of an effect. If, however, **a cause** without or **devoid of an effect** can be posited as a cause, in that case **there would be no reason** at all **for** something to be called **a "cause."** This, however, is not the case. Therefore cause and effect lack intrinsic existence.

One might ask, "In that case, how is [causal relation understood] according to you?" For the opponent who asserts that the producer and the produced exist through their intrinsic characteristics, when one inquires whether cause and effect come into contact, both alternatives lead to faults. However, according to us, for whom things come to be produced through false constructions and are posited as mere conventions by conceptual thoughts, both cause and effect are like illusions and have no intrinsic arising. Though devoid of intrinsic existence, just like the mesh of hair seen by someone with an eye disease, things are posited as mere conventions created by conceptualizing thoughts. For such a standpoint, one cannot even contemplate that the faults raised against the assertion of intrinsically existent cause and effect will equally apply. Therefore, **for us, we are not vulnerable to these objections** just outlined in terms of whether cause and effect come into contact. **Yet the things of the everyday world**—causes, effects, chariots, and so on—that are acknowledged by the world and are established without analysis **would still have existence.**

Here in the *Commentary,* objections are leveled against notions of cause and effect on the basis of qualifying the object of negation in such terms as "intrinsically," "existing in their own right," and so on. So when the objections are turned back on us, the proponent of things as devoid of intrinsic existence and as illusion-like, we need to state that these objections do not apply to us. We should not indulge in spurious responses with no appreciation for the difference between *intrinsic existence* and *existence*. [339]

Rejecting objections against this analysis

This has two parts: (1) the argument that the same faults apply to the refutation of intrinsic existence of cause and effect and (2) the response that the same faults do not apply to us.

The argument that the same faults apply to the refutation of intrinsic existence of cause and effect

Here, in response to our refutation of intrinsic existence of cause and effect, some charge back and assert the following:

> "Does your refutation refute by coming into contact with what is being
>   refuted?
> Or does it do so without coming into contact? So are you not guilty of
>   the same fault?" 6.171ab

This analysis of whether cause and effect come into contact applies equally to you. How so? For example, **does your refutation refute by coming into contact with what is being refuted? Or does it do so without coming into contact** with it? **So are you not guilty of the same fault?** Indeed, you are. Now if the refutation takes place on the basis of coming into contact, then they [what is refuting and what is being refuted] will become one, in which case what is refuting what? On the other hand, if the refutation takes place without coming into contact, then everything else that equally does not come into contact should also effect such a refutation, which is illogical. And apart from these two horns of the inquiry, there exists no third possibility.

In view of the above, your refutation does not possess any capacity to refute what is being refuted. Your own refutation is in fact refuted. This implies that entities such as cause and effect are indeed established as intrinsically existent. To state this the text says:

"Indeed when you speak in such a manner, you undermine your own
   position,
and your refutation will not have the power to refute what you are
   refuting. 6.171cd

"Since your objections rebound to your words as well, you are committing a logical fallacy;
and so with no sound logic, you deny the existence of all phenomena.
The sublime ones will never agree with you; and with no position of
   your own,
you are also simply abusing the norms of refutation." 6.172

Indeed when you speak in such a manner, presenting phony refutations, **you undermine your own position, and your refutation will not have the power to refute what you are refuting**—namely, the opponent's position. Furthermore, **since your objections** leveled against your opponent **rebound** equally **to your** own **words as well, you are committing a logical fallacy.**[805] **And so with no sound logic, you deny the existence of all phenomena.** [340] **The sublime ones will never** approve or **agree with you.** How is this so? What logic is there to the argument that "If [the cause] produces [the effect] without coming into contact with it, then everything that equally does not come into contact with the effect would produce it as well?" For example, a magnet attracts metal objects not in actual contact but suitably located but it does not attract everything that is not in contact with it. The eyes too see forms, without coming into contact with them, that are suitably located, but the eyes do not see everything not in contact with them. Similarly, in the case of causation too, although a cause produces an effect without coming into contact with it, this does not mean that it will produce everything not in contact with it. It will produce only those that are suitable to be its effects. Furthermore, **you are simply abusing the norms of refutation**—for a protagonist who has **no positions of his own** and indulges only in refuting others' positions is labeled an abuser of logic. You, for one, seem to be doing just that.

The response that the same faults do not apply to us

This has four parts: (1) how refutation and proof statements are tenable within our own system, (2) explaining clearly why such consequences do not equally apply to us, (3) the lack of intrinsic existence can be established, but the opponent cannot establish the contrary, and (4) how to understand other refutations not presented in the text.

How refutation and proof statements are tenable within our own system

This has two parts: how the refutation of others' positions is accepted on the conventional level and how the establishment of our own position is accepted.

How the refutation of others' positions is accepted on the conventional level

> The objection you have just raised—"Does your refutation refute
> what is to be refuted without coming into contact or by contacting
>   it?"—
> will certainly apply to someone who has a thesis.
> Since I have no such thesis, these consequences do not follow. 6.173

We will say this in response. **The objection you have just raised—"Does your refutation refute what is to be refuted without coming into contact or by contacting it?"—will certainly apply to someone who has a thesis:** namely, a protagonist who upholds the thesis of intrinsic existence. **Since I have no such thesis** of intrinsic existence, **these consequences** revealing faults to both possibilities of coming into contact and not coming into contact **do not follow** for me. [341] As for us, we maintain that both the refutation as well as what is being refuted have no intrinsic existence.

When stating the reason why the fault stemming from the analysis of whether a cause produces its effect on the basis of coming into contact with it does not equally apply to ourselves, the *Commentary* points out how the opponent accepts cause and effect to have intrinsic existence while we accept them to be illusion-like with no intrinsic existence. Here too, when giving the reason why the fault charged against the opponent does not rebound on us, it states, "what is being refuted and the refutation have no intrinsic existence."[806] So we must undoubtedly accept that the reason the fault does not apply to us equally is because we do not assert the intrinsic existence of both positions [of coming into contact or not coming into contact]. We should understand in this way statements such as the following in *Averting the Objections*, where [Nāgārjuna] speaks of having no thesis and no position:

> For if I have some thesis,
> then I will be open to that fault.
> Since I have no such thesis,
> I am without fault only.[807]

This is also stated extensively in the Mother Perfection of Wisdom sutras, such as in the following:

> "Subhūti, is unborn attainment attained through an arisen phenomenon, or is unborn attainment attained through an unarisen phenomenon?"
>
> Subhūti replied, "Śāriputra, I do not assert that unborn attainment is attained through an arisen phenomenon; nor do I assert that unborn attainment is attained through an unarisen phenomenon."
>
> Śāriputra stated, "What? Is there then no attainment and no realization?"
>
> Subhūti replied, "Attainment exists and realization exists, but they do not exist in such dualistic terms. Śāriputra, attainment and realization exist on the level of conventions of the world. [Similarly] stream enterer, once-returner, nonreturner, arhat, pratyekabuddha, and bodhisattva too exist on the level of conventions of the world. On the ultimate level, however, there is no attainment and no realization."[808]

Here, up to "I do not assert that unborn attainment is attained" explains how if one were to search for the object of attainment as well as the means by which it is attained by seeking the referents of their terms, attainment would become nonexistent. So the sutra negates attainment in terms of both possibilities when subject to such analysis. Since the object of attainment [found] through such binary analysis [342] for entities that have intrinsic existence is untenable for something that is nonexistent, one accepts attainment on the level of unanalyzed worldly convention. This is explained in the section that begins "Attainment exists" up to "they do not exist in such dualistic terms." "Attainment" here refers to attainment of the object of attainment and to the realizations. So just as these two do not exist on the ultimate level yet are accepted on the conventional level, likewise although the refuting argument does not refute what is to be refuted on the ultimate level, we should understand that it does refute what is to be refuted on the conventional level.

How the establishment of our own position is accepted

Just as the characteristics present in the sun can be seen
in its reflection, such as when there is an eclipse,
yet one can't speak in terms of whether the sun touches its reflection,
nonetheless, things originate through dependence as mere conventions.
    6.174

Also, though unreal, a mirror image exists to help make up one's face.
In just the same way, understand that through reasoning,
which has the power to cleanse the face of wisdom,
one can realize the conclusion even with no objective evidence. 6.175

Furthermore, for example, in dependence upon seeing **its reflection, the characteristics present in the sun** as well one's face, **such as when there is an eclipse, can be seen. Yet** if one were to analyze, in the fashion of searching for true referents of the terms, **whether** the reflection of **the sun** or one's face arise on the basis of **touching its reflection, one can't speak** of their arising. **Nonetheless, things** such as reflections **do originate as mere conventions through dependence** on the sun or one's face. They in turn help secure the desired aim [of people of the world]. **Also, though unreal, a mirror image exists** with the capacity **to help make up one's face. In just the same way,** here too, **understand that through reasoning,** such as that of *dependent origination* or *the absence of one and many,* **which has the power to cleanse the face of wisdom, one can realize the conclusion**—namely, the absence of intrinsic existence. Here, **with no objective evidence**—that is, with intrinsic existence—is the logical reason. The adverb **"even"** indicates that we should understand that refutations can refute what is to be refuted even without objective intrinsic existence. [343]

It would be inappropriate for us, who speak of existence in name only, to employ such dualistic terms based on searching for the referents behind designations. Therefore those who employ refutations based on dualistic terms and respond [to objections] in such a manner will find no opportunity to refute us Mādhyamikas. Hence *Four Hundred Stanzas* says:

> "Exists," "does not exist," [both] "exists and does not"—
> against he who has no such positions,
> even if attempted for a long time,
> no objections can ever be raised.[809]

Fundamental Wisdom too says:

> When attacked by [the logic of] emptiness,
> whatever replies might be put up in defense,
> none will be effective,
> for they would be just like the thesis.[810]

On this basis of explaining the analysis of whether refutation takes place by coming into contact with what is being refuted, we should also understand the argument about causal production by means of analyzing whether cause comes into contact with its effect. On this point, Bhāviveka says that here in [Nāgārjuna's] *Treatise on the Middle Way*, the context [when he speaks of causation] is that of a *producing cause* and not of an *explanatory cause*. And the analysis of whether [cause and effect] come into contact is relevant in the case of an explanatory cause, not in relation to a producing cause. Therefore there is no possibility at all that our own words suffer from logical fallacy.[811]

This statement that the analysis of whether cause and effect come into contact with each other applies not to a producing cause but only to an explanatory cause, such as a reasoning proof, does not constitute an effective response. For if we respond to the opponent's objection by allowing the possibility of further objections, the other side will not remain patient. So just as the faults apply to the view that accepts a producing cause to have true existence, the [same] fault would persist in the case of an explanatory cause if one accepts it to have intrinsic existence. So in rebutting the objections raised by the opponent to the reasoning presented in the *Treatise on the Middle Way* to establish the absence of intrinsic existence, Bhāviveka only offers a response that suffers from logical fallacy. Such a response deserves only to be refuted by the opponent. So in our response, we concede that the faults stemming from the analysis of whether cause and effect come into contact with each other applies equally to both a producing cause and an explanatory cause so long as one accepts intrinsic existence, but we do not accept such a thesis. Such a response is far more elegant.

Explaining clearly why such consequences do not equally apply to us

> If our proof inferring the thesis possessed real existence,
> and if the thesis being proven had real existence as well, [344]
> then the arguments about contact and so on could apply.
> Since this is not the case, you are only frustrating yourself. 6.176

If our proof inferring the thesis possessed real or essential **existence, and if the thesis being proven had real** intrinsic **existence as well, then the arguments about contact and so on** between the reason and the thesis **could apply** to us. The words "and so on" includes whether they do not come into contact with each other. **Since this is not the case**—that is to say, since no such intrinsic existence remains—the arguments you are leveling against us are pointless, and **you are only frustrating** or disappointing **yourself.**

For example, when one refutes the various standpoints connected with the mesh of hair seen by someone with an eye disease—a single strand of hair, multiple strands of hair, a ball [of hair], black hair, and so on—none of this can undermine [the perception of] someone who does not suffer from such visual impairment. Similarly, when one examines cause and effect devoid of intrinsic existence, the opponent's arguments analyzing in dualistic terms searching for the true referents of the terms will not cause any harm. In light of this, we should discern how [Candrakīrti's response here] also rejects the examples cited by the opponent, about the eyes and magnet operating without coming into contact. For if one accepts them to be intrinsically existent, the consequences stemming from [the analysis of] whether they come into contact apply equally to these examples. Having abandoned the correct path that is the absence of intrinsic existence, you take joy in traveling on the twisted path of false conceptualization, paved by the unskilled road builder that is your own fantasizing mind and obstructing the path to perfect truth. What purpose does such hard labor serve for you?[812]

That lack of intrinsic existence can be established, but the opponent cannot establish the opposite

> It is easy for us to make others realize
> that all things lack real existence, but you cannot
> easily make others apprehend intrinsic existence.
> So why ensnare the world in a web of flawed logic? 6.177

Furthermore, on the basis of examples like an illusion, a mirage, and so on, which are established for the opponents as well, **it is easy for us** Mādhyamikas **to make others realize that all things** of the world **lack intrinsic existence.** [345] **But you cannot**, in an equal manner, **easily make others**, the wise Mādhyamikas, **apprehend** that things have **intrinsic existence.** This is because there are no examples acknowledged by both parties as having true existence. This suggests that in the case of a logical reasoning such as dependent origination establishing the absence of true existence, so long as the entailment—whatever is dependently originated necessarily lacks true existence—is not established on the basis of a concordant example, there is simply no way to ascertain the absence of true existence on the basis of the subject.[813]

Thus, I, Candrakīrti, am able to avert all the arguments presented by the proponents of real entities. Furthermore, no one [among those proponents of intrinsic existence] will be able to propose any suitable defense. Who is urging or forcing you, the opponent, to cause such injury to the world? **So why ensnare the world**—in which the beings are already enveloped in a thicket of their own inferior concepts and afflictions, like a silkworm trapped inside a cocoon—**in a web** woven tightly with threads **of flawed logic?** Give up this argument of yours based on grasping at true existence. With respect to that which resembles reflections and are false, what kind of individual characteristics or general characteristics as established by direct perception or inference exist by virtue of intrinsic nature? In this sense, there is only one direct perception with respect to the entire realm of knowledge, the Buddha's omniscient gnosis.[814]

How to understand other refutations not presented in the text

> Understand other remaining refutations from what has been said above.
> Rebut too others' response to our argument about whether [a cause]
>   contacts [its effect] and so on,

and recognize also how ours is not an instance of flawed refutation.
In brief, understand all other refutations from what we have already
outlined. 6.178

With respect to the refutations presented against the proponents of real
entities in the context of defining *dependent origination*, such as a sprout
arising in dependence on its seed, and *dependent designation*, such as conceiving a person in dependence on the aggregates, there are **other remaining refutations**, such as the argument about whether a cause produces
its effect by coming into contact with it.[815] You should **understand** these
from what has been said above. And **rebut too others' response to our
argument about whether a cause contacts its effect and so on**, such as
when they ask [346] whether the refutation refutes what is to be refuted
by coming into contact with it. We should point out how such an analysis
does not equally apply to us. What is stated here represents only a single
example.

[Candrakīrti's] intention here is to state that [Nāgārjuna's] purpose of
engaging in refutation and positing [one's own standpoint] in his treatise *Fundamental Wisdom* is only to eliminate conceptualization of true
existence. This we have already explained above in the section beginning
"Ordinary beings are chained by conceptualization" (6.117). So how can
there be an abuse of the rules of refutation in [Nāgārjuna's] treatise? The
one who abuses the rules of refutation is the one who, fearing that positing his own standpoint will make him vulnerable to faults, engages only in
refuting others' positions. Here our elimination of the opponent's positions
has no existence on the ultimate level, for on the ultimate level, nothing
whatsoever exists. So how can we be abusing the rules of refutation? The
correct characterization of someone abusing the rules of refutation is that
he does not posit his own standpoint but takes the refutation of other's
standpoints to take place on the ultimate level. As for the Madhyamaka,
there is none who meets these two criteria of not positing one's own positions on the conventional level and of taking refutation of the opponent's
position to take place on the ultimate level. So there is no abuse of the rules
of refutation by the Madhyamaka. Such [violation of the rules of refuta-
tion] would be inappropriate in all contexts. So, **in brief, understand all
other** remaining **refutations from what we have already outlined above.**

From "Not originating from itself" (6.8) up to "one swiftly attains freedom" (6.119) have elucidated the selflessness of phenomena. And from

"Seeing . . . that all faults and afflictions stem from the view grasping at the perishable collection" (6.120) up to this point (6.178) have elucidated the selflessness of persons.

19. Enumerations of Emptiness

Enumerations of emptiness, the established conclusion

This has two parts: (1) a brief presentation of the enumerations of emptiness and (2) an extensive explanation of the specific types of enumerations. [347]

A brief presentation of the enumerations of emptiness

Wishing to present the enumerations of emptiness, the text reads:

> To help free beings, the Buddha taught no-self
> in twofold terms, that of phenomena and that of persons,
> and again for the sake of diverse trainees, he expounded these two
> in other diverse terms through further enumerations. 6.179

> After teaching in an elaborate way
> sixteen kinds of emptiness,
> the Buddha summarized these into four,
> and he held these to be the great way as well. 6.180

The Buddha taught no-self, which is the absence of intrinsic existence of phenomena, **in twofold terms**, the divisions of selflessness of persons and selflessness of phenomena. This twofold classification is not made on the basis of distinguishing two distinct kinds of nonexistent selfhood in relation to two bases, persons and phenomena. As for the selfhood with no existence whatsoever, this is none other than intrinsic existence. Therefore, it is from the point of view of two bases—**that of phenomena**, the aggregates and so on, **and that of persons**—that [the two selflessnesses] are distinguished. "Why were these two taught?" one might ask. The Buddha taught the no-self of persons **to help free** beings such as śrāvakas and pratyekabuddhas from the cycle of existence. And the Buddha taught both selflessnesses to benefit bodhisattva beings so that they may attain total freedom through attaining [a buddha's] omniscience.

As stated above, śrāvakas and pratyekabuddhas do possess insight into suchness in terms of the truth of the mere conditionedness of dependent origination. Nonetheless, they lack the realization of the no-self of phenomena presented above in terms of its varied classifications and vast timescale. However, these two do possess adequate means to abandon the seeds of the afflictions of the three realms of existence. Thus we do accept that they possess full meditative realization of the no-self of persons in terms of the absence of intrinsic existence of persons. So although śrāvakas and pratyekabuddhas may not generate the wisdom born of limitless varieties of reasoning negating the true existence of persons, they do possess a complete practice of the antidote to eliminate the seeds of the afflictions [i.e., the afflictive obscuration]. What they lack is the meditative cultivation of the antidote to eliminate the cognitive obscurations.

Again, for the sake of diverse trainees, the Buddha **expounded these two** kinds of no-self **in an elaborate way, in other diverse terms through further enumerations.** How so? In the Mother of the Conquerors [the Perfection of Wisdom sutras], for example, **after teaching sixteen kinds of emptiness,** once again **the Buddha summarized these into four. And he held** or stated **these to be the great way as well.** Thus the Buddha taught the condensed enumeration of two, the intermediate enumeration of four, and the elaborate enumeration of sixteen. As the sutra states:

> Subhūti, again the great way of the bodhisattvas is thus: [348] emptiness of the inner, emptiness of the outer, emptiness of both inner and outer, emptiness of emptiness, emptiness of great immensity, emptiness of the ultimate, emptiness of the conditioned, emptiness of the unconditioned, emptiness of beyond extremes, emptiness of what is beginningless and endless, emptiness of not to be discarded, emptiness of intrinsic nature, emptiness of all phenomena, emptiness of defining characteristics, emptiness of the unobservable, and the emptiness of essence that is the absence of entity.[816]

Having thus presented the sixteen kinds of emptiness, once again, the sutra presents four kinds of emptiness:

Subhūti, furthermore, entity is devoid of entity, nonentity is devoid of nonentity, intrinsic nature is devoid of intrinsic nature, and other-derived entity is devoid of other-derived entity.[817]

These kinds of emptiness are referred to as the "great way" as well. Whether it is emptiness itself or something other than emptiness, nothing has the slightest degree of intrinsic existence. What are subsumed within these diverse kinds of emptiness are labeled as such because they exist on the conventional level alone. *Fundamental Wisdom* states, for example:

If there is something that is nonempty,
there will then be something that is empty.
Since nothing is nonempty,
how can something be empty?[818]

We do not say "It is empty,"
nor do we say "It is nonempty,"
nor that it's both, nor that it's neither.
We speak of it for the purpose of indication.[819]

The preceding lines [of the second stanza] have the meaning that we, the Madhyamaka, do not speak in terms of inherent existence, with the final line declaring that what is indicated by the terms does exist on the conventional level.

An extensive explanation of the specific types of enumerations

This has two parts: an extensive explanation of the sixteen kinds of emptiness and an extensive explanation of the fourfold enumeration of emptiness.

An extensive explanation of the sixteen kinds of emptiness

This has four parts: (1) the first set of four, the emptiness of the inner and so on, (2) the second set of four, the emptiness of great immensity and so on, (3) the third set of four, the emptiness of beyond extremes and so on, and (4) the fourth set of four, the emptiness of all phenomena and so on.

The first set of four

This has two parts: (1) the emptiness of the inner and (2) the three remaining kinds of emptiness. [349]

The emptiness of the inner

The first has two parts: (1) the actual point and (2) showing, as an aside, the manner in which intrinsic nature is accepted.

The actual point

> Since their very nature is emptiness,
> the eyes are devoid of eyes;
> so are the ears, nose, and tongue;
> the body and mind too are thus defined. 6.181

> Because they do not endure eternally
> and because they do not disintegrate,
> the absence of intrinsic existence of the six senses
> such as eyes is *inner emptiness*. 6.182

The absence of intrinsic existence of the six senses such as eyes is held to be *inner emptiness*. For example, **the eyes are devoid of** inherently existing **eyes since the emptiness** of existing in its own right **is the very nature of** eyes. Just as explained for the eyes, **so are the ears, nose, and tongue,** and **the body and mind too are thus defined.** The reason they are thus empty is **because they do not,** in an ultimate sense, **endure eternally and because they do not disintegrate** [in such sense].

Here, Patsab translates [the *Commentary*] as follows:

> "Not enduring eternally" should be understood as not discarding its nature. This is because they do not disintegrate through [first] enduring for a little while and then ceasing. So it is taught [in the sutras]. This indicates that without doubt, an entity that possesses intrinsic existence cannot be eternal or unceasing.[820]

This is an erroneous translation. For this reading incurs the consequence that the opposite of the predicate [something possessing no intrinsic existence] must be pervaded by the reason [it is eternal and unceasing].[821] The translation of this passage is better in Naktso's rendering:

> Any entity that exists through its own intrinsic nature will become either something that endures eternally or something subject to destruction.[822]

It is clear, therefore, that the first version erred in its reading of the negative particle. *Explanation of the Commentary* reads the lines as "As they do not endure eternally / and as they do not disintegrate" and explains their meaning in the following:

> If eyes and so forth were to possess intrinsic nature, given that intrinsic nature is devoid of manifestations and disintegration, these things [eyes and so forth] too will be devoid of manifestations and disintegration. Since they do not possess these [characteristics], they are thus devoid of intrinsic existence.[823]

This too is incorrect. For if it is correct then, instead of the line "because they do not disintegrate," one would have to read it as "because they are subject to disintegration." [350] This contradicts the statement in the sutra that reads, "because they do not disintegrate."

The meaning of the phrase "they do not endure eternally" too should be understood as rendered in Naktso's version, where it reads, "'Eternal' refers to that which has the nature of not being subject to destruction." Thus, when permanence is negated [for eyes and so forth] in the sense of enduring eternally, one might conclude that eyes and so forth endure for a short period of time and then undergo truly existent disintegration. To negate this [possibility] the sutra states, "because they do not disintegrate."[824] In brief, the meaning here is this: the eyes and so forth do not possess true existence either as permanent or as impermanent. There is in *Light on Twenty-Five Thousand Lines* a presentation [of these two reasons, "they do not abide eternally" and they do no disintegrate"], which is different from what is found here.[825]

As for the intrinsic nature of phenomena, this is as stated in *Fundamental Wisdom*:

It's illogical that intrinsic nature
is produced by causes and conditions.
An intrinsic nature produced
by causes and conditions would be a product.

But how could there be
an intrinsic nature that is produced?
Intrinsic nature is not fabricated;
it's not dependent on others.[826]

Showing, as an aside, the manner in which intrinsic nature is accepted

[The *Commentary* says:]

[*Question:*] Now listen. Is there an intrinsic nature that the master himself accepts, such as the one characterized by Nāgārjuna is his treatise [*Fundamental Wisdom*] as not produced by causes and conditions?

[*Reply:*] There does exist what is called the *ultimate nature of things* (*dharmatā*), which the Buddha refers to when he states, "Whether tathāgatas appear in the world or not, this ultimate nature of phenomena will remain." What is this ultimate nature of phenomena? It is the *intrinsic nature* of phenomena such as that of the eyes. What is their intrinsic nature? It is the nature of the eyes and so on that is *not fabricated* and *not dependent on others*, such as a producer. This is the *reality* to be realized by a cognition that is free of ignorance's impairment.[827]

These lines effectively refute those who assert that this master [Candrakīrti] does not accept the existence of ultimate truth and the ultimate nature of things and that, when the contamination of ignorance comes to an end, no cognitive states remain.[828]

So does the ultimate nature of things exist? Who would say that it does not exist? For if it does not exist, to what end do bodhisattvas practice the path of the six perfections? [351] They would not do so. Were there no ultimate truth, there would be no perfecting of the realization of such a truth; and were this not possible, there would be no point to the meditative cul-

tivation of the path. In that case, why do the bodhisattvas initiate hundredfold effort to realize the ultimate nature of things and attain its final
attainment?[829]

This paragraph shows that those who initiate fulsome efforts on the path
while maintaining that the ultimate truth is not an object of any cognition
are quite deficient in their intelligence. That there is ultimate truth is stated
most clearly in the *Cloud of Jewels Sutra*:

> O child of the lineage, the ultimate truth has no arising, no ces-
> sation, no disintegration, no coming, and no going. It cannot
> be expressed in words, it cannot be defined thoroughly through
> words, nor can it be realized through conceptual elaboration.
> O child of the lineage, the ultimate truth is ineffable, it is tran-
> quil, and it is to be realized by the āryas through their own
> personal experience. O child of the lineage, the ultimate truth
> is such that whether tathāgatas appear in the world or not, for
> its sake the bodhisattvas shave their head and beard, clad them-
> selves in saffron robes, and through their perfect faith renounce
> the householder life and adopt that of the homeless. Following
> their renunciation, they strive with diligence as if their hair or
> clothes were on fire to attain this ultimate nature of things, and
> [this truth] abides without destruction. O child of the lineage,
> if there is no ultimate truth, engaging in pure conduct would be
> pointless; the appearance of tathāgatas in the world would also
> be pointless. Since the ultimate truth does exist, the bodhisattvas
> are referred to as those who are versed in the ultimate truth.[830]

The phrases "ineffable" and "cannot be realized through conceptual elaboration" should be understood to mean that ultimate truth as it is perceived
by the nonconceptual gnosis [of āryas] cannot be experienced as an object
of language and conceptual thought. This does not mean that it cannot be
cognized at all. And in this sutra, objections have been raised against the
nonexistence of ultimate truth, and also, when [unwanted] consequences
are revealed to the opposing standpoint, the sutra speaks of the existence of
ultimate truth. The sutra declared the ultimate truth to be existent earlier
too, so those who attempt to make distinctions between "nonexistent" and
"not being existent" only reveal the extreme inferiority of their intellect.[831]

Although Patsab's translation in numerous instances reads, "whether tathāgatas appear in the world or not, for its sake," in Naktso's translation one reads, "Whether tathāgatas appear in the world or not, the ultimate truth remains undestroyed." This latter version seems better since it accords well with the sutra cited in an earlier context in the commentary, [352] "Whether tathāgatas appear in the world or not, this ultimate nature of phenomena will remain."[832]

Some may object and say, "Alas! You assert that nothing has intrinsic existence, yet you accept an intrinsic nature that is not an adventitious creation and is not dependent on others. Your statements are contradictory."

[*Reply:*] This objection stems from a failure to understand the intention of the *Treatise on the Middle Way*. The intention of the treatise is this: If the reality of dependently originated things such as eyes and so on that can be perceived by the childish person is itself the intrinsic nature and the ultimate mode of being of these things, then since this nature is something perceived directly by a distorted cognition, the practice of pure conduct will be pointless. However, since the dependent origination of eyes and so forth is not their intrinsic nature and not their true mode of being, the practice of pure conduct for the sake of seeing that [true mode of being] comes to have a purpose.[833] So Candrakīrti responds.

So the negation of intrinsic nature involves the negation of eyes and so forth as constituting their own essential nature. The intrinsic nature that is accepted, on the other hand, relates to the recognition that the very negation of intrinsic existence is the ultimate nature of things like eyes and so forth. There is therefore not the slightest contradiction between rejecting the intrinsic existence of things, on the one hand, and accepting an intrinsic nature that constitutes things' ultimate nature.

Such an ultimate nature of things is something that we speak of, within the framework of conventional truth or mere nominal existence, as unfabricated and as not dependent on others. This ultimate nature of things not perceivable by the childish is certainly fit to be an intrinsic nature; and the simple acceptance of its existence on the conventional level does not entail its intrinsic existence as something real or unreal on the ultimate level. It's in fact the pacification of intrinsic existence itself. So this intrinsic nature, the nature of things, is something that is not only accepted by the master Nāgārjuna himself, it is a truth we can enable others to accept as well. So this intrinsic nature is presented as something that would be established, at the end of the debate, for both sides.[834] This [last] statement needs to be appreciated with special emphasis.

If, as some assert, one were to view heat and so forth as the intrinsic nature and ultimate mode of being of fire and so forth, this is wholly untenable. Heat and so forth are dependently arisen, and hence they are solely fabrications. They are also things that have arisen owing to their causes and conditions. [353] It would therefore be illogical to assert that eyes and so forth do not exist as contrivances, that they are not dependent on other causes and conditions. "This is because the phrase 'they are' indicates that there exist no entities that can be apprehended as supreme, and that things such as these are revealed on the conventional level."[835] This is how it appears in Patsab's translation. In Naktso's translation, however, this passage reads: "Here, there is no such apprehension of things as supreme, and facts are established as they are on the conventional level." This latter reading seems better. The meaning of the remaining part [of the passage] is this: the conceived object of clinging at true existence has no reality, and things are revealed on the conventional level to have the character of being fabricated and dependent on others.

On the basis of this demonstration of how the master Nāgārjuna accepts intrinsic nature, we should also understand the following from *Praise to the Ultimate Expanse*:

> The sutras that teach emptiness,
> all taught by the Conqueror,
> they all help cease the afflictions
> but do not undo the natural element.[836]

This text states how the sutras that teach emptiness demolish the objectified focus of the affliction of grasping at true existence. Such teachings do not undermine or indicate the nonexistence of the natural element of the tathāgata—namely, emptiness—which is the very negation of such objectified focus.

In brief, the sutra statement that the eyes and so forth are devoid of eyes and so forth elucidates the fact that eyes and so forth are empty of intrinsic existence. This is not the same as the assertion of the Śrāvaka school that the eyes are devoid of a self that is the inner [eternal] agent; nor is it the same as the Cittamātra statement that the eyes are devoid of subject-object duality, whereby they speak of an emptiness not as the absence of intrinsic existence of the eyes and so forth but an emptiness of one thing being absent in another.

The three remaining kinds of emptiness

> Because such is their nature,
> form is devoid of form;
> sound, smell, taste, touch,
> and mental objects are likewise empty. 6.183

> That form and so forth have no intrinsic nature
> is accepted as *outer emptiness*.
> The lack of intrinsic existence of both
> is *inner and outer emptiness*. 6.184

> That all things lack intrinsic existence,
> this the wise describe as emptiness.
> Emptiness itself is in turn held
> to be devoid of essential emptiness. 6.185

> This emptiness of what is called emptiness
> is known as the *emptiness of emptiness*.
> It was taught to counter the grasping thought
> that emptiness is something real. 6.186

[354] **That form and so forth**, factors that are not part of a person's continuum, **have no intrinsic existence**, this emptiness of intrinsic existence **is accepted as *outer emptiness*. Because such is their nature**, these outer **forms are devoid of** existing through **form's** own essence. In this way, the manner in which **sound, smell, taste, touch, and mental objects are likewise empty** should be understood. In the sutra, the two statements "They do not endure eternally" and "They do not disintegrate" are applied both in this context [of the three remaining emptinesses of the first set of four] and in connection with all remaining enumerations of emptiness. Their significance should be understood just as explained above in the context of inner emptiness.

The physical base of a sense organ, for example, is encompassed within a person's continuum, yet it is not the actual sense organ itself. Hence it is **both** inner and outer. And the **lack of its intrinsic existence**—the fact that it has no intrinsic reality—**this is *inner and outer emptiness*.** The meaning of the remaining [part of the stanza] is the same as before.

That all things, both outer and inner, lack intrinsic existence as described above, this alone the wise describe as emptiness. This emptiness of the intrinsic existence of inner and outer phenomena itself is in turn held to be devoid of a truly existing essential emptiness. Hence, this emptiness of what is called *emptiness*—namely, the emptiness in relation to which emptiness itself is the basis of being emptied—is known as *emptiness of emptiness*. It was taught in the Mother Perfection of Wisdom sutras to counter the grasping thought that emptiness or ultimate nature is something real, that it has true existence. This point is clearly stated in the following in *Hymn to the World Transcendent*:

> To help dispel all conceptualizations,
> you revealed the ambrosia of emptiness.
> He who clings to that
> you have verily denounced.[837]

These statements indicate that the Conqueror denounced both the following kinds of assertions. In the first, some, taking ultimate truth to be the elimination of essential existence, assert it to possess true existence. In the second, some, taking the ultimate nature of things to be some kind of real autonomous entity—not a mere elimination—conceive it in affirmative terms, like a blue or yellow color, and say that it possesses true existence.[838] [355]

The second set of four, the emptiness of great immensity and so on

> Space pervades all the worlds
> and also the beings these worlds contain,
> and it exemplifies the immeasurable thoughts.
> Space is a great immensity in all directions. 6.187

> That space itself is devoid of all ten directions,
> this is the *emptiness of great immensity*.
> It was taught to counteract
> clinging to great immensity as real. 6.188

Since nirvana is the supreme goal,
it is the ultimate and the transcendence of sorrow.
That it is devoid of itself
is *emptiness of the ultimate.* 6.189

To counter the grasping thought
that nirvana is something real,
the knower of the ultimate truth
taught this emptiness of the ultimate. 6.190

The three realms, coming from their conditions,
are described with certainty to be conditioned.
That they are empty of themselves
was taught as *emptiness of the conditioned.* 6.191

That which has no arising and duration
and lacks impermanence is unconditioned.
That it is empty of itself
is *emptiness of the unconditioned.* 6.192

Since no container world and no contained world of sentient beings exists other than in **space** such as eastern direction and so on, **it pervades all the worlds and also the beings these worlds contain.** Furthermore, when one cultivates the four **immeasurable thoughts** such as loving kindness, one does so in relation to the entirety of sentient beings throughout space, and such meditations are defined as "immeasurable" from the point of view of their objects. Just as space **exemplifies** immeasurability, these meditations also have an immeasurable aspect. In brief, **space is a great immensity in all ten directions. That space itself is devoid of** inherent existence of **all ten directions**, such as the east, **this is the *emptiness of great immensity*. It was taught to counteract clinging to** space **as** intrinsically **real great immensity.** Distorted clinging to space includes, for example, the non-Buddhist Vaiśeṣika view that holds space to constitute a permanent substance.

[In general] the term *truth* in the context of ultimate truth can refer to (a) a purpose, as in the sentence "There is a purpose to this statement," or it can refer to (b) a fact or an object of knowledge, as in the expression "five objects of the senses." Of these two, here [in this context of emptiness of the ultimate] the term *truth* refers to that which is **the ultimate and the tran-**

scendence of sorrow—namely, the buddha's truth body (*dharmakāya*). And since nirvana is the supreme goal to be attained, emptiness, which is this truth body being devoid of itself existing through an essence, is *emptiness of the ultimate*. Here too the Buddha, the knower of the ultimate truth, taught this emptiness of the ultimate to counter the grasping thought that nirvana, the dharmakāya, is something truly real. [356]

The three realms, coming from their causes and conditions, are described with certainty to be conditioned. That they are empty of themselves, this emptiness of intrinsic existence of the three realms, was taught as *emptiness of the conditioned*. That which has no arising and duration and lacks impermanence—namely, cessation or disintegration—such a phenomenon is unconditioned. That it is empty of itself—namely, of intrinsic existence—is taught as *emptiness of the unconditioned*.

The third set of four, the emptiness of beyond extremes and so on

> That which is free of extremes
> is referred to as beyond extremes.
> That it is empty of itself is referred to as
> *emptiness of beyond extremes.* 6.193
>
> Since samsara has neither
> a beginning point nor a final end,
> it's referred to as beginningless and endless.
> With no coming and going, it is dream-like. 6.194
> That this existence is empty of itself
> is described with certainty
> in the treatises as *emptiness*
> *of what is beginningless and endless.* 6.195
>
> "To discard" means to reject
> and definitely refers to casting aside.
> "Not to discard" means to not abandon,
> meaning not to be shunned at all. 6.196
> And what is not to be discarded
> is, in turn, empty of itself,
> and this is therefore called
> *emptiness of not to be discarded.* 6.197

> Since the essence of things
> such as those that are conditioned is not invented
> by śrāvakas and pratyekabuddhas,
> nor by bodhisattvas or tathāgatas, 6.198
> the essence of conditioned things and so on
> is termed their intrinsic nature.
> And this being empty of itself
> is *emptiness of intrinsic nature.* 6.199

The "extremes" are the positions of eternalism or nihilism, the holding of which leads one to fall into an abyss of error. It does not refer to positions such as maintaining that unconditioned phenomena are permanent or that arhats experience the annihilation of the continuum of birth and death conditioned by karma. So a distinction should be drawn between upholding eternalism or annihilationism on the one hand, which leads to falling into an adverse abyss, and holding something to be permanent or annihilated in general on the other.

That which is free of the extremes of eternalism and nihilism, the holding of which leads to falling into a grasping at an extreme, **is referred to as beyond extremes. That this is empty of itself**—that is to say, empty of the intrinsic existence of its own being—**is referred to as** *emptiness of beyond extremes.* This is as found in the *King of Meditations Sutra*, [357] where it states that having abandoned the two extremes of existence and nonexistence, of purity and impurity, one must not abide in the middle either.[839] This was taught to counter the clinging to true existence that leads to conceiving the middle, that which is free from the [two] extremes, as possessing real existence. For instance, the Cittamātra school asserts that the mind, taken to be the middle free from the two extremes, is truly existent.

The cycle of existence lacks temporal limits. **Since samsara has neither a beginning point**, such that one could say, "It did not exist prior to this point," **nor a final end**, such that one could say, "It would not exist after this point," samsara **is referred to as beginningless and endless. With no** intrinsically existing **coming and going**, this cycle of existence **is dream-like. That this existence is empty of itself**, in the sense of intrinsic existence, **this** emptiness **is described with certainty in the treatises**—namely, the Perfection Mother of Conquerors sutras—**as** *emptiness of what is beginningless and endless.*

"To discard" means to reject and definitely refers to casting aside. "Not

to discard" means to not abandon, meaning not to be shunned at all, such as the Great Vehicle. What is not to be discarded is empty of itself—it is devoid of its own being; and this emptiness of inherent existence is therefore called *emptiness of not to be discarded.*

The essence of things, such as those that are conditioned, is termed their intrinsic nature. This is because the essence or the ultimate nature of conditioned things and so on is not invented by śrāvakas and pratyeka-buddhas, nor by bodhisattvas or tathāgatas. They only bring to light such nature; it abides primordially as the essential nature of these things. And this being empty of itself, being devoid of its own being, is *emptiness of intrinsic nature.*

One might wonder, "Hasn't this point already been made in the context of the emptiness of emptiness?" Yes, this is indeed true. Nonetheless, the purpose in the prior context was to dispel the doubt that since emptiness of outer and inner phenomena is established by rational cognition perceiving suchness, it might possess true existence. This [emptiness of intrinsic nature] here, however, is presented to help dispel the thought that essential nature might possess true existence because no one has created it. So this is not a redundancy. The grounds for both of these doubts do exist in relation to the ultimate nature of things. If one were to understand how there is no contradiction in nonetheless rejecting its true existence, [358] this would help remove all misconceptions related to holding the view that ultimate truth is not cognizable by any kind of cognition.

The fourth set of four, the emptiness of all phenomena and so on

This has three parts: (1) the emptiness all phenomena, (2) the emptiness of defining characteristics, and (3) the emptiness of the unobservable and of nonthings.

The emptiness of all phenomena

> The eighteen elements, six sensory contacts,
> and six feelings that arise therefrom,
> all things both material and nonmaterial,
> all phenomena both conditioned and unconditioned—6.200
> that all these phenomena are empty
> of themselves [is *emptiness of all phenomena*]. 6.201ab

"All phenomena" refers to **the eighteen elements**—the six sense faculties of the eyes and so on, which are the support, the six types of consciousness such as eye consciousness, which are the supported, and the six objects such as form. It encompasses also the **six sensory contacts**—from contact arising from convergence in relation to the eyes up to contact arising through convergence in relation to the mind—**and** the **six feelings** that derive from these six contacts, **all things both material and nonmaterial,** and likewise **all phenomena both conditioned and unconditioned.** That all these phenomena are empty themselves—namely, of their own beings—is *emptiness of all phenomena.*

The emptiness of defining characteristics

This has three parts: a brief presentation, an extensive explanation, and a summary of the points.

A brief presentation

> The formable and so on lack their own beings;
> this is *emptiness of defining characteristics.* 6.201cd

The defining characteristic of the aggregate of form is that which is **formable** (or suitable to be a form); "**and so on**" includes all phenomena up to a buddha's omniscience.[840] The defining characteristics of all these phenomena, those of both the unenlightened and enlightened classes, **are empty of their own beings,** and **this is *emptiness of defining characteristics.*** [359]

An extensive explanation

This has three parts: (1) defining characteristics of the factors of the ground, (2) defining characteristics of the factors of the path, (3) defining characteristics of the factors of the result.

Defining characteristics of the factors of the ground

> *Form* is defined as capable of materiality;
> *feeling* has the nature of an experience;

discrimination apprehends the signs;
mental formations construct. 6.202

Awareness of specific objects
is the defining mark of *consciousness*.
Aggregates are characterized by suffering,
and the *elements'* nature is akin to a venomous snake. 6.203

Sense fields, the Buddha said,
are the doorways to the arising [of suffering].
All that is dependently originated is
characterized by composition. 6.204

Again, one might ask, "What are defining characteristics of form and so on?" **Form is defined as capable of materiality**, something that is able to assume form. For example, a sutra states:

O monks, because they exist as forms and are suitable for taking on forms, they are called "the appropriated aggregate of form."[841]

There is no necessity for these specific characteristics to constitute the definitions of the things characterized. They are mentioned here primarily to highlight the principal attributes of these specific phenomena. **Feeling has the nature of an experience**, such as of joy, pain or neutrality; **discrimination apprehends the signs**, such as external signs like blue and yellow colors and inner signs like joy, pain and so on. "Signs" refer to specific attributes of the object. **Mental formations construct** conditioned phenomena, and it is an aggregate distinct from the other four aggregates. **Awareness of specific objects** such as forms, sounds, and so on **is the defining mark of consciousness. The aggregates are characterized by suffering**, while **the elements' nature** is to sustain cyclic existence, **akin to a venomous snake** that seizes others and brings them harm. As for **the sense fields, the Buddha said** they **are the doorways to the arising** and emergence **of suffering.** Here, these three (aggregates, elements, and sense fields) are spoken of from the point of view of things belonging to the cycle of existence. **All that is dependently originated is characterized by composition** through the coming together of causes and conditions. [360]

Defining characteristics of the factors of the path

Giving is what defines the perfection of *generosity*,
discipline is the absence of torment,
forbearance is the absence of anger,
diligence is the absence of unwholesome action. 6.205

Meditative absorption is characterized by focus,
wisdom by the absence of attachment.
These then are the defining characteristics
of the six perfections. 6.206

Meditative absorptions and the *immeasurables*,
likewise the absorptions of the *formless states*—
the knower of perfect truth said these
are characterized by unperturbed serenity. 6.207

Thirty-seven factors lead to enlightenment;
their nature is to decisively drive forth from samsara.
The nature of *emptiness* is unobjectifiable;
as such it is utter absence. 6.208

Signlessness is peace itself.
The nature of the *third door*
is the absence of suffering and delusion.
The nature of the *liberating factors* is utterly freeing. 6.209

Giving, the thought of giving away entirely one's body, material resources, and roots of virtue, **is what defines the perfection of generosity**. Discipline **is** defined as cooling off or **the absence of** the afflictions' **torment**. **Forbearance is** defined as **the absence of anger**, the ability to maintain mind's composure. The defining characteristic of **diligence is** to have joy in upholding the virtues with **the absence of unwholesome action**. **Meditative absorption is characterized by** single-pointed **focus** of the mind on a virtuous object with the aim of gathering all virtuous factors. **Wisdom is** defined **by the absence of attachment**, which refers to negating or bringing attachment or clinging to the true existence of things to an end with the goal of traveling to nirvana. **These then**, as described above, **are** stated in the sutras as **the defining characteristics of the six perfections.**

The four **meditative absorptions** of the first level and so forth, the four **immeasurables** of immeasurable loving kindness and so forth, and likewise the **four formless states** of limitless space and so forth, which are distinct from the first two sets, the Buddha, **the knower of perfect truth, said these are characterized by unperturbed serenity**—that is, the absence of disequilibrium. For these are attained through abandonment of disequilibrium.

The nature of the **thirty-seven factors** that **lead to enlightenment** is to **decisively drive forth from samsara. The nature of** the liberation door of **emptiness is** [361] **unobjectifiable,** and **as such it is utter absence** in that it is untainted by the stain of objectifying conceptualizations that grasp at true existence. The liberation door of **signlessness is** defined as **peace itself** attained through nonobjectification of the signs [or the attributes of things]. **The nature of the third** liberation **door,** which is wishlessness, **is the absence of suffering and delusion.** Through it one correctly views those that have the nature of conditioned suffering as suffering, and viewing the conditioned nature of existence with the wisdom realizing suchness, one does not wish for the excellences of cyclic existence. One also does not wish for the supramundane state on the basis of holding it to possess true existence.

The nature of the eight **liberating factors is utterly freeing** in that they bring about total freedom from the five hindrances to meditative attainment.[842] Of the eight liberating factors, the first two—(1) viewing external forms while not dismantling the perception of form inside and (2) viewing external forms while dismantling such perception of form inside—are antidotes for the impediments to conjuring emanations. In many copies of the *Commentary*, the text of the second liberating factor reads, "having the perception of inner as form"; this is an error. (3) The liberating factor [viewing] appealing [forms] and belonging to the fourth level of absorption is defined as the third. This serves as an antidote for such afflictions as enjoying the conjuring of attractive forms and disliking the conjuring of unattractive forms. Within the path that brings about bliss in this very lifetime, there are two kinds: (4–7) the path that accords with liberation, the liberating factors of the four formless absorptions, and (8) the path of abiding in peace, the attainment of cessation wherein discrimination and feeling have ceased—the last two being one liberating factor.[843]

Defining characteristics of the factors of the result

The *ten powers* of the Buddha are defined
as that which bring utter certainty,
while the Savior's *four fearlessnesses*
have the nature of total firmness. 6.210

His *perfect knowledge of specific domains*
is defined by absence of deficiency in confidence and so on.
That which brings about beings' welfare,
is described as his *great loving kindness.* 6.211

That which protects those who suffer
defines his *great compassion*;
his *sympathetic joy* is defined by utter joy;
his *equanimity* is unadulterated. 6.212

The *unshared attributes* of the Buddha,
described as eighteen in number,
are defined as irremovable,
since they cannot be stolen from the Buddha. 6.213

The Buddha's *wisdom of omniscience*
is defined as direct perception. [362]
Since all other knowing remains partial,
it is not held to be direct perception. 6.214

The ten powers, to be explained below,[844] should be perceived as **characterized** or defined **as that which brings utter certainty**. In that they engage
their domains without any obstruction, they are defined as "powers." The
Buddha made four pronouncements—(1) "I am fully awakened and have
perfectly realized without distortion all objects of knowledge," (2) "I have
brought to an end all pollutants together with their residual imprints," (3)
"I say that attachment and so on are factors that obstruct liberation," and
(4) "If one endeavors in these levels and paths [I have shown], suffering will
come to an end." With respect to these four pronouncements, no legitimate
opponents can be found who can counter them and assert, "They are not
true." So **the Savior's four fearlessnesses have the nature** or characteristic

of total firmness. For no opponent can prove these pronouncements to be otherwise.

His perfect knowledge of specific domains—of Dharma, its meaning, etymologies, and confidence—is defined by absence of deficiency or exhaustion of these four of confidence and so on. That which clearly brings about beings' welfare and happiness is described as his great loving kindness. That which thoroughly protects those sentient beings who suffer defines his great compassion; his great sympathetic joy is defined by utter or supreme joy; while his great equanimity should be understood as unadulterated with being attached to some and averse toward others. It's free from [such biases].

The unshared attributes of the Buddha, described as eighteen in number, are defined as unremovable by others. The reason is that the Buddha is free from the error that is the opposite of these unique attributes; hence he is not vulnerable to those who might seek to refute him. In other words, these attributes cannot be stolen from the Buddha by others.

The *eighteen unshared attributes* are the following three sets of six:[845] (1) his body is free of error, (2) his speech is free of senseless chatter, and (3) his mind is free of forgetfulness, (4) free of absence of meditative equipoise, (5) free of conceptualization apprehending samsara and nirvana as different, and (6) free of apathy failing to discriminate natures of phenomena. This is the first set of six. Being free of impairment in the domains of (1) aspiration, (2) diligence, (3) mindfulness, (4) concentration, (5) wisdom, and (6) liberation—this is the second set of six. With respect to the deeds of (1) Buddha's body, (2) speech, and (3) mind, [363] these are preceded by [the attainment of] wisdom and follow after wisdom; and in relation to the temporal stages of (4) past, (5) future, and (6) present, he engages with them through his wisdom free of attachment and unimpeded. This then is the third set of six. "Unshared" means that these attributes are present only in a buddha and not in other attainments. Thus they remain unshared in terms of their possessor. The explanations of these attributes should be understood on the basis of the *Questions of King Dhāraṇīśvara Sutra,* which is cited in the *Commentary.*[846]

The Buddha's wisdom of omniscience is defined as direct perception with respect to all objects of knowledge. Since all other knowing apart from this omniscience remains partial with respect to its spheres of knowledge, it is not held to be direct perception of all phenomena.

The defining characteristics of phenomena presented here, from the aggregate of form up to omniscience, relate specific attributes that simply define these phenomena. There is a world of difference between these types of *defining characteristics*, on the one hand, and *intrinsic characteristic*, which constitutes the object of negation, on the other.

A summary of the points

> That which defines the conditioned
> and that which defines the unconditioned
> are devoid of themselves.
> This is *emptiness of defining characteristics*. 6.215

That which defines the conditioned and that which defines the unconditioned, these characteristics that define phenomena, **are devoid of themselves,** or empty of existing in their own right. This is *emptiness of defining characteristics*.

The emptiness of the unobservable and of nonthings

> This present moment does not endure;
> the past and future have no existence;
> in that the three cannot be perceived anywhere,
> they are referred to as the "unobservable." 6.216

> This unobservability is
> itself empty of its own being;
> it does not endure eternally nor disintegrate;
> so this is *emptiness of the unobservable*. 6.217

> Since they originate from their conditions,
> things lack existence as composites.
> The composite is itself empty of composite,
> and this is *emptiness of nonthings*. 6.218

[364] **This present moment does not endure** beyond its own time of existence; **the past** that has already occurred **and the future**, which is yet to be and has not arisen at present, **have no existence. In that the three**—that which has already occurred, that which is yet to be, and the present—are, in

their respective order, disintegrated, unarisen, and not enduring—they **cannot be perceived anywhere**. Hence **they are referred to as the "unobservable." This unobservability is itself empty of its own being**, for **it does not endure eternally nor disintegrate. So this is emptiness of the unobservable.**

Since they, things, originate from their causes and **conditions,** they **lack** intrinsic **existence as composites.** This fact about them is referred to as "nonthing," **and the composite is itself empty of composite's own essence. This** emptiness **is emptiness of nonthings.**

The presentation of these sixteen kinds of emptiness is not from the point of view of applying diverse avenues of reasoning to help negate true existence. For the same two reasonings—"that it does not endure eternally" and "that it does not disintegrate"—are used in establishing emptiness in all instances. They are also not meant, in general, to help prove the absence of true existence for a single person. For when a person has validly established the absence of true existence with respect to a specific thing, say the eyes for example, the moment he directs his mind to other things, he will be able to terminate all relevant doubts through his own extension of the reasoning, without depending upon someone stating a proof. In view of these, we should understand that this presentation is from both the perspective of a single person as well as from the perspective of specific individuals who may possess stronger clinging to the true existence of particular bases.

An extensive explanation of the four kinds of emptiness

> In brief, the term *thing* is used
> to refer to the five aggregates.
> They are empty of themselves,
> and this is called *emptiness of things.* 6.219

> In brief, *nonthing* is used
> to refer to unconditioned phenomena.
> These nonthings are empty of themselves,
> and this is called *emptiness of nonthings.* 6.220

> The absence of intrinsic nature
> is *emptiness of so-called nature.*
> In that nature is never contrived,
> *intrinsic nature* is the name ascribed to it. 6.221 [365]

Whether the buddhas appear in the world
or whether they do not appear in the world,
all things are empty, and this is proclaimed
to be their transcendent reality. 6.222

This is the "perfect endpoint" and "suchness"
and *emptiness of transcendent reality.*
This is how these enumerations of emptiness
are proclaimed in the Perfection of Wisdom sutras. 6.223

In brief the term *thing* **in** the phrase "emptiness of things" **is used to refer to the five aggregates,** and they are indicated here briefly without specifying them individually. **They,** these five aggregates, **are empty of themselves** as inherently existent, **and this** emptiness **is called** in the sutras the *emptiness of things.* Again, **in brief,** *nonthing* **is used to refer to unconditioned phenomena** without specifying them, and these include space, nirvana, and so on. That **these nonthings are empty of** inherent existence as **themselves is** referred to as the *emptiness of nonthings.* The word **"nature"** here refers to the ultimate nature of things. Such a **nature is never contrived** by śrāvakas and so on [pratyekabuddhas, bodhisattvas, buddhas] but abides as the essential nature of things. **That this nature,** the ultimate nature of phenomena, **is devoid of intrinsic existence is ascribed the name** *emptiness of intrinsic nature.* **Whether the buddhas appear in the world or whether they do not appear in the world, all things are empty, and this** empty nature **is proclaimed to be their transcendent reality.**

In Naktso's translation, there are the following readings: "whether they do or do not appear as for nature" (6.222b) and "it has been proclaimed as emptiness, the transcendent reality" (6.222d). This latter rendering seems to read better.

The Sanskrit term for "transcendent reality" (*parabhāva*) refers to three things—"supreme," "other," and "transcendent." In the first sense, [emptiness] is the suchness that is most excellent. Being most excellent has the meaning that it exists as never deviating from the defined meaning of what suchness is. In the second sense of the term, "other" here connotes something that is other than of the mundane world; so the term refers to the supramundane wisdom that is most excellent—namely, the nonconceptual wisdom [of the āryas]. And "entity" or "reality" here refers to what is being cognized by that wisdom. In the third sense of the term, what is on the other side is understood to be the "transcendent reality." The other side of cyclic existence **is**, because it transcends samsara, the **"perfect endpoint."** Here the "endpoint" is nirvana, which is the ending of cyclic existence. Since it never deviates from the defined meaning of what suchness is, such as by turning into something other [this emptiness], **this is "suchness."** It is devoid of itself, **and** this absence of intrinsic existence is called the *emptiness of transcendent reality*.

Although the emptiness of intrinsic nature and so on [366] were already explained above [among the sixteen kinds of emptiness], there is no fault of redundancy for presenting them again here. They are explained here from the perspective of enumerating emptiness within a medium-scope elaboration. The two last explanations [the emptiness of intrinsic nature and emptiness of transcendent reality] appear repeatedly both in the extensive enumerations as well as in the medium-length enumeration of emptiness. The significance of this is to help remove the doubt that if the ultimate nature is accepted as being the essential nature of things, that it exists at all times, and that it exists as the object of knowledge of nonconceptual wisdom, it must then possess true existence. It is therefore critical to understand that there is no contradiction in accepting these [and at the same time rejecting the true existence of emptiness]. The way we have presented them here [Candrakīrti says] **is how these enumerations of emptiness are proclaimed** or explained **in the Perfection of Wisdom sutras**, the Mother of Conquerors.

A conclusion stating the qualities of the ground

Now to conclude the section on the perfection of wisdom by way of presenting the unique qualities of the bodhisattva who especially aspires for the perfection of wisdom, the text says:

> Thus illuminated by the rays of wisdom's light,
> the bodhisattva sees as clearly as a gooseberry on his open palm
> that the three realms in their entirety are unborn from their very start,
> and through the force of conventional truth, he journeys to cessation.
> 6.224

Thus illuminated by the rays of wisdom's light, emerging from analysis undertaken in terms outlined above, and light that destroys the darkness obstructing the vision of suchness, **the bodhisattva sees as clearly as a** fresh **gooseberry on his open palm that the three realms in their entirety are unborn from their very start, and through the force of conventional truth, he journeys to cessation**—which is to say, he will enter into the absorption of true cessation.

To indicate that although the bodhisattva reaches the state of cessation, he never forsakes his thought to save sentient beings, the text says:

> Though his mind may rest continuously in cessation,
> he also generates compassion for beings bereft of protection.
> Advancing further, he will also outshine through his wisdom
> all those born from the Buddha's speech and the middle buddhas. 6.225

> And like a king of swans soaring ahead of other accomplished swans,
> with white wings of conventional and ultimate truths spread wide,
> propelled by the powerful winds of virtue, the bodhisattva would
>   cruise
> to the excellent far shore, the oceanic qualities of the conquerors. 6.226

This bodhisattva on the sixth level, **though his mind may rest continuously in cessation** or clear light, **also generates** and enhances his **compassion for beings bereft of protection.** [367] Thus his actions remain within the domain of samsara while his mind remains within the domain of nirvana. **Advancing further,** this bodhisattva on the sixth level **will** later **also outshine through his wisdom all those born from the Buddha's speech and the middle buddhas.**[847]

And this bodhisattva of the sixth level, who, **like a king of swans,** will **spread wide** his two **white wings**—the right and left wings—of the stages of the path **of conventional** truth, which is the vast dimension of the path, and the stages of the path of profound **ultimate truth,** he will **soar ahead of other accomplished swans,** the excellent swan-like trainees. And **propelled by the powerful winds of virtue** he had gathered in the past, **the bodhisattva would cruise to the excellent far shore, the oceanic qualities of the conquerors,** the buddhas.

Thus those of us who aspire to follow in the footsteps of such a bodhisattva, we too must travel with the wings of both aspects of the path. We should not be content with any path that appears to have neither of the two wings, nor should we be content with an incomplete path, which is like having one wing broken. We should instead travel to the stage of buddhahood on the basis of a path where both method and wisdom are complete.

This concludes exposition of the sixth ground of the ultimate awakening mind from *Illuminating the Intent: An Exposition of Entering the Middle Way.* [368]

Part III: The Final Grounds

20. The Seventh Ground, Gone Afar

Explaining the remaining four grounds, such as Gone Afar

This has four parts: (1) explaining the seventh ground, (2) explaining the eighth ground, (3) explaining the ninth ground, and (4) explaining the tenth ground.

Explaining the seventh ground

> Here on Gone Afar, the bodhisattva will enter cessation
> instantly and within a single moment.
> He attains as well blazing perfection of skillful means. 7.1

Here on the seventh ground of **Gone Afar, the bodhisattva will enter cessation instantly and within a single moment**—that is, all at once in an instant, cessation that he had attained on the sixth level. "Entering the cessation" refers here to entering into absorption of the perfect endpoint [i.e., emptiness]. So thusness (*tathatā*) is referred to here as "cessation," the point being that during an ārya's meditative equipoise [on emptiness], all perceptions of dualistic elaboration come to an end within the sphere of thusness. The *Ten Grounds Sutra*, for example, states:

> O children of the conquerors, beyond the sixth bodhisattva level one enters into the bodhisattva's absorption into cessation. So the bodhisattva who abides on the seventh bodhisattva ground enters and exits from cessation even within a single instance of a mind moment. This is not to say, however, that he has actualized cessation.[848]

On this ground **he attains as well blazing perfection of skillful means**, which means that it has become for him perfectly refined. The manner in which this perfect refinement takes place should be understood on the basis of the reasons explained above in the context of other bodhisattva levels.[849] It's on the basis of the superiority of specific facets of the perfection of wisdom itself that the last four perfections are defined.[850] It's the dimension that pertains to the thorough discrimination of phenomena that is the perfection of wisdom itself, not in relation to some other facet.

As for the "skillful means" in what is defined as the perfection of skillful means, the *Bodhisattva Grounds* speak of two sets of six types of skillful means.[851] The first six skillful means, those that accomplish the qualities of the buddha, are that (1) bodhisattvas view all sentient beings with compassion, (2) they understand the nature of all mental formations exactly as they are, (3) they desire the unexcelled wisdom of enlightenment, [369] (4) seeking the welfare of sentient beings, they do not forsake cyclic existence, (5) they revolve in cyclic existence not through an afflicted mind but through perfectly understanding the conditioning factors exactly as they are, and (6) their diligence is set ablaze because of their wish to attain buddhahood. The six skillful means for maturing the minds of other sentient beings are that (1) bodhisattvas help cultivate the minor roots of virtue of sentient beings so that they may produce immeasurable fruits, (2) they help beings plant great roots of virtue with minimal difficulty, (3) they help dispel the anger of those who are hostile toward the Buddha's teaching, (4) they help those who remain in a neutral state of mind enter the teaching, (5) they help those who have entered the teaching gain maturity, and (6) they help those who have matured attain the true freedom [of liberation]. These together are the twelve skillful means.

This concludes exposition of the seventh ground of the ultimate awakening mind, from *Illuminating the Intent: An Exposition of Entering the Middle Way.*

21. The Eighth Ground, The Immovable

Explaining the eighth ground

This has three parts: (1) how aspiration excels on this ground and how he is roused from cessation, (2) showing that all the afflictions have ceased, and (3) showing that ten types of mastery have been achieved.

How aspiration excels on this ground and how he is roused from cessation

> To attain again and again virtues superior to the earlier ones,
> the great being will enter The Immovable
> and thereby attain the state of irreversibility.
> His aspirations become perfectly refined,
> and he'll be roused by the buddhas from his cessation. 8.1

The great being, this bodhisattva on the seventh ground, **to attain again and again virtues superior to the earlier ones, will enter** the eighth level, **The Immovable, and thereby attain** the state of **irreversibility.** [370] The way in which he attains again and again virtues superior to those compared to the seventh level is explained in the *Ten Grounds Sutra*:

> O child of the conquerors, it is thus. A great sailing ship requires manual propulsion until it reaches the open ocean. However, once it reaches the great ocean, manual propulsion is no longer necessary because the wind would propel it. The distance a ship covers in a single day on the open sea far exceeds what can be covered in a hundred years through that earlier laborious way of moving. It is likewise, O child of the conquerors, with the bodhisattva who has amassed the great collections of roots of virtue and perfectly cultivated the Great Vehicle too; the progress he

will make toward omniscient wisdom within a short time by voyaging on the ocean of bodhisattva deeds through spontaneous wisdom, such distance cannot be covered by the prior intentional, laborious activity even in a hundred thousand eons.[852]

Here, "until reaching the open ocean" is the analogy for those on the seventh ground and below; entering and then voyaging on the open ocean is the analogy for traveling the path after attaining the eighth ground.

This bodhisattva on the eighth ground, all of **his aspirations become perfectly refined**, from the first generation of supramundane aspiration up to the ten great aspirations, all the countless hundred thousand aspirations he has made. Thus, he comes to greatly excel in the perfection of aspiration on this ground.

This level is characterized as the level of the youthful prince, whereas on the ninth one attains the status of a regent and on the tenth one is consecrated by the buddhas in the manner of a universal monarch. When the bodhisattva on this Immovable ground enters cessation, the ultimate nature of things, **he'll be roused from that** absorption into **cessation** by the buddhas. The *Ten Grounds Sutra* states:

> O child of the conquerors, the bodhisattva who is residing on this Immovable ground—one who has generated the power of aspiration and is abiding within that continuum of the door of Dharma—he will be urged by the blessed buddhas to accomplish the Tathāgata's wisdom. They will speak to him thus, "O child of lineage, well done! Well done! This [Immovable] indeed constitutes the ultimate forbearance with respect to the realization of the qualities of buddhahood. This said, O child of lineage, you still do not possess the perfect unique attributes of the Buddha, such as my ten powers and four types of fearlessness. [371] So strive in the practices to seek these perfect attributes of the Buddha, apply your perseverance, and do not forsake this door of forbearance.
>
> O child of lineage, although you have attained abiding in the tranquility of liberation, think about the child-like beings who remain bereft of peace, utterly bereft of peace, who are plagued by the emergence of all sorts of afflictions, and whose minds are stupefied by all kinds of conceptualization. O child of the lin-

eage, think also of your past aspirations, the welfare of sentient beings that needs to be accomplished, and the inconceivable nature of the doors of [the Buddha's] wisdom.

O child of lineage, this is the ultimate nature of all phenomena. Whether tathāgatas appear in the world or not, this ultimate expanse will remain. Thus all phenomena are empty, all phenomena are unobservable. This is not something that defines the tathāgatas only; for śrāvakas and pratyekabuddhas too will attain this concept-free ultimate nature.[853]

Also:

If, on the other hand, the blessed buddhas were not to urge this bodhisattva to enter the doors that lead to the attainment of omniscient wisdom, the bodhisattva could enter nirvana on that [Immovable] ground alone. His activity of bringing about of the welfare of all sentient beings could also then come to an end.[854]

These [passages from the sutra] state how on the eighth ground, when the bodhisattva, having mastered nonconceptual wisdom, remains equipoised on that alone, he is roused from this state and is urged to accumulate merit in post-equipoise intervals to gather the accumulations for attaining the buddha's powers and so on. The sutra speaks also of how śrāvakas and pratyekabuddhas also attain concept-free wisdom of direct realization of ultimate nature. In light of these, the assertions that the realization of suchness alone is sufficient and one need not strive in gathering the other accumulations are the mere blather of an unlearned person.

Showing that all the afflictions have ceased

Free of attachment, his mind no longer remains with faults;
thus all stains are destroyed on the eighth ground along with their
    roots.
With afflictions ceased, he becomes unrivaled in the three realms,
yet a buddha's boundless space-like resources lie beyond his reach. 8.2

[372] The reason the bodhisattva on this eighth level is roused from cessation by the conquerors is because on this ground, **free of attachment, his**

mind—that is, his wisdom mind—**no longer remains with** the **faults** of afflictions such as attachment. **Thus on the eight ground**, given that the sun of nonconceptual wisdom has risen, **all stains**, which resemble darkness—all the afflictions that have emerged in the past, which serve as causes for taking birth in the cycle of existence and whose fruits could have been experienced in the three realms—**are destroyed along with their roots.** In this way, **with** all the **afflictions ceased, he becomes unrivaled in the three realms,** or spheres of existence. Yet at this stage when all afflictions have ceased for the bodhisattva, a **buddha's boundless space-like** qualities and **resources lie beyond his reach.** So, to attain these resources, the eighth-level bodhisattva needs to endeavor further.

How is it known that all afflictions have ceased on this ground? The *Ten Grounds Sutra* states, "At this stage the bodhisattva thoroughly transcends to nirvana."[855] So one's mind on this ground is free of attachment to all three realms, for without the freedom from attachment that is the cessation of afflictions, the bodhisattva would not be able to actualize nirvana.

Showing that ten types of mastery have been achieved

> Though samsara has ceased, he displays himself for samsaric beings
> through diverse forms gained through ten controlling powers. 8.3

One might ask, if one attains freedom from attachment to the three realms on this level, birth in cyclic existence will come to an end. How then does the bodhisattva complete all the causes for attaining the attributes of the buddha?

[*Response:*] **Though** birth in **samsara** through karma and affliction **has ceased** for the eighth-ground bodhisattva, **he displays himself for samsaric beings though diverse forms** on the basis of assuming the mental body **gained** on this ground **through ten controlling powers** such as mastery of wisdom, just as explained in the *Śrīmālādevī Sutra.*[856] It is in such bodies the bodhisattva will complete his accumulations, so there is no contradiction. [373]

The ten controlling powers are described extensively in the *Ten Grounds Sutra:*

> (1) As he has transformed his lifespans across countless incalculable eons, he has gained controlling power over *lifespan*; (2) as

he has engaged in the wisdom of incalculable contemplations of concentration, he has gained controlling power over the *mind*; (3) as he displays the entirety of world systems as adorned with an incalculable array of ornaments, he has gained controlling power over *material resources*; (4) as he displays the fruits of karma in perfect accord with time, he has gained controlling power over *action*; (5) as he displays birth in all world systems, he has controlling power over *birth*; (6) as he continuously displays total realization of whatever is wished for at any time, he has gained controlling power over *aspiration*; (7) as he continuously displays the entirety of world systems as filled with the buddhas, he has gained controlling power over *intention*; (8) as he displays miraculous emanations in all buddha fields, he has gained controlling power over *supernatural feats*; (9) as he continuously displays [similitudes of] the tathāgatas' powers, their fearlessness, the unique qualities of the buddhas, the major ārya marks, the minor ārya marks, and the full awakening of buddhahood, he has gained controlling power over *wisdom*; and (10) as he continuously emanates the light that opens the doors to the Dharma free from the boundaries of center and edges, he has gained controlling power over *Dharma*.[857]

This concludes exposition of the eighth ground of the ultimate awakening mind, from *Illuminating the Intent: An Exposition of Entering the Middle Way*. [374]

22. The Ninth Ground, Perfect Intellect

Explaining the ninth ground

On the ninth the bodhisattva's power becomes perfectly refined,
and he attains the spotless qualities of four kinds of perfect knowledge.

9.1

On the ninth ground, **the bodhisattva's power**—all aspects of his perfection of power—**becomes perfectly refined**. Ten types of power are described in the context of the perfection of power, as for example in the *Ornament of the Sage's Intent*:

(1) The *power of intention* refers to the total absence of indulgence in the afflictions; (2) the *power of altruistic resolve* refers to being thoroughly trained in the wisdom of the bodhisattva levels; (3) the *power of retention* refers to never forgetting the teachings; (4) the *power of meditative concentration* refers to being always utterly free from distraction; (5) the *power of perfect resources* refers to being versed in clearly discerning the activities of beings of the limitless and infinite world systems; (6) the *power of influence* refers to realizing everything his mind hopes; (7) the *power of confidence* refers to being versed in detailed discernment of the experiences of all attributes of a buddha; (8) the *power of aspiration* refers to never forsaking the act of engaging in the deeds of all the buddhas; (9) the *power of the perfections* refers to bringing the attributes of a buddha to maturation, bringing sentient beings to their maturation, and never forsaking activities that are beneficial to all sentient beings; (10) the *power of great loving kindness* refers to being dedicated to connecting all sentient beings to safety; (11) the *power of great compassion* refers to dispelling all the sufferings of all sentient beings; (12) the *power*

of the ultimate nature of things refers to directly realizing the ultimate nature of things, such as their illusion-like character; and
(13) the *power of being blessed by all tathāgatas* refers to being face
to face with the wisdom of omniscience. These are as explained
in the sutras.[858] [375]

Just as in the case of the perfection of power, the bodhisattva also **attains
the spotless qualities of four kinds of perfect knowledge** of phenomena,
their significance, etymologies, and confidence. Here the *Commentary* states
that with the first one knows the specific characteristics of each phenomenon; with the second one knows the differentiations among attributes of all
phenomena; with the third one knows how to speak about these phenomena without confusion; and with the fourth one knows, without any gaps,
the continuum of the concordant causes of these phenomena.[859] In other
texts, these are explained in terms of the knowledge of (1) the Dharma, (2)
its subject matter, (3) the etymological meaning of the terms, and (4) limitless confidence [to speak].

This concludes exposition of the ninth ground of the ultimate awakening
mind, from *Illuminating the Intent: An Exposition of Entering the Middle
Way.* [376]

23. The Tenth Ground, Cloud of Dharma

Explaining the tenth ground

> On the tenth ground he will receive supreme empowerment from all
>   the buddhas,
> and his superior gnosis will reach here its perfection as well.
> As a heavy downpour descends from water-laden clouds, so from him,
> the Dharma rain will fall freely to water the crop of beings' virtues. 10.1

On the tenth ground he, the bodhisattva, **will receive** the **supreme empowerment** of great light **from all the buddhas** of all directions. The way in which this empowerment is received is as stated in the *Ten Grounds Sutra*:

> At the end of having attained a millionfold countless concentrations, this bodhisattva will actualize a concentration known as "conferring the empowerment," which is no different from [buddha's] omniscient wisdom. Immediately afterward, a great lotus of jewels will appear, equal in size to a quadrillionfold world system known as Endowed with All Supreme Aspects . . . surrounded by countless smaller lotuses equal to the number of atoms that exist in a million billionfold world systems. The bodhisattva's body too remains commensurate with such a size. The instant the bodhisattva attains that concentration, he will appear seated upon this lotus. As he sits on it, light rays would emerge from the mid brows of the buddhas that have converged from all the buddhafields, and they will confer empowerment upon him.[860]

For this bodhisattva, among the ten perfections, **his superior gnosis will reach here its perfection as well**—that is to say, his gnosis will become perfectly refined. As for the nature of this gnosis and how it differs from the perfection of wisdom, *Bodhisattva Grounds* says:

> The knowledge of the presentations of all phenomena as they are represents the perfection of gnosis. Regarding this, the gnosis that penetrates ultimate truth is the perfection of wisdom, while the gnosis that penetrates conventional truth constitutes the perfection of gnosis. This then is the difference between these two perfections.[861]

Just as heavy downpour descends from water-laden clouds to help nurture the crops of worldly people, **so from him,** [377] this son of conquerors on the tenth ground, **the Dharma rain will fall freely to water the crop of beings' virtues.** This ground is therefore called Cloud of Dharma.

This concludes exposition of the tenth ground of the ultimate awakening mind from *Illuminating the Intent: An Exposition of Entering the Middle Way.* [378]

24. Qualities of the Ten Grounds

Presenting the qualities of the ten grounds

This has three parts: (1) the qualities of the first ground, (2) the qualities of the second up to the seventh ground, and (3) the qualities of the three pure grounds.

The qualities of the first ground

On the first ground the bodhisattva sees a hundred buddhas
and knows as well that he is blessed by them all.
At that point he can endure for a hundred eons,
and he will know perfectly what came before and what will follow. 11.1

This wise one will enter and exit a hundred meditative absorptions;
a hundred world systems he can tremble and illuminate;
through his supernatural feats he can ripen a hundred beings to
    maturity;
he will journey to a hundred buddhafields. 11.2

This offspring of the Sovereign Sage will open a hundred Dharma
    doors,
and within his body he will display a hundred other forms.
Those hundred bodhisattva forms thus displayed
will each match his beauty, wealth, and retinue. 11.3

On the first ground of the ultimate awakening mind, **the bodhisattva** who has attained the first ground (1) **sees** instantly—that is, in a single moment—**a hundred buddhas** and (2) **knows as well that he is being blessed by all** those hundred buddhas. **At that point,** (3) the lifespan of the one abiding on the first ground will **endure for a hundred eons**; and during these hundred eons (4) **he will know perfectly what came before and what will follow.** This means that the vision of his gnosis will penetrate the bounds of past and future for up to a hundred eons. (5) **This wise one,** the bodhisattva, **will enter** into **a hundred meditative absorptions and** will **exit** out of these. (6) This bodhisattva **can cause a hundred world systems to tremble,** and (7) he will be able to **illuminate** hundred world systems. (8) Likewise, **through his supernatural feats,** this bodhisattva **can ripen hundred** sentient **beings to maturity.** (9) **He will journey to a hundred buddhafields,** one buddhafield for each buddha. (10) This bodhisattva **will open a hundred Dharma doors,** [379] and (11) **this offspring of the Sage will display within his body a hundred other forms** as well. (12) And surrounding each of these hundred bodies, **each of those hundred bodhisattva forms displayed will match his beauty, wealth, and retinue.**

The qualities of the second up to the seventh ground

> The wise one on Perfect Joy, having attained such qualities,
> attains the same on The Stainless but increased a thousandfold,
> and on the next five grounds these qualities expand.
> His qualities increase first to a hundred thousand, 11.4
> and then increasing a thousandfold on the next;
> next a hundred million, then ten billion,
> then one trillion, and after this ten million trillion.
> He thus attains perfectly all these qualities. 11.5

The wise one abiding **on the** ground of **Perfect Joy, having attained** a hundredfold of twelve **such qualities,** as he progresses to the second ground, just as described in relation to the first ground, this bodhisattva abiding **on** second ground, **The Stainless, attains** perfectly **the same** set of twelve **qualities increased a thousandfold. And on the next five grounds**—the third, fourth, fifth, sixth, and seventh—the bodhisattva will attain **these** very set of twelve **qualities** in such a way that they **expand** in their respective order, **first by increasing** them **to a hundred thousand, and then increasing a thousandfold on each** of the next **grounds to a hundred million, then ten billion, then one trillion**—that is, one trillion sets of twelve qualities—**and after this ten million trillion.** Thus, in this way, **he attains perfectly all these qualities.** [380]

The qualities of the three pure grounds

Since the qualities from the eighth ground cannot be counted, they are described in terms [comparable to the counts] of subtle atoms. The text reads:

> The one on the Immovable ground,
> who is free of concepts, attains such a magnitude
> of qualities they equal the number of atoms
> in a hundred thousand billionfold worlds. 11.6

> The bodhisattva residing on Perfect Intellect
> attains qualities thus described
> increased to the count of all the atoms
> in ten times a hundred thousand countless worlds.[862] 11.7

> On the tenth ground, to say the least, his qualities
> lie beyond the bounds of speech;
> equaling the count of all atoms.
> Such a total is a countless quantity indeed. 11.8

> Such a bodhisattva can, within every pore,
> display countless buddhas together with bodhisattvas.
> Likewise, he can display within every single instant
> celestial beings, demigods, humans, and so on. 11.9

The one abiding **on the** eighth **ground, The Immovable,** one **who is devoid of conceptualization** of self-grasping at both persons and phenomena, **attains such a magnitude of qualities they equal the number of atoms** that exist **in a hundred thousand billionfold worlds**—namely, in all three realms of the entire trichiliocosm.

The bodhisattva who is **residing on** the ninth ground, **Perfect Intellect,** **attains** these twelve **qualities thus described** above, **increased to the count of all the atoms in ten times a hundred thousand countless worlds**—namely, one million countless trichiliocosms.

On the tenth ground, the **qualities** of this ground are such that the number of the twelve qualities **lies beyond the bounds of speech. Such a total is a countless quantity indeed,** and the qualities he attains **equal the count**

of all atoms that exist in the buddhafields even beyond what is inexpressible. The phrase "to say the least" indicates that the qualities on the tenth ground are not exhausted by what has been stated here. These are the ones "to say the least," and they signal the sequence for speaking about other qualities that will appear later [in the text]. [381]

Furthermore, such a bodhisattva can, without conscious thoughtful intention, display within every bodily pore countless bodhisattvas and forms of fully awakened buddhas, each with a retinue of incalculable bodhisattvas, even changing forms into different aspects within a single instant. Likewise, in every pore of his body, he can display within every single instant other forms as well, namely those of the beings of five realms of existence[863]—celestial beings, demigods, humans, and so on—each in their distinctness and without mixing with each other. The words "and so on" indicate those that are not mentioned. What are those unmentioned ones included here? They are Indra, Brahmā, worldly guardians, kings of the human world, śrāvakas, and pratyekabuddhas. So the words "and so on" underline the point made in the statement "For the sake of sentient beings who are ready to be tamed by the Tathāgata, he is capable of assuming the physical forms of Indra and others and teach the Dharma spontaneously."[864] For an extensive explanation of this point, consult the *Ten Grounds Sutra*.

25. The Resultant Ground

The resultant ground

This has five parts: (1) how one attains full awakening first, (2) the buddha bodies and their qualities, (3) the emanation body, (4) establishing the one vehicle, and (5) explaining the time of manifest awakening and abiding.

How one attains full awakening first

This has two parts: the actual point and rebutting the objections.

The actual point

> Just as moonlight can shine bright in a cloudless night sky,
> he strives again on the ground that gives rise to the ten powers,
> and in Akaniṣṭha he will find the object of his striving, supreme peace,
> which is unrivaled as the ultimate culmination of all qualities. 11.10

[382] **Just as**, for example, **moonlight in a cloudless sky can shine bright** for all those traveling [at night], so too the one who has found that tenth ground of awakening mind, which clears away the darkness obstructing the attainment of the buddha's qualities, knows that he can attain the qualities of the buddha by himself. So **he strives** once **again**—that is, he initiates further efforts **on** that tenth **ground**, the very **ground that will give rise to** the buddha's ground endowed with **ten powers**—so that he attains the buddha's ground. The **supreme** state of **peace, the object of his striving**—namely, the unexcelled gnosis—the Blessed One **will find in Akaniṣṭha** and in that realm alone. This gnosis is **the ultimate culmination of all qualities**: here all the qualities, such as the establishings of mindfulness, have reached their culmination and are most sublime. It **is unrivaled** as well because nothing is like it and nothing surpasses it.

To be consistent with the text of the commentary, the translation of the first line should read as I have explained above.[865] As for the second line, Naktso renders it as "Once again, having striven on that ground that precedes the arising of the ten powers." This translation actually seems better. The expression "in Akaniṣṭha alone" indicates that someone who is not yet enlightened will necessarily first attain the state of complete enlightenment is Akaniṣṭha. [In contrast] the display of attaining complete enlightenment by someone who was awakened previously takes place in the desire realm. This is the position of the Perfection Vehicle.[866]

To show that when one first attains full awakening in Akaniṣṭha, that blessed one attains the gnosis that knows everything in a single instant, the text says:

> Just as space remains indistinguishable even within different vessels,
> no differentiations of phenomena exist in suchness.
> Since he perfectly realizes everything in terms of a single taste,
> the buddha, the excellent mind, perceives the knowables in a single
>   instant. 11.11

For example, there may be many **different** types of **vessels**, such as vases, bowls, and so on, but the **space** that exists **within**, or pervades, these different containers **remains** the same, in that space is the mere negation of obstruction. Other than that, it is **indistinguishable**. Likewise, although **differentiations of phenomena exist**—such as form, feelings, and so on— created by causes and conditions, **no** such differentiations exist **in** terms of their **suchness**, their absence of arising through an intrinsic nature. Thus one should recognize that the ultimate realities of all things share the same or **a single taste**. [383] **Since he has perfectly realized** this sameness of taste with his enlightened mind in a single instant, **the buddha, the excellent mind,** has found the gnosis that **perceives** all **the knowables in a single instant.**

Rebutting the objections

This has two parts: stating the opponent's position and refuting that position.

Stating the opponent's position

> "If ultimate reality is pacification, then the mind will never perceive it,
> yet there can be no knowledge of an object without the mind as a
>   knowing subject.
> And in the absence of a *knowing* mind, what *knowledge* can there be?
>   This is a contradiction in terms.
> Also, with no knower how can you teach about it to others, saying, 'It
>   is thus'?" 11.12

[*Objection*:] You say that the absence of intrinsic arising is the suchness of form and so on, but then you also assert that this is cognized by the mind. Now **if** you posit that **pacification** of intrinsic arising **is ultimate reality,** you will **then** have to admit that **the mind,** or wisdom, **will never perceive it.** For were the mind to focus on ultimate reality—which is the absence of intrinsic arising—what kind of aspect would this mind assume? No such thing is possible. Therefore, with no aspect [of an object] to be perceived, the mind could not perceive ultimate reality. And **without** a cognizing subject, **the mind as a knowing subject, there can no knowledge of an object.** So how can this truth of ultimate reality be known at all? **And in the absence of a** *knowing* **mind, what** *knowledge* **can there be? This is a contradiction in terms.** Also, if there is no possibility for a mind that engages ultimate reality, **with no knower, how can you** say, "I have realized such ultimate reality," and **teach it to others** by **saying, "It is thus"?** This is untenable.

Refuting that position

This has two parts: (1) rebutting the objection that realization of suchness would be untenable and (2) rebutting the objection that a knower would be untenable.

Rebutting the objection that realization of suchness would be untenable

> When no-arising *is* suchness and that mind too has no arising,
> it is by assuming its aspect then, as it were, the mind perceives suchness.

Just as for you, when the mind takes the aspect of an object, it perceives it,
so in dependence on convention, we say the mind can know suchness.
11.13

[384] In the conventions of the world, when consciousness holds an aspect that resembles the form of the object, that consciousness is said to perceive that object. **Just as for you**, for example, **when the mind** arises **taking the aspect** of some blue **object**, you say that such a mind **perceives it**, the blue object. Likewise, when the knowing subject **assumes** the **aspect** that resembles **suchness**, then **in dependence on** worldly **convention, we say** that **the mind can know suchness.** Thus the manner in which the mind takes on the aspect of suchness is this: **When no-arising** through intrinsic nature *is* **suchness** of the object, **and that mind too has** likewise **no arising** through intrinsic nature, one fuses with the other in the manner of water poured into water, and it is in this manner the mind takes on the aspect of such an object. It is in this manner we define how the mind realizes suchness. So the problem you have raised in your objection above does not apply.

In Naktso's translation, we read, "The very assumption of the aspect of ultimate reality is its cognition." In this reading, the words **"as it were"** are absent; this seems more accurate.[867]

Here, the *Commentary* states:

> Therefore one speaks of realizing suchness on the basis of designation, though in fact, it is not that something is known by something. Both the cognizer and the cognized are unborn.[868]

The meaning of the phrase "on the basis of designation" is as found in the line "mind knows . . . in dependence on convention." The mind perceives [suchness] not in some intrinsically real manner but on the basis of mere designation. The meaning is not that it is an instance of ersatz knowing of suchness. The expression "in fact" and so forth indicates that there is no knowing [of suchness] other than the mere arising of the aspect of the absence of conceptual elaboration. Suchness is not known in the manner of perceiving colors like yellow or blue, where there is the appearance of their forms to the mind. This is because just as the object suchness is unarisen, the subject [the mind] too possesses the aspect of being unarisen through intrinsic nature. This is what the *Commentary* is saying.

This being so, when the opponent objects that the mind perceiving suchness is impossible based on the following arguments—the mind cannot engage with an object if its aspect cannot appear to that subject; if the mind does not engage, then it would not know that object; and it is contradictory to assert something to be a knowing subject if it does not know anything— given that Candrakīrti himself agrees with the arguments, he responds to this by rejecting the assertion that ultimate truth cannot be perceived. He furthermore explains, with the help of an example, how the aspect of suchness can appear to the mind and how [385] one can speak of the mind perceiving such an object on that basis. Given this, those who say that in this system there is no nonconceptual gnosis realizing the ultimate truth simply denigrate the supreme realization of the āryas.

Here, the line "[the buddha, the excellent mind,] perceives all knowledge objects in a single instant" (11.11d) states that it is within a single instant that a buddha attains omniscient wisdom, and there is also the statement that the gnosis pertaining to the way things really are does not know in the manner of perceiving the cognizer and cognized to be separate. With respect to these statements, it seems necessary to properly understand how a buddha knows the way things really are as well as things in their diversity. So let me offer here a brief explanation.

Until one attains buddhahood, it is not possible for a single instant of cognition to perceive multiple specific phenomena and to have direct perception of their ultimate reality at the same time. The knowledge of these two will occur in an alternating manner. However, from the point when all the residual impressions of grasping at true existence are gone and one has become fully awakened, one then abides at all times in meditative equipoise on ultimate truth. At such a stage, then, there is no alternating between equipoise and post-equipoise states on the basis of exiting or arising from that equipoise. This is as described in the autocommentary on the *Two Truths*:

> Within a single instant of wisdom,
> it pervades the entire expanse of knowledge.[869]

Therefore, since there is no post-equipoise gnosis that knows things in their diversity that is a different entity from the gnosis of meditative equipoise, you have to accept that every object of knowledge encompassed by the two truths is known by a single gnosis. So, in relation to knowing ultimate reality as a gnosis knowing the way things really are, all dualistic appearances are thoroughly calmed and gnosis rests in a single taste, like water poured into water. In relation to the buddha's gnosis knowing things in their diversity, however, the dualistic appearances of object and subject appear in all their specificity. This said, since all residual imprints of deluded dualistic perceptions have been eradicated, this dualistic perception is not erroneous with respect to what is being perceived. It is thus not an erroneous type of dualistic perception. How this is not erroneous has already been explained well elsewhere.[870]

That both equipoise and post-equipoise stages do exist on the level of the buddhahood is stated in the commentary on the following lines of the *Sublime Continuum*:

> Wisdom, gnosis, and thorough freedom,
> are [respectively] luminous, radiating, and pure.
> Devoid of differentiation, they resemble
> the light, rays, and orb of the sun.[871]

Its commentary states:

> The nonconceptual supramundane wisdom that exists in the mind of a buddha, [386] since it abides dispelling the darkness that obscures the sublime ultimate reality of objects of knowledge, it resembles a luminous light. The gnosis attained in its aftermath that knows all objects of knowledge, since it engages with every aspect of things that are objects of knowledge, resembles the radiating network of light rays.[872]

The "nonconceptual supramundane wisdom" refers here to the mind in equipoise; and how this is defined in relation to the ultimate truth is indicated by the phrase "the sublime ultimate reality." The "after" in the phrase "attained in its aftermath" should not be understood in any temporal sense of sequence, such as that it was attained after rising out of that equipoise. Its meaning is that it is attained or that it emerges through the power of that meditative equipoise. The line "objects of knowledge" and so on indicates that such post-equipoise gnosis is defined on the basis of its engagement with the entire expanse of knowledge. So the buddha's gnosis, from the point of view of the phenomena that are the bases, is not a wisdom knowing the way things really are, and from the point of view of their ultimate reality, it is not a wisdom knowing things in their diversity. If one understands this point well, one will then comprehend the significance of the following from the *Two Truths*:

> Absent of the imputed essence, ·
> all things arisen in mere dependence
> in a way that corresponds to appearances:
> these the omniscient sees directly.[873]

And:

> Signs no longer appear
> for him who does not perceive in terms
> of the knower and the known.
> With his abiding firm, he does not rise.[874]

In these lines, it is stated that a buddha directly knows all the appearances of things in their diversity and that he does so without perceiving in dualistic terms of the knower and the known. Other great ones have made similar statements. With respect to these, some assert that not perceiving any dichotomy of the knower and known is from the point of view of a buddha himself, while direct knowing of all objects of knowledge [by a buddha's mind] is a mode of knowing relevant to the perspective of other trainees. When it comes to the state of buddhahood, there is actually no gnosis at all.[875] One does not have to say such things. For [if you follow our line of explanation] you will know that there is not the slightest contradiction in the fact that a single gnosis can have two distinct modes of knowing defined from the perspectives of its two distinct objects.

"In that case," someone might wonder, "will there not be a contradiction between what is said here and the definition of the two truths presented above in the lines that begin "All entities bear two natures / as obtained by correct or false views [of them]" (6.23ab)?

There is no contradiction. The definition of the two truths presented earlier is to be understood in general. The mode of knowing of a buddha's gnosis, however, is indeed a special case, unique in comparison to the mode of knowing on the tenth level and the stages below it. Therefore, were one to formulate a definition of the ultimate truth that includes even a buddha's mode of knowing, [387] it should read: "that which is found by a valid rational cognition seeing the perfect truth and with respect to which its cognition constitutes such valid rational cognition."[876] Through this one should understand the definition of conventional truth as well. In this manner, you should understand how the ultimate truth is found by the buddha's gnosis knowing the way things really are and how it is in relation to this that such gnosis is defined as knowing the way things really are. Likewise, you should understand how conventional truth is found by the buddha's gnosis knowing things in their diversity and how it is in relation to it that such gnosis is defined as gnosis knowing things in their diversity. Here you should also recall our position presented above in the context of analyzing whether reflexive awareness is tenable.[877]

Rebutting the objection that the knower would be untenable

This has two parts: the actual point and the case that such a knower is possible.

The actual point

Now we will present our response to the objection raised above (in 11.12d), "According to you, with no knower, who would teach suchness to other trainees, saying, 'It's thus'?"

It is true that the consciousness that realizes ultimate reality on the level of buddhahood is fused in a single taste with its object—namely, ultimate truth, which is the absence of intrinsic arising. However, this does not eliminate all possibility for the world to realize ultimate reality. How so? The heart of the opponent's objection is that if a buddha abides at all times within the single taste of ultimate reality, there would then be no teacher with any intention or thought to teach the Dharma. And if there is no such intention, there can be no teaching of the Dharma. Thus the text, after raising the objection, presents the following response explaining how teaching the Dharma can be tenable even in the absence of conceptualization. Thus the root text says:

> Through his enjoyment body sustained by merit
> and through the force of his emanations from space and others,
> sounds reverberate declaring the truth of ultimate reality;
> from these the world too comes to understand suchness. 11.14

The buddha's form body—the embodiment in which the buddha actualizes the dharmakāya, which is the ultimate expanse—is **sustained** or created **by** the manifold accumulations of **merit**. It is the perfect **enjoyment body** endowed with a profusion of inconceivable forms. It is the cause for bodhisattvas' enjoyment of the wealth of the Dharma. The **sounds** that **reverberate** from this buddha body **declare the truth of** the **ultimate reality** of phenomena. **From these** [388] **the world**—that is, spiritual trainees who are suitable vessels for hearing about the way things really are—**comes to understand suchness** without distortion. Not only will such sounds emerge from the buddha body that was produced by hundredfold merits, emanations will also appear through the power of such an enjoyment body, and **through the force** of those **emanations**, sounds will issue forth even **from** inanimate things like **space, and others** such as grasses, trees, walls, and rocky cliffs, revealing the truth of reality.

The case that such a knower is possible

Someone might wonder, "When there are no thought processes of the mind and mental factors, the act of intending to teach like that is impossible. So when teachings are given, what cause could give rise to the activity of teaching the Dharma?" The root text uses an analogy to illustrate the response:

> The wheel set in motion
> through long and strenuous labor by a strong potter,
> spins freely, and pots are seen to be produced thereupon,
> even when no further immediate effort is made. 11.15

> Likewise, without exerting any immediate effort,
> thanks to his aspiration and beings' merit,
> the enlightened deeds of the one abiding in
> the dharmakāya are inconceivable indeed. 11.16

In this world a **wheel set in motion through long and strenuous labor by a strong potter** continues to **spin freely** afterward, **and pots** and so forth **are seen to be produced thereupon, even when no further immediate effort is made** to spin the wheel. **Likewise,** when someone has attained the full awakening of buddhahood, **without exerting any immediate** conscious **effort, the enlightened deeds of the** buddha **abiding in** the essence of **the**

dharmakāya will engage [spontaneously]. Like [the fruits of] a wish-granting jewel and a wish-fulfilling tree, the buddha's enlightened deeds will flow from the force of the maturation of the **merit** accumulated by the trainees for hearing the Dharma from the buddha as well as the extraordinary **aspirations** made by the buddha when he was a bodhisattva in the past. This is **inconceivable indeed**.

What types of aspirations are these? They are those such as the following: "May I too become one who is dedicated to securing the welfare of sentient beings, never wavering from the ultimate expanse for even an instant and yet never missing a timely opportunity to tame sentient beings." [389] This citation from a sutra is found in Naktso's translation.

The buddha bodies and their qualities

This has two parts: (1) the buddha bodies and (2) the qualities such as the powers.

The buddha bodies

The first has three parts: dharmakāya, the enjoyment body, and the causally concordant body.

Dharmakāya

> Burning away the tinder of all objects of knowledge,
> there is the state of peace, the buddhas' perfect dharmakāya.
> In such a state there is neither arising nor cessation,
> and with mind ceased, it is actualized by the body. 11.17

Now we will describe [the buddha body] from the point of view of the dharmakāya. The buddha body, which is or has the nature of gnosis, is the fire-like gnosis that has **burned away the tinder of all objects of knowledge** that appear in dualistic terms. Since it is immersed in the absence of intrinsic arising, which is in fact the very nature of the objects of knowledge, it is endowed with an awareness bearing this aspect of the absence of intrinsic arising. This state of **peace**, the ultimate reality, is **the buddhas' perfect dharmakāya**. It is from this perspective the *Diamond Cutter Sutra* states:

The buddhas view ultimate nature,
the saviors the dharmakāya.
Ultimate nature is not an object of knowledge
because it cannot be known.[878]

This states that buddhas remain in equipoise on ultimate reality at all times, and that although the saviors know the dharmakāya and the ultimate nature, they do not view them in terms of dualistic appearances.

As for this ultimate reality, **there is neither arising nor cessation in such a state**, and it is from this point of view that the following has been stated in the sutras: "O Mañjuśrī, that which is known as no-arising and no-cessation is designated the Tathāgata."[879] Thus, on the level of buddhahood, the conceptual processes of mind and mental factors have ceased and do not operate with respect to the truth of ultimate reality. As such the two—nonconceptual gnosis and ultimate reality—remain indivisibly fused like water poured into water. Therefore, on the conventional level, this state **is** said to be first **actualized**, or obtained, **by the** enjoyment **body**. [390] To substantiate this point, Naktso's translation appears to cite here from the *Irreversible Wheel Sutra*.[880]

With respect to the meaning of "**with mind ceased**," *Clear Words* says:

> The following statement appears in the sutras: "What is this ulti-mate truth? If, with respect to it, there is not even the turnings of thought, what need is there to speak of words?" Therefore it is the absence of conceptualization.[881]

So the text explains the meaning in terms of the absence of the turnings of thought—that is, conceptualization. Here in the autocommentary too, after explaining the meaning of the state of *peace* in terms of being free of the mind and mental factors, the analogy of wish-fulfilling tree and wish-granting jewel are provided to illustrate how although such is the state of that peace, it is capable of bringing about others' welfare. And at the end of this, the autocommentary says, "So even though there is no conceptualiza-tion, like a wish-fulfilling tree and a wish-granting jewel..."[882] Thus Candra-kīrti clearly states that it is the conceptualizing mind and mental factors that a buddha is free from. So to cite this passage as a source for the claim that there is no gnosis at the level of buddhahood is a failure to understand the meaning of the text and constitutes a grave denigration.

The enjoyment body

> This body of peace, radiant like the wish-granting tree,
> resembles the wish-granting jewel that without forethought
> grants riches of the world to beings until they gain freedom.
> It will be perceived by those free of conceptual elaboration. 11.18

This enjoyment body, the buddha body in which the dharmakāya is actualized, is the **body of peace** for it is free of conceptualizing mind and mental factors. Although it does not conceptualize, it is capable of accomplishing the welfare of sentient beings. Therefore, **radiant like the wish-fulfilling tree**, it **resembles the wish-granting jewel that without** any **forethought** serves as the cause for the realization of the aims of spiritual trainees. This body remains present constantly—that is, for a long time—**granting riches of the world to beings**, the spiritual trainees, **until they gain freedom.** In this way the buddhas engage only in the welfare of sentient beings and remain as long as the world exists and as long as space endures. This enjoyment body **will be perceived** only **by those** bodhisattvas whose minds are **free of conceptual elaboration**, only those who have attained, through their twofold accumulation, the ground on which they have found the stainless mirror of wisdom. It will not be visible to those on the ordinary stage who possess conceptual elaboration. [391] Also, *Seventy Stanzas on Going for Refuge to the Three* states:

> The form body of the buddha
> blazes with major and minor marks;
> owing to the aspirations of beings,
> it assumes varied forms.

> The body that is born from
> stores of merit immeasurable
> is seen by the Conqueror's children
> who abide on the ten grounds.

> This resource body of dharmakāya
> is indeed an enlightened act of the buddhas.[883]

The causally concordant body

This has three parts: (1) how the buddha displays all his activities within a single pore of his body, (2) how all the activities of others are displayed at that very site, and (3) how he has attained perfect mastery over his intention.

How the buddha displays all his activities within a single pore of his body

Whether emerging from the force of the dharmakāya or the form body as described above, the essence of the emanation body that is other than the enjoyment body is causally concordant with the dharmakāya and the enjoyment body. In other words, it is the buddha body that has emerged from its cause—the deeds of taming sentient beings. To express that this body too possesses inconceivable power, the root text says:

> The buddha displays within a single instant,
> and within a single causally concordant form body,
> all his previous births now ceased, clear and without error;
> all these lives he displays in their vividness. 11.19
>
> The sage in whatever buddhafields there were,
> their bodies, deeds, strengths, and powers;
> and whatsoever retinues of disciples were assembled;
> whatsoever physical forms the bodhisattvas assumed; 11.20
> whatsoever teachings he gave and ways of life he assumed;
> whatsoever deeds he had engaged in having listened to Dharma,
> and whatever quantities of offerings he made—
> all this the buddha displays within a single body. 11.21
>
> Likewise his discipline, forbearance, diligence, meditative absorption,
> and wisdom, whatever practices he had engaged in in the past,
> without any omission and in clearest detail,
> all of this he displays within a single pore. 11.22

Within a single form body that is **causally concordant** with the dharma-kāya and the enjoyment body, **the buddha displays all** the circumstances of **his previous births** in cyclic existence that have **now ceased**, from time without beginning. He spontaneously **displays within a single instant** all these past occurrences, **in vividness** and **clear without error**—that is to say, without conflating them, like a reflection in an utterly unblemished mirror. [392]

For example, a blessed one displays the following: how, when he was engaged in the perfection of generosity in the past, he made offerings to and honored such and such buddhas; how the **sage** took birth **in whatever buddhafields there** were, such as with lakes that have the nature of lapis lazuli adorned with sentient beings living therein; the specifics of **the bodies, deeds, strengths, and powers** of those buddhas; the size of the retinue of their **assembled disciples**; the many [ārya] sanghas who had become such as a result of their dedicated practice of Dharma; **whatsoever physical forms the bodhisattvas assumed** adorned with the noble and exemplary marks of whatever buddhafields; the many living there enjoying requisites like monastic robes, food, and shelter; **whatsoever teachings he gave** such as those pertaining to the single vehicle or the three vehicles; the **ways of life he had assumed**—whether as intelligent lay members of different castes like the brahmans or as a monastic—who, **having listened to the Dharma** and having taken the precepts partially or in their entirety, **engaged in whatsoever** bodhisattva **deeds**; and the length of time and the **quantities of offerings he made** of precious jeweled ornaments, monastic robes, and foodstuffs to these buddhas, bodhisattvas, and śrāvakas. **All this**, without omission, **the buddha displays within a single body.**

Just as he displays all the circumstances that occurred pertaining to his perfection of generosity, **likewise he displays** within a single body **whatever practices he had engaged in in the past**, such as the perfections of **discipline, forbearance, diligence, meditative absorption, and wisdom.** The explanation given in the context of generosity [such as the length of time and the extent] should be applied to these other perfections as well. Not only does the buddha simultaneously display all his past activities within a single body, **all of this he displays without any omission and in clearest detail within a single pore** as well.

How all the activities of others are displayed at that very site

He shows how the buddhas of the past, those yet to come,
and those in the present throughout the expanse of space

teach the Dharma in a resounding and clear voice, and
how they remain in the world to relieve beings' pain. 11.23 [393]

While aware that from first embracing the awakening mind
up to the essence of enlightenment, all their deeds share
the character of optical illusions, he displays them as his own
within a single instant and inside a single pore. 11.24

Likewise, the deeds of the bodhisattvas of three times,
and the deeds of ārya pratyekabuddhas and śrāvakas,
all these without omission as well as those of others
he displays within a single pore. 11.25

He shows how the buddhas of the past and **those yet to come** in the future,
as well as **those** buddhas now **present** residing **throughout the expanse of
space teach the Dharma in a resounding and clear voice, and how they
remain in the world to relieve beings** who are seized or tormented by **pain**.
In short, **he displays, as his own** activities, **all the deeds** of the buddhas of
the three times **from first embracing the awakening mind up to the** attainment of the **essence of enlightenment.** He is in fact capable of displaying
all this **within a single pore** of his body and **within a single instant** of time.
Now some ordinary magicians can, through the power of incantations and
substances, display various appearances of habitats and the creatures living in them on their own bodies. If that is so, how could the buddhas and
bodhisattvas who understand the **character** of things as indistinguishable
from that **of optical illusions** insofar as their truth or falsity is concerned,
and who have been familiar with this truth for numerous eons, not be capable of displaying such conjurations? Therefore what learned person would
not understand this or would harbor doubt even though he comprehends
this? There cannot be. So on the basis of this analogy [of a magician], we
should develop even greater conviction.

Just as he displays all of his own past activities, the Buddha is capable
likewise of **displaying within a single pore** in a single moment of time
all **the deeds of the bodhisattvas of the three times, the ārya pratyekabuddhas and śrāvakas** of the three times, **all these without omission as
well as those of others**—namely, the deeds during their period as ordinary
beings.

How he has attained perfect mastery over his intention

[394] Thus, after describing the three perfect buddha bodies, to present how, even without conceptualization, a buddha possesses perfect control or mastery over his intent, the root text says:

> This pure enlightened activity can, as if through a mere wish,
> display within a single atom an entire world system stretching to the
>   ends of space
> and display an atom that pervades countless world systems,
> without the atom expanding or the world contracting. 11.26

This pure enlightened activity of a buddha, which is free from all stains, engages **as if through merely wishing,** and in such a way, a buddha is capable of **displaying within** the space of **a single atom an entire world system stretching to the ends of space** itself. **And** when he **displays a** single **atom that pervades** the space of **countless** or the entire **world systems,** he does so **without** that single **atom expanding**—in other words, becoming larger— and without **the world contracting**—that is, becoming smaller.

> Free of discursive thought, a buddha can display
> in every single instant until the end of time
> deeds countless in their diversity,
> unmatched by the atoms in Jambudvīpa. 11.27

Similarly, the number of **diverse deeds that a buddha,** who is **free of discursive thought,** can **display in every single instant until the end of time** is **countless** and **unmatched by** the number of **atoms** that exist **in Jambudvīpa.**[884]

The first comparison here is in terms of space, while this latter is from the point of view of time.[885]

The qualities such as the powers

This has four parts: (1) a brief presentation of the ten powers, (2) a detailed explanation of these powers, (3) how all the qualities are inexpressible, and (4) the benefits of knowing the twin qualities.

A brief presentation of the ten powers

The state of buddhahood is clearly distinguished on the basis of the ten powers. To briefly present these categories, the root text says:

> The power to know what is correct and incorrect;
> likewise the power to know the ripening of karma;
> the power to know the diverse aspirations of beings;
> and the power to know the diverse elements. 11.28

> Likewise to know faculties, superior and not superior;
> the power to know all the different paths;
> and the power to know meditative absorptions, liberating factors,
> concentrations, and meditative attainments. 11.29

> The power to know past existences;
> likewise to know deaths and rebirths of beings;
> and to know the cessation of the contaminants—
> these then are the ten powers of a buddha. 11.30

With respect to the powers of a buddha, there is (1) **the power to know what is correct and** what is **incorrect;** [395] **likewise** there is (2) **the power to know,** of the cognition of, **the ripening of karma;** (3) **the power to know the diverse aspirations of beings;** and (4) **the power to know the diverse elements;** likewise (5) the power **to know faculties,** which are **superior and** which are **not superior;** (6) **the power to know all the paths** to be journeyed; (7) **the power** of cognition **to know meditative absorptions, liberating factors, concentrations, meditative attainments,** and so on; there is (8) **the power to know** or remember **past existences; likewise** (9) the power **to know,** to understand, **deaths and rebirths of** living **beings; and** (10) the power **to know the cessation of the contaminants. These** then are **the ten powers of a buddha.**

A detailed explanation of these powers

This has two parts: (1) presenting the five: to know what is correct and what is incorrect; and (2) presenting the five: to know all the different paths.

Presenting the five: to know what is correct and what is incorrect

"That from such and such a cause certain effects will arise
is certainly correct" has been declared by those who know such truths;
what is contrary to this statement is incorrect.
Such unobstructed knowledge of limitless facts is described as a power.
11.31

"From such and such a cause certain effects will arise," and such a cause
is indeed the basis of that effect. This **has been declared by** the buddhas—
namely, **those who know the truths.** Examples include such statements
as [396] "Undesirable effects arise from nonvirtue," "Nirvana is attained
through the ārya path on the learner's stage," and so on. **What is contrary to
this statement is** declared **incorrect.** Examples include "Undesirable effects
arise from virtue," "One who has attained the path of seeing experiences an
eighth rebirth through the power of karma,"[886] and so on. Such statements
are incorrect and [what they assert] impossible. **Such unobstructed knowledge of limitless facts** such as these of what is correct and what is incorrect
is described as the **power** to know what is correct and what is incorrect.

With respect to extremely diverse fruitional effects of these karma,
that of the desired and the undesired, their opposite, and their exhaust-
    ing factor,
the knowledge that penetrates these with unimpeded potency and
    force—
a knowledge that pervades all three times—is described as a power.
11.32

The knowledge that penetrates with unimpeded potency and force
each of these [varieties of karma]—**the desired,** which is virtue, and **the
undesired,** which is nonvirtuous karma, thus two unmixed types of karma
as well as **their opposite,** namely mixed karma; uncontaminated actions,
which are **the factors that bring about the exhaustion** of contaminated
negative karma; and also **the extremely diverse fruitional effects of these
karma**—**the knowledge that pervades** all objects of knowledge pertaining
to actions and their results throughout **all three times, is described as** the
power to know the ripening of karma.

Knowing the yearnings that emerge from factors such as attachment,
their extreme diversity, such as inferior, intermediate, and
   extraordinary,
knowing even the aspirations veiled by other factors—
such pervasive knowledge that engages all three times is a power. 11.33

Yearnings stem from the power of their seeds or **emerge from factors
such as attachment**—which here stands for other afflictions like aversion.
"Such as" includes faith and so on. There is an **extreme diversity** of such
yearnings and aspirations, **such as inferior, intermediate, and** some that are
extraordinary. And **knowing even the aspirations veiled by other factors,**
thus obscuring the seeds of such aspirations as referred to above, a **knowledge** that is **pervasive** and **engages** or penetrates **all** the facts of **the three
times** pertaining to aspirations—this **is the power** to know the diverse aspirations of beings.

The buddhas skilled in differentiating the elements have stated
that the nature of the eyes and so forth constitutes an element.
The knowledge of the fully awakened buddhas is infinite.
So that which penetrates all the diverse elements is held to be a power.
   11.34

The buddhas, who are **skilled in differentiating** all **the elements, have
stated that the nature of the eyes and so forth**—which includes the ears up
to the mind; their six objects, from shapes to phenomena; and the six types
of consciousness, from visual consciousness to mental consciousness—all
consist of inner emptiness, and this **constitutes an element. The knowledge
of a fully awakened buddha is infinite. So that which penetrates all the
diverse elements is held to be** the **power** to know the diverse elements.

Sharp acumen in thought and so on is called one with superior faculty;
the intermediate and inferior are described as not of superior faculty.
The mastery of all faculties, such as the eyes, and their correlations,
this knowing, free of attachment and impediment, is described as a
   power. 11.35

[397] Conceptualizing **thought,** which superimposes something that is
not true, **and so on** constitute faculties because they empower [the person]

to engender attachment and so on. "And so on" includes the faculty of faith and so forth. Faculties of those **sharp** in **acumen are called superior faculty**; those who are **intermediate and inferior are described as not of superior faculty.** The power to know the superior and not superior faculties as well as **the mastery of all** twenty-two[887] **faculties and their correlations**—namely, their effects—**knowing** the nature of each of these **free of attachment and impediment, is described as** the **power** to know superior and not superior faculties.

Presenting the five: to know all the different paths

> Certain path leads to buddhahood, while others
> to pratyekabuddha and śrāvaka enlightenment; yet others lead to
> the realms of hungry ghosts, animals, devas, humans, hell beings, and
>   so forth.
> The knowledge of these, free of impediment, is held to be a power.
>   11.36

A **certain path leads to** the state of **buddhahood, while others** lead **to pratyekabuddha and śrāvaka enlightenment; yet others lead to the realms of hungry ghosts, animals, devas, humans, and hell beings.** "And so forth" indicates other diverse paths that are deemed right or wrong. The **knowledge of these, free of** attachment and **impediment,** [398] **is held to be** the **power** to know all the paths to be journeyed.

> In accord with the various yogis there are in the diverse worlds,
> their meditative absorptions, eight liberating factors, and
>   concentrations,
> as well as the different meditative attainments, such as the nine—
> unimpeded knowledge of these is described as a power. 11.37

In accord with the various yogis there are in the limitless **diverse worlds,** all **their meditative absorptions**—the four meditative absorptions, **eight liberating factors, and concentrations, as well as the different meditative attainments, such as the nine**—the **knowledge of these** phenomena of both afflicted and unafflicted class, knowledge that is **unimpeded, is described as** the **power** to know the factors that are afflicted [leading to cyclic existence] and unafflicted [leading to liberation].[888]

To know the past lives of self and others across deluded existences,
knowing these lives of each and every numberless being,
their bases, places, and so on—
knowing all this is described as a power. 11.38

The power to **know the past lives of self and others across** their **deluded
existences**—namely, successive lives in beginningless existence—**knowing
these lives of each and every numberless** sentient **being** as well **their
bases**—namely, their causes—recollecting facts such as the features like the
complexions that self and others had or recollecting the **places**—how self
and others were born into such a place from such and such places—**and so
on: knowing all this is described as** the **power** to know past existences.

The births and deaths of sentient beings, each and every one,
their births inhabiting worlds reaching to the edges of space,
the knowledge that penetrates all these right at the time and in their
    varied details—
unimpeded and utterly pure, this is held to be a power. 11.39

The power to know **the deaths of each and every sentient being and
their births** through connecting with new aggregates—**their births inhabiting worlds reaching to the edges of space** and created by the craftsman
karma skilled in producing such great diversity—**the knowledge that penetrates all these right at the time and in their varied details**, which is **utterly
pure and unimpeded, this is held to be** the **power** to know the deaths and
rebirths [of beings].

Through his power of omniscience, a buddha can know
the swift ceasing of the afflictions as well as their imprints; he also
    knows
the cessation of afflictions of śrāvakas and others brought forth by their
    cognition.
This knowledge, unimpeded, is accepted as a boundless power. 11.40

**Through his power of omniscience, a buddha can know the swift ceas-
ing** or destruction **of the afflictions**—desire and so forth—**as well as their
imprints; he also knows the cessation of afflictions of śrāvakas and others**, which includes the pratyekabuddhas, **brought forth by their cognition**

that is uncontaminated wisdom. **This knowledge** of relinquishment, **unimpeded, is accepted as** the **power** to know the exhaustion of the contaminants. The word "swift" indicates how the buddha's gnosis eliminates the remaining extremely subtle residual imprints in a single moment. [399]

Here, with regard to the residual imprints of the afflictions, the *Commentary* states:

> That which percolates the mental continuum, imbues it, and makes it follow is a *habitual propensity*. The "final base" of the afflictions, their "habit," their "root," and their "habitual propensities"—these are synonyms.[889]

The text says that although śrāvaka arhats and pratyekabuddha arhats have eliminated the afflictions, they do not have the capacity to eliminate their residual imprints. And the text goes on to state, "As for the residual imprints of ignorance, they are obstacles to total knowledge of all phenomena."[890] So the imprints of afflictions are described as being obscurations to knowledge as well. Since grasping at self-existence of phenomena is understood to be an affliction in this system [of Candrakīrti], the principal obscuration to knowledge must be taken to be the habitual propensities for deluded dualistic perception. Given that the noble Nāgārjuna and his son Āryadeva do not provide any explicit identification of what an obscuration to knowledge is, we should rely entirely on the explanation found here in the *Commentary*. Again, the *Commentary* states:

> These residual imprints of attachment and so on, in turn, will cease for someone who is omniscient and fully awakened alone, not for others.[891]

In light of this, the "seed" referred to in the context of the statement that the seed of afflictions will cease for śrāvaka arhats and pratyekabuddha arhats as well from the eighth ground cannot be the same as the residual imprints of the afflictions referred to in the above citation. As for the extremely subtle form of these residual imprints, the point when they are about to cease is the exactly the same point when the *uninterrupted path* of the last stage of the tenth ground is about to arise. And the *path of release* that marks the first elimination of these extremely subtle imprints is simultaneous with the first instant of a buddha's gnosis. Candrakīrti, therefore, speaks of these [residual imprints] being destroyed through the power of omniscience.[892]

The statement that the powers [of a buddha] know all phenomena has to be understood in terms of direct perception. Since it is impossible to attribute implicit cognition to a buddha's perception, this means that a buddha must know these phenomena on the basis of directly perceiving them. It is clearly explained in Candrakīrti's *Commentary on Sixty Stanzas of Reasoning* that it is not the position of this system to accept knowing without the appearance of aspects [of the objects].[893] This means also that a buddha knows the past and future not somehow implicitly on the basis of directly perceiving the present. To be specific, with respect to the present such as this very day, for example, since the past and future defined in relation to it do not exist at this time, they are not perceived right now at this very time. There is, however, no contradiction in maintaining that a gnosis that perceives the present time also perceives all the pasts and futures as well. For example, although a sprout that exists at the time of a specific seed was not produced by that particular seed, there is no contradiction in stating that seeds do produce sprouts. [400]

How all the qualities are inexpressible

As for the entirety of a fully enlightened buddha's qualities, even if the Buddha himself were to transform his lifespan to endure for countless eons to keep declaring these qualities, putting aside other enlightened activities to do so, he would not come to the end of the qualities. So what need is there to speak of bodhisattvas being able to do so? What need is there to speak at all of pratyekabuddhas and śrāvakas being able to know or express these qualities exhaustively? To indicate this by means of an analogy, the root text says:

> Birds do not stop flying because there is no more sky;
> they do so when they have exhausted their strength.
> Likewise śrāvakas and the like, as well as bodhisattvas, cease
> declaring the buddha's qualities, infinite as space. 11.41

> Therefore how could someone like me
> know and speak of the buddha's qualities?
> Nonetheless, since the noble Nāgārjuna has described them,
> I have spoken briefly, setting hesitation aside. 11.42

For example, when **birds** with wide wingspans capable of reaching the far shores cruise the sky on the power of the wind, they **do not stop flying because there is no more sky**, because the sky has reached its end. Rather, **they do so when they have**, as a result of flying on and on, **exhausted their strength**. Likewise, śrāvakas and the like—namely, pratyekabuddhas—as **well as bodhisattvas** on the great bodhisattva grounds, will **cease declaring the buddha's qualities**, which are **infinite as space**. This is not because the qualities have been exhausted; they cease to do so because their power of mind has been defeated. Given that the qualities of a buddha cannot be expressed in their entirety, the question arises, **how could someone like me**, the author of this commentary, **know and speak of the buddha's qualities?** I cannot. So I admit that I do not possess any knowledge of my own, even partial, about the qualities of a buddha. **Nonetheless, since the noble Nāgārjuna has described them**, relying on his explanations and **setting hesitation** or doubts **aside, I have spoken briefly** about them. [401]

The benefits of knowing the twin qualities

Emptiness is the profound,
other qualities the vast.
By understanding the profound and the vast,
these [twin] qualities are obtained. 11.43

In brief, the twin qualities of a buddha presented in this treatise are the *profound* and the *vast*. **Emptiness is the profound**—namely, the dharmakāya and the emptiness of the ground and of the path. **Qualities other** than emptiness—such as the powers and so forth of the eleven grounds,[894] which have been described—are **the vast**. **By understanding** the nature of these qualities of **the profound and the vast**—by, say, understanding these two essential factors by cultivating them in meditative practice—**these** twin **qualities** of the buddha **are obtained**.

The emanation body

Now to present how the emanation body is the source for realization of the aims of śrāvakas, pratyekabuddhas, and bodhisattvas, and how it is also the source for bringing about all kinds of aims of ordinary beings, including the attainment of higher rebirth and so forth, the root text says:

> Once more, you who possess an unchanging body appear in the three
>   worlds;
> through emanations you show coming, birth, enlightenment, and turn-
>   ing the wheel of peace.
> And all beings indulging in devious behavior, ensnared in a network of
>   expectations,
> you lead them with compassion to the state beyond sorrow. 11.44

Although you, the Buddha, have already attained the dharmakāya, **once
more you who possess an unchanging body** that never wavers from equipoise on ultimate reality **appear in the three worlds**: above, under, and
on the ground. And **through emanations** you **show** the deeds of **coming**
to the human world from Tuṣita, taking **birth**, and so on, which involve a
relationship with parents and a son. You also display the deed of **turning
the wheel** of Dharma in accord with others' mental faculties to help them
enter **enlightenment**, the state of **peace** that is the city of nirvana. In this
way, without any desire for fame or reward and **with** great **compassion you
lead to** or place in **the state beyond sorrow all beings indulging in devious behavior** and **ensnared in a network of expectations** or cravings. [402]
With respect to the phrase "indulging in devious behavior," *Explanation of
the Commentary* has "indulging in varied behavior."[895] This latter reading
seems to be more in tune with Candrakīrti's *Commentary*.

Establishing the one vehicle

Having thus presented the three buddha bodies, the text explains how the presentation of three vehicles with respect to the singular vehicle is intentional:

> No other means to dispel all the stains exist apart from
> the knowledge of suchness. The suchness of phenomena admits of no
>   differentiation,
> and the subject, mind, that knows it is likewise undifferentiated.
> Thus the Buddha taught to us beings a single, unmatched vehicle. 11.45

Apart from the knowledge of the suchness of all phenomena there
exist no other principal **means to dispel all the stains** belonging to the two
obscurations—that is to say, no other principal methods. Furthermore, since
the suchness of phenomena admits of no differentiation based on distinct

features, **the subject mind**—namely, the wisdom **that knows it** [suchness]—
is likewise undifferentiated. This is to say, it does not disclose different
aspects of cognizing its object. Thus you, **the Buddha, taught to us beings**
who are the trainees **a single** undifferentiated **vehicle** that is **unmatched** by
any other vehicles. For example, we find the following:

> Kāśyapa, if all phenomena are cognized in terms of perfect
> equanimity, you have transcended to nirvana. This in turn is
> singular—not two or three.[896]

Along lines similar to *Entering the Middle Way*, the noble Nāgārjuna too
says:

> With no differentiation in ultimate expanse, [403]
> no differentiation exists in your vehicle.
> The presentation of three vehicles
> is thus to help sentient beings with their entry.[897]

Given that the cessation of all afflictions is not possible without the realization of suchness, and since there is no major differentiation when it comes
to the ultimate reality of phenomena, Candrakīrti explains here that such
presentations as the following were taught to help guide some trainees in the
immediate term: those that speak about differences among causal vehicles
with respect to the need for or lack thereof of the realization of suchness for
transcendence to nirvana, and those that speak about vehicles wherein after
having attained nirvana that consists in the mere cessation of afflictions, one
does not move onto another fruit. If we understand this properly, we will
comprehend the intention behind statements that those on the Hīnayāna
path do not realize the selflessness of phenomena.

One might ask, "If there is only one nirvana, after attaining which one
does not need to enter another vehicle, how is it that the vehicles of śrāvaka
and pratyekabuddha too have been stated to lead to nirvana?" To show that
such statements are for an intended purpose, the root text says:

> So long as degenerations engendering faults are present in sentient
> beings,
> they will not enter the profound truth, the realm of buddha's
> experience.

And so the Sugata, with his wisdom and compassionate skillful means,
has taken the pledge, proclaiming, "Sentient beings I will free." 11.46

So long as the five **degenerations are present in sentient beings**—
fellow sentient beings, era, afflictions, views, and lifespan—all of which
serve as causes for **engendering faults**—namely, the powerful afflictions
making their bodies and minds unserviceable and undermining whatever
higher aspirations they might have—[these degenerations] will prevent the
world or the trainees from generating an interest in attaining the buddha's
gnosis. **They will not enter the profound truth, the realm of buddha's
experience**, which is so difficult to fathom. **And so you, the Sugata, with
your wisdom**—which is skilled in the means of taming trainees—**and
compassionate skillful means** that never allows you to forget beings'
welfare, and with other kinds of skillful means, will most definitely fulfill
the **pledge you took** as a bodhisattva in the past, **proclaiming, "Sentient
beings I will free."**

Therefore, just as a wise [captain] conjures [images of] beautiful towns,
to relieve the frustrations of travelers journeying to an isle of gems,
you set forth vehicles to help soothe the minds of your disciples;
you spoke differently to those whose minds are trained in utter
     absence. 11.47

Sentient beings face so many barriers to entering the Great Vehicle, yet it
is vital they are definitely led to nirvana. **Therefore**, as stated in the *Sublime
Dharma of the White Lotus*, **just as a wise** captain, **to relieve the frustrations
of** a host of **travelers** on a long voyage across the ocean **journeying to an isle
of gems, conjures or** emanates images of **beautiful towns** until they reach
the land of gems, [404] **so you**, the Blessed One, **set forth vehicles** before
the shore of the Mahayana as means to attain this Great Vehicle.[898] You have
done this to help **soothe the minds of your disciples** and offer them relief;
thus you taught the two vehicles of śrāvakas and pratyekabuddhas (who
are included here as well). Then **you spoke differently**, in a distinct manner, **to those whose minds are trained in** the **utter absence** of afflictions
of cyclic existence; for them you taught the Great Vehicle alone. And just
like the buddhas [of the past], they will without doubt attain buddhahood
after completing their accumulations. This establishment of the singular-
ity of vehicle should be understood on the basis of statements such as the

following from the *Compendium of Sutras*: "That the vehicle is limited to only one is taught in a multitude of sutras."[899]

Explaining the times of manifest awakening and abiding

This has two parts: the time of manifest awakening and the time of abiding [in that awakening].

The time of manifest awakening

> As many as the atoms in all the worlds
> within the sphere of the sugatas, however many there might be,
> for that many eons you've entered the enlightened state,
> but this secret of yours should not be divulged in words. 11.48

The atoms in all the worlds of all ten directions—**however many there might be**—that are **within the sphere of the sugatas, for that many eons you have entered the enlightened state.** Though this is so, it is difficult for those who have not already gathered the roots of virtue to be convinced, and so **this secret of yours should not be divulged in words.** I have spoken about them here, however, to help gather merit by those who have extraordinary admirations for these [enlightened deeds].

Here, the author of the *Explanation of the Commentary* says, "It is stated thus because the dharmakāya of all the buddhas is one; otherwise, no other buddhas could emerge."[900] This is incorrect because the *Commentary* explains this [stanza] from the point of view of emergence of the emanation body.[901] [405] It is also incorrect to interpret the [*Commentary*'s] phrase "the cause for the emergence of the emanation body" as referring to the dharmakāya, for if one accepts this to be the extent of the time for entering the dharmakāya, the fault of there being no opportunity for others to attain buddhahood would still stand for us as well. Furthermore, if the dharmakāya of all the buddhas is one, the dharmakāya of those who have not previously attained buddhahood and those who are attaining buddhahood would all have already been attained, thus entailing such extreme contradictions. This passage, therefore, indicates the measure of having departed to the essence of awakening; and with respect to this too, it is not presenting the length of time since the Buddha attained full awakening in the past. Rather, it is showing the extent of the number of times the Buddha displayed the deed of attaining full awakening as the emanation body after having already attained buddhahood. The following rendering, Naktso's translation, seems better:

> The number of atoms in all the realms,
> which are within the spheres of the buddhas of all ten
>   directions,
> that many times you, the supreme Sugata, will come forth
> to enlightenment . . .

If we explain this stanza as is done by the *Explanation of the Commentary*, we ourselves would become the ones to whom, as the root text says, this secret should not be divulged.

The time of abiding [in that awakening]

> As long as all beings have not gone to the state of supreme peace,
> and as long as space itself remains undestroyed,
> how can there be an entry into supreme peace for you, Conqueror,
> you who were brought forth by mother wisdom and nursed by
>   compassion? 11.49

The future lifespan of **you, the Conqueror,** will last **as long as all beings** or trainees **have not gone to the** state of **supreme** or total **peace**—that is, until they have become buddhas—**and as long as** unconditioned **space itself remains undestroyed.** You, the Buddha, [406] act in the manner described above because you **were brought forth** by **mother wisdom,** which is the perfection of wisdom, and were **nursed by** the wet nurse of great **compassion.** So **how can there be** the possibility of **entry into supreme peace** of one-sided nirvana **for** someone like **you?** None at all.

> The extent to which you are compassionate toward worldly beings,
> beings who feed on poisoned food because of the defect of their
>   ignorance,
> such is not found even in the pain of a mother whose child has just
>   consumed poison.
> So Savior, do not journey to supreme peace. 11.50

What kind of compassion do the buddhas who care for limitless sentient beings and work toward bringing about the welfare of all these beings have? Sentient beings, **because of the defect of their ignorance** clinging to true existence, **feed on poisoned food**—that is to say, they cling to the five sense objects and consume them, which in turn becomes the cause for great suffering. **The extent to which you are compassionate toward worldly beings**— feeling their pain like one whose family member has just eaten poisoned food—**such is not found even in the pain of a mother whose** only **child has just consumed poison** and is in mortal danger. And **so, Savior, do not journey to** the **supreme** one-sided **peace.**

> Through their unskillfulness, beings cling to notions of *things* and
> *nonthings*,
> which give rise to the pains of birth and destruction, and of loss and
> gain of wanted and unwanted;
> beings also fall to evil destinies. So this world finds itself within your
> tenderness.
> Through your compassion, Blessed One, you turn from peace and for-
> sake your nirvana. 11.51

Through their unskillfulness with respect to suchness, there are **beings** who **cling to** the **notions of** the true existence of *things* and, on that basis, owing to their conviction in the law of karma and its effects, view existence in terms of births as celestial gods or as humans. This in turn definitely **gives rise to the pains of birth and destruction**—namely, death—as well as the suffering that arises from the **loss of the wanted,** such as a loved one, **and gain of** what is **unwanted.** There are **beings also** who cling to the notion of *nonthings*, such as the nonexistence of causality, and thus **fall to evil destinies,** such as unfortunate births like those in the hell realms. Given that sentient beings meet with sufferings described previously, **this world** of beings **finds itself within** the sphere of **your** great heart's **tenderness. Through your** great **compassion, Blessed One, you turn** away **from** one-sided **peace,** and **forsaking** such one-sided peace of **nirvana,** you remain in the world.

The manner in which the treatise was composed

> This system has been explained by the monk Candrakīrti
> drawing from the *Treatise on the Middle Way,*

in perfect accord with the scriptures,
and in accord with oral instructions. 11.52

Just as outside this [tradition of the] *Treatise*,
no scriptures set forth this teaching as it is,
likewise the system found here is not found elsewhere.
O learned ones, be sure of this fact! 11.53

[407] **This system** of interpreting the intention of the savior Nāgārjuna without distortion **has been explicated by the monk**, the glorious **Candra-kīrti, drawing from** *Fundamental Wisdom*, **the** *Treatise on the Middle Way*, among others. It is **in perfect accord with** the definitive **scriptures and in** perfect **accord with** the **oral instructions** of the noble Nāgārjuna. **Just as outside this** tradition of the *Treatise on the Middle Way*, **no** other **scriptures set forth this teaching** known as emptiness unerringly **as it is, likewise the system** that is **found here** wherein emptiness has been presented on the basis of critical analysis and responses to objections **is not found elsewhere** in any other treatises. So I appeal, "**O learned ones, be sure of this fact!**"

Here, the *Commentary* states:

> Some of those Mādhyamikas who say that what the Sautrānti-kas and Vaibhāṣikas assert to be ultimate realities are accepted as conventional realities by the Madhyamaka do so because they fail to understand the true intent of the *Treatise on the Middle Way*. For it is illogical to speak of the world-transcending truth as equivalent to worldly truths.[902]

All presentations of everyday conventions in this system are made solely on the basis of the absence of existing through intrinsic characteristics. As such, the tenets of essentialist schools such as the Sautrāntika and Vai-bhāṣika, which are postulated entirely on the assumption that things exist through their intrinsic characteristics, cannot be said to exist even on the conventional level, let alone on the level of the ultimate truth. Such is the standpoint of this tradition [of Candrakīrti]. Thus Candrakīrti urges us to understand that not only is his system distinct from Cittamātra, it is unique even among other Mādhyamikas who interpret the intent of savior Nāgār-juna and Āryadeva. Since our master accepts Buddhapālita's commentary to be authoritative, he is not expressing disapproval of him here. It appears that the position of bodhisattva Śāntideva is also highly compatible with the system our master Candrakīrti. [408]

As for how, in this approach of presenting the two truths as premised on the lack of existing through intrinsic characteristics even on the conventional level, there exist numerous unique tenets—such as the rejection of the tenet of autonomous syllogism and the denial of foundation consciousness—I have explained these in some detail in *Differentiating the Definitive and Provisional Meanings* and elsewhere.[903] So I will not elaborate further here.

Some say that the phrase "world-transcending" refers to the opponent's position, interpreting it as going beyond the conventions of the world, and that the phrase "worldly truths" refers to one's own standpoint. This reading, however, would contradict the statement in the *Commentary* where it reads, "since you would be abandoning this world-transcending truth . . ."[904] In fact, the meaning has to be understood in the exact opposite way. So the meaning of the phrases "world-transcending" and "worldly" must be understood in terms of having realized suchness exactly as it is or not.

Since this system of explaining the intention of the noble Nāgārjuna is unique, those who fail to understand the noble [Nāgārjuna's] intent and lack certainty about the truth of the scriptures will be terrified by the words that reveal emptiness and will thus shun the world-transcending truth. So to present suchness, which is the meaning of the *Treatise on the Middle Way*, without any distortion, [Candrakīrti says,] "I composed this *Entering the Middle Way*." To indicate this, the root text says:

> Terrified by the blinding color of the utterly vast ocean of Nāgārjuna's
>   wisdom,
> some have shunned and kept their distance from this most wonderful
>   tradition.
> Yet moistened by the dew, these stanzas opened like the buds of water
>   lilies.
> Thus the hopes of Candrakīrti have now been realized. 11.54

Terrified by the blinding color of the utterly vast ocean, so difficult to fathom, **of** the noble **Nāgārjuna's wisdom** realizing the profound [emptiness], **some** people, such as the proponents of Mind Only, **have shunned and kept their distance from this most wonderful tradition** of Nāgārjuna. **Yet moistened by the dew, these stanzas** on the Middle Way **opened like the buds of water lilies. Thus the hopes of Candrakīrti,** the one who opened the buds of such water lilies, **have now been realized**. [The *Commentary* says:]

> If this is so, were the elders Vasubandhu, Dignāga, Dharmapāla, and so on—authors of treatises who appeared in the past—terrified of merely hearing the sound of the words prompting them to completely abandon this undistorted presentation of the truth of dependent origination? Yes indeed, I would say.[905]

With respect to this statement of Candrakīrti, it is true that in their undisputed treatises, Vasubandhu and Dignāga have interpreted the meaning of the scriptures in accordance with the consciousness-only standpoint. Nonetheless, it is extremely difficult for someone like us to determine what exactly these masters' own personal views were. [409]

"Who then will realize this profound truth?" one might ask. Here the text says:

> This suchness just explained is most profound and terrifying,
> yet people with past habituation will certainly realize it;
> others, however, despite vast learning, will fail to comprehend.
> Thus, seeing those other traditions as constructed by the authors' own
>   minds
> as akin to the treatises that set forth propositions on self,
> forsake admiration for treatises and systems contrary to this one. 11.55

This truth of **suchness most profound and terrifying**, which has already been explained, **will certainly be realized by** those **people** who in other lifetimes in the **past** gained propensities of **habituation** to extraordinary admiration for emptiness. Here, in Naktso's translation it reads, "Even from among those who view the inferior non-Buddhist treatises as true, some realize emptiness owing to the power of causation." This rendering seems better than Patsab's translation.

One might find among non-Buddhists, who fail to imprint propensities for extraordinary admiration of emptiness in their mind, that some temporarily relinquish the manifest levels of affliction as defined in the Abhidharma texts, afflictions associated with the three realms of existence except the peak of existence. They may also be able to engage with diverse philosophical tenets. Even so, they are incapable of generating extraordinary admiration for the teaching of emptiness—the ultimate truth of emptiness as taught by the Buddha. Thus these **other** masters, **despite** their **vast learning** from having studied many scriptures, **will fail to comprehend** this profound truth. **Thus,** since the traditions besides the Madhyamaka that present ultimate truth do not reach the Buddha's enlightened intention, **seeing those other traditions as constructed by the author's own minds, as akin to the** way in which you would relate to the **treatises that** elucidate or **set forth propositions of self-**existence of persons, **forsake admiration for treatises and systems** of other masters that are **contrary to this one** tradition of Madhyamaka. Do not be amazed by systems that are fabrications of their own minds; rather, feel only a sense of wonder at our own view of emptiness, and engender profound admiration for it.

Dedicating the merits of having composed the treatise

> May the merit of speaking about the excellent tradition of the master
>   Nāgārjuna extend to the edges of space itself,
> may such merits shine bright as autumn stars amid the mind's sky dark-
>   ened by afflictions,
> and through the force of having obtained merits resembling a shining
>   gem on a serpent's hood,
> may the entire world realize suchness and swiftly travel to the Sugata's
>   ground. 11.56

May the vast **merit of speaking about the excellent tradition of the master Nāgārjuna,** extremely clearly on the basis of scriptures and reasoning— merit that **extends to the edges of space itself—**[410] **may such merits shine bright as autumn stars amid the mind's sky** turned indigo or **darkened by** masses of **afflictions. And through the force of** the author's mind **having obtained merits resembling a shining gem on a serpent's hood, may** every sentient being in **the entire world realize suchness** exactly as it is **and swiftly travel to the Sugata's ground** known as Constant Light. Naktso's translation [in the first line of the stanza] reads, "Through merit obtained from commenting on the beautiful system of Nāgārjuna renowned in all directions..."

The concluding matter

This has two parts: (1) which master composed this work and (2) which translator and Indian paṇḍita undertook the translation.

Which master composed this work

> This completes *Entering the Middle Way*, which illuminates the way of the profound and the vast, composed by Master Candrakīrti, whose mind is immersed in the supreme vehicle, who is endowed with unchallengeable wisdom and compassion, and who, by milking a drawing of a cow, undoes clinging to true existence.

This completes *Entering the Middle Way* composed by the great master Glorious Candrakīrti, who was born in Samantara: the elucidator of the way of Nāgārjuna's profound and vast system, a knowledge holder, renowned as having attained the illusion-like meditative absorption, whose mind was utterly immersed in the supreme unexcelled vehicle, who possessed wisdom and compassion that cannot be stolen by hostile forces, and who, by milking the drawing of a cow, helped dispel sentient beings clinging to the true existence of things.[906]

Which translator and Indian paṇḍita undertook the translation

This text was translated in accordance with the Kashmir edition by the Indian abbot Tilaka Kalaśa and the Tibetan translator Venerable Patsab Nyima Drak at Ratnagupta Monastery located in the center of the Kashmiri town Ānuparna during the reign of King Śrī Āryadeva. Later, the Indian abbot Kanakavarma and the same Tibetan translator compared the translation with the eastern, Bengal edition and made comprehensive corrections with a final version established on the basis of teaching and study.

I have presented here one colophon, merging together the author's and translators' colophons of both the root text and its commentary. This is to indicate that I have compared and edited here two versions of the root text—one translated on its own and the other embedded in the *Commentary*. [411]

The supreme essence of all the scriptures of the buddhas
is the path of dependent origination, the profound middle way
    free of extremes.
It is the excellent Nāgārjuna who was prophesized
to reveal this truth that is free of the two extremes.

Though there exist numerous traditions of learned ones
interpreting his sublime way and the thought of Āryadeva,
it is the tradition of Buddhapālita, Candrakīrti,
and Śāntideva that expound this in its fullness.

Integrating into one the avenues of thought of these three
most accomplished masters, and by explaining well
the essential points with decisive analyses penetrating their
    words,
I have made this supreme Prāsaṅgika tradition stainless.

In this northern region, even those who admire this system
do not engage with the highly refined paths of reasoning.
And those who are unfortunate in regard to the profound truth
disparage it because of their failure to comprehend.

Seeing so many such people, I have endeavored to write this
    work
to help remove their stains, to elucidate the profound path
to those who are fortunate, and so that I too may never be
    separated
from this excellent path throughout all lives.

Through the virtue from striving in this task,
may all beings realize all the essential points of the profound
    truth.
And through their dedication to practice every day and every
    night,
may they always please the buddhas and their children.

This exposition of *Entering the Middle Way* titled *Illuminating the Intent*
was composed by the yogi of the great Middle Way, Losang Drakpai Pal, a

monk of wide learning. It was written at the strong urging of spiritual mentor Lhula Lekpa Pal, someone versed in the ten treatises, who offered a mandala of forty silver coins, and also in response to requests made by many spiritual mentors who deeply admire this teaching and possess no small capacity of intellect to comprehend its meaning. They emphatically urged me to write an exposition that is comprehensive in its explanation of the difficult points of Candrakīrti's *Commentary*, in a manner that is lucid in its explanation of the meaning of the words yet detailed in its decisive analyses of the general points. It was composed at the great mountain retreat of victorious Geden.

Appendix 1. A Complete Outline of the Text

Note: Bracketed numbers reference the pages of the Tibetan edition, which are embedded in the translation in this volume.

Illuminating the Intent
An Exposition of Entering the Middle Way

1. Preliminaries

Salutation

Preamble

The meaning of the title [4]

The translator's homage [5]

The meaning of the treatise itself

    The salutation: A means of entering into the task of composing the treatise [6]

        Praising great compassion without differentiating its characteristics [6]

            How compassion is the principal cause of bodhisattvas [6]

                How śrāvakas and pratyekabuddhas are born from sovereign sages [6]

                How buddhas are born from bodhisattvas [10]

                The three principal causes of bodhisattvas [12]

            How compassion is also the root of the two other causes of bodhisattvas [15]

        Paying homage to great compassion by differentiating its characteristics

            Paying homage to compassion that takes sentient beings as its object [16]

            Paying homage to compassion that takes phenomenal reality and takes no reference as its object [19]

2. General Presentation of the Grounds

    The actual body of the treatise

The logical proofs that establish this [absence of intrinsic arising] through reasoning [124]

Refuting self-arising [125]

Refuting self-arising through the *Commentary* author's reasoning

Refuting the views of philosophers who claimed to have realized suchness

Refuting arising from a cause that is identical in nature with its effects

If an effect arises from a cause that is identical to it in nature, its arising will be pointless. [125]

If an effect arises from a cause that is identical to it in nature, it's contrary to reason. [126]

Rejecting the defenses aimed at averting these flaws [126]

Refuting that cause and effect are identical in nature [127]

Refuting using the consequence that the seed and the sprout will not have distinct shapes and so on [127]

Refuting the responses aimed at rebutting the objections [128]

Refuting using the consequence that in both situations, its perceptibility or lack thereof would be the same [128]

Demonstrating that there is no self-arising even on the conventional level from a perspective unaffected by philosophical views [129]

Summarizing the essential points of these refutations [129]

Refuting self-arising through *Fundamental Wisdom*'s reasoning [130]

Explaining the meaning of the words of the root text [188]

Discussing related issues arising from this [190]

Why the absence of intrinsic existence in something that has ceased is a reason to reject foundation consciousness [190]

How a basis for habitual propensities is posited despite the rejection of foundation consciousness [192]

Illustrating by analogy how effects come into being from the cessation of actions [193]

Rejecting objections to this presentation [196]

Rejecting the objection that karmic acts will give forth infinite fruitional effects [196]

Rejecting the objection that we are contradicting with scriptures that present a foundation consciousness [197]

The actual meaning of the words that eliminate contradiction with the scriptures [197]

The question of whether a foundation consciousness separate from mental consciousness has been taught

Examples of scriptures taught with specific intentions [201]

13. Refuting the Cittamātra Standpoint

Refuting, in particular, the Cittamātra standpoint [203]

Refuting intrinsic existence of consciousness with no external reality [203]

Presenting the opponent's standpoint [203]

Refuting that standpoint [208]

The extensive refutation [208]

Refuting the analogy for the intrinsic existence of consciousness and the absence of external reality [208]

Refuting the dream analogy [208]

How the dream analogy does not establish intrinsic existence of consciousness [208]

How the dream analogy does not establish nonexistence of external reality [210]

How the dream analogy establishes all entities to be false [213]

Refuting the analogy of seeing floating hairs [214]

Refuting the referent, the arising of consciousness devoid of external reality through the potency of propensities [215]

Refuting the view that cognitions of external reality arise or do not from maturation or its lack [215]

15. How to Read the Sutras

Appendix 2. Table of Tibetan Transliteration

Chapa Chökyi Sengé	Phya pa Chos kyi seng ge
Chim Jampaiyang	Mchims 'Jam pa'i dbyangs
Dölpopa Sherab Gyaltsen	Dol po pa Shes rab rgyal mtshan
Drepung Gomang	'Bras sprung sgo mang
Drepung Loseling	'Bras sprung blo gsal gling
Gampopa Sönam Rinchen	Sgam po pa Bsod nams rin chen
Ganden Jangtsé	Dga' ldan byang rtse
Ganden Shartsé	Dga' ldan shar rtse
Geden	Dge ldan
Gorampa Sönam Sengé	Go rams pa Bsod nams seng ge
Gyaltsab Darma Rinchen	Rgyal tshab Dar ma rin chen
Jamchen Chöjé	Byams chen chos rje
Jamyang Chöjé	'Jam dbyangs chos rje
Jamyang Galo	'Jam dbyangs dga' blo
Jamyang Shepa Ngawang Tsöndrü	'Jam dbyangs bzhad pa Ngag dbang brtson 'grus
Jetsun Chökyi Gyaltsen	Rje btsun Chos kyi rgyal mtshan
Ju Mipham	'Ju Mi pham
Karmapa Mikyö Dorjé	Karma pa Mi bskyod rdo rje
Khedrup Jé	Mkhas grub rje
Khedrup Tenpa Dargyé	Mkhas grub Bstan pa dar rgyas
Kumbum	Sku 'bum
Lama Umapa	Bla ma Dbu ma pa
Lhula Lekpa Pal	Lhu la Legs pa dpal
Lochen Kyabchok Palsang	Lo chen Skyabs mchog dpal bzang
Lodrö Rinchen	Blo gros rin chen
Losang Drakpai Pal	Blo bzang grags pa'i dpal
Losang Tamdrin	Blo bzang rta mgrin
Maja Jangchup Tsöndrü	Rma bya Byang chub brtson 'grus
Naktso Lotsāwa	Nag tsho lo tsā ba
Ngok Loden Sherab	Rngog Blo ldan shes rab
Ölkha	'Ol kha
Panchen Losang Chögyen	Paṇ chen Blo bzang chos rgyan
Panchen Sönam Drakpa	Paṇ chen Bsod nams grags pa

Patsab Lotsāwa   Pa tshab lo tsā ba
Radreng   Rwa sgreng
Rendawa Shönu Lodrö   Red mda' ba Gzhon nu blo gros
Sakya Paṇḍita   Sa skya paṇḍi ta
Sera Jé   Se ra byes
Sera Mé   Se ra smad
Shakya Chokden   Shā kya mchog ldan
Taktsang Lotsāwa   Stag tshang Lo tsā ba
Tashi Lhunpo   Bkra shis lhun po
Thangsakpa   Thangs sag pa
Tokden Jampal Gyatso   Rtogs ldan 'Jam dpal rgya mtsho
Tsek Wangchuk Sengé   Rtsegs Dbang phyug seng ge
Tsongkhapa Losang Drakpa   Tsong kha pa Blo bzang grags pa

Notes

1. Numerous textbooks (*yig cha*) focusing on Tsongkhapa's *Illuminating the Intent* appeared over time. The earliest known are two works of Lodrö Rinchen, a student of Tsongkhapa, who later became the fifth abbot of Sera Monastery: *Summary Outlines of Illuminating the Intent* and *Light on the Principles of the Exposition Entitled Illuminating the Intent*. The most well-known textbooks on Tsongkhapa's *Illuminating the Intent* are those by Jetsun Chökyi Gyaltsen (for Sera Jé and Ganden Jangtsé), Panchen Sönam Drakpa (for Drepung Loseling and Ganden Shartsé), Jamyang Shepa Ngawang Tsöndrü (for Drepung Gomang), and Khedrup Tenpa Dargyé (for Sera Mé).

2. On the ten perfect equanimities, as presented in the *Ten Grounds Sutra*, see the beginning of chapter 9.

3. Strictly speaking, Candrakīrti shows no awareness of Dharmakīrti, who was possibly a contemporary, so his object of critique when he is taking key tenets of Buddhist epistemology to task seems to be mainly Dignāga.

4. By listing these together, I am not suggesting that there is a consensus among Candrakīrti's commentators on what constitutes his unique views. In fact, there is a range of divergent opinions on what constitutes Candrakīrti's unique reading of Nāgārjuna, from some seeing his as a faithful orthodox reading to others viewing it as radical and nihilistic.

5. For a brief study of Chapa's critiques of Candrakīrti's Madhyamaka, see Tauscher, "Phya pa chos kyi seng ge as a Svātantrika."

6. Jayānanda was an Indian author who hailed from Kashmir and at one point served as a priest at the Tangut court; he visited central Tibet in the twelfth century.

7. This question of whether any cognitive processes, including mind and mental factors, remain for buddhas seems to have been a major topic of debate in Tibet from the twelfth century, suggesting a relation to the appearance of Candrakīrti's writings in Tibet. For two examples from classical Tibetan sources on this debate, see Gampopa, *Ornament of Precious Liberation*, 363–69, and Sakya Paṇḍita, *Clarifying the Sage's Intent*, 573–77.

8. On this question of the near silence about Candrakīrti and his writings in India before the tenth century, see Vose, *Resurrecting Candrakīrti*, especially chapter 1.

9. For a detailed analysis of Candrakīrti's critique of Dignāga's epistemology, especially the latter's two key ideas—ultimate existents referred to as *unique particulars* and perception defined in terms of nonconceptuality—see Arnold, *Buddhists, Brahmins, and Belief*, chapters 6 and 7. Among classical Tibetan sources, Jamyang Shepa (1648–1721) wrote an extensive commentary on the critique of foun-

dationalist epistemology in Candrakīrti's *Clear Words* entitled *Exposition of Prasannapadā's Summary on Epistemology* (*Tshig gsal stong thun gyi tshad ma'i rnam bshad*). Jamyang Shepa's commentary is based, in turn, on Khedrup Jé's outline of this section of *Clear Words*.

10. This is part of a twenty-eight-stanza text; see Apple, *Jewels of the Middle Way*, 117–22.

11. The translation of the root text that I have inserted is based on the Tibetan translation of Patsab Lotsāwa, which appears in all editions of the Tengyur. It is important to note when reading Tsongkhapa's glosses on the words of the root text that every now and then, he uses Naktso Lotsāwa's translation instead. This creates some discrepancies between the root text included in our volume and Tsongkhapa's gloss. Although a translation of the root text attributed to Naktso does appear in the Peking edition of Tengyur, as its colophon indicates, it is a version that was revised by Patsab. Naktso's original translation of the both root text and autocommentary—both of which Tsongkhapa had at his disposal—do not appear to be extant today. Naktso's translation of the autocommentary is cited extensively in Lodrö Rinchen's *Light on the Principles*.

12. Ruegg, *Buddhist Philosophy of the Middle*, 384.

13. *Commentary* lists the additional consequence that it would have been inappropriate for the Buddha to teach that phenomena are void of intrinsic existence.

14. Rendawa, *Lamp Illuminating Suchness*, 128–32, and Lochen, *Brilliantly Illuminating the Suchness*, 179–84. Lochen's commentary, completed in 1399, appears to be the first known Tibetan commentary on the entire text of Candrakīrti's *Entering the Middle Way*. This was followed by Rendawa's commentary, completed sometime in the beginning of the fifteenth century, making Tsongkhapa's the third known commentary on the important Indian text. That these three authors, famed in their time as "the three Dharma masters of Ütsang," or central Tibet, were close colleagues who engaged in conversations with each other is evident from both Tsongkhapa and Rendawa's biographies. See my *Tsongkhapa: A Buddha in the Land of Snows*, 78–82. A careful comparative study of the three commentaries, especially the first two, is required to fully understand how Madhyamaka philosophy as understood through Candrakīrti became such an important part of the Tibetan monastic curriculum in the fourteenth century. We know from critiques of Tsongkhapa's Madhyamaka by Taktsang Lotsāwa, Shākya Chokden, and the Eighth Karmapa Mikyö Dorjé that Lochen's interpretations of Candrakīrti's *Entering the Middle Way* were perceived by some as offering a more credible alternative to Tsongkhapa's innovative readings.

15. See, for example, Tsongkhapa's *Ocean of Reasoning* (trans.), 494. This question of how a buddha's gnosis perceives conventional truth is listed as a difficult point and explained in Gyaltsab's notes on Tsongkhapa's Madhyamaka teachings, entitled *Memorandum on the Eight Difficult Points of Fundamental Wisdom*, 13b4–14a5.

16. On Tsongkhapa's prolonged quest to "find the view," see Jinpa, *Tsongkhapa*, especially chapter 8.

17. Ibid., especially chapter 5.

18. *Four Hundred Stanzas on the Middle Way* (*Catuḥśatakaśāstra*), 12.23.

19. *Fundamental Verses on the Middle Way* (*Mūlamadhyamakakārikā*), 24.11.

20. Although Tsongkhapa does not name the proponents of these readings, it is clear from Lochen's commentary on *Entering* (119–23 and 193) that he, for one, attributes versions of these views to Candrakīrti.

21. See note 7.

22. For an analysis of Tsongkhapa's synthesis of Madhyamaka and Buddhist epistemology, see Ruegg, *Three Studies*, section 3.

23. The list of sources for these key points found in this present volume, with a few additional sources found in Tsongkhapa's other Madhyamaka writings, is meant to be illustrative, not exhaustive.

24. For a careful analysis of Tsongkhapa's understanding of how the views of Bhāviveka and other Svātantrikas entail a degree of realism, see Tillemans, "Metaphysics for Mādhyamikas."

25. For a translation of the important section of Tsongkhapa's analysis in *Essence of True Eloquence* of Bhāviveka's critique of Cittamātra's three-nature theory, see Eckel, "Satisfaction of No Analysis," 179–82.

26. On this limited differentiation between veridical and distorted conventional truths, from the perspective of the everyday world, see page 18.

27. *'Jig rten pa kho na la dri bar bya yi/ kho bo la ni ma yin no //*, *Śūnyatāsaptativṛtti*, 294b6.

28. *'Jig rten pa'i tha snyad kho bos khas blangs la / de'i yul dang shes pa yang 'jig rten pas shes kyi/ kho bos ni ma yin no // . . .*, Ibid., 273a7.

29. See, for example, Tsongkhapa, *Great Treatise*, 3:178. For a collection of papers by modern scholars on the status of conventional truths according to Candrakīrti and Tsongkhapa, see the Cowherds, *Moonshadows: The Conventional Truth in Buddhist Philosophy* (New York: Oxford University Press, 2010).

30. For an alternative translation of this passage, see Tsongkhapa, *Great Treatise* (trans.), 3:178.

31. On the challenges of defining conventional truth according to Candrakīrti and Tsongkhapa, see Tillemans, *How Do Mādhyamikas Think?*, especially chapters 1 and 2. In commenting on Tsongkhapa's contribution on Madhyamaka, Tillemans writes (p. 5) "a fourteenth-century Tibetan philosophy may have been, in certain significant respects, clearer and even much better philosophy than that of the Indian thinkers on which it was based."

32. Interestingly, Tsongkhapa's teacher Rendawa maintained the view that one of the key distinctions between Svātantrika and Prāsaṅgika is their differing views on conventional truth. Arnold, *Buddhists, Brahmins, and Belief*, especially pages 158–74, presents an interpretation of Candrakīrti's deference to the world when it comes to conventional truth that is strikingly similar to Tsongkhapa's in important ways.

33. *Essence of True Eloquence*, 214. Thurman (*Central Philosophy*, 369) renders the passage this way: "(And here finally,) while being completely out of touch with the way in which a common person accepts the referents of conventional designations, if one nevertheless says '(such and such) exists as a social convention,' this is no more than (empty) talk, since one does not (in fact) accept the meaning."

34. *Essence of True Eloquence*, 136; Thurman, *Central Philosophy of Tibet*, 291. There is, in fact, a fourth way in which *svalakṣaṇa* is used in Buddhists sources—in the

sense of *unique attributes,* such as specific characteristics of the body, as opposed to *general, shared attributes* like impermanence, when describing the meditation on the fourfold applications of mindfulness. Tsongkhapa perhaps understood this usage to be very similar to the first usage.

35. For example, see Arnold, *Buddhists, Brahmins, and Belief,* 268.

36. *Dngos po rnams kyi (kyang) rang gi mtshan nyid de. Commentary on Entering the Middle Way (Madhyamakāvatārabhāṣya),* 257b6, and *Commentary on Seventy Stanzas on Emptiness (Śūnyatāsaptativṛtti),* 299b1.

37. *Rang gi sde pa gang dag dngos po rnams la rang gi mtshan nyid khas blangs nas. Commentary on Four Hundred Stanzas (Catuḥśatakaṭīkā),* 173a1.

38. *Dngos po rnams rang gi mtshan nyid kyis dus gsum du yang gnas par 'gyur na. Commentary on Seventy Stanzas on Emptiness (Śūnyatāsaptativṛtti),* 292b3.

39. *'Phags pa sa bcu pa de nyid las/ rnam par shes pa ma rig pa dang 'du byed kyi rgyu can du gsungs kyi/ rang gi msthan nyid kyis grub pa ni ma yin no //. Commentary on Entering the Middle Way (Madhyamakāvatārabhāṣya),* 278a2. Similar instrumental usage can be found on numerous occasions, especially in *Commentary on Sixty Stanzas of Reasoning, Commentary on Seventy Stanzas on Emptiness,* and *Commentary on Four Hundred Stanzas.*

40. See Mabja Jangchub Tsöndrü, *Ornament of Reason,* 115 and 160.

41. Taktsang Lotsāwa's critiques of aspects of Tsongkhapa's Madhyamaka are found in his *Establishing the Freedom from Extremes on the Basis of Understanding All Philosophical Systems (Grub mtha' kun shes nas mtha' bral grub pa),* a work containing both a root text in verse and an autocommentary, on pages 147–67. On Taktsang's critiques and subsequent Geluk rebuttals, see Cabezón, "On the *sGra pa Rin chen pa'i rtsod lan,*" and Hopkins, *Maps of the Profound.* For a more nuanced understanding of Taktsang's attitude toward Tsongkhapa, see Jinpa, *Tsongkhapa,* especially pages 357–58.

42. Most of Gorampa's important critiques of Tsongkhapa's Madhyamaka are found in his *Distinguishing the Views (Lta ba'i shen 'byed),* translated in Cabezón and Dargyay, *Freedom from Extremes,* in which he accuses Tsongkhapa of falling to the extreme of nihilism and Dölpopa for falling into eternalism. Volume 4 of the collected works of Shākya Chokden contains three specific texts all targeting Tsongkhapa's Madhyamaka: (1) *Grand Summary of Points (Don gyi mdo chen),* listing what the author views as 108 conceptual fabrications (*rtog ges btags pa*) in "others' Madhyamaka" (*gzhan gyi lugs kyi dbu ma*), (2) a critical analysis in verse of Tsongkhapa's *Praise of Dependent Origination,* and (3) *Short Summary Entitled Indra's Scepter (Stong thun chung ba dbang po'i rdo rje).* Although the author does not name whose views he has in mind in the first text, the context makes it clear that most if not all of the views on the list are those attributed to Tsongkhapa.

43. Tibetan commentators on Madhyamaka like Shākya Chokden and the nineteenth-century Nyingmapa Ju Mipham insist that Candrakīrti's rejection of foundation consciousness and reflexive awareness must be confined to the ultimate level, that it does not reject these on the conventional level. For the latter's view on this, see Padmakara Translation Group, *Introduction to the Middle Way,* 248.

44. *Commentary on Entering the Middle Way (Madhyamakāvatārabhāṣya),* 347a5.

45. *Samādhirājasūtra* 9.36–37, Toh 127 Kangyur, *mdo sde, da,* 27a7, as quoted

by Tsongkhapa in his *Great Treatise on the Stages of the Path*; see trans., 3:22. "Udraka" here likely refers to one of the Buddha's early meditation teachers who attained the highest formless-realm absorption but was unable to escape cyclic existence.

46. See page 272.

47. *Guide to the Bodhisattva Way* (*Bodhicaryāvatāra*), 9.151–52.

48. For an explanation on what uniqueness Vajrayāna brings to the meditation on emptiness, see Jinpa, *Tsongkhapa*, 269–75.

49. This is a reference to Buddhapālita (ca. fifth century CE), Candrakīrti (seventh century), and Śāntideva (eighth century). Tsongkhapa sees these three Indian Buddhist masters as the key proponents of the Prāsaṅgika Madhyamaka reading of Nāgārjuna's thought. The expression "great charioteer" (*shing rta chen po*) is an abbreviation of the full expression "great chariot-way maker" or "the great trail-blazer," invoking the idea of someone who opens a roadway for chariots to pass where before there was either no path at all or only a small trail.

50. *Commentary* here is Candrakīrti's own commentary on his *Entering the Middle Way*. Given that Tsongkhapa makes extensive reference to this autocommentary, the *Madhyamakāvatārabhāṣya*, for brevity's sake, I will refer to it in my notes simply as *Commentary*.

51. *Commentary*, Toh 3863 Tengyur, dbu ma, 'a, 220a1. The *Treatise on the Middle Way* (*Madhyamakaśāstra*) is an alias of Nāgārjuna's *Fundamental Verses on the Middle Way* (*Mūlamadhyamakakārikā*). Candrakīrti sees his own work to be a kind of a primer or guide to this text of Nāgārjuna, hence the title *Entering the Middle Way*.

52. *Rtsa ba shes rab*; this is how Tibetans customarily refer to Nāgārjuna's *Fundamental Verses on the Middle Way*.

53. *Prajñāpradīpa*, Toh 5853 Tengyur, dbu ma, *tsa*, 230b4. *Lamp of Wisdom* is an extensive commentary on Nāgārjuna's work by the sixth-century Indian master Bhāviveka.

54. *Commentary*, 347b1.

55. *Prasannapadā*, Toh 3860 Tengyur, dbu ma, 'a, 23a6.

56. *Commentary*, 228b1.

57. This is a reference to a royal decree proclaimed during the eighth century whereby, to help immediately identify which of the three baskets (*tripiṭaka*)—discipline (*vinaya*), discourses (*sūtra*), and "higher knowledge" (*abhidharma*)—a given text might belong to, different objects of homage were to be chosen by the translators. In the case of a Vinaya text, the Omniscient One is chosen as the object of homage; for a text pertaining to Sutra, the buddhas and bodhisattvas; and finally, for an Abhidharma text, homage is to be paid to Mañjuśrī. The three baskets were in turn correlated to the three higher trainings: the training in morality for Vinaya, in concentration for the Sutra basket, and in wisdom for Abhidharma.

58. The final two sections here appear at the end of the treatise. See the outline in the appendixes for relative location of subheadings within this work.

59. The Blessed Mother is the perfection of wisdom, realization of which liberates beings from cyclic existence.

60. *Madhyamakāvatāra* 1.1. This is a reference to the first line in the first verse of the

salutation stanza of Candrakīrti's *Entering the Middle Way*, which appears below. From here on, all references to the lines of *Entering the Middle Way* cited by Tsongkhapa will have the relevant chapter and stanza numbers provided in parentheses in the body of the translation rather than in the notes.

61. For an example of this expression in the scriptures, see the first chapter of the *Basis of Discipline* (*Vinayavastu*), Toh 1 Kangyur, 'dul ba, *kha*, 36b7.

62. *Saddharmapuṇḍarīka*, chapter 4, Toh 113 Kangyur, mdo sde, *ja*, 46a4; cited also in the *Commentary*, 221a5.

63. *Commentary*, 221a5. The three categories of persons are (1) śrāvakas, (2) pratyeka-buddhas, and (3) fully enlightened buddhas. Rendawa (*Lamp Illuminating Suchness*, 37) explains the meaning of *buddha* in the context of "middle-level buddha" in the manner Tsongkhapa refers to here.

64. Tsongkhapa is here referring to a bilingual Sanskrit-Tibetan lexicon, but I have not been able to identify the actual text.

65. This paragraph is, except for an additional word or two, reproduced from the *Commentary*, 221a6.

66. Jayānanda, *Madhyamakāvatāraṭīkā*, Toh 3870 Tengyur, dbu ma, *ra*, 7b3. Here, Jayānanda is citing Maitreya's *Ornament of Realizations* 2.8, which presents key characteristics of the pratyekabuddha path.

67. Tsongkhapa is pointing out an inconsistency in the position of Jayānanda. He is saying that Jayānanda, who explains that pratyekabuddhas have a higher realization of suchness than śrāvakas on the basis of the line from *Ornament of Realizations*, is a follower of Candrakīrti and thus must also uphold the tenet that both śrāvakas and pratyekabuddhas possess the wisdom realizing emptiness.

68. Haribhadra, *Abhisamayālaṃkāravṛtti-Sphuṭārthā*, Toh 3793 Tengyur, shes phyin, *ja*, 91a7.

69. Āryadeva, *Catuḥśatakaśāstra* 8.22, Toh 3846 Tengyur, dbu ma, *tsha*, 10a2.

70. Nāgārjuna, *Fundamental Stanzas on the Middle Way* (*Mūlamadhyamakakārikā*) 18.12, Toh 3824 Tengyur, dbu ma, *tsa*, 11a5.

71. *Commentary*, 220a6.

72. This is a reference to Jayānanda, *Explanation of the Commentary on Entering the Middle Way* (*Madhyamakāvatāraṭīkā*), Toh 3870 Tengyur, dbu ma, *ra*, 5b1.

73. Tsongkhapa is likely critiquing the reading of an earlier Tibetan commentator, but who that is remains unclear.

74. Here too, Tsongkhapa is likely referring to the interpretation of an earlier Tibetan commentator.

75. *Discourse for Kāśyapa* (*Kāśyapaparivarta*), Toh 87 Kangyur, dkon brtsegs, *cha*, 137a1.

76. *Perfectly Gathering the Teachings Sutra* (*Dharmasaṃgītisūtra*), Toh 238 Kangyur, mdo sde, *zha*, 79b2.

77. *Commentary*, 222b6.

78. *Commentary*, 223b6.

79. This is a reference to Jayānanda's *Madhyamakāvatāraṭīkā* Tengyur, dbu ma, *ra*, 11a2.

80. Maitreya, *Abhisamayālaṃkāra* 1.19, Toh 3786 Tengyur, shes phyin, *ka*, 2b5.

81. Nāgārjuna, *Ratnāvalī* 2.73, Toh 4158 Tengyur, spring yig, *ge*, 113b1.

82. *Adhyāśayasaṃcodana*, Toh 69 Kangyur, dkon brtsegs, *ca*, 146a4.

83. See page 53.

84. *Commentary*, 222a4.

85. This is a critique of Jayānanda's reading, which interprets the "nondual awareness" here in terms of the ultimate awakening mind. The point Tsongkhapa is making is that since ultimate awakening mind, requiring direct realization of emptiness, is only present for āryas, then for Jayānanda, the statement that nondual awareness is a cause of the bodhisattva would become untenable.

86. *Ratnāvalī* 4.52, Toh 4158 Tengyur, spring yig, *ge*, 122b4.

87. *Vinayavastu*, Toh 1 Kangyur, 'dul ba, *ka*, 87b2.

88. Candrakīrti, *Catuḥśatakaṭīkā*, chap. 2, Toh 3865 Tengyur, dbu ma, *ya*, 45a4–65b5. This chapter contains an extensive contemplation on the nature of suffering and its causes. Tsongkhapa is making the point that our capacity for empathy is rooted not only in our sentient nature but also in our natural dislike of suffering.

89. *Catuḥśatakaṭīkā*, chap. 2, Toh 3865 Tengyur, dbu ma, *ya*, 57a5.

90. *Śiṣyalekha*, Toh 4183 Tengyur, spring yig, *nge*, 52a1, and *Bhāvanākrama* 1, Toh 3915 Tengyur, dbu ma, *ki*, 23b5.

91. This is a reference to Tsongkhapa's own *Great Treatise on the Stages of the Path*; see English translation, 2:51–60. These two approaches are known also as the two instructions for cultivating awakening mind, the seven-point cause-and-effect (*rgyu 'bras man ngag bdun*) method and the equalizing and exchanging of self and others (*bdag gzhan mnyam brje'i man ngag*) method. Tsongkhapa understands these in more specific terms as two distinct approaches to engendering what he calls "a sense of endearment" (*yid 'ong gi blo*), which crucially involves a feeling of connection and sense of identification with the object of one's concern.

92. See page 51.

93. Tsongkhapa is making the point that even with respect to the second and the third types of compassion, sentient beings remain the focal object, albeit qualified in terms of moment-by-moment change and the absence of intrinsic existence.

94. This paragraph is reproduced from the *Commentary* (*) with a few additional explanatory words interspersed.

95. *Commentary*, 223b6.

96. Śāntarakṣita, *Madhyamakālaṃkāravṛtti*, Toh 3885 Tengyur, dbu ma, *sa*, 83a4. In the Dergé edition of the Tengyur, these stanzas are found toward the end of the autocommentary but not in the root verses.

97. The phrase "purpose and connections" (*dgos 'brel*) is an abbreviation of the expression "Stanza expressing the purpose, connections, and so on" (*dgos 'brel ngag*), which expresses a classical Indian and Tibetan Buddhist approach to textual exegesis, especially when commenting on a root verse text. According to this, an authoritative text must possess four key elements—(1) its subject matter (*brjod bya*), (2) purpose (*dgos pa*), and (3) goal (*nying dgos*), and (4) the connections (*'brel ba*) among the first three in that the latter must be dependent on the former.

98. Tsongkhapa is referring to the passage above where, in explaining the title, he spoke of how Candrakīrti's distinctive purpose in composing this work was to develop an authoritative interpretation of Nāgārjuna's *Treatise on the Middle Way* as well as to present a sustained critique of the Cittamātra standpoint.

99. These refer to the first four stages of the path—the paths of accumulation, preparation, seeing, and meditation.

100. See the citations on pages 43 and 46 above.

101. Nāgārjuna, *Ratnāvalī* 5.35–39, Toh 4158 Tengyur, spring yig, *ge*, 123a7.

102. *Dharmadhātustava*, verse 68, lists four factors that enhance the natural sphere (*dhātu*), these being wisdom endowed with (1) skillful means, (2) aspiration, (3) power, and (4) gnosis. Incidentally, these are also the last four in the list of ten perfections. See Toh 1118 Tengyur, bstod tshogs, *ka*, 43a5. The *natural sphere* (*khams*; Skt. *dhātu*) is analogous to the concepts of buddha nature (*gotra*) and buddha essence (*garbha*) found in Maitreya's works. Although Tsongkhapa takes the Tibetan tradition's attribution of *Praise to the Ultimate Expanse* to Nāgārjuna for granted, this is, to say the least, problematic.

103. Nāgārjuna, *Sūtrasamuccaya*, Toh 3934 Tengyur, dbu ma, *ki*, 153a2.

104. Ibid., 158b2.

105. Tsongkhapa's collected works (vol. *pha*) contains a lengthy summary of Śāntideva's *Compendium of Training* based on lecture notes from a teaching he gave on the text at Radreng Monastery. In this summary, Tsongkhapa correlates the structure and content of Śāntideva's text closely with Nāgārjuna's *Compendium of Sutras*, which he sees as the basis of the former.

106. This is a reference to Tsongkhapa's *Great Treatise on the Stages of the Path to Enlightenment*. Dīpaṃkara is the personal name of the Bengali Indian Buddhist master widely known as Atiśa, who came to Tibet in the first half of the eleventh century. For a brief account of Atiśa's legacy in Tibet, see my introduction to *The Book of Kadam*.

107. Nāgārjuna, *Sūtrasamuccaya*, Toh 3934 Tengyur, dbu ma, *ki*, 207a3.

108. *Tha snyad kyi rnam gzhag thams cad gzhan ngo kho na la skyel ba.* A version of these views can be found in Lochen Kyabchok Palsang's *Brilliantly Illuminating the Suchness*, 11–23.

109. Nāgārjuna, *Ratnāvalī* 5.40, Toh 4158 Tengyur, spring yig, *ge*, 123b2. The "eight śrāvaka grounds" referred to here are the grounds (1) of the lineage (*rigs*), (2) of the eighth (*brgyad pa*), (3) of seeing (*mthong ba*), (4) of thinning (*srab pa*), (5) of freedom from attachment (*'dod chags dang bral ba*), (6) of cognizing what is done (*byas pa rtogs pa*), (7) of the śrāvaka (*nyan thos*), and (8) of the pratyeka-buddha (*rang rgyal*). The first six grounds relate to progressive stages of development on the path, beginning with the awakening of one's lineage through to becoming the eighth level of person (counting backward from first-level arhats), then attaining the path of seeing, through to progressive thinning of obscurations on the path. The last two are the final arhat stages on the paths of the śrāvaka and pratyekabuddha.

110. *Commentary*, 224b2.

111. Tsongkhapa is here referring to Vasubandhu's *Abhidharmakośa* 1.4 (Toh 4089 Tengyur, mngon pa, *ku*, 1a5), where the text defines what it means to be contaminated.

112. Candrakīrti, *Prasannapadā*, Toh 3860 Tengyur, dbu ma, *'a*, 13a3.

113. *Commentary*, 224a6.

114. According to Tsongkhapa, any gnosis realizing emptiness, such as an inferential

one, is free of the two extremes, but only an ārya's direct realization of emptiness is free of dualistic perception.

115. *Gang gis mthong bar 'gyur zhe na.* The version of this line that Candrakīrti quotes differs from the version in the Kangyur, which reads, *Gang gyis sems mthong 'gyur zhe na* ("What is it that sees the mind?").

116. Nāgārjuna, *Ratnāvalī* 4.63d–64a, Toh 4158 Tengyur, spring yig, *ge*, 120b3.

117. Nāgārjuna, *Dharmadhātustava*, verse 20, Toh 1118 Tengyur, bstod tshogs, *ka*, 64b1.

118. This is a reference to Jayānanda's *Madhyamakāvatāraṭīkā* (Toh 3870 Tengyur, dbu ma, *ra*, 53b2), which Tsongkhapa critiques here.

119. *Daśabhūmikasūtra*, Toh 44 Kangyur, phal chen, *kha*, 174a4.

120. This is *Bhadracaryāpraṇidhāna*, which is part 4 of the *Avataṃsaka Sūtra*. In the Tibetan canon this prayer is also cataloged as a self-standing work in Toh 1095 Kangyur, gzungs 'dus, *vam*.

121. Śāntideva, *Śikṣāsamuccaya*, Toh 3940 Tengyur, dbu ma, *khi*, 162b5. The two stanzas read: "Just as the heroic Mañjuśrī knows, / and just as Samantabhadra knows likewise, / I will follow after all such [heroic bodhisattvas] / and thoroughly dedicate all of the these merits. // All conquerors past, present, and future / praise this dedication as most supreme, / so I dedicate thoroughly all my roots of virtue / so that all beings may master good conduct."

122. *Commentary*, 224b2. Candrakīrti is pointing out here that just as someone who is on the śrāvaka path of preparation cannot be said to have entered the first of the four fruits—stream entry, once-return, nonreturn, and arhatship—similarly, someone on the last stage of the bodhisattva's path of preparation would be on a stage where the ultimate awakening mind has not yet arisen. "The greatest of the great stage" (*chen po'i chen po*) is the last of the nine stages of "supreme mundane dharma"—small of small, medium small, great small, and so on—with supreme mundane dharma being the fourth stage of the path of preparation, the preceding three being "heat," "peak," and "patience." The phrase "engaging by means of imagination" (*mos pas spyod pa*) indicates that, until one has reached the path of seeing, one's engagement with the ultimate truth remains at the level of concepts and imagination. The first two of the five paths—the path of accumulation and the path of preparation—belong to this stage and are thus collectively referred to as "the ground of engagement by imagination" (*mos pas spyod pa'i sa*).

123. Asaṅga, *Abhidharmasamuccaya*, Toh 4049 Tengyur, sems tsam, *ri*, 107b6. Each of the four fruits has two phases—entry and abiding. Thus the opponent is saying that the point of entry to stream entry is still on the path of preparation and not an ārya ground, whereas the actual fruit of abiding in stream entry occurs on the path of seeing.

124. Nāgārjuna, *Sūtrasamuccaya*, Toh 3934 Tengyur, dbu ma, *ki*, 160b1. The "person of the eighth stage" (*'phags pa brgyad pa*) here is one on the entry stage of stream entry, the eighth stage if one lists the "eight āryas" as starting from the arhat and descending.

125. *Ratnameghasūtra*, Toh 231 Kangyur, mdo sde, *wa*, 47a7.

126. *Pañcaviṃśatisāhasrikāprajñāpāramitā*. Toh 9 Kangyur, shes phyin, *ka*, 30b6.

127. Vasubandhu, *Abhidharmakośa* 5.44, Toh 4089 Tengyur, mngon pa, *ku*, 17b3.

128. Asaṅga, *Abhidharmasamuccaya*, Toh 4049 Tengyur, sems tsam, *ri*, 65a2.
129. This story comes from the *Adornment of Trees Sutra* (*Gaṇḍavyūhasūtra*), Toh 44 Kangyur, phal chen, *cha*, 239b.
130. Ibid., 218b5.
131. Jayānanda, *Madhyamakāvatāraṭīkā*, Toh 3870 Tengyur, dbu ma, *ra*, 68a4. "Verbally derived awakening mind" (*brda las byung ba'i sems skyed*) is a simulated awakening mind that remains at the level of an intellectual understanding rather than a felt spontaneous experience.
132. Maitreya, *Mahāyānasūtrālaṃkāra* 5.2, Toh 4020 Tengyur, sems tsam, *phi*, 4b3.
133. The "awakening mind of pure altruistic intention" (*lhag bsam dag pa'i sems bskyed*) is one of three types of awakening mind according to a system of distinguishing the different stages of the development of awakening mind presented especially in Maitreya's *Mahāyānasūtrālaṃkāra*. The other two are the "awakening mind at the level of imaginative engagement" (*mos pas spyod pa'i sems bskyed*)—identified with the level of awakening mind on the first two paths of accumulation and preparation—and the "fruitional awakening mind" (*rnam par smin pa'i sems bskyed*), the awakening mind from the eighth to the tenth bodhisattva grounds.
134. *Adornment of Trees Sutra* (*Gaṇḍavyūhasūtra*), Toh 44 Kangyur, phal chen, *ka*, 223a5.
135. Śāntideva, *Śikṣāsamuccaya*, Toh 3940 Tengyur, dbu ma, *khi*, 7b7.
136. *Daśabhūmikasūtra*, Toh 44 Kangyur, phal chen, *kha*, 234a1.
137. The *perfect endpoint* (*yang dag pa'i mtha'*; Skt. *bhūtakoṭi*) is where all contaminated conditioning has ended, often used as a synonym for emptiness or ultimate truth.
138. See pages 239–44.
139. Jayānanda, *Madhyamakāvatāraṭīkā*, Toh 3870 Tengyur, dbu ma, *ra*, 68a4.
140. This is a reference to Rendawa Shönu Lodrö, Tsongkhapa's principal teacher. Rendawa, *Lamp Illuminating Suchness*, 54.
141. This is a reference to a passage in the *Commentary* (226b5).
142. In this classification, each of the four ārya truths is subdivided into four aspects. For instance, the aspects of the first truth, the truth of suffering, are impermanence, suffering, emptiness, and selflessness. For more, see Hopkins, *Meditation on Emptiness*, 292–304.
143. This is a reference to the reasoning outlined in the second chapter of Dharmakīrti's *Exposition of Valid Cognition* (*Pramāṇavārttika*), especially 2.121–31, establishing how what is initially an inferential knowledge could culminate in a direct realization.
144. Asaṅga, *Abhidharmasamuccaya*, Toh 4049 Tengyur, sems tsam, *ri*, 58a2.
145. Dharmakīrti, *Pramāṇavārttika* 2.254, Toh 4210 Tengyur, tshad ma, *ce*, 117a6.
146. Here Tsongkhapa is referring to Indian authors such as Śāntarakṣita and Jitari who interpret this citation from Dharmakīrti's *Pramāṇavārttika* in terms of the view that defines emptiness as the absence of true existence.
147. The "two Abhidharma systems" are Asaṅga's system, especially as presented in his *Compendium of Abhidharma*, and Vasubandhu's Sarvastivāda system presented in the *Treasury of Abhidharma*. Both present a detailed psychology of the afflictions.
148. *Commentary*, 226b6.

149. *Bodhicaryāvatāra* 9.40ab, Toh 3871 Tengyur, dbu ma, *la*, 32a7. In these two lines, Śāntideva anticipates an argument from Buddhist essentialists against the very need to realize emptiness.

150. *Bodhicaryāvatāra* 9.40cd.

151. Prajñākaramati, *Bodhicaryāvatārapañjikā*, Toh 3872 Tengyur, dbu ma, *la*, 217a4. Of all the Indian commentaries on Śāntideva's *Guide to the Bodhisattva Way*, this one by Prajñākaramati is not only the most extensive but is also accorded the greatest authority by Tibetan commentators. To indicate this esteem, this text is often referred to simply as "the great commentary on *Guide to the Bodhisattva Way*" (*spyod 'jug grel chen*).

152. *Bodhicaryāvatāra* 9.44, Toh 3871 Tengyur, dbu ma, *la*, 32b2.

153. *Bodhicaryāvatāra* 9.45, Toh 3871 Tengyur, dbu ma, *la*, 32b3.

154. This is *Bodhicaryāvatāra* 9.40a, which Tsongkhapa cited at the outset of this discussion.

155. *Bodhicaryāvatāra* 9.45, Toh 3871 Tengyur, dbu ma, *la*, 32b3.

156. *Bodhicaryāvatāra* 9.48, Toh 3871 Tengyur, dbu ma, *la*, 32b4. "No-perception" is a meditative state of deep absorption wherein all the manifest levels of perception and discrimination have ceased. For a comparative study of the meditative states such as this, which entail states of mindlessness, in the Theravāda, Sarvastivāda, and Yogācāra traditions, see Griffiths, *On Being Mindless*.

157. *Bodhicaryāvatāra* 9.46ab, 32b3.

158. *Bodhicaryāvatāra* 9.46cd, 32b4.

159. *Bodhicaryāvatāra* 9.47ab, 32b4.

160. *Bodhicaryāvatāra* 9.99, 34b4.

161. Nāgārjuna, *Yuktiṣaṣṭikākārikā* 52ab, Toh 3825 Tengyur, dbu ma, *tsa*, 22a7.

162. Chapa Chökyi Sengé's (1109–69) *Summary Outlines of Guide to the Bodhisattva Way* (*Spyod 'jug bsdus don*) has been discovered as part of a large cache of old Kadampa texts, but this short text contains only the outlines of the text with no annotations. So Tsongkhapa must be referring to some other work of Chapa. Tsek Wangchuk Sengé was one of the eight famous students of Chapa all bearing the name Sengé. I have not been able to locate any of his work.

163. Chapa was the most vocal Tibetan critic of Candrakīrti. Being an upholder of the tradition of what is known as the "three eastern masters of Svātantrika" (*rnag rgyud shar gsum*)—Jñānagarbha, Śāntarakṣita, and Kamalaśīla—Chapa subjected Candrakīrti's interpretation of Nāgārjuna's teaching on emptiness to sustained criticism. Most famously, he threw a series of consequences against Candrakīrti, found in his *Great Summary on the Middle Way of the Three Eastern Masters* (*Dbu ma shar gsum stong thun*), 58–76.

164. Jayānanda, *Madhyamakāvatāraṭīkā*, 21a1.

165. *Sthīrādhyāśayaparivarta*, Toh 224 Kangyur, mdo sde, *dza*, 165b3, which is cited in Candrakīrti's *Prasannapadā*, chap. 1, Toh 3860 Tengyur, dbu ma, *'a*, 14b5.

166. *Bsam gtan pa'i dpe mkhyud kyi mdo* (*Dhyāyitamuṣṭisūtra*), as cited in *Prasannapadā*, chap. 24, Toh 3860 Tengyur, dbu ma, *'a*, 171b5.

167. Cited in *Prasannapadā*, chap. 24, Toh 3860 Tengyur, dbu ma, *'a*, 171b2. There, Candrakīrti gives the name of the sutra as *Demonstrating All Phenomena to Be*

Non-Entering Sutra (*Chos thams cad 'jug pa med par bstan pa'i mdo*), a sutra not found in the Kangyur.

168. Śāntideva, *Śikṣāsamuccaya*, Toh 3940 Tengyur, dbu ma, *khi*, 43b1.

169. *Vajracchedikā*, Toh 16 Kangyur, shes phyin, *ka*, 123b6.

170. Ibid., 124a1.

171. The other three abidings in the fruits are those of once returner, nonreturner, and arhat. Together, these four fruits are known as the "four fruits of śrāvaka path." See note 122 above.

172. What Tsongkhapa is stating here is this: when the *Diamond Cutter Sutra* states that the stream enterer does not apprehend with the thought "I have attained the fruit," it is saying that the stream enterer does not relate to his attainment on the basis of not having eradicated the object of apprehension of grasping at true existence. In other words, the stream enterer relates to his attainment with the realization of its emptiness. However, this does not mean that the stream enterer no longer possesses *any* innate levels of grasping at true existence, which will be eliminated only when he attains the state of arhat.

173. Prajñākaramati, *Bodhicaryāvatārapañjikā*, Toh 3872 Tengyur, dbu ma, *la*, 223b2.

174. Nāgārjuna, *Ratnāvalī* 1.35–37, Toh 4158 Tengyur, spring yig, *ge*, 108b5; these three stanzas are cited also in the *Commentary*. The "three avenues" (*lam gsum*) refer to the three afflicted factors of afflictions, karma, and birth, as Tsongkhapa mentions below. Together these lead to existence within samsara through the twelve links of dependent origination.

175. *Commentary*, 226b7.

176. Nāgārjuna, *Precious Garland* (*Ratnāvalī*) 4.65, Toh 4158 Tengyur, spring yig, *ge*, 120b4; cited also in the *Commentary*, as part of a longer quote that includes 4.57–64.

177. *Ratnāvalī* 4.66, 120b4.

178. *Perfectly Gathering the Teachings Sutra* (*Dharmasaṃgītisūtra*), Toh 238 Kangyur, mdo sde, *zha*, 39b2. This exact citation can also be found in *Saṃyutta Nikāya* III, 95(3) (translated by Bhikkhu Bodhi in *Connected Discourses*, 952). Candrakīrti cites this in his *Commentary* (227b2), which is presumably Tsongkhapa's source here.

179. Nāgārjuna, *Bodhicittavivaraṇa*, verses 11–13, Toh 1801 Tengyur, rgyud 'grel, *ngi*, 38b7.

180. Nāgārjuna, *Bodhicittavivaraṇa*, verse 72, Toh 1801 Tengyur, rgyud 'grel *ngi*, 41a3.

181. Nāgārjuna, *Ratnāvalī* 4.86, Toh 4158, Tengyur, spring yig, *ge*, 121b1.

182. Here, once again, Tsongkhapa is critiquing Jayānanda's reading as found in his *Madhyamakāvatāraṭīkā* (Toh 3870 Tengyur, dbu ma, *ra*, 75b7).

183. Ajitamitra, *Ratnāvalīṭīkā*, Toh 4159 Tengyur, spring yig, *ge*, 161a7.

184. Cited in Candrakīrti, *Yuktiṣaṣṭikāvṛtti*, Toh 3864 Tengyur, dbu ma, *ya*, 10a5; the exact name of the sutra remains unidentified.

185. Tsongkhapa is saying that here the references of the phrases "this suffering or aggregate" (*sdug bsngal lam phung po 'di*) should be understood in general terms and not in specific terms such as of the afflictions. In brief, he is stating that the exhaustion referred to in the sutra quote is not the cessation of afflictions attained

through the path; rather it is to the emptiness of the aggregates, which, as characterized in the sutra quote, is a definite elimination, a purification, and so on.

186. Maitreya, *Uttaratantra* 1.15, Toh 4024 Tengyur, sems tsam, *phi*, 55b3.

187. Ibid.

188. *Mūlamadhyamakakārikā* 15.7, Toh 3824 Tengyur, dbu ma, *tsa*, 9a1. This sutra does not exist in the Tibetan canon, but the Pali version, the *Kaccānagotta Sutta*, appears in Saṃyutta Nikāya II.12.15 (Bodhi, *Connected Discourses*, 544).

189. See note 188.

190. *Commentary*, 227b5.

191. *Buddhapālitavṛtti*, chap. 7, Toh 3842 Tengyur, dbu ma, *tsa*, 198a2.

192. *Prajñāpradīpa*, chap. 7, Toh 3853 Tengyur, dbu ma, *tsha*, 123b3. This objection is raised also in the *Commentary*, but Candrakīrti does not identify the source.

193. Nāgārjuna, *Ratnāvalī* 4.90, Toh 4158 Tengyur, spring yig, *ge*, 121b3, cited also in *Commentary*, 227b7.

194. Nāgārjuna, *Lokātītastava*, verse 25, Toh 1120 Tengyur, bstod tshogs, *ka*, 64b3. The first line of this stanza in the Dergé Tengyur edition appears as "Without entering signlessness," *mtshan ma med la ma 'jug par*. However, the version of the stanza cited in Candrakīrti's commentary accords with the one found here in Tsongkhapa's text. An English translation is in Lindtner, *Nagarjuniana*, 129–39.

195. Tsongkhapa is here thinking of the proponents of so-called *extrinsic emptiness* (*gzhan stong*), such as the early fourteenth-century Tibetan master Dölpopa, who maintained that emptiness itself is absolute, eternal, and truly existent.

196. Maitreya, *Abhisamayālaṃkāra* 2.8, Toh 3786 Tengyur, shes phyin, *ka*, 5a4.

197. Ibid. 2.29, 6a2. Here the purities that one attains on the paths of śrāvaka, pratyekabuddha, and bodhisattva are characterized distinctly in terms of three categories of obscuration—the afflictive obscurations, the knowledge obscurations, and the obscurations pertaining to knowledge of the paths of the three vehicles.

198. *Four Hundred Stanzas* (*Catuḥśatakaśāstra*) 8.16, Toh 3846 Tengyur, dbu ma, *tsha*, 9b6.

199. Tsongkhapa is saying that if one reads *Ornament of Realizations* through commentators like Haribhadra, there is indeed a striking similarity between pratyekabuddhas and Cittamātra in their basic view of reality, since both negate external reality. Those who find this unbelievable, Tsongkhapa says, reveal their ignorance of the commentarial tradition of masters like Haribhadra.

200. The "two *Differentiations*" are Maitreya's *Differentiation of the Middle and Extremes* (*Madhyāntavibhāga*) and *Differentiating Phenomena and Their Ultimate Nature* (*Dharmadharmatāvibhaṅga*). Tsongkhapa is stating that, among the five works of Maitreya, the philosophical positions of the *Ornament of Realizations* is that of Madhyamaka, while the *Ornament of the Mahayana Sutras* and the two *Differentiations* present the Cittamātra view.

201. Maitreya, *Abhisamayālaṃkāra* 1.40, Toh 3786 Tengyur, shes phyin, *ka*, 3b2.

202. Vimuktisena, *Pañcaviṃśatisāhasrikāvṛtti*, Toh 3787 Tengyur, shes phyin, *ka*, 59b1.

203. Ibid., 59b6.

204. Ibid., 59a6.

205. "Thirteen lineages" refers to specific lineages corresponding to thirteen meditative cultivations (*sgrub pa bcu gsum*) enumerated in the *Ornament of Realizations*,

which are defined in terms of progressive development on the stages of the bodhisattva's path toward buddhahood.

206. Vimuktisena, *Pañcaviṃśatisāhasrikāvṛtti*, Toh 3787 Tengyur, shes phyin, *ka*, 60b1.

207. Tsongkhapa is making the point that since the "thirteen lineages" are defined on the basis of progressive stages on the bodhisattva path, the question of suitable versus unsuitable receptacles is irrelevant because all thirteen lineages are defined on the basis of bodhisattva practitioners who are all excellent receptacles of the Great Vehicle lineage.

208. Cited in Vimuktisena, *Pañcaviṃśatisāhasrikāprajñāpāramitāvṛtti*, Toh 3787 Tengyur, shes phyin, *ka*, 60a4; and also in Haribhadra, *Aṣṭasāhasrikāprajñāpāramitāvyākhyā*, Toh 3791 Tengyur, shes phyin, *cha*, 48a1.

209. See *Vajracchedikāsūtra*, Toh 16 Kangyur, shes phyin, *ka*, 123a5.

210. This marks the conclusion of the discussion that began on page 101, where Tsongkhapa raised an objection, not mentioned in the *Commentary*, based on how the realization of pratyekabuddhas is defined in sources such as Maitreya's *Ornament of Realizations*.

211. Since Tsongkhapa is here paraphrasing the text of Candrakīrti's commentary, the sentences of the Tibetan text are quite cumbersome. The point is that even giving with a self-centered motive, where the key concern is to enjoy the future fruits of generosity, such an act will still lead to the benefits of enjoying excellent material wealth and so on.

212. Cited in the *Commentary* (229a3), this is probably a line from a sutra, but neither Candrakīrti nor Tsongkhapa identify the source.

213. Nāgārjuna, *Suhṛllekha*, 6, Toh 4182 Tengyur, spring yig, *nge*, 41a1.

214. *Gaganagañjaparipṛcchāsūtra*, Toh 148 Kangyur, mdo sde, *pa*, 257a1.

215. Nāgārjuna, *Ratnāvalī* 3.27, Toh 4158 Tengyur, spring yig, *ge*, 115b2.

216. Tsongkhapa's reading of this stanza is quite different from the standard Patsab version. This is because Tsongkhapa is relying here more on Naktso's version of the root text. See next note.

217. On numerous occasions Tsongkhapa refers to Naktso Lotsāwa's translation of *Entering the Middle Way*, and often speaks of his preference for readings from that version. The standard canonical version, found in the Tengyur, is however that of Patsab Lotsāwa, the translator who is credited with a systematic introduction of the writings of Candrakīrti in Tibet. A version of Naktso's translation of the root text of *Entering the Middle Way*, revised by comparing against Patsab's translation, is featured in Peking and Narthang editions of the Tengyur, but not in Dergé. Tsongkhapa appeared to have access to an earlier unrevised version of Naktso's translation of both the root text and the *Commentary*.

218. See, for example, *Perfection of Wisdom in Ten Thousand Lines* (*Daśasāhasrikāprajñāpāramitā*), chap. 9, Toh 11 Kangyur, shes phyin, *nga*, 96b1.

219. Tsongkhapa is explaining in this paragraph the etymology of the Sanskrit term *pāramitā*, literally "to go beyond" or "to have gone beyond," which is typically rendered in English as "perfection."

220. *Commentary*, 230a5. This passage deals with Sanskrit grammatical rules on how words should be modified when creating compounds. In explaining how the two

terms *dānasya* ("of generosity," which is the genitive form of the term *dāna*) and *pāramitā* ("perfection") are combined into the single compound *dānapāramitā*, Candrakīrti invokes here two different Sanskrit grammatical rules. The first rule justifies the retention of the accusative form *am* in the word *pāramitā* even though the genitive ending *sya* of the word *dānasya* is removed when creating the compound word. The second rule Candrakīrti invokes, which Jamyang Shepa (*Critical Analysis of Entering the Middle Way*, 137a3) identifies as from the well-known Sanskrit grammar of Pāṇini, justifies this retention on aesthetic grounds. Jamyang Shepa (136a5–138b1) explains in detail how these two grammatical rules invoked by Candrakīrti in his *Commentary* account for the formation of the compound *dānapāramitā*, "perfection of generosity."

221. Jayānanda, *Madhyamakāvatāraṭīkā*, Toh 3870 Tengyur, dbu ma, *ra*, 85a5.

222. Tsongkhapa is here referring to Jayānanda's explanation of how the compound word *pāramitā* (perfection or, literally, "to have gone beyond") is formed through the combination of the two words *pārama* (beyond) and *īta* (gone). He is suggesting that there might be a typographical error in Jayānanda's text, where the word *su* should probably read as *si*.

223. The *anusvāra* is the dot, or *bindu*, placed over a letter in Sanskrit to indicate a nasal ending. In transliteration, it changes *ra* to *raṃ*.

224. Śāntideva, *Bodhicaryāvatāra* 3.10, Toh 3871 Tengyur, dbu ma, *la*, 7a2.

225. Ibid., 3.11.

226. This distinction between "naturally reprehensible deeds" (*rang bzhin gyis kha na ma tho ba*) and "violations of rule-based precepts" (*bcas pa dang 'gal ba'i 'chal khrims*) is crucial to understanding Buddhist ethics. The morality of restraining from naturally reprehensible deeds—acts that by their very nature harm others, such as killing, stealing, and adultery—is binding for all who wish to live a moral life. In contrast, the morality of restraining from violating rule-based precepts applies only to those who have explicitly vowed to uphold a set of precepts, such as not eating after midday or not indulging in sexual intercourse. These do not entail any nonvirtuous karma for those who have not taken those vows.

227. In his commentary on these two lines of his root text, Candrakīrti cites the *Ten Grounds Sutra* at length, enumerating each of the ten nonvirtuous actions and explaining how the bodhisattva relinquishes involvement in any of these acts through his body, speech, and mind.

228. Tib. *dgag bcas* and *sgrub bcas*. This distinction here is between what could be characterized as "Thou shall not" and "Thou shall" injunctions. Generally speaking, in Buddhist ethics, the practice of morality moves from the basic level of refraining from the standard ten unwholesome actions—the three physical acts of (1) killing, (2) stealing, and (3) engaging in sexual misconduct, the four verbal acts of (4) telling lies, (5) using divisive speech, (6) speaking harshly, (7) and indulging in senseless gossip, and the three mental acts of harboring (8) covetousness, (9) harmful intent, and (10) wrong views—to more advanced disciplines involving ever more prescriptions, including positive ones. The bodhisattva ethics is an example of such advanced morality. For a detailed presentation of bodhisattva ethics in English based on Tsongkhapa's commentary on the chapter on morality from Asaṅga's *Bodhisattva Grounds*, see Tatz, *Asaṅga's Chapter on Ethics*.

229. *Discourse for Kāśyapa* (*Kāśyapaparivarta*), Toh 87 Kangyur, dkon brtsegs, *cha*, 142b2.

230. *Gal te rang bzhin tshul khrims rnam dag par / mthong na des de tshul khrims 'chal ba yin.* Tsongkhapa is saying that the pronoun "he" (*de ni*) in the first line of Patsab's version of the root text is problematic because it can be misread as referring to the subject of the preceding verse—namely, the bodhisattva on the second ground. In contrast, Naktso's translation makes it possible to read the line as making the general point that should one grasp at one's discipline to be intrinsically pure, this would be a form of moral degeneration.

231. *Daśabhūmikasūtra*, Toh 44 Kangyur, phal chen, *kha*, 190b3. The two are constantly seeking opportunities to harm others and constantly being assailed by others.

232. *Definite goodness* (*nges legs, naiḥśreyasa*) refers to the two supramundane attainments—nirvana and full enlightenment.

233. The section from the *Ten Grounds Sutra* that Tsongkhapa says is paraphrased here in the lines of *Entering the Middle Way* is *Daśabhūmikasūtra*, Toh 44 Kangyur, phal chen, *kha*, 189b7–190b4.

234. This paragraph is almost a direct quote from the *Daśabhūmikasūtra*, Toh 44 Kangyur, phal chen, *kha*, 189b1–5.

235. Nāgārjuna, *Suhṛllekha*, verse 7, Toh 4182 Tengyur, spring yig, *nge*, 41a2.

236. This is a reference to stanzas 4–7 of this same chapter of the root text.

237. Ratnadāsa, *Guṇāparyantastotra*, Toh 1155 Tengyur, bstod tshogs, *ka*, 198a7.

238. Candrakīrti, *Catuḥśatakaṭīkā*, Toh 3865 Tengyur, dbu ma, *ya*, 42b6. Edgerton's Sanskrit-English dictionary (p. 180) too states that *kālakarṇin*, literally "black-eared," is an idiom for an omen of bad luck.

239. Nāgārjuna, *Ratnāvalī* 5.45–46, Toh 4158 Tengyur, spring yig, *ge*, 123b6.

240. This is a reference to the first two lines of the root text in this chapter, which Tsongkhapa explained just above.

241. *Commentary*, 236a3. The particle referred to here is the one in the last line of the root text in the extract above.

242. *Commentary*, 236a2. Tsongkhapa is saying is that the phrase "for this reason too" in the *Commentary* parallels the phrase "by seeing thus too" here in the root text.

243. Jayānanda, *Madhyamakāvatāraṭīkā*, Toh 3870 Tengyur, dbu ma, *ra*, 47a2.

244. *Mañjuśrīvikrīḍitasūtra*, Toh 96 Kangyur, mdo sde, *kha*, 231b4.

245. *Commentary*, 236b4.

246. Nāgārjuna, *Sūtrasamuccaya*, Toh 3934 Tengyur, dbu ma, *ki*, 159b4.

247. *Bodhicaryāvatāra* 6.1, Toh 3871 Tengyur, dbu ma, *la*, 15b3. For a poignant description of the destructive impacts of anger by Āryaśūra, see Khoroche, *Once the Buddha Was a Monkey*, 137–39.

248. This is a reference to the passage in the *Maitreya's Lion Roar Sutra* cited earlier on p. 134.

249. *Prajñāpāramitāsaṃcayagāthā*, Toh 13 Kangyur, shes phyin, *ka*, 14b4. In Maitreya's *Ornament of Realizations* (4.9), the meditative cultivation of the path of preparation is characterized as the "cultivation that has received the prophecy" (*lung bstan thob pa'i sbyor ba*).

250. *Bodhicaryāvatāra* 1.35, Toh 3871 Tengyur, dbu ma, *la*, 3b2.

251. *Sarvavaidalyasaṃgraha,* Toh 227 Kangyur, mdo sde, *dza,* 187b6.

252. Cited in Śāntideva, *Śikṣāsamuccaya,* Toh 3940 Tengyur, dbu ma, *khi,* 83a3.

253. Cited in Nāgārjuna, *Sūtrasamuccaya,* Toh 3934 Tengyur, dbu ma, *ki,* 160a1. *Moon Lamp Sutra (Candrapradīpasūtra)* is an alternate title for the *King of Meditations (Samādhirājasūtra).*

254. Nāgārjuna, *Sūtrasamuccaya,* Toh 3934 Tengyur, dbu ma, *ki,* 146a5.

255. *Gaṇḍavyūhasūtra,* Toh 44 Kangyur, phal chen, *a,* 317a4.

256. *Abhidharmakośabhāṣya,* chap. 4, Toh 4090 Tengyur, mngon pa, *khu,* 94b5.

257. Bhāviveka, *Blaze of Reasoning (Tarkajvālā),* chap. 4, Toh 3586 Tengyur, dbu ma, *dza,* 185a3; critical edition, 343.

258. Nāgārjuna, *Sūtrasamuccaya,* Toh 3934 Tengyur, dbu ma, *ki,* 149a1.

259. *Ākāśagarbhasūtra,* Toh 260 Kangyur, mdo sde, *za,* 272b4.

260. Śāntideva, *Śikṣāsamuccaya,* Toh 3940 Tengyur, dbu ma, *khi,* 84a2.

261. Tsongkhapa does not include in his commentary the word "swiftly" (*myur*) as part of his gloss on this stanza, suggesting that he is reading a slightly different version of the root text.

262. Tsongkhapa is referring to the second line of the root verse, where he suggests that there is an extra particle after "attachment and aversion" (*'dod chags zhe sdang*). This comment on the conjunction "and" (*dang* in Tibetan or *ca* in Sanskrit) is found also in Candrakīrti's *Commentary,* which suggests that the Sanskrit original of the root text contains it. However, both Patsab's translation and the current version of Naktso's translation (revised by Patsab) read the line as *'dod chags zhe sdang yongs su zad par 'gyur*—that is, without the "and" (*dang*).

263. This is a reference to the *Daśabhūmikasūtra,* Toh 44 Kangyur, phal chen, *kha,* 201a3.

264. Ibid, 201a5. In the Dergé Kangyur edition, this sentence reads, "Those fetters derived from views were already purified even earlier" (*lta ba las byung ba'i bcings pa rnams ni snga nas kyang byang ba yin te*). In the version of the sutra cited in Candrakīrti's *Commentary* (240a2), this sentence appears as "These types of fetters were already eliminated previously" (*de lta bur gyur pa'i 'ching ba rnams ni snga nas spangs pa yin no*).

265. Asaṅga, *Bodhisattvabhūmi,* Toh 4037 Tengyur, sems tsam, *wi,* 175a2. Tsongkhapa is here simply providing this alternative reading of the sutra statement offered by Asaṅga. The "ground of engagement by meditation" is the paths of accumulation and preparation; see note 122 above.

266. *Daśabhūmikasūtra,* Toh 44 Kangyur, phal chen, *kha,* 201a5.

267. What is relinquished by the path of meditation is divided into nine parts: small of great, middling of great, great of great; small of middling, middling of middling, and great of middling; great of small, middling of small, and small of small. Of these, it is the first six that are relinquished from the second to the seventh grounds.

268. On the three binding factors, see the commentary on verse 1.6 of the root text at page 72.

269. Tib. *dod pa'i 'dod chags kyang [ni] rtag tu spong.*

270. Nāgārjuna, *Ratnāvalī* 4.99, Toh 4158 Tengyur, spring yig, *ge,* 122a1. Writing here

to a king, Nāgārjuna is emphasizing that the Buddha taught that the practices of generosity, morality, and forbearance are especially important for the laity.

271. *Diligence* is defined in Buddhist sources as "taking joy in virtue" (*dge ba la spro ba*), a definition Candrakīrti cites later; see page 502.

272. Nāgārjuna, *Ratnāvalī* 5.47–48, Toh 4158 Tengyur, spring yig, *ge*, 123b7.

273. The critical Tibetan edition gives the *Daśabhūmikasūtra* (Toh 44 Kangyur, phal chen, *kha*, 207a5) as the exact source for this sutra reference, but this is an error. Tsongkhapa is saying that, according to the *Ten Grounds Sutra*, the entirety of the afflictions together with their seeds are permanently eliminated only on the eighth ground. Thus, according to this sutra, the bodhisattva on the fourth ground still has innate dimensions of identity view left to eliminate.

274. In Buddhist scriptures, four principal *māras*, or obstructive forces, hinder one's path to enlightenment: (1) the māra of attachment personified here as Devaputra ("son of the gods"), (2) the māra of afflictions, (3) the māra of the psychophysical aggregates, and (4) Māra personified as the Lord of Death. A key aspect of these forces is to tempt us away from the path and toward our more negative tendencies and impulses through distraction and heedlessness. The language of the māras clearly aims to resonate with the life story of the historical Buddha, who countered the forces of Māra with his meditation on loving kindness.

275. Nāgārjuna, *Ratnāvalī* 5.49–50, Toh 4158 Tengyur, spring yig, *ge*, 124a1.

276. *Daśabhūmikasūtra*, Toh 44 Kangyur, phal chen, *kha*, 212a7.

277. *Pitāputrasamāgamanasūtra*, Toh 44 Kangyur, dkon brtsegs, *nga*, 61b4.

278. *Commentary*, 143a7.

279. Candrakīrti, *Yuktiṣaṣṭikāvṛtti*, Toh 3864 Tengyur, dbu ma, *ya*, 7b5.

280. Tsongkhapa's point here is that for Candrakīrti cessation must be ultimate truth because it is known by the wisdom directly realizing emptiness within the ārya's meditative equipoise.

281. Nāgārjuna, *Dharmadhātustava*, Toh 1118 Tengyur, bstod tshogs, *ka*, 63b3.

282. This somewhat challenging paragraph needs to be read with some familiarity with the way in which classical Buddhist thought understands the function of negation in language. There are two principal forms a negation may take: a negation that is simple, categorical, and does not imply anything in its wake, and a form of negation that casts an implication. The first is called a *nonimplicative negation* (*med dgag*) while the second is an *implicative negation* (*ma yin dgag*). What Tsongkhapa is saying is that there are, within the category of nonimplicative negations, two kinds—one whose object of negation does not exist at all (e.g., the horn of a rabbit) and another type whose object of negation does exist in general (e.g., a vase). In other words, though equal in being simple negations, the negation of the first kind—the nonexistence of a rabbit's horn—is universal, while the second negation is contingent to a specific context. In other words, we can negate the existence of vase only in contexts where there are no vases. Now, because of the universality of the first kind of negation, one can say that it permeates everywhere and everything. So, logically speaking, the nonexistence of a vase *is* an instance of the nonexistence of a rabbit's horn. However, this does not entail that what is being negated by the "nonexistence of a vase"—namely, a vase—does not exist in

general. For an explanation of the logical forms of negation and their function in language, see Jinpa, *Self, Reality, and Reason*, chap. 2.

283. In this paragraph Tsongkhapa is identifying the truth of cessation (*nirodha*) with the ultimate nature of the mind—its emptiness—characterized by the absence of the afflictions, which are the adventitious stains. Thus this emptiness that is the ultimate nature of mind has two dimensions of purity, its *natural purity* in the sense of it being free of intrinsic existence and the *purity attained* through eliminating the adventitious stains such as the afflictions. While the object of negation (*dgag bya*) of the first purity does not exist at all, the object negated by the second type of purity—the afflictions, their seeds, and residual propensities—although eliminated on the path, do exist in general.

284. Directly Facing (*mngon du phyogs pa*) is an alternative name in Tibetan for the sixth ground, the other being The Manifest (*mngon du gyur pa*).

285. Jayānanda, *Madhyamakāvatāraṭīkā*, Toh 3870 Tengyur, dbu ma, *ra*, 11b6.

286. Nāgārjuna, *Ratnāvalī* 5.51–52, Toh 4158 Tengyur, spring yig, *ge*, 124a1.

287. *Rab 'phrul ni 'phrul dga' 'o*. This is a comment on the Tibetan word *rab 'phrul* found in the translation of the above verse from Nāgārjuna's *Ratnāvalī*. Tsongkhapa is simply saying that this word *rab 'phrul* is the same as *'phrul dga'*, the latter being the more common way of referring to the Nirmāṇarati (*'phrul dga'*, "delighting in emanations") gods, one of the six classes of devas belonging to the desire realm.

288. *Prajñāpāramitāsaṃcayagāthā*, Toh 13, shes phyin, *ka*, 6a5.

289. *Vajracchedikā*, Toh 16 Kangyur, shes phyin, *ka*, 127a1.

290. *Commentary*, 244b3.

291. Here Tsongkhapa is critiquing the views of some earlier Tibetan thinkers, which entail the denial of any form of mental phenomena, including even gnosis with respect to the ultimate truth, in meditative equipoise on emptiness. For these Tibetan thinkers meditative equipoise of the āryas represent states of total mindlessness. Sakya Paṇḍita too critiques this standpoint in his *Clarifying the Sage's Intent* (trans), 573–77.

292. *Laṅkāvatārasūtra*, Toh 107 Kangyur, mdo sde, *ca*, 165b5.

293. *Suvarṇaprabhāsottamasūtra*, Toh 557 Kangyur, rgyud 'bum, *pha*, 4b6. This Licchavi youth is the key protagonist in the *Sublime Golden Light Sūtra*.

294. *Mahāmeghasūtra*, Toh 232 Kangyur, mdo sde, *wa*, 187a7.

295. *Mañjuśrīmūlatantra*, Toh 543 Kangyur, rgyud 'bum, *na*, 308b6.

296. *Mahābherīsūtra*, Toh 222 Kangyur, mdo sde, *dza*, 100b5.

297. See, for example, Bodhibhadra, *Interspersed Explanation of Heart of Wisdom* (*Jñānasārasamuccayanibandhana*), Toh 3852 Tengyur, dbu ma, *tsha*, 29a7; and Atiśa, *Open Basket of Jewels* (*Ratnakaraṇḍodghāṭa*), Toh 3930 Tengyur, dbu ma, *ki*, 114a6.

298. *Mahābherīsūtra*, Toh 222 Kangyur, mdo sde, *dza*, 100b5.

299. Nāgārjuna, *Mūlamadhyamakakārikā* 24.11, Toh 3824 Tengyur, dbu ma, *tsa*, 15a2.

300. Candrakīrti, *Prasannapadā*, Toh 3860 Tengyur, dbu ma, *'a*. 164a7.

301. Āryadeva, *Catuḥśatakaśāstra* 12.12, Toh 3846 Tengyur, dbu ma, *tsha*, 13b4.

302. Candrakīrti, *Catuḥśatakaṭīkā*, Toh 3865 Tengyur, dbu ma, *ya*, 190a7.

303. To engage in generosity in relation to the higher and lower fields means to make

offerings to such higher fields like the Three Jewels or one's teacher, and to give material aid, counsel, and psychological comfort and peace to those who are needy, such as the poor, the weak, and the frightened.

304. Nāgārjuna, *Bodhicittavivaraṇa*, verse 72, Toh 1801, Tengyur, rgyud 'grel, *ngi*, 41b4.

305. Once again Tsongkhapa is here emphasizing the critical importance of appreciating the boundary or scope of negation entailed by the Madhyamaka philosophy of emptiness. For him, all this talk of conventional truths being applicable only for the delusory perspective, all thoughts being forms of grasping at intrinsic existence, and the logic of emptiness entailing the negation of everything lead naturally to a pernicious nihilistic standpoint, which makes it impossible then to offer any rationale for taking seriously matters of either ethics or soteriology. See my introduction, pages 18–20.

306. Candrakīrti, *Catuḥśatakaṭīkā*, Toh 3865 Tengyur, dbu ma, *ya*, 188b7. The "great abyss" here probably refers to birth in the lower realms, which is a consequence of engaging in nonvirtuous deeds. "The four means of attraction" (*bsdu ba'i dngos po bzhi*) refers to a set of four principles, which are paired with the six perfections, as key deeds of the bodhisattva. The four are (1) giving what is immediately needed (especially material needs), (2) using pleasant speech, (3) giving sound spiritual advice, and (4) living in accord with what you teach.

307. Cited in Nāgārjuna, *Sūtrasamuccaya*, Toh 3934 Tengyur, dbu ma, *ki*, 205a6.

308. *Vajracchedikā*, Toh 16 Kangyur, shes phyin, *ka*, 125a1.

309. Cited in Nāgārjuna, *Sūtrasamuccaya*, Toh 3934 Tengyur, dbu ma, *ki*, 206a1.

310. This sutra is known also as the *Chapter on Magical Emanations of Mañjuśrī* (*Mañjuśrīvikurvāṇaparivarta*), Toh 97 Kangyur, mdo sde, *kha*, 251a2.

311. *Ajātaśatrukaukṛtyavinodanā*, Toh 216 Kangyur, mdo sde, *tsha*, 267b5.

312. *Commentary on the Treasury of Abhidharma* (*Abhidharmakośabhāṣya*), chap. 4, Toh 4090 Tengyur, mngon pa, *ku*, 225b6.

313. *Daśabhūmikasūtra*, Toh 44 Kangyur, phal chen, *kha*, 219a4.

314. Vasubandhu, *Daśabhūmivyākhyāna*, Toh 3993 Tengyur, mdo 'grel, *ngi*, 196a1, and Asaṅga, *Bodhisattvabhūmi*, Toh 4037 Tengyur, sems tsam, *wi*, 178a4.

315. This "first" and "second" refer to the first two perfect equanimities that make the general point about the perfect equanimity of all phenomena. Thus the two phrases, "the absence of signs" and "the absence of intrinsic characteristics" become the two general qualifications in the context of the other specific perfect equanimities.

316. *Mi skye ba'i chos la bzod pa* (Sanskrit: *anutpattikadharmakṣānti*). "Forbearance toward the unborn nature" refers to a state of mind one attains on the path that is free of any fear or apprehension with respect to emptiness, the unborn nature. The first stage of such forbearance is attained on the third level, "forbearance," of the path of preparation, while the highest is attained on the eighth ground.

317. *Bodhicaryāvatāra* 9.138, Toh 3871 Tengyur, dbu ma, *la*, 36a6.

318. *Laṅkāvatārasūtra*, Toh 107 Kangyur, mdo sde, *ca*, 174b5. The version found in the sutra itself has the first line as "Conventionally things do exist" (*kun rdzob tu ni dngos rnams yod*).

319. Kamalaśīla, *Madhyamāloka*, Toh 3887 Tengyur, dbu ma, *sa*, 228a1. This passage

from Kamalaśīla is cited by Tsongkhapa's student Khedrup Jé in his *Opening the Eyes of the Fortunate*. For Khedrup Jé's explanation of this passage as well as an alternative translation of the citation, see Cabezon, *A Dose of Emptiness*, 141–43.

320. Because of syntactic differences between the two languages, the specific words from Kamalaśīla's text cited by Tsongkhapa when glossing them do not match those in the translation here. Here, I have provided the terms from the translation.

321. Jñānagarbha, *Satyadvayavibhaṅgavṛtti*, Toh 3882 Tengyur, dbu ma, *sa*, 12a7.

322. The emphasis is mine. The italicized phrase constitutes the measure of the hypothetical "true existence," which is the object of negation according to Svātantrika Madhyamaka.

323. Kamalaśīla, *Madhyamakāloka*, Toh 3887 Tengyur, dbu ma, *sa*, 229b3.

324. Although Tsongkhapa does not identify who he sees to be the proponents of these errors, his student Khedrup Jé attributes the first error to the great translator Ngok Loden Sherab (1059–1109) and the second to the logician Chapa Chökyi Sengé (1109–69). See Cabezón, *Dose of Emptiness*, 143. Khedrup offers a crucial middle step—namely, that such proponents fail to differentiate between "something that can withstand reasoned analysis" and "something that is established by reasoning." Since even the ultimate truth cannot withstand analysis, Ngok felt compelled to admit, according to Khedrup Jé, that ultimate truth is unestablished (*gzhi ma grub*).

325. For example, on Tsongkhapa's understanding, there is no contradiction in maintaining that emptiness is the essential mode of being of things and therefore the ultimate truth, yet even the ultimate truth does not exist through its own mode of being or, for that matter, ultimately. For a clear distinction between these statements, see Jinpa, *Self, Reality, and Reason*, 46–48.

326. Tsongkhapa is pointing out that the referent of the analogy is not that though things appear as themselves—a vase as a vase—they do not exist as themselves; rather it is that although they appear as if they possess true existence, they are devoid of such existence. So to take the "vase being devoid of a vase" as the referent of the analogy misses the whole point of this special analogy.

327. Tsongkhapa is referring the reader here to such classic expositions as Vasubandhu's critique of atomism in *Thirty Verses* and Śāntarakṣita's *Ornament of the Middle Way*.

328. *Upāliparipṛcchā*, Toh 68 Kangyur, dkon brtsegs, *ca*, 129b5.

329. Nāgārjuna, *Yuktiṣaṣṭikākārikā* 37, Toh 3825 Tengyur, dbu ma, *tsa*, 21b6.

330. Candrakīrti, *Yuktiṣaṣṭikāvṛtti*, Toh 3864 Tengyur, dbu ma, *ya*, 3a6.

331. Āryadeva, *Catuḥśatakaśāstra* 8.3, Toh 3846 Tengyur, dbu ma, *tsha*, 9a6.

332. Candrakīrti, *Catuḥśatakaṭīkā*, Toh 3865 Tengyur, dbu ma, *ya*, 133a6.

333. Nāgārjuna, *Ratnāvalī* 1.80, Toh 4158 Tengyur, spring yig, *ge*, 109b7.

334. *Samādhirājasūtra*, chap. 12, Toh 127, Kangyur, mdo sde, *da*, 44a2.

335. *Prajñāpāramitāsaṃcayagāthā*, Toh 13, shes phyin, *ka*, 3a6.

336. Nāgārjuna, *Ratnāvalī* 1.81, Toh 4158 Tengyur, spring yig, *ge*, 110a1.

337. Nāgārjuna, *Ratnāvalī* 1.99–100, Toh 4158 Tengyur, spring yig, *ge*, 110b3.

338. Ibid. 2.14, 111a4.

339. This is a cross-reference to page 175 above, where when identifying the object of negation according to Svātantrika Madhyamaka, Tsongkhapa distinguished two

senses of the term *ultimate*. For philosophical implications of this distinction between the two senses of the term, see also Jinpa, *Self, Reality, and Reason*, especially 46–49.

340. In the preceding paragraph, Tsongkhapa listed six well-known ways the object of negation is understood in the context of understanding emptiness: true existence (*bden par grub pa*), ultimate existence (*don dam par grub pa*), real existence (*yang dag par grub pa*), existence by virtue of an essential nature (*ngo bo nyid kyis grub pa*), existence through intrinsic characteristic (*rang gi mtshan nyid kyis grub pa*), and intrinsic existence (*rang bzhin gyis grub pa*). Although existence in terms of any of these six remains untenable for Prāsaṅgika Madhyamaka, who rejects them all, Tsongkhapa maintains that Svātantrika Madhyamaka would allow the last three from the list to be tenable, at least on the conventional level.

341. Candrakīrti, *Catuḥśatakaṭīkā*, Toh 3865 Tengyur, dbu ma, *ya*, 190a2.

342. *Commentary*, 292a7.

343. *Commentary*, 292b7.

344. Tsongkhapa is here making an important psychological point concerning how our innate identity-view operates. He states that while our psychophysical aggregates as well as our personal possessions are instances of what we call "mine"— my body, my mind, my house, and so on—when identity view in the form of the thought "mine" occurs, it is in fact the notion of "mine" itself that is the object of our innate grasping, not the specific objects that serve as the basis for the arising of that thought "mine."

345. For Tsongkhapa's own commentary on this line, see page 47.

346. *Commentary*, 223a5.

347. Tsongkhapa is saying that when it comes to the aspect of apprehension, there is no difference between grasping at self-existence of persons and that of phenomena. They both have intrinsic existence as their object of grasping. The only difference between the two forms of grasping is their object, one takes persons as its focal object while the other takes phenomena other than persons.

348. Nāgārjuna, *Śūnyatāsaptatikārikā* 64, Toh 3827 Tengyur, dbu ma, *tsa*, 26b3.

349. Ibid. 65, 26b4.

350. Nāgārjuna, *Dharmadhātustava* 64, Toh 1118 Tengyur, bstod tshogs, *ka*, 66a3.

351. Ibid. 26cd, 64b5.

352. Āryadeva, *Catuḥśatakaśāstra* 14.25, Toh 3846 Tengyur, dbu ma, *tsha*, 16a5.

353. Ibid. 6.11, 7a3.

354. Tsongkhapa is here referring particularly to what he sees as the problem of over-negation, which he treats at length in his *Great Treatise on the Stages of the Path*. See Tsongkhapa, *Great Treatise*, 3:125–95.

355. *Fundamental Verses on the Middle Way* (*Mūlamadhyamakakārikā*) 1.1, Toh 3824 Tengyur, dbu ma, *tsa*, 1b3.

356. Candrakīrti, *Prasannapadā*, Toh 3860 Tengyur, dbu ma, *'a*, 5a1. Tsongkhapa is referring here to Patsab's translation of *Clear Words*, where one reads the phrase "'Therefore, from itself, nothing whatsoever has arising in any terms.' This is how predication of the three terms should be applied." Tsongkhapa is suggesting that this sentence reads better if rendered as "Therefore, nothing whatsoever arises in any terms from itself . . ."

357. *Commentary*, 246b7.
358. See, for example, Kamalaśīla, *Madhyamakāloka*, Toh 3887 Tengyur, dbu ma, *sa*, 190a3.
359. Candrakīrti, *Prasannapadā*, chap. 1, Toh 3860 Tengyur, dbu ma, *'a*, 11a4.
360. Ibid., chap. 15, 93b7.
361. *Commentary*, 257a1.
362. Candrakīrti, *Prasannapadā*, chap. 1, Toh 3860 Tengyur, dbu ma, *'a*, 12b4.
363. Tsongkhapa is here critiquing those interpreters who assert that Candrakīrti's goal is to simply refute others' views, such as their proposition about thing's intrinsic existence, and not to establish or prove that things do not have intrinsic existence. See my introduction.
364. Candrakīrti, *Prasannapadā*, chap. 1, Toh 3860 Tengyur, dbu ma, *'a*, 11a4.
365. Ibid., chap. 20, 127b3.
366. Nāgārjuna, *Vigrahavyāvartanī*, verse 26, Toh 3828 Tengyur, dbu ma, *tsa*, 27a6.
367. See, for example, Tsongkhapa's *Great Treatise*, 3:267–75, and *Essence of True Eloquence* in Thurman, *Central Philosophy*, 327–44.
368. For Tsongkhapa, the appreciation of the distinction between constructive and negative propositions in general and the difference between the two forms of negation—implicative and nonimplicative—is of vital importance to understanding Nāgārjuna's teachings on emptiness. Given the centrality of this point, we find treatment of the topic of negation in three of Tsongkhapa's major works on the Middle Way philosophy—namely, his *Essence of True Eloquence, Ocean of Reasoning*, and the present work. For further discussion of Tsongkhapa's take on logical analysis of the forms of negation in Madhyamaka's overall project of refuting intrinsic existence, see my *Self, Reality, and Reason*, especially 57–63.
369. Avalokitavrata, *Prajñāpradīpaṭīkā*, Toh 3860 Tengyur, dbu ma, *wa*, 63b6. To correlate these to the three types of nonimplicative negation, the first line presents what Tsongkhapa lists as the second (indirect implication), the second line the first (direct implication and negation effected by a single term), and the third line the final type, where implication is done both directly and indirectly.
370. For a concise yet comprehensive introduction to Sāṃkhya views, see "The Philosophy of Sāṃkhya" chapter in Larson et al., *Encyclopedia of Indian Philosophy, Volume 4*, 44–103.
371. The distinction being drawn here between a simple "reversal of consequence" (*bzlog pa 'phen pa*) and a "reversal of consequence in the form of an autonomous syllogism" (*bzlog pa rang rgyud 'phen pa*) relates to the fundamental disagreement between Candrakīrti's Prāsaṅgika and Bhāviveka's Svātantrika Madhyamaka. Tsongkhapa is saying that so long as the reverse of the consequence thrown does not contain an autonomous syllogism, this is not a problem for Candrakīrti.
372. Tib. *skyu ru ra* and *pi pi ling*, respectively. The technical name of the first, known as *āmlakī dhātri* in Sanskrit, is *Emblica officinalis Gaertn*, while that of the second, *pippalī* in Sanskrit, is *Piper longum L.* Both of these are understood, according to both Tibetan and Indian Āyurveda medical systems, as possessing healing properties.
373. Tsongkhapa is here drawing our attention to the need for a refined approach to understanding the intricacies of reasoning involved in critiquing the Sāṃkhya

thesis of self-arising. A key element is to understand what is meant by things being identical in nature (*ngo bo gcig pa*), and how while being identical in nature two things can yet possess conceptually distinct identities. So being identical in nature does not entail being identical in all respects. So, according to Madhyamaka, emptiness, being the ultimate nature of all things, can be said to be the ultimate nature of two entirely separate entities, such as a vase and a flower. Nonetheless, this does not mean that the emptiness of the vase *is* the emptiness of that flower or vice versa. To assert this would imply a belief in some kind of unitary, all-pervading "mother" emptiness that can be conceived as an absolute, as being *the* one and only emptiness.

374. *Lamp of Wisdom* (*Prajñāpradīpa*), chap. 1, Toh 3853 Tengyur, dbu ma, *tsha*, 49a2.

375. Nāgārjuna, *Mūlamadhyamakakārikā* 20.18, Toh 3824 Tengyur, dbu ma, *tsa*, 12a4.

376. Ibid. 10.1, 6b6.

377. Tib. *gcig yongs su gcod pa cig shos rnam par bdad pa med na med pa'i dgnos 'gal*. This phrase is actually from Kamalaśīla's *Madhyamakāloka*, and Tsongkhapa cites the passage containing it on page 228.

378. Vasubandhu, *Abhidharmakośa* 2.61d, Toh 4089, Tengyur, mngon pa, *ku*, 6a7. For a detailed presentation on these six causes according to Vaibhāṣika, see Chim Jampaiyang, *Ornament of Abhidharma*, 291–309.

379. Ibid. 2.62c, 6b1.

380. Ibid. 2.62ab, 6a7.

381. Ibid. 2.62d, 6b1.

382. Ibid. 2.49, 5b7.

383. This paragraph is found almost verbatim in Candrakīrti's *Commentary* (249a1), but he too does not specify whose view it is. Candrakīrti, however, presents the position as that of "some others" (*gzhan dag na re*), which suggests he is presenting a view different from Vaibhāṣika, possibly that of Sautrāntika.

384. *Commentary*, 249a1.

385. Candrakīrti, *Prasannapadā*, chap. 1, Toh 3860 Tengyur, dbu ma, *'a*, 28b7.

386. Ibid., 27a4.

387. *Commentary*, 244b3.

388. Bhāviveka, *Prajñāpradīpa*, chap. 1, Toh 3853 Tengyur, dbu ma, *tsha*, 53b3.

389. *Commentary on the Lamp of Wisdom* (*Prajñāpradīpaṭīkā*), Toh 3860 Tengyur, dbu ma, *wa*, 157b1.

390. Vasubandhu, *Abhidharmakośa* 2.64, Toh 4089, Tengyur, mngon pa, *ku*, 6b2. For an explanation of this somewhat cryptic stanza on how, according to Vaibhāṣika, phenomena are produced from the four conditions, see Chim Jampaiyang, *Ornament of Abhidharma*, 327–30.

391. *Śālistambasūtra*, Toh 210; mdo sde, *tsha*, 118a5.

392. Nāgārjuna, *Mūlamadhyamakakārikā* 20.19cd and 20cd, Toh 3824 Tengyur, dbu ma, *tsa*, 12a4. In his *Commentary*, Candrakīrti cites these four lines in the manner presented here by Tsongkhapa.

393. Although Candrakīrti does not explicitly address the question of whether his two consequence-revealing arguments throw their reverses, he does end each with a syllogism-style proof statement that arising from other is untenable because we do not observe that pitch darkness comes from flames, and arising from other is

untenable because we do not observe everything coming from everything else. See *Commentary*, 249a5.

394. Losang Tamdrin (*Annotations*, 94.3) says this refers to the many Tibetans who are confused by Jayānanda's critique of autonomous syllogism.

395. Tib. *ldog pa gcig pa'i phung 'phul lo*. I agree with Samten and Garfield (in Tsongkhapa, *Ocean of Reasoning*, 67n21) when they remark that this Tibetan expression is meaningless in English if translated literally, but the meaning is nicely captured by this idiom.

396. See, for example, *Essence of True Eloquence*, 90b6. For an English translation, see Thurman, *Central Philosophy*, 325.

397. Candrakīrti, *Prasannapadā*, chap. 1, Toh 3860 Tengyur, dbu ma, *'a*, 18b2.

398. This is a cross-reference to chapter 9 on "identifying the object of negation" pages 174–89.

399. Candrakīrti, *Prasannapadā*, chap. 1, Toh 3860 Tengyur, dbu ma, *'a*, 7b7.

400. Ibid., 8a2.

401. Ibid., 8a4.

402. *Buddhapālitavṛtti*, chap. 1, Toh 3842 Tengyur, dbu ma, *tsa*, 161b4.

403. The two consequences thrown are (1) that from pitch darkness can arise bright flames of fire and (2) that everything can arise from everything else. Tsongkhapa points out that the Mādhyamika can and does accept their opposites.

404. Tsongkhapa is making the observation that the conjunctive adverb "therefore" (*de'i phyir*) does not fit well with Candrakīrti's own reading of this stanza in the *Commentary*.

405. This paragraph, except for few additional words here and there, is reproduced from Candrakīrti's *Commentary*, 249b7.

406. Tsongkhapa is making the point that the Buddhist essentialists do not assert action or activity (*karma*) to be objectively distinct from substance (*dravya*), as the non-Buddhist school Vaiśeṣika does. This means for the Buddhist essentialists, given their commitment to the notion of intrinsic existence, the thing and its activity would necessarily be simultaneous.

407. *Śālistambasūtra*, Toh 210 Kangyur, mdo sde, *tsha*, 122b2.

408. *Commentary*, 251a2.

409. This is a reference to 6.19d, where Candrakīrti demonstrates how arising is illogical without its agent, the cause.

410. *Commentary*, 201b3.

411. Candrakīrti, *Prasannapadā*, chap. 1, Toh 3860 Tengyur, dbu ma, *'a*, 6a7.

412. In verse 4 of his *Seventy Stanzas on Emptiness*, Nāgārjuna presents exactly the same argument to negate intrinsic arising, examining whether what is produced is existent, nonexistent, both, or neither.

413. *Commentary*, 253a7.

414. Śāntideva, *Śikṣāsamuccaya*, Toh 3940 Tengyur, dbu ma, *khi*, 142b3.

415. Tsongkhapa is alluding to some earlier Tibetan commentators of Śāntideva who took the line "The ultimate is not an object of intellect" from *Guide to the Bodhisattva Way* (9.2c) to literally mean that the ultimate truth is not an object of any cognition. Geluk commentators of Tsongkhapa, including even Khedrup Jé (*Dose*

of Emptiness, 357), identify the great translator Ngok Loden Sherab to be one of the masters who upheld such a view.

416. Nāgārjuna, *Bodhicittavivaraṇa*, 67c–68, Toh 1801 Tengyur, rgyud 'grel, *ngi*, 41a1.

417. *Bodhicaryāvatāra* 9.2, Toh 3871 Tengyur, dbu ma, *la*, 21a1.

418. *Pitāputrasamāgamanasūtra*, Toh 60 Kangyur, dkon brtsegs, *nga*, 60b5, as cited in *Śikṣāsamuccaya*, Toh 3940 Tengyur, dbu ma, *khi*, 142b5.

419. See page 252 below for Tsongkhapa's treatment of Candrakīrti's use of this citation to comment on verse 6.29.

420. This discussion appears later in relation to the resultant ground; see pages 533–39.

421. This appears to be the subtitle of the *Meeting of Father and Son Sutra* (*Pitāputrasamāgamanasūtra*), Toh 60 Kangyur, dkon brtsegs, *nga*, 61b5.

422. *Commentary*, 243b1.

423. *Madhyamakāloka*, Toh 3887 Tengyur, dbu ma, *sa*, 191a5.

424. Ibid., 191b3.

425. In modern parlance, Tsongkhapa is stating that the suggestion that Madhyamaka rejects the law of the excluded middle is not only unfounded, but those who make such an assertion will not be able to explain how many of the reasonings presented in Madhyamaka sources that analyze in binary terms work.

426. Spelled *dhadura* in Sanskrit (*thang khrom* in Tibetan), the scientific name of this plant is *Datura stramonium*. In India, the plant is found mainly in the foothills of the Himalayan mountain range, and all three parts of the plant—the leaves, the flower, and the seeds—are used in the Ayurveda medical system as remedies. The plant is supposed to possess also strong hallucinogenic properties with high levels of toxicity. Tibetan medical sources speak of multicolored *thang khrom* (*Datura stramonium*), white *thang khrom* (*Przewalskia tangutica maxim*), and red *thang khrom* (*Anisodus tanguticus*). For identification of these individual plants, see Pasang Yonten Arya, *Dictionary of Tibetan Materia Medica*, 89–90.

427. Tsongkhapa is saying that philosophical views such as Sāṃkhya's primal substance and Vaiśeṣika's eternal indivisible atoms can be refuted without realizing suchness as emptiness in Madhyamaka terms. Even non-Mādhyamikas can demonstrate that these assertions are false.

428. Tsongkhapa is distinguishing between two objects of cognition: the *appearing object* (*snang yul*) and the apprehended or *conceived object* (*zhen yul*). With respect to deluded perceptions—imagining a mirage to be water, for example— even though the object apprehended by this perception—the mirage grasped as water—does not exist, there is still the perception of the mirage itself, which is the cognition's appearing object.

429. Tsongkhapa is here identifying the acceptance of external reality (*bāhyārtha*) in a specific manner in the light of rejecting intrinsic existence to be a unique tenet of Candrakīrti. In Gyaltsab's *Memorandum on the Eight Difficult Points of Fundamental Wisdom*, based on his notes from Tsongkhapa's teachings, it is listed also as the third difficult point.

430. *Laṅkāvatārasūtra*, Toh 107 Kangyur, mdo sde, *ca*, 274b5. This same stanza was cited above on page 174.

431. See page 235.

432. *Commentary*, 254b6.

433. *Commentary*, 255a1.

434. *Commentary*, 255a1.

435. *De yang*. In the canonical version of *Commentary*, the opening phrase of the sentence reads *de la* ("Here . . ."). Tsongkhapa is probably using Naktso's version of the commentary here.

436. Tsongkhapa is saying that to recognize something as a conventional truth entails understanding it to be false, not true, and so to say that phenomena such as vases are not conventional truths for the three classes of āryas because these beings lack grasping at true existence is to make a totally irrelevant argument. In fact, it is the contrary—it is precisely because these beings are free from grasping at true existence that for them the phenomena are ultimately false and are mere conventional truths.

437. *Commentary*, 255a1, and *Catuḥśatakaṭīkā*, chap. 14, Toh 3865 Tengyur, dbu ma, *ya*, 221b3.

438. *Catuḥśatakaṭīkā*, chap. 14, Toh 3865 Tengyur, dbu ma, *ya*, 221b6. Here bodhisattvas attaining the "forbearance toward the unborn nature" refers to those on the eighth ground and above; see also note 316.

439. Tsongkhapa is saying that just as there are two types of identity view, one defined uniquely by Candrakīrti here and the other as defined in the Abhidharma, there would be likewise two types when it comes to defining the extreme views as well.

440. Āryadeva, *Catuḥśatakaśāstra* 6.10, Toh 3846 Tengyur, dbu ma, *tsha*, 7b2.

441. *Catuḥśatakaṭīkā*, chap. 6, Toh 3865 Tengyur, dbu ma, *ya*, 112b7.

442. Tsongkhapa is alluding to stanza 6.11 from the *Four Hundred Stanzas*.: "If one sees dependent origination / then delusion will arise no more. / Therefore, with all of one's energy, / one should engage in discourse on this." *Catuḥśatakaśāstra* 6.11, Toh 3846 Tengyur, dbu ma, *tsha*, 7b3.

443. *Yuktiṣaṣṭikākārikā*, v. 51, Toh 3825 Tengyur, dbu ma, *tsa*, 22b6. In the standard Dergé Tengyur version, however, the first line of this stanza reads, "Having found a locus, one will be seized," giving a slightly different reading. In *Seventy Stanzas on Emptiness*, we find the following stanza: "Things arisen from causes and conditions, / that which conceives these to be real / the Buddha taught to be ignorance; / from this emerge the twelve links." *Śūnyatāsaptatikārikā*, v. 64, Toh 3827 Tengyur, dbu ma, *tsa*, 26b3.

444. *Yuktiṣaṣṭikākārikā*, v. 52ab, Toh 3825 Tengyur, dbu ma, *tsa*, 22b7.

445. *Yuktiṣaṣṭikāvṛtti*, Toh 3864 Tengyur, dbu ma, *ya*, 28a4.

446. Ibid., 28a7.

447. Ibid., 28b1.

448. *Bodhicaryāvatāra* 9.47cd–48c, Toh 3871 Tengyur, dbu ma, *la*, 32b4. The "meditative attainment of nondiscrimination" here refers to the highest formless absorption called *neither consciousness nor unconsciousness* (*naivasañjñānāsañjñā*). The implication is that one may achieve the most refined states of concentration, but unless one has realized the emptiness of intrinsic existence, one will eventually have to experience the afflictions again.

449. This paragraph is a careful gloss on a similar passage from Candrakīrti's *Commentary* (255a2). In brief, it states that the objects of the everyday world such as flowers are not only perceived by ordinary beings but in fact, since ordinary beings grasp

at them as existing intrinsically, sentient beings are deceived by these objects of conventional truth. In contrast, these objects of conventional truth become mere conventions and not true in any sense for the three classes of ārya beings cited above. Furthermore, says Candrakīrti, it is only during the phases outside meditative equipoise that the three classes of āryas perceive the objects of conventional truth. This is because these āryas still have residues of ignorance and its propensities, and so dualistic perceptions still persist for them during those states. In contrast, given that there is no dualistic perception during meditative equipoise, the ārya beings who remain absorbed in meditative equipoise do not perceive things of conventional truth.

450. *Commentary*, 342b6. This passage is found in fact in the final part of commentary (11.40), in connection with the final tenth power of the buddha.

451. This is a gloss on the following important sentence from the *Commentary*, 255a4: "As for the buddhas, given that they have thoroughly comprehended and realized the nature of all phenomena, we maintain that all turnings of mind and mental factors have come to cease permanently."

452. This is a reference to a passage in the *Commentary*, which Tsongkhapa already glossed above on page 244 as "They possess a form of ignorance that is not afflicted but is characterized as an obscuration to knowledge."

453. *Prasannapadā*, chap. 18, Toh 3860 Tengyur, dbu ma, *'a*, 18a3. The sutra cited is the *Teachings of Akṣayamati Sutra* (*Akṣayamatinirdeśasūtra*), Toh175 Kangyur, mdo sde, *ma*, 123b3.

454. *Commentary*, 255a5.

455. *Commentary*, 255a5.

456. *Commentary*, 255a6.

457. *Prasannapadā*, chap. 18, Toh 3860 Tengyur, dbu ma, *'a*, 119b5.

458. This following paragraph is a gloss on a relevant section of Candrakīrti's *Commentary*, 255b3.

459. Jñānagarbha, *Differentiation of the Two Truths* (*Satyadvayavibhaṅga*), Toh 3881 Tengyur, dbu ma, *sa*, 14b6.

460. "Resultant Ground" is the final chapter of Candrakīrti's *Entering the Middle Way*. Tsongkhapa's further analysis of the question of the modes of knowing of the buddha's mind can be found on pages 535–40 below. On the debate in Tibet on whether gnosis can be attributed to a buddha, see also my introduction.

461. This question and its response are adapted from the *Commentary*, 255b6.

462. *Commentary*, 283a2. In the second sentence of the citation, Candrakīrti is alluding here to the etymology of the word *buddha*, which, as observed above (page 37) in the context of commenting on the salutation verses, connotes "one who has realized suchness."

463. Kamalaśīla's *Lamp on the Middle Way* (168b4) contains this exact sentence and cites it as from the *Perfectly Gathering the Teachings Sutra* (*Dharmasaṃgītisūtra*). In the sutra itself (Toh 238 Kangyur, mdo sde, *zha*, 68b6), however, the sentence appears slightly differently as "Not seeing all phenomena is perfect seeing" (*chos thams cad ma mthong ba ni yang dag pa mthong ba'o*), a version closer to the one cited in Bhāviveka's *Blaze of Reasoning* (critical edition, 58), where it reads, "Not seeing is seeing suchness" (*mthong ba med pa ni de nyid mthong ba'o*).

464. Tsongkhapa's point is that, in reading seemingly paradoxical statements such as this, one needs to understand the contexts carefully so that one avoids blatant contradictions like "not seeing is seeing." On Tsongkhapa's reading, "not seeing" relates to the phenomena of the conventional truth, such as the aggregates, elements, and sense bases, while "seeing" should be correlated to their ultimate nature, which is their emptiness.

465. *Prajñāpāramitāsaṃcayagāthā*, Toh 13, shes phyin, *ka*, 5b2.

466. *Pratītyasamutpādasūtra*, Toh 212 Kangyur, mdo sde, *tsha*, 125b3.

467. *Saṃvṛtiparamārthasatyanirdeśasūtra*, Toh 179 Kangyur, mdo sde, *ma*, 247a4.

468. Ibid., 274a5.

469. See page 350.

470. This paragraph glosses Candrakīrti's *Commentary*, 256b4.

471. *Commentary*, 256b6.

472. Essentially, Tsongkhapa, following Candrakīrti, is saying that these are inappropriate applications of reasoning from the ultimate perspective. They attempt to undermine conventional valid cognitions by asserting their ultimate unreality, but they do so in an inappropriate context, which is to conflate two distinct domains of analysis.

473. *Commentary*, 283a4.

474. *Prasannapadā*, chap. 1, Toh 3860 Tengyur, dbu ma, *'a*, 18b1.

475. Ibid., 18b2. Tsongkhapa cited this passage above as well; see page 193.

476. Both examples are drawn from Candrakīrti's *Commentary*. The point is that, conventionally speaking, when a seed produces a sprout, although the seed itself comes to cease, its continuum remains as the sprout it has produced. But if the two are intrinsically distinct entities, they will be no different from other totally unconnected entities, like a yak and a cow, or two distinct persons, an ordinary person and an ārya. The existence of the sprout in that case would have nothing to do with the continuum of the seed.

477. *Commentary*, 257a6.

478. *Sa bon rgyun chad pa zhes pa.* Tsongkhapa is referring here to a phrase in the *Commentary* (257a5).

479. *Lalitavistarasūtra*, Toh 95 Kangyur, mdo sde, *kha*, 89b1. This citation is found also in the *Commentary* (257a7) as well.

480. Ibid., 89b1. This citation is also found in the *Commentary* (257b5).

481. Nāgārjuna, *Mūlamadhyamakakārikā* 18.10, Toh 3824 Tengyur, dbu ma, *tsa*, 8b2.

482. These three points, which are part of the demonstration of how intrinsic arising does not exist in any manner, are presented in 6.34–37. Tsongkhapa reads these as representing Candrakīrti's critique of fellow Mādhyamika Bhāviveka, who while denying ultimate arising, subscribes to some notion of arising by virtue of intrinsic characteristics. In his *Essence of True Eloquence*, Tsongkhapa speaks of three arguments presented in the root text, with one additional argument found in the *Commentary*. For a presentation of Tsongkhapa's reading of the four relevant stanzas of *Entering the Middle Way*, as developed in *Essence of Eloquence*, see Thurman, *Central Philosophy*, pp. 366–75.

483. *Commentary*, 258a2.

484. Tsongkhapa is referring in particular to Bhāviveka, who Tsongkhapa credits with

rejecting *true* existence but retaining some notion of *intrinsic* existence, at least on the conventional level.

485. See page 185. And for the later discussion he refers to, see page 267 below.

486. *Questions of Upāli* (*Upāliparipṛcchā*), Toh 68 Kangyur, dkon brtsegs, *ca*, 132a4.

487. *Commentary*, 258a2. Emptiness, signlessness, and wishlessness together constitute the "three doors of liberation" and refer, respectively, to the emptiness of things themselves, their causes, and their effects.

488. In his *Essence of True Eloquence*, Tsongkhapa lists this as the additional fourth argument presented in the *Commentary* "that the statement in the sutra that things are devoid of intrinsic existence would be incorrect." See Thurman, *Central Philosophy*, 374.

489. Āryadeva, *Catuḥśatakaśāstra* 8.7, Toh 3846 Tengyur, dbu ma, *tsha*, 9b1.

490. Nāgārjuna, *Fundamental Verses on the Middle Way* (*Mūlamadhyamakakārikā*) 13.8, Toh 3824 Tengyur, dbu ma, *tsa*, 8a6.

491. Tsongkhapa is critiquing here Tibetan Mādhyamikas who interpret "intrinsic emptiness" (*rang stong*) to mean that things are empty of themselves—e.g., "a vase is empty of vase" (*bum pa bum pas stong ba*). There are two ways in which one could make sense of a vase being empty of vase—in the sense of not *being* a vase or in the locative sense of there being no vase in a vase. Since it cannot be meant in the second, locative sense, it will have to be in the first sense. But to assert that vase is not a vase would violate all norms of everyday convention. Furthermore, such a characterization of intrinsic emptiness would leave our habitual innate grasping at intrinsic existence of things unchallenged and unscathed.

492. Tsongkhapa is here probably critiquing the view of extrinsic emptiness, especially as held by the fourteenth-century Tibetan thinker Dölpopa. Briefly, this view maintains that the view of intrinsic emptiness—the emptiness of intrinsic existence of all phenomena as propounded in the Perfection of Wisdom sutras and systematically developed in Nāgārjuna's analytic corpus and interpreted by Candrakīrti—remains essentially a nihilistic form of emptiness. The teaching of such emptiness is a mere step toward the understanding of the final view, which according to Dölpopa is embodied by the standpoint of extrinsic emptiness, which states that things are empty of all things other than emptiness itself. Dölpopa says this is presented in "definitive" treatises such as Maitreya's *Sublime Continuum* and in the hymns of Nāgārjuna.

493. This paragraph appears almost verbatim in one of Tsongkhapa's earlier works, *Essence of True Eloquence*. For an English translation of the relevant section from the *Essence*, see Thurman (1984), 357. Tsongkhapa is presenting here what he understands to be a key criterion for whether a particular view of emptiness constitutes the correct intrinsic-emptiness view of Nāgārjuna. If, despite having realized a particular understanding of emptiness, there remains room for grasping at some kind of objective existence, one has not arrived at the final understanding of emptiness. Once one has arrived, Tsongkhapa suggests, there will be no ground left for any temptation to grasp or reify, especially due to philosophical reflection, while the impact of the realization lasts. This suggestion echoes Nāgārjuna's point (*Sixty Stanzas of Reasoning*, verses 52 and 58) that as long as one's mind remained tied to an objectifiable locus, there is always an opening for afflictions to arise.

494. *Commentary*, 258a7. Jayānanda does not identify the opponent here, but Tsongkhapa reads the passage as Candrakīrti anticipating an objection from someone like Bhāviveka, according to whom arising from other is rejected on the ultimate level but not on the conventional level.

495. *Commentary*, 258b2.

496. *Yuktiṣaṣṭikāvṛtti*, Toh 3864 Tengyur, dbu ma, *ya*, 7b7.

497. Ibid., 8a7. Tsongkhapa is probably referring here to Candrakīrti's commentary on stanzas 7 and 8 of Nāgārjuna's *Sixty Stanzas of Reasoning*.

498. *Four Hundred Stanzas* (*Catuḥśatakaśāstra*) 8.19, Toh 3846 Tengyur, dbu ma, *tsha*. 9b7.

499. Nāgārjuna, *Fundamental Verses on the Middle Way* (*Mūlamadhyamakakārikā*) 24.10, Toh 3824 Tengyur, dbu ma, *tsa*, 15a2.

500. *Vigrahavyāvartanī*, Toh 3828 Tengyur, dbu ma, *tsa*, 27b7.

501. See pages 174–80 above, where Tsongkhapa explained in some detail the Svātantrika Madhyamaka criteria for what is to be negated when establishing the view of emptiness.

502. See, for example, his *Great Treatise on the Stages of the Path to Enlightenment*, 3:163–94.

503. *Commentary*, 259a3. The version here is slightly different from Patsab's canonical version; Tsongkhapa's version probably comes from Naktso's translation.

504. *Commentary*, 259a5.

505. *Prasannapadā*, chap. 1, Toh 3860 Tengyur, dbu ma, *'a*, 23a4.

506. This quote is actually more of a paraphrase of the *Commentary* (259a7) with some interpolations by Tsongkhapa, who, as indicated by the immediately following two sentences, reads this as a critique of someone like Dharmapāla.

507. That Candrakīrti was aware of Dharmapāla's commentary on *Four Hundred Stanzas* is evident from the opening section of his own commentary on the *Four Hundred*. See *Catuḥśatakaṭīkā*, Toh 3865 Tengyur, dbu ma, *ya*, 31b2; for an English translation of the relevant passage, see Lang, *Four Illusions*, 112.

508. In the critical Tibetan edition, as well as in the Tashi Lhunpo and Kumbum editions of Tsongkhapa's collected works, this reads "in *literal* interpretable terms." I believe this is a typographical error.

509. *Commentary*, 251b1. Candrakīrti is here referring to approaches such as those of Vasubandhu that read the Perfection of Wisdom sutras as being nonliteral and requiring further interpretation.

510. *Commentary*, 259b3.

511. *Catuḥśatakaṭīkā*, chap. 11, Toh 3865 Tengyur, dbu ma, *ya*, 175b2.

512. *Pitāputrasamāgamanasūtra*, Toh 60 Kangyur, dkon brtsegs, *nga*, 50b1.

513. This is a reference to 6.33c. For Tsongkhapa's exposition of this line, see page 259 above.

514. Nāgārjuna, *Fundamental Verses on the Middle Way* (*Mūlamadhyamakakārikā*) 15.11, Toh 3824 Tengyur, dbu ma, *tsa*, 9a2.

515. Ibid. 17.31, 10b4.

516. *Commentary*, 259b7.

517. *Commentary*, 260a2. "Obtainment" refers to the Vaibhāṣika notion of an attribute, a distinct entity, that one is said to acquire whenever one comes to possess

something. So a person who has committed an act and accrued a karma comes to maintain that karma through this new attribute of obtainment.

518. This list should not be confused with another list of eight found in Tsongkhapa's short work entitled *Memorandum on Eight Difficult Points*. There, the last two are replaced by (a) rejection of the notion of intrinsic characteristic, and (b) a unique explanation of the way a buddha's gnosis perceives the world. Thus this second list contains four negative tenets and four positive tenets.

519. This alludes to Tsongkhapa's own discussion in works such as the special insight section of his *Great Treatise on the Stages of the Path to Enlightenment*, 447a6 (Trans., 3:257–75), and *Essence of True Eloquence* (see Thurman, *Central Philosophy*, 321–44).

520. These four positions of other Buddhist schools, on the account of how a karmic act maintains its connection to an effect that comes into being long after the act itself has ceased to be, are listed briefly in Candrakīrti's *Commentary* (260a5), which is clearly Tsongkhapa's source here. In his *Ocean of Reasoning* (trans., 360) as well, Tsongkhapa refers the reader to these four positions as listed in Candrakīrti's *Commentary*.

521. *Commentary on the Lamp of Wisdom* (*Prajñāpradīpaṭīkā*), Toh 3859 Tengyur, dbu ma, *wa*, 203b4.

522. See, for example, *Abhidharmakośabhāṣya*, Toh 4090 Tengyur, mngon pa, *ku*, 94a7.

523. Tsongkhapa is referring to the opening sentence of this section of the *Commentary* (260a4), where Candrakīrti asks: "According to you, following the cessation of the karmic act, how does an effect come into being from the karmic act that has already ceased?"

524. *Fundamental Verses on the Middle Way* (*Mūlamadhyamakakārikā*) 17.21, Toh 3824 Tengyur, dbu ma, *tsa*, 10a6.

525. *Meeting of Father and Son Sutra* (*Pitāputrasamāgamanasūtra*), Toh 60 Kangyur, dkon brtsegs, *nga*, 51b2.

526. This is the last line of the two-stanza sutra citation immediately above.

527. *Daśabhūmikasūtra*, Toh 44 Kangyur, phal chen, *kha*, 221b7. Candrakīrti cites this and the next quote from the same sutra in chapter 7 of his *Clear Words*.

528. Ibid., 221b1.

529. Nāgārjuna, *Mūlamadhyamakakārikā* 25.13d, Toh 3824 Tengyur, dbu ma, *tsa*, 16b6.

530. Nāgārjuna, *Yuktiṣaṣṭikākārikā* 20ab, Toh 3825 Tengyur, dbu ma, *tsa*, 21a4.

531. See Tsongkhapa, *Ocean of Reasoning*, chap. 7 (trans., 212–16).

532. *Commentary*, 259b7.

533. *Commentary*, 342b4.

534. "Type continuity" (Tib. *rigs 'dra'i rgyun*, Skt. *nikāyasthiti*) refers to the persistence of identity across time owing to similarities among successive moments within a causal continuum.

535. *Commentary*, 342b4.

536. By "two types of bases" of habitual propensities, Tsongkhapa is referring to his earlier discussion about how the "mere I," which is the object of our habitual thought "I am," is the basis upon which the propensities are imbued, and also how the

mental continuum itself can be a kind of "intermittent" or temporary basis for the propensities. Tsongkhapa thus identifies two types of bases, a more enduring one and a temporary or intermittent one.

537. Here, Tsongkhapa is alluding to a standard Abhidharma classification of conditioned phenomena into the three morally significant categories: (1) virtuous, (2) nonvirtuous, and (3) neutral. The third category includes those that are neutral but defiling, such as ignorance and other afflictions, and those that are nondefiling. Tsongkhapa's point is that the standpoint upholding foundation consciousness, because it identifies the person with such consciousness, understands the person as belonging to the category of neutral nondefiling phenomena. Furthermore, such identification of persons is done on the basis of inquiring into what is the referent of the first-person "I" in a truly objective and intrinsically real sense.

538. *Bhavasaṃkrāntisūtra*, Toh 226 Kangyur, mdo sde, *dza*, 175b5.

539. Ibid., 176a1.

540. Ibid., 176a4.

541. Ibid., 176a5.

542. Ibid., 176a6.

543. This sutra is cited in the *Commentary* (262b1) without naming its source. In the ninth chapter of Vasubandhu's *Commentary on the Treasury of Abhidharma* too, a similar citation is found, which reads, "Bhikṣus, I will explain to you the burden, the taking up of the burden, the casting off of the burden, and what bears it" (Duerlinger, *Indian Buddhist Theories of Persons*, 87). In the Pali *Khandasaṃyutta* in the *Connected Discourses of the Buddha* (Bhikkhu Bodhi, 871), we find the following strikingly similar passage: "Bhikkhus, I will teach you the burden, the carrier of the burden, the taking of the burden, and the laying down of the burden."

544. Candrakīrti cites this sutra in his *Commentary* (262b1), which is clearly the source for Tsongkhapa here. Neither Candrakīrti nor Tsongkhapa identifies the sutra.

545. *Ratnāvalī* 1.26, Toh 4158 Tengyur, spring yig, *ge*, 108a1.

546. Āryadeva, *Catuḥśatakaśāstra* 5.10, Toh 3846 Tengyur, dbu ma, *tsha*, 6b1.

547. *Uttaratantravyākhyā*, Toh 4025 Tengyur, sems tsam, *phi*, 111b6.

548. Nāgārjuna, *Bodhicittavivaraṇa*, verses 33–35, Toh 1801 Tengyur, rgyud 'grel, *ngi*, 39b4.

549. Ibid., verse 39, 39b7.

550. *Commentary on the Compendium of Views on Reality* (*Tattvasaṃgrahapañjikā*), chap. 27, Toh 4267 Tengyur, tshad ma, *ye*, 105a1.

551. *Abhidharmakośa* 3.42, Toh 4089 Tengyur, mngon pa, *ku*, 8b2.

552. The same seven verses are found in the same sequence in Candrakīrti's *Commentary* (262b2). Except for the fourth stanza, all the cited stanzas are found in the *Engaging in Accordance with the World Sutra* (*Lokānuvartasūtra*, Toh 200 Kangyur, mdo sde, *tsa*), though these verses do not appear in that sutra in one continuous flow or even in this order. The six stanzas are found, respectively, at 303b7, 306a2, 305b6, 307b2, 306b2, and 306a3.

553. Bhāviveka, *Tarkajvālā*, Toh 3856 Tengyur, dbu ma, *dza*, 148a6 (critical edition, 261). Mahāsāṃghika was one of the four root schools of early Buddhism. The four schools eventually divided into what are commonly referred to as the "eighteen schools," which Buddhist historians say resulted from divergent interpretations

of the scriptures and monastic discipline following the Buddha's death. The Pūrvaśailas, often referred to as the Uttaraśailas, were a subsect of the Mahāsāṃghika that split off around the time of Aśoka and were active in the Andhra region. They appear to have disappeared by the time of Xuanzang's pilgrimage to India in the seventh century.

554. Candrakīrti's *Commentary* cites this verse as well without identifying its source. The exact quote is found also in chapter 3 of Bhāviveka's *Blaze of Reasoning* (*Tarkajvālā*, Toh 3856 Tengyur, dbu ma, *dza*, 111b4; critical edition, 178) in the context of presenting the view of the proponents of Īśvara as the world's creator. There too, the author does not specify its source.

555. Asaṅga, *Mahāyānasaṃgraha*, Toh 4048 Tengyur, sems tsam, *ri*, 3b2.

556. Ibid., 12a5.

557. Asaṅga, *Yogācārabhūmiviniścayasaṃgraha*, Toh 4038 Tengyur, sems tsam, *zhi*. This text is one of five "summaries" (*saṃgraha*) of the levels of yogic practice composed by Asaṅga.

558. Vasubandhu, *Pratītyasamutpādādivibhaṅganirdeśa*, Toh 3995 Tengyur, mdo 'grel, *chi*, 20b4.

559. This numbering of the three attributes of the dependent nature, while not present in the root text itself, has been adopted from Candrakīrti's *Commentary*.

560. This paragraph is a paraphrase of a short sentence in Candrakīrti's *Commentary* (264a2), which in turn appears to gloss a passage in Asaṅga's *Bodhisattva Grounds* and Vasubandhu's *Commentary on the Differentiation of the Middle and Extremes*. This view explains the ultimate nature of reality within the framework of the *three natures*. The *dependent nature* is the basis, and the *imputed nature* is what we conceptually superimpose on dependent phenomena. The absence, or emptiness, of the imputed within the dependent constitutes the consummate or *perfect nature*, which is the ultimate reality.

561. Respectively, Asaṅga, *Bodhisattvabhūmi*, Toh 4037 Tengyur, sems tsam, *wi*, 26b5, and Vasubandhu, *Madhyāntavibhāgabhāṣya*, Toh 4027 Tengyur, sems tsam, *bi*, 2a2.

562. Asaṅga, *Uttaratantravyākhyā*, Toh 4025 Tengyur, sems tsam, *phi*, 114a3.

563. *Madhyāntavibhāgaṭīkā*, Toh 4032 Tengyur, sems tsam *bi*, 195b.

564. Perhaps it is because the use of the dream analogy by Cittamātra is so well known that neither Candrakīrti nor Tsongkhapa provides any source for the opponent's position here. A classic source is Asaṅga's *Summary of the Great Vehicle* (*Mahāyānasaṃgraha*, Toh 4048 Tengyur, sems tsam, *ri*, 13b4), where one reads: "One might ask, 'What analogy do you have for your statement that these cognitions consist of consciousness only with no external reality?' You should see dreams and so forth as analogies for this. . . ." Dream is only one of several similar analogies presented by Asaṅga to demonstrate the cogency of the assertion that cognitions can arise without any reference to an objective external reality. The other examples in the same category include recollections, which take on past nonexistent objects, and the perceptions of two types of reflections—a reflection of a face in a mirror and a reflection of sound in the form of echoes.

565. *Commentary*, 271b2.

566. Tsongkhapa is saying that for cognitions in general, the act of *perceiving* (*dmigs pa*) an object is the *experiencing* (*myong ba*) of that object as well. For instance,

when our visual perception comes into contact with an object—say, a blue flower—it experiences the object by perceiving it. But in some specific contexts, a distinction must be made between perceiving and experiencing, such as when the Buddha's mind perceives the suffering of sentient beings. To say that the Buddha experiences the suffering would violate convention. By "specific context" here Tsongkhapa might also be thinking of Dharmakīrti's distinction (PV 3.459) between *perceiving* as referring to cognition's act of perceiving its object and *experiencing* as referring to its act of revealing itself in a reflexive manner.

567. In classical Indian logical reasoning, *analogy* or illustration plays a crucial role in facilitating a correct inference. In most cases, such analogies are what Tsongkhapa calls here "direct example," such as in the syllogism "Sound is impermanent because it is a product; just as a pot, for example"—where the example, *a pot*, illustrates on the subject *sound* the invariable relationship between something being impermanent and being a product. Such a direct analogy is not viable in the proof of past lives; the thesis, past lives, is proven only indirectly as in this typical syllogism: "The consciousness of the newborn child must have been preceded by an earlier instance of consciousness because it is an instance of consciousness; just as our present moment consciousness, for example."

568. *Commentary*, 264b6.

569. *Commentary*, 265a2.

570. *Phyogs snga'i nam ma lang pa la dgag pa'i nyi ma shar ba yin.*

571. *Blaze of Reasoning* (*Tarkajvālā*), Toh 3856 Tengyur, dbu ma, *dza*, 205a4; critical edition, 390.

572. *Commentary*, 265a5.

573. Tsongkhapa is here alluding to an important condition of a correct proof according to classical Indian system of logic, according to which a valid example in a proof must be something that is compatible with both the *reason* (*hetu*)—the proof—and the predicate to be proven or *probandum* (*sādhyadharma*). This system of proof statement is based on a structure of proposition that has three members: (1) subject (*dharmin*), (2) probandum, and (3) reason. Take the well-known proposition from Śāntarakṣita's *Ornament of the Middle Way*, for example:

    1. Self and so forth postulated by the philosophers (subject)
    2. Are devoid of true existence (probandum)
    3. Because they have no reality as one or multiple (reason or proof)
    Just like the reflection of a face in a mirror, for example.

In short Tsongkhapa is saying that as long as one fails to reject intrinsic existence, some notion of true existence will always remain. This means that one will never find a valid example that can help establish that the given subject is devoid of true existence.

574. Tsongkhapa is here thinking of the five types of mental-object forms mentioned in Asaṅga's *Compendium of Abhidharma* (*Abhidharmasamuccaya*, chap. 1, 47a): (1) forms emerging from a process of deconstruction, (2) forms of open space, (3) forms of vows derived through a rite, (4) forms that are imagined or imputed, and (5) forms arising from meditative expertise.

575. *Commentary*, 265a7. Both sutra citations are found in the *Commentary*, but neither Candrakīrti nor Tsongkhapa identify their source texts.

576. A classic example of Cittamātra's use of this analogy of the vision of floating hairs is verse 1 of Vasubandhu's *Twenty Verses*, where one reads: "All this is only consciousness; / the appearance of nonexistent external objects / is like when someone with an eye malady / sees nonexistent webs of hair." For an alternative translation of the verse, see Anacker, *Seven Works of Vasubandhu*, 161.

577. This is the second part of the actual refutation of the Cittamātra school's postulation of intrinsically real consciousness. Tsongkhapa divides this critique into two aspects—refuting the *analogy* (*dpe*) proposed to demonstrate intrinsic reality of consciousness (p. 307) and refuting the *referent* (*don*) of such analogy, the existence of consciousness in the absence of external reality. The second part of this refutation starts from here.

578. This argument seems to trade on two distinct senses of the Tibetan word *nus pa* (Skt. *śakti*), which can mean "potentiality" or "potency." In the first sense, which is how the Cittamātra opponent seems to understand it, potentiality would be the *cause* of the cognition that results from it. In the second sense, however, "potency" can be understood as an *attribute* of the cognition, such as when we speak of a "potent cognition."

579. Vasubandhu, *Abhidharmakośa* 3.17, Toh 4089 Tengyur, mngon pa, *ku*, 7b2. This is cited in Candrakīrti's *Commentary* (266b7) in the same section.

580. *Commentary*, 267a7.

581. This last sentence is a gloss on the following concluding comment in the *Commentary* (267a6): "In that case, you will become a follower of our discourse."

582. This is cited in Candrakīrti's *Commentary* (267b7) as well and may be a citation from a classical Sanskrit grammar text or lexicon.

583. These sentences, with their complex analysis of the concept of continuum as well as its associated Sanskrit term, are a word-by-word explanation of Candrakīrti's *Commentary*, 267b7.

584. On how this assertion lies at the heart of the opponent's rebuttal of Madhyamaka critique of arising from other, see page 213 above.

585. See note 395 above on the domino effect in this phrase. In brief, Tsongkhapa is saying that those who fail to appreciate the critical importance of the qualifier "by virtue of intrinsic nature" read Candrakīrti's refutation of arising from other to rest on the rejection of mere otherness—i.e., "If a rice sprout grows from rice seed because the two are distinct from each other, then everything could grow from everything else." This interpretation assumes that the force of Candrakīrti's argument comes from drawing parity between the rice seed and everything else insofar as their distinctness from the rice sprout is concerned, and when everything else is shown one by one to be not a producer of the sprout, the negation of the rice seed being the producer of the sprout would come about as a knock-on effect.

586. In his *Examination of Objects*, verse 7cd, for example, Dignāga writes: "The potentiality that empowers the coemergence [of blueness and its cognition] / is the *sense faculty* as well." In his autocommentary, Dignāga explains, "As for organs they can be inferred as potentiality on the basis of their effects; they are not composed of material elements." *Commentary on Examination of Objects* (*Ālambana-parīkṣāvṛtti*), Toh 4206 Tengyur, tshad ma, *ce*, 87a7; critical edition, 536.

587. Maitreya, *Madhyāntavibhāga* Toh 4021 Tengyur, sems tsam, *phi*, 40a3.

588. *Commentary on the Thirty Verses* (*Triṃśikabhāṣya*), Toh 4064 Tengyur, sems tsam, *shi*, 150a3.

589. *Commentary*, 265a1.

590. *Commentary*, 265a1.

591. This entire section—beginning with the Madhyamaka's own argument, followed by the three types of arguments proposed from Cittamātra as their rejoinders— are reproduced here by Tsongkhapa, almost verbatim from Candrakīrti's *Commentary*, 169b6.

592. *Laṅkāvatārasūtra*, Toh 107 Kangyur, mdo sde, *ca*, 122a2. In the Tibetan translation of the sutra, the Sanskrit term *rūpa* is translated as "intrinsic nature" (*rang bzhin*); here I have rendered it as "matter," as suggested in Tsongkhapa's explanation of these lines from the sutra.

593. *Laṅkāvatārasūtra*, Toh 107 Kangyur, mdo sde, *ca*, 85a5.

594. *Commentary*, 270a5.

595. *Pramāṇavārttika* 1.239, 103b5.

596. Cited in *Commentary*, 271a1.

597. For these five, see note 574 above.

598. Asaṅga, *Mahāyānasaṃgraha*, Toh 4048 Tengyur, sems tsam, *ri*, 16a1.

599. *Mahāyānasaṃgrahopanibandhana*, Toh 4051 Tengyur, sems tsam, *ri*, 225a5.

600. Nāgārjuna, *Suhṛllekha*, verse 95ab, Toh 4182 Tengyur, spring yig, *nge*, 45a3.

601. Nāgārjuna, *Lokātītastava*, Toh 1120 Tengyur, bstod tshogs, *ka*, 69a2.

602. Source not located.

603. Nāgārjuna, *Bodhicittavivaraṇa* 39ab, Toh 1801 Tengyur, rgyud 'grel, *ngi*, 39b7.

604. The root text embedded in Candrakīrti's *Commentary* reads this as "By what means do you know that it exists?" (*di ni yod par gang gis shes par 'gyur*).

605. Tsongkhapa is speaking possibly of Bhāviveka's critique of reflexive awareness, which is cited immediately below.

606. Tsongkhapa does not appear to be citing a specific text of the Cittamātra school so much as making a general statement about the position of that school. What is offered here is, in fact, a gloss on Candrakīrti's *Commentary*, where it says: "If a separate cognition were an object of another consciousness, the very notion of consciousness-only will be undermined." The point both Candrakīrti and Tsongkhapa are making is that according to Cittamātra, except for the fully awakened mind of a buddha, wherein a total transformation of the base has occurred with foundation consciousness transformed into a buddha's wisdom, a person cannot directly perceive the mind of a different person by taking it as the appearing object.

607. Bhāviveka, *Tarkajvālā*, Toh 3856 Tengyur, dbu ma, *dza*, 205a5; critical edition, 391.

608. *Satyadvayavibhaṅgavṛtti*, Toh 3882 Tengyur, dbu ma, *sa*, 4b2. This translation is adapted from Eckel, *Jñānagarbha on the Two Truths*, 72.

609. *Yongs su gcod pa* (Skt. *pariccheda*). Drawing from classical Buddhist epistemological thought, Tsongkhapa uses two key terms—"positive determination" (*yongs su gcod pa*) versus "negative determination" (*rnam par gcod pa*)—to characterize the epistemic function of a knowledge-engendering cognition. For example, when we perceive, say, a blue flower, the explicit content of that knowledge is the cognition of the thing as blue and flower. However, an implicit knowledge arises

simultaneously of the negative function of that cognition—that is, the elimination of the thing as being non-blue and non-flower.

610. This is a well-known sutra quote cited in numerous texts, especially those of Buddhist epistemologists like Dignāga and Dharmakīrti. However, nowhere have I seen this quote actually sourced.

611. *Commentary*, 272b3.

612. *Madhyamakāvatāraṭīkā*, Toh 3870 Tengyur, dbu ma, *ra*, 211b2.

613. *Pramāṇavārttika* 3.501cd, Toh 4210 Tengyur, tshad ma, *ce*, 137b4. The two immediately preceding lines of the same stanza, before the ones cited here by Tsongkhapa, make it clear that Dharmakīrti understands the sutra statement about simultaneous nonoccurrence of multiple streams of consciousness as referring to streams of consciousness belonging to the same class. What Dharmakīrti is saying in these two lines is this: what the sutra statement indicates is that each of the six classes of consciousness has the potential to produce a singular continuum of their own class at any given moment, not multiple streams.

614. Tsongkhapa is, most probably, referring here to *Pramāṇavārttika* 3.135 (Toh 4210 Tengyur, tshad ma, *ce*, 123b3), where Dharmakīrti rejects the suggestion that cognitive speed is the cause for our perception of simultaneity. If that is the case, he argues, then when the words *saraḥ* ("ocean") and *rasa* ("salt") are uttered quickly one after another, the listener should hear them as being simultaneous, which is not the case. Subsequent Geluk commentators distinguish between *explanatory cause* (*shes byed kyi rgyu*) versus *efficient cause* (*skyed byed kyi rgyu*) and maintain that what Dharmakīrti is rejecting is that cognitive speed is an efficient cause of our sense of simultaneity. However, Dharmakīrti does not reject cognitive speed as being an explanatory cause—i.e., an explanation—for why we sometime take what are in fact serially occurring to be simultaneous. For in *Pramāṇavārttika* 3.133, Dharmakīrti himself states how although our visual perception and subsequent mental cognition arise in a sequence, naïve worldly people conflate them as treat them as if they were the same.

615. See page 345 under the heading "How recollection arises in the absence of reflexive awareness according to our system."

616. *Mūlamadhyamakakārikā* 7.12, Toh 3824 Tengyur, dbu ma, *tsa*, 5a2. For Tsongkhapa's commentary on these lines of Nāgārjuna's *Fundamental Wisdom*, see *Ocean of Reasoning* (trans.), 189–90.

617. *Commentary*, 273a1.

618. Ibid., 273a3.

619. *Bodhicaryāvatāra* 9.23, Toh 3871 Tengyur, dbu ma, *la*, 21b5.

620. The consequence thrown by the opponent is "if no reflexive awareness, then no recollection," and its inverse refers to "because subsequent recollection, so reflexive awareness." Tsongkhapa is stating that, according to Śāntideva, there is no logical entailment in either of these instances.

621. *Prasannapadā*, chap. 1, Toh 3860 Tengyur, dbu ma, *'a*, 25b3.

622. *Averting the Objections* (*Vigrahavyāvartanī*), v. 40, Toh 3828 Tengyur, dbu ma, *tsa*, 28a6.

623. *Prasannapadā*, chap. 1, Toh 3860 Tengyur, dbu ma, *'a*, 25b3.

624. *Catuḥśatakaṭīkā*, Toh 3865 Tengyur, dbu ma, *ya*, 186b4.

625. Ibid., 180b1.

626. Ibid., 171b4.

627. *Prasannapadā*, chap. 1, Toh 3860 Tengyur, dbu ma, *'a*, 25b2.

628. *Prasannapadā*, chap. 1, Toh 3860 Tengyur, dbu ma, *'a*, 25b4.

629. See page 407.

630. *Satyadvayavibhaṅgavṛtti*, Toh 3882 Tengyur, dbu ma, *sa*, 13b3. In Eckel, *Jñānagarbha*, 98, the second part of this sentence is missing.

631. *Satyadvayavibhaṅgavṛtti*, Toh 3882 Tengyur, dbu ma, *sa*, 13b4. Eckel (*Jñānagarbha*, 99) reads this passage quite differently.

632. *Laṅkāvatārasūtra*, Toh 107 Kangyur, mdo sde, *ca*, 179b4.

633. This last sentence is a gloss on *Commentary* (274a5), where, in concluding this section on the critique of reflexive awareness as the "proof" of dependent nature, Candrakīrti mocks Cittamātra's position with an absurd consequence.

634. *Meeting of Father and Son Sutra* (*Pitāputrasamāgamanasūtra*), Toh 60 Kangyur, dkon brtsegs, *nga*, 61b4. Tsongkhapa uses an alternative name of the sutra. This quote as well as all subsequent stanzas from the same sutra cited by Tsongkhapa are in fact found in Candrakīrti's autocommentary, where they are provided in a continuous uninterrupted manner. Tsongkhapa divides them into sections and provides a helpful summary of the meaning of each.

635. Ibid., 61b5.

636. Ibid., 61b6.

637. Ibid., 62a1.

638. Ibid., 62a2.

639. Ibid., 62a2. The eight types of suffering are those of (1) birth, (2) aging, (3) sickness, (4) death, (5) getting what you do not want, (6) not being able to hold on to what you like, (7) not getting what you want, and (8) the all-pervasive suffering of conditioned existence. For a detailed presentation of the eight types of suffering, see Tsongkhapa, *Great Treatise*, 1:265–80.

640. *Meeting of Father and Son Sutra* (*Pitāputrasamāgamanasūtra*), Toh 60 Kangyur, dkon brtsegs, *nga,*, 62a4.

641. From this sentence and to the end of this section, including the citations of the *King of Meditations Sutra*, Tsongkhapa transcribes Candrakīrti's *Commentary* (275a7) with additional explanatory words interspersed.

642. Candrakīrti's *Commentary* (275b1) does not specify the exact source of this quote, and though Tsongkhapa identifies it as from the *King of Meditations Sutra*, I have been unable to locate this verse in the edition of the sutra in the Dergé Kangyur.

643. Nāgārjuna, *Mūlamadhyamakakārikā* 24.10, Toh 3824 Tengyur, dbu ma, *tsa*, 15a2.

644. Both this objection and the subsequent response are found in Candrakīrti's *Commentary* (275b4–7), and Tsongkhapa presents them here with some additional explanatory words inserted.

645. Vasubandhu, *Triṃśikā*, v. 22d, Toh 4055 Tengyur, sems tsam, *shi*, 2b5. Sthiramati's *Commentary on the Thirty Verses* interprets this line as stating that without *seeing* the ultimate nature, the dependent nature cannot be fully seen. Thus it's only the gnosis of the āryas, for whom all subject-object duality has ceased, that directly sees the truth of dependent nature. Both Candrakīrti and Tsongkhapa take this

statement in the *Thirty Verses* to indicate how Cittamātra accepts dependent nature as possessing intrinsic existence.

646. *Triśaṃvaranirdeśasūtra*, Toh 45 Kangyur, dkon brtsegs, *ka*, 94b. As identified in Tillemans (*How Do Mādhyamikas Think?*, 58), a similar passage is found in the Pali canon in Saṃyutta Nikāya III 22.94, where an important qualifier "the wise in the world" is found, making the text read: "A proponent of the Dhamma does not dispute with anyone in the world. Of that which the wise in the world agree upon as not existing, I too say it does not exist. And of that which the wise in the world agree upon as existing, I too say that it exists" (trans. Bodhi, *Connected Discourses*, 949).

647. *Śūnyatāsaptatikārikā*, v. 1, Toh 3827 Tengyur, dbu ma, *tsa*, 24a6.

648. This paragraph represents a close paraphrase from Candrakīrti's *Commentary* (276a5). This relates to an earlier challenge thrown against Madhyamaka by Cittamātra: "If you Mādhyamikas refute our intrinsically real consciousness, the dependent nature, we will then negate conventions that you accept as well." Candrakīrti responds to this by stating that since conventional truths are posited on the basis of worldly conventions, it is only within the framework of worldly conventions that they could be negated or affirmed. Such negation cannot be done from the standpoint of a philosophical system, including even his own Madhyamaka.

649. *Catuḥśatakaśāstra* 16.24, Toh 3846 Tengyur, dbu ma, *tsha*, 18a4.

650. *Daśabhūmikasūtra*, Toh 44 Kangyur, phal chen, *kha*, 220b4. The text of both the objection and the subsequent response presented here by Tsongkhapa are paraphrased from Candrakīrti's *Commentary* with only minor additions.

651. Ibid., 22b42.

652. *Mahāyānasaṃgraha*, Toh 4048 Tengyur, sems tsam, *ri*, 14a1.

653. *Viṃśatikāvṛtti*, Toh 4057 Tengyur, sems tsam, *shi*, 4a4.

654. *Laṅkāvatārasūtra*, Toh 107 Kangyur, mdo sde, *ca*, 164a2.

655. Literally "children of owl," Aulūkya (*'ug phrug*) refers to the proponents of the Indian Vaiśeṣika school, so called because they follow the teacher Ulūka, the "owl-like" sage. Digambaras, "the naked," are the proponents of the Indian Jaina school, in which nakedness is an important feature of the tradition's ascetic practice.

656. *Ratnāvalī* 1.62, Toh 4158 Tengyur, spring yig, *ge*, 109a4. These two stanzas from *Precious Garland* are cited also in Candrakīrti's *Commentary* (277b2). Nāgārjuna is stating that the teaching of emptiness, which transcends such duality of existence and nonexistence, is unique to the Buddha among the great teachers in India.

657. Although Tsongkhapa does not cite this as a direct quote from Candrakīrti's *Commentary* (277b4), this paragraph appears verbatim in that text. In his subcommentary, Jayānanda (204b5) interprets this passage as an elaboration on what Candrakīrti meant by the word *tīrthika*, as someone who propounds pernicious notions (*rtog pa ngan pa*) about substantial reality of things.

658. The Tibetan text here reads: *Dpe kha cig las sprong dkar po la sogs pa zhes kyang 'byung zhing.s.* Literally, it reads: "In some version of the text, the reading 'white *sprong*' is found as well." The term *sprong* is, as far as I know, meaningless in

Tibetan, and Tsongkhapa seems to be suggesting that it is a corrupt spelling of *spong* (pronounced *pong*), which means a renunciate.

659. *Madhyamakāvatāraṭīkā*, Toh 3870 Tengyur, dbu ma, *ra*. 204b7.

660. The reading provided here works only with the Tibetan word for buddha, *sangs rgyas*, which is composed of two syllables meaning, respectively, "awakened" and "blossomed." More accurately, especially in a manner that fits the Sanskrit term *buddha*, it should read something like the following: When the term *awakened one* (*buddha*) is used as an epithet for someone "whose mind has blossomed into suchness," the phrase "into suchness" (*de kho na nyid la*) is left implicit. This is to say that the full expression should be *tattva buddha* ("whose mind has blossomed in suchness"), yet the convention is to simply use the second part, *buddha*, while leaving the first part, *tattva*, implicit. Lodrö Rinchen (254) makes this exact observation based on listing two distinct meanings to the word *buddha*, "to awaken" and "to blossom or to realize."

661. *Daśabhūmikasūtra*, Toh 44 Kangyur, phal chen, *kha*, 228a3. Candrakīrti's *Commentary* cites extensively from the *Ten Grounds* presentation of the causal dynamics of the twelve links of dependent origination both in terms of the sequential order of origination and the reverse order of cessation.

662. Nāgārjuna, *Yuktiṣaṣṭikākārikā*, vv. 37–38, Toh 3825 Tengyur, dbu ma, *tsa*, 21b6.

663. Tsongkhapa is alluding here to the customary Abhidharma conception of the cosmos, which has the wind as its base with the remaining elements—fire, water, and earth—forming on top of each other. And it is from the "mandalas" of four elements that the entire world system comes into being. In such a cosmology, the heavenly realm of Akaniṣṭha is said to be the highest level of existence.

664. Candrakīrti's *Commentary* (279b5) too cites this stanza but, like Tsongkhapa here, does not identify its source.

665. *Commentary*, 268b7.

666. *Commentary*, 277b5.

667. Asaṅga, *Mahāyānasaṃgraha*, Toh 4048 Tengyur, sems tsam, *ri*, 9a6.

668. Tsongkhapa is citing these two fragments of sutra here exactly as they appear in Candrakīrti's *Commentary* (280b1), though neither provides the exact source. The statements are typical of those found in the Perfection of Wisdom sutras.

669. *Laṅkāvatārasūtra*, Toh 107 Kangyur, mdo sde, *ca*, 116a6.

670. Among the Buddhist schools, the Vaibhāṣika is well known for insisting that sensory cognitions perceive their objects "directly" without mediation by something called "aspect" or form (*ākāra*). Most Buddhist schools reject this view and maintain that sensory cognitions perceive their objects through mediation of such an aspect or likeness that cognition assumes.

671. *Lamp of Wisdom* (*Prajñāpradīpa*), Toh 5853 Tengyur, dbu ma, *tsa*, 245b2.

672. Tsongkhapa begins here an extensive exegesis of these two lines from the root text and their associated *Commentary*, weaving in both the text of Candrakīrti's own commentary on the line as well as the key passages from the *Descent into Laṅkā Sutra* and the *Unraveling the Intent Sutra*. In brief, based on a careful reading of the *Commentary*, Tsongkhapa identifies four types of statements from the *Unraveling the Intent Sutra* that require interpretation—those pertaining to (1) differentiation between dependent nature and imputed nature with respect to

636 *Illuminating the Intent*

their intrinsic nature or absence of intrinsic nature, (2) acceptance of foundation consciousness, (3) rejection of external reality, and (4) ultimacy of all three vehicles. The provisional nature of these four statements is demonstrated on the basis of one scripture, the *Descent into Laṅkā Sūtra*. For the benefit of the reader, I have numbered the sutra segments being demonstrated as provisional in parentheses.

673. *Saṃdhinirmocanasūtra*, chap. 7, Toh 106 Kangyur, mdo sde, *ca*, 21a4; and chap. 5, 13b7. *Commentary*, 22.1a4.

674. In the Cittamātra presentation of eight classes of consciousness, the first five are the five sensory consciousnesses, the sixth is mental consciousness, the seventh is the afflicted mental consciousness, and the eighth is the foundation consciousness. The last two are unique to the Cittamātra system. For a detailed presentation by Tsongkhapa of these last two classes of consciousness unique to Cittamātra, see Sparham, *Ocean Eloquence*.

675. This is the subtitle of Tsongkhapa's well-known *Essence of True Eloquence*. Tsongkhapa is not referring to a specific section of his text but is simply underlining the importance of appreciating the distinct interpretations of sutras like *Unraveling the Intent*, sutras that Cittamātra takes to be definitive and Candrakīrti's Prāsaṅgika takes to be provisional.

676. *Saṃdhinirmocanasūtra*, chap. 8, Toh 106 Kangyur, mdo sde, *ca*, 27a3. Cited in *Mahāyānasaṃgraha*, Toh 4048 Tengyur, sems tsam, *ri*, 14a2.

677. Tsongkhapa is probably speaking here of Śāntarakṣita and other Yogācāra-Madhyamaka thinkers who, while interpreting the teachings about foundation consciousness and the ultimacy of all three vehicles as provisional, accept the teachings on the three natures and on nonexistence of external reality as definitive. Candrakīrti does not make such distinctions but understands all four sutra segments of *Unraveling the Intent* as provisional teachings.

678. *Sūtrasamuccaya*, Toh 3934 Tengyur, dbu ma, *ki*, 188b6.

679. *Laṅkāvatārasūtra*, Toh 107 Kangyur, mdo sde, *ca*, 174a2.

680. *Commentary*, 27.1a6.

681. This is a reference to the *Commentary* passage quoted by Tsongkhapa above on page 382, where the text reads: "Likewise, there are statements such as . . ."

682. *Madhyamakāvatāraṭīkā*, Toh 3870 Tengyur, dbu ma, *ra*. 204b7.

683. *Commentary*, 28.1a6.

684. *Laṅkāvatārasūtra*, Toh 107 Kangyur, mdo sde, *ca*, 85b5.

685. Ibid., 86a3.

686. In Buddhist hermeneutics, a standard method employed in explaining a specific scriptural statement as provisional in meaning is to specify three important features of that particular statement: (1) its intended purport (*dgongs gzhi*)—that is, its actual intended point; (2) its purpose (*dgos pa*) for making that specific statement; and finally (3) what objections would follow if one were to adopt the literal meaning of the statement. See Lopez, *Buddhist Hermeneutics*, and Ruegg, "Purport, Implicature, and Presupposition."

687. Tsongkhapa is referring here to his own *Essence of True Eloquence*. For an English translation of the relevant section of that text, see Thurman, *Central Philosophy*, 347–52.

688. *Commentary*, 282a3; *Laṅkāvatārasūtra*, Toh 107 Kangyur, mdo sde, *ca*, 85b4.

689. *Commentary*, 282a4.

690. *Madhyamakāvatāraṭīkā*, Toh 3870 Tengyur, dbu ma, *ra*, 230b1.

691. *Ghanavyūhasūtra*, Toh 110 Kangyur, mdo sde, *cha*, 55b1.

692. *Laṅkāvatārasūtra*, Toh 107 Kangyur, mdo sde, *ca*, 143b6.

693. *Commentary*, 261b7.

694. This is a reference to the *Laṅkā Sutra* passage cited in a quote from the *Commentary* on page 386 above. See note 688.

695. *Laṅkāvatārasūtra*, Toh 107 Kangyur, mdo sde, *ca*, 85b5. In brief, Tsongkhapa identifies three distinct statements in the *Laṅkā Sutra*, each demonstrating the provisional nature of the first three segments of the *Unraveling the Intent Sutra*, which present (1) the notion of mind only with no external reality, (2) foundation consciousness, and (3) the intrinsic existence of dependent nature. The demonstration of the fourth statement, the ultimacy of all three vehicles, is only implied and not directly addressed.

696. Nāgārjuna, *Bodhicittavivaraṇa* verse 27, Toh 1801 Tengyur, rgyud 'grel, *ngi*, 39b1.

697. Tsongkhapa is probably referring here to the part where, immediately after presenting the core positions of Cittamātra, the text presents the final view of the Madhyamaka by way of critiquing Cittamātra (*Jñānasārasamuccaya*, Toh 3851 Tengyur, dbu ma, *tsha*, 27b3). Although the Tibetan tradition attributes the *Compendium of the Essence of Wisdom* to the Āryadeva who is the author of the famed *Four Hundred Stanzas*, given the explicit reference to the dispute over whether our sensory cognitions perceive their objects by way of bearing "aspects" (*ākāra*) of the objects, as well as the explicit listing of the key tenets of Cittamātra school, ascription of this work to Āryadeva is problematic at best.

698. Nāgārjuna, *Lokātītastava*, verse 5, Toh 1120 Tengyur, bstod tshogs, *ka*, 68b7.

699. Neither Candrakīrti nor Tsongkhapa identify the source sutra here. They just state that in the sutras, the meaning of impermanence is also explained in terms of the absence of intrinsic existence.

700. *Samādhirājasūtra*, Toh 127 Kangyur, mdo sde, *da*, 20b3. All these stanzas from *King of Meditations Sutra* cited by Tsongkhapa here in this section are found in Candrakīrti's *Commentary* as well.

701. Ibid., 104b1.

702. *Commentary*, 282b6; *Candraprabha* is an alternative name of the *King of Meditations Sutra*.

703. Tsongkhapa's *Essence of True Eloquence*. See Thurman, *Central Philosophy*, especially pages 253–64.

704. *Commentary*, 282b6.

705. *Mūlamadhyamakakārikā* 15.2, Toh 3824 Tengyur, dbu ma, *tsa*, 8b5.

706. *Commentary*, 282b6. For a translation of a slightly shorter paraphrase of this exact passage from *Commentary*, as found in Tsongkhapa's *Essence of Eloquence*, see Thurman, *Central Philosophy*, 361. These two paragraphs, separated by Nāgārjuna's quote, are notorious for being some of the most difficult and complex parts of Candrakīrti's commentary. Tsongkhapa reads the two, ostensibly, to respond to the question about whether Madhyamaka accepts the theory of three natures. Tsongkhapa addresses this question more extensively in his *Essence of Eloquence* (Thurman, *Central Philosophy*, 355–63), where he critically compares the theory

of three natures as presented in the *Unraveling the Intent Sutra* (as maintained by Cittamātra school) and a similar theory presented in the "Questions of Maitreya" chapter in the *Perfection of Wisdom in Eight Thousand Lines*.

707. *Commentary*, 282a3.

708. This is a chapter from the *Perfection of Wisdom in Eight Thousand Lines*. See note 706 above.

709. See Thurman, *Central Philosophy*, 355–63.

710. This "and so on" is a reference to the *Commentary* (283a3), where Candrakīrti explicitly lists the first six Jaina categories and indicates the remaining three with the words "and so on."

711. The argument that if something arises from itself, its arising from a cause would be meaningless was presented on page 198 above. The gist of the argument is this: The purpose of something arising is to enable an effect, which did not exist before, to come into being due to the activity of its cause. However, if things arise from themselves, this would imply that the thing in question would have already obtained its existent status at the time of its cause. In that case, causation would be pointless.

712. This entire paragraph presenting the Cārvāka account of how the entire world, both outer and inner, comes into being purely through the interaction of the four natural elements is reproduced here by Tsongkhapa from the *Commentary* (285b1), with only few explanatory expansions.

713. Both *Commentary* as well as Tsongkhapa's citation has the following line as *'jigs ma song ba ldog par mi 'gyur ro* ("What is not lost can never return"), which probably reflects a typographical error. I have read the line without the negative particle "not." This stanza, often invoked by opponents of Cārvāka school as an evidence of the school's alleged abject hedonism, is cited in Candrakīrti's *Commentary*, which is the source for Tsongkhapa. In Cowell and Gough, *Sarva-Darśana-Saṃgraha*, 2, translating from the well-known encyclopedia of Indian philosophy of Mādhava Vidyāranya, a similar Cārvāka passage is rendered as the following: "While life is yours, live joyously; / None can escape Death's searching eye: / When once this frame of ours they burn, / How shall it e'er again return?"

714. This stanza is cited in Candrakīrti's *Commentary* (185b3), which is the source for Tsongkhapa here. Bhāviveka too cites it in his *Lamp of Wisdom* (186b4) but also does not specify its exact source.

715. Tsongkhapa draws an important logical implication from Candrakīrti's response to the Cārvāka's possible rejoinder that the example cited by Candrakīrti—"Just as when one asserts self-existence of the elements, one views reality in a distorted manner"—does not work because the predicate "one views reality in a distorted manner" does not apply to it. The implication is that, even within our own Madhyamaka system, when we use a valid reasoning, the predicate must be something that can be established in the example. He then combines this point with an earlier statement of Candrakīrti (p. 343), where it was stated that the following is an instance of unestablished proof: *Sound* (subject) is *impermanent* (predicate), because it is *a visible object* (reasoning sign). From these two points, Tsongkhapa concludes that, even according to Candrakīrti, a correct proof statement must possess the three marks as defined in the system of Dignāga and Dharmakīrti.

Roughly stated, there are three elements to a syllogism—subject (A), predicate (B), and a reasoning sign or proof (C). The "three logical marks" (*trairūpya*) capture the logical relationship between these three elements represented in the following: A is C. If C then B, and if not B then not C, therefore A is B.

716. This way of extending the same argument presented in verse 102 above against the views that reject the possibility of buddhahood, based on modifying the wording of the first line, is actually suggested by Candrakīrti himself in *Commentary* (86b4). Responding to the opponent's charge that the Madhyamaka view too would be open to the same objection, Candrakīrti shows how in fact it's the exact opposite that will be true if one upholds the correct views pertaining to the afterlife and to omniscience.

717. *Commentary*, 287a2. Here Candrakīrti appears to be making a point about the possibility of the knowledge of all things (*sarvajñatā*) beyond the more specific point about the possibility of a buddha's omniscience (*sarvajñā*).

718. This entire paragraph represents a close paraphrase of Candrakīrti's *Commentary* (187a7), with few explanatory words interspersed by Tsongkhapa.

719. *Rice Seedling Sutra* (*Śālistambasūtra*), Toh 210, Kangyur, mdo sde, *tsha*, 116b2.

720. *Prajñāpāramitāsaṃcayagāthā*, Toh 13, shes phyin, *ka*, 16b2. Literal translation of the last line reads, "He will destroy the darkness of ignorance and attain self-origination." I have chosen to translate the word *rang 'byung* instead as "freedom," reading the phrase "self-origination" in the sense of self-mastery or mastery over one's own situation—that is, freedom from conditioned existence dictated by karma and afflictions.

721. This paragraph and the subsequent one, including the sutra citation in between, are reproduced here by Tsongkhapa from Candrakīrti's *Commentary* (288a7), with only a few explanatory words interspersed.

722. *Pitāputrasamāgamanasūtra*, Toh 60 Kangyur, dkon brtsegs, *nga*, 48b3.

723. Ibid., 50b1. "Druma" (Tib. *ljon pa*) is the name of the king of the Kinnaras, who is an interlocutor in the *Meeting of Father and Son Sutra*.

724. Drawing on Candrakīrti's rebuttal of the opponent's charge, if things do not possess arising by virtue of their intrinsic nature they will be no different from nonexistent things like the son of a barren woman, Tsongkhapa brings up the point that for a Mādhyamika like Candrakīrti, there has to be some criteria of conventional existence that could help differentiate between the existential status of objects of everyday experience and utterly nonexistent things like the son of a barren woman. For if conventional existence were defined purely in terms of being an object of an erroneous or deluded cognition, then even nonexistent things like the son of a barren woman, the horn of a rabbit, and so on would possess conventional existence.

725. *Ratnameghasūtra*, Toh 231 Kangyur, mdo sde, *wa*, 9b4.

726. *Abhidharmakośa* 6.4, Toh 4089 Tengyur, mngon pa, *ku*, 18b6.

727. Vasubandhu, *Abhidharmakośabhāṣya*, Tengyur, mngon pa, *khu*, 7b1.

728. All these possible metaphysical views about arising of things listed here are reproduced from Candrakīrti's *Commentary* (190b2). Theistic non-Buddhist Indian schools propose the view that it's Īśvara or God that is the cause of all things, with Vaiśeṣikas proposing indivisible atoms and Sāṃkhyas asserting primal substance

(*prakṛti*) to be this cause. The proponent of Nārāyaṇa as the cause, being referred to here, is probably the now vanished Indian school known as Ājīvikas, who are often referred to as the "worshipers of Nārāyaṇa."

729. *Story of Origins Sutra* (*Abhiniṣkramaṇasūtra*), Toh 301 Kangyur, mdo sde, *sa*, 85b3. In the Dergé edition of the canon, the first sentence reads, "Here are what are designated as phenomena" (*chos kyi brdar btags pa ni 'di yin te*).

730. *Ratnāvalī* 1.48, Toh 4158 Tengyur, spring yig, *ge*, 108b5.

731. *Mūlamadhyamakakārikā* 8.12–13, Toh 3824 Tengyur, dbu ma, *tsa*, 6a7.

732. *Yuktiṣaṣṭikākārikā*, v. 19, Toh 3825 Tengyur, dbu ma, *tsa*, 21a4. This stanza from *Sixty Verses* and the ones that follow from *Fundamental Wisdom* and from the sutra are all cited in Candrakīrti's *Commentary*.

733. *Mūlamadhyamakakārikā* 24.18, Toh 3824 Tengyur, dbu ma, *tsa*, 15a6. In the Dergé canonical edition of Nāgārjuna's *Fundamental Wisdom*, the third line reads slightly differently as "This too is dependently designated" (*de ni brten nas brtags pa ste*).

734. *Questions of Nāga King Anavatapta* (*Anavataptanāgarājaparipṛcchāsūtra*), Toh 156 Kangyur, mdo sde, *pha*, 230b2. Tsongkhapa cites this sutra as well as the subsequent one from *Laṅkā Sutra* and offers extensive explanations of these two important scriptural citations in his *Great Treatise* (trans. 3.188–89).

735. *Laṅkāvatārasūtra*, Toh 107 Kangyur, mdo sde, *ca*, 84b5; cited in *Prasannapadā*, chap. 24, Toh 3860 Tengyur, dbu ma, *'a*, 166b1.

736. *Catuḥśatakaśāstra* 16.23, Toh 3846 Tengyur, dbu ma, *tsha*, 18a4.

737. *Catuḥśatakaṭīkā*, chap. 16, Toh 3865 Tengyur, dbu ma, *ya*, 238a1.

738. *Madhyamakāloka*, Toh 3887 Tengyur, dbu ma, *sa*, 158a4. This passage appears in the context of commenting on an important quotation from the *Discourse for Kāśyapa* concerning the meaning of the phrase "the middle way." Kamalaśīla points out that if, as maintained by Cittamātra, there do exist ultimately real entities that are mental in nature, then viewing them in terms of permanence cannot constitute falling to an extreme view; ultimate existence would imply permanence. This would mean the sutra statement that to view in terms of "this is permanent" constitutes falling to the extreme of eternalism would be incorrect.

739. This paragraph, including the quote from Kamalaśīla, and the next two paragraphs appear verbatim in Tsongkhapa's earlier work, his commentary on Nāgārjuna's *Fundamental Stanzas on the Middle Way*. See Tsongkhapa, *Ocean of Reasoning* (trans.), 22–24. In brief, Tsongkhapa differentiates between two types of nihilistic extreme. The first is nihilism in the form of denigration, which involves denying what actually does exist, such as the denial of afterlife, karma and its effects, and so on. The second is nihilism in the form of reification—namely, absolutizing the negation of intrinsic existence. This latter is equivalent to grasping at emptiness as something ultimately real, absolute, and eternal, the prevention of which is the purpose behind the teaching on the emptiness of emptiness.

740. Tsongkhapa is saying that, in general, ultimate existence constitutes the extreme of existence according to Madhyamaka, and this is how such extreme is defined in the texts. Tsongkhapa says, however, that if one grasps at emptiness itself to have intrinsic existence, this would in fact constitute falling into a special kind of nihil-

ism, which he characterizes as falling into the extreme of nonexistence through reification.

741. Āryadeva, *Catuḥśatakaśāstra* 12.15, Toh 3846 Tengyur, dbu ma, *tsha*, 13b6.

742. *Yuktiṣaṣṭikākārikā* Verse 50, Toh 3825 Tengyur, dbu ma, *tsa*, 22a6. In the Dergé edition of *Sixty Stanzas* translated by Patsab, the first lines of the stanza reads: "For these great beings, / there is no position, no dispute; / ..." (*che ba'i bdag nyid can de dag / rnams la phyogs med rtsod pa med / ...*)

743. *Catuḥśatakaśāstra* 8.10, Toh 3846 Tengyur, dbu ma, *tsha*, 7b2.

744. *Samādhirājasūtra*, Toh 127 Kangyur, mdo sde, *da*, 69b3.

745. Tsongkhapa is referring here to the following statement in *Commentary*, 313a2: "From the line 'Not originating from itself' (MA 6.8) up to the line 'and engaging in analysis that one swiftly gains freedom' (MA 6.119), the text has made clear the selflessness of phenomena."

746. Tsongkhapa is referring to Nāgārjuna's *Dharmadhātustava*, v. 64, and Āryadeva's *Catuḥśatakaśāstra* 14.25, cited above on page 188.

747. *Śikṣāsamuccaya*, Toh 3940 Tengyur, dbu ma, *khi*, 132a7. The sutra quote is found at *Tathāgatacintyaguhyanirdeśasūtra*, Toh 47 Kangyur, dkon brtsegs, *ka*, 171a1.

748. *Ratnāvalī*, Toh 4158 Tengyur, spring yig, *ge*, 108a5.

749. Tsongkhapa cites this as it appears in Candrakīrti's *Commentary*, 292b7. Neither Candrakīrti nor Tsongkhapa identify its source. The citation is in fact stanza 3 of the *Sāṃkhya Verses* (*Sāṃkhyakārikā*) attributed to one Īśvarakṛṣṇa (ca. 350 CE). The stanza presents in a summary the Sāṃkhya ontology of twenty-five categories of reality: (1) primal substance (*prakṛti*), (2) intellect (*buddhi*), (3) I-maker (*ahaṃkāra*), (4–8) five sense objects, (9–13) four elements plus space, (14–18) five action faculties of speech, hands, legs, anus, and genitals, (19–23) five sense organs of eyes, ears, nose, tongue, tactile sense, (24) mental organ, and (25) person (*puruṣa*).

750. Tsongkhapa here uses "self" (*bdag*) and "person" (*skyes bu*) interchangeably to render the Sanskrit term *puruṣa*, which is effectively the Sāṃkhya equivalent of self (*atman*).

751. *Commentary*, 294b3.

752. Here is the syllogism embedded in Candrakīrti's lines: "The self postulated by the non-Buddhist schools" (*subject*) "does not exist as they conceive" (*probandum*) because "it is devoid of arising" (*logical reason*), like, for example, the son of a barren woman. For a standard syllogism to be valid, the logical reason must be established in the subject of the syllogism. For example, for "being a product" to be a logical proof to establish an earthen jar as "impermanent," the proof itself must be first establishable in the subject—namely, the earthen jar. To not do so would entail what is known as "the fallacy of non-establishment." Tsongkhapa is making the point that in certain types of argument, where both the logical reason and the probandum are mere negations, it's not necessary for the logical reason to be established in the stated subject of the syllogism. This is particularly true when refuting metaphysical postulations that have no reality even on the conventional level. The issue here relates to the larger debate within classical Indian logic and epistemology on the validity or invalidity of forms of logical proof where nonexistent entities are taken as subjects of syllogism. Tsongkhapa takes up this

debate extensively in a later unfinished work, his commentary on Śāntarakṣita's *Ornament of the Middle Way*, based on his analysis of the text's opening syllogism refuting the postulations of non-Buddhists and Buddhist essentialist schools. For a study of Tsongkhapa's treatment of this question, based on Alaksha Tendar Lharam's (1756–1840) interpretation, see Tillemans and Lopez, "What Can One Reasonably Say about Nonexistence?"

753. *Ngo bo dang khyad par rnams bsal bar rig par bya'o.* Although the critical Tibetan edition as well as standard versions of Tsongkhapa's collected works have the penultimate verb of this sentence as "illuminate" (*gsal bar*), matching the Dergé edition of the *Commentary*, I have corrected it to read as "eliminate" (*bsal bar*), choosing the reading found in the Peking and Narthang Tengyur editions of the *Commentary*.

754. Tsongkhapa is referring here to the influential idea of Dharmakīrti that, from a logical point of view, there are only two kinds of invariable relations between two things: a causal relation (*tadutpatti*), such as between a fire and smoke, and an identity relation (*tādātmya*), such as between "being an oak" and "being a tree," which allows correct inference to take place.

755. *Mūlamadhyamakakārikā* 27.07, Toh 3824 Tengyur, dbu ma, *tsa*, 18a2.

756. Ibid. 18.1, 10a6.

757. This sutra quote is cited in Candrakīrti's *Commentary*, 295b6. Neither Candrakīrti nor Tsongkhapa identifies the source. The same quote is also cited in the ninth chapter of Vasubandhu's *Commentary on the Treasury of Abhidharma*. For a translation and study of this important chapter from Vasubandhu's text, which contains a lengthy treatment of the views of Vātsīputrīyas, see Duerlinger, *Indian Buddhist Theories of Persons*.

758. *Collection of Aphorisms* (*Udānavarga*) 23.14, Toh 326 Kangyur, mdo sde, *sa*, 229b4. In the Dergé edition of the canon, the third line reads, "He who has become his own savior" (*bdag nyid bdag gi mgon gyur pa'i*).

759. Ibid. 31.1cd, 243a1.

760. Bhāviveka, *Tarkajvālā*, Toh 3856 Tengyur, dbu ma, *dza*, 80b4; critical edition, 113.

761. *Commentary*, 296a4.

762. Cited also in the *Commentary*, 296a6. Neither Candrakīrti nor Tsongkhapa provides the source.

763. In other words, for these schools (unlike for the Madhyamaka), the aggregates are substantially real, and so to identify the self with them would render the self substantially real as well, though as he goes on to note, the scriptures of this school say that the self, or person, is a mere designation.

764. This sutra quote is cited in the *Commentary* (296a7) as well as in Vasubandhu's *Commentary on the Treasury of Abhidharma*, but neither identifies the sutra.

765. This is cited in Candrakīrti's *Commentary* (296b1) without naming the source, and Tsongkhapa cites it in his *Essence of True Eloquence* as "from the Śrāvaka scriptures" (*nyan thos kyi sde snod las*). What appears in the *Bhikkhunisaṃyutta* in the Pali *Saṃyutta Nikāya* as verse 554 of the collection appears to be the scriptural source. See Bhikkhu Bodhi, *Connected Discourses*, 220.

766. This paragraph is a gloss on Candrakīrti's *Commentary* (296b2) with a few explan-

atory words added by Tsongkhapa. In essence, it says that just as perceptions of blue or yellow color are not distorted cognitions for these Buddhist schools— they are veridical cognitions in that what they perceive does exist as real—the identity view would also be an undistorted mental state. Now if identity view is undistorted, then when Buddhist teachings speak of its elimination, this can be understood only in terms of relinquishing one's *attachment* to identity view, not in terms of eliminating the view itself. It is akin to relinquishing one's attachment to blue color, since it makes no sense to speak of eliminating the blue color itself.

767. Cited in *Commentary*, 296b6. Candrakīrti is here probably referring to the Buddha telling the story of himself as King Māndhātṛ or Māndhātā, as found in chapter 6 of the *Basis of Discipline* (*Vinayavastu*, Toh 1 Kangyur, 'dul ba, *kha*, starting on 169b6).

768. *Mūlamadhyamakakārikā* 27.6, Toh 3824 Tengyur, dbu ma, *tsa*, 18a1.

769. Ibid. 18.1, 10b6.

770. Candrakīrti is pointing out that the opponent's views would have the undesirable consequence of violating two basic norms of the theory of karma, which are (1) a person never reaps the result of a karma not created by himself, and (2) karma once accumulated never disintegrates owing to the mere passage of time.

771. Nāgārjuna, *Mūlamadhyamakakārikā* 27.10–11, Toh 3824 Tengyur, dbu ma, *tsa*, 18a3.

772. Ibid. 27.16, 18a6.

773. These fourteen views pertaining to the "unanswered questions" (*lung du ma bstan pa*) all relate to metaphysical questions pertaining to the beginning or end of the world and to the identity relation between body and the self. These are questions the Buddha refused to either affirm or deny. Candrakīrti's formulates these the same way Vasubandhu does in his *Commentary on the Treasury of Abhidharma* (5.22). Vasubandhu situates these in the context of four types of answers the Buddha gives in response to questions: (1) answering categorically in a straightforward manner, (2) answering through qualifying one's response, (3) asking counter questions, and (4) leaving the question unanswered. The Theravada tradition, based on the *Connected Discourses* (*Saṃyutta Nikāya*) 44, lists ten instead of fourteen unanswered questions, these being as follows: Is the world eternal? Is it not eternal? Is it finite? Is it not finite? Is the body same as the self? Is the body one thing and the self another? Does the Tathāgata exist after death? Does he not exist after death? Is it both? Is it neither?

774. This paragraph together with the analogy of a bird feeding on a flower is a gloss on the *Commentary*, 298b2. The texts of both the *Commentary* and Tsongkhapa's gloss here are quite dense, and the lines of argument difficult to follow. The gist of the argument is this: Just as the presence of a bird feeding on a lotus stamen is incidentally connected to its taste being sweet, belief in the existence of a permanent self as conceived by the non-Buddhist schools is merely incidental to the arising of afflictive emotions like attachment. Furthermore, if the absence of a permanent self alone is what the yogi with the wisdom of no-self has realized, such a yogi as understood by the essentialist Buddhist schools will continue to experience the arising of afflictions. There will also be no means available to such a yogi to eliminate attachment and other afflictions, since insight into selflessness

remains the only means and, according to the Buddhist essentialists, absence of a permanent self exhausts the meaning of selflessness. In that case, the yogi who has realized selflessness according to these Buddhist essentialist schools will be no different from the non-Buddhist yogis who have attained mere temporary respite from attachment and other afflictions.

775. This sutra quote was cited earlier. See page 429.

776. This stanza is cited in Candrakīrti's *Commentary* (299b3) as well, but no source is given. The first line is a well-known line found in the *Dhammapada* and in *Collection of Aphorisms* (*Udānavarga*, 23.14a), but the source for rest of the stanza remains unidentified.

777. *Collection of Aphorisms* (*Udānavarga*) 23.14cd, Toh 326 Kangyur, mdo sde, *sa*, 229b4. The entire verse was cited above on page 432.

778. See page 437 above.

779. This second stanza was cited above on page 432. See note 765. Both stanzas are cited also in Vasubandhu's *Commentary on the Treasury of Abhidharma* (*Abhidharmakośabhāṣya*), chap. 9, 86a6.

780. Nāgārjuna, *Mūlamadhyamakakārikā* 10.11, Toh 3824 Tengyur, dbu ma, *tsa*, 6b6.

781. Ibid., 10.15, 7a6.

782. Ibid., 8.13, 6a4.

783. Candrakīrti, *Prasannapadā*, Toh 3860 Tengyur, dbu ma, '*a*. 64b4.

784. This passage concerning technical grammatical issues about the meaning of the word *upādāna* (Tib. *nye bar len pa*), which I have rendered as "appropriation," is an almost verbatim reproduction of a passage from the *Commentary* (300b4).

785. Nāgārjuna, *Mūlamadhyamakakārikā* 10.11, Toh 3824 Tengyur, dbu ma, *tsa*, 6b6.

786. This sutra passage was not located in the Kangyur. The quote is cited here as it appears in Candrakīrti's *Commentary* (301a1); Tsongkhapa also cites this in his *Essence of True Eloquence*, where he says it comes from Vasubandhu's *Rules of Exposition* (*Vyākhyāyukti*); see note 788 below.

787. *Dependent Origination's First Division Sutra* (*Pratītyasamutpādasūtra*), Toh 211 Kangyur, mdo sde, *tsha*, 123b4.

788. *Vyākhyāyukti*, Toh 4061 Tengyur, sems tsam, *shi*, 109b4.

789. *Pitāputrasamāgamanasūtra*, Toh 60 Kangyur, dkon brtsegs, *nga*, 127b3.

790. Extending the same four possibilities of relationship—of (1) identity, (2) ownership, (3) being located in, and (4) being the locus—to the remaining four aggregates gives the number twenty.

791. Nāgārjuna, *Mūlamadhyamakakārikā* 22.1, Toh 3824 Tengyur, dbu ma, *tsa*, 13a3.

792. Cited in the *Commentary* (302b5) as well, but the source sutra remains unidentified.

793. Although the root text speaks of only of negating the aggregates as the support of self, the *Commentary* (303b5) explicitly mentions the need to negate both self as the support of the aggregates and vice versa, as read here by Tsongkhapa.

794. This paragraph as well as the subsequent question and response appear in Candrakīrti's *Commentary* (304a6). The "further objection" seems to be that if the shape is what actually constitutes the chariot, then there will be no chariot beyond the mere shape. And if there is no chariot that is the whole or the bearer of the chariot

parts, the chariot parts too can have no existence. Hence the suggestion that shape is the chariot is illogical.

795. *Commentary*, 105b5.

796. *Commentary*, 106b1.

797. Nāgārjuna, *Mūlamadhyamakakārikā* 18.1, Toh 3824 Tengyur, dbu ma, *tsa*, 10b1. The same verse was cited above on page 433.

798. The "four attributes" are permanence, impermanence, both, and neither.

799. Nāgārjuna, *Mūlamadhyamakakārikā* 22.12, Toh 3824 Tengyur, dbu ma, *tsa*, 13b2. The other two, included in the words "and so on," are that the Tathāgata is *both* permanent and impermanent and *neither* permanent nor impermanent.

800. This sutra quote is found also in Candrakīrti's *Commentary* (308a2), which is the source for Tsongkhapa here. Neither Candrakīrti nor Tsongkhapa identifies the source sutra.

801. Nāgārjuna, *Mūlamadhyamakakārikā* 18.4, Toh 3824 Tengyur, dbu ma, *tsa*, 10b7.

802. In Tsongkhapa's text, the last two lines of verse 167 are extracted here rather than after all four lines of stanza 6.166 are explained. In his *Commentary* (308a1 and 4) too, Candrakīrti cites these two lines of stanza 167 as part of his commentary on both stanzas 166 and 167.

803. Tib. *shing rta phran*.

804. *Triśaṃvaranirdeśasūtra*, Toh 45 Kangyur, dkon brtsegs, *ka*, 94b. This quote already appeared above; see note 646.

805. "Logical fallacy" (*jāti* in Sanskrit and *ltag chod* in Tibetan) refers to specific types of flaws identified in classical Indian logic of debate, such as in chapter 6 of Dignāga's *Compendium of Valid Cognition* (*Pramāṇasamuccaya*). The one being charged against the Madhyamaka by the opponent is the one known as *kārya samā* (*'bras mtshungs kyi ltag chod*), where the objection raised against one's opponent equally applies to one's own position.

806. *Commentary*, 311a1.

807. *Vigrahavyāvartanī*, Toh 3828 Tengyur, dbu ma, *tsa*, 28a1.

808. *Perfection of Wisdom in Eighteen Thousand Lines* (*Aṣṭadaśasāhasrikāprajñāpāramitā*), Toh 10 Kangyur, shes phyin, *ka*, 234a3.

809. Āryadeva, *Catuḥśatakaśāstra* 16.25, Toh 3846 Tengyur, dbu ma, *tsha*, 18a5.

810. Nāgārjuna, *Mūlamadhyamakakārikā* 4.8, Toh 3824 Tengyur, dbu ma, *tsa*, 3b7.

811. Candrakīrti raises this objection in the *Commentary* (311b7), where he prefaces it with the phrase "Some say . . ." Tsongkhapa identifies it to be Bhāviveka but does not provide an exact source. One would expect to find it in Bhāviveka's *Lamp of Wisdom*, his commentary on Nāgārjuna's *Fundamental Wisdom*, but I was unable to locate it there.

812. This entire paragraph is a recapitulation of Candrakīrti's *Commentary* (312a4), with only a few explanatory words added by Tsongkhapa.

813. Once again Tsongkhapa is drawing our attention to an important point he wishes to emphasize throughout his exposition of Candrakīrti—namely, that the master does not reject valid logical argument that can lead to genuine inference. The form of logical argument Tsongkhapa has in mind here is this: A *sprout* [subject] is *devoid of intrinsic existence* [probandum] because it is *dependently originated* [logical reason], just like the reflection of a face in a mirror [*example*]. Tsongkhapa

is pointing out here that, even according to Candrakīrti, the inference that a sprout lacks intrinsic existence based on the reason that it is dependently originated can only take place after the entailment has been established between the logical reason and the probandum in relation to an example, which is agreed upon by both parties in the discourse.

814. This paragraph as well as the preceding one closely mirrors the text of Candrakīrti's *Commentary* (312b4), with only few explanatory words added.

815. Both Candrakīrti's *Commentary* and Tsongkhapa's interpretation agree on the "remaining refutation" as referring to the analysis of whether a cause comes into contact with its effect, which was presented in 6.169–70. Rendawa's commentary (*Lamp Illuminating Suchness*, 273) identifies the phrase "what has been said above" as referring to the extensive refutation of intrinsic arising by means of rejecting arising from any of the four possibilities—from self, from other, from both, and no cause—presented earlier in the sixth chapter. Thus he characterizes the particular refutation, of analyzing in terms of whether the cause comes into contact with its effect, to be a further refutation presented by Candrakīrti.

816. This passage is found in the *Perfection of Wisdom in Twenty-Five Thousand Lines* (*Pañcaviṃśatisāhasrikāprajñāpāramitā*), Toh 9 Kangyur, shes phyin, *ka*, 221a7.

817. Ibid., 223b4.

818. Nāgārjuna, *Mūlamadhyamakakārikā* 13.8, Toh 3824 Tengyur, dbu ma, *tsa*, 8a6.

819. Ibid. 22.11, 13a1.

820. *Commentary*, 314a3.

821. The error in Patsab's translation, according to Tsongkhapa, lies in the final sentence of the quoted passage. The text should read thus: "An intrinsically existent entity must, without doubt, be eternal and something that will cease to exist."

822. On the question of locating Naktso's translation of both *Entering the Middle Way* and the *Commentary*, see note 217 above.

823. Jayānanda, *Madhyamakāvatāraṭīkā*, Toh 3870 Tengyur, dbu ma, *ra*, 288b4.

824. See, for example, *Perfection of Wisdom in Eighteen Thousand Lines* (*Aṣṭadaśasāhasrikāprajñāpāramitā*), Toh 10 Kangyur, shes phyin, *ka*, 144a2.

825. Haribhadra, *Commentary on the Perfection of Wisdom in Twenty-Five Thousand Lines* (*Pañcaviṃśatisāhasrikāprajñāpāramitāṭīkā*), Toh 3790 Tengyur, shes phyin, *ga*, 215–217a, provides a gloss on each of the sixteen kinds of emptiness, extending to each these two lines "because they do no abide eternally" and "because they do not disintegrate." In each class of emptiness, Haribhadra formulates the reasoning in the following: "Because they do not abide eternally, and because they do not disintegrate, eyes are devoid of eyes. Why? Because this is their true nature."

826. Nāgārjuna, *Mūlamadhyamakakārikā* 15.1–2, Toh 3824 Tengyur, dbu ma, *tsa*, 8b4. These stanzas are cited also in Candrakīrti's *Commentary*.

827. *Commentary*, 314a5. Here there is an important equation made between the following terms: "ultimate nature" (*chos nyid*), "intrinsic nature" (*rang bzhin*), "that which is not fabricated and not dependent on other producers" (*bcos ma ma yin pa dang skyed byed gzhan la ltos pa med pa*), and "reality" (*ngo bo*). They all refer to emptiness, and such intrinsic nature of the ultimate nature of things does exist.

828. Tsongkhapa is here critiquing earlier Tibetan commentators of Candrakīrti, some of whom make these assertions. The first type of assertion involves read-

ing Candrakīrti's views on emptiness as a form of agnosticism with respect to the question of ultimate truth. In contrast, the second type of assertion relates to questions of soteriology and has to do with whether or not the entire continuum of cognition ceases when all afflictions and obscurations of ignorance are cleansed. See my introduction.

829. This paragraph is a gloss on Candrakīrti's *Commentary*, 314a7, with few additional phrases and words from Tsongkhapa.

830. *Ratnameghasūtra*, Toh 231 Kangyur, mdo sde, *wa*, 99a4. This entire sutra passage is cited in the *Commentary* (314b1) as well.

831. Tsongkhapa is pointing out that there is no difference at all between "nonexistence" (*med pa*) and "not being existent" (*yod pa ma yin pa*). So if someone says that the ultimate truth is not existent, they will be saying that it is nonexistent. Here he has in mind possibly those Tibetans who uphold what is referred to as the "not existent and not nonexistent view" (*yod min med min gyi lta ba*).

832. Tsongkhapa is referring to the quote from the *Cloud of Jewels Sutra* cited above on page 491.

833. This hypothetical objection and its response are adapted from Candrakīrti's *Commentary* (314b5) with only few additional explanatory words from Tsongkhapa. At the heart of Candrakīrti's response to the charge of possible contradiction is a distinction between two senses of the term *intrinsic nature* (*svabhāva*). In the context of negating intrinsic nature, *svabhāva* is an essence—something independent, self-defining, and unique—by virtue of which things are thought to obtain their existence. In the second sense, *svabhāva* is simply emptiness, which is nothing but the absence of intrinsic existence and things' ultimate mode of being. For this distinction and its implications, especially as understood by Tsongkhapa, see Jinpa, *Self, Reality and Reason*, 93–104.

834. This entire paragraph is reproduced from Candrakīrti's *Commentary*, 315a2, with only few additional words from Tsongkhapa.

835. This is a reference to Patsab's translation of Candrakīrti's autocommentary.

836. Nāgārjuna, *Dharmadhātustava*, v. 22, Toh 1118 Tengyur, bstod tshogs, *ka*, 64b2.

837. Nāgārjuna, *Lokātītastava*, v. 21, Toh 1120 Tengyur, bstod tshogs, *ka*, 69b1.

838. What Tsongkhapa has in mind here are probably the views, respectively, of the Tibetan logician Chapa Chökyi Sengé and Dölpopa, the latter a key thinker of the Jonang school. Dölpopa is known for his advocacy of a cataphatic or affirmative approach to defining what ultimate truth is and for his criticism of what he saw as nihilistic interpretations of Indian Madhyamaka masters like Candrakīrti. Chapa, on the other hand, is an enthusiastic advocate of the apophatic or *via negativa* approach to defining emptiness, arguing that mere negation of true existence constitutes the ultimate truth and the final truth of the Buddha's teaching on emptiness. Being an upholder of the so-called Svātantrika subdivision of Madhyamaka school, as opposed to Candrakīrti's Prāsaṅgika, there is a way to read Chapa as arguing that emptiness possesses a kind of intrinsic existence.

839. *Samādhirājasūtra*, Toh 127 Kangyur, mdo sde, *da*, 27a1.

840. There is an allusion here to the phrase "from form to a buddha's omniscience," which refers to a well-known enumeration of 108 items used in Mahayana sources such as *Ornament of Realizations* as a way of speaking of all phenomena. The list

consists of two classes of phenomena, those of unenlightened existence (fifty-three items) and those of the enlightened stage (fifty-five items). It begins with the five aggregates, thus with the aggregate of form, and ends with three types of knowledge, with a buddha's omniscience being the final item on the list.

841. Source unidentified.

842. The five hindrances to meditative attainment are (1) sensory desire, (2) ill will, (3) sloth and torpor, (4) excitation and remorse, and (5) doubt.

843. In brief, Candrakīrti (*Commentary* 317b7) describes the eight liberating factors (*rnam thar brgyad, aṣṭavimokṣa*) as the following: (1) a physical being viewing physical forms, (2) viewing a physical form with a perception of form inside, (3) viewing an appealing form and belonging to the third concentration level, (4–7) the four formless absorptions, and (8) the meditative attainment of the cessation of feeling and discrimination. The classification of these eight liberating factors functionally into three categories—the path of antidotes, the path that accords with liberation, and the path of abiding in peace—is not found in Candrakīrti's *Commentary*. Tsongkhapa is likely introducing this from the commentarial tradition on Maitreya's *Ornament of Realizations*, where the eight are organized around these three functions. A slightly different presentation of the eight liberating factors can be found in Vasubandhu's *Treasury of Abhidharma* (8.32–33).

844. Both the *Commentary* and Tsongkhapa's text contains this phrase "to be explained below," referring to 11.28–30. The ten powers of the buddha are the powers of knowing (1) what is correct and what is incorrect, (2) the effects of karma, (3) diverse domains of aspiration, (4) multitudes of world systems, (5) superior and inferior mental faculties, (6) all the paths of transmigration, (7) both enlightenment and afflicted states of existence, (8) past lives, (9) death and rebirth, and (10) the cessation of pollutants. For a detailed explanation of each of these ten powers in Asaṅga's *Bodhisattva Grounds*, see Engle, *Bodhisattva Path*, 622–39.

845. Non-Mahayana sources appear to identify "the eighteen unshared attributes of the Buddha" differently. For example, in chapter 7 of the *Treasury of Abhidharma*, Vasubandhu identifies the eighteen as the ten powers of the Buddha's mind, plus the four perfect knowledges of specific domains and the four fearlessnesses.

846. The entire section of the *Dhāraṇīśvararājaparipṛcchāsūtra* describing the eighteen unshared attributes of the Buddha is cited in Candrakīrti's *Commentary* (391a1). Though well known in the Tibetan tradition—for example, Tsongkhapa cites its famous analogy of washing clothes with cleansing agents to gradually eliminate the pollutants on the path—the sutra itself is not found in any existing editions of the Kangyur. However, a very similar presentation of the eighteen unshared attributes can be found in the *Definite Teaching on the Tathāgata's Great Compassion Sutra* (*Tathāgatamahākaruṇanirdeśasūtra*, Toh 147 Kangyur, mdo sde, *pa*, 205b4).

847. See the discussion on pages 75–79 on the distinction between a bodhisattva outshining śrāvakas and pratyekabuddhas through the power of his lineage, which is through the conventional awakening mind, versus outshining them through the power of his wisdom. As stated in the line "When at Gone Afar, he will also surpass them with his intelligence" (1.8d), this second form of outshining takes place

for the bodhisattva only at the seventh level. Hence the statement "Advancing further, he will also outshine them through his wisdom."

848. *Daśabhūmikasūtra*, Toh 44 Kangyur, phal chen, *kha*, 234b1.

849. See, for example, page 107.

850. Tsongkhapa is referring to the final four of the *ten* perfections, the perfections of (7) skillful means, (8) aspiration, (9) power, and (10) gnosis, which all follow the perfection of wisdom and are correlated with the final four of the ten bodhisattva grounds. They are defined in terms of the "specific facets" or dimensions of the perfection of wisdom.

851. *Bodhisattvabhūmi*, Toh 4037 Tengyur, sems tsam, *wi*, 228a7; Engle, *Bodhisattva Path*, 436–37.

852. *Daśabhūmikasūtra*, Toh 44 Kangyur, phal chen, *kha*, 242a1. This and the two subsequent citations from the *Ten Grounds Sutra* are quoted exactly in Candra-kīrti's *Commentary* as well.

853. Ibid., 240b3.

854. Ibid., 241a7.

855. Ibid., 306b7.

856. *Śrīmālādevī*, Toh 92 Kangyur, dkon brtsegs, *cha*, 264b7.

857. *Daśabhūmikasūtra*, Toh 44 Kangyur, phal chen, *kha*, 45a5–b3. Numbers in parentheses have been added to assist the reader.

858. Abhayākaragupta, *Munimatālaṃkāra*, Toh 3903 Tengyur, dbu ma, *a*, 254b3. Although Tsongkhapa's text has the phrase "ten types of power" (*stobs bcu*), unless there is a way of grouping these powers to make the overall number ten, this is a scribal error. The text should probably read "thirteen types of power" (*stobs bcu gsum*) instead. Abhayākara himself does not number these powers; the numbers have been added by the translator.

859. *Commentary*, 307b3.

860. *Daśabhūmikasūtra*, Toh 44 Kangyur, phal chen, *kha*, 262a2.

861. Asaṅga, *Bodhisattvabhūmi*, Toh 4037 Tengyur, sems tsam, *wi*, 191a6; Engle, *Bodhisattva Path*, 602.

862. "Countless" (*grangs med*) is a numerical unit defined in the Abhidharma system as equivalent to 10^{59}.

863. When birth in cyclic existence is counted in terms of five realms of existence, birth as a hungry ghost is included within the realm of birth as animals.

864. *Daśabhūmikasūtra*, Toh 44 Kangyur, phal chen, *kha*, 274a4.

865. Tsongkhapa is pointing out the first line as it appears in Patsab's translation of the root text, *gang phyir nam mkha' dri ma med la zla snang gsal bar 'gyur ba'i phyir*, should be modified to read *ji ltar nam mkha dri ma med la zla snang gsal bar nus pa bzin*.

866. Tsongkhapa is saying that it is a teaching of the Sutra or Perfection Vehicle that while an already enlightened buddha might display the deed of enlightenment in the desire realm, such as the Buddha did under the Bodhi tree, one can first attain full enlightenment only in Akaniṣṭha, the highest heaven of the form realm. According to Vajrayāna, however, buddhahood can be attained even in the desire realm.

867. Tsongkhapa is here referring to the phrase "as it were" in the second line. He is

saying that Naktso's version, which does not contain this, gives a more straightforward statement, instead of suggesting a more figurative sense of knowing suchness.

868. *Commentary*, 330b2.

869. Jñānagarbha, *Commentary on the Differentiation of the Two Truths (Satyadvayavibhaṅgavṛtti)*, Toh 3882 Tengyur, dbu ma, *sa*, 14b6. For an alternative translation, see Eckel, *Jñānagarbha's Commentary*, 102.

870. See, for example, Tsongkhapa's *Ocean of Reasoning*, 243a9 (trans., 490–93).

871. Maitreya, *Uttaratantra*, 1.93, Toh 4024 Tengyur, sems tsam, *phi*, 55b5.

872. Asaṅga, *Commentary on Sublime Continuum (Uttaratantravyākhyā)*, Toh 4025 Tengyur, sems tsam, *phi*, 105b7.

873. Jñānagarbha, *Differentiation of the Two Truths (Satyadvayavibhaṅga)*, v. 37, Toh 3881 Tengyur, dbu ma, *sa*, 3a5.

874. Ibid., v. 39, 3a5.

875. Tsongkhapa is here chiming in, once again, on the long-standing debate among Tibetan scholars on the question of whether gnosis exists at the level of buddhahood—whether the buddha possesses anything comparable to the mind. For a brief discussion of this question by Sakya Paṇḍita, see the translation of his *Clarifying the Sage's Intent*, 573–77.

876. Tsongkhapa's point is that when, in 6.23, a definition of ultimate truth was provided in terms of "what is found by a rational cognition seeing the perfect truth," this definition was from the perspective of unenlightened beings. A buddha's mind, being omniscient, directly perceives both ultimate truth and the conventional truth of the world of multiplicity, so the definition requires a second component—"with respect to which its cognition constitutes such valid rational cognition." In other words, although the buddha's gnosis pertaining to the way things really are, being omniscient, does perceive conventional truth, it is only in relation to ultimate truth that such gnosis is defined as such.

877. See page 357.

878. *Vajracchedikā*, Toh 16 Kangyur, shes phyin, *ka*, 131b1.

879. This is cited in Candrakīrti's *Commentary* (332a1), where the source sutra is not named.

880. This is *Avaivartacakrasūtra*, Toh 240 Tengyur, mdo sde, *zha*. Lodrö Rinchen appeared to have cited Naktso's passage Tsongkhapa is referring to here, but unfortunately the page containing this specific sutra citation is missing in the current available version of his *Light on the Principles* commentary on *Entering the Middle Way*.

881. *Prasannapadā*, Toh 3860 Tengyur, dbu ma, *'a*, 120a3.

882. *Commentary*, 332a3.

883. Candrakīrti, *Triśaraṇasaptati*, Tengyur, dbu ma, *gi*, 251a4.

884. Jambudvīpa is the southern continent surrounding Mount Meru in ancient Indian cosmology according which there is a specific continent in each of the four cardinal directions of the great mountain. Deriving its name from the *jambu* tree, this continent is the closest correlate to our world, earth.

885. Tsongkhapa is distinguishing here between two distinct ways, spatial and temporal, in which the comparison to atoms is being made. In the first, a buddha as part of his enlightened activity, which engages as if by mere wish, can display the entire

universe within the space of a single atom; in the second example, the infinity of a buddha's enlightened activities that can occur in a single moment of time is unmatched by the number of atoms in the universe.

886. Once a person has reached the path of seeing, at the most, he is said to take rebirth through karma only seven times. That there will be no eighth rebirth is definite. So to state that such a person will have an eighth rebirth through karma would be incorrect and contrary to what is true.

887. The twenty-two faculties (*indriya*) are referred to in the opening of chapter 2 of Vasubandhu's *Treasury of Abhidharma*. See Chim Jampaiyang, *Ornament of Abhidharma*, 175: "the faculties of eye, ear, nose, tongue, body, mental faculty, female, male, life force, pleasure, pain, mental satisfaction, mental dissatisfaction, equanimity, faith, effort, mindfulness, concentration, wisdom, producing complete knowledge of the unknown, complete knowledge, and possessing complete knowledge."

888. This is the seventh power named above on page 547 as "the power to know meditative absorptions, liberating factors, concentrations, meditative attainments, and so on."

889. *Commentary*, 342b4. This citation appeared above as well as part of a larger quote; see page 285.

890. *Commentary*, 342b6.

891. *Commentary*, 342b7.

892. *Madhyamakāvatāra* 11.40a: "Through his power of omniscience, a buddha can know."

893. Tsongkhapa is referring here possibly to *Yuktiṣaṣṭikāvṛtti* (Toh 3864 Tengyur, dbu ma, *ya*), 9a3, where it reads: "Others define cognitions of blueness that perceive aspects concordant with their objects, which are unique particulars, as direct perceptions (*pratyakṣa*). The cognition [we are speaking of here] too has such a characteristic, so there is no contradiction in acknowledging that this is an instance of direct perception." Candrakīrti accepts the epistemological theory that proposes that when sensory consciousnesses directly perceive objects, they do so by assuming an aspect (*ākāra*) resembling the form of the object. If this is so, since implicit knowledge cannot be attributed to a buddha's omniscience, whatever a buddha perceives must be perceived by way of aspects of the objects.

894. "Eleven grounds" refer to, in addition to the ten bodhisattva grounds (the ten causal grounds) the resultant of ground of buddhahood.

895. Jayānanda, *Madhyamakāvatāraṭīkā*, Toh 3870 Tengyur, dbu ma, *ra*, 352b3. Tsongkhapa is commenting here on two slightly different Tibetan translations of one and the same phrase in the root text, as *gyo bag can* ("indulging in devious behavior") or as *sna tsogs spyod can* ("indulging in varied behavior").

896. This is cited in Candrakīrti's *Commentary*, 345a2, the likely source for Tsongkhapa's citation here. Neither source identifies the sutra.

897. *Praise to the Peerless One* (*Nirupamastava*), Toh 1119 Tengyur, bstod tshogs, *ka*, 68a7.

898. This story of the skillful means used by a wise captain is found in *Saddharmapuṇḍarīka*, Toh 1405, mdo sde, *ja*, 71b6.

899. *Sūtrasamuccaya*, Toh 3934 Tengyur, dbu ma, *ki*, 118b6.

900. Jayānanda, *Madhyamakāvatāraṭīkā*, Toh 3870 Tengyur, dbu ma, *ra*, 359b5. Jayānanda is saying that the statement in the stanza that Buddha Śākyamuni, the historical buddha, entered the enlightened state for so many eons should be understood in terms of his sharing the same dharmakāya with all the countless other buddhas. Otherwise, were this statement taken at face value, the distinctness of the individual buddhas would collapse, and there would be no other buddhas.

901. *Commentary*, 346a3.

902. *Commentary*, 347a5.

903. Tsongkhapa is referring here to the section on Prāsaṅgika views in his *Essence of True Eloquence*, especially Thurman, *Central Philosophy*, 306–44.

904. *Commentary*, 347a7.

905. *Commentary*, 347b1.

906. This is a reference to the legend of how Candrakīrti once served fellow monastics a porridge he prepared from milk extracted from the drawing of a cow.

Glossary

affliction(s) (*nyong mongs, kleśa*). Dissonant mental states, both thoughts and emotions, that have their root in ignorance. The term has been translated elsewhere as "delusion" or "defilement." Classical Buddhist texts list six root afflictions—attachment, aversion, conceit, afflicted doubt, ignorance, and afflicted view—out of which attachment, aversion, and ignorance are referred to also as the *three poisons* of the mind. Associated with these root afflictions, especially the three poisons, Abhidharma lists twenty secondary or derivative afflictions. They are called *afflictions* because they disturb the individual from deep within.

ārya (*'phags pa*). In all Buddhist traditions, a practitioner whose enlightenment is certain, usually because of his or her direct insight into the ultimate nature of things with a mind that is deeply concentrated. In the five-path schema, whether of Hīnayāna or Mahayana, the point at which one becomes an ārya (literally, "noble being") is one's entrance into the third path, the path of seeing. The term is often contrasted with *ordinary being* (*so so'i skye bo*), someone who had not yet attained the vision of directly seeing the ultimate nature of things.

awakening mind (*byang chub kyi sems, bodhicitta*). In the Mahayana, a state of mind cultivated by a bodhisattva. The *conventional* awakening mind is the generation of the aspiration to attain enlightenment for the sake of all beings, and the *ultimate* awakening mind is the direct realization of emptiness of all phenomena, including especially of the enlightened mind.

cessation (*'gog pa, nirodha*). The third among the four noble truths, the others being the truths of suffering, of its origin, and of the path that leads to cessation of first two. In this sense, *cessation* refers to a state defined by the ending of specific factors brought about by the power of their antidote, such as the elimination of ignorance through the wisdom of emptiness, the highest such cessation being nirvana. When used as referring to one of the three characteristics of the condition—arising, enduring, and cessation—the term refers to the fact that conditioned phenomena never remain static but undergo moment-by-moment change that entails cessation of preceding instances. In Tibetan texts, this second meaning of the word is captured by rendering the Sanskrit term *nirodha* distinctly as *'gag pa* and not as *'gog pa*.

Cittamātra (*sems tsam pa*). Literally, "mind only," this is the name of a well-known Mahayana Buddhist philosophical school that is also called Yogācāra or Vijñānavāda. Its founding figures include Asaṅga (fourth century) and Vasubhandu (fourth century).

concentration (*ting nge 'dzin, samādhi*). A meditative state in which one's mind abides in deep equipoise. Often used interchangeably with *meditative absorption* (*bsam gtan, dhyāna*), a key feature of concentration is the heightened quality of focus and absorption and absence of distraction. The term need not always connote a meditative state. In the Abhidharma taxonomy of mental factors, for example, concentration is one of the five object-determined factors and is defined as the mind's natural capacity for single-pointedness and focus.

concept/conceptualization (*rtam rtog, vikalpa*). The constructive mental activity that dominates the inner life of sentient beings and obstructs them from seeing things as they really are. For humans in particular, such activity entails processes of interpreting their experience of the world shaped by language-based thought, perspectives, and attitudes. Like conceptual elaboration, it involves a process of superimposition on reality that must be eliminated before enlightenment can be attained.

conceptual elaboration (*spros pa, prapañca*). Conceptual elaborations occur in the domain of thought and language and include all forms of dichotomizing conceptualization, such as subject-object duality as well as grasping at objects and their characteristics. The ultimate truth and its direct realization are marked by total freedom from such conceptual elaborations.

conventional truth (*kun rdzob bden pa, saṃvṛtisatya*). *See* two truths.

dependent origination (*rten 'brel, pratityasamutpāda*). The general causal law in Buddhist thought that asserts that whatever arises does so in dependence upon causes and conditions. Sometimes taken to be the essential Buddhist teaching, it is given specific instantiation in the twelve links of dependent origination, which explains how it is we continually take birth in cyclic existence. Dependent origination is also explained by Nāgārjuna as equivalent to, and as a major proof of, emptiness.

dharmakāya (*chos sku*). In earlier traditions, the corpus of the Buddha's teaching; in Mahayana, the aspect of buddhahood that is equivalent to the enlightened mind and the basis of the two form bodies. Literally "truth body," it is sometimes singular and sometimes divided into a *natural* dharmakāya (*ngo bo nyid chos kyi sku, svabhāvikadharmakāya*), which is the buddha's emptiness or suchness, and a *gnostic* dharmakāya (*ye shes chos sku, jñānadharmakāya*), which is the buddha's perfect knowledge, compassion, power, and other qualities. When dharmakāya is differentiated into these two dimensions, a buddha's embodiment (*kāya*) is explained to be fourfold: (1) natural dharmakāya and (2) gnostic dharmakāya (the two truth bodies), and (3) enjoyment body and (4) emanation body (the two form bodies).

disintegration (*zhig pa, vināśa*). Tsongkhapa is using this term as the past tense of "disintegrating" or "ceasing" (*'jig pa, bhaṅga*), one of the three characteristics of the conditioned, the other two being arising (*utpāda*) and enduring (*asthiti*). So, just as disintegrating is a conditioned phenomenon, according to Tsongkhapa, *disintegration* (*zhig pa*) as the outcome is also a conditioned phenomenon in that it is a caused event. Tsongkhapa sees disintegration as a conditioned phenomenon to be an important feature of Candrakīrti's Madhyamaka, in that it accounts for the causal connection between a past karma and the maturation of its effect, even after a long lapse of time.

emanation body (*sprul sku, nirmāṇakāya*). Within the buddha's form embodiment, the aspect that appears for the sake of ordinary sentient beings. A single buddha may have multiple emanation bodies, which may be in human, animal, or inanimate forms. The historical Buddha Śākyamuni is generally regarded as an emanation body.

emptiness (*stong pa nyid, śūnyatā*). According to the Madhyamaka school, all things and events, including our own existence, are empty or devoid of any independent, substantial, and intrinsic existence. This emptiness of intrinsic existence is the ultimate truth, the ultimate mode of being of all phenomena—the way they actually are—hence referred to also by such epithets as *suchness* or *thatness*. As such, according to Madhyamaka, the realization of this truth, emptiness, is indispensable for the attainment of enlightenment.

enjoyment body (*longs sku, saṃbhogakāya*). Within the buddha's form embodiment, the glorified aspect of a buddha that appears only to select disciples. The enjoyment body is said to possess the major and minor marks of a buddha and to teach Mahayana Dharma in Akaniṣṭha heaven to high-level bodhisattvas for as long as cyclic existence lasts.

exhaustion (*zad pa, kṣaya*). Often used as an equivalent to *cessation*, the term can refer to (1) the cessation or elimination of afflictions and suffering that enlightened beings have attained through the path, (2) emptiness, the fact that all things are primordially clear or free of intrinsic existence, or (3) the mundane fact of something having been used up, such as the oil in a lamp consumed through burning.

extrinsic emptiness (*gzhan stong*). A controversial view of emptiness propounded especially by Dölpopa (fourteenth century) and a major object of critique by Tibetan Madhyamaka thinkers like Rendawa, Tsongkhapa, and Gorampa. The view asserts that samsaric phenomena are empty of intrinsic existence, but a buddha's dharmakāya is empty of everything extrinsic to it—namely, all samsaric phenomena—but is itself eternally replete with all the buddha qualities. In this view, emptiness itself, which is defined as dharmakāya and buddha nature (*sugatagarbha*), is absolute and possesses intrinsic existence.

foundation consciousness (*kun gzhi rnam shes, ālayavijñāna*). A unique concept within the Yogācāra theory of mind, which asserts eight (as opposed to six) classes of consciousness—the five sensory, the sixth mental, with the addition of afflicted mental consciousness and foundation consciousness. Defined as the basis as well as the repository of all of our experiences, it is said to be morally neutral, the basis of our identity thought "I am," and ever present until the attainment of nirvana without residue.

gnosis (*ye shes, jñāna*). Tibetan authors differentiate between *shes pa* (cognition) as a generic term referring to all mental events, including those of ordinary people, and *ye shes* (gnosis), referring specifically to realizations of ārya beings pertaining to the nature of things that are profound and liberating. The Sanskrit term *jñāna*, in fact, captures the meaning of both Tibetan terms.

Hīnayāna (*theg dman*). Literally "lesser vehicle," the term is used by the Mahayana tradition to refer to the systems of Buddhist practice based exclusively on the teachings expounded by the Buddha in his first turning of the wheel of Dharma. Such a vehicle sets as its ideal the attainment of nirvana, the arhat's state of freedom from personal suffering, while the Mahayana upholds as its vision the attainment of buddhahood for the benefit of all beings. When the term is used in the context of philosophical schools, the first two—Vaibhāṣika and Sautrāntika—are recognized as Hīnayāna schools, while Yogācāra and Madhyamaka are Mahayana schools.

identity view (*'jig tshogs lta ba, satkāyadṛṣṭi*). Literally "view of the transitory collection," the term refers to our innate sense of self-identity as individuated beings. This identity view can take the form of the thought "I am" when it is based on an underlying assumption of an intrinsically existing self that is the referent of such a "self" or "I." By extension, the identity view can take the form of the thought "mine" in relation to people and things that we appropriate as part of our identity. According to Buddhist thought, the identity view—an important subclass of grasping at self-existence—constitutes a fundamental ignorance and hence a root of all our afflictions.

intrinsic characteristic (*rang gi mtshan nyid, svalakṣaṇa*). In Tsongkhapa's usage in the context of Madhyamaka thought, the term refers to a kind of fixed, defining essence by virtue of which a given thing is thought to acquire its existence and identity. In this sense, *intrinsic characteristic* becomes equivalent to *intrinsic nature* (*svabhāva*), an important object of critique for Nāgārjuna's Madhyamaka. In general, the Sanskrit term *svalakṣaṇa* and its Tibetan equivalent can also connote (1) a defining characteristic, such as heat in relation to fire, (2) unique attributes, such as attributes unique to the body as opposed to a general attribute like impermanence, and (3) unique particulars in the context of Dignāga and Dharmakīrti's Buddhist epistemology.

intrinsic emptiness (*rang stong*). The view of emptiness that insists that all phenomena, of both samsara and nirvana, are empty in the same way—as devoid of intrinsic existence—and that denies any notion of absolute, independent reality defined by virtue of intrinsic nature. This is stated in contradistinction to the *extrinsic emptiness* view, in which nirvanic phenomena are seen to be empty in a different way than samsaric phenomena. This *intrinsic emptiness* view is emphasized by Tsongkhapa in his interpretation of Nāgārjuna's philosophy of emptiness as read through Candrakīrti.

intrinsic existence (*rang bzhin gyis grub pa, svabhāvasiddhi*). Existence by virtue of some kind of intrinsic nature, something categorically rejected by Nāgārjuna as read through Candrakīrti and Tsongkhapa.

intrinsic nature (*rang bzhin, svabhāva*). Chapter 15 of Nāgārjuna's *Fundamental Verses on the Middle Way* defines intrinsic nature as "unfabricated" and "not dependent on something else." There are two senses in which the term is used in the Madhyamaka context: (1) something intrinsic in things, an essence by virtue of which a given thing obtains its existence and identity, and (2) a thing's absence of intrinsic existence—its emptiness—which, in an objective sense, is the only true nature that things have. In the first sense, intrinsic nature is categorically rejected, while in the second sense, intrinsic nature is accepted.

Madhyamaka (*dbu ma pa*). With Cittamātra, one of the two major philosophical schools of Mahayana Buddhism. Founded by Nāgārjuna (second century CE), it focuses on the doctrine of emptiness expounded in the Perfection of Wisdom literature. Madhyamaka was the most influential single philosophical tradition in Tibet and spread throughout the Mahayana world as well. The Tibetan tradition recognizes two subschools of Madhyamaka philosophy: Svātantrika and Prāsaṅgika.

Mādhyamika (*dbu ma pa*). A person who propounds the Madhyamaka philosophical standpoint.

Mahayana (*theg chen, mahāyāna*). Literally "great vehicle," the term is contrasted with Hīnayāna and refers to the system of Buddhist path based on the teachings that are part of the second and third turnings of the wheel of Dharma. Mahayana became the dominant form of Buddhism in medieval India as well as many countries in east and central Asia, including Tibet, Bhutan, and Mongolia.

meditative absorption (*bsam gtan, dhyāna*). Meditative absorption refers to the state where the mind is focused single-pointedly. Used as a general term, a paradigmatic example of meditative absorption is the state of *tranquility* (*zhi gnas, śamatha*), where the person has attained a deep state of effortless focused attention marked by absence of mental excitation or laxity. When used technically in the context of "four meditative absorptions," however, the term refers to four progressively subtler states of mind defined by progressive diminishing of feelings and discriminations, with tranquility being the gateway into such states. Meditative absorption is also the term used for one of the six perfections in Mahayana Buddhism. The term is often used interchangeably with *concentration* (*ting nge 'dzin, samādhi*).

meditative attainment (*snyoms 'jug, samāpatti*). Advanced meditative states characterized by single-pointed focus, absence of distraction, and tranquility accompanied by physical and mental pliancy. Typically, three distinct types of such meditative attainments are mentioned in the texts: (1) meditative attainment in the form of states of absorption (*bsam gtan snyoms 'jug*), (2) meditative attainment devoid of discrimination (*'du shes med pa'i snyoms 'jug*), and (3) the meditative attainment of cessation (*'gog pa'i snyoms 'jug*).

mode of being (*gnas lugs*). A synonym for *essential mode of being* (*gshis lugs*), the terms refer to the way in which things are understood to exist from the perspective of their ultimate truth. Often an epithet for emptiness.

nirvana (*mya ngan las 'das pa, nirvāṇa*). Liberation from cyclic existence, hence the extinction of suffering and its causes—the afflictions and karma. Typically, nirvana is defined as a highest form of cessation, with a distinction drawn between *nirvana with residue*, the first stage of the attainment of nirvana when the person still possesses his psychophysical aggregates, and *nirvana without residue*, when even the aggregates no longer remain.

nominal existence (*btags yod, prajñaptisat*). The existence of things on the level of a truth defined not in an objective sense, as independent facts, but from the perspective and shared norms of thought, language, and everyday experience and conventions.

nonreferential compassion (*dmigs med snying rje, anālambanākaruṇā*). Rendered also as "objectless compassion," the term refers to an advanced level of compassion where there is not even the slightest degree of grasping at objectively real sentient beings. In other words, it refers to compassion that is powerfully accompanied by awareness of the emptiness of all beings.

obscuration (*sgrib pa, avaraṇa*). Sometimes rendered also as "defilement," the term refers to factors that obscure and obstruct our attainment of enlightenment. Typically, two classes of obscuration are identified— afflictive obscuration (*nyon sgrib, kleśāvaraṇa*), which refers to all the afflictions and their seeds, and knowledge obscuration (*shes sgrib, jñeyāvaraṇa*), the subtle residue of dualistic thinking that obstructs perfect wisdom and omniscience and thus is eliminated only by buddhas. Sometimes, two additional classes of obscuration are added: (3) obscuration to concentration (*ting nge 'dzin gyi sgrib pa, samādhyāvaraṇa*), referring to the five hindrances to meditation—sensory desire, ill will, sloth and torpor, restlessness and remorse, and doubt—and (4) karmic obscuration (*las kyi sgrib pa, karmāvaraṇa*).

path of release (*rnam grol lam, vimuktimārga*). This is the second phase, the first phase being the *uninterrupted path*, in meditative equipoise such as on the path of seeing characterized by nondual direct realization of emptiness. The first phase consists of applying the direct antidote against the relevant afflictions being eliminated, while this second phase represents the freedom characterized by attainment of the relevant cessation.

Prāsaṅgika (*thal 'gyur ba*). According to Tibetan scholarly tradition, the school of Madhyamaka philosophy that (1) stresses the use of *reductio ad absurdum* reasoning to reveal unwanted consequences (*prasaṅga*) when establishing emptiness as the ultimate nature of all phenomena and (2) denies that phenomena possess intrinsic characteristics even on the conventional level. Buddhapālita and Candrakīrti are the most well-known representatives of Prāsaṅgika.

pratyekabuddha (*rang sangs rgyas*). Literally "solitary realizer" or "self-enlightened one," a pratyekabuddha is an adept who seeks liberation on the basis of autonomous practice. Along with the vehicle of the śrāvaka, the vehicle of the pratyekabuddha belongs to the Hīnayāna path, requiring a thorough realization of the truth of dependent origination. *See also* śrāvaka.

rational cognition (*rigs shes*). An important term in Tsongkhapa's Madhyamaka thought referring to a form of reasoned knowledge with respect to ultimate truth—i.e., emptiness. Such cognition can be nonconceptual, such as a yogi's direct, nondual realization of emptiness, or it could take the form of an inferential cognition of emptiness derived from prolonged reflection and meditation.

reflexive awareness (*rang rig, svasaṃvedana*). A dimension of mental states, according to Cittamātra and Sautrāntika, that makes it possible for our experiences to be self-aware in a nondual manner. Its proponents argue that, without such reflexive awareness, there can be no credible account of memory. Reading Nāgārjuna, Madhyamaka figures like Bhāviveka, Candrakīrti, and Tsongkhapa reject reflexive awareness as defined by Cittamātra and Sautrāntika.

Sautrāntika (*mdo sde pa*). A Hīnayāna school whose name means "followers of the sutras." The Sautrāntikas emerged as a reaction to the Vaibhāṣika, preferring to follow the original discourses of the Buddha rather than the great Abhidharma compendium the *Mahāvibhāṣa*.

self (*bdag, ātman*). The Sanskrit term *ātman* and its Tibetan equivalent *bdag* have multiple overlapping senses so require different renderings in different contexts. In two distinct but related senses of the term, it is rendered as "self": the sense of an individual, as in "self and others," and the sense of personal identity, especially the sense that assumes some kind of enduring principle like an eternal soul. However, when the term is used more broadly as an ontological concept, attributing an objective existence whereby both persons and things are thought to possess independent reality, the term is rendered as "selfhood" or "self-existence." In this latter sense, the term then becomes synonymous with true existence, intrinsic existence, and objective independent existence, all of which are categorically rejected by Madhyamaka.

selflessness (*bdag med, anātman*). The absence or negation of self-existence. The negation of such self-existence in relation of persons is called the *selflessness of persons* and its negation in relation to phenomena other than persons is called the *selflessness of phenomena*. These two forms of selflessness, according to Candrakīrti, are the two basic divisions of emptiness taught by the Buddha. *See also* self.

self-sufficient substantial reality (*rang rkya thub pa'i rdzas yod*). One of the three levels of selfhood, according to Tsongkhapa: (1) the notion of self conceived in non-Buddhist Indian schools as eternal, unitary, and autonomous; (2) the notion of self as self-sufficient and possessing substantial reality; and (3) the notion of self as existing by virtue of an intrinsic nature. The grasping at the first type is present only in those whose mind have been conditioned by philosophical thinking, while the last two can be found in all beings, the latter progressively subtler than the preceding one.

śrāvaka (*nyan thos*). Literally "hearers," śrāvakas are disciples of the Buddha whose primary objective is to attain liberation from cyclic existence. They are often paired with pratyekabuddhas as spiritual trainees on the Hīnayāna path, as distinct from the bodhisattvas, who embark on the Mahayana path to full enlightenment.

substantial existence (*rdzas yod, dravyasat*). Contrasted with nominal existence, substantial existence is the way Buddhist essentialists conceive things as possessing an objective existence that can be defined in terms of underlying substance. A well-known Abhidharma definition states that a thing is substantially existent if it retains its identity even when it's destroyed (as when a clay pot is smashed) or mentally deconstructed (as when a chariot is considered in terms of its individual parts). In Madhyamaka writings, the term is often a synonym for true existence, intrinsic existence, or objective independent existence, all of which are objects of negation in the philosophy of emptiness.

suchness (*de kho na nyid, tathatā*). The reality of things as they are. Having the same meaning as *thatness* (*de bzhin nyid, tattva*) and *ultimate nature* (*chos nyid, dharmatā*), the term is often a synonym for emptiness.

Svātantrika (*rang rgyud pa*). According to Tibetan scholarly tradition, the school of Madhyamaka philosophy that, following the interpretation of Nāgārjuna's thought by Bhāviveka, emphasizes the use of autonomous syllogistic reasoning to establish the truth of emptiness. The term literally means "proponent of autonomous syllogism." The school is subdivided into Sautrāntika-Svātantrika (represented by Bhāviveka and Jñānagarbha) and Yogācāra-Svātantrika (represented by Śāntarakṣita and Kamalaśīla).

things in their diversity (*ji snyed pa, yāvabhāvikatā*). A synonym for *conventional truth*, characterized by differentiation and multiplicity. The term is used in contrast with another term, the *way things really are* (*ji lta ba, yathābhāvikatā*), the latter being a synonym for ultimate truth, which is characterized by oneness, unity, and absence of conceptual elaboration. In Madhyamaka texts, including especially of Tsongkhapa, these two terms—things in their diversity and the way things really are—are used mostly in relation to the buddha's gnosis pertaining to the two truths.

tīrthika (*mu stegs pa*). A term used in classical Indian and Tibetan Buddhists texts to refer to the upholders of non-Buddhist Indian philosophical tenets.

true existence (*bden par grub pa, satyasiddhi*). *See* intrinsic existence.

two truths (*bden pa gnyis, dvayasatya*). Conventional truth (*kun rdzob bden pa, saṃvṛtisat*) and ultimate truth (*don dam bden pa, paramārthasat*). According to the Madhyamaka school, *ultimate truth* refers to emptiness—the absence of intrinsic existence of all phenomena. In contrast, *conventional truth* refers to the empirical aspect of reality characterized by diversity and differentiation and experienced through perception, language, and thought.

ultimate expanse (*chos dbyings, dharmadhātu*). In Madhyamaka writings, *dharmadhātu* is an epithet for emptiness and used as a synonym for *suchness* and *thatness*. Emptiness is called an "expanse" (*dhātu*) to convey the idea of it as a "field," "sphere," "realm," or "element" in which (metaphorically, at least) all phenomena, both of cyclic existence and nirvana, naturally reside.

ultimate nature (*chos nyid, dharmatā*). A term defined in contrast with *dharma* (phenomena) to refer to the true nature of things, hence *dharma* and *dharmatā*. In Mahayana thought, the term is used invariably as a synonym for terms like *suchness* and *thatness*, and like those terms, refers to emptiness.

ultimate truth (*don dam bden pa, paramārthasat*). *See* two truths.

uninterrupted path (*bar chad med lam, anantaryamārga*). *See* path of release.

Vaibhāṣika (*bye brag smra ba*). Literally "the proponents of differentiation," the school derives its name from its emphasis on the authority of the great Abhidharma compendium the *Mahāvibhāṣa*.

way things really are (*ji lta ba, yathābhāvikatā*). *See* things in their diversity.

wisdom (*shes rab, prajñā*). The Sanskrit term and its Tibetan equivalent are also translated as "insight," "understanding," or "intelligence" depending on the context. In the Abhidharma taxonomy of mental factors, *prajñā* is a mental factor that helps evaluate the attributes of an object, and as such the term can refer to basic intelligence or mental aptitude. In the Mahayana, *prajñā* is the wisdom aspect of the path, consisting primarily of deep understanding of the emptiness of all phenomena. It is also the name of the sixth perfection. *See also* gnosis.

worldly convention (*'jig rten gyi tha snyad, lokavyavahāra*). An important term in Madhyamaka thought, especially according to Candrakīrti and Tsongkhapa, *worldly convention* refers to a perspective as well as a framework—defined through intersubjective experience, shared norms, and practice—that enable us to make sense of our experience of the world. It is the standpoint from which the conventional truth is defined, as opposed to ultimate truth, which is defined from the perspective of the perfect vision of the āryas. Tsongkhapa stresses the point that such worldly convention must include the perspectives of both ordinary people as well as āryas pertaining to everyday experience of the lived world.

Bibliography

Works Cited by the Author

CANONICAL SCRIPTURES (*KANGYUR*)

Adornment of Trees Sutra. Gaṇḍavyūhasūtra. Sdong po rgyan pa'i mdo. Toh 44, Kangyur, phal chen *cha*; the final chapter (45th) of the *Flower Ornament Sutra* (*Avatataṃsakasūtra*).

Ajātaśatru Sutra. Ajātaśatrukaukṛtyavinodanā. Ma skyes dgra'i 'gyod pa bsal ba. Toh 216, mdo sde *tsha*.

Ākāśagarbha Sutra. Ākāśagarbhasūtra. Nam mkha'i snying po'i mdo. Toh 260, mdo sde *za*.

Basis of Discipline. Vinayavastu. 'Dul ba gzhi. Toh 1, 'dul ba *kha*.

Candraprabha Sutra. See *King of Meditations Sutra*.

Chapter on Magical Emanations of Mañjuśrī. Mañjuśrīvikurvāṇaparivarta. 'Jam dpal rnam par 'phrul ba'i le'u. Toh 97, mdo sde *kha*. A.k.a. *Chapter on Defeating the Māras*.

Cloud of Jewels Sutra. Ratnameghasūtra. Dkon mchog sprin. Toh 231, mdo sde *wa*.

Collection of Aphorisms. Udānavarga. Tshoms. Toh 326, mdo sde *sa*.

Condensed Perfection of Wisdom. Prajñāpāramitāsaṃcayagāthā. Shes rab kyi pha rol du phyin pa bsdus pa. Toh 13, shes phyin *ka*.

Definite Teaching on the Tathāgata's Great Compassion. Tathāgatamahā-karuṇanirdeśasūtra. De bzhin gshegs pa'i snying rje chen po nges par bstan pa. Toh 147, mdo sde *pa*.

Densely Arrayed Sutra. Ghanavyūhasūtra. Sdong po bkod pa'i mdo. Toh 110, mdo sde *cha*.

Dependent Origination Sutra. Pratītyasamutpādasūtra. Rten cing 'brel bar 'byung ba'i mdo. Toh 212, mdo sde *tsha*.

Dependent Origination's First Division Sutra. Pratītyasamutpādādi-vibhaṅganirdeśasūtra. Rten cing 'brel bar 'byung ba dang po dang rnam par dbye ba bstan pa'i mdo. Toh 211, mdo sde *tsha.*

Descent into Laṅkā Sutra. Laṅkāvatārasūtra. Lang kar gshegs pa'i mdo. Toh 107, mdo sde *ca.*

Diamond Cutter Sutra. Vajracchedikā. Rdo rje gcod pa. Toh 16, shes phyin *ka.*

Discourse for Kāśyapa. Kāśyapaparivarta. 'Od srung gi le'u. Toh 87, dkon brtsegs *cha.*

Discourse for Sthīrādhyāśa. Sthīrādhyāśayaparivarta. Lhag bsam brtan pa'i le'u. Toh 224, mdo sde *dza.*

Engaging in Accordance with the World Sutra. Lokānuvartasūtra. 'Jig rten gyi rjes su mthun par 'jug pa. Toh 200, mdo sde *tsa.*

Entering the Two Truths Sutra. Saṃvṛtiparamārthasatyanirdeśasūtra. Bden pa gnyis la 'jug pa'i mdo. Toh 179, mdo sde *ma.*

Gathering All Fragments Sutra. Sarvavaidalyasaṃgrahasūtra. Rnam par 'thag pa thams cad bsdus pa'i mdo. Toh 227, mdo sde *dza.*

Goddess Śrīmālā Sutra. Śrīmālādevīsūtra. Dpal phren gyi mdo. Toh 92, dkon brtsegs *cha.*

Great Clouds Sutra. Mahāmeghasūtra. Sprin chen po'i mdo. Toh 232, mdo sde *wa.*

Great Drum Sutra. Mahābherīsūtra. Rnga bo che'i mdo. Toh 222, mdo sde *dza.*

Heap of Jewels Sutra. Ratnakuṭa. Dkon brtsegs. This is a collection of discourses comprising one section of the canon, Toh 45–93.

Invoking the Altruistic Resolve Sutra. Adhyāśayasaṃcodana. Lhag pas bsam pa bskul ba'i mdo. Toh 69, dkon brtsegs *ca.*

Irreversible Wheel Sutra. Avaivartacakrasūtra. Phyir mi ldog pa'i 'khor lo'i mdo. Toh 240, mdo sde *zha.*

King of Meditations Sutra. Samādhirājasūtra. Ting nge 'dzin rgyal po'i mdo. Toh 127, mdo sde *da.*

Liberating Story of Maitreya Sutra. Byams pa'i rnam par thar pa'i mdo. This is part of the *Adornment of Trees Sutra (Gaṇḍavyūhasūtra).*

Manifestations of Mañjuśrī Sutra. Mañjuśrīvikrīḍitasūtra. 'Jam dpal rnam par rol pa'i mdo. Toh 96, mdo sde *kha.*

Mañjuśrī's Root Realizations Tantra. Mañjuśrīmūlatantra. 'Jam dpal gyi rtsa ba'i rtogs pa brjod pa. Toh 543, rgyud 'bum *na.*

Meeting of Father and Son Sutra. Pitāputrasamāgamanasūtra. Yab sras mjal ba'i mdo. Toh 60, dkon brtsegs *nga.*

Perfection of Wisdom in Eighteen Thousand Lines. Aṣṭadaśasāhasrikāprajñā-pāramitā. Shes rab kyi pha rol tu phyin pa khri brgyad stong pa. Toh 10 Kangyur, shes phyin *ka.*

Perfection of Wisdom in Ten Thousand Lines. Daśasāhasrikāprajñāpāramitā. Shes rab kyi pha rol tu phyin pa khri pa. Toh 11, shes phyin *nga.*

Perfection of Wisdom in Twenty-Five Thousand Lines. Pañcaviṃśatisāhasrikā-prajñāpāramitā. Shes rab kyi pha rol tu phyin pa nyi khri. Toh 9, shes phyin *ka.*

Perfectly Gathering the Teachings. Dharmasaṃgītisūtra. Chos yang dag par bsdus pa'i mdo. Toh 238, mdo sde *zha.*

Play in Full Sutra. Lalitavistarasūtra. Rgya cher rol pa'i mdo. Toh 95, mdo sde *kha.* P763, *ka.*

Presenting the Three Vows Sutra. Triśaṃvaranirdeśasūtra. Sdom pa gsum bstan pa'i mdo. Toh 45, dkon brtsegs *ka.*

Questions of Gaganagañja Sutra. Gaganagañjaparipṛcchāsūtra. Nam mkha' mdzod kyi mdo. Toh 148, mdo sde *pa.*

Questions of Maitreya. Maitreyaparipṛcchā. Byams pas zhus pa. Toh 85, dkon brtsegs *cha.*

Questions of Nāga King Anavatapta. Anavataptanāgarājaparipṛcchā. Ma dros pas zhus pa. Toh 156, mdo sde *pha.*

Questions of Upāli. Upāliparipṛcchā. Nye bar 'khor gyis zhus pa. Toh 68, dkon brtsegs *ca.*

Rice Seedling Sutra. Śālistambasūtra. Sa lu ljangs pa'i mdo. Toh 210, mdo sde *tsha.*

Secrets of the Tathāgata Sutra. Tathāgatacintyaguhyanirdeśasūtra. De bzhin gshegs pa'i gsang ba bsam gyis mi khyab pa bstan pa'i mdo. Toh 47, dkon brtsegs *ka.*

Story of Origins Sutra. Abhiniṣkramaṇasūtra. Mngon par 'byung ba'i mdo. Toh 301, mdo sde *sa.*

Sublime Dharma of White Lotus. Saddharmapuṇḍarīka. Dam pa'i chos pad ma dkar po. Toh 113, mdo sde *ja.*

Sublime Golden Light Sutra. Suvarṇaprabhāsottamasūtra. Gser 'od dam pa'i mdo. Toh 557, rgyud 'bum *pha.*

Teachings of Akṣayamati Sutra. Akṣayamatinirdeśasūtra. Blo gros mi bzad pas bstan pa'i mdo. Toh 175, mdo sde *ma.*

Ten Grounds Sutra. Daśabhūmikasūtra. Sa bcu pa'i mdo. Chapter 31 of the *Avataṃsaka Sutra.* Toh 44, phal chen *kha.*

Transferring to Another Existence Sutra. Bhavasaṃkrāntisūtra. Srid pa 'pho ba'i mdo. Toh 226, mdo sde *dza,* 175b5.

Unraveling the Intent Sutra. Saṃdhinirmocanasūtra. Dgongs pa nges par 'grel pa'i mdo. Toh 106 Kangyur, mdo sde, *ca.*

Vows of Good Conduct. Bhadracaryāpraṇidhāna. Bzang po spyod pa'i smon lam. Toh 1095, gzungs 'dus *vam.*

Canonical Treatises (Tengyur)

Abhayākaragupta (eleventh–twelfth century). *Ornament of the Sage's Intent. Munimatālaṃkāra. Thub pa dgongs rgyan.* Toh 3903, dbu ma *a.*

Ajitamitra (d.u.). *Commentary on the Precious Garland. Ratnāvalīṭīkā. Rin po che phreng ba'i 'grel pa.* Toh 4159, springs yig *ge.*

Āryadeva (second century). *Compendium of the Heart of Gnosis. Jñānasārasamuccaya. Ye shes snying po kun las btus pa.* Toh 3851, dbu ma *tsha.*

———. *Four Hundred Stanzas. Catuḥśatakaśāstra. Bstan bcos bzhi brgya pa.* Toh 3846, dbu ma *tsha.*

Asaṅga (ca. fourth century). *Bodhisattva Grounds. Bodhisattvabhūmi. Byang chub sems dpa'i sa.* Toh 4037, sems tsam *wi.*

———. *Commentary on Sublime Continuum. Uttaratantravyākhyā. Rgyud bla ma'i 'grel pa.* Toh 4025, sems tsam *phi.*

———. *Compendium of Abhidharma. Abhidharmasamuccaya. Mngon pa kun las btus pa.* Toh 4049, sems tsam *ri.*

———. *Summary of the Explanations of the Levels of Yogic Practice. Yogacārabhūmiviniścayasaṃgraha. Rnam grangs bsdu ba.* Toh 4038, sems tsam *zhi.*

———. *Summary of the Great Vehicle. Mahāyānasaṃgraha. Theg pa chen po bsdus pa.* Toh 4048, sems tsam *ri.*

Asvabhāva (sixth century). *Interspersed Explanation of the Summary of the Great Vehicle. Mahāyānasaṃgrahopanibandhana. Theg pa chen po bsdus pa'i bshad sbyar.* Toh 4051, sems tsam *ri.*

Atiśa (982–1054). *Open Basket of Jewels. Ratnakaraṇḍodghāṭa. Rin po che'i za ma tog kha phye ba.* Toh 3930, dbu ma *ki.*

Avalokitavrata (eighth century). *Commentary on the Lamp of Wisdom. Prajñāpradīpaṭīkā. Shes rab sgron ma rgya cher 'grel pa.* Toh 3859, dbu ma *wa, zha,* and *za.*

Bhāviveka (sixth century). *Blaze of Reasoning. Tarkajvālā. Rtog ge 'bar ba.* Toh 3856, dbu ma *dza.* Critical edition in *Dbu ma snying po'i 'grel pa rtog ge 'bar ba (Tarkajvālā: An Autocommentary on the Madhyamakahṛdaya),* edited and introduced by Thupten Jinpa. New Delhi: Institute of Tibetan Classics, 2019.

———. *Essence of the Middle Way. Madhyamakahṛdaya. Dbu ma snying po.* Toh 3855, dbu ma *dza.*

———. *Lamp of Wisdom. Prajñāpradīpa. Shes rab sgron me.* Toh 5853, dbu ma *tsa.*

Bodhibhadra (eleventh century). *Interspersed Explanation of Heart of Wisdom. Jñānasārasamuccayanibandhana. Ye shes snying po kun las btus pa'i bshad sbyar.* Toh 3852, dbu ma *tsha.*

Buddhapālita (ca. fifth century). *Buddhapālitamūlamadhyamakavṛtti. Dbu ma rtsa ba'i 'grel pa buddha pā li ta.* Toh 3842, dbu ma *tsa.*

Candragomin (ca. seventh century). *Letter to a Student. Śiṣyalekha. Slob ma la springs pa.* Toh 4183, spring yig *nge.*

Candrakīrti (ca. seventh century). *Clear Words: A Commentary on Root Treatise on the Middle Way. Prasannapadā. Dbu ma rtsa ba'i 'grel pa tshig gsal.* Toh 3860, dbu ma *'a.*

———. *Commentary on Entering the Middle Way. Madhyamakāvatārabhāṣya. Dbu ma la 'jug pa'i bshad pa.* Toh 3862, dbu ma *'a.*

———. *Commentary on Four Hundred Stanzas. Catuḥśatakaṭīkā. Bzhi brgya pa'i 'grel pa.* Toh 3865, dbu ma *ya.*

———. *Commentary on Seventy Stanzas on Emptiness. Śūnyatāsaptativṛtti. Stong nyid bdun cu pa'i 'grel pa.* Toh 3867, dbu ma *ya.*

———. *Commentary on Sixty Stanzas of Reasoning. Yuktiṣaṣṭikāvṛtti. Rigs pa drug cu pa'i 'grel pa.* Toh 3864, dbu ma *ya.*

———. *Entering the Middle Way. Madhyamakāvatāra. Dbu ma la 'jug pa.* Toh 3861, dbu ma *'a.*

———. *Seventy Stanzas on Going for Refuge to the Three. Triśaraṇasaptati. Skyabs 'gro bdun cu pa.* Toh 3971, dbu ma *gi.*

Dharmakīrti (seventh century) *Exposition of Valid Cognition. Pramāṇavārttika. Tshad ma rnam 'grel.* Toh 4210, tshad ma *ce.* Critical edition in *Dpal chos kyi grags pa'i tshad ma sde bdun (Seven Pramāṇa Works of Dharmakīrti),* edited and introduced by Thupten Jinpa. New Delhi: Institute of Tibetan Classics, 2015.

Dignāga. See below among works cited by translator.

Haribhadra (eighth century). *Clear Words: A Commentary on Ornament of Realizations. Abhisamayālaṃkāravṛtti-Sphuṭārthā. 'Grel pa don gsal.* Toh 3793, shes phyin *ja.*

———. *[Commentary on] the Perfection of Wisdom in Twenty-Five Thousand Lines. Pañcaviṃśatisāhasrikāprajñāpāramitāṭīkā. Shes rab kyi pha rol tu phyin pa stong phrag nyi shu lnga pa'i 'grel bshad.* Toh 3790 Tengyur, shes phyin *ga.*

———. *Exposition on the Eight-Thousand-Line Perfection of Wisdom. Aṣṭasāhasrikāprajñāpāramitāvyākhyā. Mngon par rtogs pa'i rgyan gyi snang ba.* Toh 3791, shes phyin *cha.*

Jayānanda (twelfth century). *Explanation of the Commentary on Entering the Middle Way. Madhyamakāvatāraṭīkā. Dbu ma la 'jug pa'i 'grel bshad.* Toh 3870, dbu ma *ra.*

Jñānagarbha (eighth century). *Commentary on the Differentiation of the Two Truths. Satyadvayavibhaṅgavṛtti. Bden gnyis rnam par 'byed pa'i 'grel pa.* Toh 3882, dbu ma *sa.*

———. *Differentiation of the Two Truths. Satyadvayavibhaṅga. Bden pa gnyis rnam par 'byed pa.* Toh 3881, dbu ma *sa.*

Kamalaśīla (ninth century). *Commentary on the Compendium of Views on Reality. Tattvasaṃgrahapañjikā. De kho na nyid bsdus pa'i dka' 'grel.* Toh 4267, tshad ma *ze.*

———. *Light of the Middle Way. Madhyamakāloka. Dbu ma snang ba.* Toh 3887, dbu ma *sa.*

———. *Stages of Meditation. Bhāvanākrama. Sgom pa'i rim pa.* Toh 3915, dbu ma *ki.*

Maitreya (fourth century). *Differentiation of the Middle and Extremes. Madhyāntavibhāga. Dbu mtha' rnam 'byed.* Toh 4021, sems tsam *phi.*

———. *Differentiation of Phenomena and Their Ultimate Nature. Dharmadharmatāvibhaṅga. Chos dang chos nyid rnam 'byed.* Toh 4022, sems tsam *phi.*

———. *Ornament of the Mahayana Sutras. Mahāyānasūtrālaṃkāra. Theg pa chen po mdo sde rgyan.* Toh 4020, sems tsam *phi.*

———. *Ornament of Realizations. Abhisamayālaṃkāra. Mngon rtogs rgyan.* Toh 3786, shes phyin *ka.*

———. *Sublime Continuum. Uttaratantra (Ratnagotravibhāga). Rgyud bla ma.* Toh 4024, sems tsam *phi.*

Nāgārjuna (second century). *Averting the Objections. Vigrahavyāvartanī. Rtsod pa bzlog pa.* Toh 3828, dbu ma *tsa.*

————. *Commentary on the Awakening Mind. Bodhicittavivaraṇa. Byang chub sems kyi 'grel pa.* Toh 1801, rgyud 'grel *ngi.*

————. *Compendium of Sutras. Sūtrasamuccaya. Mdo kun las btus pa.* Toh 3934, dbu ma *ki.*

————. *Friendly Letter. Suhṛllekha. Bshes pa'i springs yig.* Toh 4182, springs yig *nge.*

————. *Fundamental Verses on the Middle Way* (a.k.a. *Fundamental Wisdom; Treatise on the Middle Way*). *Mūlamadhyamakakārikā. Dbu ma rtsa ba'i tshig le'ur byas pa* (*Rtsa ba'i shes rab*). Toh 3824, dbu ma *tsa.*

————. *Hymn to the World Transcendent. Lokātītastava. 'Jig rten las 'das par bstod pa.* Toh 1120, bstod tshogs *ka.*

————. *Praise to the Peerless One. Nirupamastava. Dpe med par bstod pa.* Toh 1119, bstod tshogs *ka.*

————. *Praise to the Ultimate Expanse. Dharmadhātustava. Chos kyi dbyings la bstod pa.* Toh 1118, bstod tshogs *ka.*

————. *Precious Garland. Ratnāvalī. Rin chen phreng ba.* Toh 4158, springs yig *ge.*

————. *Seventy Stanzas on Emptiness. Śūnyatāsaptatikārikā. Stong nyid bdun cu pa.* Toh 3827, dbu ma *tsa.*

————. *Sixty Stanzas of Reasoning. Yuktiṣaṣṭikākārikā. Rigs pa drug cu pa.* Toh 3825, dbu ma *tsa.*

————. *Treatise on the Middle Way.* See *Fundamental Verses on the Middle Way.*

Prajñākaramati (950–1030). *Exposition of "Guide to the Bodhisattva Way." Bodhicaryāvatārapañjikā. Byang chub sems pa'i spyod pa la 'jug pa'i dka' 'grel.* Toh 3872, dbu ma *la.*

Ratnadāsa (d.u.). *Praise to the One with Infinite Qualities. Guṇāparyantastotra. Yon tan mtha' yas par bstod pa.* Toh 1155, bstod tshogs *ka.*

Śāntideva (eighth century). *Compendium of Training. Śikṣāsamuccaya. Bslab pa kun las btus pa.* Toh 3940, dbu ma *khi.*

————. *Guide to the Bodhisattva Way. Bodhicaryāvatāra. Byang chub sems dpa'i spyod pa la 'jug pa.* Toh 3871, dbu ma *la.*

Śāntarakṣita (ninth century). *Commentary on Ornament of the Middle Way. Madhyamakālaṃkāravṛtti. Dbu ma rgyan gyi 'grel pa.* Toh 3885, dbu ma *sa.*

————. *Ornament of the Middle Way. Madhyamakālaṃkāra. Dbu ma rgyan.* Toh 3884, dbu ma *sa.*

Sthiramati (sixth century). *Commentary on Differentiation of the Middle and Extremes. Madhyāntavibhaṅgaṭīkā. Dbus mtha' rnam 'byed pa'i 'grel bshad.* Toh 4032, sems tsam *bi.*

———. *Commentary on the Thirty Verses. Triṃśikabhāṣya. Sum cu pa'i bshad pa.* Toh 4064, sems tsam *shi.*

Vasubandhu (ca. fourth century). *Commentary on the Dependent Origination Sutra. Pratītyasamutpādādivibhaṅganirdeśa. Rten cing 'brel bar 'byung ba dang po'i rnam par dbye ba bshad pa.* Toh 3995, mdo 'grel *chi.*

———. *Commentary on the Differentiation of the Middle and Extremes. Madhyāntavibhāgabhāṣya. Dbus mtha' rnam byed kyi 'grel pa.* Toh 4027, sems tsam *bi.*

———. *Commentary on the Ten Grounds Sutra. Daśabhūmivyākhyāna. Sa bcu pa'i rnam par bshad pa.* Toh 3993, mdo 'grel *ngi.*

———. *Commentary on the Treasury of Abhidharma. Abhidharmakośabhāṣya. Chos mngon pa mdzod kyi bshad pa.* Toh 4090, mngon pa *ku.*

———. *Commentary on Twenty Verses. Viṃśatikāvṛtti. Nyi shu pa'i 'grel pa.* Toh 4057, sems tsam *shi.*

———. *Rules of Exposition. Vyākhyāyukti. Rnam par bshad pa'i rigs pa.* Toh 4061, sems tsam *shi.*

———. *Thirty Verses. Triṃśikā. Sum cu pa.* Toh 4055, sems tsam *shi.*

———. *Treasury of Abhidharma. Abhidharmakośa. Chos mngon pa mdzod.* Toh 4089, mngon pa *ku.*

———. *Twenty Verses. Viṃśatikā. Nyi shu pa.* Toh 4056, sems tsam *shi.*

Vimuktisena (sixth century). *Light on Perfection of Wisdom in Twenty-Five Thousand Lines. Pañcaviṃśatisāhasrikāvṛtti. Nyi khri snang ba.* Toh 3787, shes phyin *ka.*

Works Cited by the Translator

Anacker, Steven. *Seven Works of Vasubandhu: The Buddhist Psychological Doctor.* Delhi: Motilal Banarsidass, 1984.

Apple, James. *Jewels of the Middle Way: The Madhyamaka Legacy of Atiśa and His Early Tibetan Followers.* Somerville, MA: Wisdom Publications, 2018.

Arnold, Dan. *Buddhists, Brahmins, and Belief: Epistemology in South Asian Philosophy of Religion.* New York: Columbia University Press, 2005.

Bodhi, Bhikkhu, trans. *The Connected Discourses of the Buddha: A New Translation of the Saṃyutta Nikāya.* Boston: Wisdom Publications, 2000.

Cabezón, José Ignacio. *A Dose of Emptiness: An Annotated Translation of the sTong thun chen mo of mKhas grub dGe legs dpal bzang.* Albany: State University of New York Press, 1992.

———. "On Sgra pa shes rab rin chen pa'i rtsod lan of Paṇ chen blo bzang chos rgyan." *Études Asiatiques* 69.4 (1995): 643–69.

Cabezón, José, and Geshe Lobsang Dargyay. *Freedom from Extremes: Gorampa's "Distinguishing the Views" and the Polemics of Emptiness.* Boston: Wisdom Publications, 2006.

Chapa Chökyi Sengé (1109–69). *Great Summary on the Middle Way of the Three Eastern Masters. Dbu ma shar gsum gyi stong thun.* Vienna: Arbeitskreis für Tibetische und Buddhistische Studien, Universität Wien, 1999.

———. *Summary Outlines of Guide to the Bodhisattva Way. Spyod 'jug bsdus don.* In *Bka' gdams gsung 'bum phyogs bsgrigs,* 7:135–48. Sichuan: Dpal brtsegs bod yig dpe rnying zhib 'jug khang, 2006.

Chim Jampaiyang (1245–1325). *Ornament of Abhidharma: A Commentary on Vasubandhu's Abhidharmakośa.* Translated by Ian James Coghlan. Library of Tibetan Classics 23. Boston: Wisdom Publications, 2018.

Cowell, E. B., and A. E. Gough, trans. *The Sarva-Darśana-Saṃgraha, or Review of the Different Systems of Hindu Philosophy, by Mādhava Ācārya* [partial translation]. London: Trübner & Co., 1882

Cowherds, The. *Moonshadows: The Conventional Truth in Buddhist Philosophy.* New York: Oxford University Press, 2010.

Dignāga (ca. 480–540). *Commentary on Examination of Objects. Ālambanaparīkṣāvṛtti. Dmigs pa brtag pa'i 'grel pa.* Toh 4206 Tengyur, tshad ma *ce.* Critical edition in *Phyogs glang gi tshad ma'i gzung phyogs btus* (*Dignāga's Pramāṇa Texts*), edited and introduced by Thupten Jinpa. New Delhi: Institute of Tibetan Classics, 2016.

———. *Examination of Objects. Ālambanaparīkṣā. Dmigs pa brtag pa.* Toh 4205 Tengyur, tshad ma *ce.* Critical edition as in previous entry.

Dreyfus, Georges B. J., and Sara L. McClintock, eds. *The Svātantrika-Prāsaṅgika Distinction: What Difference Does a Difference Make?* Boston: Wisdom Publications, 2003.

Duerlinger, James. *Indian Buddhist Theories of Persons.* London: Routledge-Curzon, 2005.

Eckel, Malcolm David. "The Satisfaction of No Analysis: On Tsong-kha-pa's Approach to Svātantrika-Madhyamaka." In Dreyfus and McClintock, *Svātantrika-Prāsaṅgika Distinction*, 173–203.

———. *Jñānagarbha's Commentary on the Distinction between the Two Truths*. Albany: State University of New York Press, 1987.

Edgerton, Franklin. *Buddhist Hybrid Sanskrit Grammar and Dictionary*, vol. 2. Delhi: Motilal Banarsidass, 1993 (1953).

Engle, Artemus, trans. *The Bodhisattva Path to Unsurpassed Enlightenment*. Boulder: Snow Lion Publications, 2016.

Gampopa Sönam Rinchen (1079–1153). *Ornament of Precious Liberation. Thar pa rin po che'i rgyan*. Translated by Ken Holmes and edited by Thupten Jinpa in *Stages of the Buddha's Teachings: Three Key Texts*. Library of Tibetan Classics 10. Boston: Wisdom Publications, 2015.

Gorampa Sönam Sengé (1429–89). *Distinguishing the Views. Lta ba'i shen 'byed*. Collected Works of Goram Sönam Sengé, vol. *ca*. Dehradun, India: Sakya College, 1979. Translation in Cabezón and Dargyay, *Freedom from Extremes*.

Griffiths, Paul J. *On Being Mindless: Buddhist Meditation and the Mind-Body Problem*. LaSalle, IL: Open Court, 1986.

Gyaltsab Darma Rinchen (1364–1432). *Memorandum on the Eight Difficult Points of Fundamental Wisdom. Rtsa ba shes rab kyi dka' gnad brgyad kyi brjed byang*. Collected Works of Tsongkhapa, vol. *ka*. Kumbum edition.

Hopkins, Jeffrey. *Meditation on Emptiness*. Boston: Wisdom Publications, 1996.

———. *Maps of the Profound: Jam-yang-shay-ba's "Great Exposition of Buddhist and Non-Buddhist Views of the Nature of Reality."* Ithaca, NY: Snow Lion Publications, 2003.

Huntington, C. W., with Geshe Namgyal Wangchen. *The Emptiness of Emptiness: An Introduction to Early Indian Mādhyamika*. Honolulu: University of Hawaii Press, 1989.

Jamyang Shepa (1648–1721). *Critical Analysis of Entering the Middle Way. Dbu ma'i mtha' dpyod*. Collected Works of Kun mkhyen 'Jam dbyangs bzhad pa, vol. *da*. Tashi Khyil edition.

Jinpa, Thupten, trans. *The Book of Kadam: The Core Texts*. Library of Tibetan Classics 2, Boston: Wisdom Publications, 2007.

———. "Delineating Reason's Scope for Negation," *Journal of Indian Philosophy* (1998), 27: 275–308.

———. *Self, Reality and Reason in Tibetan Philosophy: Tsongkhapa's Quest for the Middle View*. London: RoutledgeCurzon, 2002.

———. *Tsongkhapa: A Buddha in the Land of Snows*. Boulder: Shambhala Publications, 2019.

Khedrup Jé (1385–1438). *Opening the Eyes of the Fortunate: A Treatise Illuminating the Truth of Emptiness. Zab mo stong pa nyid kyi de kho na nyid gsal bar byed pa'i bstan bcos skal bzang mig 'byed (Stong mthun chen mo)*. Collected Works of Khedrup Gelek Palsang, Kumbum edition, vol. *kha*. Translation in Cabezón, *Dose of Emptiness*.

Khoroche, Peter, trans. *Once the Buddha Was a Monkey: Āryaśūra's Jātakamālā*. Chicago: University of Chicago Press, 1989.

Lang, Karen C. *Four Illusions: Candrakīrti's Advice to Travelers on the Bodhisattva Path*. New York: Oxford University Press, 2003

Larson, Gerald James, Ram Shankar Bhattacharya, and Karl Potter. *The Encyclopedia of Indian Philosophy, Volume 4: Sāṃkhya*. Princeton, NJ: Princeton University Press, 1987.

Lindtner, Christian. *Nagarjuniana: Studies in the Writings and Philosophy of Nāgārjuna*. Copenhagen: Akademisk Forlag, 1982.

Lochen Kyabchok Palsang (d. 1412). *Brilliantly Illuminating the Suchness of the Ocean of Scriptures: An Extensive Exposition of Entering the Middle Way. Dbu ma la 'jug pa'i rgya cher bshad pa gsung rab rgya mtsho'i de kho na nyid rab tu gsal ba*. Typeset edition. Sichuan: Si khron mi rigs dpe skrun khang, 2002.

Lodrö Rinchen (fifteenth century). *Light on the Principles of the Exposition Entitled Illuminating the Intent. Rnam bshad dgongs pa rab gsal gyi de nyid gsal byed*. In *Kun mkyen blo gros rin chen seng ge'i gsung rtsom*. Typeset edition. Beijing: Krung go bod rig pa'i dpe skrun khang, 2007.

———. *Summary Outlines of Illuminating the Intent. Rnam bshad dgongs pa rab gsal gyi snying po'i bsdus don*. In the above volume, pp. 1–53. Typeset edition. Beijing: Krung go bod rig pa'i dpe skrun khang, 2007.

Lopez, Donald, ed. *Buddhist Hermeneutics*. Honolulu: University of Hawaii Press, 1988.

Losang Tamdrin (1867–1937). *Annotations on the General Presentation on the Middle Way. Dbu ma'i spyi don gyi mchan 'grel zab don rab gsal sgron me*. Collected Works of Blo bzang rta mgrin, vol. *nga*. New Delhi: Guru Deva, 1975.

Mabja Jangchub Tsöndrü. *Ornament of Reason: The Great Commentary to Nāgārjuna's Root of the Middle Way*. Translated by the Dharmachakra Translation Committee. Ithaca, NY: Snow Lion Publications, 2011.

Mipham, Ju (1846–1912). *A Rosary of Pure Crystal: A Commentary on Entering the Middle Way. Dbu ma la 'jug pa'i 'grel pa zla ba'i zhal lung dri med shel phreng.* Translation in Padmakara, *Introduction to the Middle Way.*

Padmakara Translation Group, trans. *Introduction to the Middle Way: Candrakīrti's Madhyamakavatara with Commentary by Jamgön Mipham.* Boston: Shambhala, 2002.

Pasang Yonten Arya. *Dictionary of Tibetan Materia Medica*. Translated and edited by Dr. Yonten Gyatso. Delhi: Motilal Banarsidass, 1998.

Rendawa Shönu Lodrö (1349–1412). *Lamp Illuminating Suchness: An Exposition of Entering the Middle Way. Dbu ma la 'jug pa'i rnam bshad de kho na nyid gsal ba'i sgron me.* Collected Works of Rendawa, vol. 5. Sichuan: Old Tibetan Texts Printing, 2015.

Ruegg, David Seyfort. *The Buddhist Philosophy of the Middle*. Boston: Wisdom Publications, 2010.

———. "The Indian and Indic in Tibetan Cultural History, and Tsong-kha-pa's Achievement as a Scholar and Thinker: An Essay on the Concepts of 'Buddhism in Tibet' and 'Tibetan Buddhism.'" *Journal of Indian Philosophy* 32 (2004): 321–43. Republished in *Buddhist Philosophy of the Middle*, 375–98.

———. "On the Thesis and Assertion in the Madhyamaka/Dbu ma." In *Contributions on Tibetan and Buddhist Religion and Philosophy*, edited by E. Steinkellner and H. Tauscher, 205–41. Weiner Studien zur Tibetologie und Buddhismuskunde 11. Vienna: Arbeitskreis für Tibetische und Buddhistische Studien, Universität Wien, 1983.

———. "Purport, Implicature, and Presupposition: Sanskrit *abhiprāya* and Tibetan *dgongs pa / dgongs gzhi* as Hermeneutical Concepts." In *Buddhist Philosophy of the Middle*, 195–211.

———. *Three Studies in the History of Indian and Tibetan Madhyamaka Philosophy: Studies in Tibetan Madhyamaka Thought*, part 1. Vienna: Arbeitskreis für Tibetische und Buddhistische Studien, Universität Wien, 2000.

Sakya Paṇḍita (1182–1251). *Clarifying the Sage's Intent. Thub pa'i dgongs pa rab tu gsal ba.* Translated by David P. Jackson in *Stages of the Buddha's Teachings: Three Key Texts.* Library of Tibetan Classics 10. Boston: Wisdom Publications, 2015.

Shākya Chokden (1428–1507). *Grand Summary of Points. Don gyi mdo chen.* Collected Works of Shākya Chokden, vol. 4. Beijing: Krung go bod rig pa'i dpe skrun khang, 2013.

Sideris, Mark, and Shōryū Katsura. *Nāgārjuna's Middle Way.* Boston: Wisdom Publications, 2013.

Sparham, Gareth, trans. *Ocean of Eloquence: Tsong Kha pa's Commentary on the Yogācāra Doctrine of the Mind.* Albany: State University of New York Press, 1993.

Taktsang Lotsāwa (b. 1405). *Establishing the Freedom from Extremes on the Basis of Understanding All Philosophical Systems. Grub mtha' kun shes nas mtha' bral grub pa.* Beijing: Mi rigs dpe skrun khang, 1999.

Tatz, Mark. *Asaṅga's Chapter on Ethics with the Commentary by Tsong-Kha-Pa.* Lewiston, NY: Edwin Mellen Press, 1986.

Tauscher, Helmut. "Phya pa chos kyi seng ge as a Svātantrika." In Dreyfus and McClintock, *Svātantrika-Prāsaṅgika Distinction,* 207–55.

Thakchoe, Sonam. *The Two Truths Debate: Tsongkhapa and Gorampa on the Middle Way.* Boston: Wisdom Publications, 2007.

Thurman, Robert F. *The Central Philosophy of Tibet: A Study and Translation of Jey Tsong Khapa's Essence of True Eloquence.* New York: Columbia University Press, 1984.

———, ed. *The Life and Teachings of Tsongkhapa.* Dharamsala: Library of Tibetan Works and Archives, 1981.

Tillemans, Tom J. F. *How Do Mādhyamikas Think?* Boston: Wisdom Publications, 2016.

———. "Metaphysics for Mādhyamikas." In Dreyfus and McClintock, *Svātantrika-Prāsaṅgika Distinction,* 93–123.

Tillemans, Tom J. F., and Donald S. Lopez Jr. "What Can One Reasonably Say about Nonexistence? A Tibetan Work on the Problem of *Āśryāsiddha.*" *Journal of Indian Philosophy* 26 (1998): 99–129.

Tsongkhapa Losang Drakpa (1357–1419). *Essence of True Eloquence: Differentiating the Provisional and Definite Meanings. Drang ba dang nges pa'i don rnam par 'byed pa legs bshad snying po.* Collected Works of Jé Tsongkhapa, Kumbum edition, vol. *pha.* English translation in Thurman, *Central Philosophy.*

———. *The Great Treatise on the Stages of the Path to Enlightenment,* 3 vols. Translated by the Lamrim Chenmo Translation Committee. Ithaca, NY: Snow Lion Publications, 2000–2004.

————. *Illuminating the Intent: An Exposition of Entering the Middle Way.* *Dbu ma la 'jug pa rgya cher bshad pa dgongs pa rab gsal.* Collected Works of Jé Tsongkhapa, Kumbum edition, vol. *ma.*

————. *Memorandum on Eight Difficult Points. Dka' gnas brgyad kyi zin bris.* Collected Works of Jé Tsongkhapa, Kumbum edition, vol. *ba.*

————. *Notes on Compendium of Training. Bslab btus zin bris.* Collected Works of Jé Tsongkhapa, Kumbum edition, vol. *pha.*

————. *Notes on the Ornament of the Middle Way. Dbu ma rgyan gyi zin bris.* Collected Works of Jé Tsongkhapa, Kumbum edition, vol. *ba.*

————. *Ocean of Reasoning. Rtsa ba shes rab kyi ṭik chen rigs pa'i rgya mtsho.* Collected Works of Jé Tsongkhapa, Kumbum edition, vol. *ba.*

———— [rJe Tsong Khapa]. *Ocean of Reasoning: A Great Commentary on Nāgārjuna's Mūlamadhyamakakārikā.* Translated by Geshe Ngawang Samten and Jay L. Garfield. New York: Oxford University Press, 2006.

Vose, Kevin A. *Resurrecting Candrakīrti: Disputes in the Tibetan Creation of Prāsaṅgika.* Boston: Wisdom Publications, 2009.

Williams, Paul. *The Reflexive Nature of Awareness: A Tibetan Madhyamaka Defence.* London: Curzon, 1998.

Yoshimizu, Chizuko. "Tsong kha pa's Reevaluation of Candrakīrti's Criticism of Autonomous Inference." In Dreyfus and McClintock, *Svātantrika-Prāsaṅgika Distinction,* 257–88.

Index

About the Translator

THUPTEN JINPA LANGRI was educated in the classical Tibetan monastic system and received the highest degree of *geshé lharam* from Ganden Shartsé Monastery. Jinpa also holds a BA in philosophy and a PhD in religious studies, both from Cambridge University, where he also worked as a research fellow. Since 1985, he has been the principal English translator to His Holiness the Dalai Lama, translating and editing many of his books. Jinpa's own writings include translations of major classical Tibetan texts, scholarly articles and books, with the latest book being *Tsongkhapa: A Buddha in the Land of Snows*. He is the chair of the Mind and Life Institute, the president of the Compassion Institute, the founder and president of the Institute of Tibetan Classics, and the general editor for the *Library of Tibetan Classics* series. He is married with two daughters and lives in Montreal, Canada.

The Institute of Tibetan Classics

THE INSTITUTE OF TIBETAN CLASSICS is a nonprofit, charitable educational organization based in Montreal, Canada. It is dedicated to two primary objectives: (1) to preserve and promote the study and deep appreciation of Tibet's rich intellectual, spiritual, and artistic heritage, especially among the Tibetan-speaking communities worldwide; and (2) to make the classical Tibetan knowledge and literature a truly global heritage, its spiritual and intellectual resources open to all.

To learn more about the Institute of Tibetan Classics and its various projects, please visit www.tibetanclassics.org or write to this address:

Institute of Tibetan Classics
304 Aberdare Road
Montreal (Quebec) H3P 3K3
Canada

The Library of Tibetan Classics

"This new series edited by Thupten Jinpa and published by Wisdom Publications is a landmark in the study of Tibetan culture in general and Tibetan Buddhism in particular. Each volume contains a lucid introduction and outstanding translations that, while aimed at the general public, will benefit those in the field of Tibetan Studies immensely as well."

—Leonard van der Kuijp, Harvard University

"This is an invaluable set of translations by highly competent scholar-practitioners. The series spans the breadth of the history of Tibetan religion, providing entry to a vast culture of spiritual cultivation."

—Jeffrey Hopkins, University of Virginia

"Erudite in all respects, this series is at the same time accessible and engagingly translated. As such, it belongs in all college and university libraries as well as in good public libraries. *The Library of Tibetan Classics* is on its way to becoming a truly extraordinary spiritual and literary accomplishment."

—Janice D. Willis, Wesleyan University

Following is a list of the thirty-two proposed volumes in *The Library of Tibetan Classics*. Some volumes are translations of single texts, while others are compilations of multiple texts, and each volume will be roughly the same length. Except for those volumes already published, the renderings of titles below are tentative and liable to change. The Institute of Tibetan Classics has contracted numerous established translators in its efforts, and work is progressing on all the volumes concurrently.

1. *Mind Training: The Great Collection*, compiled by Shönu Gyalchok and Könchok Gyaltsen (fifteenth century). NOW AVAILABLE

2. *The Book of Kadam: The Core Texts*, attributed to Atiśa and Dromtönpa (eleventh century). NOW AVAILABLE

3. *The Great Chariot: A Treatise on the Great Perfection*, Longchen Rapjampa (1308–63)

4. *Taking the Result As the Path: Core Teachings of the Sakya Lamdré Tradition*, Jamyang Khyentsé Wangchuk (1524–68) et al. NOW AVAILABLE

5. *Mahāmudrā and Related Instructions: Core Teachings of the Kagyü Schools.* NOW AVAILABLE

6. *Stages of the Path and the Whispered Traditions: Core Teachings of the Geluk School of Tibetan Buddhism*

7. *Ocean of Definitive Meaning: A Teaching for the Mountain Hermit*, Dölpopa Sherap Gyaltsen (1292–1361)

8. *Four Tibetan Lineages: Core Teachings of Pacification, Severance, Shangpa Kagyü, and Bodongpa*, Jamgön Kongtrül (1813–90). NOW AVAILABLE

9. *Sutra, Tantra, and the Mind Cycle: Core Teachings of the Bön School*

10. *Stages of the Buddha's Teachings: Three Key Texts.* NOW AVAILABLE

11. *The Bodhisattva's Altruistic Ideal: Selected Key Texts*

12. *The Ethics of the Three Codes*

13. *Sādhanas: Vajrayana Buddhist Meditation Manuals*

14. *Ornament of Stainless Light: An Exposition of the Kālacakra Tantra*, Khedrup Norsang Gyatso (1423–1513). NOW AVAILABLE

15. *A Lamp to Illuminate the Five Stages: Teachings on the Guhyasamāja Tantra*, Tsongkhapa (1357–1419). NOW AVAILABLE

16. *Studies in the Perfection of Wisdom*

17. *Treatises on Buddha Nature*

18. *Differentiations of the Profound View: Interpretations of Emptiness in Tibet*

19. *Illuminating the Intent: An Exposition of Candrakīrti's Entering the Middle Way*, Tsongkhapa (1357–1419). NOW AVAILABLE

20. *Tibetan Buddhist Epistemology I: The Sakya School*

21. *Tibetan Buddhist Epistemology II: The Geluk School*

22. *Tibetan Buddhist Psychology and Phenomenology: Selected Texts*

23. *Ornament of Abhidharma: A Commentary on the "Abhidharmakośa,"* Chim Jampaiyang (thirteenth century). NOW AVAILABLE

24. *A Beautiful Adornment of Mount Meru: Presentation of Classical Indian Philosophies*, Changkya Rölpai Dorjé (1717–86). NOW AVAILABLE

25. *The Crystal Mirror of Philosophical Systems: A Tibetan Study of Asian Religious Thought*, Thuken Losang Chökyi Nyima (1737–1802). NOW AVAILABLE

26. *Gateway for Being Learned and Realized: Selected Texts*

27. *The Tibetan Book of Everyday Wisdom: A Thousand Years of Sage Advice.* NOW AVAILABLE

28. *Mirror of Beryl: A Historical Introduction to Tibetan Medicine*, Desi Sangyé Gyatso (1653–1705). NOW AVAILABLE

29. *Selected Texts on Tibetan Astronomy and Astrology*

30. *Art and Literature: An Anthology*

31. *Tales from the Tibetan Operas.* NOW AVAILABLE

32. *A History of Buddhism in India and Tibet*, Khepa Deu (thirteenth century)

To receive a brochure describing all the volumes or to stay informed about *The Library of Tibetan Classics*, please write to:

support@wisdompubs.org

or send a request by post to:

Wisdom Publications
Attn: Library of Tibetan Classics
199 Elm Street
Somerville, MA 02144 USA

The complete catalog containing descriptions of each volume can also be found online at wisdomexperience.org.

Become a Benefactor of the Library of Tibetan Classics

THE LIBRARY OF TIBETAN CLASSICS' scope, importance, and commitment to the finest quality make it a tremendous financial undertaking. We invite you to become a benefactor, joining us in creating this profoundly important human resource. Contributors of two thousand dollars or more will receive a copy of each future volume as it becomes available, and will have their names listed in all subsequent volumes. Larger donations will go even further in supporting *The Library of Tibetan Classics*, preserving the creativity, wisdom, and scholarship of centuries past, so that it may help illuminate the world for future generations.

To contribute, please either visit our website at wisdomexperience.org, call us at (617) 776-7416, or send a check made out to Wisdom Publications or credit card information to the address below.

Library of Tibetan Classics Fund
Wisdom Publications
199 Elm Street
Somerville, MA 02144
USA

Please note that contributions of lesser amounts are also welcome and are invaluable to the development of the series. Wisdom is a 501(c)3 nonprofit corporation, and all contributions are tax-deductible to the extent allowed by law.

If you have any questions, please do not hesitate to call us or email us at support@wisdompubs.org.

To keep up to date on the status of *The Library of Tibetan Classics*, visit the series page on our website, and subscribe to our newsletter while you are there.

About Wisdom Publications

Wisdom Publications is the leading publisher of classic and contemporary Buddhist books and practical works on mindfulness. To learn more about us or to explore our other books, please visit our website at wisdomexperience.org or contact us at the address below.

Wisdom Publications
199 Elm Street
Somerville, MA 02144 USA

We are a 501(c)(3) organization, and donations in support of our mission are tax deductible.

Wisdom Publications is affiliated with the Foundation for the Preservation of the Mahayana Tradition (FPMT).